Politics in the

USSR

The Little, Brown Series
in Comparative Politics

Under the Editorship of
GABRIEL A. ALMOND
LUCIAN W. PYE

A COUNTRY STUDY

Politics in the
USSR
Third Edition

Frederick C. Barghoorn
Yale University

Thomas F. Remington
Emory University

LITTLE, BROWN AND COMPANY
Boston   Toronto

Library of Congress Cataloging-in-Publication Data

Barghoorn, Frederick Charles, 1911–
    Politics in the USSR.

    (Little, Brown series in comparative politics.
A Country study)
    Includes index.
    1. Soviet Union—Politics and government—1917–
I. Remington, Thomas F., 1948–   II. Title.
III. Series: Little, Brown series in comparative
politics.   Country study.
JN6531.B3   1986   320.947   85-24043
ISBN 0-316-08091-8

Library of Congress Catalog Card No. 85-24043

ISBN 0-316-08091-8

9 8 7 6 5 4 3 2 1

ALP
Published simultaneously in Canada
by Little, Brown & Company (Canada) Limited

Printed in the United States of America

Preface

It seems to us that the structural-functional approach to the study of contemporary political systems developed by Gabriel Almond and some of his associates is especially suitable for comparative political analysis. Analytical categories such as political culture and interest articulation focus our attention on structures, functions, and processes common to political systems that differ from one another in many ways because of their divergent origins and historical cultural experiences. In the first and second editions of this book, in 1966 and 1972, these categories were applied to data derived from widely varying primary Soviet sources, studies of the Soviet system produced by Soviet official scholarship, and works by Western Sovietologists and journalists and Soviet dissidents and emigrants. The results, we believe, were significant contributions to understanding of political life in the USSR. These two editions benefited in particular from paths broken by Almond and G. Bingham Powell in their *Comparative Politics, A Developmental Approach* (1966).

This third edition also benefits greatly from Almond and Powell's second, fundamentally revised treatment of comparative politics in their *Comparative Politics: System, Process, and Policy* (1978). Among other new features in this study, Almond and Powell focused on decisionmaking and policymaking and on performance of the political system. In the present work, too, we have stressed how policy is made and implemented, as well as performance, and we include a chapter, absent in the first two editions, on Soviet foreign policy. In other ways, too, we have sought to take account of how domestic and foreign policies interact in the political life of the USSR. We examine the growing influence in Soviet policy-making of foreign policy and security specialists, and we assess evidence in Soviet sources of apprehension about foreign influences on Soviet citizens. We have wholly rewritten chapters retained from the earlier edition, in which we deal with political culture and socialization, communications, social structure and political subcultures, elite recruitment, policymaking and implementation, and rule adjudication. Though we retain the theoretical framework from the earlier books—the structural-functional organization — the third edition is an entirely new book.

We believe that this is the only textbook on Soviet politics in which the Soviet political system is analyzed from the perspective of modern comparative political theory. We emphasize, however, that this book is grounded in Soviet and Russian history and in writings of Western Sovietologists that we consider to be particularly relevant, as well as, in appropriate instances, works by Soviet authors or Soviet dissidents and emigrants. From our extensive study of new literature and data, then, we undertake to describe and analyze the structures, functions, and processes of Soviet politics, duly attending to the differences and similarities between the prerevolutionary tsarist system and the new one created by Leninist revolutionaries, as well as to Stalin and the post-Stalin leaderships. We describe in detail the urbanizing, industrializing, and modernizing that in a few decades have deepened Soviet society's complexity and aroused new expectations and demands; obviously the new Gorbachev leadership is absorbed in coping with these pressures. Among the methods available to all Soviet leaderships for guiding the sociopolitical life of their vast country are those of political socialization, citizen participation, and elite recruitment, as well as rule adjudication and the role of law generally, including use of law to curb dissent that the Soviet authorities regard as objectionable. To each of these subjects we devote a chapter. In the final chapter we attempt to capture the dynamics of the Gorbachev leadership, which after only months in office seemed well launched not only in consolidating power but also in demonstrating confidence in its ability to convince the Soviet people that it would be able to solve.problems with which previous leaderships had failed to cope. In a way the Gorbachev regime appeared to combine elements of sensible reform with respect for tradition. Like a modern Peter the Great, Gorbachev sought to use Western technology to revive the Soviet economy and make it competitive, while claiming, as is traditional in Russian and especially Soviet Russia, moral, even spiritual superiority over the "capitalist" West and particularly the "imperialist" United States.

It is a pleasure to acknowledge our gratitude to several people who helped in various ways during preparation of this edition of *Politics in the USSR*. At Little, Brown, Don Palm, John Covell, and Jayna Pike have been unfailingly helpful. At Emory, Karen Salsbury, Linda Boyte, and Joan Loeb have made innumerable copies of the text along the way, and students in Remington's course on Soviet politics over two years have offered comments on draft portions of the manuscript in a constructive and generous spirit. Judith Record McKinney made valuable suggestions about Chapter X. Bing Powell's sharp-eyed editing of our chapter "Politics in the USSR," which appeared in *Comparative Politics Today: A World View,* 3rd ed., offered incisive comments useful in writing this longer work. To Paul K. Cook we owe special acknowledgment for generosity with his time and for patient and expert assistance and guidance in identifying data. Among his many helpful acts was providing organization charts of the Soviet Communist Party and government.

We are greatly in the debt of the scholars and journalists who in the years since the second edition of *Politics in the USSR* appeared have produced works on Soviet politics and society that have greatly advanced the study of the Soviet system. Much of the newer literature has produced deeper understanding of the policy-making processes in the USSR, which is, we hope, reflected in the greater emphasis on policy issues in this book. They have challenged the younger generations of political scientists to match their ingenuity and rigor in analyzing a system that, though considerably more open than in Stalin's era, remains closed and secretive by comparison with our own.

The junior author would like to express his appreciation to the senior author for the invitation to collaborate in writing the new edition of *Politics in the USSR,* the two previous editions of which piloted him through his study of Soviet politics as an undergraduate and in graduate school. It has been a privilege and a pleasure to share in producing a book that we hope is a worthy successor to the earlier volumes.

Finally, both of us consider ourselves fortunate to have been associated with Gabriel Almond in a project that owed its origin to his creative imagination and to the successful completion of which his friendship and enthusiasm contributed enormously.

Contents

CHAPTER I

Analytic Framework: Soviet Politics in Historical and Comparative Context

THE TSARIST AUTHORITARIAN HERITAGE AND THE SOVIET SYSTEM: LINKS, CONTINUITY, AND CHANGE

To understand the political system of the USSR (Union of Soviet Socialist Republics), now almost seventy years old, requires knowledge of the main features of the eleven-century history of the pre-Soviet Russian state. Why is it important for us to know at least the rudiments of Russian history prior to what is officially known as the Great October Socialist Revolution? (Although it occurred on October 25, 1917, the October Revolution has been celebrated on November 7 since change from the Russian Old Style to the Western calendar on February 1, 1918.)

A brief answer is that the historical record sheds light on vulnerabilities of the authoritarian — or more harshly put, autocratic or despotic — Russian empire that enabled the Russian communists led by Vladimir Lenin to engineer its overthrow in 1917. (Lenin was the name taken by the most potent of communist leaders, Vladimir Ulyanov.) More important, but also more speculative, is that knowledge of the essential characteristics of the tsarist regime can help explain the ways in which tsarist authoritarianism influenced the authoritarianism of the USSR. Later in this chapter we indicate why in this study we characterize the Soviet system as authoritarian, rather than *totalitarian,* at least since the death of Joseph Stalin (Iosif Djugashvili) on March 5, 1953. As we examine relevant characteristics of the tsarist system, it will be useful to keep in mind a pertinent statement by that greatest of revolutionary thinkers, Karl Marx. Marx asserted that although men make their own history, they do not do it under circumstances chosen by themselves "but under circumstances directly found, given and transmitted from the past." He added that "the tradition of all the dead generations weighs like a nightmare on the brain of the living."[1]

By an authoritarian political system we mean one with the following attributes: The power and influence of the state, and particularly of the ruler or chief executive, vis-à-vis other elements of the political system and the society are overwhelming. Interest articulation and aggregation and policy making (these and other terms used in this book will be defined later in this chapter) are the prerogatives of a restricted circle of leaders and their carefully selected assistants, and policy implementation is restricted to a centralized hierarchy of bureaucrats, controlled by the supreme political authorities. Local government agencies are weak in comparison with the central administration. Clearly, in such systems checks and balances against the arbitrariness of centralized power — such as effective legislatures, relatively autonomous religious institutions, competitive political parties, relatively free and uncensored communications media, professional associations and other interest groups, free universities and research organizations, and an independent judiciary — are lacking or poorly developed.

Perhaps the most noteworthy characteristic of Russian foreign policy was what Robert Tucker, in an extraordinarily insightful study, described as "the drive of the autocratic power to aggrandize the national territory," its "gathering of lands," through which "Muscovy expanded from an original area of a few thousand square miles to one fifth of the earth's surface in 1917."[2] Tucker quoted the great Russian historian Vasili Klyuchevski on the baneful impact on the Russian people of their rulers' successful expansionist policy. Klyuchevski wrote that in the period from the sixteenth century on "the expansion of the state territory, straining beyond measure . . . the resources of the people

[1]Karl Marx, "The Eighteenth Brumaire of Louis Bonaparte," in Robert Tucker, ed., *The Marx-Engels Reader* (New York: Norton, 1972), p. 437.

[2]Robert Tucker, "The Image of Dual Russia," in Cyril Black, ed., *The Transformation of Russian Society* (Cambridge, Mass.: Harvard University Press, 1960). pp. 587–605. Quotation p. 590.

only bolstered the power of the state without elevating the self-consciousness of the people. . . . The state swelled up, the people grew lean."[3]

The views of Klyuchevski and Tucker on the sources and effects of Russian expansionism are, to our knowledge, shared by most informed students of Russian history. Many also stress other factors, including the opportunities, temptations, and perhaps the justification for territorial aggrandizement provided by Muscovy's location within a vast territory stretching from the White Sea and the Arctic Ocean to the Black and Caspian Seas, to Persia, Afghanistan, India, and China, and from the Baltic Sea to the Pacific Ocean. As the historian Michael Florinsky noted, Russian geography "presents remarkable features that seem to have predetermined its political future" — largely because of the lack of natural barriers to the movement of armies along either its north–south or its east–west directions.[4]

Russia's lack of access to the sea was a major obstacle to the development of trade. It inhibited economic development and contributed to the economic backwardness of Russia relative to the West European states that became her rivals and partners, largely as the result of successful diplomatic and military exploits by Peter the Great and Catherine the Great in the eighteenth century. Even Russia's European rivers flow (as in the case of the mighty Volga) into the Caspian Sea and into the Baltic and Black Seas — and the Baltic area was not acquired until the eighteenth century. The great Russian Siberian rivers have their outlet in the Arctic Ocean. The foregoing helps to explain the centuries-long Russian effort to acquire territories and ports to the west and south of a land-locked country.

There is little doubt that the struggle, lasting many centuries, in which the rulers of Muscovy gradually overcame the dominance of the Mongol khans who had in the thirteenth century

---

[3]Ibid., pp. 589–90.

[4]Michael Florinsky, *Russia: A History and an Interpretation,* 2 vols., vol. 1 (New York: Macmillan, 1953), pp. 1–2. Florinsky's views on the role of the topography, the Russian rivers, and the struggle between the forest-dwelling Russians and the steppe-dwelling Ukrainians and other peoples who came under Russian control beginning in the seventeenth century are widely accepted. We have derived much of the information on which this section is based from historical surveys such as Florinsky's and the useful recent survey, *The Making of Modern Russia* by Lionel Kochan and Richard Abraham, 2nd ed. (London: Penguin, 1983).

destroyed the first Russian state (which had been established in the ninth century by the Varangians, Scandinavian adventurers) taught the Russians a great deal about state building. As Kochan and Abraham put it, with some exaggeration, "Mongol rule provided future Russian rulers with a model: a state with universalist ambitions, subordinating everything to efficiency in matters of military administration and relying on a class of servicemen bound to serve their khan with absolute obedience."[5]

This statement should be understood within the context of the intense hostility characterizing the relationship between the sedentary, mainly Slavic (Russian, Ukrainian, and, further west, Polish and non-Slavic Lithuanian) populations, and their largely Mongol and Turkic-steppe nomad enemies. It was not until the late eighteenth century, during the reign of Catherine the Great, that the Russians achieved security against the last powerful Tatar (a more accurate term than Mongol to describe the steppe peoples) state. John Armstrong quotes his fellow historian Alexandre Eck on the terror inspired among the Russians by the Tatars, which "was transmitted to their descendants."[6]

As Armstrong also points out, after the conversion of the Tatars to Islam, the centuries of warfare between the Slavs and the steppe nomads reflected not only ethnic but also religious conflict. In the course of this conflict, the Russian tsars claimed not only to be fighting to gather and unify all the Orthodox population and to be the protectors of Orthodox peoples everywhere, especially after the Ottoman Turks conquered Constantinople in 1453, but also to be the heirs to the steppe heritage of their Moslem antagonists. Still, the "Polish-Lithuanian Catholics were, however, perceived as enemies by the Russian Orthodox princes, who often preferred Tatar alliances."[7]

The capability of the Russians to form alliances with Tatar elements when it was expedient reflected not only the rich experience in statecraft acquired by the Russian princes in a very long struggle to build imperial power and learn how to deal effectively with a variety of ethnic groups, but also the sense of alienation that has often characterized relations between Russia and both

[5]Kochan and Abraham, *Making of Modern Russia,* p. 24.

[6]John Armstrong, *Nations Before Nationalism* (Chapel Hill: University of North Carolina Press, 1982), p. 76.

[7]Ibid.

Catholic and Protestant Europe. A famous episode illustrates the complex interweaving of ethnic and religious elements in Russian history. Alexander Nevsky, Prince of Vladimir, whose victory in battle over the Livonian Knights of the Sword, an affiliate of the Catholic Teutonic Order, saved the city of Novgorod and made him a legendary Russian hero, paid tribute to the Mongols.[8] As one scholar remarks, "This victory over the Catholic crusaders from the West was achieved at the price of submission to the Mongol infidels in the East. Alexander seems to have justified this choice as necessary for the preservation of Russian Orthodoxy, which had less to fear from the Mongols than from the Catholicism of the Teutonic Order."[9]

According to recent scholarship the Russian Orthodox church, and in particular its Byzantine heritage, seems to have been a less important component of the Russian imperial myth than has often been suggested. The first component, writes Armstrong, was "in gathering of the Russian lands." Because of the sharp split between the Eastern Orthodox and the Western Roman Catholic churches, by the fifteenth century, however, "emphasis on Orthodoxy constituted a second major theme of the Russian myth." Third, incorporation of the Tatar city of Kazan on the Volga by Ivan the Terrible (Dread) in 1552, according to Armstrong, quoting Jaroslav Pelenski, "signalled the transformation of Muscovite Russia from a centralized national state into a multi-national empire. . . . The two other strands in this interwoven fabric were, respectively, the conception of "a Russian emperor as national ruler" as a result of the decline and fall of Byzantium after the Turkish capture of Constantinople in 1453 and the struggle of Russian rulers in the sixteenth, seventeenth, and eighteenth centuries for "acquisition of the Rurikid heritage. Through this struggle the Russian tsars aimed to regain the lands once held by the first, Kievan Russian (or Rus) rulers and subsequently incorporated into the Polish kingdom. Thus Russia emerged in early modern times as an empire with a vast but far from universal

---

[8] Nevsky was celebrated, incidentally, in an Eisenstein film used by Joseph Stalin to steel Soviet resolve against Hitlerite Germany and also to justify Stalin's attempt to steer clear of a military conflict with any of the major power groupings confronting one another on the eve of World War II.

[9] Reinhard Bendix, *Kings or People* (Berkeley: University of California Press, 1978), p. 96.

mission and with a conception of a very strong autocratic power based on Tatar-Mongol, Byzantine Orthodox, and other elements. According to Armstrong, "Absence of a Roman law tradition like the one that had restrained the Byzantine emperor enabled the Russian rulers to become more complete autocrats than the Byzantine emperors. . . . "[10] "The tsar's drastically enhanced power over the church, as evidenced by even a weak tsar's ability to depose a patriarch in 1667, constituted an important component of autocracy. Peter I's [Peter the Great's] elimination of the patriarchate [established in 1589] . . . suggested the attainment of Caesaropapism [union of temporal and ecclesiastical authority in the person of the temporal ruler] such as the Byzantine myth had only adumbrated."[11]

Of course the church continued to play an important role in Russian social and political life even after its subordination under Peter the Great to a branch of the government bureaucracy headed by a lay official who had the title of chief procurator of the Holy Synod. Count Uvarov, one of Nicholas I's education ministers, proclaimed the slogan "Orthodoxy, Autocracy, and Nationality" the ideological basis of education and of social and political life generally. Konstantin Pobedonostsev, the most influential of all procurators of the Holy Synod (because of his access to Alexander III and Nicholas II, the last two Russian tsars) promoted an increasing role for the Orthodox clergy in elementary education. According to Florinsky, while the number of church schools grew rapidly, "their educational standards remained, with rare exceptions, deplorably low."[12]

It seems that even in the last decades of the declining empire of the tsars, the influence of the church remained considerable, at least among the peasants. The upper and middle classes, however, appear to have become indifferent to its teachings, and the

[10]Armstrong, *Nations Before Nationalism,* pp. 148–51.

[11]Ibid, p. 151.

The weak tsar mentioned by Armstrong in the above quotation was Tsar Alexis, and the patriarch was the strong-willed Nikon, apparently the only head of the Russian church who ever defied a tsar. Nikon's reforms, largely confined to matters of ritual, aroused the bitter opposition of archpriest Avvakum, a traditionalist dissident of great courage, whose followers, known as Old Believers, split from the official church. Some of them in the nineteenth and early twentieth centuries were to become wealthy merchants. Avvakum was burned at the stake in 1681.

[12]Florinsky, *Russia* 2: 1116.

vast majority of the intelligentsia displayed varying degrees of skepticism or hostility toward all forms of religion; in the case of Lenin and most of his Bolshevik followers, this amounted to fanatical hatred.

The Russian Orthodox church was on the whole an intellectually and spiritually weak institution, incapable of acting as a counterweight, morally or politically, to the autocracy. It appears that many of the clergy were "sincerely devoted to their parishioners, and beloved by them. But their attitude to the civil power often verged on the servile, and their culture was seldom high."[13] That it could not cope with the antitsarist radicalism that became an increasingly powerful intellectual force in Russia from the 1850s on is indicated by, among other things, the tendency of sons of Orthodox parish priests to become revolutionaries. A notable example was Nikolai Chernyshevski, who probably influenced Lenin's thinking more than anyone else except Karl Marx. It is worth noting that Joseph Stalin, whose politics combined Marxist justifications with medieval tsarist methods, revived the institution of the patriarchate during World War II. He thus sought to tap the Russian peasantry's residual devotion to the traditional values represented by the Russian Orthodox church. Although for the most part that church's clergy have repaid the Soviet authority for the limited breathing space allowed to them, there has been more resistance, at any rate since Stalin, than was the case under the tsars.

In the remainder of this historical overview we offer some necessarily speculative answers to two questions, or rather to two sets of questions. First, why, in 1917, did a mighty empire, hundreds of years in the making and for additional hundreds of years one of the great powers of Europe and the world, so suddenly collapse? Second, what features of tsarism survived in the new Soviet system, whose creators proclaimed the intention of smashing the old Russian regime and moving to its replacement by at least the first stage of a new and better order in Russia and eventually throughout the world?

The peculiar character of the Russian state and of state-citizen relations in Russia provides a clue to answering both questions.

[13]Hugh Seton-Watson, *The Decline of Imperial Russia* (New York: Praeger, 1952), p. 13.

Robert Tucker, in a study cited earlier, pointed out: "The fact that the state, by virtue of its role in Russian historical experience, had come to be widely regarded as an alien "abstract entity" is of great importance for an understanding of the turbulent course of events in Russia between 1855 [when after the Crimean War, which went badly for Russia, a new tsar, Alexander II, began a process of reform that created more problems than it solved] and 1917." In this connection Tucker quotes the distinguished Russian emigrant historian Michael Karpovich, who wrote, "A few days of street disorders in St. Petersburg, and the refusal of the soldiers of the city garrison to put them down, were enough to topple the tsarist regime. It made no real attempt to defend itself, for *it proved to have no supporters.*"[14]

Among Western historians and to a degree among their Russian counterparts in the pre-Soviet period, there has long been a considerable measure of agreement on a number of factors to which the collapse of the Russian empire in 1917 can be attributed. One of these factors was the lack of a politically powerful bourgeoisie and the interest groups and other channels by which society as a whole might have pressured the autocracy to shape policies that could have resolved problems posed by modernization, especially in the nineteenth and early twentieth centuries. There was also growing discontent, especially in the last thirty or forty years of imperial rule, among many of the non-Russian nationalities, who were increasingly irked by the Russification policies adopted by the last two tsars (Alexander III, 1881–1894; Nicholas II, 1894–1917) in an effort to contain centrifugal forces springing from the spread of nationalism from Western to Eastern Europe. To the Russian liberals' petitions for changes in the relationship between the imperial power and society and particularly for the gradual introduction of representative political institutions, the tsars, including Alexander II (1856–1881), the liberator of the serfs and prime mover in introducing the other major reforms of the 1860s, of course turned a deaf ear. The tsars and their upper-level bureaucratic advisers had good reason to think that in a country in which a series of increasingly radical oppositional groups engaged in underground antigovernment agitation and political assassination, relaxation of repression would invite social and political disintegration. It is true, of course, that

---

[14]Quoted in Tucker, "Image of Dual Russia," p. 591. Italics in original.

the reforms of the 1860s constituted first steps: the beginnings of a legal system like that of the West, and limited local self-government institutions in the *zemstvos*. On the basis of these, gradual progress toward the building of a constitutional order might have been made if the tsars had given a freer hand to able and loyal statesmen who might have been able to reverse the deterioration culminating in the catastrophe of 1917. Unfortunately, probably all of the Russian rulers after Peter the Great and certainly those after Catherine the Great were unequal to the tasks with which history confronted them. They were all, even the most responsive and adaptive of them, under the spell of what Hugh Seton-Watson called the "dogma of autocracy."[15]

A few years before the abortive 1905 revolution, which Lenin called the "dress rehearsal" for the revolution of 1917, destroyed the tsarist system (both revolutions, like the reforms of the 1860s, were in large part the results of Russian military defeats), the incompetent but stubborn Nicholas II had spurned as "senseless dreams" the request of some patriotic citizens, members of local government bodies, that they be "given the right to state their desires to the Tsar." The great Russian historian Klyuchevski thereupon predicted that Nicholas II would be the last Russian tsar.[16] If even patriots like Klyuchevski with good contacts in court circles foresaw doom ahead for the monarchy, radicals like Lenin of course perceived opportunity in the crisis-torn situation confronting Russia under Nicholas, especially during World War I, although even Lenin found himself surprised by Nicholas's abdication on March 15 (New Style), 1917.

Russia lacked the infrastructure of social and political institutions that in Western Europe enabled the civil society, partly in opposition to but also partly in cooperation with the political authorities, to create a relatively flexible, relatively stable sociopolitical order.[17] As Hugh Seton-Watson pointed out in a major work:

[15]Seton-Watson, *Decline of Imperial Russia,* pp. 378ff. Seton-Watson here insightfully compares the political instability of Russia in the last sixty years of imperial rule with the revolutionary situation generated in many of what are now called less developed countries, of which Russia in many ways was one.

[16]George Vernadsky, *Russian Historiography* (Belmont, Mass.: Nordland, 1978), p. 131.

[17]For an insightful comparison of the far greater success in creating a "civil society" in the West than in Russia and the disastrous impact on Russia of this gap see Marc Raeff, *The Well-Ordered Police State* (New Haven, Conn.: Yale University Press, 1983).

Yet it was [in the declining years of the empire] still unrealistic to apply West European categories to Russia and to speak of a *bourgeoisie,* of a single homogeneous middle class. Russian bureaucrats, businessmen and intelligentsia did not share a common ethos. . . . The capitalists of Russia were drawing nearer in outlook to their European or North American counterparts . . . but they mostly retained their indifference to political rights. . . . Finally, the intelligentsia remained . . . rebellious, rejecting . . . the values of a European *bourgeoisie.* For the most part they . . . believed themselves resolutely opposed to autocracy in principle, yet in many cases the objection was to an autocracy which served the existing social system rather than to autocracy as such.[18]

We round out our survey of the possible factors involved in the collapse of the tsarist system with a brief summary of Richard Pipes's argument that the concept of *patrimonialism,* as he applies it, provides the best approach to explaining the early success and the later failures of that system.[19] Pipes defines patrimonial states as those in which "political authority is conceived and exercised as an extension of the rights of ownership, the ruler (or rulers) being both sovereign of the realm and its proprietor. The difficulty of maintaining this type of regime in the face of steadily increased contact with a differently governed west has brought about in Russia a condition of permanent internal tension that has not been resolved to this day."[20]

In early Russia the locus of political authority was the private domain of the prince or tsar. Gradually Muscovy became the most powerful of the Russian principalities and transformed Russia into "a giant royal state." Pipes finds differences between the ancient medieval Russian state and the feudal West, where the contractual relationship between lord and vassal "produced a whole network of dependencies," and similarities between Russia and the Hellenistic states of the late ancient world.[21] By the middle of the seventeenth century, according to Pipes, the tsars had succeeded "in transforming Russia into a gigantic royal domain."[22] The system created by this process of territorial aggrandizement in-

[18]Hugh Seton-Watson, *The Russian Empire* (Oxford: Clarendon Press, 1967), p. 538.

[19]Richard Pipes, *Russia Under the Old Regime* (New York: Scribners, 1974).

[20]Ibid., p. xxii.

[21]Ibid., pp. 20, 52.

[22]Ibid, p. 85.

cluded "the crown's monopoly on political authority, its ownership of nearly all the landed, commercial and industrial wealth,
its tight grip on the social classes and its ability to isolate the country from unwanted foreign influences. . . . " Increased contact
with the West, however, made Russia's rulers realize that the system their forebears had built "set strict limits on what they could
accomplish because it deprived them of support from a freely acting society."[23] Their response was the well-known reforms of Peter I and Catherine II, which set in motion developments that by
the end of the eighteenth century had virtually freed the aristocracy from obligatory service to the state and opened up the country to Western cultural influences. The monarchy, however,
retained and never formally relinquished a monopoly of political
power.[24]

We shall not summarize Pipes's treatment of the peasant question except to note that he stresses not peasant poverty but the
"inherent arbitrariness" of serfdom, "that is, the serf's permanent subjection to the unbridled will of other men."[25] Like many
other historians, Pipes reports a steady deterioration in the economic situation of the peasants in the decades after the emancipation in 1861; their condition, he believes, was worse in 1900
than in 1800. This was due partly to the aftereffects of the onerous
terms of the emancipation but even more to the growing rural
overpopulation. Economic misery was not compensated for by any
substantial improvement in the majority of the peasants' political
rights or social status, although increasingly as the nineteenth century wore on, relatively well-off peasants were acquiring lands that
impoverished smaller holder noblemen were forced to sell. The
mood of the peasants generally was worsening and their disrespect
for authority was growing. By the beginning of the twentieth century, there was "a situation ripe for violence," and "the events
of 1905 [Russia's defeat in war with Japan, the 1905 revolution,
and the tsar's grant of a limited form of parliamentary government, quickly followed by reverse moves] gave the peasants a sense

[23]Ibid, pp. 112–13.
[24]Ibid, pp. 112–14. See the impressive description of the still vast powers held,
according to law at least, by the monarch as of the beginning of the twentieth
century in Robert Tucker, *Stalin as Revolutionary* (New York: Norton, 1973), pp.
1–2.
[25]Ibid, p. 169.

of power such as they had never possessed before. When in 1917 Nicholas II suddenly abdicated, there was no force left to restrain them.''[26] Moreover, Russia at this juncture lacked the other sociopolitical forces that in England, France, and other Western countries had — not without turbulence, to be sure — succeeded in substituting representative, constitutional government for absolute monarchy.

In his concluding chapters Pipes argues that even in the period of the autocracy's final fumbling decline the Russian nobility was incapable of adapting to the capitalist economy beginning to develop in late nineteenth-century Russia (economic growth rates in the period roughly from 1890 to 1914 were high). This group and what he calls the ''missing'' bourgeoisie were still inclined to fawn on the autocracy, which for centuries had been ''the ultimate source of all material benefits'' (and, one might add, the ultimate symbol of national unity and identity). As for the autocracy itself, it displayed a measure of creativity and originality only in the area of political repression. Alexander III's regulation on ''protection . . . of government and public tranquility'' — dated August 14, 1881 — was, says Pipes, ''the most important piece of legislation in the history of imperial Russia between the abolition of serfdom in 1861 and the October Manifesto of 1905 (when Nicholas II sanctioned the Duma, or limited legislature).'' Pipes calls the system of rule by emergency decree introduced under this regulation — which included such measures as requiring police permission for establishing a newspaper, consulting various (including scientific) books in libraries, surveillance of citizens whom the police considered unreliable, and elaborate censorship — a protopolice state. It constituted the first stage, he argues, of the type of state that was to be established by Lenin's Bolsheviks. Its severity was mitigated by loopholes resulting from the existence of private property, relative ease of getting permission to travel abroad, and the Western influences that pervaded the court and upper bureaucracy. Its ''principal if unintended accomplishment,'' according to Pipes, was ''to radicalize Russian society.''[27]

Many who might have supported the government or at least remained neutral were driven to join the revolutionary move-

---

[26]Ibid, p. 169.
[27]Ibid,, p. 315.

ments because of sometimes brutal and more often incompetent and unjust official policies. Contemplating the political scene in the last decades of old Russia, one thinks of Professor Michael Karpovich's description (one of the authors of this book recalls it from a description by Karpovich in a lecture at Harvard in the 1930s) of the tsarist political system as one of "despotism tempered by inefficiency." The main beneficiary of this system was Lenin's Bolsheviks. One of the justifications offered by Lenin for the military or combat structure of the new cadre political party that he designed as his instrument to wage political warfare against the tsarist government was that only such a centralized, disciplined, and secretive party could cope with the tsar's secret police. As Leonard Schapiro has argued in an important book, Lenin, like some Russian revolutionaries before him, sought not so much to destroy autocracy in Russia as to "capture it and make it work in the interests of a different class."[28]

Also stressing continuity between the Bolsheviks and tsarist autocracy but focusing particularly on the police machine as the essence of aristocracy in its last phase, Pipes sees Lenin's Cheka (the earliest name of the Soviet political police) as continuator but "with much vaster powers" of the imperial police apparatus. Pipes credits both Lenin and his fellow revolutionaries and the imperial government with believing that when they instituted repressive measures these moves were temporary emergency measures. He attributes the persistence of repression under both tsarist and Soviet regimes to the "unenforceable" idea that politics can be monopolized by one group or one ideology. He concludes his book with the emphatic and perhaps overly optimistic assertion that "any government that persists in this notion must give ever wider berth to its police apparatus and eventually fall victim to it."[29]

The preceding remarks lead logically to the last point to be discussed in this historical introduction: the question of continuity and similarity, as well as of change and dissimilarity, between the tsarist and Soviet polities. Among the most important similarities between tsarist autocracy and Soviet communism is the existence under both systems of bureaucracies answerable to powerful chief

---

[28]Leonard Schapiro, *Rationalism and Nationalism in Nineteenth Century Russian Political Thought* (New Haven, Conn: Yale University Press, 1967), p. 167. See also pp. 130–142.

[29]Pipes, p. 318.

executives. In the former case the executive was the emperor; in the latter, it is the General Secretary of the Communist Party of the Soviet Union (usually hereafter referred to as CPSU or simply the party), who can promote or demote bureaucrats arbitrarily. Another similarity is a social stratum — we avoid the term *class* because of definitional and conceptual problems associated with it — that enjoys extensive material privileges and a life-style significantly different from that of the vast majority of the population.[30]

Both the pioneering article by Edeen and the impressive monograph of Pintner, Rowney, and their collaborators present evidence indicating that even in the 1920s and increasingly from about 1930 on, the Soviet leaders were engaged in restoring the "traditions of hierarchy and precedence" first formally codified in Peter the Great's Table of Ranks and abandoned during the few idealistic-utopian years of the regime, though even then not completely.[31]

Matthews ends his sober, well-documented study of privileges in the USSR with a few pages of comparison between American and Soviet elite living standards and life-styles. He finds that "the Soviet elite family in the early seventies enjoyed a standard of living roughly equal to . . . an average American household."[32] He concludes that "after more than sixty years of avowedly egalitarian social engineering Soviet society may still have a hiatus between average and elite levels, not greatly unlike that observable in the world's first capitalist land."[33] Not very surprisingly,

---

[30]On bureaucratic continuities, see, for example, Alf Edeen, "The Civil Service: Its Composition and Status," in Black, *Transformation of Russian Society,* pp. 274–92; Walter Pintner and Don K. Rowney, *Russian Officialdom* (Chapel Hill: University of North Carolina Press, 1980) and on the Soviet elite's privileges, Mervyn Matthews, *Privilege in the Soviet Union* (London: Allen & Unwin, 1978).

[31]Quotation above in Pintner and Rowney, *Russian Officialdom,* p. 371. Edeen traces the tortuous process of forming a new bureaucratic hierarchy under Soviet rule with many characteristics of the tsarist one but open to entry by social strata largely excluded before the revolution. According to him, "Peter's rejected table of ranks was in fact re-established, with its ostentatious titles, rank distinctions and uniforms. . . . " Edeen, "Civil Service," p. 287. Edeen, as far as we know, was the first scholar to mention the Soviet institution of the "nomenklatura," or list of official positions, about which we shall have more to say, especially in the chapter on elite recruitment. (See Edeen, p. 286.)

[32]Matthews, *Privileges in the Soviet Union,* p. 177.

[33]Ibid, p. 183.

Matthews finds that "party and state bureaucrats, managers of large productive enterprises, representatives of the technical and artistic intelligentsia . . . and military, security and diplomatic services" are the materially most favored groups in the USSR.[34]

Many other areas of resemblance between the tsarist and Soviet polities and societies come easily to mind. One of the most obvious and important is the proneness of the two systems to apply arbitrary coercion against persons regarded by the political leaders and their agents as subversive. Of course, the extent of such coercion has been infinitely greater under the Soviet than it was under the tsarist regime. Vastly more people have been executed or perished in Soviet labor camps in the sixty-six years of communist rule than died under persecution in the many centuries of tsardom. Other parallels between the two regimes include the notion of the sacredness of the state and its boundaries (the incident of the downing of an unarmed Korean passenger jetliner on September 1, 1983, exemplified Soviet attitudes about this sphere), venality and corruption among public officials, aversion of the two regimes to emigration by their citizens, and the conviction that one of the prerogatives of government is the right and duty to decide what books their subjects may read, what paintings they may view, etc. In these and other spheres current Soviet norms are stricter than those prevalent under the tsars but much less strict than the policies imposed by Joseph Stalin, who, not so incidentally, apparently believed that "the Russian people is a tsarist people."[35]

Most of the continuities we have identified so far between tsarism and Sovietism refer to attributes that most Westerners would perceive as negative. We should, however, take note of the "altruistic devotion to ideas and to visions of social betterment" among some members of the Russian pre-Soviet intelligentsia and of the late Max Hayward's opinion that "the majority of Soviet writers have acquitted themselves with honor in a situation which

---

[34]Ibid, p. 27.

[35]Anton Antonov-Ovseyenko, *The Time of Stalin* (New York: Harper & Row), p. 223. In *The Marquis de Custine and His Russia in 1839* (Princeton, N.J.: Princeton University Press, 1975), George Kennan described striking continuities, especially in controls over contacts of Russians and foreigners, between the rule of Nicholas I and that of Stalin and, to a lesser degree, that of Brezhnev.

required more courage, patience, intelligence and fortitude than could ever be imagined by people who live in more fortunate circumstances."[36]

Basic traits of the new Soviet state and society — perhaps most of all its vastly enhanced powers of penetration of society and of mobilization and domination over the mass of the citizenry — confirm the belief of twentieth-century comparative students of revolution such as Crane Brinton and Theda Skocpol who, despite differing viewpoints, agreed that one of the most important results of great social revolutions, such as that which began in France in 1789 or in Russia in 1917, was a great increase in the centralization and efficiency of state power.[37] In the Russian communist case, military and police power grew as the new regime defended itself against foreign and domestic foes, including large elements of the non-Russian population that resisted continued Russian rule (in some cases, such as that of the Poles, successfully) and also a substantial portion of both Russian and non-Russian peasants, whose primary concern was to be able to freely sell whatever portion of their crops they did not need to feed themselves and their families. By forced collectivization of agriculture Stalin put the regime in control of grain, drove millions of peasants off the land and into factories, and sent to labor camps millions of so-called kulaks (peasants categorized as rich often only because they owned a few animals or had been denounced to the police by hostile or frightened neighbors). Thus he was responsible for enormous losses of life and for a deep fear of the authorities that is by no means dead even today.

Thus the peasants, who until the 1950s comprised the largest socioeconomic group in the country, were tamed in a process probably as rigorous as any that has occurred in modern history. This process included such episodes as the famine in Ukraine in 1932–1933, in which millions of peasants died partly because of the regime's manipulation of food supplies in order to suppress

---

[36]Max Hayward, *Writers in Russia,* ed. and with introduction by Patricia Blake (New York: Harcourt Brace Jovanovich, 1983), pp. 44, 117.

[37]Crane Brinton, *The Anatomy of Revolution* (New York: Vintage, 1965); Theda Skocpol, *States and Social Revolutions* (London: Cambridge University Press, 1979). Very early, the insightful Tocqueville had pointed to the association between revolution and enhanced state power. See Alexis de Tocqueville, *The Old Regime and the French Revolution* (Garden City, N.Y.: Doubleday Anchor Books, 1955. Originally published in 1856.)

resistance to collectivization. The landed aristocracy and most of the old business and professional classes had already been crushed during the turbulent years of civil war and foreign intervention (1917–1921). Some members of these classes, in some cases out of patriotic motives, did not join fellow members of their class in the unsuccessful armed resistance to the new regime of those years, and many of them proved useful to the new rulers in their efforts to restore the economy and government service to a level of effectiveness adequate to lay the foundations for the forced-draft industrialization program launched by the communists in 1929–1930.

Mention of the subjection of those members of the old elite who were not killed in civil war or did not flee after defeat of the anti-Bolshevik armies reminds us that the differences as well as the similarities between communist and tsarist Russia are profound. The ideological-symbolic perspectives of the Bolsheviks who came to power in 1917–1921 differed drastically from those of the tsarist elite. Despite the surging growth of capitalism in the last decades of the empire, tsarist Russia was still a deeply traditional country. Its main institutions were divine right monarchy and a state-dominated Russian Orthodox church. Its elite still consisted largely of landed aristocrats and courtiers, many with a pedigree of centuries of exalted titles, as well as, to an increasing degree, newly rich merchants and manufacturers. The tsarist elite was culturally cosmopolitan and sophisticated and in some cases effete. Suddenly this partly hereditary, partly self-made, and very much state-dominated elite was replaced by a much tougher, coarser cadre that was, despite its "internationalism," more parochial, dedicated to its self-chosen mission of the revolutionary transformation first of Russia and then of the world. Lenin's Bolsheviks quickly established dominance over their Menshevik rivals in the Russian Social-Democratic Labor Party and also over the Left Socialist Revolutionary Party. For a time, into 1918, members of the latter group had cooperated uneasily with the Bolsheviks in a coalition government that fell apart in 1918 partly because its minority non-Bolshevik members found the harassment and persecution inflicted upon them by their dictatorial Bolshevik partners intolerable. By 1921 at the Tenth Congress of the Soviet Communist Party (which, however, still retained in its official name the designation Bolshevik in small letters until its Nineteenth

Congress in October 1952), pretensions to monolithism were officially asserted when at Lenin's insistence a resolution was adopted against formation of fractions within the party.

CLASSIFYING THE SOVIET POLITICAL SYSTEM

Although some social scientists apply the concept *totalitarian* to the Soviet political system, this term has been the subject of heated debate. Some scholars doubt whether the post-Stalin Soviet political system can be meaningfully studied as totalitarian, and others reject the very utility of the concept. First introduced into the language by fascist writers and their opponents, the term *totalitarian* lacks precise definition but normally has referred to political systems in which a unified and centralized political organization — the state — dominates the society typically by using a terroristic police apparatus and a single, monopolistic party that demands unqualified acceptance by the populace of the rulers and their ideology. Often totalitarianism has been distinguished from less oppressive but still nondemocratic systems, which are given the broader and less emotionally loaded label of *authoritarian.* The author of a recent study of comparative political systems differentiates between totalitarianism and authoritarianism by stressing, in the first case, the important role played by a comprehensive, messianic, and mandatory ideology; the concentration of unaccountable power in a single individual or a small group, who are unremovable except by force; and the attempt to mobilize the entire society in channels of directed participation. He defines authoritarian systems, by contrast, as those that have a limited degree of political pluralism and lack an elaborate guiding ideology (are guided rather by general, open-ended mentalities), in which the populace is largely inactive or unmobilized except on certain ceremonial occasions such as national elections and in which there are relatively predictable limits on the rulers' power.[38]

Unlike earlier writers on totalitarianism, such as Hannah Arendt, Linz does not insist on mass terror as one criterion of such a system. Other scholars have questioned, however, whether ideological belief and indoctrination are of sufficient importance in

[38]See Juan J. Linz, "Totalitarian and Authoritarian Regimes," in Fred I. Greenstein and Nelson W. Polsby, eds., *Handbook of Political Science,* 8 vols. Vol. 3, *Macropolitical Theory* (Reading, Mass.: Addison-Wesley, 1975), pp. 175–411 at pp. 188–89 and 264.

fascist or communist systems to warrant their classification as totalitarian. One writer, for example, asserts that it is ''the skillful use of political power, not ideology, [that] determines the success of failures of modern authoritarianism. . . . Mussolini, Hitler, Lenin and Stalin confidently believed in totalitarian solutions and in the ultimate success of totalitarian systems. This does not mean that they achieved it or that it could be accomplished. After all, they have left a legacy of authoritarian instruments: the single authoritarian party, the political police, and the parallel and auxiliary structures in charge of mobilization and control.''[39]

The discussion of totalitarianism is a dispute over language and only partly a discussion of the actual, empirical nature of power relations in communist or fascist regimes. Still, insofar as the Soviet political system has undergone significant change since the death of Stalin and the dismantling of some of the more dysfunctional features of his rule, we are likely to find that use of the concept of totalitarianism, however we define it, makes us insufficiently attentive to such processes as the increased role of subcentral elites and specialists in articulating interests. It may be more accurate, therefore, to regard the Soviet system as a modernized variant of authoritarianism. In it open opposition is illegitimate, but extensive popular participation initiated by the leadership and supervised by the party is encouraged. In the end, the general label that we use to characterize the Soviet political system matters less than a proper understanding of the reality to which the label refers.[40]

SOVIET POLITICS IN COMPARATIVE PERSPECTIVE

The Soviet political system cannot be understood solely in terms of the historical experiences that have shaped it. To explain its political processes we must also locate the system in the universe of political systems by applying a more general comparative framework. In this book we use the framework of analytic concepts developed by Almond and Powell in their pioneering work *Comparative Politics: A Developmental Approach* and more recently in

---

[39]Amos Perlmutter, *Modern Authoritarianism* (New Haven, Conn.: Yale University Press, 1981), p. 65.

[40]Jerry F. Hough, ''Pluralism, Corporatism and the Soviet Union,'' in Susan Gross Solomon, ed., *Pluralism in the Soviet Union* (New York: St. Martin's Press, 1983), pp. 57–58.

the same authors' *Comparative Politics: System, Process, and Policy,*
2nd ed.[41]

Use of this body of comparative political theory and terminology does not imply that all political systems are more alike than
they are different or that the differences separating the Soviet
from, say, the British political system are negligible. Rather, the
comparative approach looks beyond ideological and organizational differences to identify those common processes by which
any political system maintains its identity through time while coping with pressures emanating from the domestic and international
environments with which they interact. The varied methods by
which parties, governments, and peoples select their leaders, decide on policies, deal with opposition, and shape the attitudes and
values of their youth reflect variation in their responses to certain
universal needs shared by all political systems. These needs determine the functions performed by the processes and institutions
of the system. Stable patterns of institutional behavior are called
structures. The structural-functional theory, then, presumes the
existence of a universally applicable set of political processes that
may be described as functions served by particular structures of
political systems. In the remaining portion of this section we shall
define the terms used to analyze the structures and functions of
the Soviet political system.

POLITICAL CULTURE AND POLITICAL STRUCTURE

Political culture is a basic component of our conceptual framework. As Verba says, it refers to "fundamental beliefs about the
nature of political systems." Almond and Powell define political
culture as the totality of "attitudes, beliefs, values, and skills that
are current in a population," and they note as well the existence
of currents of attitudes among certain groups of the population,
such as ethnic groups, that may reflect distinct differences from
the political culture of the nation.[42] The degree to which the dominant values and beliefs of the society as a whole are shared among

[41]Gabriel A. Almond and G. Bingham Powell, *Comparative Politics: A Developmental Approach* (Boston, Mass.: Little, Brown, 1966); idem, *Comparative Politics:
System, Process, and Policy,* 2nd ed. (Boston, Mass.: Little, Brown, 1978).

[42]Lucian W. Pye, "Introduction: Political Culture and Political Development," in Lucian W. Pye and Sidney Verba, *Political Culture and Political Development* (Princeton, N.J.: Princeton University Press, 1965), p. 518; Almond and
Powell, *Comparative Politics,* p. 13.

all of its members varies widely among different political systems. In nations such as Russia that have experienced rapid and drastic social and political change there are likely for a long time to be ideological, political, and cultural cleavages between the champions of the revolutionary ideology from among whom the new political elite is recruited and members of the society, especially in older age brackets, who cling to traditional patterns and may try to raise children or grandchildren in accordance with them. When the revolutionary elite seeks to make over the political culture of the society by the use of force and mass political indoctrination, individuals in various occupational, ethnic, or religious categories whose beliefs the rulers regard as inimical to the fulfillment of their revolutionary aspirations may be classified as counterrevolutionaries and suppressed.

In an effort to inculcate a new and revolutionary political culture rapidly and effectively, the elite employs with special intensity and vastness of scope the techniques of political mobilization. Political mobilization in some forms is characteristic of all modern political orders.[43] At a minimum, political mobilization refers to the activation of the energies and loyalties of the population for political goals by making members of the society available to play new roles in political life or by making groups previously outside active politics into committed participants. Some political systems — particularly those in which political institutions or national identity are weakly rooted because of revolutionary change — devote extraordinary effort toward mobilizing the society. They may direct intense ideological appeals to the populace or spread organizers out among towns and villages. In communist and other revolutionary societies, mobilization of the public is an especially important priority of the rulers.[44]

In their early phases, to consolidate their goals revolutionary elites often attempted to break the power of social attachments that weaken their grip on power. Through coercive means they suppress religious, educational, political, and other associations that articulate interests contrary to the elite's self-proclaimed revolutionary mission. Characteristic of a mobilizing revolutionary

[43]J. P. Nettl, *Political Mobilization* (New York: Basic Books, 1967), esp. chs. 5,6.
[44]See David Apter, *The Politics of Modernization* (Chicago, Ill.: University of Chicago Press, 1965), ch. 10.

regime in this phase is the subordination of the legal system to the political demands of the ruling elite. In addition, through control of the arts, the mass media, schools, and other instruments of communication and socialization, the rulers manipulate the flow of facts and ideas so as to generate a political culture that legitimates their power.[45]

With time, the attempt to reshape the political culture of society by creating a *new person* often assumes rigid and stultifying forms. Doctrines that once legitimated the aims of the revolutionary party in overthrowing the old ruling classes become the orthodoxy of a new elite. That something like this has evidently happened in the USSR is reflected in the ritualistic political practices by which the regime seeks to foster the impression among its populace and in the world outside its borders of unshakable unanimity and solidarity within its society. These ceremonial customs include the preoccupation with concealing differences of opinion within the party, the practice of recording unanimous decisions when groups vote, and the parades marking the anniversaries of the October Revolution, in which the population pays homage to Lenin, the Communist Party of the Soviet Union, and the state and party rulers. These and like practices would suggest that the political culture of the Soviet Union possesses remarkable stability, consensus, and conservatism. This apparent stability, however, like that of all established patterns in an era of unsettling technological, intellectual, and emotional change, may be more apparent than real. As we shall see in this book, the Soviet system may be no more able to contain the long-term effects of social change than can the open societies of the advanced industrial West.

Within the Soviet society, the effects of the denunciation of Stalin by his successor in power, Nikita Khrushchev, together with the effects of higher educational levels, wider internal communications, and contacts with the West, have already been felt in the form of challenges to the reigning orthodoxy of Marxist-Leninist doctrine. Intellectual dissent is by no means homogeneous,

---

[45]Two articles that offer a comparative analysis of mobilizing one-party regimes are Chalmers Johnson, "Comparing Communist Nations," in Chalmers Johnson, ed., *Change in Communist Systems* (Stanford, Calif.: Stanford University Press, 1970), and Samuel P. Huntington, "Social and Institutional Dynamics of One-Party Systems," in Samuel P. Huntington and Clement H. Moore, eds., *Authoritarian Politics in Modern Society* (New York: Basic Books, 1970), pp. 3–47.

but most of the dissidents have come from sectors of the population likely to be relatively cosmopolitan in outlook and to have relatively close links to foreign reference groups. Scientists, writers, artists, and members of non-Russian ethnic groups such as Jews, Ukrainians, and Lithuanians — especially younger members of these groups — comprise much of the dissident subculture. The dissenters share in worldwide intellectual culture. In much of their criticism of established Soviet beliefs and policies is an underlying belief that the Soviet system, even in its scientific and economic achievements, threatens important moral and political values. Not all challenges to the official political culture have emanated from the articulate and educated segments of society. Recently, despite the extreme sensitivity that the authorities display toward unauthorized working class activity, blue-collar workers have protested against their onerous working conditions and lack of political power by organizing strikes and even forming small and quickly suppressed labor unions.[46]

The official political culture of the USSR represents a set of operating principles and rationalizations of the political monopoly enjoyed by the ruling elite. These are presented to all citizens of the country as a set of precepts flowing from the universal truth of Marxism as developed and applied by the founder of the Soviet state, Vladimir Ilyich Lenin. This body of doctrine, called Marxism-Leninism, is said to be the core of the consciousness of every faithful Soviet citizen. An elaborate system of formal *political socialization,* meaning the acquisition of political beliefs, values, and attitudes by individuals, is organized and run by the ruling CPSU and embraces preschool institutions, schools and youth groups, and indoctrination of individuals and groups through oral, print, and broadcast media. Political socialization is a universal political process: every political system must shape the outlooks of each new generation that rises to maturity. In few political systems, however, is the effort to mold character and personality as elaborate or consistent as in the Soviet case. In the Soviet system, learning about politics is an overt and highly organized activity conducted under the direction of persons specially trained and authorized by the political authorities. In other types of systems,

[46]Marshall Goldman, *USSR in Crisis* (New York: Norton, 1983), pp. 108–12; Betsy Gidwitz, "Labor Unrest in the Soviet Union," *Problems of Communism* 31 (November-December 1982): 25–42.

such as those of Britain and the United States, attitudes about nonpolitical objects may affect attitudes toward the political system without extensive direction by schools and officials. In the Soviet case, political socialization is direct and sharply defined by the authorities; in democratic systems it is more indirect, diffuse, and casual. We must take care, however, not to assume that all individuals fully accept the norms adumbrated by Marxism-Leninism or that official doctrines are the only influences on socialization. Values and beliefs inherited from the prerevolutionary past, from religious faiths, from the democratic societies of the West, or from other sources, may, despite the regime's efforts to weaken or eliminate them, serve as important countercurrents to the official doctrine.[47]

THE POLITICAL SYSTEM AND FUNCTIONAL ANALYSIS

Almond and Powell distinguish among three levels of analysis of any political system: the level of the system itself, the level of the political processes that convert demands and supports into decision and action, and the level of the actual outputs of the political system as they interact with the foreign and domestic environments. Since political socialization is the process by which members of a polity acquire the knowledge, attitudes, and skills that enable the system to persist, Almond and Powell term it a *system-level function:* it relates to the maintenance of the political system and its adaptation to change.

A second system-level function is that of political recruitment, which refers to the selection of individuals to fill particular political roles — such as judge, policeman, or government minister — as well as to their assimilation of the knowledge and rules that govern appropriate performance in those roles. Since each political system needs to find, train, and distribute personnel for the enormous range of roles that comprise it, this function is performed in all political systems, but the Soviet system again reveals certain peculiarities. A highly organized set of procedures for selecting and training personnel in key positions has been developed to ensure party dominance over political recruitment and to create incentives among the incumbents of official posts to remain loyal

---

[47]We shall devote most of Chapters IV and V to a discussion of the official instruments of political socialization and shall leave an assessment of their effectiveness to those chapters.

to the political elite.[48] Thus, the highly organized and directed character of the structures performing this function distinguishes the Soviet system from those in which political recruitment reflects the pluralistic and competitive features of liberal democracy.[49]

A final system-level function is political communication, the process by which elites convey information and ideas to the general public, the public relates demands and supports to elites, and members of the political system exchange information with one another. Many channels of communication perform this function — the mass media, visits and letters from ordinary citizens to their representatives and other officials, promulgation of laws, court decisions, and other official decisions, and the voices of religious leaders, trade unions, scholars, businessmen, and other representatives of societal associations. Once again, however, the Soviet case is distinctive in the organization of structures that serve the communication function. Although the network of mass media and the techniques of parochial contacts resemble those of Western democracies in some respects — particularly the saturation of the society by newspapers, magazines, radio, and television — all such channels, as well as those within the ruling bureaucracies, are under close supervision by party officials. This supervision is intended to ensure that messages continually reaffirm the validity of Marxist-Leninist doctrine, support the decisions of the country's leaders, and exclude messages that would contradict these precepts. Since no private publishing or broadcasting is allowed and since all published communication is in principle subject to censorship, the Soviet authorities effectively ensure that they can expand or retract the limits of acceptable public communication according to their preferences. To be sure, private communication, restricted to members of primary social groups such as families, friends, and colleagues at work, largely lies outside the explicit political direction of the party. Frequently such channels convey values and ideas that counter the official

[48]See T. H. Rigby and Bohdan Harasymiw, *Leadership Selection and Patron-Client Relations in the USSR and Yugoslavia* (London: Allen & Unwin, 1983).

[49]A recent study of political elites that distinguishes between politicians and bureaucrats discusses elite recruitment as well as other characteristics of elite groups in Western Europe and the United States. See Joel D. Aberbach, Robert D. Putnam, and Bert A. Rockman, *Bureaucrats and Politicians in Western Democracies* (Cambridge, Mass.: Harvard University Press, 1981).

political culture, and they may serve as settings for the generation and dissemination of dissent.[50] By their nature, however, such settings of private communication cannot be used as channels through which to mobilize larger publics for alternative courses of political action. When dissension moves outside the zones of private communication and into the public realm — soliciting signatures on a protest petition, for example — the authorities act swiftly to suppress it.[51]

At the next level, Almond and Powell distinguish four general *process functions.* These are the processes by which the *inputs* to government — such as legal claims, contributions to candidates, demands for action, rallies of support or protest, publicity campaigns, and the like — are converted into the authoritative acts of political officials — or the *outputs* of politics. The four process functions include the articulation of interests, aggregation of interests, policy making, and policy implementation. Interest articulation refers to the formulation and expression of demands presented to political leaders, whether by individual citizens or by organized groups. Interest aggregation is the combination and generalization of such demands into platforms of broader application and with broader bases of support. Policy making is the selection among alternative courses of proposed action and the authoritative adoption of decisions about the use of governmental power for the accomplishment of particular ends. Policy implementation refers to execution or carrying out of policy, typically by bureaucratic government agencies.[52]

As we discuss the Soviet political system by means of the structural-functional framework, we shall call attention to structures in the Soviet case that take the place of the competitive parties and interest groups of democratic systems in formulating and articulating policy proposals. The differences between the functions performed by formally analogous structures — for example, the single party in the Soviet political system and the competitive mass parties in liberal democracies — reinforce the premise underlying

[50]See Jonathan Mark, "The Private Zone," Ph.D. diss., University of Oklahoma, 1981; Thomas Remington, "The Mass Media and Public Communication in the USSR," *Journal of Politics* 43 (August 1981): 803–17.

[51]See Chapter V for detailed discussion of political communication, together with references to the scholarly literature on the subject.

[52]See Almond and Powell, *Comparative Politics,* pp. 14–15.

functionalist theory that different types of political systems at different levels of development perform differently the functions we have named.

Some political scientists have called attention to the multiplicity of functions performed by such structures as the party, youth groups, trade unions, and soviets, adapting to functionalist framework to isolate some of the distinctive features of the Soviet system. In a radical adaptation of Almond and Powell's approach, the Australian scholar T. H. Rigby has offered a scheme emphasizing the dynamic and developmental character of the Soviet system. Aware, like most Soviet specialists, of the extreme concentration, scope, and dynamism of Soviet power, Rigby asserts that in the Soviet setting socialization and recruitment also influence the performance of the functions of internal and external order maintenance, legitimation, and policy implementation. Moreover, stressing the regime's preoccupation with accumulating and wielding unrestricted political power, Rigby identifies a set of transformation and adaptation functions, including political initiation, power realization, and appropriation and deployment of power, as well as political mobilization. In all Rigby identifies three general categories of functions performed by the system — those by which the system maintains itself and integrates its parts, those by which it transforms resources and adapts to its environment, and those through which it generates and exercises power. These categories are in turn broken down into eleven more specific functions.[53]

Other scholars have employed the functionalist perspective to analyze the nature of mass political participation in the Soviet system. Robert Sharlet has pointed out that participation in the Soviet context contributes to such functions as interest articulation — initiated by the party, not by the individual or the group — socialization, mobilization, and political communication. He has in effect identified participation as the major dependent variable of a sequence of stages of economic and political development in communist political systems. With greater modernization comes an expansion of the individual's social responsibility in the society. In communist systems, however, the ultimate goal of mass

---

[53]See T. H. Rigby, *Communist Party Membership in the USSR, 1917-1967* (Princeton, N.J.: Princeton University Press, 1968), pp. 18-44.

participation is to produce the "new man" who is expected to
internalize the political and social norms of the emerging communist society rather than "the autonomous individual of democratic systems."[54]

Theodore H. Friedgut, in a study of neighborhood-level citizen
organizations in the Soviet Union, showed the importance of participatory structures in the output side of the political system —
activities contributing to the implementation of policy — rather
than in the articulation and aggregation of policy demands or other
inputs. Such *mobilized participation,* besides being useful to the regime in legitimating its decisions, may also have unintended feedback effects on the regime itself, for example, by creating
community pressures for change. Thus, although mass-level participation in the Soviet Union is not a channel for the organization
of autonomous forces in the political arena and serves in the first
instance to mobilize and socialize citizens, it may have the effect,
among some citizens, of creating desires for more active participation.

Friedgut's observations alert us to the importance of studying
political systems at the third and final level of analysis outlined
by Almond and Powell: that which pertains specifically to the behavior of the political system in interaction with the domestic and
international environments in which it is situated. This is the policy level, which deals with the policy outputs of political systems,
the effects of policy upon the economy, the political culture, and
the international community, and the actual outcomes of policy.
The analysis of policy outputs and outcomes requires that we assess the performance of the system in three broad areas: the regulation of behavior of members of the society, the extraction of
resources from the economy, and the distribution of goods and
services to various segments of the population. Regulation, extraction, and distribution have short- and long-term consequences
for the effectiveness and legitimacy of the ruling elite; in turn,
effects altering the environment through policy have consequences
for the political system. This direction of influence — from the

[54]Robert S. Sharlet, "Systematic Political Science and Communist Systems"
and "Concept Formation in Political Science and Communist Studies: Concep-
tualizing Political Participation," in Frederic J. Fleron, Jr., ed., *Communist Studies
and the Social Sciences* (Chicago, Ill.: Rand-McNally, 1969), pp. 207–12, 244–53.

[55]Theodore H. Friedgut, *Political Participation in the USSR* (Princeton, N.J.:
Princeton University Press, 1979), ch. 1.

environment back to the political system — is called *feedback,* and we shall be discussing here the feedback effects of the Soviet political system's heavy emphasis upon political structures specializing in regulation and resource extraction for the sake of expanding the power and wealth of the state.

The studies by Rigby, Sharlet, and Friedgut cited above can stimulate our ingenuity in applying the structural-functional approach to the USSR. The framework is flexible and must be applied judiciously. It directs attention to essential features of an ensemble of related activities, the performance of each of which is necessary to the continued existence and effectiveness of the political system. At the same time, it points out that certain norms or structures may have negative, or *dysfunctional,* consequences for the system as a whole, registered through immediate or lagged feedback effects. However, the performance of functions may vary in accordance with historical circumstances within a fairly wide range. Moreover, because the functions are related, changes in the performance of one or more can affect the ways in which others are performed. Thus changes in performance, such as a reduction in regulatory capacity, would lead logically to a change in the performance of the interest articulation function. Such a change in the regulative performance of the system seems to have occurred after the death of Stalin. It made possible the limited articulation of hitherto suppressed demands and at the same time rendered less functional for the Soviet polity the methods of policy implementation used by the party and police agencies under Stalin.

What is meant by the term *political system?* What is distinctive about politics that allows us to compare all political systems? Almond and Powell observe that most definitions of politics and political systems link the political system with the legitimate use of physical coercion. Most imply "the rightful power to punish, to enforce, to compel. . . . [L]egitimate force is the thread that runs through the action of the political system, giving it special importance and coherence as a system. The political authorities, and only they, have some generally accepted right in a given territory to utilize coercion and to command obedience based upon it."[56]

According to David Easton, who pioneered in developing the

[56]Almond and Powell, *Comparative Politics,* p. 4.

concept of political system, an adequate definition "will reveal
. . . the life processes of political systems — those fundamental
functions without which no system could endure — together with
the typical modes of response through which systems manage to
sustain them."[57] Easton adds that "a political system can be designated as those interactions through which values are authori-
tatively allocated for a society." According to Easton, the
"essential variables of political life are the allocation of values and
the relative frequency of compliance with allocations made by the
Authorities."[58] The basic components of his analytic framework
are inputs of demands and supports, outputs of policies, and feedback, or information, about the results of past policy outputs, by
the use of which future adaptive outputs may be produced.

Like other recent theorists, Easton emphasizes that political
systems interact with and must cope with stresses, or pressures,
emanating from domestic or intrasocietal and international or ex-
trasocietal environments.[59] Leaders of revolutionary political parties and regimes, especially Marxist-Leninist ones, are almost
obsessively conscious of the dangers to the consolidation and prosperity of their regimes that may be posed by inputs from imperialist forces in the international environment. In our era of instant
worldwide electronic communication and military confrontation
all political systems face unprecedentedly complex problems of interaction with external environments, in terms both of military
security and of alien ideological influences.

We need now to provide a least a basic definition of another
related term, *subsystem*. Subsystem are components of the system
as a whole. They perform tasks related to the higher goals and
values of the systems to which they are subordinate. In the functionalist theory developed by Talcott Parsons, the political subsystem, a component of the social system, performs "goal
attainment" functions while the economy performs the function
of "resource adaptation."[60] If subsystems are highly differentiated one from another and specialized in function so that performance of the roles through which they act requires special

[57]David Easton, *A Systems Analysis of Political Life* (New York: Wiley, 1965), p.
17.
[58]Ibid., p. xx.
[59]Ibid., pp. 21, 22, 24.
[60]Talcott Parsons, *The Social System* (New York: Free Press, 1951).

training, attitudes, and norms that are not readily transferable to other spheres of life, they are said to be autonomous. In the United States political and economic subsystems are relatively autonomous. If, however, as in the USSR, the complexity and differentiation of structures performing distinct functions — such as the educational, communications, economic administrative, elite recruitment, and many other hierarchical agencies — do not also acquire values and perspectives distinct from those of the ruling political authorities, then subsystem autonomy is said to be weakly developed. Members and officials of the CPSU are strategically deployed in the command posts of all institutions and organizations and from them dominate political, economic, and cultural life. Moreover, within the dominant political institution, the CPSU, the lowest levels of territorial organization have no formal and little informal autonomy. There is a similar relationship between the CPSU and other organizations within society such as the government.

Despite minor semantic difficulties, the use of the political culture concept, together with the concepts of system and structure, offers substantial benefits. Because these categories are tools of comparative analysis, they enable us not only to relate polities to one another but also to perceive the special properties of particular political orders. The notion of political culture draws on the insights of history and anthropology. It invites us to perceive the present situation of a political community as the product of that community's past experience and as a dynamic, evolving product. Political culture is a diachronic (across time), or developmental, concept; political system and political structure are synchronic, or cross-sectional, concepts, orienting us to the relationships among elements of a polity at any given time. In combination, these analytical tools encourage us to view the polity as a persisting pattern of interdependent elements. To survive, it must often adapt to the stresses and strains of unpredictable environments, but, especially in systems of the Soviet type, it possesses the ability to influence its environments to a significant degree.

Insights derived at least in part from political culture, structural-functional, and systems concepts help us to ask relevant questions about the nearly seventy years of dominance by the communist party in the USSR and about the country's prospects for the future. Questions about persistence and change in political culture will draw our attention to significant aspects of tsarist autocracy that helped to shape the Russian version of Marxism and its application to Soviet Russia.

The notion of system helps us to understand the capacity of polities both to endure and to change. By successfully resisting external and internal pressures, by coping with stresses and strains emanating from their environments, but in so doing by altering without necessarily dismantling or abandoning their essential structures and practices, systems are constantly changing, yet persisting. They retain their identity and distinctiveness, their special pattern of continuity with past and future. The idea of the interdependence of the parts and functions of a system, when applied to politics, helps us to understand how changes in the CPSU's performance of its functions in the Soviet system, in particular at supreme leadership levels, have affected and been affected by recruitment of political leadership, the operations of government administration, cultural policy, relations with foreign powers, and other aspects of the system.

CHAPTER II

Political Culture

IN CHAPTER I, among other things, we briefly outlined the conception of political culture developed by Gabriel Almond and Sidney Verba and further refined by Almond and G. Bingham Powell. Before describing the political culture underlying and also justifying political behavior in the USSR, we need to provide some further definitional and contextual observations on political culture in general and on Soviet political culture specifically. In particular, it is necessary to realize how difficult it is for the outside observer to know just what are the "attitudes, beliefs, values and skills that are current in a population," as Almond and Powell put it in a statement already quoted in our first chapter.[1] Even for countries such as Britain or the United States where sophisticated attitudinal surveys are easy to conduct, there is much difference of opinion regarding basic pattens of political beliefs. However, despite the difficulties posed by official Soviet secrecy, Soviet citizens' fear of speaking candidly to foreigners about political matters, and other hindrances to observation and communication characteristic of the relatively closed Soviet system, much can be learned by patient study.

In certain respects, indeed, it is perhaps easier to study Soviet political culture than that of more open, loosely organized societies. This is perhaps particularly true in respect to the elite Soviet political culture of the Soviet leaders, or ruling few, who control the Soviet communications media and use them to socialize and

---

[1]Gabriel A. Almond and G. Bingham Powell, *Comparative Politics: A Developmental Approach* (Boston, Mass.: Little, Brown, 1966), p. 23.

mobilize the Soviet public. In so doing they are forced at least to some degree to reveal some of the assumptions underlying the commands and directions they constantly issue in the form of May Day and November 7 slogans, speeches on the anniversary of Lenin's birthday, and editorials in *Pravda* intended to rally the workers, peasants, and intelligentsia behind the CPSU in the struggle to perfect socialism and eventually communism in the USSR. Of course, one must weed out the elements of propaganda distortion, outright falsification, doubletalk, fantasy, and ritual contained in the official Soviet media and this can be a difficult operation. The task of interpreting the official sources, with respect to political culture, institutions and practices, and policies, is of course rendered easier by the use of the voluminous writings of foreign scholars and in recent years by the increasing availability of the writings and statements of the nearly 300,000 emigrants from the USSR now in Western Europe, Israel and the United States. The excellent works of journalists such as Hedrick Smith, Robert Kaiser, and David Shipler are also helpful.

Another topic worthy of attention is the degree to which ordinary, low-ranking Soviet people accept the Soviet official political culture. One author, who has produced the only relatively comprehensive book-length treatment of Soviet political culture, defines as the regime or official culture that which refers "to the ideology and practices which are prescribed and promoted by the regime," but he notes that the acceptance of this official culture by the citizenry "must remain a matter for empirical investigation." In addition, there is a "mass" political culture, "applying to the population at large," and an "elite" one, "characteristic of the political decision-makers and other such groups."[2]

Contrary to White, who states the intention of focusing on "mass" political culture in the USSR, we shall emphasize what we regard as major themes of the elite culture, realizing as we do

---

[2]Stephen White, *Political Culture and Soviet Politics* (London: Macmillan, 1979), p.14. White's study is particularly valuable for its effort to trace the historical roots of contemporary Soviet political culture, which according to him "is rooted in the historical experience of centuries of absolutism"(p. 21). Without rejecting this view, which tallies with the emphasis placed on continuities in Soviet and tsarist politics in our chapter, we feel that it underplays such distinctive features of the Soviet period, particularly in the Stalin era, as extreme coercion and terror and extraordinarily tight control of information and political participation by the central political leadership. Despite this shortcoming, White's book should be read by all those interested in Soviet political culture.

so that some of what we present could well be regarded as regime culture, since our data are drawn in substantial measure from official Soviet sources. With these themes, however, we seek to demonstrate how official statements reflect predispositions toward politically significant actions. We believe, for example, that when the Kremlin demands or asserts the existence of "unity" between Soviet leaders and people or among the USSR, the communist leadership of Eastern Europe, and nonruling communist parties everywhere, such a demand reflects the existence of a major operational political value. It can also, of course, reflect concern that this value is not at the moment being taken as seriously by the audiences to which the Politburo's messages are addressed as the latter considers desirable.

We regard as extremely pertinent to the study of Soviet political culture the judgment that "It makes sense to picture Soviet leaders as convinced and thoroughgoing Hobbesians, so persuaded of the precariousness of social cohesion and so appalled at the prospect of social breakdown, as to rate the absolute position of the sovereign as a supreme value in politics. They are Hobbesians, moreover, not Machiavellians, because they seek the bulwark against social breakdown in an institutional arrangement, the Communist Party of the Soviet Union, and not in the personal quality of the sovereign. If we imagine Soviet leaders proceeding from a serious conviction of the actual superiority of one-party (absolute) government over other forms, we find a great many of the familiar but characteristic features of Soviet politics taking their place in a coherent pattern."[3]

The author of the above quoted propositions finds that the Soviet leaders' main "principles of government" are "beliefs about

[3]John H. Miller, "The Communist Party: Trends and Problems," in Archie Brown and Michael Kaser, eds., *Soviet Policy for the 1980's* (Bloomington: Indiana University Press, 1982), pp. 1–34, at 1-2. Miller cites Archie Brown as a source of material "on the fear of social breakdown as a salient theme in Russian political thought." See A. H. Brown, *Soviet Politics and Political Science* (London: Macmillan, 1974), pp. 93–94, especially his quoting the eloquent words of Nadezhda Mandelshtam on "fear of chaos" as a source of support by the Soviet intelligentsia for a political system that restrains what some Soviet intellectuals perceive as a dangerous potential for anarchy among the common people. More recently David Shipler in his perceptive, insightful book *Russia: Broken Idols, Solemn Dreams* (New York: Times Books, 1983) has chosen as one of his major themes Russian fear of disorder *(besporiadok)*. See especially Chapter 6, "Order and Truth."

how organized society holds . . . together," such as "the vanguard role of the party" and the ban on factions in the party. These, he holds, are the "operative" aspects of ideology.

Second, "stylistic" features of Soviet politics, "such as the intense (and utterly non-Marxist) concern with security, control and social order," and other fundamentals of Soviet political life, "are features that should be expected of politics conducted by, and within, a single and sovereign political organization." Finally, and again briefly, summarizing, the same author sees as crucial to assuring the party's "vanguard" role: (1) the licensing of all non-party organizations and meetings; (2) centralized control, via the nomenklatura system, of all political recruitment; (3) penetration of other organizations and meetings by party members; (4) control of communications.[4]

Since most of the remainder of this chapter will be devoted to what we regard as major themes of the Soviet official political culture, what seems to be known about the mass political culture will now be summarized briefly. Stephen White has presented the most systematic available account of the mass culture. Running through his account is the view, which on the whole we share, that insofar as the Soviet regime has been successful in shaping the belief system of the Soviet peoples, especially the Russians, and to a considerably lesser degree that of the non-Russian peoples, this has been largely due to the high degree of compatibility between traditional Russian beliefs and practices and important Bolshevik goals. There are striking correspondences between the tsarist and Soviet systems in terms of what they have in common and what they lack, according to Western democratic criteria. At the same time, as we have already noted, we feel that White, although by no means oblivious to the differences between Soviet objectives and traditional Russian values, mutes these differences. He fails for example, to bring out as vividly as he might have the vastly greater scope and intensity of terror, coercion, fear, and in general the grimness of Soviet political life — despite its undeniable success in modernization and development — as compared both with the tsarist past, and with political life in Western democracies.[5]

---

[4]Ibid. p. xx.

[5]Some scholars believe that not merely beliefs and values but also the entire mass of behavior reflecting cultural learning should be taken as constituent elements of a political culture. If this broad view of political culture is adopted, then,

Despite obvious differences, however, such as the change in the status of organized religion (or indeed of all manifestations of religion) from a major political instrument of the tsarist government to a barely tolerated and continuously vilified negative phenomenon in the USSR, continuities between the two opposing systems abound. White's description of the tsarist "pattern of orientations to government" would fit its Soviet counterpart quite well. Thus, representative institutions were "weakly articulated and ineffective," popular political attachments "were highly personalized," and political knowledge and experience were confined to "an extremely limited circle." In addition, the scope of government was unusually broad, extending into fields in which Western governments tended not to interfere, such as "economic entrepreneurship and control, religion and morals, and the detailed administration of justice."[6]

In his discussion of the contemporary Soviet political culture, based on, among other sources, data obtained from interviews with Soviet emigrants and research done by Soviet social scientists in the USSR, White finds much evidence that, as he sums up in a chapter entitled "The Contemporary Political Culture," it is "as a blend of conformity and dissent, of genuine commitment to the Soviet system and pride in its achievements combined with considerable cynicism with regard to those presently responsible for its management" that this political culture may be characterized.[7]

---

as Robert C. Tucker shows, political culture cannot be accounted an *explanation* for behavior. The task of the political analyst, in this case, is *political ethnography*—that is, it consists in tracing and describing the entire pattern of political attitudes, views, values, and actions through which a political system reproduces and transforms itself. The basic statement of this view is by Robert C. Tucker, "Culture, Political Culture, and Communist Society," in *Political Science Quarterly,* 88, (June 1973): 173–90. Although this argument has some validity, it overlooks the possibility of tension and incongruence between the value orientations and beliefs characteristic of a prerevolutionary society and those which resulted from a revolutionary elite's adoption of a radical revolutionary ideology. The resulting amalgam of cultural outlooks may well be powerful explanatory factor in the resulting institutional system. See the stimulating discussion of this point in Archie Brown, ed. *Political Culture and Communist Studies* (Armonk, NY: M. E. Sharpe, 1985).

[6]White, *Political Culture and Soviet Politics,* ch. 2, "The Imprint of Autocracy," and ch. 3, "The Social Fabric of Absolutism." Quotations on p. 64.

[7]Ibid, pp. 84–112. Quotation on p. 111. Much of White's data is drawn from the now partly outdated but still useful study of Soviet emigrant attitudes conducted in the late 1940s and early 1950s by Alex Inkeles and Raymond Bauer.

White also finds that although such forms of political participation as "attendance at meetings or conferences," "lecturing
within the party educational system and acting as an unpaid police auxiliary" have vastly expanded the scope of participation in
public affairs as compared with the tsarist period, the available
forms of political participation and the vast official program of
indoctrination in Marxist-Leninist theory have failed to "bring
about a commitment to Marxist-Leninist values" in the Soviet
population "which would be sufficient" to legitimate Soviet rule.[8]

Contemporary Soviet political culture derives much — perhaps
most — of its emotional force from a broad spectrum of patriotic
and nationalistic sentiments, some of them contained in material
passed by the Soviet censors and some circulated in samizdat in
the USSR or published abroad (as in the case of most of the writings of Alexander Solzhenitsyn before his forced exile in February
1974, and those of other proponents of religious and "nationalist"
beliefs) or published abroad. The historian Roman Szporluk has
classified these patriotic-nationalistic beliefs and perspectives as
primarily "political" or primarily "cultural" in content. Political
nationalist attitudes, as long as they do not openly challenge basic
tenets of official "Marxist-Leninist," Soviet ideology, can be articulated in the USSR and indeed appear to have strong support
from powerful elements in the Soviet political elite. Culturally or
religiously oriented Russian patriotism, on the other hand, is often
subject to censorship and in some cases its proponents —
Solzhenitsyn, Leonid Borodin, Vladimir Osipov, and many others — have been subject to severe persecution and ultimately to
imprisonment.[9]

Actually, the roots of official Soviet patriotism, exalting the
workers' fatherland over the decadent, imperialist, and aggressive
world of capitalism, can be traced almost to the very beginnings

[8]White, *Political Culture and Soviet Politic,* p. 142. White, correctly in our opinion, foresees the possibility "that the Soviet political culture may not be unaf-
fected by the unpalatable choices, economic and otherwise, which future decades
appear likely to place before it." Ibid., p. 189.
[9]See Roman Szporluk, "History and Russian Ethnocentrism," in Edward
Allworth, ed., *Ethnic Russia in the USSR* (New York: Pergamon, 1980), pp. 41–
54; Frederick Barghoorn, "Four Faces of Soviet Russian Ethnocentrism, in Allworth, ed., *Ethnic Russia,* pp. 55–66; and, on Borodin, Shipler, *Russia,* ch. 6. Also
see John Dunlop, *The Faces of Contemporary Russian Nationalism* (Princeton, N. J.:
Princeton University Press, 1983).

of the Soviet state in 1917–1918, but full acceptance of the traditional tsarist concepts of *fatherland (otechestvo)* and *motherland (rodina)* did not occur until after Stalin gave the signal in the early 1930s.[10] In our time, David Shipler was able to say, without exaggeration we think, that "of all the ideas and beliefs and forces of allegiance that crisscross through Soviet society, patriotism is the most pervasive and the most powerful."[11]

Another of Shipler's observations with which it is difficult to disagree seriously, this one in regard to Soviet education, is that "it is the inflated regard for country that stands as the centerpiece of all that can be called political in Soviet education."[12] As he further notes, "It is ok to be both a nationalist and a communist; in fact, it is desirable because since the Soviet Union is at the vanguard of the Communist movement, devotion to the country becomes devotion to the cause." He found that the official efforts "at the blurring of nationalism and communism" found general acceptance among Soviet young people.[13]

Given the concern about Soviet national security presumably generated by memories of past life-and-death struggles kept alive

[10]On the early development of official Soviet patriotism and its relationship to Russian nationalism, see Frederick Barghoorn, *Soviet Russian Nationalism* (New York: Oxford University Press, 1956).

[11]Shipler, *Russia,* p. 278. Shipler stresses, again correctly, we believe, as a focus of Soviet patriotism, "the legacy of World War II, the Great Patriotic War." (See pp. 278–83.) Our reading of Soviet press in recent years yields the impression that patriotism based on memories of the events that decided whether or not the USSR was going to survive and become a superpower, vying with the United States for world leadership, has steadily grown more intense, even strident, since the last year of Jimmy Carter's presidency and especially during the years of Ronald Reagan's administration. For a particularly vivid manifestation, see Pravda's lead editorial for December 3, 1983. Entitled "Turning to History" (*Obrashchenie k istorii),* this editorial said, among other things, that while the United States and NATO were complicating the international situation to the utmost, Soviet peoples' memories of "the events of military history," especially of "the struggle against the dark forces of fascism" were growing sharper. It struck notes common in such messages, such as the need for heightened vigilance *(bditel'nost')* and for "military-patriotic instruction of youth" on a level appropriate to "the present dangerous developments of the international situation." In this connection, Professor Seweryn Bialer's article in the *New York Times,* 5 February 1984, reporting "fear" among ordinary Soviet people and "anger" against the United States among elites, is of interest, whether or not one agrees with his interpretation of the reasons for and significance of these attitudes. Although the focus and intensity of patriotic attitudes shift in response to events, their basic content has remained relatively unchanged over the years.

[12]Shipler, *Russia,* p. 106.

[13]Ibid., pp. 108–9.

in the propaganda described by Shipler, it is not surprising that evidence is available that Soviet foreign policy actions that have aroused alarm and indignation in the West, such as the intervention against the reformist Czechoslovak government led by Alexander Dubček in 1968, have in fact been "quite popular." It seems, however, that intervention in Czechoslovakia was more favorably received by both ordinary citizens and members of the elite than was the invasion of Afghanistan begun at the end of 1979.[14]

As the foregoing remarks about Soviet policy in Czechoslovakia and Afghanistan indicate, public response seems to have been either silent consent or, more likely in our opinion, apathy, which, considering the tightness of Soviet political controls, amounts to assent. This judgment, however, must be qualified in at least two ways. In the first place, as always in the study of Soviet public opinion, what can be learned about it by outside observers is so limited that it amounts all too often to no more than intelligent speculation. Second, it seems certain in view of what is known about the fate of dissenters and oppositionists in the USSR that the relative lack of resistance to intervention in Czechoslovakia

[14]On indications, based on interviews with Soviet emigrants in Israel, of Soviet attitudes toward the invasion of Czechoslovakia, see White, *Political Culture,* p. 106. See also Victor Zaslavsky, *The Neo-Stalinist State* (Armonk, N.Y.: M. E. Sharpe, 1982), ch. 2, "Adult Political Socialization." There was, of course, significant opposition to Soviet policy toward the Prague Spring in Czechoslovakia among Soviet dissidents, and this apparently was shared by many who, unlike academician Andrei Sakharov, did not openly criticize the intervention. On negative attitudes expressed not only in public statements but also in street demonstrations, see Peter Reddaway, "Policy towards Dissent since Khrushchev," in T. H. Rigby, Archie Brown, and Peter Reddaway, *Authority, Power and Policy in the USSR* (New York: St. Martin's Press, 1980); also Frederick Barghoorn, *Détente and the Democratic Movement in the USSR* (New York: Free Press, 1976), pp. 46–47. Jiri Valenta argues "uncontrolled reformism" in Czechoslovakia "would infect the other members" of the Warsaw Pact, "and perhaps in the long run the Soviet Union itself." See his *Soviet Intervention in Czechoslovakia, 1968* (Baltimore, Md.: Johns Hopkins Press, 1979), p. 136. Regarding responses to Moscow's military intervention in Afghanistan, Henry Bradsher in *Afghanistan and the Soviet Union* (Durham, N.C.: Duke University Press, 1983), pp.214–17, presents evidence that, among other things, service in Afghanistan had caused "grumbling in the ranks" of the Soviet troops sent there and by 1981 was "beginning to cause a heroin addiction problem" for Soviet soldiers, and also that by the second year of the war the Soviet leadership was finding it "increasingly difficult to ignore public opinion." However, he also points out that the Soviet government's tight control of information regarding the situation in Afghanistan greatly reduced the impact of that brutal war on both Soviet and world public opinion.

and Afghanistan, as well as other major foreign ventures or even domestic policies, is at least partly the result of fear of official reprisals in the event of failure to comply with explicit or implicit official commands. Compliance, or apparent acceptance, can also be regarded as in part the result of effective censorship and information control. It would also be unrealistic to overlook the possibility that, at least in the area of foreign relations, widespread patriotic and nationalistic attitudes, especially among the dominant Russian component of the population, provide a basis for a considerable element of willing support for the Soviet leadership's actions. Perhaps one of the most significant beliefs shared by Soviet elites, especially but by no means only at the level of the national leadership, is pride in the superpower role of the USSR gained by the country's extremely costly victory in World War II and by skill in political exploitation of Soviet military power. As one historian wrote some thirty years ago, "Out of the confidence acquired by successful prosecution of the war, something like a sense of community emerged in the party leadership and persisted in spite of Stalin's postwar efforts to destroy it." He adds: "Parallel with this sense of community in the leadership of the Soviet Union, the war created a larger sense of community as well. Relatively vague and ill-defined, it consisted nevertheless of a feeling shared by a large number of people that the validity of the common war experience was something quite different from the official pronouncements of validity."[15]

Let us briefly round out the foregoing condensed treatment of the patriotic-nationalist component of Soviet political culture. The attitudes described represent recent, overt manifestations of latent, long-dormant sentiments that Stalin and his successors found it expedient to strengthen but also to a considerable degree

[15]Sidney Monas, "The Political Police," in Cyril Black, ed., *The Transformation of Russian Society*, Cambridge, Mass. Harvard University Press, 1960), p.186. On the Soviet leadership's frequently manifested insistence on bringing to the attention of the world the superpower role of the USSR see, for example, Morton Schwartz, *The Foreign Policy of the USSR: Domestic Factors* (Encino, Calif.: Dickenson, 1975). Schwartz notes Soviet appreciation for the recognition of the USSR's greater power role by U.S. presidents Kennedy and Nixon. (See pp. 87, 88.) In this connection it is interesting that Seweryn Bialer, in his earlier cited article in the *New York Times*, 5 February 1984, attributed much of the resentment he found among the Soviet people he had recently been in contact with to their perception that the U.S. government was not according to the USSR the respect to which its status as one of the two leading world powers entitled it.

shared. On one level, these sentiments are part of the common set of perspectives shared by regime and nonregime elements of the population, by elites and masses, and even probably by most members of the Soviet intelligentsia. There are many exceptions among the latter group, however, such as Academician Sakharov and other Soviet liberals. It should also be kept in mind that although in official propaganda Soviet and socialist patriotism is held to be the universal cement binding together the entire "Soviet people" in devotion to a single homeland, there is evidence that in fact the word *Soviet* really is roughly equivalent to the tsarist term *Rossiiski,* translated by Edward Allworth as *Russia-wide.* In tsarist usage it referred to the imperial span of great Russian power and in ethnic terms to Russians and Russianized non-Russians.[16]

Without further developing here a very complex theme, we should also note that there is a continuum of exponents of nationalism, ranging from those who emphasize pre-Soviet Russian achievements, especially in war and diplomacy, and the contemporary leading role of Russian people among the Soviet family of nations (references to Russian help to the non-Russians are, incidentally, required actions for non-Russian political leaders) through a few "Russites" prominent in the late 1960s and early 1970s. The latter, while politically loyal and ideologically orthodox, nevertheless were embarrassing to a leadership intent on at least outwardly proving its devotion to Marxist-Leninist "internationalism" because they seemed to derive Bolshevism as much from Russian as from Marxist roots. At the far end of the spectrum are such people as the imprisoned art historian Leonid Borodin or the exiled writer Alexander Solzhenitsyn, whose version of a traditionalist Russian perspective explicitly rejected Marxism and exalted such values as religious faith and other elements of the Russian tradition totally incompatible, if sincerely held, with official Soviet ideology. We leave for later treatment the important and very difficult problems of Russian–non-Russian relations and the cultures, or subcultures, of the non-Russian ethnic groups.

Events surrounding the death of the Soviet leader, CPSU Central Committee General Secretary Yuri Andropov, on February 9, 1984, also reminded the world of the persistence of some fun-

---

[16]See, for example, Oleh S. Fedyshin, "The role of Russians among the New, Unified 'Soviet People'," in Allworth, ed., *Ethnic Russia in the USSR,* pp. 149–58.

damental aspects of Soviet political culture. These traits are among those that render the study of Soviet political culture and indeed of all the important aspects of Soviet politics difficult. Moscow correspondents of the *New York Times* reported that the line of mourners for Andropov headed for the Hall of Unions in downtown Moscow was a mile long, but in their reports there were indications — such as the fact that the people in the long cold lines had been officially recruited — that the apparent grief of the mourners was not necessarily spontaneous. Accompanying reports of praise by some of the mourners for Andropov's sternness and his crackdown on corruption reflected, however, a traditional Russian yearning for firm, strong, and efficient rule. A less positive impression, at least in terms of Western democratic values, is made by the revelations in the official government medical bulletin on Andropov's death indicating that from almost the beginning of his leadership and especially from the day in August 1983 when he disappeared from public view, he had been so ill that no return to normal personal or political functioning was possible; yet the world, including of course the Soviet public had been systematically kept in the dark about this state of affairs.[17]

Similarly, the seriousness of Konstantin Chernenko's illness was concealed from the public. After nearly two months of absence from public view, Chernenko was shown on Soviet television on February 24, casting a ballot in the elections to the RSFSR Supreme Soviet. This image, together with a scene broadcast four days later evidently in the same room but with the balloting par-

[17]On December 30, 1983, the *New York Times* reported that officials at the Supreme Soviet sessions in Moscow were assuring diplomats and Western reporters that Andropov's illness was no more than a matter of advancing age, and they denied specifically that he had kidney problems. Earlier, on the fifth of December at an unusual press confrence, Chief of Staff Ogarkov, Deputy Foreign Minister Kornienko, and Head of the Central Committee's International Information Department Zamyatin answered a question concerning the absent leader's health. Reporters were informed that Andropov was recovering from a cold and was fully in command of his responsibilities in party and state affairs (*Pravda,* 6 December 1983). As we know now from the official medical bulletin issued after Andropov died, these assurances were flat falsehoods. (See *Pravda,* 11 February 1984, where the official announcement of Andropov's death appeared.) The medical bulletin describing his illness and the cause of death indicated that he had suffered from "chronic renal insufficiency," diabetes, and other ailments, and that since February of 1983 he had needed dialysis treatment. He had felt well and was capable of work, the bulletin continued, until the final and fatal crisis of his kidneys in late January 1984, which brought about death on February 9.

aphernalia removed, was probably designed to counteract the impression left by the announcement that Chernenko had declined to deliver the customary address to his constituents "on his doctors' advice." The televised pictures of Chernenko casting his ballot, and then receiving congratulations upon his election showed so enfeebled a leader that they can hardly have had the reassuring effect that was intended.[18] In any case, they were quickly superseded by the announcement, on March 11, 1985, of Chernenko's death the previous day.

Deception about the state of the leaders' health may well reflect the exaggerated fear of chaos and disorder among Soviet leaders, who perhaps feared that any indication that the supreme political leader of the country was on his deathbed could have somehow shaken the firmness of the party's rule and particularly its strength vis-à-vis "imperialist" America. It should be noted, however, that during the periods of seclusion by both Andropov and Chernenko, there was an absence of the publicly stated indications that had been voiced after Stalin died in March 1953 that the danger of "panic and disorder" faced the nation.

The contrasts between the tough-minded and impatient discipline of Andropov and Chernenko's more permissive attitude were blurred by the continuation under Chernenko of several investigations into corruption involving high-ranking officials, especially in certain national republics, the partial expansion of the modest economic reform introduced under Andropov, but above all by the short duration of each man's rule and the signs of physical incapacity, which neither could entirely conceal, that cast doubt on the ability of either to accomplish major policy objectives.

SUBJECT-PARTICIPATORY ASPECTS OF OFFICIAL POLITICAL CULTURE

Almond and Powell's discussion of political culture focuses mainly on three aspects: system culture, relating to the bases of a system's legitimacy and to national identity; *process culture*, concerned with citizens' roles in politics, particularly with citizens' perceptions of their possible influence on the political system and their obligations toward it; and finally, *policy culture*, pertaining

[18]See *New York Times*, 25 February 1985 and 1 March 1985.

to preferences as to how such public goods as welfare, liberty, and security are, or should be, provided by the political system.[19]

Our treatment thus far of Soviet political culture has, in its references to Soviet and Russian patriotism, and to continuities between tsarist and Soviet practices and policies, touched on some aspects of the Soviet *mass* culture and also to some extent, on characteristics of *official* culture. In what follows, we focus on what we consider a relatively easy way to document aspects of the official, or ideal, culture, keeping in mind that this ideal culture is also shaped by and to some extent reflects the values of the Soviet political elite. We begin with and emphasize a type of political participation that we call *subject-participatory*. By this we mean participation directed ultimately from the political center at the top of the CPSU command structure. As Rigby has put it, in the Soviet system "command becomes the overwhelmingly predominant determinant of social action, and all groups are linked together . . . such that there is a direct chain of command from the supreme political authorities to those operatively responsible in every sphere of social activity."[20]

Our use of the term *subject-participatory* should not be taken to mean that the participatory activities in which millions of Soviet citizens engage (for example, in carrying on agitational work connected with elections to the soviets at levels from the local soviets up to those for the USSR Supreme Soviet) are meaningless. As the author of the best study to date of political participation in the Soviet Union points out, at the local level the Soviet citizen "has the greatest opportunity to exercise some degree of what Gabriel Almond and Sidney Verba have termed 'citizen competence.' "[21] This is because "the citizen's ability to make himself

[19]Almond and Powell, *Comparative Politics,* pp. 34–46.

[20]T. H. Rigby, "A Conceptual Approach to Authority, Power and Policy in the Soviet Union," in Rigby, Brown, and Reddaway, eds., *Authority, Power and Policy in the USSR,* p. 19. Rigby also argues in the section already cited that the Soviet regime "is primarily concerned not with regulating activities" in accordance with law but with "directing" them and setting them "tasks." The worth of most officials is judged by their success in fulfilling their tasks.

[21]Theodore Friedgut, *Political Participation in the USSR* (Princeton, N.J. Princeton University Press, 1979), p. 8. Friedgut borrows the term *citizen competence* from G. Almond and S. Verba, *The Civic Culture* (Boston, Mass.: Little, Brown, 1965), pp. 168–69.

heard in matters affecting him most closely and most often may offset any dissatisfaction he feels over his lack of high-level competence."[22]

In evaluating the elections to the work of the local soviets — the aspect of political participation on which Friedgut focuses — it is important to remember that these elections are, like most elections in the USSR, one-candidate elections and that the process and the campaign preceding election are directed from behind the scenes by appropriate CPSU agencies that organize, for example "public parades or rallies, lectures and agitation meetings."[23] Interestingly enough, there are genuine elections in the Politburo when it selects new members or chooses a new general secretary of the CPSU. It is also important to bear in mind that individuals who fail to demonstrate to the authorities who oversee their conduct a conscientious attitude toward the elections can face sanctions "ranging from public opprobrium to eviction from housing, and possible loss of advancement, employment, or study opportunities."[24] Friedgut also points out that the satisfaction that citizens might derive from participation in public affairs is diminished by "unsatisfactory operation of public services," especially in rural areas.[25]

A more basic factor is the failure of the Soviet leadership to encourage "maximal development of citizen participation," largely by substituting voluntary activity for that of professional administrators.[26] There are, however, mitigating and perhaps justifying considerations. It is often pointed out by Soviet emigrants and Western journalists with experience in the USSR that although failure of citizens to put in an appearance at political propaganda sessions is likely to be reported to superiors, the atmosphere at such sessions is often casual; for example, attendees may spend time knitting during these meetings. In explaining the failure to go beyond slogans in elevating citizen participation to the level that Almond and Verba have described in a pathbreaking 1965 work entitled *The Civic Culture,* one may cite the continued underdevelopment of Soviet society, particularly the very large

[22]Friedgut, *Political Participation,* p. 309.
[23]Ibid., p. 19.
[24]Ibid., p. 309.
[25]Ibid., p. 280.
[26]Ibid., p. 63.

proportion of the population still engaged in agriculture, as well as the continued influence of traditional centralism inherited from the tsarist regime. Finally, it is necessary to point out that even an author as skeptical as Friedgut (whose views we tend to share) regarding the nature of political participation in the USSR finds that for some Soviet citizens, particularly pensioners, participation gives "a place to prominence in the community, assuring status and occupation." More important, of course, are CPSU members — constituting about 10 percent of the adult Soviet population — whose participation can advance their careers, and non-party people, particularly when the kind of participation available to them is "connected with the individual's immediate welfare, thus compensating him in some degree for whatever effort is demanded."[27]

It is clear from the foregoing that as a rule the only participation permitted in the USSR is that which complies with customs and directions prescribed or approved by the Soviet authorities. This kind of participation is to be expected in a system in which overt dissent, not to mention organized opposition, has no legitimate place in political life. This is not, of course, to say that there is no element of political group and individual rivalry in the USSR or that opposing points of view regarding important issues are not vigorously discussed. Such activity will be discussed subsequently, especially in the chapter on interest articulation and aggregation. The Soviet system, however, allows a very limited space for the sort of open clash of opinion that is the very stuff of politics in what Soviet officials contemptuously label *bourgeois* democracies. Invoking the Leninist demand for "unity," Konstantin Chernenko set forth the official attitude toward both legitimate and illegitimate and punishable forms of participation in the USSR:

> Not ideological and organizational amorphousness,but ideological and organizational unity. . . . In that Lenin saw an integral characteristic of the party of the new type, and in it, he also was convinced, lay the best guarantee that it would always behave as a truly revolutionary, organized and organizing force in the struggle for socialism.

[27]Ibid., pp. 308–10.

Chernenko went on to attack "opportunists" in various countries, who, he asserted, shared the common characteristic of denying the necessity of unity, and frequently even defended "ideological" and "organizational" "pluralism."[28]

The longest section of Chernenko's above-quoted book is, interestingly, devoted to "The CPSU and the Rights of Man." [29] This may indicate, in part, Politburo concern about damage done to the USSR's image abroad and embarrassment at home caused by the harsh antidissident measures applied in the Soviet Union from the late 1970s on, when most of the significant figures in the Soviet protest movement who had not been sent to forced labor camps, internally exiled, or forced to leave the country fell victim to intensified repression. Of particular interest is Chernenko's defense of the official Soviet doctrine enshrined in the 1977 Constitution and implicit in articles of the criminal codes of the Russian Republic and the other union republics: that the exercise of rights and freedoms must not damage the interest of state and society. This doctrine, in the absence in the USSR of a communications network or a judiciary and legal profession not controlled and directed by the CPSU, leaves no real scope for independent political thought or action. It should, however, be borne in mind that the contemporary Soviet control mechanism is more sophisticated and flexible than was that directed by Joseph Stalin. The control of objectionable articulation of opinions and interests is effected by a wide range of methods, with outright force and coercion playing a lesser role than formerly. As Friedgut and many other authors have pointed out, coercion is applied as a rule only after persuasion, social pressure — often exercised through the ubiquitous collectives within which the vast majority of Soviet citizens work — and other methods have failed to elicit desired compliance.[30]

[28]K. U. Chernenko, *Avangardnaya rol partii kommunistov* (The Communists' Vanguard Role) (Moscow: Mysl, 1982), p.16.

[29]Ibid., pp. 174–347.

[30]See, for example, Friedgut, *Political Participation,* pp. 309–14; Frederick Barghoorn, "The Post-Khrushchev Campaign to Suppress Dissent," in Rudolf Tökés, ed., *Dissent in the USSR* (Baltimore, Md.:Johns Hopkins Press, 1975), pp. 35–95, discussing symbolic controls, censorship, and extra-judicial and judicial repression of dissent, and the criminal code statutes relied on in connection with the latter. (See also Barghoorn's "Factional, Sectoral and Subversive Opposition in Soviet Politics," in Robert Dahl, ed., *Regimes and Oppositions* (New Haven, Conn.:Yale University Press, 1973), pp. 27–88, and his "Regime-Dissenter Re-

In fact, insofar as possible, the party and police authorities involved in controlling behavior deemed undesirable — and this is true whether such behavior has a prominently political or only an ordinary criminal content — regard it as undesirable that knowledge of its existence become known in the capitalist world or indeed that it be disseminated widely among Soviet citizens. We can be pretty sure that many, perhaps most, cases of dissident behavior never come to the attention of non-Soviet publics.

ELITIST-HIERARCHICAL ASPECTS OF SOVIET POLITICAL CULTURE

Every informed student of Soviet politics and society is aware that rank and status and the struggle to achieve them and the material and psychological rewards associated with them are at least as salient features of life in the USSR as in the capitalist world. In fact, elites may well be more highly developed in the socialist USSR and in other systems of the Soviet type than in Western societies, in which markets determine the distribution of wealth and other values; in the former systems this function is performed by administrative methods. In the centrally managed, monoorganizational USSR, as the introduction to a recent study points out, "all social entities are incorporated into various hierarchical chains of command integrated by the apparatus of the Communist Party." This requires "constant attention by the political leadership" to problems of "cadres," or in Western parlance, personnel administration, and the basic instrument for this is the *nomenklatura,* "the schedule of posts, changes in the tenure of which require the nomination or approval of a particular unit in the party hierarchy."[31] The exact number of nomenklatura workers is not of special significance here, nor do we intend at this point to discuss in detail the methods and structure of elite

---

lations after Khrushchev: Some Observations," in Susan Solomon, ed., *Pluralism in the Soviet Union* (London: Macmillan, 1983), pp. 131–68. Perhaps the most sophisticated treatment is Peter Reddaway's "Policy towards Dissent Since Khrushchev," in Rigby, Brown, and Reddaway, *Authority, Power and Policy in the USSR,* pp. 158–92. Professor Reddaway's forthcoming book-length treatment of this subject will be of great importance.

[31]T. H. Rigby and Bohdan Harasymiw, *Leadership Selection and Patron-Client Relations in the USSR and Yugoslavia* (London: Allen & Unwin, 1983), pp. 2–3. Apparently there are some 2 million nomenklatured workers, according to Rigby and Harasymiw.

recruitment, which is the subject of a later chapter. What is important here is that "with a handful of exceptions (mainly scientists and artists) an individual's material rewards, power and status" in Soviet-type societies "are overwhelmingly a function of the official position to which he or she has been appointed under the nomenklatura system."[32] Academician Andrei Sakharov, doubtless the most honored of Soviet dissidents in the West — though he and his wife have been harassed and vilified in their own country for years, especially since Sakharov was forcibly transported to the provincial town of Gorky for protesting the invasion of Afghanistan in early 1980 — has made the following statement, which sheds light on the way of life and to some extent the perspectives of the nomenklatura workers:

> This stratum has its own life-style, its own sharply defined position in society, that of the "boss" or "the head," and its own language and way of thinking. The nomenklatura is virtually inalienable and is now becoming hereditary. Thanks to the complex system of secret and open privileges . . . and to high salaries these people enjoy the opportunity of living in far better housing and of eating and dressing better — often for less money in special 'closed' shops . . . or again by virtue of journeys abroad (in our circumstances a special and supreme form of reward for loyalty).[33]

Years before he wrote the above-quoted statement, Sakharov had experienced the angry condescension of Nikita Khrushchev, then first secretary of the CPSU and chairman of the USSR Council of Ministers, in response to Sakharov's lobbying against Khrushchev's intended plan to test in the atmosphere a particularly enormous and "dirty" hydrogen bomb. In effect, Khrushchev treated the scientist as a hired hand of the party, a "good scientist" but a person who should not inject himself into the "tricky business" of making foreign policy.[34] Although nothing like a full, coherent, and systematic account of the beliefs of the Soviet political elite that underlie and rationalize its tutelary and condescending, not to say domineering, attitude toward both the

[32]Ibid., p. 4.

[33]Quoted and translated by Rigby and Harasymiw, *Leadership Selection*, p. 5, from Andrei Sakharov, *O strane i mire* (New York: Khronika Press, 1976), pp. 33–34.

[34]See Andrei Sakharov, *Sakharov Speaks* (New York: Vintage Books, 1974), pp. 32–34.

Soviet intelligentsia and the mass of ordinary folk in the USSR is available, scattered illuminating fragments of information can be found, for example, in some autobiographical accounts by former Soviet citizens now in emigration. Interesting are the reflections of the distinguished literary scholar Efim Etkind, before his emigration a leading member of the Leningrad Writers' Union, who was forced out of his position as a professor of French literature.[35] Etkind describes the rector of the higher educational institution where he taught in Leningrad as a "baron." It was his task, assigned by the Leningrad provincial committee of the party to stage-manage Etkind's dismissal from his professional post. Etkind develops the conception suggested by this word as follows:

> "Baron" is not a slip of the pen but possibly the best term for a man like B., a manager very typical of his age and country. A baron is bound to obey his overlord unquestioningly, since he is a vassal, but then too he is an overlord with power over vassals of his own. This peculiarly feudal psychological complex—a combination of unconditional subordination and authority—is characteristic of a considerable number of Soviet bosses; each one is at the same time vassal and tyrant.[36]

Etkind, noting that "Soviet bosses" can be ordered about and shouted at like "naughty boys" but can also force their subordinates to wait uncomplainingly for an audience, suggests that that is why "you can often spot in the facial expression, the habits and the voice of the Soviet manager a striking mixture of humility and despotism, bootlicking and bullying."[37]

Etkind also describes how the Leningrad Writers' Union forbade its members to invite foreigners to their homes, instructing them instead to take foreign guests to restaurants for fear of having the visitors see the crowded conditions in which their Soviet hosts lived. This practice—an example of *pokazukha,* or make-believe — made him feel bitter shame, he writes. Again we have an

---

[35]See Efim Etkind, *Notes of a Non-Conspirator* (Oxford: Oxford University Press, 1978), a brilliant account of the process of removing Etkind, who had run afoul of party and KGB policies for his subversive association with Alexander Solzhenitsyn, his moral support for the poet Joseph Brodsky, and especially for allegedly urging young Soviet Jews to struggle against anti-Semitism in the USSR.

[36]Etkind, *Notes,* p. 10.

[37]Ibid.

example of a requirement imposed by superiors on subordinates — in this case, one that can generate hostile impulses toward the Soviet political elite among proud and honest individuals. This practice, however, perhaps also reflects the embarrassment of even high-ranking members of the Soviet elite over the inferiority of Soviet living standards to those in advanced Western countries, as well as the habit of concealing disagreeable sides of Soviet life from the putatively inquiring and hostile West.

Another of the elitist and hierarchical aspects of political culture manifested in the methods by which political elites are recruited concerns the personalized bonds of loyalty that develop between officials of unequal rank, a practice called *clientelism*. Rising officials with the ability to promote ambitious subordinates and to facilitate the latter's careers in return for their support serve as patrons for willing political clients. Although the obscurity within which cadre affairs and other decisions are handled limits the results of the several painstaking studies that have been undertaken on these matters, it is clear that cliques such as those to which followers of Brezhnev, who rose with their patron from Dnepropetrovsk and Moldavia, or those of Podgorny, who came from Kharkov, belonged play an important role in determining, to borrow the words of the late Harold Lasswell, who gets what, when, and how. Perhaps the most conspicuous contemporary example of a client who derived benefits from the favor of a patron is Konstantin Chernenko, whose loyalty to Brezhnev was doubtless as important as any factor in bringing about his ultimate selection as successor to Yuri Andropov as head of the CPSU in February 1984. It seems clear that membership in a network of powerful leaders such as that put together by Brezhnev, not least the absence of hostility on the part of such a group, is one of the prerequisites for achievement of supreme power in the USSR.[38] Although the support of other powerful leaders can help an aspirant to supreme power to achieve his goal, however, he must, once at the pinnacle, "build authority" to achieve his policy goals, as one political scientist has persuasively argued.[39]

[38]That there are, in addition to patron-client relations, other sources of political advancement, particularly "functional career specialization," is the argument, ably presented, of Joel C. Moses in his chapter in the Rigby and Harasymiw, *Leadership Selection,* pp. 15–61.

[39]See George Breslauer, *Khrushchev and Brezhnev as Leaders* (London: Allen & Unwin, 1982).

Still, barring overly ambitious goals, excessive impatience, and other qualities that can generate fear and anger in the Politburo, and of course fatal illness, possession of the post of general secretary of the central committee of the CPSU confers a kind of authority, at least formally, that is unique. It is symbolized, for example, in pattern of publicity accorded to the principal leader. To a much lesser but still stunning degree, of course, in comparison with practice in Western democracies, all Politburo full members and even the nonvoting alternate members (in Russian, *kandidaty*) are spotlighted in a fashion far exceeding anything comparable in bourgeois democracies. When Leonid Brezhnev was general secretary of the CPSU, at least in his later years, he was often quoted twice in the daily *Pravda* editorials.Once Yuri Andropov had reached this level of rank, he was quoted once per editorial, and immediately after Chernenko's installation his views and pronouncements began receiving almost daily prominence in *Pravda* editorials. As quotations from Chernenko replaced Andropov's utterances immediately upon Chernenko's appointment as general secretary, so Chernenko's former prominence as a source of guidance on all policy questions ended upon his death. Interestingly, Mikhail Gorbachev, in the early months of his rule, has been very rarely quoted in *Pravda* editorials.

Perhaps the most impressive public display of the towering status of Soviet political leaders occurs on occasions such as the vast spectacles staged to honor the anniversaries of the great October Socialist Revolution and May Day, when Politburo members, together with a number of top military commanders, review from atop the Lenin Mausoleum the parades and demonstrations of the Soviet masses. Funerals of leaders such as Brezhnev and Andropov are of course also solemn displays of political pomp and ceremony.[40]

While the rulers thus dominate the Soviet scene (and as the media keep pointing out in reporting funerals of leaders, May Day, and November 7 parades, they are also at the focus of attention of progressive humanity everywhere, ordinary working

---

[40]*Pravda,* 15 February 1984, published at the top of its front page a photograph showing Chernenko delivering the funeral oration honoring Andropov and at the bottom left, Chernenko leading the procession of Politburo members and other mourners. On the right side of the page was a picture of two goose-stepping military servicemen marching beside a rocket launcher.

people play a role more like that of extras on a movie lot than that of the ruling class they are sometimes told they are. A statement by David Shipler neatly catches the essence of the ruler-citizen relationship: "The parades on the anniversary of the 'Great October Revolution' . . . and on May Day are pageants of military might and worker solidarity, done in the name of the common man, but not open to him. Admission is by ticket only, a ticket carefully provided to those deemed worthy."[41]

MARXIST IDEOLOGY AND SOVIET POLITICAL CULTURE

One could hardly call the Soviet political culture an ideological one in the sense that any meaningful effort is being made in the USSR to achieve the avowedly egalitarian and libertarian objectives proclaimned by Marx and Engels, or even Lenin, or that progress in that direction appears likely in the foreseeable future, or that Marxism still inspires widespread enthusiasm among any significant proportion of the Soviet population. It is, however, an ideological culture if by that one means that the leadership in speeches, slogans, and a steady stream of messages and claims in the mass media justifies its practices and policies by reference to what has become the official creed of Marxism-Leninism. To be sure, Marxist-Leninist symbols are invoked in a rather formal, ritualistic style. Good examples can be found in the official Soviet announcement of Yuri Andropov's death.[42] This document, addressed by the CPSU Central Committee to "all communists and to the Soviet people," began with a paragraph hailing Andropov as "an outstanding figure of the Leninist party and the Soviet state," and an "ardent patriot of the socialist Motherland," as well as a "tireless fighter for peace and communism." Its seventeen paragraphs contained eight references to Lenin or the Leninist cause, the Leninist foreign policy of the USSR, the Leninist Central Committee, and the like. Marx and Engels each rated one mention, both in the next-to-last paragraph, which asserted that Andropov would always be remembered by all communists and by all other Soviet people for his dedication to "the teaching of Marx, Engels and Lenin."

All but three paragraphs explicitly contained references to the CPSU or a variant of that expression. Since the CPSU officially

[41]Shipler, *Russia,* p. 250.
[42]See *Pravda,* 11 February 1984, p. 1.

describes itself as a Marxist-Leninist party, this can be construed as implicitly an equivalent of identification with Marxism-Leninism, but the attention given to the CPSU suggests the dominant role of the party and its members, especially its leaders, in all matters political, including decisions as to who are to be considered genuine Marxist-Leninists and how the official doctrine is to be interpreted. To a considerable extent, Marxism-Leninism can be said to have become a body of symbols a function of which is rationalization and legitimation of CPSU rule. Since there are in the USSR only one party and only one official ideology, and a Soviet citizen's good standing in the community depends on the extent to which he is indoctrinated in or gives lip service to this ideology (requirements more exactingly applied as his education, status, and rank increase), it is easy to understand that official Marxism is a powerful instrument of social and political control. Especially as applied to experts, specialists, and professionals, particularly but by no means only sensitive fields such as art, literature, philosophy, history, and the social sciences, an individual's perceived attitude toward the ways in which Marxism-Leninism is being currently interpreted can play an important part in an official decision as to whether he or she will be promoted to a responsible post — or even whether a coveted opportunity to travel abroad will become available.

It would, however, be incorrect to say that Marxism-Leninism functions only as an instrument of political control in the USSR, although we are inclined to consider that to be its most important function, along with the closely related one of justifying whatever policy line the top political leader — often in a struggle against opposing factions in the party — is pushing at a particular time.[43]

[43]For excellent analysis of changes in interpretation of Soviet official ideology as policy changed — but without explicit discussion of Marxism-Leninism as a factor being taken for granted — see Breslauer, *Khrushchev and Brezhnev*, pp. 25, 59, 109–10, 174, 189. The well-known self-proclaimed Marxist dissident Roy Medvedev, in his book *On Socialist Democracy* (New York: Knopf, 1975), p. 90, reported that because of the intellectual deterioration of official Soviet Marxism, increasing reliance would be placed on nationalism in the indoctrination of Soviet youth. The Andropov obituary commented on above perhaps confirms the correctness of Medvedev's view. It contains a considerable number of references to such emotionally charged terms as *motherland (rodina), Great Fatherland War,* and *might of the Soviet state.* The most extreme form, but one not without deep insight, of the argument that official Soviet ideology has become a mere rationalization of the power and privilege of the Soviet elite is contained in such writings as Dmitri Nelidov's "Ideocratic Consciousness and Personality," first published in the em-

To conclude that the only remaining functions of Marxism-Leninism in the era of *developed* or *mature* socialism — as the Soviet sociopolitical order has been frequently characterized since about 1970 — are opinion control and system and policy legitimation would perhaps be something of an exaggeration. In a diffuse way, probably even today's Soviet leaders — a great many of whom, not excluding Mikhail Gorbachev, are of peasant origin — identify with the aspects of official ideology that stress class struggle. The Soviet elite as a whole is still close enough to farmer and working class origins for residues of class consciousness, reinforced by ideological indoctrination to play a role in shaping the elite's political mentality. In this connection it is interesting that official Soviet documents, such as Chernenko's speech at Andropov's funeral, often contain sections stressing the importance of the party's maintaining close links with the working masses, and heeding their thoughts. Such statements, like the party leadership's assurances that one of its main concerns is to promote popular welfare, can be dismissed as demagogy, but even as such they might be politically useful demagogy, derived in part from Marxist-Leninist doctrine. Perhaps even more important are the aspects of doctrine that stress the importance of unity, control, and holding

---

igrant journal *Vestnik RSKhD,* no. 106, pp. 175–93, in 1973, and in English in Michael Meerson-Aksenov and Boris Shragin, eds., *The Political, Social, and Religious Thought of Russian "Samizdat"* (Belmont, Mass.: Nordland, 1977), pp.256–59. Nelidov argues that this state credo replaced "Marxism (as a force exploding all of the traditional social ties, and as a concentrated revolutionary will) by means of contemporary Marxist-Leninist ideology (as the maximum hardening, the preserving of the definite social system in the capacity of an ideology)." Meerson-Aksenov and Shragin, p. 263. He adds that "truth for man became a coercive objectivity, and when the data of experience does not correspond to this truth . . . it is all the worse for the facts" (p. 264). Under Soviet communism, argues Nelidov, man lives by instincts which . . . are trained within him by constant ideological pressure" (p.267). People acquire an "alienated consciousness," a "system of conditioned reflexes . . . in response to a system of corresponding ideological signals" (p. 271). A system of "mass double-think" develops (p. 278). The author goes on to argue that the dissident "Democratic Movement" manifested a "norm of mental health which turned out to be intolerable to a society infected by a spiritual epidemic" (p. 286). This is a reference both to the salutary nature of democratic dissent, which at least partially exposed the realities concealed by Soviet propaganda myths, as Nelidov sees them, and to the limited success of an effort conducted under enormously difficult conditions. The article concludes on a qualifiedly optimistic note, calling the Democratic Movement "a form of expressing the humane in an environment where human nature was perverted and suppressed," and quoting the French writer Saint-Exupery on spirituality as the source of human freedom and dignity (p. 290).

fast to other basic elements of this extremely power-oriented doctrine, such as the superiority of public state property over private property as the basis of the elite's power and as a means of assuring social and political cohesion.

If Marxist ideology still has some significance in shaping policy in relations with the capitalist world, or at least in making the official Soviet case that Soviet policies and practices are fundamentally different from and superior to those of capitalist states, it is probably far more important in the area of foreign affairs than in that of domestic policy. The two spheres are logically interconnected, and to a very striking degree Soviet doctrine emphasizes this interconnection: it claims, for example, that the USSR needs military and state security agencies only because of the existence of foreign class enemies.[44]

In the areas of state security and foreign policy there is a great deal of continuity between the Soviet attitudes of the Stalin era and current perspectives and even between present-day attitudes and those that shaped Lenin's outlook on foreign relations. It should not be forgotten that in 1921 Lenin, Trotsky, and other Soviet leaders of the time disseminated the legend that the rebellion of Soviet sailors at the Kronstadt naval base (they had played an important role in helping the Bolsheviks to seize power and only finally rebelled after their legitimate grievances had been ignored for years) was instigated by bourgeois intelligence services. Those who have governed the USSR, from Lenin to Gorbachev, have, as the foregoing discussion indicates, employed what they believe or say they believe to be Marxist doctrine as justification for whatever action seemed appropriate against threats to political stability, elite privilege, and their personal power. However dubious the Stalinist and post-Stalin doctrine that tends to equate dissent with treason may be and however irrelevant its applica-

[44]See, for example, the important book, *Sovetskoe administrativnoe pravo: Upravlenie v oblasti administrativno-politicheskoi deyatel'nosti* (Soviet Administrative Law: Administration in the Sphere of Administrative-Political Activity) (Moscow: Juridical Literature, 1979), sections I and II. See p. 66, quoting a 1967 *Pravda* article by then chairman of the KGB, Yuri Andropov, asserting that "with the liquidation of hostile classes the center of gravity more and more moves from the struggles against internal class enemies to the struggle against external enemies." See also p. 82, asserting that the activity of the KGB is determined by the fact that "relations in the sphere of socialism and imperialism are primarily relations of class struggle."

tions have been to historical reality, they may well lend a certain plausibility to official Soviet propaganda both at home and abroad. In additions, of course, such interpretations serve as potent warnings to Soviet citizens that the boundries of permissible political expression are narrow indeed.

Numerous significant aspects of the body of purportedly Marxist propositions, claims, evaluations, commands, and demands presented by the Soviet leaders to describe their world and the world outside and to prescribe what in their opinion needs to be done in the interests and improvement of socialism and for the ultimate ellimination of capitalism have been omitted from the preceding account. Nothing has been said, for example, about the content and justification of the militant anti-religious indoctrination that the Soviet educational system provides from elementary grades through university or about the continued claim that a new person is being created in the USSR. In foreign relations, besides endless claims that Soviet-like people's democracies by their very nature are peace-loving in contrast to bourgeois regimes, there are numerous other important claims. One of the most significant of these is the current version of Lenin's doctrine of imperialism according to which the USSR is the friend and champion of national liberation movements and of countries that have gained political sovereignty but are exploited and threatened by their former colonial masters.

The Soviet leaders continue to extol the Leninist path as blueprint of mankind's future. The propositions and prescriptions of official ideology are presented as a seamless web of goals and commitments to be supported unreservedly. There is no place in the official creed for partial, selective, or qualified commitment. This is a set of perspectives designed to encourage, reflecting what David Shipler calls "the willing suspension of disbelief."[45] The official political culture is not only utopian and idealistic in style but is also laced with realism and pragmatism. If it promises a golden age in the hazy future — the achievement of communism

[45]See Shipler, *Russia,* ch. 2, esp. pp. 94–97. Shipler writes that "in the political dimension" of Soviet education, "reality and truth are not investigated but constructed." Although in parts of his book he reports meeting almost nobody who believed that communism would be achieved in his or her lifetime or in any foreseeable future, nevertheless he writes that suppression of disbelief "helps keep many, perhaps most, adults in a spirit of political comfort with their country and their system. To disbelieve is to destroy."

has again and again been put off to a more and more distant future — it also warns that the way to the classless, coercion-free future is difficult and dangerous. In the meantime, far more attention is paid to means than to ends, to strategies for surviving in a world divided among clashing powers and forces, and to principles of management and incentives designed to promote efficiency and productivity. The official culture, though it succeeds perhaps in eliciting prudent conformity from the majority of the population, engenders boredom and skepticism in some individuals, efforts in others — including some of the best writers and natural scientists — to carve out spheres of limited creative freedom for themselves, and usually after a tortuous process of self-emancipation from official ideology, outright rebellion in others. Usually the process of intellectual self-emancipation involves breaking with Marxism, at least with what passes for Marxism in the USSR. As Lev Kopelev, a leading dissident emigrant who was the model for Rubin, the idealistic front-line propagandist in Alexander Solzhenitsyn's novel *The First Circle,* put it in a conversation with David Shipler, ''The most dangerous thing here would be Marxism. Not just propaganda, not just slogans, but Marxism as a system of historical analysis.''[46]

Thus Marxism has been ritualized and incorporated as one ele-

---

[46]Shipler, *Russia,* p. 265. Another well-known and outstanding dissenter, former Soviet General Petro Grigorenko, began his dissent in 1963 as a deeply committed Marxist. In fact he took the lead in organizing in 1963 a group whose objective was the revival of a Marxism that in its official version had, Grigorenko thought, become ossified and irrelevant. For his pains, Grigorenko was declared insane and committed to his first confinement in a mental institution — a fate that has befallen a number of other committed Marxist dissenters. Finally, after a stormy and dangerous career as a dissenter, which included a long second period of psychiatric incarceration. (Grigorenko's thinking grew similar to a Western-style democratic position.) One of the main themes of Ferdinand Feldbrugge's valuable study *Samizdat* (Leyden: Sijthoff, 1975) is the progression of Soviet dissenters from official Marxism to non-Marxist democracy. George Schoepflin in his article ''Eurocommunism, Socialism, Modernization,'' in *Studies in Comparative Communism* 16 (Winter 1983): 275–86, at 277, quoted a political emigrant from Czechoslovakia who writes that in the contemporary Soviet-dominated Eastern Europe, ''Marxism is no more than a portrait carried over the heads of the workers at the First of May parades.'' The same can be said, in our opinion, of the USSR itself. In connection with the above, it is interesting that the former dissident and camp inmate Boris Vail expresses a kind of antiregime Marxism in his memoir, *Osobo opasny* (Extremely Dangerous) (London: Oversees Publications Interchange, 1980), when he argues that widespread theft of state property in the USSR can be justified, since the state itself steals from the people by extracting surplus value from them. See, for example, p. 18.

ment of an authoritarian political culture, the most potent ingredient of which is statist nationalism; and yet the Soviet leaders seem doomed because they cannot afford to break with their revolutionary origins or to admit that they are in fact great power nationalists, for obvious reasons of domestic and foreign politics. Instead they continue to profess allegiance to ideas and concepts increasingly irrelevant in the modern world.

CHAPTER III

Social Structure
and Political Subcultures

A MULTINATIONAL, INDUSTRIALIZING SOCIETY, the Soviet Union comprises a great diversity of ethnic, occupational, and other societal groupings representing multiple social interests and political subcultures. Although Soviet doctrine has held since Stalin's time that relations among social groups under socialism are mutually friendly and nonantagonistic, in contrast to the struggle between classes that is said to dominate social relations under capitalism, the conversion of aspirations and grievances held by various social groups into inputs into the political system is extremely difficult to examine because of the shroud of secrecy that the Soviet authorities lay over the political process. Certain social problems that are of exceptional sensitivity, including such issues as attitudes on the part of non-Russian ethnic minorities toward the dominant Russian nationality or the political values and beliefs of the intelligentsia, are rarely discussed openly or objectively in the public media. In other cases, Soviet scholars and party officials have published empirical data — for example, on occupational structure and mobility or career aspirations of youth in different occupational groups — that allow us some insight into the effect of a group's social status on its political interests. Soviet scholars have been increasingly willing to acknowledge the multiplicity of group interests in Soviet society and the possibility of divergence and even conflict among them.[1]

[1]See A. P. Butenko, "Protivorechiia razvitiia sotsializma kak obshchestvennogo stroia," (Contradictions in the Development of Socialism as a Social Or-

GENERAL CHANGES IN SOCIAL STRUCTURE

Before considering particular social groups and political subcultures, it is useful to examine the changes that are acting to
transform the society as a whole. Above all because of the rapid
progress of industrialization, Soviet society has become more urban (that is, a larger proportion of its population lives in cities
rather than the countryside); a much larger proportion of its population derives its livelihood from industrial or service occupations and a much smaller segment from working the land; and a
much larger proportion of the population has secondary or higher
education. We must bear in mind how recently these changes have
affected the Soviet population. American society reached the point
at which half its population lived in cities and half in the countryside in 1920. The Soviet population did not reach this point
until 1961.[2] From 1950 to 1980, the size of the population classified as urban rose by nearly 100 million persons while the rural
population declined by about 11 million, or about 10 percent. The
largest share of the growth of the urban population has been due
to migration from rural areas; smaller shares of the growth are
due to natural increases and the expansion of existing cities.[3] The
transition of the Soviet society from predominantly rural to predominantly urban is continuing, although the pace is slowing. The
latest Soviet census, conducted in 1979, found that 63.4 percent
of the population was urban. Urbanization has grown in all parts
of the country, although it has been slower in some areas of Central Asia, partly because the rural population there continues to
experience very high birthrates and also because of the pro-

---

der), *Voprosy filosofii,* no. 10 (1982): 16–29. Western literature on social structure
includes Mervyn Matthews, *Class and Society in Soviet Russia* (New York: Walker,
1972); Alex Inkeles and Raymond Bauer, *The Soviet Citizen* (New York: Athe-
neum, 1968); Mervyn Matthews, *Privilege in the Soviet Union* (London: Allen &
Unwin, 1978); Alex Inkeles, *Social Change in Soviet Russia* (New York: Simon &
Schuster, 1968); Walter Connor, *Socialism, Politics and Equality* (New York: Columbia University Press, 1979); David Lane, *The End of Social Inequality?* (London: Allen & Unwin, 1982); Ellen Mickiewicz, ed., *Handbook of Soviet Social Science
Data* (New York: Free Press, 1972). Citations to works discussing particular social
groups will be supplied below.

[2]Murray Feshbach, *The Soviet Union: Population Trends and Dilemmas* (Washington, D.C.: Population Reference Bureau, 1982), pp. 36–37.

[3]Stephen Rapawy and Godfrey Baldwin, "Demographic Trends in the Soviet
Union: 1950–2000," in Joint Economic Committee of the United States Con-
gress, *Soviet Economy in the 1980's: Problems and Prospects* (Washington, D.C.: U.S.
G.P.O., 1983), pp. 273–74.

nounced unwillingness of many Central Asians to leave the familiarity and security of their rural homes.

Soviet social structure has changed markedly as a result of the expansion of job openings in industry and in white-collar occupations. As a result of these changes, the proportion of the population, including dependents, whose livelihoods are derived from industrial occupations has risen from 44.2 percent in 1959 to 51.3 percent in 1979. The proportion classified as white-collar workers (*sluzhashchie,* in Russian, sometimes translated as *employees*) has also risen significantly and at an even faster rate, from 20.1 percent in 1959 to 25.1 percent in 1979. At the same time the peasant population has declined. Overall, the proportion of the population making its livelihood from farming has fallen from 35.4 percent in 1959 to 23.6 percent in 1979. The picture formed by these statistics is one of a society that in its occupational and social structure is beginning to resemble the industrialized countries of Europe or North America, where similar changes occurred in earlier decades of this century.[4]

Soviet authorities assert that Soviet society is divided into two basic social classes, workers and collective farm peasants, with a stratum of white-collar employees forming a distinct part of the working class. The category of employees has grown rapidly as the economy has generated a larger number of jobs for technical, administrative, professional, and clerical personnel. This is a loosely defined category, however, encompassing party secretaries and nuclear physicists along with bookkeepers and watchmen. If we separate from the employee category a smaller category of *employee-specialists,* we find that those so classified form the most rapidly growing segment of the Soviet economy. From 50 percent of the employee stratum in 1960 they now comprise 65.5 percent of it in 1980.[5] The specialist category is also a loose and broad grouping. A *specialist* is defined as anyone with specialized secondary or higher education who is employed (even in a blue-collar position) or who is employed in a position requiring equivalent specialized training or experience. The diversity of this grouping is

---

[4]Figures are taken from *Razvitie rabochego klassa v sotsialisticheskom obshchestve* (The Development of the Working Class in Socialist Society) (Moscow: Nauka, 1982), p. 460; Alex Pravda, "Is There a Soviet Working Class?" *Problems of Communism* (November–December 1982): 4.

[5]*Razvitie rabochego klassa,* p. 462.

therefore so wide that we need to break it down into more homogeneous subgroups. A prominent Soviet sociologist, M. N.
Rutkevich (a corresponding member of the Academy of Sciences
and head of a department in the Academy of the National Economy under the Council of Ministers), divides the specialists into
three groups, the first consisting of those with only secondary educations; the second, of those with a higher education; and the
third (a very small group) of persons who are in senior or executive positions in science, technology, management, government,
law, and the media, or who are members of the *creative intelligentsia*
(writers, artists, musicians, and the like). About 58 percent of the
specialists are in the first group, about 35 percent in the second,
and about 6 percent in the third. The third group numbers no
more than 1.5 million people. Of these, about a quarter are scientists and another quarter are managers, technical professionals,
lawyers, journalists, or members of the creative arts.[6]

This last small segment of the specialist group together with
most of the second group might properly be termed the Soviet
intelligentsia. Although ideological considerations, particularly the
need to pay homage to the working class as the creator of social
values, prompt Soviet writers to employ a broad, loose definition
of the intelligentsia, a more precise usage would isolate this group
from the larger category of those whose occupations involve labor
of a primarily nonmanual or white-collar type. The intelligentsia
would consist of those with higher education who occupy positions
of responsibility in the social and political system. The key to at-
taining intelligentsia status, therefore, is obtaining a higher education. Within the intelligentsia we can distinguish groups
according to the nature of their roles within the society. The cultural or creative intelligentsia, for example, consisting of writers,
poets, artists, musicians, and other practitioners of the fine arts,
help create artistic and cultural values for the society at large,
working, to be sure, within the bounds set by party ideological
watchdogs. The scientific and technical intelligentsia work in basic
and applied research, developing and applying methods for meeting the society's goals.

Although the two long-term social changes we have noted —

[6]See M. N. Rutkevich and F. P. Filippov, *Sotsial'naia struktura razvitogo sotsialisticheskogo obshchestva v SSSR* (The Social Structure of Developed Socialist Society in the USSR) (Moscow: Nauka, 1976), pp. 87–89.

the shift of the population from rural to urban residence and the emergence of an occupational hierarchy characteristic of an industrial economy — are of enormous importance in understanding the relationship between the official political culture and the subcultures that interact with it, perhaps the single most significant long-term change in the domestic environment of the political system is the rise in the educational attainments of the total population. Although the intelligentsia proper is a small segment of the population, a far larger proportion of Soviet citizens have obtained the skills and knowledge corresponding to secondary or specialized secondary schooling. In large measure this development reflects the commitment of the Soviet leadership since the revolution to provide the means of universal secondary education as well as to create a large system of technical and vocational schools aimed at providing the technical expertise needed to run and expand the nation's economy.

The first step on the way toward raising the educational qualifications of the populace on a large scale was the campaign undertaken by the Bolsheviks in the first decade of their rule to eradicate illiteracy. The census of 1926 recorded that throughout Soviet Russia, about 77 percent of adult males and 46 percent of females were literate and that in the other national Soviet republics, particularly those comprising the territory today called Central Asia, literacy even among males was confined to small minorities of the population.[7] By the time of the first postwar census in 1959, illiteracy had been all but wiped out throughout the Soviet Union. The regime's early stress on diffusing literacy was consistent with its aim of raising the political consciousness of the population and with distributing the tools for economic development as widely as possible.

It took the regime longer to establish universal secondary education and to decide on the appropriate mixture of general and technical skills that the primary and secondary schools should impart. Having instituted the *unified labor school* as the basic unit of schooling — it provided schooling that was mandatory, coeducational, and polytechnical in curriculum — the Bolsheviks expanded enrollments immensely through the 1920s and 1930s. By the mid-1950s probably all children in the relevant ages attended

[7]Mickiewicz, ed., *Handbook of Soviet Social Science Data,* p. 139.

TABLE 1:   *Distribution of Eighth-grade School-leavers (by Percentage)*

Those completing eighth grade		Went to work	Admitted to study in day division of:			
			Vocational-technical schools		Ninth grade	Tekhnikum
			Conventional	Secondary		
1965:	100%	42.5	12.3	—	40	5.2
1975:	100%	2.3	21.4	10.2	60.9	5.2
1980:	100%	.5	13.8	19.3	60.2	6.2

Source: M. Rutkevich, "Reforma obrazovaniia, potrebnosti obshchestva, molodezh' " (The Reform of Education, the Needs of Society, and Youth), *Sotsiologicheskie issledovaniia,* no. 4 (October-December 1984): 24.

at least the first four grades of school (now called the *general educational labor polytechnical school);* of them about two-thirds succeeded in completing seven grades; and of these about 20 percent finished the complete course of ten grades.[8] Under Khrushchev and Brezhnev, enrollments in higher levels of secondary and higher education continued to grow, and by 1976 virtually all youths were receiving at least eight grades of education, although only about 60 percent of the children leaving the eighth grade at that time continued in the general school to the ninth.[9] Virtually all who leave the general school in the eighth grade go on for some form of continued schooling: most go to vocational-technical schools (many of these today receive a secondary school diploma in the course of their schooling), and a smaller number go to *specialized secondary* schools *(tekhnikumy),* which offer more advanced education and typically lead to higher-paying occupations than do the vocational-technical schools.

The figures indicate that the Soviet authorities have succeeded in raising the educational qualifications of nearly all school-leavers as nearly all go on for some form of schooling after the eighth grade. The most dramatic change in this regard came between 1965 and 1975, when the sizable proportion that went to work directly after leaving eighth grade was cut back substantially. A change almost equally dramatic came as the regime reorganized the schooling given in vocational-technical schools, in many cases

[8]Mervyn Matthews, *Education in the Soviet Union* (London: Allen & Unwin, 1982), ch. 1. This is probably the best recent study of the Soviet educational system.

[9]*Sovetskaia intelligentsiia i ee rol' v stroitel'stve kommunizma (The Soviet Intelligentsia and Its Role in the Construction of Communism)* (Moscow: Nauka, 1983), p. 195; Matthews, *Education,* p. 41.

TABLE 2: *Distribution of Secondary School Graduates (by Percentage)*

Those completing tenth or eleventh grade:		Admitted to study in day division of:			
	Went to work	Voc.-tech. schools	Tekhnikum	VUZ
1965: 100%	16.2	—	42.4	41.4
1975: 100%	55.3	12.9	16.0	15.8
1980: 100%	41.2	26.9	15.6	16.3

Source: M. Rutkevich, "Reforma," p. 24.

lengthening the term of study and including more general subjects that would qualify the graduate for a secondary diploma. This is the distinction between the two types of vocational-technical schools indicated on the table, the traditional or conventional type (which is seen as a direct feeder to industrial and service jobs) and the more demanding *secondary* type. When all forms of completion of secondary school are considered, around 80 percent of youth today receive complete secondary educations.[10]

Table 2 examines the careers of those who do go on in the general school and finish the final or tenth (in some schools, eleventh) grade. Traditionally thought of as the preparatory ground for admission to an institution of higher education (often referred to as *VUZ*, standing for *vysshee uchebnoe zavedenie*, which can be either a university or an institute), completion of the secondary education through the tenth grade is today more likely to lead to a job than to higher education. A large proportion, 42.5 percent, also continue their educations in specialized secondary or technical schools.

Table 2 shows that the older patterns have broken down to a considerable extent. The technical schools have grown in the quality and sophistication of the training they offer to the point that they attract a sizable proportion of secondary school graduates, but this growth has largely been the compensation for the decline in the opportunities secondary school graduates have to go on to higher education. This latter squeeze is the result of the rapid growth in the 1960s and 1970s of enrollment in the upper grades of secondary school at the same time that the number of openings in *VUZ'y* has grown only slowly.

[10]Murray Yanowitch, "Schooling and Inequalities," in Leonard Schapiro and Joseph Godson, eds., *The Soviet Worker: Illusions and Realities* (New York: St. Martin's Press, 1981), p. 133.

Thus overall the last decades have witnessed a considerable rise in the educational qualifications of the population but much less growth in the number of persons with higher educations. Soviet figures indicate that between 1959 and 1970, the proportion of individuals ten years of age and older who had completed general secondary school nearly doubled, from 6.1 percent to 11.9 percent; the proportion almost doubled again between 1970 and 1979, from 11.9 percent to 20.7 percent. The proportion in the same age group with specialized secondary education rose over those two decades from 4.8 percent to 10.7 percent. Similarly, the proportion with complete higher education nearly tripled, from 2.3 percent to 6.8 percent. Overall, therefore, the proportion of the population ten years of age and older with *at least* complete secondary education rose from 14.3 percent in 1959 to 39.7 percent in 1979. If we add the percentage of those with incomplete secondary education, the figures rise from 36.1 percent to 63.8 percent. [11]

However, wide gaps between the educational levels of urban residents and those in the countryside remain. Although 9.3 percent of the urban population 10 years old and older has a complete or partial higher education, only 2.5 percent of the equivalent rural population does; 63 percent of the urban population of the same age bracket has a partial or complete secondary education, contrasted with only 46.7 percent of the rural populace. The difference in educational levels between city and country has proven to be rather stable and difficult to overcome, in large measure because rural youths who do get complete secondary or specialized secondary educations tend to leave the village, with its lower standard of living and bleak cultural life, and to seek jobs in cities. Meanwhile, the regime's efforts to induce graduates of specialized secondary or higher educational institutions to settle down in the countryside often fail. Although Soviet graduates do face a job-assignment system upon graduation requiring the graduate to accept a job — often in a rural area — and remain in it for at least three years, many who spend three years in their assigned positions then leave, and many others find ways of avoiding the fulfillment of their obligation. [12]

[11] *Narodnoe khoziaistvo SSSR: 1922–1982* (National Economy of the USSR: 1922–1982) (Moscow: Finansy i statistika, 1982), p. 42.
[12] Matthews, *Education,* p. 172.

It is instructive to compare these figures with statistics on educational attainments in the United States. About three-quarters of American pupils graduate from high school (in 1955 the figure was about 55 percent), and about 45 percent go on to enter college. By contrast, fewer than 60 percent of Soviet youth graduate from the secondary general school (though, as we have seen, another 20 percent or so receive the equivalent of a secondary degree through their technical school), and only around 10 percent enter a VUZ. If we compare the proportions of the population who have secondary or higher educational degrees, we find higher levels among the American population. Among Soviet citizens ten years of age or older in 1982, 7.6 percent had a complete higher education. Among Americans ten years of age or older, the proportion with at least four years of college was 11.2 percent in 1980. Among Soviets at least ten years of age in 1982, the proportion with at least complete secondary or specialized secondary education was 45.1 percent. For Americans in 1980 the corresponding proportion was 45.5 percent. Thus, although the Soviet regime has succeeded in diffusing secondary education or its equivalent to a roughly equal proportion of its population, the United States continues to expose a larger proportion of its youth to general secondary school and college education. In the United States in 1981–1982 about 7.2 million persons were enrolled as full-time students in colleges and universities, of whom about one-quarter were in two-year institutions. In contrast, in the Soviet Union in the same year, some 5.3 million students were studying in institutions of higher learning, and of them only 3 million, or 57 percent, were full-time students. The rest were enrolled in evening or part-time courses. In contrast, only about a quarter of the American students are enrolled part time.[13]

Although these raw comparisons tell us nothing about the quality of the education students receive in either system, they do suggest that youth in the United States have a greater opportunity to obtain general secondary and postsecondary educations even though the Soviet regime has made rapid strides to expand places in schools and to equalize chances for mobility through education

[13]*Narodnoe khoziaistvo SSSR*, p. 506; Maurice Friedberg, "Culture and Intellectual Life," in Robert F. Byrnes, ed., *After Brezhnev* (Bloomington: Indiana University Press, 1983), p. 270; Matthews, *Education*, Appendix A; Andrew Hacker, ed., *U/S: A Statistical Portrait of the American People* (New York: Viking Press, 1983), pp. 237, 241, 251.

for the offspring of all social groups. Another factor is the far greater attention that the Soviet regime has given to providing various forms of occupationally oriented terminal secondary degrees on a mass scale while restricting enrollment in higher education to a relatively small segment of the student population. Some 8.1 million Soviet citizens are enrolled full or part time in vocational-technical or specialized secondary schools, receiving education heavily oriented toward occupational skills. Finally, the comparison also underscores the relative affluence of American society and the much larger proportion of its national wealth that it has invested in education: it is estimated that the percentage of GNP that the United States spends on education is about one-third higher than that of the USSR.

The expansion of technical and specialized schooling has in turn raised new questions concerning the correlation between the educational qualifications of the population and the assortment of jobs available in the economy. Social scientists have referred to a widely held view that many blue-collar workers are overeducated for their jobs, the consequence of nearly universal secondary schooling combined with slow technological advancement of industry. The relative overqualification of many workers for their jobs has led, many believe, to frustration and discontent. Another of the problems is the inadequate scientific and technical background many persons receive in the schools, which is often thorough but narrow and outdated. This lack of basic or general technical knowledge is frequently blamed for holding up the progress of scientific and technical development. Another line of criticism that has been voiced in recent years by the party authorities is the low level of ideological knowledge and conviction that students acquire in school, partly a product of outdated texts and dogmatic or formalistic teaching. The sociologist M. N. Rutkevich recommended that only 25–30 percent of the pupils leaving eighth grade continue to ninth; the rest, he proposed, should immediately receive specialized training in the basic sciences.[14]

In response to these criticisms, the Andropov regime called for major educational reform. On January 4, 1984, the authorities announced a set of changes affecting the entire Soviet educational

[14]M. Rutkevich, "Put Labor into the Secondary School Graduation Certificate," *Sovetskaya Rossia,* 21 September 1983, in *Current Digest of the Soviet Press* (hereafter CDSP), 35, no. 4 (2 November 1983): 3.

system. Unwilling to allow the extension of secondary school to come at the expense of the already inadequate supply of young eligible workers, the regime declared that an extra year of school would be added by having children start school at the age of 6 rather than, as in the past, at age 7. To improve the preparation for work that schools impart, the reform called for increased exposure to industrial labor in the early grades, through such measures as school visits to factories, and increased study of technical subjects in the later grades.[15] The reform also included other provisions, such as the demand that all school graduates demonstrate satisfactory competence in the Russian language and measures to increase the length of study in teachers' training schools from four years to five. Although the objectives of the current reform are evidently to improve the productivity of existing labor resources and to raise the quality of technical education, the reform is not likely to bring about any marked changes in the schooling process. Similar reforms under Khrushchev in 1958 and under Brezhnev in 1972 and 1974 were hampered by the difficulty of quickly improving schools' technical facilities, establishing training programs at local factories, and raising teachers' qualifications.[16] Moreover, the extension of complete secondary schooling from 10 to 11 years is likely to intensify the problem mentioned earlier of overeducation of many whose jobs demand less than the level of general and technical knowledge they acquired in school.

ETHNICITY

One of the most important traits differentiating groups in Soviet society is ethnicity, affiliation with an ethnic or national group. Although Marxists hold that ethnicity is a characteristic that declines in salience as socialism advances, ethnic or national identity matters both to the Soviet authorities, who require that every adult's internal passport indicate the nationality of the bearer, and to citizens, who, as recent research among émigrés has ascertained, continue to be intensely conscious of their own nationality and that of others with whom they come into contact.[17] The Soviet Union comprises well over one hundred indigenous

---

[15]"Soviet Revamping School System," *New York Times,* 5 January 1984.

[16]See Mervyn Matthews, *Education,* pp. 21–28, 53–54.

[17]Zvi Gitelman, "Are Nations Merging in the USSR?" *Problems of Communism* 32, no. 5 (September–October 1983): 41.

nationalities, of which twenty-two contain at least one million people. The most populous ethnic group, of course, is the Russians, who, with 137.4 million as of the 1979 census, made up 52.4 percent of the total. Taken together with the other major Slavic nationalities, the Ukrainians and Belorussians, they comprise a dominant though declining majority of the country. In 1959 Slavs made up 77 percent of the total, in 1979 about 73 percent. While the Slavs' share has been declining, that of the groups in the Central Asian region (the territory made up of the Soviet republics of Uzbekistan, Tadjikistan, Turkmenistan, Kirgizia, and Kazakhstan) has been gaining. The ethnic groups residing here are of primarily Turkic and Persian extraction and share a cultural and religious heritage similar to that of some of their neighbors in the Middle East. Their relatively faster growth over the past twenty years has increased their proportion in the total Soviet population. Between 1959 and 1979, the Moslem population of the Soviet Union increased from 24.7 million to 43.8 million, or from 11.8 percent to 16.7 percent of the population.[18]

The Slavic and Moslem groups are far from the only main ethnic or religious groupings in the population. In the northwest of the country, on the Baltic littoral, are the Estonians, Latvians, and Lithuanians, whose republics were forcibly joined with the Soviet Union first as a result of the Soviet-German pact of 1939 and then, once war broke out, as the Red Army reconquered the territories claimed by the agreement with Hitler. These small nationalities (1, 1.4, and 2.85 million in population, respectively) retain the influence of their long contact with Western Europe and are Protestant or Catholic by religious orientation. In the southwest live the Moldavians, 2.97 million in number, whose territory, like that of the Baltic peoples, was annexed to the Soviet Union by Stalin. They are closely related to the Romanians, and their territory was a province of Romania until Stalin declared them to be ethnically and linguistically distinct. To the south, in the Transcaucasian region, between the Black and Caspian seas, live the Armenians, Georgians, and Azerbaijani (4.15, 3.57, and 5.48 million in population, respectively). The first two of these groups are Christian by heritage, the third Moslem. A large number of smaller groups, nearly all Moslem, also reside in Trans-

[18]Rapawy and Baldwin, "Demographic Trends," pp. 278–83.

caucasia, having been subjugated by the Russian empire in the last century. In the Far East live a large number of small ethnic groups of mixed religious affiliation, some Orthodox, reflecting their contact with the expanding Russian empire of the eighteenth and nineteenth centuries; others, practicing traditional faiths.

Of the lands and peoples incorporated into the tsarist Russian empire as of the eve of World War I, only Finland and Poland, which were provinces of Russia through the nineteenth century, are not today part of the Soviet Union. In territory and ethnic composition, the Soviet Union bears a close resemblance to its tsarist predecessor and thus shares with it the challenge of maintaining political integration over a vast and extremely diverse territory. In contrast, however, to tsarist Russia, in which national resentments of Russian imperial domination and of forced assimilation of Russian culture fed the grievances of revolutionary movements, the Soviet authorities claim to have developed a highly effective formula for building harmonious and friendly relations among the peoples of the country. Often this is referred to as the Leninist nationality policy. This policy asserts the equality of all peoples under Soviet law and demands mutual friendship and respect among all nationalities. *Internationalism* — meaning tolerance and brotherly affection for peoples other than one's own in the Soviet Union — is a cornerstone of political indoctrination. Moreover, under the constitution the nations of the Soviet Union are considered to share a "unitary, federal and multinational state, formed on the basis of the principle of socialist federalism and as the result of the free self-determination of nations."[19] The constitution provides that each large national group should have a territorial-governmental unit located in the region of the greatest concentration of that population. Thus, the Russian nationality is represented by the Russian Soviet Federated Socialist Republic (RSFSR), while fourteen other major nationalities also lend their names to Soviet socialist republics. These fifteen republics, called *union republics,* together comprise the Union of Soviet Socialist Republics, or USSR. Moreover, smaller national groups are similarly represented by other territorial-governmental units: sixteen autonomous republics exist for ethnic groups of medium size, all

[19]Robert Sharlet, *The New Soviet Constitution of 1977* (Brunswick, Ohio: King's Court, 1978), p. 78.

of which are located on the territory of a union republic; in addition, there are eight autonomous *oblasti* (provinces) and ten national *okruga* (circuits) for smaller nationalities, most of them located in Siberia, the Far East, or mountainous areas.[20] The constitution provides residents of each of these *ethnoterritories* the right to elect a fixed number of deputies to the Council of Nationalities, one of the two chambers in the Soviet parliament.

Although law and doctrine grant equality of rights and status to all national groups and thus aim at eliminating any grounds for ethnic prejudice or hostility, substantial reason exists for questioning the degree of success achieved by Soviet nationality policy. Soviet policy is directed toward the long-term *merger*, or *fusion* (*sliyanie*) of the nationalities. Recognizing that the elimination of national customs and culture in the creation of a homogeneous Soviet nation is a process of protracted duration the pace of which cannot be forced, Soviet authorities consider that for the foreseeable future the nationalities will be in the process of *drawing together* (*sblizhenie*) so that opportunities, occupations, and values increasingly converge. At the same time, the diversity of language and culture continues to be a point of pride, taken as a sign of the success of the Soviet system in allowing nations to *flourish* (*rastsvetat'*). For many, the principle of flourishing, suggesting that each nation retains rights as a group to develop socially and culturally, is contradicted by the regime's efforts to forge a common Soviet people out of the multiethnic population through education and the suppression of any manifestation of nationalist attitudes that, in the authorities' eyes, pose a threat to the security of the state. Despite the homage paid in doctrine to the equality and harmony of nations, two sets of cleavages in nationality relations persist. The first is the continuing prevalence of national distinctions and prejudices in the relations among all the nationalities. The second, certainly the most important in determining the future stability of the Soviet political and social order, is the predominance of the Russians among the Soviet population generally.

With respect to the first point, survey research has made it clear that almost seven decades of exposure to Soviet doctrine concerning national relations and common participation in the social and

[20]See Ralph S. Clem, "The Ethnic Dimension of the Soviet Union, Part I," in Jerry G. Pankhurst and Michael Paul Sacks, eds., *Contemporary Soviet Society: Sociological Perspectives* (New York: Praeger, 1980), p. 20.

political structures of the system have not abolished consciousness of national differences, and in many cases traditional stereotypes have continued to thrive. Research conducted by Zvi Gitelman and others among individuals who emigrated from the Soviet Union during the 1970s (most of them Jewish, others Russian, and a sizable minority Soviet Germans) has discovered the strength of ethnic identity and the persistence of ethnic prejudice in Soviet society. Gitelman concludes that "sensitivity to ethnic identification seems to be shared by the population. People know one another's nationality, inquire about it, and, in many cases, feel it is significant." He explains that this awareness is justified in light of the belief by most people that ethnic identity is a factor in determining an individual's opportunity to acquire a higher education, a good job assignment, and an apartment. On the other hand, most of his respondents believed that in the armed forces, the nationalities were treated equally. Perhaps most telling is his finding that when his respondents were asked to what extent they believed that "friendship of peoples" characterizes the actual relations among national groups, a majority answered "hardly at all," and only 20 percent felt that it existed to some or a great degree.[21]

Among the subjective attitudes that have survived formal political socialization to the contrary are ethnic stereotypes. Many Russians, for example, consider their culture superior to that of the rest of the peoples of the Soviet Union. A Russian mechanic and party member in his forties made the following comment in an informal interview:[22]

> We cannot let an Armenian or a Georgian impose his authority on us. The last time that happened, it led to the cult of personality [i.e., the Stalinist regime]. We should learn the lessons of history. The Russian is more vigilant and has more of a sense of justice towards the other peoples of the USSR.

A Russian engineer in his thirties expressed a similar belief in the natural superiority of the Russians:

---

[21]Gitelman, "Are Nations Merging in the USSR?", pp. 41–43.

[22]These quotations are cited from interviews conducted under the auspices of the Soviet Area Audience and Opinion Research project of Radio Liberty. See "Demographic Evolution in the USSR: Russian and Non-Russian Perspectives," SAAOR AR#5-83 (December 1983).

The Russian will always play a dominant role in our society. This is due to the fact that he is more just, more loyal and more responsible than the other peoples of the USSR.

By the same token, attitudes of suspicion and animosity among ethnic groups still persist:

The greater part of the non-Slavic population is poorly educated if not completely uncivilized. Look at the Buryats, Kabardinians, Gypsies, etc. One can't really expect a great deal from people like that. [From a Russian cook and party member in his forties.]

Many ethnic groups, such as the Uzbeks, Estonians and Azeris, still do not live like normal Soviet people. They have considerable influence on Russians, teaching them all about corruption and nationalism. [From a Jewish housewife in her forties.]

In some cases, animosity among groups is fed by economic competition. In Georgia, the oversupply of highly skilled technical workers for the number of jobs available has been linked to manifestations of hostility toward members of other nationalities, presumably Russians.[23] Thus frictions among ethnic groups may be fed both by the perpetuation of traditional attitudes and by tensions induced through the groups' direct contact with one another.

Of far greater significance, however, in determining the impact of ethnicity on political life is the relationship between Russians and non-Russians. This cleavage is characterized above all by the superior position of the Russians in the political and social life of the USSR. To understand the preponderance of power at the disposal of the Russians, it must be remembered that as of the 1979 census only seven nationalities numbered more than 5 million people (the Russians, the Ukrainians, the Uzbeks, the Belorussians, the Kazakhs, the Tatars, and the Azerbaijani). The Russians, with 137.4 million, are more numerous than these six combined. In addition, more than other groups, the Russians have moved out of the Russian republic and settled in other republics in large numbers (a pattern that some non-Russian nationalists regard as colonialism). Russians outside their own republic normally live in cities, where they occupy key managerial and ad-

---

[23]L. M. Drobizheva, "Mezhlichnostnye natsional'nye otnosheniia: Osnovnye cherty i osobennosti" (Interpersonal Nationality Relations: Basic Traits and Peculiarities), *Sotsiologicheskie issledovaniia* (Sociological Research), no. 4 (October–December 1982): 37.

ministrative positions, enabling them to dominate political, economic, and cultural affairs. (In Central Asia this problem is compounded by the fact that many of the indigenous nationality continue to live in the countryside while the cities are Russianized, a pattern resembling classical colonial imperialism.) Finally, Russian is the language of politics, economics, and science for the Soviet Union as a whole, giving native Russian speakers an additional cultural advantage in mobility. The regime has made vigorous efforts to ensure that members of non-Russian nationalities are exposed to Russian language education in school, which has resulted in a steady rise in the number of non-Russians who claim to command Russian as either their first or second language (this figure rose from slightly under 50 percent to over 60 percent between the 1970 and 1979 census points). These attempts are regarded, depending on the observer's viewpoint, either as cultural *Russification* (the coercive imposition of Russian culture upon subordinate peoples) or as testimony to the success of Soviet nationality policy in creating a *lingua franca* for the society.[24] The rates of Russian in-migration to the national republics serve also as an irritant in relations between Russians and non-Russians.[25] In addition, the geographic location of most of the non-Russians in politically and strategically sensitive borderlands and the memories still alive among many non-Russians of conquest by tsarist Russian troops or of forced annexation to Russia are important parts of the background of tension and friction between Russians and non-Russians.

In the political sphere, the centralization of power through the party undercuts the nominal federalism of the system. It was Lenin's strict policy that any concessions made to the principle of national self-determination be confined to the governmental structure, not to the party structure. From the earliest point in Bolshevik party history, Lenin conceived the party as a monolithic instrument for exercising the power of the socialist movement.[26] Therefore, he adamantly refused to accept the demands for fed-

[24]I. B. Dzhafarov, "Prevrashchenie russkogo iazyka vo vtoroi rodnoi iazyk narodov SSSR," (Conversion of Russian Language into the Second Native Language of the Peoples of the USSR), *Sotsiologicheskie issledovaniia,* no. 3 (July–September 1982: 11–16.

[25]On rates of in-migration, see Ann Sheehy, "The All-Union Census of 1979 in the USSR," RL 123/80 (Radio Liberty Research Bulletin) (September 1980).

[26]Leonard Schapiro, *The Communist Party of the Soviet Union* (New York: Vintage Books, 1960), esp. part 1: "The Formative Years."

eralism within the party or any form of local autonomy for party branches in ethnic regions. Lenin acknowledged the right of national self-determination (including the right for a national republic to secede from the Soviet Union if it chose to do so) as an important gesture demonstrating the complete absence of imperial or chauvinistic motives on the part of the party leadership in Moscow in their treatment of the nationalities, but he also insisted on a model of political power in which the party would direct all major political affairs throughout the country. The party was open to all committed communists of any nationality, but the use of party power to advance local or ethnic interests was treated as being incompatible with the goals and spirit of socialism. Stalin went even further in dismissing the nominal rights of the nationalities under Soviet federalism as expedient but hollow window-dressing. In his view, the national republics enjoyed the right of secession from the union, but any move to assert that right would be counterrevolutionary and was therefore unacceptable. The formal governmental autonomy of the nationalities continues to be countered in practice by the centralization of power in the party, which reflects the general line set by party officials in Moscow.

Reflective of this gap between party and government structure is the fact that though an identical set of governmental structures exists in each of the fifteen union republics and another at the federal level (much like the relationship between the fifty state governments and the federal government in the United States), the party lacks a separate party organizational apparatus in the Russian Republic. The other fourteen republics have party organs at the republican level modeled after the organs at the all-union level in Moscow. The absence of a separate Russian party organization testifies not to the weakness of the Russians but to their power, for Russian party officials thereby possess a greater opportunity to supervise political affairs for the entire Soviet Union from their vantage point in the Kremlin in Moscow.

Russian dominance of the Soviet Union is also facilitated by Russian dominance within the party. Although the proportions of national representation in the party are gradually growing more equal, Russians continue to comprise about 60 percent of the party's membership. Perhaps more important, party officials of Russian nationality dominate all important decision-making organs in the party, government, military, and security apparatuses. Of the members of the party Central Committee named in 1981, two-thirds were Russian. Another 14 percent were Ukrainians. (Ukrainians are often treated as the younger brothers of the Russians in political structures: in the military, for example, the officer corps tends to be composed of Russians and the NCO's are often Ukrainians, while the enlisted ranks are filled with members of all nationalities.) David Lane's analysis of the ethnic composition of the one hundred most powerful figures in the Soviet political system determined that sixty-nine were Russian and another thirteen were Urkainian.[27] At lower levels of the political system, representation of non-Russians is much more prevalent; political life in each national republic is conducted primarily by members of the indigenous nationality. The first secretary of each national republic is a member of the indigenous nationality of that republic. Even at this level, however, the assurance of Russian dominance is maintained by the practice of vesting certain key powers, reputedly including power over personnel appointments, in the second secretary, the number two official in the republic's party apparatus, who is usually Russian (or Ukrainian) by nationality.[28] In addition, many of the controlling positions of the military and security forces of each national republic are occupied by Russians. All these political patterns help reinforce the cleavage between Russians and non-Russians in the Soviet Union and strengthen the hand of Russians in maintaining political supremacy despite their declining share in the population.

In light of these patterns, it is understandable that many members of non-Russian nationalities view the regime's efforts to forge a new Soviet people or nationality (*sovetskii narod*) as a thinly disguised form of Russification and regard the extension of central control and political uniformity from Moscow as the post-1917 equivalent of tsarist imperialism. The Kremlin, however, sternly suppresses any expressions of such a view. (It also suppresses, though less strenuously, manifestations of excessive overt Russian chauvinism.) In the Ukraine, for example, waves of protests against Russification have been met with harsh measures of repression. In the fall of 1965 some thirty Ukrainian intellectuals

[27]David Lane, *The End of Social Inequality?* (London: George Allen & Unwin, 1982), p. 93.

[28]See Hélène Carrère d'Encausse, *Decline of an Empire* (New York: Newsweek Books, 1979), p. 142.

were arrested in the capital city, Kiev, and in the main city of Western Ukraine, Lvov (Lviv, in Ukrainian), on charges of conducting anti-Soviet agitation and propaganda. Other leading Ukrainian intellectuals were subjected to press attacks, police harassment, and the like but were not arrested. In 1972 there was a much bigger wave of arrests. From 1978 to the present there have been still further arrests, directed in particular at members of the Ukrainian Helsinki group (an independent group attempting to monitor Soviet fulfillment of its obligations under the Helsinki Agreement of 1975). Perhaps the best way to indicate the intellectual content of some of the resistance and protest is by quoting a few passages from what is probably the resistance movement's most important single published manifesto, the literary critic Ivan Dzyuba's major work, *Internationalism or Russification?*, published in English in London in 1968. Writing from an avowedly Leninist perspective, Dzyuba denounced what he regarded as Moscow's economic exploitation of the Ukraine. "Overcentralization," he said, "fetters the existing possibilities of development of a number of republics, the Ukraine in particular." He linked Soviet centralized administration, the flooding of the Ukraine with Russian economic-administrative cadres, and linguistic Russification as instruments of a policy that threatened the Ukrainian people with "denationalization."[29]

Other nationalities have also produced a substantial outpouring of nationalistic protest. It is important to note that the relative material well-being of a nationality in the USSR is poorly correlated with contentment with its situation as an ethnic group. There is abundant evidence that the Jews, the Baltic peoples, and the Georgians and Armenians are much more privileged peoples in terms of percentages of their group with higher education and other factors making for social mobility than are the politically dominant Slavs. However — and here we mention a factor that probably goes far to explain discontent among the Georgians and Armenians — the relative advantages enjoyed by the groups declined sometime after the death of Stalin. Of course, as far as the Jews are concerned, covert and even overt anti-Semitism extends well back into the Stalin era. Presumably the deterioration in re-

[29]See Frederick C. Barghoorn, "Soviet Dissenters on Soviet Nationality Policy," in Wendell Bell and Walter Freeman, eds., *Ethnicity and Nation-Building* (Beverly Hills, Calif.: Sage, 1974), pp. 122–23.

cent years of the Georgians' relative position in the Soviet nationalities' pecking order exacerbated well-established Georgian beliefs that their culture was superior to that of the Russians and that it was threatened by political-administrative pressures emanating from Moscow.

In 1978 new republic constitutions were drafted for the fourteen non-Russian republics. Traditionally the three Transcaucasian republics (Georgia, Armenia, and Azerbaijan) — and only these three — had a clause in their constitutions declaring the indigenous language the state language of the republic. The Georgians and Armenians had also been permitted to continue to write and publish in their beautiful and distinctive alphabets, although all the other major non-Russian languages had been converted to the Cyrillic alphabet used by the Russians. The question of the alphabet was not raised in 1978 or at any other time so far as we are aware, but the local party and state authorities in the three Transcaucasian republics mounted campaigns purporting to show that public opinion there favored eliminating the state-language status of the local languages. The effort met with an angry response among wide circles of the population, at least in Georgia and Armenia. According to one report, "as many as 20,000" people demonstrated in Tbilisi, the capital of Georgia, on April 14, 1978, against the plan to drop Georgian as the republic's state language. The then first secretary of the Georgian communist party, Eduard Shevardnadze, now USSR Foreign Minister, was permitted (or ordered) to state, though not in public media, that the nationality clause would remain in the Georgian constitution. In fact it did remain, almost identical with its equivalent in the 1937 Georgian constitution.[30]

The failure of the plan to deprive the three Transcaucasian republics of their state languages — despite the fact that the issue was more symbolic than substantive — reflected both the touchiness of segments of the local populations concerned, especially their most educated members, and a measure of flexibility in official policy. In subsequent years there has been evidence, again mainly from Georgia, of anxiety, resentment, and protest

[30]See dispatches by Craig Whitney in the *New York Times* 15 and 18, April 1978; RL 81/78, "The Georgian Language and National Pride Prevail," 18 April, 1978; and RL 97/78, "The National Languages and the New Constitutions of the Transcaucasian Republics," 3, May 1978.

over such matters as Moscow's attempts to "extend the use of the Russian language in educational establishments," particularly after adoption in 1975 of a statute requiring that dissertations for higher degrees be submitted in Russian.[31]

Nationality discontent is probably even stronger in Lithuania than in Georgia. The attitudes of Lithuanians toward the Soviet Union seem to resemble closely those of their fellow Roman Catholics, the Poles. Of course, in the stricter political environment of the Soviet Union, the Lithuanians have been unable to develop forms of resistance as massive and challenging as the Polish Solidarity movement. As in Poland, religious and national resistance and dissent are partly fused. Lithuania is notable for a profusion of samizdat journals unmatched anywhere else in the Soviet Union and for the large number of signatures on protest petitions. In January 1972 more than 17,000 people signed a petition protesting failure of the Lithuanian Soviet authorities to abide by their obligations under Soviet law to allow a measure of autonomy to the Lithuanian Catholic Church to carry out its religious functions. Although much of the within-system dissent in Lithuania has by Soviet standards been unusually bold, however, it should be noted that the Lithuanian Helsinki group has suffered the same fate as the Moscow, Ukrainian, Georgian, and Armenian groups as the result of police action and forced emigration.[32]

We shall not deal at length with relations between the Kremlin and Soviet Jews, since there is such a vast literature on this subject and it has been so fully reported in the Western press. Regarded by the Kremlin as an ethnic group (and to the extent that they are Zionists, as a political group seeking world domination), they vividly illustrate the failure of Soviet nationality policy to achieve its goals of friendship of peoples and ultimate assimilation into a common Soviet nationality. Aside from a few small nations, such as the Crimean Tatars, Soviet Jews are perhaps the most totally alienated Soviet nationality. They are officially categorized as a nationality, not a nation, because they do not meet Joseph Stalin's criterion of being located primarily in a common national territory. In the 1920s and 1930s, despite Stalin's covert anti-Semi-

---

[31]See, for example, Anthony Austin, "Georgians Wary of Moscow over Language Rights," *New York Times,* 21 December 1979.

[32]See V. Stanley Vardys, *The Catholic Church, Dissent and Nationality in Soviet Lithuania* (New York: Columbia University Press, 1978).

tism, it was probably true that Soviet Jews who served the regime loyally benefited more than any other ethnic group in the USSR in terms of access to education, social mobility, and other opportunities made available by rapid economic development. As a result of the increasingly open appeal by Stalin and his successors during and after World War II to Russian nationalism as a means of tapping the loyalty of the largest Soviet ethnic group, along with numerous other factors (such as the Kremlin's belief that Arab hostility to the West in the oil-rich Middle East could be profitably exploited), the situation of the Soviet Jews deteriorated and their discontent increased.

The catalyst, however, for overt protest and extensive efforts to emigrate, at first primarily to Israel and in the middle and late 1970s often to the United States, was the Arab-Israeli war of 1967, which both bolstered national consciousness and pride among Soviet Jews and triggered anti-Zionist propaganda that all too often was a cover for the dissemination of crude anti-Semitism. The right of Soviet Jews to emigrate of course became a major theme of the writings and appeals of Soviet human rights activists in the 1970s and a thorny issue in Soviet-Western relations. As of late 1983, about a quarter of a million Soviet Jews had emigrated, nearly all between 1971 and 1981. Of all the Soviet peoples, the Soviet Jews had been most successful in achieving their objective of emigration, but as the authorities began sharply restricting the numbers granted exit visas in the early 1980s, the future of Jews who remained in the USSR looked increasingly uncertain, even bleak.

Lest readers conclude that Soviet Jews have lost all status or influence, it should be noted that quite a few Jews still hold high positions, although it might be doubted that such a situation could long persist, in view of increasing restrictions being placed on the access of Jews to higher education or their recruitment to sensitive fields of work.[33] Among Soviet nationalities, Jews continue to show one of the highest rates of national representation in the communist party, to have one of the highest rates of educational attainment, and to have one of the highest proportions of employed specialists in the economy. These facts should be seen, however, in the context of, first, a declining trend in each of these

[33]See Carrére d'Encausse, *Decline of an Empire,* pp. 202–8.

indicators; second, the fact that as a nationality Jews are the most highly urbanized group; and third, the fact that they have one of the oldest age structures of any nationality. In part, the high rates of participation in education and politics reflect their activation into social life in the earlier decades of the revolution, when an orientation to education and advancement combined with their liberation from traditional tsarist barriers to allow them exceptional social mobility. As the generations of the 1930s and 1940s grow older and younger cohorts experience anti-Jewish discrimination in education and employment, the overrepresentation of Jews in higher education and high-status occupations will continue to decline. Finally, it should be noted that Jews are one of the most rapidly shrinking groups in the population, according to the census records of 1959, 1970, and 1979. From around 2.27 million in 1959, their numbers had declined to 1.81 million as of the 1979 census. Low birthrates are failing to replace those whom death or emigration has taken.[34]

AGE AND SEX

There are two other broad forms of social differentiation that we need to take into account in order to understand the diversity of Soviet social structure — age and sex. Both of these variables, important in any society in explaining how status and power are distributed among the population, show up in distinctive patterns in Soviet society.

In common with other largely industrialized societies in which birthrates are slowing and life expectancies are relatively high, the average age of the Soviet Union's population is slowly increasing. The median age in the USSR has been steadily rising, as it has in the United States and other countries of the West. Between 1950 and 1980 the median age (the midpoint in the distribution at which the number of all those younger equals that of all those older) rose from 24 to 29 years. In the United States, between 1970 and 1980, it rose very similarly, from 28 to 30.[35] Median

[34]See Ellen Jones and Fred W. Grupp on the importance of taking into account the age structure of a nationality in determining its rates of participation in education and other indicators of mobility. "Measuring Nationality Trends in the Soviet Union: A Research Note," *Slavic Review* 41, no. 1 (Spring 1982): 112–22; idem, "Modernisation and Ethnic Equalisation in the USSR," *Soviet Studies* 36, no. 2 (April 1984): 159–84.

[35]Hacker, *U/S,* p. 30; Rapawy and Baldwin, "Demographic Trends," p. 269.

age measures the change in the number of older and of younger people, and in the Soviet Union, as in the United States, there have been proportionately more and more people in the older age brackets and fewer in the younger brackets. The pension age population in the Soviet Union — women 55 and older and men 60 and older — rose between 1959 and 1980 from 12.2 percent of the total to 15.5 percent. Among other things, this increase means that the pension burden on the economy is growing, much in the way that the proportion of the U.S. federal budget that goes to Social Security rises as the proportion of the population eligible for retirement benefits rises. The overall trend in the Soviet population, therefore, is toward the "graying" of the society.[36]

This aggregate trend has been more powerful than a contrary trend among certain groups in the population in the direction of increasing youthfulness. Demographers speak of a *demographic transition* that occurs in all societies in the course of economic development: it refers to a shift in child-bearing patterns as a population adjusts to falling death rates (mortality rates) and families begin to have fewer children. Where mortality rates are high, birthrates tend also to be high as families look on their progeny as an economic asset. When improved sanitation and health care bring death rates down, populations tend, after a lag, to experience lower birthrates as well. This shift is called the demographic transition. It has occurred in most regions of the Soviet Union but is only now beginning to set in among some of the ethnic groups of Moslem background, whose birthrates are two and three times those of the European populations. The result of this difference in birthrates is that it is the population in the Slavic (Russian, Ukrainian, and Belorussian) national republics and in the Baltic (Estonian, Latvian, and Lithuanian) republics that is aging, while the populations in Central Asia — especially in Uzbekistan, Kirgizia, Turkmenistan, and Tadjikistan — are characterized by large numbers in the lowest age brackets. In those four last-named republics, the proportion of the population aged 15 and under rose over the last 20 years, in contrast to the trend everywhere else in the Soviet Union. This segment represents over 40 percent of the Central Asian population but makes up just un-

---

[36]See Stephen Sternheimer, "The Graying of the Soviet Union," *Problems of Communism* 31 (September–October 1982): 81–87.

der a quarter of the population of the USSR as a whole.[37] Growth
of the population in these age brackets places quite a different
strain on the economy, requiring the addition of child care facilities, medical and educational institutions, and in the future the
provision of job opportunities as these young people enter the labor force.

The changing age structure of the population has several significant implications for the policy choices the leadership will face
in the next decade. Because the number of people entering the
labor force during that period is increasingly going to fall short
of the economy's need for labor and because those who will be
entering working ages will comprise an increasingly large proportion of non-Europeans, the regime will need to decide where
it will concentrate new investment in productive capital. Should
it choose the developed regions of European Russia, where labor
is scarce but administrative control is centered, or regions farther
to the south and east, where the labor will be more abundant but
less fully integrated into the Soviet political culture? Or can the
regime count on labor to migrate to the remote and inhospitable
regions of Siberia and the Far East, where the greatest sources of
natural mineral wealth are located? The shrinking of the labor
force relative to the economy's need for new labor is striking at
a time when larger numbers of people will be entering retirement
age and thus become eligible for pension benefits. A Soviet de-
mographer has estimated that in the 1986–1990 period, the numbers of people of working age in the population will actually
decrease by one percent.[38] One solution to the growing labor
shortage often proposed in Soviet discussions is to encourage retired persons to continue to work, drawing at least some of their
pensions along with a salary. Whether this solution can resolve
the pressing needs for manual labor in an economy still heavily
dependent on physical work to supplement machines is question-
able. The retired population is likely to become a more important
segment of the population, both because it is becoming a proportionately larger group and because the generations that came
of age after World War II and thus were not decimated by the

[37]Rapawy and Baldwin, "Demographic Trends," p. 271.

[38]V. I. Perevedentsev, "Vosproizvodstvo naseleniia i sem'ia" (The Reproduction of the Population and the Family), *Sotsiologicheskie issledovaniia,* no. 2
(1982): 81.

war's ravages will be entering the retirement ages in the next decade. These groups have larger shares of men and hence are unlikely to be as politically quiescent as the World War II generation was.

In addition, the differences among the nationalities in age structure mean that to the extent that equalization of opportunity for higher education and higher status occupations across the nationalities increases, national groups with larger cohorts in the younger age brackets will gain disproportionate advantages. Here it is important to bear in mind Jones and Grupp's admonition that in comparing the proportions of each nationality that are party members or have higher educations, we must compare groups similar in age. When the appropriate age cohorts are compared, the evidence shows that the 1960s and to a lesser extent the 1970s saw a substantial narrowing in the differences among the nationalities in educational attainments, party membership, and occupational opportunity. This equalization of the nationalities, caused by the rapid catching up of the younger generations of the less developed nationalities to the levels of social development reached by the Slavic and other groups, will have the effect in the future of increasing the political weight of the Central Asians in particular as their rapidly growing population begins to assert its increasing power in the social and political spheres. On the other hand, the disproportionate pressure of numbers on the party, educational, and occupational hierarchies will increase the competition among national groups for access to the means of status and influence. Already in the late 1970s the earlier trend toward equalization of opportunity began to slow down and to be reversed. According to Jones and Grupp, "Relative enrolment of young Muslims in higher educational institutions and specialized secondary schools declined. . . . Relative party participation rates, which had continued to grow until the mid-1970s, began to decline in the latter half of the decade."[39] In the coming decades, competition for places in institutions of higher education, party membership, and white-collar jobs between Central Asians with large populations in the age brackets of the twenties and thirties and Russians and other Slavs whose relative ages are older is likely to increase ethnic tensions.

[39]Jones and Grupp, "Modernisation and Ethnic Equalisation in the USSR," p. 179.

The final issue, less tangible than the economic questions that the aging of the population poses, concerns the impact that the different age structures that characterize different ethnic groups will have on the political culture of the society. The population that confronted German invasion in the 1940s was more dominated by Russians and other Slavs; this population experienced a common trauma and rallied to the cause of national defense. As the population's composition increasingly shifts away from the numerical preponderance of these Slavic and other European groups, the assertion of national and cultural identity by the southern and eastern populations is likely to exert a centrifugal pull on the cohesion of the society. Political generations are often defined by common experience as much as by common age, and the experiences that will be salient to the younger generations of the non-Slavic population are growing increasingly remote from the era of revolution, terror, and war. Leaders drawn from these groups are unlikely to place as much emphasis on obedience to Moscow as did their elders, and the political culture will need to accommodate their interests in the goals of preserving the harmony of the multinational Soviet state.

The final variable to be discussed is that of sex. As we observed above, the cataclysmic events of the twentieth century pressed with great force on the Soviet population, and above all on its men. The 1959 census showed that in the 35 to 49 year old age group (people who would have been 21–35 years old in the war) there were only 63 males to every 100 females. The disparity in the numbers of the sexes has narrowed considerably but is still greater than in other countries. Now in the USSR there are 87 males per 100 females (compared with 94.5 in the United States).[40] The gap in the numbers reflects not only the war but also the disproportionately severe impact of Stalin's terror on the male population, as well as the privations and disruptions of the revolutionary era of the teens and twenties.

This difference in numbers together with other factors has tended to draw women into the labor force in exceptionally large numbers. Most Soviet and Western analysts agree that the participation of women in the labor force is virtually at the saturation point: the number of women in the Russian republic who are not

---

[40]Rapawy and Baldwin, ''Demographic Trends,'' p. 272; Hacker, *U/S*, p. 31.

employed in the economy is less than one-fifth, and most of these women are prevented from entering the labor force by poor health or the need to care for a large number of children. At the same time, the absence of abundant household conveniences and appliances, the poor and uneven distribution of food and other consumer goods, and the slow pace at which traditional patriarchal attitudes have broken down combine to impose a significant double burden on women. The double burden refers to the necessity for most women to hold full-time jobs and in their nonworking hours to spend a roughly equal amount of time on housekeeping, shopping, and childrearing tasks. It is estimated that men spend two to three times less time on housekeeping and child care than do women; women who work on average spend 41 hours a week on the job and another 36 hours in domestic chores.[41] Another factor contributing to the hard circumstances Soviet women face is the rising divorce rate and the difficulty single women have (particularly those raising a child) in coping with the combined demands of work and home. Divorce rates have shot upwards: from three per hundred marriages in 1950, they have now reached thirty-four per hundred in 1980, a rate comparable to that reached in the United States in 1970 (it was forty-nine per hundred in 1980)[42]. The plight of the single woman and single mother has become one of the most widely discussed themes in the Soviet media, not only because it puts to the test the claims of the humanism of the Soviet society but also because it is directly linked to the serious economic problem of excessively low birthrates.

The perpetuation of these patterns has put men in an advantageous position as far as political and occupational advancement is concerned. Women predominate in certain occupations, such as the textile industry, sales, teaching, and medicine. Women comprise 69 percent of the doctors and 71 percent of the teachers of the Soviet Union.[43] Although such highly feminized occupations require a higher educational degree, they are, not coincidentally, the lower-status occupations in the society and pay accordingly low wages. As we move up the status ladder, however — examining the composition, for example, of the medical workers engaged in research as opposed to clinical practice — we

---

[41]Perevedentsev, "Vosproizvodstvo naseleniia," pp. 86–87.
[42]Hacker, *U/S,* p. 106.
[43]David Lane, *The End of Inequality?,* p. 76.

find that men predominate. Only around 9 percent of enterprise directors are women.[44] The same principle holds true in directly political careers. One-quarter of the CPSU is made up of women, but no women are first secretaries of provincial-level party organizations, none are members of the Central Committee Secretariat or of the Politburo, and only about 3 percent of the members of the Central Committee itself are women. Of David Lane's hundred top officials mentioned above, none is a woman, nor is any of the over one hundred members of the USSR Council of Ministers.[45] Much of the reason for these disparities is that the party's expectation of a high volume of volunteer responsibilities taken on by party members is frequently difficult for women of working ages to meet, with the result that men are more likely to be given openings for advancement to influential posts in the economy, government, and party. In turn, the perpetuation of this gender-based division of labor reinforces the traditional notions of patriarchy and women's place. Rhetorical commitment to equality of the sexes, long a vital element of socialist doctrine, does little to overcome a gap that the structure of the economy itself helps to maintain.

SOVIET SOCIAL STRATIFICATION

Let us examine how the forms of social differentiation that we have considered above separately — urban vs. rural residence, occupation, education, ethnicity, age, and sex — relate to one another. To a large extent, it is the fundamental task of the Communist Party of the Soviet Union to prevent these and other social groupings from acquiring the self-consciousness and political techniques that would enable them to articulate group demands. The party oversees the processes for integrating the populace into a united, harmonious "Soviet people," all of whose citizens are "productive" rather than "nonproductive," or parasitical, in their occupational position and all of whom enjoy equal social and political rights. In 1936 Stalin declared the great revolutionary struggle of the working class and to a lesser degree the peasantry against capital to have been consummated with the completion of the construction of socialism. Resentment by non-Russian nationalities of Russian domination likewise is considered long since

[44]Ibid., p. 80.
[45]Ibid.

replaced by the successful implementation of the Leninist nationality policy. The old society's unfair treatment of women has given way, according to Soviet doctrine, to their full and equal participation in social life.

In fact, though frictions among classes, nationalities, and other groupings of the population have not been eliminated by the imposition of socialist political and social institutions, in practice they have not proved insuperable obstacles to the party's policies or power. To a considerable extent this testifies to the party's ability to inculcate acceptance of the legitimacy of the regime among most segments of the population. Of no less importance is the fact that these cleavages are not mutually reinforcing: nationality discontent tends to cut across class differences and often is directed against other nationalities, and working class resentment of the power and privilege of the rulers tends to undermine national self-consciousness. The situation stands in sharp contrast to the crisis that existed in the Russian empire on the eve of 1917, when organized and doctrinally armed working class unrest in the cities coincided with a widespread revolt by peasants in the countryside as well as with revolutionary nationalistic stirrings among many of the ethnic minorities. The present-day Soviet society is far from experiencing so severe a breakdown of social authority. Recognizing the potential for conflict among diverse social interests, the regime appears adept at playing classes and groups off against one another — fostering fears among the intelligentsia, for example, of working class discontent while tacitly appealing to working class authoritarianism and xenophobia through disguised or open anti-Semitic, chauvinistic, or anti-intellectual propaganda. One of the important sources of the regime's stability, therefore, is the cross-cutting character of social cleavages.

To prevent social development from reinforcing existing inequalities, the authorities seek to diffuse opportunities and benefits among all regions and classes and to ensure that working class and peasant children enjoy high rates of social mobility by means of an expanding industrial occupational system and a universal educational system. Probably the single most important social change under Soviet rule has been the movement of millions of peasants into urban life and industrial or related occupations. This form of mobility is both horizontal and vertical as peasants have left the tedium of farm labor and entered higher-paying jobs with better prospects in the cities. The movement of peasants into the cities has made up by far the largest share of growth of cities since the inception of the regime. Of the 129 million people added to the urban population between 1927 and 1976, 73 million (56.6 percent) were migrants from the countryside; individuals born into urban families numbered about half that figure, while the rest were added as a result of redefining areas as urban.[46] The main reason for this large-scale exodus from the countryside was the desire to seek a better way of life in the city.[47] For most, this meant the hope for improvement in material circumstances and the wish to acquire a better education as well as the desire to escape the routine and hardship of rural life. For rural boys, one of the major routes of mobility is military service, which provides exposure to training and discipline and often weakens the ties to the village. Surveys in the late 1960s revealed that no more than 30 percent of peasant youth returned to their villages after military service.[48] For girls and boys both, the fact that most specialized secondary and higher educational institutions are located in the cities means that students wishing to advance their education beyond the eighth- or tenth-grade level must leave the village to do so.

The shift of the population from the villages to the cities has often resisted planning and control. Various problems have resulted from the rapid and massive nature of this transformation. One has been the quality of rural labor left behind. As a result of the tendency for the able-bodied, educated, and highly motivated to leave, the elderly, the less skilled, and often the women stay behind.[49] The persistence of this problem is one reason for the difficulties Soviet planners have in raising productivity among farm workers. A second consequence is the strain imposed on the cities by trying to provide adequate housing, transportation, shopping, educational, and occupational facilities. Although the extreme overcrowding of the cities that was characteristic of the Stalin era — when it was common for several families to crowd into a single apartment — has been alleviated by the construction

[46]Rapawy and Baldwin, "Demographic Trends," p. 273.

[47]See Mervyn Matthews, *Class and Society in Soviet Russia* (New York: Walker, 1972), p. 198.

[48]Victor Zaslavsky, *The Neo-Stalinist State*, p. 31.

[49]Ann Goodman and Geoffrey Schleifer, "The Soviet Labor Market in the 1980's," in Joint Economic Committee, *Soviet Economy in the 1980's*, p. 333.

of apartment houses on a large scale since the 1950s (over the three decades from 1950 to 1980, urban population rose 2.4 times, while the quantity of urban housing space rose 4.3 times), urban overcrowding and the shortage of housing are still problems. Only about 80 percent of the urban population lives in individual family apartments. The provision of other amenities such as shops, transportation, communal services, and goods continues to be a problem as well, particularly in newer towns and those enjoying lower national status than the showcase cities of Moscow or Leningrad. The relative shortage of such facilities imposes various forms of inconvenience on the population, such as the prevalent need to wait in long lines to buy scarce goods.[50]

Perhaps more significant in this rapid influx of new residents to the cities is the question of their social integration into the fabric of urban life. Though the problem of inculcating the new urbanites with the habits and culture of an urban working class has become less acute since the Stalin era, it remains a serious challenge. The isolation and alienation of individuals, often young and relatively unskilled, who have settled in the cities but have not assimilated its norms are often linked in Soviet discussions to such social maladies as low labor productivity, disciplinary infractions, alcohol abuse, and crime.[51] Nevertheless, though low agricultural labor productivity, urban overcrowding, and unsuccessful social integration of "yesterday's peasants" remain serious problems, there can be little doubt that the shift of the population into urban and industrial ways of life has given force to the regime's claims that it is dynamic in achieving its aim of building socialism.

The great movements of social leveling, equalization, and upward mobility have not been spread evenly across the nearly seven decades of Soviet rule. Three waves of social mobilization can be distinguished. The first occurred during the revolutionary turmoil

[50]Soviet scholars calculated that in one smaller city with a population of 167,000, the time spent just standing in lines at the cafeterias at work, during work hours, took 4.3 million man-hours a year. Eliminating the time lost to the economy by waiting in these lines would, it was estimated, raise the economic productivity of the city by 7 percent, the equivalent of adding 3000 workers to the labor force. "Aktual'nye voprosy politiki KPSS i pressa" (Current Questions of Party Policy and the Press), *Zhurnalist,* no. 3 (1983): 32.

[51]See Ellen Propper Mickiewicz, *Media and the Russian Public* (New York: Praeger, 1981), ch. 7, "Pocket of Isolation: Migrants to the City."

of the war communism period, when the Bolshevik assault on the administrative and economic elites of the old regime — the "Red Guard attack on capital," as Lenin called it — thrust workers into leading political and administrative positions in the party and state apparatuses and to a lesser degree in industrial management. The destructiveness of the Civil War and other calamities, such as epidemics and famine, however, also decimated the working class, while the economic retreat of the New Economic Policy slowed the social gains of the workers and peasants.

The period of the first two Five Year Plans, beginning in 1928, was the second major phase of rapid and sustained social transformation. Millions of peasants entered urban, industrial occupations while millions of workers advanced to higher occupations in the economy or in the burgeoning economic, governmental, security, or party bureaucracies. Alex Inkeles noted that the total number of workers and white-collar employees more than doubled in the 1930s, while the intelligentsia grew 3.8 times between 1926 and 1937. The ranks of enterprise managers grew more than 4 times in this period and the number of scientists and scholars rose almost 6 times.[52] Expansion of the educational system, especially through crash technical schooling, enabled many to acquire the skills for better-paying occupations almost overnight.[53] Combined with the effects of terror and purges, which struck most heavily at those in higher echelons of the party and state, the period of Stalin's "revolution from above" propelled millions into higher-status positions in society. Many of the Brezhnev generation of leaders shot upwards from modest working class or peasant backgrounds into senior party or government positions at the regional or even national levels. Survivors and beneficiaries of the Stalin revolution, they were in many ways its most loyal servants. Well into the 1970s the men of the Stalin generation continued to form the senior elite group in the party, government, military, and security apparatuses.[54]

[52]Alex Inkeles, "Social Stratification and Mobility in the Soviet Union," in Alex Inkeles, *Social Change in Soviet Russia* (New York: Simon & Schuster, 1971), pp. 154–55.

[53]The number of students in higher technical education nearly doubled, from 53.3 million in 1926–1927 to 108.5 million in 1936, and the percentage of workers enrolled in these schools rose from one-third to 57.2 in the same period. See Nicholas Lampert, *The Technical Intelligentsia and the Soviet State* (New York: Holmes & Meier, 1979), p. 70.

[54]Jerry F. Hough, *Soviet Leadership in Transition* (Washington, D.C.: Brookings Institution, 1980), pp. 40–48.

The social revolution wrought under Stalin, profound as the upheaval was, nonetheless left serious inequalities in its wake. For one thing, it tended to be concentrated more in Russia and the Ukraine than in the more backward parts of the Soviet Union. In Central Asia and other borderlands, agriculture continued to dominate the local economies until well after World War II. As of 1939, the peasantry still made up around 80 percent of the population among Uzbeks, Turkmens, Tadjiks, and Kirgiz, whereas the share of white-collar employees among them was around 5 percent. As late as 1970, when only 12 percent of the Russians were classified as collective farm peasantry, between 40 and 50 percent of the Central Asian peoples were still *kolkhozniki*. Another of the effects of the Stalin revolution was severe rural poverty, especially among collective farm peasants. In industry, Stalin's deliberate use of wage differentials as an incentive left wide gaps between the highest-paid and lowest rungs of the income ladder. Under Khrushchev and Brezhnev, these gaps were steadily reduced. Collective farm income rose as the prices paid for farm produce increased and, in 1966, when a fixed annual minimum income from the state was provided for farmers. In industry, though income for middle- and higher-level strata was gradually increased, wages at the lower end of the scale were increased by a higher rate, reducing overall wage differences. From the mid-1950s to the mid-1970s, therefore, incomes in the population underwent significant equalization.

In addition, educational expansion under Khrushchev and Brezhnev also helped to equalize social status across classes and nationalities. One major development was the universalization of secondary schooling: if in the early 1950s only about 10 percent of the pupils were entering the ninth and tenth grades, by the late 1970s, as we have seen, virtually all pupils were receiving complete secondary educations, either through the general school or in a vocational-technical school.[55] The spread of secondary and technical schooling benefited the working class and peasantry most of all and particularly those in the non-Russian republics. The effect of rapidly expanding educational opportunity in the outlying regions has meant that in the 1960s and 1970s, the social and educational makeup of the less developed nationalities grew

[55] Murray Yanowitch, *Social and Economic Inequality in the Soviet Union* (White Plains, N.Y.: M. E. Sharpe, 1977), p. 80.

closer to that of the more developed European nationalities.[56] By
the late 1970s, when this process slowed down noticeably, the
younger generations of the Central Asian nationalities (as well as
Moldavian and other late-developing groups) had gone far to catch
up with the Russians in such indicators as the proportion of the
group with higher education or the share among them of employed specialists. Between 1962–1963 and 1976–1977 the absolute numbers of students in specialized secondary schools from the
six major Moslem nationalities (Azeri, Kazakh, Kirgiz, Tadjik,
Turkmen, and Uzbek) increased by nearly three times, and the
number in institutions of higher learning rose nearly two and a
half times, while both figures rose by less than 60 percent for the
whole country.[57] Two American scholars who compared like age
groups among the various nationalities found a "substantial narrowing of the educational gap in the 1960's" and concluded that
"the 1960's, then, were a time of rapid gains by the late-mod-
ernizing minority groups."[58] A similar pattern was revealed in
respect to other measures of social and political development, such
as party membership by ethnic group, the number of specialists
employed in the economy, and mastery of the Russian language.
In all measures, a trend toward convergence of the level of development of the Soviet nationalities occurred in the 1960s and
1970s as a result of the unequally rapid gains made by the younger
age cohorts of the minority groups.

Taken together, these changes in income and educational levels
among the population amount to a third great wave of social mobility and equalization, less dramatic but more protracted than
the revolutionary shifts of the Bolshevik and Stalinist era. On the
other hand, the slowing economic growth of the late 1970s and
the heavy pressure of rapid population growth among the Moslem
nationalities had the effect of slowing the pace of this trend, leaving inequalities between social classes and among more developed
and less developed nationalities in place.

[56]Iu. V. Arutiunian, "Korennye izmeneniia v sotsial'nom sostave sovetskikh
natsii" (Fundamental Changes in the Social Makeup of Soviet Nations), *Sotsiologicheskie issledovaniia,* no. 4 (October–December 1982): 21–27.

[57]John L. Scherer, ed., *USSR Facts and Figures Annual,* vol. 6 (Gulf Breeze,
Fla.: Academic International Press, 1982), pp. 301–2.

[58]Jones and Grupp, "Modernisation and Ethnic Equalisation in the USSR,"
p. 166.

If social equalization and mobility are important props of the regime's legitimacy, periods of stagnant growth and low opportunity pose dangers for the stability of the regime by hardening class and ethnic inequalities. As existing social groups grow more stable in composition, they may develop a sharper sense of collective interests, and pluralistic tendencies may gain ground at the expense of the homogenizing and centralizing processes pursued by the regime. Paradoxically, the most acute conflicts are likely to emerge within the most privileged sector of the society, the intelligentsia, which is a diverse and composite group, and the one whose members are most likely to articulate demands either in acceptable, within-system forms or in the form of illegitimate expression or dissent. We now turn to a more detailed examination of the social composition and political interests of this segment of the population.

PRIVILEGES AND PROBLEMS OF THE INTELLIGENTSIA

Earlier we proposed a relatively restrictive definition of the *intelligentsia* as the class formed of those with a higher education and holding positions of authority or responsibility within the social and political systems. All holding senior-level executive positions in the party, government, industry, trade, medicine, agriculture, education, planning, and similar spheres would be included (perhaps 5 million); so would members of the scientific-technical intelligentsia and the creative intelligentsia. All in all, between seven and eight million persons may be said to comprise the Soviet intelligentsia, although this figure is but a rough estimate.[59]

The members of intelligentsia perform several vital functions essential to maintaining the system. They administer and develop economic production, organize and oversee cultural life, conduct

[59]See Matthews, *Class and Society in Soviet Russia,* p. 145, who takes as his yardstick the number of specialists with higher educational degrees employed in the economy, or about 6 million as of 1968; also see M. N. Rutkevich and F. P. Filippov, *Sotsial'naia struktura razvitogo sotsialisticheskogo obshchestva v SSSR* (The Social Structure of the Developed Socialist Society in the USSR) (Moscow: Nauka, 1976), pp. 89–90. The latter source gives a figure of 7.44 million as of 1974 for the number of specialists with VUZ degrees employed in the economy plus another 1.36 million who are the most highly placed and highly educated in the society; L. G. Churchward, in *The Soviet Intelligentsia* (London: Routledge & Kegan Paul, 1973), occupies a middle ground, defining as the intelligentsia all with higher educational degrees or equivalent experience. Today by his definition between nine and ten million individuals would be classified as the intelligentsia.

research, voice criticism, advance theory, and help conduct the political socialization of the population.[60] The intelligentsia is a complex and diverse group, however. One major cleavage within it runs between those who enjoy privilege and status as a consequence of their position in the political system, such as full-time party functionaries, and those who hold influential posts in economic planning, administration, and management or in the sphere of culture, including the fine arts and the mass media. Following the German specialist Boris Meissner, we might term the former group the *power elite* and the second the *prestige elite*.[61] The core of the power elite is the party apparatus, and taken together with the top echelons of the military, state bureaucracy, and security forces, it probably numbers between half a million and a million persons. Much larger, then, than the power elite are the groups whose status derives from their importance in managing the complex modern society. To minimize tensions between these groups, the party leadership has followed a strategy of incorporation or co-optation of social elites, allowing them a variety of privileges to contain discontent and infusing them with a sense of privilege and responsibility. The self-esteem of intelligentsia is further bolstered by superior access to inside information and Western books and periodicals and by opportunities to travel abroad and have contact with Western colleagues. Their children have substantially better than average chances of securing admission to the best higher educational institutions and to pursue high-status careers.

In return for these privileges, the political authorites demand not only good professional performance but also ideological orthodoxy and political fidelity. To cultivate these qualities, the regime subjects the intelligentsia to particularly intensive forms of political indoctrination through the adult political education system (see Chapter VI) and also requires nearly universal participation in spare-time social and political work. At the same time, the power elite has itself grown closer in educational attainments to the groups it oversees. By the beginning of the 1970s, virtually all party secretaries above the primary party organization level

[60]Churchward, *Soviet Intelligentsia*, p. 93.

[61]Boris Meissner, ed., *Social Change in the Soviet Union: Russia's Path toward an Industrial Society*, trans. Donald P. Kommers (Notre Dame, Ind.: University of Notre Dame Press, 1972), pp. 134–38.

(see below) possessed higher educations.[62] In addition, the party recruits heavily from among the members of the intelligentsia, ensuring that sizable proportions of every important category of jobholder will be party members. Nearly a third of the specialists with higher or specialized secondary educations are party members; so are a quarter of all engineers and technicians, a quarter of all teachers, half of all scholars holding the graduate degrees of candidate or doctor of science, half of all writers, and three-quarters of all journalists.[63]

Nevertheless, despite these measures, many members of the intelligentsia have voiced serious criticism of the policies and even the very ideological basis of the regime. Much criticism has been couched in terms acceptable to the censors, while much has appeared in unpublished manuscript form (samizdat) or has been transmitted to the West. Many members of the intelligentsia think of themselves as heirs and custodians of the prerevolutionary Russian tradition in which members of the intelligentsia, somewhat like Western intellectuals, were critical thinkers, concerned with fundamental moral, cultural, and political issues and imbued with aspirations toward social justice and the betterment of mankind. Men such as Andrei Sakharov and Alexander Solzhenitsyn are clearly faithful to this tradition. When such intellectuals speak out against moral and political evil or on behalf of the public good, they do so not as spokesmen of their professional group but as representatives of enlightened public opinion. In other cases intellectuals are also likely to articulate the interests of the professional or occupational groups to which they belong.

Undoubtedly the greatest stimulus to political activism among the intelligentsia came from Khrushchev's campaign of de-Stalinization, which included his denunciation of the "crimes" of the Soviet dictator and an attempt to expunge Stalin's "cult of personality" — as Khrushchev termed the state-sponsored adulation of the power and authority of Stalin — from the Soviet political culture. In the course of undoing many though not all of the wrongs committed by Stalin against the Soviet people, Khrushchev awakened intense social criticism from among many ele-

---

[62]"KPSS v tsifrakh" (The CPSU in Figures), *Partiinaia zhizn'*, no. 14 (July 1981): 25.

[63]*Pravda*, 26 September 1983, in CDSP 35, no. 39 (26 October 1983): 6.

ments of the intelligentsia for whom the oppression of the Stalinist system was intolerable. In his own precarious efforts to retain and expand power, Khrushchev resorted to the risky task of allying himself with some of these intellectuals, hoping thereby to discredit those of the old Stalinist political elite still entrenched in the party and state bureaucracies. Thus Khrushchev personally succeeded in authorizing the publication of Solzhenitsyn's powerful, simply written story of the Stalinist labor camps, *One Day in the Life of Ivan Denisovich* in 1962. Publication of this story in the journal of the liberal intelligentsia, *Novy mir* (The New World), proved to be a bombshell, and it in turn stimulated attempts by many more authors to win publication for their own memoirs and fiction dealing with the hitherto taboo subject of the widespread incarceration of innocent people in concentration camps.[64] Frustrated by the resistance of entrenched conservatives in the party and state bureaucracies to his de-Stalinization campaign, at one point in this phase Khrushchev even agreed with the intellectuals' demand that censorship be abolished.[65]

Khrushchev's tolerance for the attack by the liberal-minded intelligentsia on the values and institutions associated with Stalin was not consistent and in any case did not outlive his own tenure in power. The Brezhnev leadership, assuming power in October 1964 after a bloodless coup against the isolated Khrushchev, signaled its attitude toward intellectual dissent with the arrest in 1965 of two writers and critics, Andrei Sinyavsky and Yuli Daniel. Nevertheless, while this tolerance lasted, intellectuals divided over the Stalin issue, which became the litmus test of the political and social attitudes of the intelligentsia. Those aligned on the liberal side of this cleavage espoused values of intellectual freedom, the absolute moral value of truth, critical and self-aware openness toward the past, and the moral dignity and worth of the individual, all of which were trampled underfoot in the Stalin era. On the conservative side were those adhering to the older Stalinist doctrines of worldwide class antagonism and incompatibility between socialism and capitalism, the necessity for centralized rule and social solidarity, and acceptance of the moral compromises ac-

[64]Zhores A. Medvedev, *Ten Years after One Day in the Life of Ivan Denisovich,* trans. Hilary Sternberg (London: Macmillan, 1974).

[65]On these and other episodes, see Dina R. Spechler, *Permitted Dissent in the USSR: Novyi mir and the Soviet Regime* (New York: Praeger, 1982), p. 158.

companying communist party rule.[66] Also lining up on the anti-Stalinist side were reformists who sought to rationalize the rigid and dysfunctional aspects of the system Stalin and his associates had created. Legal specialists contributed to the reform of the codes of criminal law and criminal procedure and economists advanced ideas, which formerly would have been impossible to voice publicly, about the utility of some measure of profitability of capital investment and enterprise performance.[67] They shared with the moralists among the intelligentsia an interest in promoting a climate of personal security and political toleration that would permit relatively open discussion of major issues.

Analyzing the evolution of within-system criticism (''permitted dissent,'' in her term), Dina Spechler has identified three streams of intellectual dissent in the immediate post-Stalin period: social pragmatism, which was concerned with improving existing structures though not subjecting them to a more searching ethical examination; cultural liberalism, interested in pushing back the intrusive power of the party and state from the sphere of personal and professional action; and moral humanism, seeking to restore the ethical values that intellectuals considered the only valid ends of human existence. As intellectuals, at first largely through the medium of fictional literature, dealt with questions that had been suppressed under Stalin or treated accepted subjects in new ways, the critiques they advanced were deepened and developed. A new spirit of *critical realism* toward actual social problems, such as the demoralization of youth or the poverty of the countryside, grew up. Finally writers began dealing with the Stalinist past itself, in some ways the most ideologically threatening subject of all and the one that prompted the sharpest reaction from among the leadership.[68]

Many of the liberal intellectuals had an outlet in the literary journal *Novy mir,* which became the basis for a wing or grouping among the intelligentsia. As it became known for publishing daring, risky works that questioned Stalinist practices and values, it

[66]See Stephen F. Cohen, ''The Stalin Question since Stalin,'' in idem, *An End to Silence: Uncensored Opinion in the Soviet Union* (New York: Norton, 1982), pp. 22–50.
[67]See H. Gordon Skilling and Franklyn Griffiths, eds., *Interest Groups in Soviet Politics* (Princeton, N.J.: Princeton University Press, 1971).
[68]Spechler, *Permitted Dissent,* pp. 4, 21, 49, 60, 131–45.

attracted a wide readership among all groups of the intelligentsia, reaching tens of thousands of readers. It published not only fiction but also works reflecting unorthodox thinking in fields such as history and economics.[69] In this case the bonds formed across the professional lines within the intelligentsia over the liberal-conservative cleavage were stronger than those uniting members of occupational or professional categories. The solidarity among anti-Stalinist, democratically minded intellectuals that was generated in the late 1950s and early 1960s continued well into the Brezhnev period, when the regime's crackdown on forms of dissent it considered unacceptable often provoked protest petitions and actions by the intelligentsia. The wide reaction to the regime's arrest of Sinyavsky and Daniel in 1965 and their trial and conviction in 1966 on charges of having disseminated "anti-Soviet propaganda" through their fiction indicated both the willingness of intellectuals to group together to defend liberal values and the wide impact that the journal *Novy mir* had, since both writers had been contributors to the journal.[70]

The crackdown on intellectual dissent that the Brezhnev regime initiated — reinforced, no doubt, by the example of political liberalization in neighboring Czechoslovakia during the Prague Spring — succeeded by the late 1970s in driving most forms of dissenting thought and activity underground or into exile abroad. (The success of this campaign may well have improved Yuri Andropov's own political prospects during his tenure as KGB head from 1967 to 1982.) Within-system social criticism, however, continues to be articulated, reaching small and elite audiences through scholarly or small-circulation periodicals or in the closed setting of high-level meetings and conferences. Much of this expression comes not from literary intellectuals but from social scientists, whose commentary is generally couched in scholarly or ideological jargon. Nevertheless, the range of published (if ignored) reformist thinking can be surprising.

Following a major national conference on the problems of the economy held in April 1983, a memorandum prepared for the conference was (no doubt deliberately) leaked to the West. Written by Tatiana Zaslavskaya, a social scientist working under the

[69]Ibid., pp. 199, 247.
[70]Ibid., p. 262.

Siberian branch of the Academy of Sciences, it laid out a sweeping analysis of the problems of the economy. In cautious language the report asserted that the contemporary social institutions established in the Stalin era were no longer justifiable on either practical or ethical grounds. In the 1930s, Zaslavskaya observed, "people were in fact viewed as little 'cogs' in the economic machine and they behaved almost as obediently and passively as machines and materials." In place of the overcentralization of economic planning and administration, which, the author held, was a fetter on further economic progress, "economic" (market-type) incentives were needed to stimulate better enterprise-level management and worker productivity. If adopted, these proposals would necessitate sweeping changes in the political system and would strike above all at the power of the planning and ministerial bureaucracy in Moscow, a fact that the memo flatly acknowledged and deplored.[71]

A journal entitled EKO (standing for *Ekonomika i organizatsiia promyshlennogo proizvodstva* — Economics and the Organization of Industrial Production), also published by the economists based in Novosibirsk under the editorship of the renowned, independent-minded member of the Academy of Sciences, A. G. Aganbegyan, became known as a forum for the articulation of moderately reformist specialist opinion on a variety of significant social and economic themes. Many of its contributors call for wider use of economic levers in economic management. A round-table discussion published in August 1983, involving economists, industrial managers, and planners, voiced a call by Aganbegyan for "a radical restructuring of the economic mechanism" and sharp attacks on the overcentralized planning system, the quality of which, one manager claimed, had "deteriorated markedly in recent years."[72]

An interesting book published in 1984 provides some indication of the outer limits of permissible demands for reform. Its author, M. I. Piskotin, calls for extensive changes — he is careful to avoid

[71]A full text of the report will be found in RFE/RL "Materialy Samizdata," AS no. 5042, vyp. no. 35/83 (26 August 1983), Tat'iana Zaslavskaia, "Doklad o neobkhodimosti bolee uglublennogo izucheniia v SSSR sotsial'nogo mekhanizma razvitiia ekonomiki" (Report on the Necessity for More Profound Study in the USSR of the Social Mechanism of Economic Development). Excerpts of the report and an analysis were published by the *New York Times* on 5 August 1983.

[72]CDSP 35, no. 48 (28 December 1983): 1-5.

using the provocative word "reform" — in the structure of the economy. Although he vehemently denies that what he aims at is market socialism, he calls for the introduction of widespread use of "economic," essentially market-oriented, levers to regulate the economy. Administrative devices such as production output targets should be minimized, he argues, and such economic devices as self-financing and rational pricing should be expanded. This inevitably would entail widened enterprise autonomy and less power for the central ministerial bureaucracies, and he outlines the reasons that the Moscow officialdom resists any such changes. Together with his strong plea for administrative decentralization, he calls for greater use of material incentives to rationalize the system of material distribution and to stimulate production. The cost of living would rise, as would wages, but the overall effect, as he readily acknowledges, would be to reduce the egalitarianism of official distributive policy. Yet it would strengthen social justice by weakening the force of the "shadow economy," which runs on privilege and connections. Although the presentation of these and other ideas in Piskotin's book is relatively bold in the context of current Soviet social science literature, their force is diluted by the abstract and general level of the book's discussion. Rarely does the author descend to particulars, and he refrains from exploring in greater depth some of the self-contradictory elements of his analysis. No attention is given to the effect of his proposed reforms on the existing regulative controls over the society, notably the party and the security police. Nevertheless, despite these reservations about the practicality of the changes Piskotin envisages, it must be said that the book represents a major statement of the reform-minded current in contemporary Soviet social science circles, and an important assault on the conservative assumptions behind existing social institutions.[73]

Relations between social scientists and the party authorities continue to be troubled. Despite full political loyalty on the part

[73]M. I. Piskotin, *Sotsializm i gosudarstvennoe upravlenie* (Moscow: Nauka, 1984). In a recent article, the British scholar Archie Brown calls attention to Piskotin's book, and notes that he offers acknowledgments to four other scholars, including Tatiana Zaslavskaya, in the preface. According to Brown, this suggests the existence of a kind of informal opinion grouping, which is counterposed to informal groups of conservatives and dogmatists. See Archie Brown, "Gorbachev: New Man in the Kremlin," *Problems of Communism,* 34, no. 3 (May–June 1985): 19.

of the senior echelons of the sociological, economic, and political science professions, the institutionalization of professional norms and standards has repeatedly led to strivings for autonomy on the part of social scientists.[74] Although each research project nominally forms part of larger institutional plans and must be justified on the grounds of utility to the state, social science research frequently touches sensitive subjects or reveals unwelcome results. A major purge of the sociological establishment in 1973 failed to prevent developments troublesome to the party authorities.[75] Although a tightening of party control over sociological research resulted from this purge, party authorities have not always succeeded in obtaining the results they desire from it. An example is the field of public opinion research. Party authorities at republican and provincial levels sometimes turn to pollsters to provide findings that the public supports policies that are already decided upon (the Georgian party's institute for public opinion research often performs this role). Even though much of the best research goes unpublished, that which is published often reveals such undesirable phenomena as low knowledge and interest on the part of large segments of the population in political affairs, high rates of apathy and alienation among the working class, and critical attitudes toward the regime on the part of the intelligentsia.[76] That the existing state of social science research is not altogether to the party overseers' liking was attested by criticism made at the June 1983 Central Committee plenum by Politburo member Konstantin Chernenko:

> We expected much [he commented] from the Institute of Sociological Research and the Central Economic-Mathematical Institute of the Academy of Sciences of the USSR, founded back in the 1960s.

[74]The former two but not the third discipline are recognized as academic subjects, but political scientists have won permission to form a professional association whose members are drawn from among those with backgrounds in philosophy, law, or other specialties. See Ronald J. Hill, *Soviet Politics, Political Science and Reform* (Oxford: Martin Robertson, 1980); Archie H. Brown, *Soviet Politics and Political Science* (New York: St. Martin's Press, 1974).

[75]On the development of the sociological profession and the effect of the shake-up of 1973, see Edward Beliaev and Pavel Butorin, "The Institutionalization of Soviet Sociology: Its Social and Political Context," *Social Forces* 61, no. 2 (December 1982): 418–35.

[76]Thomas Remington, "Soviet Public Opinion and the Effectiveness of Party Ideological Work," *Carl Beck Papers in Russian and East European Studies* (Pittsburgh, Pa.: University of Pittsburgh, 1983).

But we still have not seen any substantial applied investigations of social phenomena and current economic problems. The activity of these institutes has graphically revealed defects that are characteristic in greater or lesser degree of several other scientific establishments: self-enclosure within "dissertation" and group interests, triviality of themes, weak party influence.

Chernenko charged party and scholarly authorities with the task of strengthening their control over social science.[77]

If continuing tension characterizes relations between the thoroughly domesticated social science elite and the party authorities, even greater conflict attends the position of the literary establishment in the intelligentsia. As the above discussion suggested, the literary intelligentsia articulated the intellectuals' critique of Stalinism more sharply than any other group, often using the medium of fiction to dramatize the pragmatic and moral dilemmas of Stalinism. The work that probably did more than any other to bring the truth about Stalinist terror into the public realm, Solzhenitsyn's *One Day in the Life of Ivan Denisovich,* was given the green light by Khrushchev for obviously political reasons, but it allowed Solzhenitsyn for a short while to enjoy remarkable esteem in the literary establishment. In what in retrospect seems an amazing stroke, Solzhenitsyn was even nominated for the Lenin Prize in literature. A few of his short stories were published in *Novy mir* between 1962 and 1964. While many other anti-Stalinist writers also produced major works in this period, the power of Solzhenitsyn's prose and the uncompromising moral stance he took became a major influence on other writers. Together with other writers, Solzhenitsyn helped set two trends in motion that became significant currents in literature well after the crackdown on liberalizing and anti-Stalinist literature of the mid- and late 1960s.

The first was a turn to the peasant as a protagonist in fiction. Presented as the sturdy, enduring preserver of traditional moral values, the peasant, his unenviable lot, and the rural community of which he was the center became the symbol of something vital and essential in Soviet culture and the last repository of the values that might still redeem the Soviet society, lurching thoughtlessly

[77]*Pravda,* 15 June 1983, p. 1.

into the spiritually bankrupt materialism of the West.[78] The second element was a rediscovery of the Russian cultural heritage. Treated properly, nationalistic love of the Russian soil and people could be presented compatibly with the tame forms of national pride and identification that Soviet authorities allow all the Soviet national groups. Several of the most popular and ideologically tolerated writers, such as Valentin Rasputin, Viktor Astafyev, and the late Vasili Shukshin, have set their novels and stories in Siberia, treating traditional Siberian customs with honor and lamenting their passing.[79] In more zealous hands, the Russian theme was politically explosive, because it called attention to the element of Great Russian chauvinism and imperialism that even Lenin had found it necessary to warn his colleagues against and that had provoked resentment against the Russians under Stalin and later. For a time in the late 1960s, a major wing of the literary intelligentsia was given the opportunity to articulate highly emotional defenses of Russian national qualities and culture until the top leadership at a meeting in November 1970 at which Brezhnev spoke, made it clear that overt expression of Russian nationalism must be curbed.[80]

Rural, or countryside, prose has, however, continued to flourish, possibly because it corresponds to the more conservative and inward-looking cultural climate of the 1970s. Its values are not those of the democratic intelligentsia of the early 1960s, but they

[78]See Gleb Zekulin, "The Contemporary Countryside in Soviet Literature: A Search for New Values," in James R. Millar, ed., *The Soviet Rural Community* (Urbana: University of Illinois Press, 1971), pp. 376–404.

[79]See Maurice Friedberg, "Cultural and Intellectual Life," in Byrnes, *After Brezhnev*, pp. 282–83; Klaus Mehnert, *The Russians and Their Favorite Books* (Stanford, Calif.: Hoover Institution, 1983).

[80]See "Osuzhdenie linii zhurnala 'Molodaya gvardiya'," (Condemnation of the Line of the Journal "Young Guard") in *Politicheskii dnevnik* (Political Diary), II (Amsterdam: Alexander Herzen Foundation, 1975), p. 702. *Molodaya gvardiya* is a monthly publication of the Komsomol Central Committee appearing in some half a million copies. As John Dunlop, author of the most comprehensive recent study of Russian nationalism, has indicated, the action taken by the Politburo against the journal, including the removal of its editor, was part of a drive in the late 1960s and early 1970s against all forms of dissent, from the Democratic Movement to nationalism. See John B. Dunlop, *The Faces of Contemporary Russian Nationalism* (Princeton, N.J.: Princeton University Press, 1983), esp. p. 43. See also the chapters by Frederick C. Barghoorn and Roman Szporluk in Edward Allworth, ed., *Ethnic Russia in the USSR* (New York: Pergamon, 1980).

are implicitly anti-Stalinist to the extent that Stalinism is portrayed as depriving the countryside, through the brutality of farm collectivization, of the strength and integrity from which the entire country drew sustenance. That this implied criticism of one of the fundamental institutions of Soviet rule, collectivized agriculture, could trouble the party authorities was evident when Chernenko in the speech cited above also fired a shot over the bows of the rural writers:

> It is disquieting that in several works [of literature] deviations from historical accuracy are permitted, for example with respect to the evaluation of collectivization; God-seeking motifs slip through along with idealization of the old patriarchal family order.[81]

It was not only the writers who sought through their fiction to portray the search for absolute ethical standards and the greatness of the Russian spirit who invoked the wrath of the party. In 1979 a major conflict shook the literary establishment when a group of twenty-three writers, many of them enjoying full political favor, attempted to compile an anthology of works, most of which had been previously rejected by the Soviet censors. In general the works, which included poems, stories, plays, criticism, and art, were not directly political but touched on sore points or employed risky "pornographic" techniques. The compilers of the anthology entitled it *Metropol* (or Metropolis), suggesting perhaps the differences between their urban-centered, cosmopolitan concerns and those of the rural school. After publication of the collection was ruled out by the leadership of the Writers' Union, various forms of repression followed against the contributors. Most were pressured to renounce their participation in the venture. Sharp attacks on it were published. One of the best known contributors, Vasili Aksyonov, resigned from the Writers' Union in protest over the harassment and emigrated to the West.[82] Thus by its response both to the ethical searchings of the countryside writers and to the recognized figures involved in the Metropol' affair, the regime leadership has made it clear that the range of tolerated expression in literature is very narrow and that party control cannot be violated. In recent years a number of prominent Soviet writers have

---

[81]*Pravda,* 15 June 1983, p. 2.

[82]A review of the Metropol affair is given in Elizabeth C. Scheetz, "More Repercussions of the *Metropol'* Affair," RFE/RL, RL 27/80 (18 January 1980).

emigrated (and lost their citizenship in the process): Georgi Vla-dimov, Vasili Aksyonov, Lev Kopelev, Alexander Zinoviev, Vla-dimir Voinovich, Viktor Nekrasov, and others. Alexander Solzhenitsyn, winner of the 1970 Nobel Prize for Literature, was forcibly expelled from the country in 1974. Despite the steady regime pressure for works that are politically conformist, the his-tory of the past three decades suggests that there will continue to arise writers whose devotion to the literary profession will bring them into conflict with the political leadership.

THE STATUS OF WORKERS

A basic theme in Soviet doctrine is the claim that production workers in factories, mines, transport, and the like constitute the leading class of Soviet society. Its "revolutionary ideology and morality" and its "collectivist spirit" are considered to shape the political culture of the entire society.[83] This claim, however, is largely a myth both in political and social terms and has been so since the revolution, when, acting on Lenin's precept that without organization and indoctrination by a vanguard party of profes-sional revolutionaries, the workers would advance merely to "trade union consciousness," the Bolsheviks subjected the work-ing class and its organizations to thorough regimentation. Despite the considerable gains made by workers in social mobility within and across generations, the intelligentsia continues to occupy nearly all positions of esteem or influence in the society. Perhaps more disturbing to the party's leaders is evidence that despite strenuous efforts to equalize social and political opportunity made, as we have seen, from the late 1950s until the late 1970s, class lines are beginning again to ossify, diminishing the chances that working class children might rise to the intelligentsia.

In order to give force to the claims of the working class's lead-ing role among the social groups, various types of preference have been given to workers in such key avenues of mobility as party membership and admission to VUZy. Concerned that the party was becoming a body of white-collar employees and social elites, the party leaders issued a directive in September 1974 requiring local party committees to admit four or five blue-collar workers

---

[83]See *Pravda,* 26 September 1983, translated in CDSP 35, no. 39 (26 October 1983): 6.

for every white-collar employee they took in.[84] This policy has given rise to numerous complaints from the intelligentsia about reverse discrimination and the greater difficulty they have in entering the party. The use of quotas to ensure a high influx of blue-collar candidates to the party has increased the numerical weight of workers among all admitted to the party to about 60 percent. These figures are also probably inflated, however; some young VUZ graduates, for example, were reported to have taken temporary factory jobs to increase their chances of party admission.[85] The quota system, moreover, gives rise to disparities between the admissions rate among high-skilled workers and workers employed in lower-level administrative jobs (such as brigade chiefs or foremen) and those with lower skill levels or employed in more purely manual occupations. Miners working in underground operations, for example, are seriously underrepresented. The British social scientist Alex Pravda describes these differences as follows.

> Approximately one in eleven workers is a Communist; among male industrial blue-collar workers this rises to one in five. And since party ranks include relatively few unskilled manuals, membership among skilled industrial workers — at around one in three — equals saturation levels found among the ITR [engineering-technical personnel] and many professional groups. Among worker-technicians, a majority are party members, which places them on a par with college graduates. Thus, while accentuating the lowliness of the unskilled, party membership elevates the skilled working class and pinpoints the working middle class as an influential group.[86]

With respect to VUZ admissions, children of the working class are statistically much less likely to obtain a higher education than are the offspring of the intelligentsia, with the result that in large measure the intelligentsia passes its superior social and political position on to its heirs. At each of several points in the educational process, youth from blue-collar backgrounds are less likely to move on into those educational settings that afford a faster track to advancement. Blue-collar children are about half as likely as professionals' children to go on from eighth grade into the ninth and tenth grades of the general school. Those who do are between a

---

[84]*New York Times,* 10 November 1974.
[85]Ibid.
[86]Alex Pravda, ''Is There a Soviet Working Class?'' *Problems of Communism* 31 (November–December 1982): 19.

quarter and a third as likely to enter a VUZ as a professional's child. Even in the VUZy, blue-collar students are more likely to drop out than are white-collar students. Overall, children from working class backgrounds are about a third as likely as those from the employee stratum to obtain a higher education. Part of the reason lies in the aspirations transmitted by parents, and part lies in the tangible and intangible social and cultural assets that parents of the intelligentsia pass on in addition to their superior ability to obtain tutoring help for their youngsters and their greater connections with educational officials.[87]

Efforts under Khrushchev to tilt the balance in favor of working class children through direct and overt reverse discrimination, particularly a measure that reserved most spaces in VUZy for those who were applying from a job in production with tenure as a production worker of at least two years, met stiff opposition from educators concerned about weakening standards and from most segments of the intelligentsia, resentful over losing their privileged status. These measures were soon watered down and, when Khrushchev fell, dropped.[88] The Brezhnev regime, however, faced with the same problem of the reinforcement of class distinctions in Soviet society that could lead to unsettling political disquiet, instituted a partial remedy — closer in spirit to affirmative action than to reverse discrimination. In 1969 special preparatory departments at VUZy were created to give worker and peasant children the opportunity to ready themselves for VUZ admission. After courses lasting up to one year, these students take exams on which passing grades qualify them for VUZ admission without the need to take the stiff VUZ entrance exams. Perhaps 15 percent of all VUZ entrants come via this route, a figure too small to affect significantly the social advantages that the white-collar groups enjoy over the blue-collar sudents in seeking VUZ degrees. Moreover, the working class students who attend these preparatory courses are then more likely to enter the less prestigious agricultural and polytechnical institutes.[89]

[87]Pravda, "Working Class," pp. 11–12; Yanowitch, "Schooling and Inequalities," pp. 139–45.

[88]See Matthews, *Education,* pp. 24–33; Joel J. Schwartz and William R. Keech, "Group Influence and the Policy Process in the Soviet Union," *American Political Science Review* 62, no. 3 (September 1968): 840–51.

[89]Yanowitch, "Schooling and Inequalities," pp. 147–148; *Pravda,* "Working Class," pp. 12–13; L. Ia. Rubina, "Izmeneniia v sotsial'nom sostave studenchestva (Changes in the Social Makeup of the Student Body)," *Sotsiologicheskie issledovaniia,* no. 3 (July–September 1982): 108.

The need to prevent acute dissatisfaction among workers and the ideological homage given to their leading position in society prompt the regime to adopt palliative measures such as those described above and to maintain what is probably the single most important element in the social contract between regime and working class — the assurance of job security.[90] Through propaganda continually drawing attention to the problem of unemployment in the capitalist states of the West, the regime reinforces the promise of full employment and the Soviet worker's constitutional right to a job. The promise occupies a prominent place in the 1977 Constitution, as part of Brezhnev's effort to call attention to the importance of the "social rights" enjoyed by the population under socialism. In addition, job security is a de facto consequence of the problem of an inadequate labor supply: workers and managers alike know that a worker who leaves or is fired from one job can easily find a job elsewhere. This fact of life gives rise to a set of attitudes that the Soviet press constantly deplores: the belief by workers that they cannot be punished for poor performance and the belief by managers that they have no effective means of disciplining workers.[91]

Recent attempts by the leadership to raise the productivity of labor by altering this pattern but without provoking overt worker protest have not been especially effective. One of the most interesting developments in this regard is the *Shchekino experiment.* Introduced in 1967, it was a local, small-scale trial of a potentially significant reform in the powers and incentives of enterprise managers. In essence, the method consists of a grant of power to a manager to release workers whom he considers redundant or underemployed (he is not obliged to find them another job); meantime, the enterprise's wages and bonus fund remains constant, so that those workers who are retained can then be given substantial raises. At the enterprise where the method was first tried, per-worker productivity more than doubled in the first four years. Then, as all sources agree, the experiment largely fizzled out. One problem was that the planners chipped away at the manager's prerogatives. Another was that the greater profits the enterprise

[90]George W. Breslauer, "On the Adaptability of Soviet Welfare-State Authoritarianism," in Karl W. Ryavec, ed., *Soviet Society and the Communist Party* (Amherst: University of Massachusetts Press, 1978), p. 4.

[91]*Zhurnalist,* no. 2 (1983), p. 3.

now received could not be readily invested in new plant and equipment because of the shortage of needed goods. But perhaps the single greatest obstacle, which has not been openly discussed, is the fear that widespread worker resistance to the reform would increase tension between the regime and the working class. Success in the case of the Shchekino combine was largely due to the fact that the branch was expanding and the released workers easily found new jobs in the same combine. Overall, despite constant pressure in the press to adopt the method, only about 3 percent of the Soviet work force as of 1975 was working on this basis and further diffusion of the method in its original form appeared unlikely.[92]

The other notable attempt by the authorities to crack down on the problem of slack productivity and poor discipline among workers came with the installation of Yuri Andropov as general secretary of the party in November 1983. Accepting what had become a consensus among managers and economists that low productivity was one of the critical bottlenecks impeding further economic growth, Andropov launched a relatively ambitious campaign to emphasize to workers that their well-being depended upon honest labor of high quality. To drive home the point that the campaign was not a war by the authorities on the workers, he pointedly called for an end to corruption and foot-dragging by bureaucrats in the government and sacked twenty high officials, including three government ministers, during his first two months in office.[93] In January Andropov visited a Moscow factory for a widely publicized chat with the workers; he exhorted them to work harder for their own sake and for that of the country. "You understand yourselves," he told them, "that the government can give only so many goods as are produced. The growth of wages — if it is not accompanied by needed wares of good quality, if, finally, services are suffering — cannot give a real improvement in material well-being."[94] At the same time, the police initiated a series of identity checks on citizens found in movie theaters, bars, baths, and markets during the day to catch those who were away from their jobs without authorization. Newspapers printed letters

[92]David A. Dyker, "Planning and the Worker," in Schapiro and Godson, eds., *The Soviet Worker,* p. 58.

[93]*New York Times,* 7 February 1983.

[94]*New York Times,* 1 February 1983.

to the editor complaining about poor workplace discipline, one writer even suggesting that the worker's right to leave his job be abrogated. The authorities acknowledged that illegal absenteeism was in fact rising and worker discipline decreasing. Among workers performing predominantly manual labor in the metallurgical industry, half the work force were caught illegally absent from the jobs at some point.[95]

Although the steam quickly went out of the crackdown on labor absenteeism, the party did institute measures aimed at stiffening penalties for workplace violations, particularly when these were accompanied by alcohol abuse.[96] Figures for industrial production in 1983 showed that the campaign had some effect, with productivity rising noticeably. Further progress on this front was clouded, though, not only by Andropov's illness in the second half of the year but also by the difficulty of shifting the economy quickly to a more consumer-oriented assortment of outputs. The recent memory of the Solidarity movement in Poland still stands as a deterrent to any changes that abruptly worsen the relative living standards of the working class.

How likely is a repetition of the Polish experience of 1980–1981, when a broad, national working class movement aligned with the country's intelligentsia forced significant concessions and political liberalization from the leadership? The Soviet worker is still far from such extreme steps. The Polish society is unusually homogeneous in ethnic and linguistic makeup, quite unlike the diverse and multinational Soviet society in which, as we noted earlier, social cleavages tend to cut across one another. Second, the Solidarity period in Poland was notable for the alliance that was struck between the intelligentsia and the workers who enjoyed, in addition, the powerful benefit of the Catholic church's moral backing. The Soviet working class is still cut off from and often hostile to the intelligentsia. Two separate unofficial opinion polls among Soviet citizens found, for example, that blue-collar workers were indifferent or hostile to Andrei Sakharov; only about one in seven expressed a positive opinion about him.[97] When on two occasions in 1977 and 1978 a few workers did attempt to form

[95]"Aktual'nye voprosy," *Zhurnalist,* no. 3, pp. 31–32.

[96]See *Pravda,* 7 August 1983.

[97]REF/RL SAAOR "Attitudes of some Soviet to Andrei Sakharov," AR#11–81, p. 7.

independent trade unions and to contact Western reporters to publicize their organization, they were quickly arrested or incarcerated in psychiatric hospitals.[98] Third, the prevalence of authoritarian attitudes, together with apathy, cynicism, and demoralization, leaves workers indifferent to political organization or questions of high politics. Workers were overwhelmingly likely to support the Soviet invasion of Czechoslovakia in 1968 (three-quarters in one unofficial internal poll did so).[99] Their attitudes toward the Solidarity movement in Poland were generally negative, although nonparty members were considerably more likely to be sympathetic than were working class party members.[100] What working class protest there has been in recent years has taken the form of anomic unrest, such as wildcat strikes. Such actions have been reported in a variety of cities in the late 1970s and early 1980s, always concentrated in particular enterprises.[101] Workers are too closely overseen by the security police and the party to develop the means for their own national organization.

Nonetheless, the events in Poland and the potential for serious Soviet worker discontent have prompted the authorities to respond by admonishing the largely quiescent Soviet trade union organization to deal with grass-roots worker interests more effectively. In March 1982 the chairman of the All-Union Central Council of Trade Unions (AUCCTU), Aleksei Shibaev, was removed and replaced by Stepan Shalaev, a career trade union official who was, according to Blair Ruble, "the first trade union official to rise to the head of the Soviet Union hierarchy in over fifty years."[102] At the same time, the press carried numerous complaints about the bureaucratized role that the unions played; one comment published in *Pravda* accused the unions (justly) of simply serving as an appendage of management.[103] The response that the

[98]RFE/RL, RL 453/82, Julia Wishnevsky, "The Rise of Dissidence in the Brezhnev Era" (15 November 1982), p. 7.

[99]Victor Zaslavsky, *The Neo-Stalinist State* (Armonk, N.Y.: M. E. Sharpe, 1982), p. 26.

[100]RFE/RL AR#6-82, SAAOR, "Soviet Citizen Attitudes Toward Poland since Martial Law: *Agitprop,* Western Radio and the Evolution of Opinion," p. 5.

[101]Betsy Gidwitz, "Labor Unrest in the Soviet Union," *Problems of Communism* 31 (November–December 1982): 25–42.

[102]Blair A. Ruble, "Soviet Trade Unions and Labor Relations after 'Solidarity'," in Joint Economic Committee, *Soviet Economy in the 1980's,* p. 350.

[103]Ibid., p. 352.

post-Brezhnev regime settled upon, however, the campaign for higher productivity, seems more representative of the actual view among the party elite as to the desirable relationship between the working class and the state.

THE STATUS OF THE PEASANTRY

Of all social strata, the Soviet peasantry, particularly those employed on collective farms (*kolkhozy;* the peasants employed by them are called *kolkhozniki*) are probably the least thoroughly integrated into Soviet political culture. Although the modernization of the countryside has reduced inequalities between town and country to a certain degree, gaps in income and educational levels remain. The average income of a person employed on a collective farm is a little over half of that of the average state employee, although the differential is closing.[104]

The low productivity and low standard of living of the peasantry testify to the rapidity and brutality of the collectivization campaign conducted in the early years of Stalin's "revolution from above," when millions of peasant families were deprived of their land, stock, and tools and were forced to become members of agricultural cooperatives. Peasants on collective farms, as opposed to state farms, were legally considered to be leasing the land collectively from the state in perpetuity, with their income wholly dependent on the output of the farm and the prices paid by the state for their products. Since the state could manipulate the prices set in the contracts between procurement agencies and the farms, the peasants' welfare, especially in less productive regions, was often extremely low. Resistance to collectivization was broken by several means of coercion, including violence, arrests, and deportations of those considered to be class enemies of the state, the monopoly of farm machinery in state-owned machine-tractor stations (MTS), and the manipulation of food and seed supplies, which contributed to a massive famine in the Ukraine in 1932 costing millions of lives but effectively smashing the last remnants of opposition to the collectivization drive.

When the initial wave of agricultural collectivization was complete, Stalin tempered the harshness of rural life by allowing farm-

---

[104]Ann Lane, "USSR: Private Agriculture on Center Stage," in Joint Economic Committee, *Soviet Economy in the 1980's,* p. 38.

ers to cultivate small plots for their family's subsistence. The private plot remains a vital adjunct of collective farming to this day. Vegetables can be raised and animals kept on these private plots, subject to various limitations. Surpluses from the plots are sold at farm markets in the cities at prices substantially higher than the prices offered by the state. In effect, the duality of farm sectors, one collective and oriented to state procurements and the other private and directed to small-scale production and sale, has enabled the regime to squeeze the peasants economically while ensuring that they would survive; the dysfunctional consequence of this system, however, has been to reinforce the peasant attitude of indifference toward the work that was for the state. To this day, although procurement prices are far higher and farm conditions greatly ameliorated since Stalin's day, the productivity of private plots is many times higher than that of the collective acreage. It is often pointed out that while private plots comprise only 3 percent of the sown land of the USSR, they yield about 60 percent of the country's potatoes, around 30 percent of its vegetables, meat, and milk, over half of its fruits and berries, and around a third of its eggs.[105] Whereas traditional Soviet doctrine held that the private plots were a vestige of capitalist ways grudgingly tolerated in the socialist present, the Brezhnev regime, in decrees of 1977 and 1981, made a concerted effort to encourage increases in their production by decreeing greater access to fertilizer, fodder, and credit. Clearly this was a pragmatic means of compensating for low productivity in the socialist sector of agriculture rather than a step toward the acceptance of capitalist principles in agriculture generally.[106]

The peasantry consists of those employed by collective farms and those employed on state farms. The essential difference is that the state farm is considered, as Khrushchev once put it, a "factory in the fields," meaning that state farmers (*sovkhozniki*) are directly employed by the state and are paid regular wages. They are subject to the same regulations and benefits as are industrial workers,

[105]Anton F. Malish, "The Food Program: A New Policy or More Rhetoric?" in Joint Economic Committee, *Soviet Economy in the 1980's,* p. 52; Roy D. Laird and Ronald A. Francisco, "Observations on Rural Life in Soviet Russia," in Jerry G. Pankhurst and Michael Paul Sacks, eds., *Contemporary Soviet Society: Sociological Perspectives* (New York: Praeger, 1980), p. 145.

[106]See Lane, "Private Agriculture," pp. 23–40.

including sick leave, vacation, and retirement benefits. Frequently the state farm is rather highly mechanized, exposing the farmers to the discipline of factory life. Because of the differences in their occupational situation, sovkhozniki are considered to be ''workers'' in their social status, even though many of them do many of the same tasks as their kolkhoz cousins. Particularly in the 1950s and 1960s, the regime converted many *kolkhozy* into *sovkhozy,* which automatically brought about the reclassification of many farmers from *kolkhozniki* to *sovkhozniki.* Thus while the peasantry as a whole has been declining, the collective farm population has been shrinking at a rapid pace while the number of workers on farms has risen slightly. In 1970 there were 16.7 million *kolkhozniki* and 8.9 million *sovkhozniki;* in 1980 there were 13.3 million *kolkhozniki* and 11.6 million *sovkhozniki.* [107] Therefore the actual drop in the size of the peasantry is not so sharp as official figures would suggest. [108]

The process of unifying the population by reducing the disparities between peasants and workers is slow because of the prevalent tendency for more ambitious and motivated peasants to seek education and employment in the cities. Whereas the regime blocked undesired flight from the countryside in the past by denying peasants the right to bear internal passports without special permission and thus forbade them to leave their farms without explicit authorization, the Brezhnev regime alleviated their lot in 1966 by granting collective farm peasants the right to bear passports and thus legally to seek work in other regions. In addition, in 1967 the regime guaranteed a minimum annual income to collective farmers and included them in the state retirement pension fund for the first time. Although the minimum wage and retirement benefits are lower than those accorded workers in the state sector, they have contributed to increasing the average income of

[107] Ibid., p. 38.

[108] See Alexander Vucinich, ''The Peasants as a Social Class,'' in Millar, ed., *The Soviet Rural Community,* pp. 311–18. As a proportion of the Soviet population, the share of collective farmers and their families has shrunk from 65.56 million in 1959 to 36.8 million in 1981 while the percentage of those working in agriculture, including dependents, has declined only from about 74.3 million to about 62 million in the same period. See Alex Pravda, ''Working Class,'' p. 4. Vucinich makes the important observation that the de jure mobility of collective farm peasants to state farm workers considerably outstrips their actual integration into urban industrial society; most state farm workers, he points out, remain an integral part of rural culture. Vucinich, ''Peasants as a Social Class,'' p. 318.

the collective farm peasantry. Together with the substantial increases in the procurement prices the state pays for collective farm produce, these changes have had the effect of monetarizing the farm economy — that is, putting farm activity more on a money basis and less on an in-kind basis. This change creates new pressures: when farmers receive less in-kind payment from the farm, they have greater difficulty feeding their families and the livestock on their private plots, and the state must seek to satisfy the increased demand for foodstuffs in the stores.[109] The exceptional string of poor harvests in 1979, 1980, 1981, and 1982 led to food rationing in many rural regions and limits on the amount of food any family could purchase in many farm stores. Often rural residents visit large cities, taking advantage of excursions and tours or other opportunities, in order to stock up on food provisions.

Soviet policy in the long term aims at raising the material and culture level of the countryside to that of the cities by increasing the level of technological advancement of agriculture and the educational levels of rural inhabitants. One Soviet social scientist declared, rather optimistically: "A new type of peasant is increasingly in evidence in the countryside, a person with secondary education, a high cultural standard, and a good knowledge of technology, literature and music. More and more educated young people remain on their collective farm."[110] The writer cited no figures, however, on how many peasants in fact approximated the "new type." Clearly the difficulty of transforming the peasant to conform with the socialist new person of Soviet doctrine has been greater than the regime expected. The success Hungary has enjoyed in giving private individual and collective enterprise in agriculture free rein has often been discussed by Soviet officials, and the late Brezhnev-era decrees strengthening private agricultural production indicate that the political authorities, at least for now, see the route to greater agricultural output as lying through encouragement of the private sector.

Of all Soviet social groups the peasantry is least well represented in party and state bureaucracies and has least access to political power. Even today, rates of party membership among

---

[109]Lane, "Private Agriculture," p. 38.

[110]N. A. Aitov, "An Analysis of the Objective Prerequisites for Eliminating the Distinctions between the Working Class and the Peasantry," in G. V. Osipov, ed., *Town, Country and People* (London: Tavistock Publications, 1969), p. 134.

peasants, particularly those in the lowest-paying occupations, are extremely low — among milkmaids, swineherds, and similar groups, no more than 2–4 percent are party members.[111] Partly because of their lower educational levels and the lack of institutional levers available to them for articulating interests, peasants have less opportunity than any social group to affect party policy. The historical pattern in Russia in which members of other social groups, particularly the cultural intelligentsia, spoke *for* the peasants — voicing their problems and complaints — tends to continue into the present, as the example of today's countryside writers indicates. The peasantry's isolation and alienation from the state have been alleviated to a considerable degree by the rising level of rural well-being made possible by the sustained investment in agriculture undertaken by the Brezhnev regime. The stagnation and apathy so apparent among the peasants after Stalin's death are perhaps less severe now. On the other hand, the low economic productivity of the peasantry attests to the continuing backwardness of the countryside relative to the city. In addition, among some nationality groups, the resistance by the peasants to control by the state is reinforced by ethnic and religious ties. In regions of Soviet Central Asia, where out-migration of peasants to the city is far slower and birthrates much higher than in the European regions of the country, the rural community maintains its cultural and economic traditions and resists the penetration of the Soviet regime.

THE COMMUNIST PARTY OF THE SOVIET UNION: COMPOSITION AND STRUCTURE

The Communist Party of the Soviet Union (CPSU), numbering today nearly 18.5 million persons, represents a cross-section of the most influential members of all occupational and class groups. In keeping with its aim of being the ''leader, the vanguard of the Soviet people,''[112] the party does not represent all social groups equally. A considerable proportion of its members are drawn from the most highly educated, those in executive positions in government, the economy, and occupations exerting ideologi-

[111]*Pravda,* 11 February 1983.

[112]*Spravochnik sekretaria pervichnoi partiinoi organizatsii* (Handbook of the Secretary of the Primary Party Organization), 2nd ed. (Moscow: Izdatel'stvo politicheskoi literatury, 1980), p. 11.

cal influence on the population. According to a specialist on the party, the Australian scholar John Miller, the party's role requires that it take in people in certain categories:

(1) All (or virtually all) persons who take, or interpret, decisions at any level in society, plus those who might be needed to replace them, and a substantial proportion of those who influence or communicate decisions. This will give the party a commanding presence, inter alia, among people who appoint or supervise the work of others; communicators in the media and education; the armed forces, police and security; and people in a position to affect economic output.

(2) A second, much larger group whose function is to permeate all walks of ordinary, non-party life, to gather and report information, to mobilize local opinion and lead local activity, and to verify performance.[113]

The party uses recruitment policy to maintain its elite character in two ways. First, it ensures that a substantial proportion of the most educated and influential in every occupational sector are party members. As a result the proportion of such persons in the party is far greater than in the population generally. Second, it takes pains to distribute its members in occupations, regions, and activities considered critical to the party's task of social control.[114] The party normally recruits anyone who, by reason of position or ability, enjoys considerable social esteem, while at the same time party membership also confers elite status on the individual who is a member. Rigby and other writers on the party have often called attention to the tension in party recruitment between the need to make the party representative of the major social groupings in the Soviet population, and hence to act as an integrating device in society, and the need for the party to guide and direct the society by serving as its advance guard.[115]

In keeping with its representative role, the party carefully follows policies designed to ensure that no major social group is greatly underrepresented. Party admissions rules stress that entrants to the party should include sizable proportions of blue-col-

---

[113]John H. Miller, "The Communist Party: Trends and Problems," in Archie Brown and Michael Kaser, eds., *Soviet Policy for the 1980s* (Bloomington: Indiana University Press, 1982), pp. 3–4.

[114]T. H. Rigby, *Communist Party Membership in the U.S.S.R., 1917–1967* (Princeton, N.J.: Princeton University Press, 1968), pp. 510–11.

[115]Ibid., Introduction.

lar workers (currently the share of workers among new members is about 60 percent) as well as collective farm peasants and white-collar employees (their shares among new members are about 10 percent and 30 percent, respectively). Beyond these rules of representation, the party is concerned to equalize the proportion of women who are members with the share of women in the population. Thus, although only about 28 percent of the party is made up of women, women make up about one-third of new members. Similarly, the party endeavors to take in members from each ethnic group, seeking to overcome the historical domination of the party by Russians, Georgians, and certain other groups. In the non-Russian republics, the party has taken in members of the indigenous nationalities at rates faster than in the Russian republic. At the same time, the overrepresentation of Georgians in the party has moderated somewhat, probably because of tacit instructions from Moscow to Georgia to slow down the growth of the party in that republic.[116] The effect of the competing imperatives of social representativeness and social elitism is to raise party saturation (membership rates) to high levels among those within every occupational category who have high technical qualifications or who hold especially important administrative positions.

According to a comprehensive analysis of party recruitment by Bohdan Harasymiw, the high admission rate of manual workers has been accompanied by an apparent policy of setting a threshold level for educational qualifications; the more highly educated manual workers have a far greater likelihood of becoming party members than do their less educated comrades.[117] Although as a group manual workers are still somewhat underrepresented in the party compared with their strength in the general population, and the technical and scientific intelligentsia somewhat overrepresented, recruitment policies are giving unequal advantages in admission to manual workers at the expense of the intelligentsia. This means that some nonproductive sectors of the economy are becoming underrepresented in the party, and, perhaps more significant, there will probably be friction over access to party membership, with the career advantages it brings, on the part of skilled white-collar groups whose growing numbers in the society are not

[116]Miller, "The Communist Party," p. 15.

[117]Bohdan Harasymiw, *Political Elite Recruitment in the Soviet Union* (New York: St. Martin's Press, 1984), p. 75.

matched by a corresponding growth of their representation in the party.[118]

From a tool for the mobilization of the population for the purposes of building socialism, the party has today become the principal means for managing and coordinating the continued development of the society. Certain important features of the party's organization and operating principles have remained constant, however, since Lenin's time. It was Lenin's remarkable prescience as a political leader to envision the party as a flexible instrument both for overturning and seizing political power in the revolution and for exercising political power after the revolution. Lenin's conception of the party as a united, centralized, and doctrinally disciplined yet pragmatic body has proved to be adaptable to a variety of functions in the succeeding decades of economic transformation, war-time mobilization, post-war reconstruction, and post-Stalinist social management.

Lenin's formula for party organization, *democratic centralism,* has remained in force over this period. The term *democratic centralism* refers to the nominal rights of every party member to participate in party discussions and decisions and to elect delegates to conferences that in turn name the leaders of higher-level party bodies; at the same time, the centralism element of the formula remains uppermost, since it dictates stern and unquestioning subordination to the policies adopted in the name of the party. Under the rule forbidding factionalism adopted by the Tenth Party Congress in 1921, a party member may not caucus or combine with others in groups opposing the line followed by the party. Violation of the rule is punishable by expulsion. Just as unwavering obedience to party commands is demanded of every party member, so within the political system the party enjoys a monopoly of political power. No competing group may form. To ensure that existing social organizations never pose a threat to the party's exclusive grasp on power, the party has a licensing power over all other social organizations, authorizing them or demanding that they disband, according to its judgment of their political activity. For example, Marxist study circles among university students deemed threatening to the party's monopoly of control over ideological interpretation have been broken up. Unofficial peace groups, such as

[118]Ibid., pp. 187–92.

the Group for the Establishment of Trust between the United States and USSR, or human rights monitoring groups, such as the Helsinki Group, have been suppressed and their leaders imprisoned, exiled, or committed to psychiatric hospitals. Only social groups whose goals and activities support regime policies are permitted.

To preserve the disciplined, centralized character of the party, admission rules are stringent. Consistent with Lenin's early opposition to the mass party model advanced by his opponents in the Russian Social Democratic Workers' Party and his preference instead for a small, tightly bound party of professional revolutionaries, today's party recruiters seek to admit only individuals who will be politically reliable and competent in their jobs, submitting them to a thorough screening before and after they are accepted as members. Each recruit spends a year as a *candidate* member of the party, during which time he does not vote in party meetings and his conduct is carefully scrutinized before he is accepted to full membership. Today an increasing proportion — now nearly three-quarters — of the party's new members are accepted out of the youth league attached to the party, the Komsomol. By this means the party has the opportunity to identify individuals who are likely to make worthy party members as attested by their volunteer work in the Komsomol and their records in school and on the job. Once in the party, each member is expected to spend a substantial amount of time performing volunteer services for it by serving, for example, as an agitator, or by heading a neighborhood committee. It is also expected that each member will periodically attend a party school in order to update his knowledge of party theory and doctrine. Such schools (which will be discussed in detail in Chapter VI) are held in the evenings and on weekends and, though often tedious, are considered important for the ideological molding of party members, especially those involved in police and intelligence work.

As compensation for the obligations they bear, party members also enjoy privileges and benefits that are, however, kept unpublicized. These may include superior access to housing, scarce goods, and medical service as well as brighter career prospects. Indeed, many individuals join the party precisely because membership is a prerequisite of advancement in most fields of endeavor leading to privileged social status. As an individual rises to more responsible positions, the prequisites accompanying his position grow correspondingly more impressive. Depending on the city in which the individual lives, his rank, personal connections, and other factors, these benefits include unreported cash bonuses, access to restricted retail shops selling better and cheaper food, clothing, and other goods, larger and better-situated housing, access to better hospitals and doctors, access to tickets to concerts, plays, and other cultural productions, access to closed information media, and the opportunity to travel abroad.[119] These benefits serve as incentives for loyalty and good performance to those seeking advancement and help instill a sense of responsibility for the security and well-being of the regime.

The party itself is run by an inner core of full-time party functionaries, often called apparatchiki. Their number, exact duties, and salaries are carefully concealed from public view. Most Western scholars estimate that at most there are 200,000 or so full-time officials.[120] They include secretaries, deputy secretaries, department and section chiefs, and instructors of party committees, which are the seat of party decision-making power in every territorial-administrative jurisdiction in the country. The party committees are divided into four basic levels — (in descending order) central, regional, local, and primary. At the central level, the Central Committee of the CPSU, through its Secretariat, oversees the day-to-day functioning of the party throughout the Soviet Union. At the bottom level, the Primary Party Organizations (PPO's) are the nuclei of the party's organization, its building blocks, based in every workplace. In between are the committees of the party in each union republic except the Russian Republic and the committees of each province, rural district, city, and city district. At each of these levels, the party committee consists of a group of prominent party members working in top levels of government, the media, the economy, and the party itself, in whose hands is vested decision-making power over party affairs in its jurisdiction. A smaller group called the party bureau meets regularly to review and set general policy, and the full-time func-

[119]Mervyn Matthews, *Privilege in the Soviet Union* (London: Allen & Unwin, 1978), ch. 2.

[120]See Matthews, *Privilege,* p. 30; Alex Simirenko, *Professionalization of Soviet Society,* ed. C. A. Kern-Simirenko (New Brunswick, N.J.: Transaction Books, 1982), p. 37.

tionaries carry out party policy and link the party leaders of the committee with the network of subordinate party organizations and economic and cultural agencies that they supervise. Each level is guided and supervised by the next-higher level of party organization. Stalin in 1937 likened this hierarchy of command to that of an army, and the analogy is still valid.

At the top level of this army are the powerful secretaries of the Central Committee of the CPSU in Moscow and their deputies and assistants. The lower ranks of the officer corps are the secretaries and their staffs in the republics and provinces, and below them are equivalent officials in the districts and cities. Heading the PPO's in the workplaces are secretaries, working on a paid full-time basis if the PPO is large enough and on a spare-time basis otherwise, who oversee party work in their workplace. The lower enlisted ranks are composed of the rank-and-file party members, each of whom belongs to the PPO where he or she works. In this way, no party member is outside a chain of command of party authority that stretches all the way to the Kremlin, and each party official has a designated sphere of responsibility and a place in the hierarchy.

Within the party apparat, or bureaucracy, officials tend to specialize by function. The main career lines involve industry, agriculture, personnel, and ideology, whereas another group of officials consists of "mixed generalists," in Joel Moses' terms.[121] Party officials tend to concentrate on one of these areas and often continue specializing in it when they are reassigned to a new party committee. The secretaries work through functional departments of the committee. The department overseeing ideological work (which includes supervision of schools, the media, the arts, youth work, and the observance of holidays), for example, is called the *agitation-propaganda department.* The department, in turn, is divided into sections for specific duties. The press section of the agitation-propaganda department works closely with the newspapers and other media in the province to ensure that all publications correspond with current party policy. Each department and each section have a head, and their staff includes responsible instructors

[121]See Joel C. Moses, "Functional Career Specialization in Soviet Regional Elite Recruitment," in T. H. Rigby and Bohdan Harasymiw, eds., *Leadership Selection and Patron-Client Relations in the USSR and Yugoslavia* (London: Allen & Unwin, 1983), pp. 15–61.

who perform the legwork for the committee and maintain liaison with the organizations under the party committee's charge. By means of close and continuous oversight, the party instructors see to it that the general interests represented by the party are served by each organization under the committee's jurisdiction.

In keeping with the complexity of the tasks that party members must perform, the educational attainments of the party's membership have risen steadily. Among all party members, about 30 percent have a complete higher education and only about 10 percent have no more than an elementary education.[122] This means that a high proportion of the country's intelligentsia belongs to the party. When we take into account the overrepresentation of men in the party and combine the factors of age, sex, and education, we find that the rate of membership among men over thirty with complete secondary education is 30 percent and that of men over thirty with higher education is 50 percent.[123] These figures suggest that the party is close to being a mass party of the most socially privileged members of the society. In contrast to the early Bolshevik period, when technically untrained but politically dedicated party cadres asserted the revolution's authority over all spheres of social life, the party today tends to recruit extensively from among social elites.[124] Some theorists have claimed, in fact, that the importance of technical and administrative expertise in an industrial society weakens the special authority enjoyed by purely *political* elites, and hence that the ideologically grounded power of the party apparatchiki must give way as society develops to managers and experts representing important institutional sectors.

Two important considerations should be taken into account, however, before accepting uncritically the view that the continuing modernization of society is transforming the party. First, party admission policies since the late 1960s have shifted the emphasis back from technical criteria to a combination of technical

[122]"KPSS v tsifrakh," (The CPSU in Figures) *Partiinaia zhizn'*, no. 15 (August 1983): 17.

[123]Jerry F. Hough and Merle Fainsod, *How the Soviet Union Is Governed* (Cambridge, Mass.: Harvard University Press, 1979), p. 345.

[124]Zygmunt Bauman, "The Party in the System-Management Phase: Change and Continuity," in Andrew C. Janos, ed., *Authoritarian Politics in Communist Europe: Uniformity and Diversity in One-Party States* (Berkeley: Institute of International Studies, University of California, 1976), pp. 81–108.

and political qualifications.[125] The formerly common practice of co-opting technical specialists in mid-career into the party declined in the 1970s while the admission rate of new members drawn from the Komsomol, where young people could be politically tested and trained, increased.[126] Although the proportion of party members with higher education has kept pace with the proportion of the population who possess higher education despite the much slower overall growth of the party, this has occurred to a large extent by party members' upgrading their educational qualifications through evening or correspondence courses.[127] Thus although the party's recruitment policies stress educational criteria, the emphasis on political reliability and representation of manual workers means that some highly educated sections of the population are falling behind in their representation in the party.

Second, as Richard Lowenthal has persuasively argued, the party has generally succeeded in adapting itself to change without making major political concessions. Party apparatchiki have become technically expert and specialized in particular spheres of responsibility and create channels for consultation with qualified experts without necessarily granting them independent political power. It is the party's prerogative to draw the line between acceptable and unacceptable disagreement with current policy. Though the flow of policy-relevant information necessarily becomes somewhat uneven as a result, the party has shown its capacity to make tactical changes in policy without giving up its domination of the political process.[128] Though the party's saturation by educated and elite members of society is high, we should also bear in mind the considerable proportions of the intelligentsia that remain outside the party — half and more of the members of such professions as engineering, agronomy, science, law, medicine, and the arts are *not* party members. T. H. Rigby points out that the party does not so much *incorporate* society's elites into its ranks as it overlaps with them.[129] Preservation of the party's

---

[125]Harasymiw, *Political Elite Recruitment,* pp. 45–46.

[126]Ibid., p. 190.

[127]Ibid., p. 115.

[128]Richard Lowenthal, ''The Ruling Party in a Mature Society,'' in Mark G. Field, ed., *Social Consequences of Modernization in Communist Societies* (Baltimore, Md.: Johns Hopkins Press, 1976), pp. 92–96.

[129]Rigby, *Communist Party Membership,* p. 453.

unique role therefore requires a delicate balance between inclusion into the political elite of a broad and representative selection of social groups and the restriction of privileged status to as small a segment of the population as possible so as to preserve the independence of the political elite from society's demands. Intensive indoctrination within the party and of society by the party, together with careful rules governing party recruitment, is the key to reconciling these imperatives.

CHAPTER IV

Political Socialization

"Political socialization is the process by which political cultures are formed, maintained and changed."[1] The high priority assigned by Soviet leaders to socialization is reflected in the extent to which the party has invested resources in socialization programs. Fiercely determined to transform a backward society into the model for mankind's future, the leaders have sought to inculcate in the rising generations devotion to the agencies of revolutionary transformation, especially the CPSU. The party has initiated, proclaimed, and supervised the fulfillment of all major decisions affecting the generation and transmission of political ideology. It has set in motion one of the most systematic overt political indoctrination programs to which any population has ever been subjected. Through it, every citizen is exposed from early childhood to a coordinated array of influences intended to mold his character and determine his outlook.[2]

POLITICAL SOCIALIZATION IN THE SCHOOL SYSTEM

The most important instrument of political socialization in the Soviet Union has always been its system of educational institu-

[1]Gabriel A. Almond and G. Bingham Powell, *Comparative Politics: System, Process and Policy* (Boston, Mass.: Little, Brown, 1978), p. 79.

[2]On Soviet political indoctrination and socialization, the following may be considered fundamental: Alex Inkeles, *Public Opinion in Soviet Russia: A Study in Mass Persuasion,* rev. ed. (Cambridge, Mass.: Harvard University Press, 1958), which is, however, based on materials dating from the 1940s and 1950s. A more recent and highly comprehensive source is Gayle Durham Hollander, *Soviet Political Indoctrination: Developments in Mass Media and Propaganda since Stalin* (New York: Praeger, 1972). On the Komsomol and policies toward the youth, see Allen Kassof, *The Soviet Youth Program* (Cambridge, Mass.: Harvard University Press, 1965).

tions, beginning with the primary schools and including schools through the university level. After the consolidation of communist power around 1921 and especially after the start of rapid industrialization and the collectivization of agriculture in 1928, Soviet educational institutions embarked on an immense and increasingly complex effort to impart traits such as orderliness, punctuality, and discipline to a population that was (and to a certain extent still is, especially outside the European heartland) preindustrial in outlook. Millions of village children were made conscious of national and international political events, policies, and leaders, mobilized from the status of *parochials* to that of *subjects* and even *participants* in the new Soviet order. Simultaneously, Soviet educators had to provide training in Marxist-Leninist concepts of history, political economy, and philosophy for the relative few who went all the way through secondary school and on to higher education. The content of the curriculum was adapted, of course, to changing domestic and international pressures. It was heavily influenced by wars and expectations of wars; as a result of external threats, patriotic themes permeated history instruction.

In the primary and secondary schools, the character of political socialization developed in three main phases. The first coincided with the hopeful years following the revolution, when some teachers experimented with American-style progressive educational methods and with a polytechnical approach designed to acquaint their pupils with underlying principles of modern industry. (This approach differed from the narrowly vocational one later sponsored by Khrushchev.)[3] Visiting the Soviet Union in 1928, John Dewey, the pioneer of American progressive education, was favorably impressed.

The second phase of Soviet educational development extended from about 1929 until the late 1950s. The inculcation of loyalty and support for the polity, the party, its leaders, and their policies remained the major tasks of political socialization. At the same time, the methods and spirit by which these objectives were implemented changed drastically. Belief in the moral superiority of socialism over capitalism and in the historically inevitable triumph of the former over the latter remained prominent in classroom

[3]See George Z. F. Bereday, William W. Brickman, and Gerald H. Read, eds., *The Changing Soviet School* (Boston, Mass.: Houghton-Mifflin, 1960), pp. 64–67.

teaching. These themes were increasingly overshadowed, however, by two others, which reflected Stalin's pessimism about the international situation of the 1930s and his "revolution from above" in agricultural collectivization and rapid, coercive industrialization.

One of these themes consisted of emotionally charged accusations that the international bourgeoisie was plotting war to destroy the USSR and of calls for vigilance, military preparation, and patriotism to counter a mortal threat to the survival of the socialist motherland. The other was the demand for developing a communist version of puritanism — ascetic, self-sacrificing, and goal-directed. Stalin demanded that schools inculcate citizens from childhood with disciplined initiative to achieve collective goals. His successors reiterated this theme. He emphasized that economic progress and national survival could not be entrusted to the operation of historical laws alone. The laws of history would work only in favor of those who served them with disciplined, informed, and purposeful action. Teachers were called upon to proclaim an implacable struggle not only against the class enemy abroad and his spies in the USSR and against traditional group attitudes such as religious beliefs and ethnic prejudices, but also against laziness, apathy, lack of discipline, impulsiveness, and other traits incompatible with the beliefs and moral values prescribed by the party for the New Soviet Person it professed to be creating.

In the 1930s and 1940s aspects of prerevolutionary culture, including even religion, were selectively tolerated or given official encouragement. In Stalin's effort to rally the Soviet people against the foreign threat, priority went to revival of pride in Russian military tradition. History texts exalted the heroism of Russian troops in battles against Tatars, Swedes, Frenchmen, and Germans. Tsarist generals such as Suvorov and Kutuzov and admirals such as Nakhimov were honored. Literature of course also served to instill in the rising generation love of country. Tolstoy's *War and Peace,* for example, was very suitable for this purpose. Citizens were encouraged to take pride in all Russian as well as Soviet achievements in science, technology, and other spheres of endeavor. Prerevolutionary as well as Soviet positive heroes were held up as models to schoolchildren. In the campaign to revive patriotism and thus generate support, the party relied heavily on tsarist pedagogical methods, including standardization of curriculum and regimentation of pupils together with strict classroom discipline and rote learning.[4]

Concurrently, symbols of rank, status, and achievement reminiscent of the tsarist era, such as uniforms with distinctive and elaborate insignia of rank and branch for millions of state employees were reintroduced.[5] Probably many Soviet people would have agreed with the émigré sociologist Timashev's characterization of these conservative measures as a "great retreat." Others doubtless shared Leon Trotsky's view that they constituted a "betrayal" of the 1917 revolution in favor of a new elite of party, state, and economic "bureaucrats."[6] Nevertheless, the educational system instituted under Stalin achieved enormous successes. It allowed millions to rise rapidly into the new industrial organizations and political bureaucracies. The emphasis on discipline and obedience, on patriotism and heroism served the country well when it was put to the terrible test of World War II. Jeremy Azrael observes that the system "helped socialize a predominantly tradition-oriented population into the cultural patterns of an industrial society" and, among many other achievements, "was instrumental in producing enough highly motivated, ideologically committed, and politically active young people that the regime was able to institutionalize tremendously rapid social and economic change . . . without losing its essential political continuity."[7]

On the other hand, the system created serious difficulties that Stalin's successors were left to solve. By the 1950s it had ceased to give working class and village children a wide opportunity to rise to higher-status occupations. Universities and the better technical schools were filled with the offspring of the new Soviet elite. Those able to complete their secondary educations expected to enter a VUZ and thus acquire a nonmanual technical or administrative post after graduation. The tendency to look down on

[4]See Jeremy R. Azrael, "The Soviet Union," in James S. Coleman, ed., *Education and Political Development* (Princeton, N.J.: Princeton University Press, 1965), pp. 239–42.

[5]See Alex Inkeles, *Social Change in Soviet Russia* (New York: Simon and Schuster), p. 159.

[6]Nicholas Timashev, *The Great Retreat* (New York: Dutton, 1946); Leon Trotsky, *The Revolution Betrayed* (New York: Pathfinder Press, 1972).

[7]Azrael, "The Soviet Union," p. 247.

manual jobs sharpened the class distinction between white-collar and blue-collar groups. A kind of careerism developed that put personal advancement ahead of the interests of the society and thus deepened the gulf between those who had advanced and the masses of the population. The result was widespread apathy and disaffection.

Stalin's successors, and particularly Khrushchev, regarded reform of the educational system as essential to revive its egalitarian promise, reinspire loyalty and faith in socialism, and bring the curriculum closer to the actual political and economic needs of the society. Khrushchev's denunciation of the late dictator and his effort to hold up Lenin and the party as alternative symbols for popular loyalty were part of a major ideological reorientation. Paradoxically, widespread popular indifference toward high politics helped ease Khrushchev's de-Stalinization campaign by enabling most youth to adjust easily to the dethronement of the former idol. Although he succeeded in generating idealism and activism among a section of the youth, many of whom later became dissident intellectuals, the problem of political apathy continues to be widespread, if one judges by frequent statements in the Soviet press. One likely reason is the contradiction between demands for conformity and obedience to commands issued by the authorities in the name of the people and the demands for initiative, innovativeness, and purposefulness. We may surmise either that the subject and participatory elements of the political culture are mutually incompatible or that insufficient resources and skill are devoted to synthesizing them.

Khrushchev's 1958 educational reforms, which were aimed at giving all pupils greater exposure to manual labor and technical training, had many implications, both pedagogical and economic. Perhaps the most important aspects were the attempt to strengthen the production-oriented, polytechnical content of the curriculum and the decision to improve the chances for a higher education for working class and peasant youth at the expense of the children of white-collar and professional strata. Under Khrushchev's version of vocational training, the polytechnical element was added to the academic workload in the lower grades; students in the upper secondary grades had to spend one-third of their time working in agricultural or industrial production. Probably the most irritating measure from the standpoint of Khrushchev's opponents was the decision that 80 percent of the places in institutions of higher education would be reserved for secondary school graduates with at least two years of work experience after graduation. This measure was not to apply to the most gifted students in mathematics and the physical sciences, however.[8] Khrushchev also introduced a system of boarding schools (*internaty*) designed to "become the new schools of communist society." They were intended to weaken familial influence over the youth, and some educational authorities believed that they would come to dominate or even eventually monopolize the educational system.[9]

Khrushchev's reforms were strongly opposed by groups of parents, educators, and educational administrators. Opponents resorted to such tactics as expressing, though cautiously, their reservations in the press and seeking to weaken the implementation of the reforms.[10] It became apparent even before Khrushchev was expelled from the leadership that the attempt to add a heavy dose of labor training and actual factory and farm work to the secondary school curriculum was adversely affecting the quality of education. Subsequent decrees ostensibly clarifying the reforms in fact watered them down. They were never fully implemented, and where implemented they had little effect either on pupils' career choices or on their attitudes. As soon as Khrushchev was removed from the party Presidium in October 1964, his educational reforms were dropped.[11]

The Brezhnev leadership brought with it a new approach to education, combining a conservative, stable ideological line with increased rationalism, as evidenced by greater attention to explaining concepts and demanding high levels of performance. A 1966 decree criticizing superficiality of learning and inadequate standards reduced the total number of hours of course work required of secondary school pupils, added elective subjects, and reintroduced military training for boys.[12] At the same time the principle of polytechnical education, in which classroom schooling

[8]Ibid., p. 259; Mervyn Matthews, *Education in the Soviet Union* (London: Allen and Unwin), pp. 18–32.

[9]Azrael, "The Soviet Union," p. 257.

[10]See Philip D. Stewart, "Soviet Interest Groups and the Policy Process: The Repeal of Production Education," *World Politics* 22, no. 1 (October 1969): 29–51.

[11]Matthews, *Education in the Soviet Union*, pp. 31–32.

[12]Ibid., p. 46.

in basic and applied subjects was supplemented with vocational and practical education, was preserved as the regime tried to expand the availability of shop facilities in schools and to mobilize pupils during summer holidays and other times for production work on farms, in forestry, construction brigades, or other jobs. Still, in such key areas as the formality of instruction, the emphasis upon mastery of ideological doctrine, course requirements, and subject matter, the curriculum changed little from Khrushchev's time.[13] The authorities' continuing dissatisfaction with the performance of the system is attested by the reform of January 1984, which added a year to the secondary program and intensified study in technical subjects. (See the following section.)

COMMUNIST UPBRINGING: THE INDIVIDUAL AND THE COLLECTIVE

According to Nadezhda Krupskaya, Lenin's spouse and a leading educational theorist of the Soviet regime, the aim of political socialization is as follows:

> Society is interested in the common aim of primary, secondary and higher education — the upbringing of multi-dimensional people who possess conscientious and organized communal instincts, who possess a purposeful and well-thought out world view, who clearly understand everything that occurs around them, in nature and communal life, people who are prepared in theory and in practice for any kind of labor — be it physical or mental and who are capable of building a rational, full of meaning, beautiful and happy communal life. These are the people that are needed for socialist society. Socialism without them cannot be fully realized.[14]

Communist upbringing (*vospitanie*) has a broad scope and explicit objective: it is directed toward the creation of a new, socialist society by molding individuals' values, beliefs, and attitudes and inculcating a collectivist mentality in every individual. The collective, a concept that may be applied to one's place of work or smaller groups as well as to Soviet society at large or even the well-being of progressive mankind, is treated as both the agent of socialization and its beneficiary. As individualism is a cornerstone

[13]Ibid., pp. 64–65.
[14]Quoted in Joseph I. Zajda, *Education in the USSR* (Oxford: Pergamon Press, 1980), p. 27.

of classical liberalism, so Soviet Marxism-Leninism treats collectivism as the basis of social morality as well as of all individual values. Both the structure and the content of political socialization reinforce this principle.

Formal political socialization has three main directions: political-doctrinal education, moral education, and labor education.[15] Though all agencies of political socialization, including public organizations, mass media, oral agitation, and the like, are expected to emphasize these three areas in their ideological work, schools are expected to concentrate especially on moral education at all levels and political-doctrinal and labor education in the upper grades. Political instruction includes inculcating mastery of political theory and doctrine, including basic lessons from the works of Marx, Lenin, and the current leaders. It involves the study of original texts and party documents as well as the biography of Lenin. Both the number of hours devoted to such studies and the level of complexity of the subject matter increase as students reach higher grades.[16] In the tenth grade, students ordinarily must take a 2-hour-per-week course dealing specifically with social studies, and a good deal of the instruction in such subjects as history, literature, and military training also covers explicitly political matter.[17]

In the VUZ, a significant expansion of the hours devoted to political-doctrinal instruction occurred under Khrushchev and again under Brezhnev. In 1974 the regime decreed that in each of the five years of higher education the student must take a full-time course on a specific ideological subject. Students take courses on dialectical materialism, historical materialism, party history, scientific communism, and the stages of capitalism and social-

[15]See the important party decree covering all aspects of party ideological work published on May 6, 1979, entitled "O dal'neishem uluchshenii ideologicheskoi, politiko-vospitatel'noi rabote" (On the Further Improvement of Ideological, Political-Upbringing Work), *Pravda*, 6 May 1979, pp. 1-2. This decree has been widely cited by party leaders in calling for more vigorous and effective political socialization. Also see the report on the methods and goals of political socialization among youth by Sergei Zamascikov, who until leaving the Soviet Union in 1979 was first secretary of the Komsomol organization in a city in Latvia and had previously worked as a political officer in the armed forces and as a journalist. "Ideological Indoctrination of Soviet Youth," Radio Liberty, RL 300/83 (10 August 1983), pp. 7-8.

[16]Zajda, *Education in the USSR*, pp. 128-29.

[17]Matthews, *Education in the Soviet Union*, p. 48.

ism.[18] By formalizing and standardizing the curriculum in ideological subjects in the upper secondary and tertiary levels, the authorities seek to ensure that all who enter the ranks of the Soviet intelligentsia are exposed to an equal and heavy dose of explicit doctrinal instruction. After-hours political education, tailored to the job roles of individuals in most occupational categories and effectively required of virtually everyone in the intelligentsia, continually reinforces and updates this ideological knowledge after individuals leave school.

Labor education includes both familiarizing youth with the technology of various branches of production and inculcating appropriate attitudes toward labor: zeal in achieving work targets, conscientiousness and devotion toward the job, respect for all engaged in productive labor, and understanding of the principles of socialist economic organization. Labor education is conducted through both classroom instruction and practical work experience in factories, farms, and other workplaces. As with all types of communist upbringing, the specific content of labor education varies depending on the current problems and needs of the economy as interpreted by the leaders. A staple of labor education, both in schools and in labor collectives, is the organization of *socialist competition* (*sotsialisticheskoe sorevnovanie*) among similar groups. Two factories might compete to achieve the highest output, to meet plan targets in the shortest time, to achieve the highest savings in scarce raw materials, or to fulfill other objectives. Komsomol groups in school may organize socialist competitions among detachments of their class to achieve the best grade average. Such forms of rivalry are considered socially constructive, since the techniques and esprit of the winners are held up as models for all collectives — in contrast, it is claimed, to the destructive character of competition in a capitalist society. Another means of linking school with labor is through *patronage* (*shefstvo*), a practice by which the workers of a leading enterprise adopt a school, meeting with the students and providing an orientation to the workplace. By the same token, a Komsomol unit may adopt a lagging enterprise in order to raise morale and performance standards.[19]

[18]Zajda, *Education in the USSR,* p. 98; Matthews, *Education in the Soviet Union,* p. 125.

[19]Zamascikov, ''Ideological Indoctrination,'' p. 7.

Besides seeking to instill appropriate attitudes toward work as well as to give youth the knowledge and skills needed by the economy, labor education is often used as a justification for drafting large numbers of young people into temporary jobs in the economy at times when extra labor at low cost is needed. School-organized holiday labor, especially in helping bring in the harvest or in finishing a construction project, is justified as a useful form of labor education. It is common for secondary school pupils to give uncompensated labor to local factories and construction sites or, in rural areas, to collective farms. VUZ students often form student construction units and work at less than minimum wage during the summer.[20] Such labor not only furthers ideology but is also a useful and even indispensable source of revenue for the state. In impoverished areas the economic need for cheap student labor may outstrip the desire to give students practical exposure to productive labor.

Many managers and economists have complained about the poor preparation students receive in both applied and basic knowledge in school and decry as well the prevalence of undesirable attitudes among youth such as unwillingness to take on manual jobs. At the June 1983 Central Committee plenum, Politburo member Chernenko referred to these difficulties:

> The party also sees negative phenomena among the youth. Late civic maturation and political naivete, parasitical idleness of some young people, their unwillingness to work where they are needed by society today are worrisome. We cannot help but be concerned at the aspiration among a section of the youth to acquire not knowledge and a love of labor, but expensive things bought with their parents' money. . . . Our enemy seeks to use for his purposes the special traits of the psychology of youth. By solely its own personal experience it does not know the cruel trials of class struggle and wars, when the true face of imperialism, its hatred for the peoples of our country, towards the socialist order, were utterly exposed.[21]

The 1984 education reform, promulgated in draft form on January 5, 1984 and adopted by the USSR Supreme Soviet on April 12, devotes considerable attention to several aspects of labor education. Reiterating the purpose of labor education in instilling a

[20]Ibid., p. 8.
[21]*Pravda*, 15 June 1983, p. 2.

love and respect for labor as well as acquaintance with industry, agriculture, and other economic branches and the formation of good work habits, the reform envisions a "significant expansion" of the time given to labor education in school as well as the time given to on-the-job training and holiday work experience.[22] Specific training for occupations will be concentrated in the tenth and eleventh grades of the general secondary school and will be completed with another year of vocational training in a professional-technical school or more advanced training in a specialized secondary school or a VUZ. The reform envisions setting aside one day a week in the tenth and eleventh grades for vocational education. Beyond its specific provisions, the long-range policy goal is to unify general education with occupational education, though without major cost either to the breadth and quality of general education or to the depth of knowledge needed for vocational education. To accomplish this aim, an extra year of education will be added for all youth by requiring them to begin school at age 6 rather than age 7, as in the past. In recognition that any meaningful improvement in the content of labor education will require substantial revision of the curriculum as well as more effective cooperation with local economic managers, the proposal calls for a comprehensive restructuring of the program of study, starting with the first grade. It must be borne in mind, however, that past efforts to increase the polytechnical content of general education have foundered on the difficulty of providing schools with adequate equipment for training in new technologies and the unwillingness of local managers to divert scarce resources to training unskilled schoolchildren.

The final branch of communist upbringing is called moral education. It is the broadest of the categories of ideological work, since it deals with the transmission of general moral values as well as desired attitudes toward such things as the Soviet homeland, military service, socialist property, or the threat posed by world imperialism. According to Zamascikov, "this form of indoctrination has recently begun to receive increasing attention in both Party and Komsomol documents and also in the press because of the importance being given to 'military-patriotic' values and the current state of 'Socialist morality' in the young generation."[23]

---

[22]*Pravda*, 4 January 1984, pp. 1–2.
[23]Zamascikov, "Ideological Indoctrination," p. 8.

Communist morality is an open-ended concept. Elements of it include humanism, collectivism, internationalism, patriotism, and atheism, as well as values associated with a communist attitude toward labor.[24] Along with the last-named, probably the single most emphasized area of communist morality in the 1970s and 1980s has been military-patriotic education. Here the aim of indoctrination is to link the emotions associated with love of the socialist homeland with explicit military and protomilitary training. Under the aegis of military-patriotic education, military values, doctrine, and organization pervade Soviet schooling. Many believe, indeed, that the militarization of education is intensifying.[25]

Within the school curriculum, ninth- and tenth-grade boys are required to take 2 hours a week of military instruction. Some 50,000 military instructors, mostly retired officers and reserve officers, are attached to schools for this purpose. Many schools have their own shooting ranges for rifle practice; others make arrangements with local military garrisons for shooting practice.[26] After ninth grade, boys go out for 5 days of summer field training. Local units of DOSAAF or the Voluntary Society for Assistance to the Army, Air Force and Navy — a nationwide paramilitary organization — cooperate with school, local military district, and Komsomol authorities in instructing youth in a variety of military-related skills and activities that raise their physical fitness and technical knowledge, such as radio operation and repair, navi-

---

[24]Zajda, *Education in the USSR,* p. 117.

[25]One author argues that militarization of society is growing in four particular areas: the increase in the number of officer-training colleges (one in seven or eight VUZy trains military officers), the increase in military training in secondary school since 1967, the increased role of DOSAAF (Dobrovol'noe obshchestvo sodeistviia armii, aviatsii i flotu) in providing specialized military training to civilians, and the intensification of civil defense. See William E. Odom, "The 'Militarization' of Soviet Society," *Problems of Communism* 25 (September–October 1976): 34–51. Also see Timothy J. Colton, "The Impact of the Military on Soviet Society," in Seweryn Bialer, ed., *The Domestic Context of Soviet Foreign Policy* (Boulder, Colo.: Westview Press, 1981), pp. 125–30. Colton describes the intensification of military and military-related training in civilian society in recent years but cautions against viewing it as part of an effort to "militarize" society. Rather, he sees the authorities using military values to achieve their own political ends.

[26]Matthews, *Education in the Soviet Union,* p. 53; L. N. Ul'ianov, *Voenno-patrioticheskoe vospitanie i traditsii* (Military-Patriotic Education and Traditions) (Leningrad: Lenizdat, 1983), p. 43.

gation, truck driving, and target shooting.[27] Schools commonly maintain museums and halls of military glory and organize field trips to local monuments commemorating the heroes of the "Great War of the Fatherland," as World War II is commonly called. Pupils are encouraged to join clubs (Young Warriors or Red Scouts) that perform such tasks as helping reunite families separated by the war or locating the gravesites of the fallen. Their activities have a quasi-religious and sentimental quality, and help keep the memory of foreign invasion and national sacrifice alive both for the generations that experienced the horror of the war and, more important, for those that did not.

The youth groups, Pioneers and Komsomol (which will be discussed more fully below), actively aid in the organization of activities serving military-patriotic education. Both groups run summer camps and summer games emphasizing military skills in which boys and girls participate. For 12–14-year-olds there are the *Zarnitsa* (Summer Lightning) games. Groups are organized along military lines, maintain military discipline, and are taught drill and ceremony and other military skills. For 16–17 year olds, Komsomol runs the *Orlyonok* (Little Eagle) games, a final phase of preinduction training. Typically they run over a period of two years. Final competitions are held in such skill areas as running 100 meters with a gas mask, assembling an AK-47 rifle, erecting a tent, passing through a 50 meter infected zone, driving an army truck, operating a portable radio transmitter, target shooting, throwing grenades, and giving first aid.[28]

Upon graduation from secondary school, or reaching the age of 18 if they are not in school, boys are conscripted for 2 to 3 year terms of service in the armed forces, unless they enter a VUZ. Very few escape induction: 88 percent of 18 and 19 year old boys enter the service.[29] The 10 percent or so of the male boys who do enter a VUZ continue to receive military training and indoctrination. Although the pattern varies, male students commonly take 4 to 5 hours a week of instruction in military science in their third,

[27]Harriet Fast Scott and William F. Scott, *The Armed Forces of the USSR,* 2nd ed. (Boulder, Colo.: Westview Books, 1981), pp. 309–10.

[28]See Zajda, *Education in the USSR,* pp. 219–22; Scott and Scott, *The Armed Forces of the USSR,* pp. 314–15.

[29]Murray Feshbach, *The Soviet Union: Population Trends and Dilemmas* (Washington, D.C.: Population Reference Bureau, 1982), p. 2.

fourth, and fifth years of study. Summer field training complements classroom instruction: 20 day summer camp is held after
the second and fourth years. After final examinations, a longer
summer camp is required (as much as 7 weeks long), followed by
an examination on military subjects. Passing the exam gives the
graduate the status of a reserve officer and normally exempts him
from further active service. Failure can mean conscription.[30]

Military service itself is a powerful agency of political socialization as well, particularly for rural youth. The former Soviet
social scientist Victor Zaslavsky, who conducted official and unofficial opinion surveys within the Soviet Union, found that military service was one of the most significant factors affecting
political attitudes. The Soviet invasion of Czechoslovakia in 1968
provides one example. Young workers who had not yet served
were markedly more likely to question the invasion than workers
of the same age who had been exposed to the intense influence
of military training and indoctrination.[31] The strong effect is due
both to the constancy and consistency of indoctrination in a closed
setting where virtually no countermanding ideological influences
can penetrate and to the residual impact of life in a tightly regi-
mented, highly structured society that places absolute value on
severe discipline and unquestioning obedience to authority. Both
manifest and latent socialization contribute to the internalization
and reinforcement of patriotism, loyalty, hierarchy, and fear and
hostility toward the country's external and internal enemies.[32] In
addition, for peasant youth the military offers escape from the
restrictive circumstances of village life. These factors help to explain the importance of military service as a source of political
values and attitudes for the civilian population, particularly the
youth. In a state as diverse as the Soviet Union, with Russian and
Slavic domination of the population declining because of rapid
increases of the non-European population, military service is perhaps the single most important means by which the leadership
seeks to inculcate a common sense of loyalty among all ethnic
groups to the Soviet party and state and the ideological values

[30]See Matthews, *Education in the Soviet Union,* p. 129.

[31]Victor Zaslavsky, *The Neo-Stalinist State* (Armonk, N.Y.: M. E. Sharpe, 1982),
pp. 30–31.

[32]See Colton, ''The Impact of the Military,'' pp. 123–25.

that support them. The usefulness of military training in transmitting such values as patriotism, discipline, and obedience, which are central to communist morality, together with the regime's desire for a national pool of ready manpower in case of war, accounts for the pervasiveness of military instruction in the schools.

Although the content of communist morality corresponds to the political interests of the regime as interpreted by the political elite, it nevertheless must be shown to be logically consistent with Marx's and Lenin's pronouncements. At times the effort to reconcile Soviet doctrine with Marxism produces further dilemmas. An example is the stress on military-patriotic education. The glorification of values associated with the Soviet state, such as national defense and loyalty to the fatherland, implicitly erodes the identification of Soviet society as one based upon a working class revolution. For both Soviet Russians and non-Russians, the propaganda of Soviet patriotism is not very different in its implications from the tsarist propaganda relating to Russian (*Rossiiskii*, or *Greater Russian*) imperialism. It certainly does not dampen Russian ethnic self-awareness.[33] This contention finds confirmation in the propaganda surrounding the Soviet character and the Soviet way of life, which, although it is avowedly non-national, is nevertheless clearly rooted in Russian literary and historical models.[34]

A second contradiction is the clash between the aim of creating a new Soviet person, an active and independent individual serving the society with all his energies, and the insistence upon inculcating subservience to higher authority. Lenin called on Soviet youth to take a critical attitude toward received learning rather than simply mastering it by rote.[35] Reviving this principle after the stultifying Stalin years, Khrushchev's party program adopted at the Twenty-second Party Congress in 1961 defined the goal of socialist construction as "a highly organized society of free and conscious producers, in which social self-government is con-

[33]See Oleh Fedyshin, "The Role of Russians among the 'New, Unified' Soviet People," in Edward Allworth, ed., *Ethnic Russia in the USSR* (New York: Pergamon, 1980), pp. 149–58.

[34]See such works as Mikhail Shkerin, *Sovetskii kharakter* (Soviet character) (Moscow: Sovietskii pisatel, 1963), and F. Lutoshkin, "Sovetskii kharakter," *Literaturnaia gazeta*, 31 July 1974.

[35]V. I. Lenin, *Polnoe sobranie sochinenii* (Complete Collected Works), (Moscow: Gosudarstvennoe izdatel'stvo politicheskoi literatury, 1958–1965), vol. 41, p. 305.

firmed.''[36] At the same time, individual moral autonomy is subordinated to the needs of the collective. As Gayle Durham Hollander wrote, "Soviet citizens are not encouraged to be open-minded, fair, independent, self-reliant, or to exhibit a spirit of compromise, all traits which would put them in good standing in a democratic society. . . . Soviet politics is not oriented even in an ideal sense toward mediation and problem-solving by an association of rational, equal citizens.''[37]

Third, contemporary ethical teaching resembles official propaganda of the church-dominated tsarist propaganda of the nineteenth century much more closely than it does the Marxist views of the Russian Bolsheviks. In words never repudiated and often quoted with approval, Lenin stated at the Third Congress of the Komsomol that "our morality is completely subordinated to the interests of the class struggle of the proletariat.''[38] Yet the values taught through political indoctrination emphasize the universality of the traits of the New Soviet Person, described in the *Moral Code of the Builder of Communism,* adopted in 1961, as including "honesty and truthfulness, moral purity, intolerance toward injustice" and similar precepts. A Soviet critic claims that recent Soviet fiction reflects "the highest and eternal spiritual values of humanity — the search for the meaning of life, inspiration, honor, truth, good, the struggles of conscience." Seeking to reconcile the rhetoric of moral absolutism with the Marxist belief that there is no eternal morality since class interests dictate all morals, the same writer asserts that "this is all ours, precisely ours, these values of real, i.e. socialist, humanism.''[39] Thus, although Soviet moral philosophy was shaped in large part by Lenin's experience of revolutionary conspiracy, political combat, and propaganda manipulation, contemporary ideology has reverted to older, traditional moral values as a firmer foundation for upbringing than the values of class struggle. This contradiction between moral absolutism and moral relativism and utilitarianism is said to be resolved in

[36]*KPSS: Spravochnik* (The CPSU: A Handbook) (Moscow: Izdatel'stvo politicheskoi literatury, 1982), p. 295.

[37]Hollander, *Soviet Political Indoctrination,* p. 9.

[38]Lenin, *Polnoe sobranie sochinenii,* vol. 41, p. 309.

[39]F. Kuznetsov, "Rol' nravstvennykh nachal" (The Role of Moral Principles), in N. Ts. Stepanian, comp., *Povesti, rasskazy* (Novellas, Stories) (Moscow: Sovetskaia Rossiia, 1981), p. 387.

socialist humanism, a form of humanism unique to political systems of the Soviet type. As described by G. L. Smirnov, the true humanism of Soviet society is manifested in the rights and freedoms enjoyed by Soviet citizens, the new type of personality they display, and the fulfillment of human nature that only socialism permits. Socialism, because it is free of the amorality, greed, inflation, crime, unemployment, and imperialism intrinsic to capitalism, is the only type of society that achieves true humanism.[40]

It would be unwise to overstate the problems these logical contradictions cause in the socialization process. The emphasis upon the more universalistic aspects of communist morality, however, may establish ethical values against which youth judge the institutions and norms of Soviet political life. The late Soviet dissident Andrei Amalrik believed that the older Christian ethic had been "driven out of the popular consciousness" and the attempt to replace it with a utilitarian, politically centered morality had only succeeded in demoralizing society and depriving it of any "nonopportunistic moral criteria." Although there may be some truth in this view, it is nevertheless notable that several thousand political dissidents such as Amalrik have been willing to sacrifice themselves for the sake of moral values they regard as absolute.[41] Soviet youth who have absorbed the idealistic and utopian elements of the political culture may experience a shock when they experience greater contact with the norms of the adult world.[42] On the other hand, those who have developed great skill in reconciling the contradictory values offered in the socialization process may have relatively little difficulty in adjusting to the demands of the economy and the polity and may go more smoothly from

[40]G. L. Smirnov, *Sovetskii chelovek: Formirovanie sotsialisticheskogo tipa lichnosti* (The Soviet Person: Formation of the Socialist Type of Personality), 3rd ed. (Moscow: Izdatel'stvo politicheskoi literatury, 1980), pp. 1–30.

[41]See Peter Reddaway, "Dissent in the Soviet Union," *Problems of Communism* 32, no. 6 (November–December 1983): 1–15.

[42]One of the authors of this book remembers the result of his efforts to arrange for an American singing group to visit his Leningrad University graduate student dormitory while he was an exchange student there in 1977. He was assisted by the leader of the Komsomol organization in the dormitory, who was sure that her influence could overcome bureaucratic resistance to the event. At a certain point in her dealings with the university administration, including the office responsible for contacts between foreigners and Soviets, she came up against authorities opposed to the visit whose power could not be overruled, and she was genuinely surprised and dejected at the outcome.

success in school to success in their careers. Of course, such youths, though they may become competent officials and experts, are perhaps unlikely to be imbued with the selfless dedication and other qualities embodied in the Leninist ideal.

EARLY POLITICAL MOBILIZATION

The Soviet educational pattern has a special feature that may be described as the politicization of personality formation through the collectivization of upbringing. In the preschool and early school years, unique mechanisms, the product of prerevolutionary Russian cultural patterns combined with Soviet ideological and industrialization requirements, come into play. In part, they operate through agencies we might expect to have to central role, such as the family — but a family the CPSU seeks to convert into its agent. They also operate through structures and programs specially designed and directed to carry out collective upbringing.[43] The home and especially the classroom-based collective are expected to imbue even the very young with the goals codified as communist morality.[44]

According to Soviet sources a collective (*kollektiv*) is not merely a group of individuals associated more or less spontaneously for some purpose; it is a group organized for particular work or tasks, with its own organs of administration and coordination and relationships of subordination, responsibility, and mutuality. Lyalin refers to the "children's collective" as the "foundation of the system of communist education, through which the teacher should exercise his leadership role."[45] It is both the object and the subject of education. Its usefulness is enhanced when it is drawn into practical activity and directed toward the attainment of goals that are clearly defined and attractive to its members. Citing the noted Russian physiologist and psychologist Ivan Pavlov and the famous Soviet educator of the 1920s and 1930s Anton Makarenko as theoretical mentors, contemporary Soviet educators assert that personality and behavior are produced not by the whims of a free spirit but through the influence of demands made upon the in-

---

[43]See Urie Bronfenbrenner, *Two Worlds of Childhood* (New York: Russell Sage Foundation, 1970), pp. 37–49.

[44]Ibid., pp. 26–37, 151.

[45]N. A. Lyalin, *Kollektiv i razvitie lichnosti shkol'nika* (The Collective and the Development of the Schoolchild's Personality) (Leningrad: Leningradskoe gosudarstvennoe pedagogicheskoe izdatelstvo, 1962), pp. 25–29.

dividual by society and the state.[46] The collective, therefore, must be organized and its socializing influence upon the individual formalized and directed. As Makarenko formulated the goal of upbringing, it must be *"in* the collective, *through* the collective, *for* the collective."[47]

It follows that the party devotes considerable effort to emphasizing the priority of the collective interest over the individual and the power of the collective to regulate the social behavior of its members. The values promoted are those that strengthen the well-being of the collective: respect and consideration for parents, other children, and teachers; discipline and self-discipline; a sense of responsibility toward the collective and toward larger units. They also include praise for those who placed the good of the regime ahead of their own or their family's welfare. One such hero was the still-idolized martyr Pavlik Morozov, who during the collectivization drive of the 1930s was killed by villagers after he had denounced his father to the authorities as a collaborator with kulaks who opposed collectivization. The methods employed to foster conformity to official norms stress not punishments but rewards — for groups, not for individuals. Corporal punishment is rejected in favor of withdrawal of affection by parents, teachers, and members of the collective. Nevertheless, transgressions are sometimes punishable by severe psychological pressure. Bronfenbrenner says, "Deviance is interpreted as emotional betrayal and is responded to by withdrawal of acceptance and mobilization of guilt."[48] This system produces highly dependent children, who are much less prone than their Western counterparts to antisocial behavior but who also give less importance than children in Western societies "to telling the truth and seeking intellectual understanding."[49]

Outside the formal curriculum of the schools the most important agency of collective upbringing for youth is the network of organized youth groups operated under the supervision of the party: the Komsomol and its junior affiliates, the Pioneers and Octobrists. Each is, for its respective age cohort, the official and sole organization for youth. The groups are regarded officially as

[46]Ibid., p. 30.
[47]Smirnov, *Sovetskii chelovek,* p. 214.
[48]Bronfenbrenner, *Two Worlds,* p. 69.
[49]Ibid., pp. 77–81.

mass or public organizations (*obshchestvennye organizatsii*), to emphasize their voluntary and nongovernmental character. Membership in the Pioneers (the group embracing 10–14 year olds) and the Octobrists (*Oktiabriata*) — which is not a formal organization and seeks largely to give 7–9 year old children a foretaste of the more institutionalized extracurricular life to be enjoyed as a Pioneer — is virtually universal.[50] At the same time, all three youth groups stress the special nature of membership in the group, the obligations and commitments borne by members, and the high responsibility that must be earned in order to pass to the next stage. Komsomol members (who enter at age 14 or 15 and may remain members through age 28) are groomed for party membership. The party's success in using Komsomol as a training ground and pool of candidates for recruitment to the party may be gauged by the fact that when Brezhnev addressed the Twenty-third Party Congress in 1966, he observed that 45 percent of all new party members in the preceding 5 years had entered directly from Komsomol; when he addressed the Twenty-sixth Congress in 1981, that figure had risen to close to 75 percent.[51]

In the Pioneers, the importance of collectivism in social and political life is emphasized by the quasi-military structure of the organization. Each grade in school is called a detachment, and the classroom groups comprising the detachment are termed links. All the detachments together form a brigade. A commander heads each link, and elected councils with chairmen head each detachment and each brigade. The military analogy is carried further with the use of special uniforms and insignia indicating organizational rank. Entrance is marked by an elaborate ceremony in which the gravity of membership is impressed upon the pupils and initiates take an oath pledging loyalty to the Pioneer organization, Lenin, the party, and the homeland. This symbolism and the formal organizational structure reinforce the individual's awareness of the collective's power and strengthen the desire to achieve good results in school in order to reflect credit upon the collective. Members are expected to enforce rules of conduct, discipline, scholastic performance, and grooming in order that the link, detachment, and brigades of which they form a part will succeed in

[50]Nigel Grant, *Soviet Education,* 4th ed. (New York: Penguin Books, 1979), pp. 72–73.
[51]*Pravda,* 24 February 1981, p. 8.

the *socialist competitions* (*sotsialisticheskie sorevnovaniia*). By under-scoring the privileged and even somewhat elitist character of membership, the authorities make each Pioneer a monitor of the behavior of each member of the group and reinforce awareness of the group's power over the individual. The sanctions available to the group, which include reprimands and ultimately expulsion, represent powerful tools of moral influence over children at such an age, and it is a rare child who can withstand the organized peer pressure to conform exerted by his fellows. A teacher also uses the collective power of the Pioneer group in order to diffuse his or her disciplinary power and strengthen the effect of his or her lessons.[52]

The Pioneers offer children a wide variety of spare-time activities that integrate pleasurable social activity and play with political socialization. Tens of millions of Pioneers each year visit summer camps that teach a variety of athletic, military, and technical skills.[53] During the school year clubs and hobby groups, often based in Pioneer Homes and Palaces, offer after-school instruction in such subjects as the life of Lenin, the teachings of the party, and other political themes, as well as sports, chess, music, and other arts. On special holidays the Pioneers organize honor guards at memorials and hold parades. Participating in these activities strengthens the sense of identification with the political system and offers the beginnings of training in leadership.

Of far greater importance in political socialization of youth as well as social control is the Komsomol. Founded in the heat of the civil war in 1918, the All-Union Leninist League of Communist Youth, or Komsomol, is regarded as the reserve and helper of the party. The wide range of the Komsomol's functions is described by Sergei Zamascikov, formerly first secretary of the Komsomol organization of Jurmala, Latvia:

> Working under the strict control of the Communist Party, the Komsomol has at its disposal a vast, elaborate ideological machine that includes newspapers, radio stations, and publishing houses and that uses all the major languages of the Soviet Union. Charged by the CPSU with indoctrination of Soviet youth, Komsomol in fact plays

---

[52]Zajda, *Education in the USSR,* pp. 155–63; Zamascikov, "Indoctrination," pp. 3–4.

[53]Zamascikov, "Indoctrination," p. 4.

the role of a kind of "Ministry for Youth Affairs," and its vast bureaucracy includes numerous departments dealing with such subjects as propaganda and agitation, military-patriotic education, culture and art, athletics, student affairs, foreign tourism, etc. The widespread net of primary Komsomol organizations and committees that exists in every factory, institution, and educational establishment places the young Soviet person in a situation where on every important issue of his life — from acquiring an obligatory recommendation for university admission to obtaining a ticket to the local disco — he has to deal with the Komsomol, and, in one way or another, to conform with its ideology.[54]

Over half the youth in the 15–28 age bracket are members of Komsomol. Most youth enter Komsomol when they reach the requisite age, and membership rates fall off progressively in the older ages as youths leave school and enter the work force. Rates of membership are high in the armed forces, however, and virtually universal among VUZ students.[55] A good reference from one's Komsomol committee is essential for admission to a competitive VUZ and for getting a good job assignment afterward. Moreover, for individuals interested in pursuing careers in party or government work or other responsible spheres, it is desirable to take on leadership positions in Komsomol organizations. In keeping with the group's effort to model its organization upon that of the party, each Komsomol member is expected to take on volunteer social or political service, such as tutoring, supervising a Pioneer organization, or serving on the governing committee of the local Komsomol organization. The Komsomol also publishes an extensive array of newspapers, periodicals, and books. Every union republic, territory, and province publishes a Komsomol newspaper. As of 1974, Komsomol was publishing 131 newspapers and 28 Pioneer newspapers as well as 66 magazines for youth of various ages and interests.[56] In addition to periodicals, Komsomol publishes a large number of book titles through its publishing house, *Molodaia gvardiia* (Young Guard). As part of their volunteer service activity, individual Komsomol branches also put out wall

[54]Ibid., p. 5.

[55]Jerry F. Hough and Merle Fainsod, *How the Soviet Union Is Governed* (Cambridge, Mass.: Harvard University Press, 1979), p. 300.

[56]V. I. Ganichev, *Molodezhnaia pechat': istoriia, teoriia, praktika* (Youth Press: History, Theory, Practice) (Moscow: Mysl', 1976), p. 99.

newspapers, which are a kind of bulletin board containing exhortation and information for intramural reading.

The Komsomol also assists the authorities in educational institutions, military units, and enterprises in the conduct of physical education, sports, and military training. In cooperation with DOSAAF (which Komsomol members are urged to join), Komsomol organizes sports and military skill competitions aimed at preparing members to meet national physical fitness standards. Komsomol members are also expected to engage in political study through the Komsomol's own adult education classes and circles. Komsomol is considered the repository of the society's political idealism, having organized volunteer groups to fight in the civil war and World War II and to go into remote wilderness areas to work on some of the great development projects of the Soviet period such as the Virgin Lands campaign in the mid-1950s. It still helps form volunteer groups to spend time working at sub-minimum wages on such arduous projects as construction of the new Baikal-Amur Mainline (BAM), the rail trunk line linking Lake Baikal with the Pacific north of the existing Trans-Siberian Railroad. These acts of self-sacrificing social labor rank high on the regime's scale of values.

One of the important functions of the Komsomol in higher education is its contribution to the early stages of recruitment into the Soviet political elite. The Komsomol assists the party in identifying and training activists. These are persons who distinguish themselves in community activity, such as propaganda and assistance in welfare and recreational programs, and who often also exercise surveillance over fellow students and submit reports on their attitudes and behavior to Komsomol and party organizations. Foreign visitors to Soviet institutions of higher education are likely to meet members of Komsomol organizations who, because their propaganda and administrative duties in the Komsomol occupy so much of their time, are permitted to study part time and are allowed extra time to complete their studies. Frequently philosophy majors who are Komsomol activists go on to careers as professional propagandists or as teachers of political courses in higher education. Activists who are students of journalism can hope someday to become editors of leading Soviet newspapers such as *Pravda, Izvestiia,* and *Komsomol'skaya Pravda.*

Other Komsomol activists, whether in universities or in industrial establishments, can expect to enter paid positions in the

Komsomol organization itself. A few achieve this status while still in university and eventually rise to the highest posts of the party apparatus. The most prominent contemporary example is that of Mikhail Gorbachev. Gorbachev, whose rise to supreme power was meteoric, is the first member of the postwar generation to assume command of the party. Born in 1931, he entered the juridical faculty of the highly competitive Moscow State University in 1950 and became a Komsomol secretary there during his final year, 1954–1955. Upon returning to his native region of Stavropol after graduation, he became a full-time official in the local Komsomol organization, rising to senior positions in the city and territorial Komsomol committees before being transferred to full-time party work in 1962.[57] Another Komsomol leader who entered the ranks of the party apparat is the late party general secretary, Yuri Andropov. In 1936 Andropov left the Technical School for Water Transport in Rybinsk and became a Komsomol official in a local shipyard. The following year he became a secretary of the Komsomol committee of Yaroslavl province (where Rybinsk is located) and rose in 1939 to become first secretary of the provincial Komsomol committee. The following year he was made first secretary of the Komsomol of the entire Karelo-Finnish Republic, which is now defunct. He remained in that post until 1944, when he transferred to full-time party positions in the republic before being brought to Moscow in 1951 to work in the apparatus of the CPSU Central Committee. Doubtless his experience in handling youth problems in a sensitive border republic in wartime as well as his later service as ambassador during the uprising and suppression of the Hungarians in 1956 qualified him for the position of chairman of the KGB in 1967. These examples attest to the usefulness of Komsomol experience in the recruitment of party apparatchiki as well as the significance of the Komsomol itself as an instrument of rule.

THE ROLE OF THE FAMILY

Although in the early years of the revolution, Soviet policy aimed at the weakening of the family unit (Marxists saw the family as an institution of bourgeois society), Soviet policy since the

[57]See Jerry F. Hough, "Soviet Succession: Issues and Personalities," *Problems of Communism* 31 (September–October 1982): 35–36. Hough points out that to be a successful Komsomol leader in 1954–1955 at the country's most elite university would have been a major test of Gorbachev's political skills.

1930s has generally assigned the family an honored place in the upbringing of Soviet citizens. The family has been viewed as an important instrument for promoting social stability by teaching basic moral principles. The education reform of 1984 restates the government's interest in strengthening the family as an agency of socialization:

> It is necessary to strengthen aid to the family and at the same time to raise its responsibility for the upbringing of the rising generation. The upbringing of children is a constitutional obligation of citizens of the USSR. Parents are called upon to elevate the authority of the school and teacher in all ways, to bring up children in the spirit of respect and love for labor, to prepare them for socially useful activity, to instill a sense of order, discipline, observance of the norms of our society's life, to watch out for their physical development and the strengthening of their health, to create the necessary conditions for their acquisition of general secondary and occupational education, and through their attitude to labor and their social obligations to set children an example in everything. In their turn, children are obliged to care for their parents, and those older. "To honor and respect them, to be concerned for them," remarked Iu. V. Andropov, "is the obligation of the young person of our country. . . ."[58]

Although Soviet social scientists have expressed concern at the evidence — such as rising divorce rates, premature male mortality, and falling marriage rates — that the family is under growing strain in the contemporary society, it remains a powerful agent of political socialization.[59] Recent measures aimed at improving the incentives to mothers to have second and third children confirm the regime's interest in raising birthrates by relieving some of the burden borne by families. Nevertheless, despite the growth in the network of preschool day care and kindergarten facilities, only about half the children in the corresponding ages attend preschool institutions; the rest are under the care of parents or grandparents

---

[58]*Pravda,* 4 January 1984, p. 2.

[59]On this point, see G. L. Smirnov, *Sovetskii chelovek* (The Soviet Person), 3rd ed. (Moscow: Politizdat, 1980), pp. 202–9; see Gail Warshofsky Lapidus, "Social Trends," in Byrnes, ed., *After Brezhnev,* pp. 186–249. Lapidus makes the startling observation that, despite the rapid increase in divorce rates, premature deaths of males now exceed divorce as the leading cause of the breakup of families. Ibid., p. 217.

until they start school at age 7. The regime's current intention to have children start school at age 6 rather than 7 will be phased in over a period of several years because new facilities must be constructed. It is unlikely to diminish materially the family's ability to shape children's attitudes and beliefs.

The family seems to have acted as a mediating and steadying influence in socialization during periods in which official indoctrination reflected rapidly shifting changes in the official political culture. Studies of Soviet émigrés have shown that during the Stalin era, parents tended to reduce the incidence of generational conflict between radicalized youth and conservative parents by "adaptive-conforming responses to the regime's ideology."[60] Often the family serves as a sanctuary of relatively nonpolitical or depoliticized private life, leading to official complaints that families do too little to emphasize the civic responsibilities of the young. A *Pravda* editorial stated:

> Few fathers and only some mothers talk with their children on civic themes, apparently believing that our Soviet reality itself molds one's Communist world view. Some parents even forget to ask their sons or daughters what assignments he or she is fulfilling in the Youth Pioneer detachments or the Young Communist League and rarely take an interest in children's public activities in school. But after all, this is extremely important — detailed conversations about the small citizens' doings, joint excursions to historical sites, family discussions on new books and motion pictures, and many other things that go into moral upbringing.[61]

The family's role has often tended to strengthen pluralistic tendencies generated by regional, cultural, religious, and occupational differences. Such variations impede the party's drive for uniformity and are not conducive to identification with the official political culture. One significant family influence at variance with official interests is reflected in differing levels of interest in education shown by children of different social strata. Children of white-collar and particularly intelligentsia backgrounds are significantly more likely to desire and attain higher education than

[60]Alex Inkeles and Kent Geiger, *Soviet Society* (Boston, Mass.: Houghton-Mifflin, 1961), p. 557; see also Alex Inkeles and Raymond A. Bauer, *The Soviet Citizen* (Cambridge, Mass.: Harvard University Press, 1959), chs. 8–9.

[61]Cited in Hollander, *Soviet Political Indoctrination,* pp. 11–12.

are children of blue-collar workers, and lowest educational aspirations are found among children of peasant families. Besides the intangible advantages higher-status parents pass on to their children are the more material forms of help. A letter to *Literaturnaya gazeta* (*Literary Gazette,* the official weekly paper of the Writers' Union) complained about the difficulties rural inhabitants faced in competing with more well-to-do urban and intellectual families in procuring tutoring for their children:

> What should we, the villagers, do? Young men and women who grow up here also dream about one or another institute and also deserve to receive a higher education. Where are they to find coaches? We have no professors or Ph.D. candidates in our villages. Here it is difficult just to find good teachers. Who will prepare our children for entrance to the institute?
>
> Even without this [coaching], the village school is behind the city schools. Here the people often complain: the teacher is not as good, and the equipment is not the same, and the libraries do not compare at all with those in the city. The village children, especially those who live far away from the regional roads, are deprived of museums, theaters, lectures. Consequently their preparation is already worse. But in addition to all these other things, one must add "the competition of the purse . . . "[62]

Thus patterns of education, social mobility, and standard of living established by parents of different social strata tend to be repeated in their children's generation.

In all regions of the Soviet Union, the family tends to be the main transmitter of religious belief. This is perhaps a more pronounced and politically significant phenomenon outside the predominantly urban, industrial Russian communist culture. Religiosity varies widely, reaching high levels in Catholic Lithuania and Moslem Central Asia, somewhat lower levels among the Russian Orthodox peasants of Russia, and lowest levels among workers and intellectuals of the cities of European Russia. Among particular denominations and sects, such as the evangelical Protestants and the Old Believers among the Russian Orthodox, religious fervor is sustained by a history of official harassment. Current estimates of the proportion of religious believers among

[62]Cited in Richard B. Dobson, "Education and Opportunity," in Jerry G. Pankhurst and Michael Paul Sacks, eds., *Contemporary Soviet Society: Sociological Perspectives* (New York: Praeger, 1980), p. 129.

the population overall range from 10 to 15 percent of the adult urban population and 20 to 30 percent of the rural population.[63] Since religious organizations are not permitted to operate private schools to teach religious doctrine to the young, and the party actively propagates atheist doctrine in schools and youth groups, the home becomes the primary site of religious education. Believing parents confront the dilemma of deciding whether to expose their children to the opprobrium of school and youth group authorities by teaching their religious values and beliefs at home.

Many parents, particularly in areas where religion is deeply rooted in the culture of the national community, continue to preserve religious traditions in the family. Soviet social scientists studying the prevalence of religious belief conducted a survey among fourth-year students at Samarkand University in the Uzbek Republic and found that parents' religious belief had a continuing hold on the students. Nine and four-tenths percent responded that they were still influenced by believing members of their families.[64]

The regime seeks to undercut the influence of religion both by frontal assault in the form of antireligious propaganda and selective persecution of believers and by popularizing a variety of holidays and rituals that borrow from folk or prerevolutionary religious customs but that emphasize modern and Soviet values. In this way devotional rites and sacred symbols are displaced from the family's religion to collective, state-sponsored activity. Examples of officially encouraged votive rituals include wedding ceremonies at state-run wedding palaces, where, in order to produce some of the same effect of solemnity and grandeur created in religious weddings, attendants pronounce vows attesting to the dignity and importance of marriage in the eyes of the state. A widespread current practice after weddings is for the newlyweds to visit the local tomb of the unknown soldier to lay a wreath commemorating the sacrifices made by past generations of Soviet citizens to secure the blessings of life for their heirs. Many similar customs, together with a calendar of official holidays (such as the

[63]Jerry G. Pankhurst, "Religion and Atheism in the USSR," in Pankhurst and Sacks, *Contemporary Soviet Society*, p. 200.

[64]A. B. Bazarov, "Osobennosti musul'manskikh religioznykh perezhitkov (Traits of Moslem Religious Survivals)," *Sotsiologicheskie issledovaniia* (Sociological Research), no. 2 (1982): 173.

anniversaries of victory in Europe in 1945, the October Revolution, Lenin's birthday, International Women's Day, and May first, the International Worker's Day), have come into official usage as part of the effort to channel the desire for religious expression into an official political religion.[65] Nonetheless, although many of the state-sponsored rites have caught on, observers believe that in most parts of the Soviet Union a revival of religious faith and practice is under way, concentrated particularly among that section of the population whom Soviet social theory least expected to be susceptible to religious influences: the young, urban, and educated.[66] Rooted in the family, which the political leadership encourages for its contribution to basic political socialization and social stability, sentiments at variance with official doctrine, particularly nationalism and religious belief, have withstood the regime's efforts to eradicate them.

RESULTS OF THE SOCIALIZATION EFFORT

To assess the relative success of this immense effort to shape the "New Soviet Person" is extremely difficult because of the shortage of reliable empirical data. As the regime acknowledges, the task of socialization is "not among those that are ever resolved once and for all."[67] Each new generation needs to be imbued with the political-ideological lessons, the moral values and attitudes associated with the official political culture. Complicating the effort at comprehensive socialization is the growth of political awareness among the population as education levels increase and urbanization proceeds. Noting that society had become more demanding and critical in its receptivity to official propaganda, the major ideology resolution of 1979 declared:

[65]A recent study of this subject is Christel Lane, *The Rites of Rulers: Ritual in Industrial Society — The Soviet Case* (Cambridge, England: Cambridge University Press, 1981).

[66]See Paul A. Lucey, "Religion," in James Cracraft, ed., *The Soviet Union Today* (Chicago, Ill.: *Bulletin of the Atomic Scientists,* 1983), pp. 293–303; David K. Shipler, *Russia* (New York: Times Books, 1983), pp. 265–77. Shipler quotes the deputy chairman of the Council on Religious Affairs, which regulates organized religion, on the growth of religious interest among the youth: "We see with our own eyes how such fads disappear. This is a temporary and passing phenomenon, like the flu, which comes and goes." pp. 272–73.

[67]Smirnov, *Sovetskii chelovek,* p. 347.

In our ideological-upbringing and informational work we still have not a few deficiencies, including extremely substantial ones. The main one is that the quality of this work is far from always meeting the more mature educational and cultural level and needs of the Soviet people. . . . Major defects, essentially reducing the impact of upbringing work on the consciousness and feelings of people, are the common phenomena of formalism, the inclination to verbal noise, all sorts of propagandistic clichés, a dry, 'official' style of writing, frequent mechanistic repetition of platitudes. . . ."[68]

The gap between the repetitive, ritualistic nature of communist upbringing and the habits and values prevalent among youth is especially problematic for the political authorities, judging from the urgency of recent statements about the deficiencies of labor education and other forms of indoctrination. A report commenting with unusual frankness on problems of labor discipline in various age groups and occupational categories of the population acknowledged that, in the case of the construction industry, the popular view that the youth, and especially those fresh from the villages, pose the worst disciplinary problems was partially correct: "It is true that youth under 18 are truly 'unfavorable' . . . but 41–50 year olds are 'entirely unfavorable'."[69] Note that the latter generation came of age during the period of Khrushchev's de-Stalinization campaign, which is held to have had a disorienting effect on the population. Smirnov writes that this generation had to experience "complicated political changes tied with criticism of the cult of personality and subjectivism" (that is, not only Khrushchev's denunciation of Stalin but also the denunciation of Khrushchev by *his* successors) while they were in a formative period. They tended to look critically at the past, and not all, says Smirnov, could cope with these strains. In general, however, they came through these trials successfully.[70] The report notes that those youth entering the work force out of the Soviet Army or with prior work experience are among those with the fewest discipline problems.

---

[68]*Pravda,* 6 May 1979.

[69]"Aktual'nye voprosy politiki KPSS i pressa," *Zhurnalist,* no. 3 (March 1985), pp. 30–33.

[70]Smirnov, *Sovetskii chelovek,* p. 344.

Frequently press discussions of youth problems center on the seemingly insatiable appetite of youth for the products of Western popular culture, such as the perennial favorite, American blue jeans, as well as records of Western rock music. A characteristic commentary, illustrating the moral degradation caused by the pursuit of such tastes, appeared in the newspaper *Sovetskaia Latvia*. Discussing a particular gang, the paper stated:

> Base instincts gradually brought these dissipated fellows together. The need for tape-recording so-called pop music gave rise to a great interest in the broadcasts of foreign radio stations hostile to us. What seemed at first glance harmless buffoonery and the desire thoughtlessly to imitate all kinds of 'hippies' and the Beatles led these young fellows into the filthy morass of moral dissipation and alienation from real life. . . . They preferred to loaf, to be a burden on others. It took a long time to prove to them that in our time one cannot live as a deadbeat, that our society does not tolerate parasites or apostates from the established rules of our socialist community.[71]

On the other hand, before concluding that a youth problem of particular severity has arisen in the post-Khrushchev period, it is important to consider that youthful interest in forbidden fruits of Western popular culture has been a persistent complaint of ideological overseers since the founding of the regime. Tracing the history of jazz in Soviet popular culture since 1917, S. Frederick Starr has shown that despite periods of regime disapproval and sometimes harsh repression, popular interest in jazz remained strong. What seems to have finally reduced the popularity of jazz has been the growth of rock and roll since the late 1960s, to which the authorities have slowly and grudgingly accommodated by means of Komsomol-supervised rock groups, clubs, discos, and concerts.[72] In short, it appears that the taste for officially disdained cultural wares imported from the capitalist West has managed to coexist in uneasy tension with the official political culture in each generation.

It is evident, however, that the assimilation of Marxist-Leninist doctrine falls well short of the regime's wishes. Levels of activism and political study are unsatisfactory, even among Komsomol

[71]Cited in Stephen White, *Political Culture and Soviet Politics* (London: MacMillan, 1979), p. 178.

[72]S. Frederick Starr, *Red and Hot: The Fate of Jazz in the Soviet Union* (New York: Oxford University Press, 1983).

members. Among those who do take on sociopolitical volunteer activity, many engage in it rather intermittently and without conviction. In this respect, youth are not markedly different from other sections of the populace.[73] At the same time, Stephen White warns against concluding that alienation among the younger generation will lead to the growth of political disaffection among the population generally.[74] Other socializing influences besides direct political-ideological indoctrination help to create a generalized acceptance of the system and some of its fundamental values. These influences include the military-patriotic education and military training received in secondary school and, for the approximately 1.6 million youths inducted annually into the armed forces, in military service. Frequent repetition of rudimentary principles and the idealization of Lenin, parts of the upbringing process from earliest childhood, leave a residue of uncritical support for socialism, homeland, and collectivism, as well as a measure of xenophobia and chauvinism. For many, the socialization process does bring about the internalization of a benevolent, altruistic value system and identification with a corresponding image of what authority should be, although for a few who take this value system most seriously, the discovery that reality may be considerably different may contribute to alienation and disaffection. Among young activists in the Komsomol, most appear to be imbued with the peculiar mixture of anticapitalism and nationalism known as Soviet patriotism. Many young people are convinced not only that socialism is morally superior to capitalism but that it is destined to replace capitalism throughout the world, both by the unfolding of the dialectic of history and by the determined application of Soviet power.

As time separates current Soviet generations from the historical events that helped shape earlier generations' political consciousness — the October Revolution, the drive to construct socialism in the 1930s, the trauma of World War II, and the revival of Leninist idealism in the 1950s (the latter, as we saw, with some counterproductive results) — the political authorities will face increasingly complex and subtle problems in shaping the outlook of emerging generations. Their major task will be either to reinvigorate Marxist-Leninist doctrine as a unifying and motivating moral force for a population increasingly stratified by occupational and educational differences or to turn to alternative sources of legitimacy for their political monopoly. Can Marxism-Leninism incorporate enough empiricism and pragmatism to satisfy new managers and specialists called upon to resolve the problems of declining productivity and technical modernization? These persons are likely to judge the validity of ideas by their effectiveness in action rather than by accepting on faith the doctrine's claim to universal and scientific validity. The official creed is also likely to be further attenuated by increasing preoccupation with computer technology, consumer goods, and numerous other aspects of the mature industrial economy that is beginning to develop. On the other hand, the loss of belief in the more idealistic aspects of the doctrine in favor of concentration on the more practical and immediate problems it is called upon to solve has created, according to many Soviet citizens and outside observers, a vacuum of moral values that various ideological faiths are competing to fill. Among non-Russian ethnic populations, the growth of nationalistic and patriotic beliefs among the Russian nationality has stimulated national identification and even separatism. The revival of nationalistic religiosity among groups such as the Lithuanians has been noted. Some observers have found that among the Moslem population certain forms of religious fervor are increasing, as evidenced by the growth of mystical Sufism in Central Asia. Certainly a mixture of Moslem and national self-consciousness and pride is being expressed more among intellectuals in the Central Asian republics.[75] The large-scale emigration movements in the 1970s — a quarter of a million Jews, 80,000–90,000 citizens of German extraction, and 15,000 Soviet Armenians — suggest a substantial failure to encourage these three nationalities to identify with the Soviet regime.

In other respects the socialization process has been more effective, as studies among many of the émigrés have shown. The legacy of Russian imperialism, autocracy, and industrialism has

[75]See James Critchlow, "Uzbek Studies and Uzbekistan," *Problems of Communism* 29, no. 6 (November–December 1980): 75–76; Daniel C. Matuszewski, "The Turkic Past and the Soviet Future," *Problems of Communism* 31, no. 4 (July–August 1982): 76–82; Martha Brill Olcott, "Soviet Islam and World Revolution," *World Politics* 34 (July 1982): 487–504.

eased the task of inculcating acceptance of multinational unity, centralized and undemocratic political rule, and state ownership of the basic means of production.[76] These and other empirical surveys suggest that at the mass level, the intrusive and all-encompassing character of the Soviet state may not be the threat to the power and stability of the political authorities that we might expect. Although some of the specific doctrinal tenets of Marxism-Leninism and particularly the attention of a universalistic working class interest may claim little hold on the minds of Soviet citizens, others, such as the hostility to private enterprise and market competition or the positing of an omnipresent imperialist threat, may be congruent with traditional values deeply embedded in Russian culture.

A second factor to consider in judging the effectiveness of the socialization effort is the importance of support for the central political authorities among middle- and lower-level political and social elites.[77] Their continued political loyalty and the quality of their performance determine in large measure the cohesion of the political system. To this end party officials take numerous measures to secure the support of the managers, scientists, scholars, teachers, editors, intellectuals, and other authority figures who work in close contact with rank-and-file citizens.[78] As we saw in Chapter III, these groups are recruited extensively into the party. In addition, as the next chapter will show, they are also subjected to intensive theoretical indoctrination through party schools and meetings. An array of material and other benefits further reinforces their sense of identification with the interests of the central leadership. How loyal are members of the broadly defined political elite to the principles of Marxism-Leninism? A variety of surveys, including some that are scientifically designed but not officially sponsored, has suggested that party members and those

[76]See Stephen White, "The USSR: Patterns of Autocracy and Industrialism," in Archie Brown and Jack Gray, eds., *Political Culture and Political Change in Communist States* (New York: Holmes & Meier, 1977), pp. 25–65; also Zvi Gitelman, "Soviet Political Culture: Insights from Jewish Emigres," *Soviet Studies* 29, no. 4 (October 1977): 543–64.

[77]Seweryn Bialer, *Stalin's Successors* (Cambridge, England: Cambridge University Press, 1980), p. 183.

[78]See John H. Miller, "The Communist Party: Trends and Problems," in Archie Brown and Michael Kaser, eds. *Soviet Policy for the 1980s* (Bloomington: Indiana University Press, 1982), p. 4.

of higher political status tend to express positions on political issues consistent with the official line of the party. A large, unauthorized survey of opinion on the invasion of Czechoslovakia in 1968, for example, revealed that party membership was strongly correlated with support for the invasion.[79] Similar findings have been reported for surveys of opinion toward the Polish Solidarity movement and the dissident scientist Andrei Sakharov. By processes of self-selection and official screening, together with the mechanisms and benefits that serve to reinforce the loyalty of elites, the political authorities are fairly successful in generating attitudes and beliefs on the part of opinion leaders throughout society that resist the forces of ideological pluralization and disintegration.

---

[79]Zaslavsky, *Neo-Stalinist State,* pp. 22–23; other studies are cited in Thomas Remington, ''Sources of Support for the Soviet Regime,'' paper presented at the 1983 meeting of the American Political Science Association, September 1983.

CHAPTER V

Political Communication
and Public Opinion

Despite their similar paths of technological development, probably no single sector of political life more clearly distinguishes liberal democracies from those of polities of the Soviet type than their respective systems of political communication. Soviet citizens visiting the United States are astonished and often disturbed at the diversity, sensationalism, and commercialism pervading the media here. Americans in the USSR remark at the massiveness of the effort to ensure that every citizen perceives the world as the rulers see fit. The market societies confront the citizen with the dilemma of making choices, often ill-informed, among a variety of facts and interpretations; the socialist societies surround the individual with messages of often stultifying uniformity bent on shaping his views and molding his character to satisfy the demands of the state.

Media organizations in capitalist societies are competitive business enterprises, treating news, advertisement, opinion, and entertainment as commodities for sale in the marketplace. Particularly in a society such as that of the United States, which in comparison with many European polities has a low degree of government control over the content of mass communications, media firms pander to public tastes for triviality and sensation. People who value individual political freedom, however, regard such defects as part of the cost of maintaining a wide range of information sources on which to base judgments about the policies of their own and foreign governments. From the Leninist point of view the Western ideal of freedom of information and opinion is an illusion through which a ruling class guards its monopoly over power, whereas the party-state monopoly over information under socialism is an instrument of popular rule. In addition, the Soviet approach to mass communications stresses the use of the media for political-psychological conditioning. It was Lenin's belief that the press under Soviet rule should cease covering day-to-day political news and gossip and concentrate instead on being a "serious organ of economic education of the masses."[1] Lenin's advice is realized today in the didacticism and repetitiveness of much of the content of the media and its avoidance of any mention of conflicts or disagreements among those in power making decisions.

Of course we should acknowledge areas of similarity between democratic and Soviet patterns of communication. In both, the audience for political messages is stratified according to levels of attentiveness, participation, and understanding. High-status groups, those with higher levels of education and income, tend to be more avid consumers of media products than others and have greater access to communication channels. In both systems the cards are stacked against dissemination of information or opinion deemed by elite groups to be subversive. Obviously, however, the range of permissible disclosure and advocacy is vastly broader in democracies built on the principles of individual liberties than in systems of the Soviet type. A political culture valuing the individual's right to acquire and express knowledge about the political system allows a much greater variety of information in the public media than is the case when a relatively small political elite with a permanent claim to power monopolizes the right to grant access to the media and can exclude some ideas or categories of fact from public discourse altogether. At its Stalinist extreme, this type of control is represented in the Orwellian expressions "double-think" and "newspeak," in which the very nature of language is twisted inside out.

The functions performed by the Soviet and Western press, radio, and television are probably more similar than the content. Although in both, information, entertainment, and commentary

[1]V. I. Lenin, *Polnoe sobranie sochinenii* (Moscow: Gosudarstvennoe izdatelstvo politicheskoi literatury, 1958–1965), Vol. 36, pp. 146–47.

make up much of the content, the Soviet media emphasize the need to instruct the audience far more than do Western media systems. The result is a style of content that Westerners often consider dry, pedantic, and arid. In addition, the media often use the particular to illustrate the general: stories on leading workers, successful collectives, or hidebound administrators are common because they are considered useful object lessons to society. A story about a juvenile delinquent who falls in with the wrong gang and becomes a threat to society might appear in order to allow the writer to draw out conclusions of an edifying and uplifting nature. On the other hand, aggregate factual data on sensitive subjects, such as figures on the number of crimes committed by juvenile delinquents, are rarely published.

The system of communication has made some concessions to the changes in the levels of public taste and the greater ability of the public to choose among media sources.[2] A much larger number of Soviet citizens have higher or specialized secondary education than was the case under Stalin. Moreover, until Khrushchev expanded the range of permissible contacts between Soviet citizens and foreigners, the seals on information flowing to and from the West were much tighter. As a consequence, the national public is more demanding in its consumption of official information, with the most critical appraisals of media performance clustered at the two ends of the educational and status spectrum. Those with lowest levels of education continue to find the media difficult to understand and use, remote from their needs and interests, and not a major source of the information they use in daily lives; those with highest levels of education, and particularly members of the intelligentsia, are critical because they find the media banal and uninformative.[3] Both groups gather news and form opinion by word of mouth to a greater extent than do the groups in the middle of the social spectrum. Intent on making the means of public communication into effective instruments of opinion formation and social control, editors and party leaders have used the insights into audience interests gained through such means as audience research surveys to modify format and con-

[2] A major study of the nature of the media-consuming Soviet public is Ellen Propper Mickiewicz, *Media and the Russian Public* (New York: Praeger, 1981); also see Mark W. Hopkins, *Mass Media in the Soviet Union* (New York: Pegasus, 1970).
[3] Mickiewicz, *Media and the Russian Public*, p. 134.

tent, such as by adding radio programs that compete for audience favor with popular Western radio broadcasts.[4]

In addition, some media organizations have faced market pressures as subsidies from the state budget have been reduced. Although competition among independent media organizations within the same market is absent, as is commercial advertising (the main source of revenue for most Western media firms), some paid advertising of the wares of state-owned enterprises does appear. In the local press, the major sources of revenue are sales and subscriptions and classified advertising, notices placed by citizens and enterprises about such things as sales, coming events, and deaths. (A survey determined, moreover, that over 90 percent of the readers of the local press begin reading the newspaper by reading the classified ads.) A local paper in Latvia, for instance, earns nearly half its annual revenue from advertisements and notices, of which nearly half come from government agencies and enterprises.[5] Commercial success, as measured by advertising revenue, income from subscriptions and sales, and audience ratings, is not, however, the major criterion by which the success of media organs is measured. Although theater and cinema organizations are expected to raise revenues from ticket sales sufficient to cover expenses, the same is not true of newspapers, periodicals, radio stations, and television stations, which are the major formal carriers of political messages to the masses. Ideological orthodoxy and consistency with the policy line of the party form the principal grounds for party evaluations of media performance. Reporters and editors take their cues about what and how to write far more from the party's agitation-propaganda specialists than from their audiences.

STRUCTURE OF THE POLITICAL COMMUNICATION SYSTEM

Although Soviet citizens have access to much the same mixture of print and broadcast information sources that citizens in the West use, the Soviet political communication system differs from that of noncommunist societies in its continued heavy reliance on a broad national network of nonprofessional, spare-time oral communicators who relate officially approved information and com-

[4]Victor Zaslavsky, *The Neo-Stalinist State* (Armonk, N.Y.: M. E. Sharpe, 1982), p. 178.
[5]*Zhurnalist,* no. 11 (1982), p. 58.

mentary to the population. By segmenting the society into numerous small live audiences, the authorities supplement the formal media of newspapers, magazines, television, and radio with interpersonal influence through face-to-face communications. The present-day system of oral communications grows out of the use of agitators and propagandists by the Bolsheviks and other socialist parties to organize a revolutionary movement around a common program. In earlier days it was an essential adjunct to the party press and party pamphlets, since many of the people the party sought to reach were illiterate and since the tsarist gendarmes confiscated revolutionary printed matter. Today *mass-political work,* the term given to all forms of direct mass oral communication, consists of a wide spectrum of activity with well-differentiated functions.

AGITATION

The most basic form of mass-political work, agitation, defined as simple, emotional political messages directed toward immediate and relatively concrete goals, has changed as the regime's needs and the audience's knowledge have changed. No longer stirring the masses to strikes and protest, agitators now exhort their fellow citizens to achieve higher production targets or to vote in elections of deputies to the soviets. Still a useful form of direct contact between regime and society, agitation today continues to work in the settings of small groups (typically between eleven and twenty-five persons), normally in the workplace, and enables the agitator (who is usually a leading member of the work collective in which he or she conducts agitation) to maintain personal ties to the individuals in the audience.[6] Agitation individualizes and personalizes the regime's political messages and, by receiving and responding to the queries of the audience, mediates between the general public and the political authorities. Agitation has also been adapted to more specialized needs. It may consist of counseling for troubled families, religious believers, alcoholics, lawbreakers,

[6]V. P. Vasiliev, "Ustnaia politicheskaia agitatsiia v sisteme ideologicheskoi raboty trudovogo kollektiva" (Oral Political Agitation in the System of Ideological Work in the Labor Collective), *Voprosy teorii i metodov ideologicheskoi raboty* (Questions of the Theory and Methods of Ideological Work), no. 9 (Moscow: Mysl', 1978), p. 69.

and other social deviants.[7] Despite the continuing growth and technical advancement of the print and broadcast media, the usefulness of this flexible and fundamental form of communication has been proved by its application to increasingly specialized purposes.

POLITICAL INFORMATION

In the Brezhnev period another form of face-to-face address grew up alongside agitation, changing the functions performed by agitation. Agitators are generalists who do not need or use a large store of specialized information.[8] Political information developed to meet the audience's need for information in greater depth on topics connected with domestic and international affairs. In practice, political information is not always clearly distinguished from agitation, since it also is normally based in the workplace and is carried out by members of the same labor collective. An official definition of political information calls it "a major part of social information, which especially covers facts, events, and phenomena of the political sphere of social life — relations among classes, nations, states. It includes economic and social events which have political significance."[9] Thus it concentrates on news about current events. Political information sessions are briefings for general but intimate audiences where more or less prepared speakers survey the current situation in the economy, national politics, foreign affairs, or cultural life. Normally offered at the end of the workday, most sessions are 20 to 30 minutes long, and most occur at least every 2 weeks. Variations of political information include *question and answer evenings, information conferences,* or *oral journals.* A factory may organize a *political information club* that sponsors regular meetings devoted to particular topics, all under the guidance of the party committee of the factory.[10]

The information transmitted in such sessions may be highly detailed and may consist of facts not readily found in published

---

[7]*Kompleksnyi podkhod v ideologicheskoi rabote* (The Complex Approach in Ideological Work) (Moscow: Izdatel'stvo politicheskoi literatury, 1976), p. 220.

[8]Gayle Durham Hollander, *Soviet Political Indoctrination* (New York: Praeger, 1972), pp. 157–60.

[9]*Kompleksnyi podkhod,* p. 155.

[10]B. Podkopaev, "Klub politicheskoi informatsii" (The Political Information Club), *Partiinaia zhizn',* no. 12 (1979): 65–67.

sources available to general audiences. The facts themselves are selected carefully to illustrate larger lessons, such as the continuous progress of socialism in overcoming the reactionary forces of imperialism in the Third World. Sessions are usually accompanied by question and answer periods in which listeners can obtain fuller explanations of various points. Thus despite the formalistic and ritualized character of many sessions, they are relatively popular because they offer the possibility of satisfying the hunger for objective information that is normally not filled by the print and broadcast media. At the same time, as is the case with agitation, the comments and questions from the audience are a crucial means by which party officials in each jurisdiction can monitor public opinion, spotting sources of discontent or identifying potential political opposition.

POLITICAL DAYS

In recent years the use of *unified political days* — and variations on the form — has become widespread. It consists of sending a large number of party, government, and other officials into workplaces and residences to give speeches on a common theme and to answer questions from the public. In some cases the authorities solicit questions beforehand so that the speaker can respond to them. Afterward, speakers summarize the comments made by their audiences and forward the results to party committees and other agencies. This form of contact between the political elite and the masses serves several useful purposes from the standpoint of the leadership. It fosters the impression that local leaders are informed and competent to discuss problems with local citizens. The leaders help to coordinate the flow of information from higher levels of the party and state bureaucracies to lower levels, reducing unintended leaks and rumors and unifying the approach taken by the authorities in dealing with current issues. Public opinion can be judged in a relatively controlled and large-scale way by comparing questions received on similar topics in different factories and institutions. As a result, low morale in a particular workplace or a poor performance by a given leader will stand out more clearly. It is understandable, as a result, that the party authorities charged with managing ideological work have smiled upon this form of oral communication.

A related type of communication employs the immediacy of

radio and television for the same purpose. In many areas local television stations air regular call-in and discussion programs with ranking officials. Reports indicate that such shows are highly popular. A program of this type broadcast monthly on Moscow television entitled ''Problems, Searchings, Answers'' elicits floods of phone calls and letters from viewers, who have the opportunity to ask responsible bureaucrats such questions as why consumer products continue to be of low quality, why so few spare parts for automobiles are produced, or whether conservation efforts are retarding economic growth. In response to a listener's question, on one program the minister of the fishing industry explained that the reason cod liver oil had disappeared from the stores was that ocean pollution had reduced catches.[11] When a similar program on Estonian television invited the republican minister of agriculture to appear, 600 questions poured into the studio.[12] A major function of such shows, as of all forms of direct contact between officials and citizens, is to combat rumors. When food shortages prompted hoarding and discontent in Lvov in 1981, the head of the provincial trade board appeared on television to explain the new system of limiting purchases of milk and meat to fixed quantities, reassuring the public that rationing ensured sufficient supplies for all. The success of this program convinced the authorities to air the show monthly.[13]

Political days and talk shows reflect ingenuity in modernizing what is still a largely closed and downward flow of political information from elites to masses. The prevalence of rumor, a response to unsatisfied public interest in news, has stimulated authorities to expand the means for gauging and selectively responding to currents of public opinion. Traditional methods of popular feedback, particularly the letters addressed from citizens to public figures, media organizations, and government and party offices, which because of the absence of other institutionalized means of articulating demands became more prominent in Soviet political life than elsewhere, have been supplemented by more di-

---

[11]*Zhurnalist,* no. 11 (1982): 13; ''Avtoritet peredachi'' (The Authority of a Broadcast), *Televidenie i radioveshchanie* (Television and Radio Broadcasting), no. 5 (1982): 6–9.

[12]K. Vaino, ''Delovoi nastroi (A Business-like Attitude),'' *Zhurnalist,* no. 2 (1982): 12.

[13]*Zhurnalist,* no. 7 (1982): 11–12.

rect and immediate forms of contact between elites and ordinary citizens. These methods do not, however, increase the degree of accountability by officials to citizens because they center on *individualized* and parochial forms of expression. The political balance still tilts heavily in favor of the authorities in choosing which demands to respond to and which to ignore. Group interests and demands must overcome many obstacles to gain access to the public media. In part, this pattern also reflects the older traditions of Russian patrimonialism, which left room for the individual to petition the tsar for redress of grievances and cultivated an image of the tsar as the all-seeing judge of the needs of his subjects.

LECTURES

One of the more well-established forms of regular oral communication is the nationwide series of lectures organized under the auspices of the *Znanie* (Knowledge) Society, which serves as a kind of national speakers' bureau offering nearly 30 million lectures a year.[14] Znanie Society lecturers deal with a variety of topics, some political and philosophical (antireligious propaganda has always been one of its main branches), others on scientific themes. In 1980, for example, the Leningrad branch of the Znanie Society organized 720,500 lectures, of which over 60 percent dealt with social and political themes. A third of these were attacks on bourgeois ideology, Maoism, or revisionism, and another quarter were specifically aimed at youth. Over 15,000 lectures concerned scientific atheism.[15] Typically work as a Znanie Society lecturer is part of the social work performed by high-ranking administrators, technical experts, scientists, and intellectuals, who are represented in it much more widely than are workers and peasants. (Lecturers are, however, paid for their work, and are paid at a higher rate if they belong to one of the creative unions, such as the Union of Writers.[16]) Attendance at lectures tends to be wide-

---

[14]I. Kapitonov, "Osnova partii, politicheskoe iadro trudovogo kollektiva (The Foundation of the Party, the Political Core of the Labor Collective)," *Kommunist,* no. 7 (1982): 10.

[15]B. A. Barsukov, "Propaganda sovetskogo obraza zhizni" (Propaganda of the Soviet Way of Life), in V. I. Korzhov, ed., *Voprosy ideologichekoi raboty: o kompleksnom podkhode k problemam kommunisticheskogo vospitaniia trudiashchikhsia Leningrada i oblasti* (Questions of Ideological Work: On a Complex Approach to the Problems of Communist Upbringing of the Toilers of Leningrad and Leningrad Province) (Leningrad: Lenizdat, 1982), pp. 77, 87.

[16]*Zhurnalist,* no. 7 (1983): 65.

spread: a survey in one province determined that 80 percent of the population attended at least one lecture in the course of a year and over half attended three or more.[17]

PARTICIPATION IN MASS-POLITICAL WORK

All the forms of mass political work just described are performed by individuals who volunteer their services to the party. Individuals who take on agitating, organizing, or similar responsibilities outside their regular occupations are called *activists*. Every party member and Komsomol member is expected to be an activist, and the party took particular pains in the 1970s to see that all members had at least one spare-time assignment. Many nonparty members take on social commissions as well, those in higher-status posts because it is expected of them and others out of a combination of altruistic concern for society and more instrumental motives. The party's aim in soliciting wide participation in oral agitation and propaganda is to enlist leading members of work collectives and neighborhoods to serve as opinion leaders and sources of authoritative information and to channel questions back up the party chain. Their work helps keep the intensive political socialization efforts taken by the authorities from becoming too impersonal and remote. In turn, activists are encouraged to feel part of the political elite and are privy to somewhat better information about the state of domestic and foreign affairs than the ordinary citizen.

The scope of volunteer ideological work is impressive, at least on paper. Soviet sources claim that some 4 million citizens serve as agitators, 2.1 million as political information specialists, 3.2 million as Znanie Society lecturers, and 2.3 million as teachers in the party's adult political education programs.[18] Although these figures should not be taken too literally, they reflect a sizable amount of activist participation in ideological work by the citizenry.

All forms of oral communication by activists are closely supervised by party officials working in each party committee. In each

[17]*Kompleksnyi podkhod*, p. 96.

[18]*Pravda*, 17 August 1979 and 29 September 1979; E. N. Marikhin, "Nekotorye voprosy sovershenstvovaniia partiinogo rukovodstva ustnoi politicheskoi agitatsii," (Certain questions of the perfection of party direction of oral political agitation), in *Voprosy teorii i metodov ideologicheskoi raboty* no. 12 (Moscow: Mysl', 1980, p. 193.

primary party organization, the deputy PPO secretary normally supervises mass political work in his or her workplace. At district and higher levels of the party organization, full-time secretaries, department heads, and "instructors" do the massive job of organizing and coordinating all lectures, agitation and political information sessions, political days, and the like while also processing and analyzing the reports that come back about comments and questions from the public. Frequently the committees carrying out various forms of this activity are headed by full-time party officials or propagandists, who keep tabs on the contacts between activists and citizens. So great a reliance by the party officials upon volunteer activists requires, however, a constant and massive effort to maintain the loyalty of those citizens who guide and conduct ideological work.

THE FORMAL MEDIA

All forms of media — press, periodicals, books, cinema, broadcasting, news services, all forms, indeed, of publicly disseminated information — fall under the ideological supervision of the party. Its agitation and propaganda officials at every level of party organization guide and screen the output of the mass media and the oral political work that has been discussed. This supervision is organized through the agitation-propaganda department of each party committee, overseen by a secretary in charge of ideological affairs. Direct party supervision is supplemented by parallel lines of control, including high party saturation of the publishing and media professions and the national censorship machinery. In the more specifically political forms of communication, such as newspapers, radio, and television, the content is further subject to party influence by the use of the two news and feature services, TASS and APN, which help centralize the gathering and dissemination of information on social and political subjects. In addition, radio and television production is a function of the broadcasting department of each soviet executive committee. The combined effect of these methods of control ensures that the content of the mass media reflects — to a remarkable degree — unanimity of outlook and purpose. The aim of the communications system is to saturate the social environment with an immense variety of information sources and channels, all of which carry a consistent set of messages about the Soviet homeland and the world outside.

From the earliest period of Soviet history, the political leadership has laid heavy emphasis on the mobilizing and socializing roles of the communications media. Lenin, with his prescient insight into the importance of the press in shaping a mass political movement, saw the Bolshevik newspapers both as the means for reaching and activating the working masses of Russia and as the basis for the organization of the party.[19] By bringing the workers into the production and distribution of the newspaper, he also made them activists who tied the party leaders with the nuclei of the party's organization in the factories and mines.[20] Hence it was unthinkable that the press be independent of the party or not organizationally linked with it.[21] The tasks of the press were an indispensable outgrowth of the party's role in mobilizing society and centralizing power within it. Lenin's writings on the press, except for comments holding that censorship was at best a temporary and unfortunate necessity,[22] are frequently cited today as authority for the organization and policies of all the mass media. Lenin's description of himself as a "publicist" is commonly referred to in order to demonstrate the proud and honored position of the journalist in the socialist order.

Under Lenin several important structural features of the Soviet media were established, including the political monopoly held by media outlets loyal to and dependent on the regime. During the civil war the regime suppressed all opposition press organs and established a party monopoly on publishing.[23] In addition, during the same period, the party took pains to render the language of the media as simple and accessible for the untutored masses as possible and made heroic efforts to broaden the distribution network of the press despite overwhelming difficulties in procuring newsprint, ink, and transportation. Lenin established the tradition of *worker-peasant correspondents* (*rabochie i sel'skie korrespondenty*) who worked as free-lance, volunteer contributors to the press, writing about daily life and problems in their factories and farms.

[19]Lenin, *Polnoe sobranie sochinenii,* vol. 4, p. 192; vol. 47, p. 100.

[20]Ibid., vol. 25, pp. 104–5.

[21]Ibid., vol. 11, p. 163.

[22]See Roy Medvedev, *On Socialist Democracy,* trans. Ellen de Kadt (New York: Norton, 1975), pp. 186–88.

[23]Paul Roth, *Sow-Inform: Nachrichtenwesen und Informationspolitik der Sowjetunion* (Duesseldorf: Droste Verlag, 1980), pp. 37–49.

Lenin also welcomed letters and materials from readers, frequently exhorting editors and officials to pay more attention to the voice of the masses. This populist tradition has had, however, a side effect that may not be entirely unwelcome. Journalism is one of the most weakly developed professions, and its claims to specialized expertise or standards of performance are undermined by the emphasis given, on the one hand, to popular participation in the generation of material and, on the other, to the intense politicization to which media personnel are subjected. These factors, together with Stalin's demand for total ideological uniformity, help to explain the fact that no distinct union of journalists existed until Khrushchev authorized the foundation of a union in 1956.[24]

Under Stalin, the leadership placed even greater emphasis upon *mobilizing* the population and less on informing it than in the 1920s. The most sharply formulated expression of Stalinist policy — and one still quoted today with approval if some qualification — was given by V. V. Kuibyshev, chairman of the State Planning Agency, in February 1931, the time of the height of collectivization and of the First Five Year industrialization plan. Speaking to delegates from branches of the news agency from various parts of the country, Kuibyshev explained that Lenin had considered the press a vital weapon of propaganda and political organization and asserted that this view was still valid. The general task of the press today, according to Kuibyshev, was to struggle for the party's line on all fronts, not only by extending the regime's authority downward but also by serving as the "antennae" of the public in monitoring the performance of officials. Thus the press must lead campaigns and retain the capacity to react quickly to events. The information component of messages had to remain subordinate to the persuasive and mobilizing goal. Lenin, Kuibyshev recalled, had called news "agitation by means of facts." Following from this, Kuibyshev explained how the press should make use of information:

> The information part of our press is a sector of this agitation by means of facts. And in these two words is essentially contained the whole Bolshevik definition of the tasks of information. Above all

[24]Christine Kunze, *Journalismus in der UdSSR* (Munich: Verlag Dokumentation Saur KG, 1978), pp. 100–102.

this is agitation — i.e., not the toothless, dispassionate transmittal of facts, but the selection of facts in such a way, in such an order, that they themselves shout out for us, for our cause.

Kuibyshev stressed the great opportunities opened to the regime through the unity of political doctrines and the political centralization of the press. The content of the information would be dictated entirely by the needs of the regime: domestic information should assist socialist construction; foreign affairs coverage, the struggle of the world proletariat. The speed with which the press can transmit information down the bureaucratic chain of command also commended it; it could inform lower levels of the state apparatus about current policy much more directly than if the same information passed through bureaucratic channels. On the other hand, the further the regime went in building socialism, the greater would be the challenges facing the press. As society became more complex, the political leadership would make yet greater demands on the press because, as Kuibyshev explained, "we must know everything that happens below, so as to be able to steer the ship of our economic policy." At the same time, the local and intermediate levels of the state would also require more information "because they are being drawn more and more into the general policy of the country, because they are more and more tightly bound with all the rest of the organism of our Union."[25]

Kuibyshev's stark description of the absolute subservience of information to the party's political demands continues to stand, though in somewhat softer form, as the basic statement of the relationship between the content of the media and political authority. A contemporary professor of journalism, referring to Kuibyshev's speech, explains that a given newspaper article might contain more propaganda or more agitation, but that there should in every case be at least a dose of one of these qualities in all materials relating to regime ideology.[26] Though editors and jour-

[25]V. V. Kuibyshev, "Bor'ba za general'nuiu liniiu partii protiv vsiakikh uklonov i izvrashchenii — osnovnoe politicheskoe soderzhanie raboty pechati" (The Struggle for the General Line of the Party against Any Deviations and Distortions Is the Fundamental Political Content of the Work of the Press), *Izvestiia,* 24 February 1931, p. 2.

[26]V. A. Shandra, *Gazeta, propaganda, zhizn': voprosy teorii i metodiki* (The Newspaper, Propaganda, Life: Questions of Theory and Methodology) (Moscow: Mysl', 1982), p. 30.

nalists bear responsibility for seeing to it that all content meets these demands, Soviet writers underline the party's ultimate responsibility for the content of mass communications. Party direction, according to M. V. Shkondin, docent in the department of the theory and practice of the party-Soviet press of the journalism faculty at Moscow State University, is, above all, *political* in nature. The party imposes its political interests on the media just as it imposes them on ''all spheres of public life.''[27] The party's concern with the media therefore extends to all aspects of media work: the planning of coverage from day to day, quarter to quarter, and year to year; the conduct of campaigns and other forms of special coverage; the quality and accuracy of content.

The close attention devoted by the party to the media and the overriding importance of politically correct expression in content do not prevent conflicts between the political authorities and the media. These arise when media personnel seek to perform the advocacy role of people's tribune that is part of the ideological tradition of the Soviet press. Though journalists more commonly published materials critical of established policies or individuals in the 1960s than in the 1970s and 1980s, controversies do arise, usually centering on local issues. Most disputes arise when a newspaper exposes an injustice in the work of an economic enterprise or government agency; it is less common for the press to take on party officials directly. When, however, local party officials take the side of officials accused of impropriety, higher-level party and media organs may intervene to settle the issue. Often such incidents concern rather trivial matters in which the exposure of malfeasance on the part of officials does not impugn the good name of the party or state.

Another category of press controversies concerns policy questions on which no clear political line exists. Disputes over environmental protection offer a good example. A reporter's horror at finding severe pollution in a formerly clear stream or lake may provoke an extended series of articles and letters, some deploring the depredation caused by uncontrolled industrial development and others defending economic growth and attacking environ-

---

[27]M. V. Shkondin, *Pechat': Osnovy organizatsii i upravleniia* (The Press: Fundamentals of Organization and Management) (Moscow: Izdatel'stvo moskovskogo universiteta, 1982), p. 68.

mental extremism.[28] Problems of popular culture and morality —
for example, whether society should encourage unwed women to
have children or whether the love of rock music among the young
is a social threat — regularly evoke long exchanges of views in
the press. The party often encourages a press discussion to develop, since it serves as a safe and often useful outlet for popular
opinion as long as it does not touch upon taboo topics such as the
party leaders, Leninist doctrine, or the leading role of the party
in the Soviet state. Moreover, the exposure of corruption or in-
eptitude among lower-level officials supplements the party's other
methods for monitoring bureaucratic performance and is considered an important example of the practice of criticism and self-
criticism by which the regime adjusts to feedback information
about its behavior.

The organization of the communications media varies slightly
with the types of media — book publishing, newspapers, periodicals, and broadcasting. State committees under the direction
of the USSR Council of Ministers oversee the specific functions
of book publishing (the State Committee for the Affairs of Publishing Houses, Printing and the Book Trade, often referred to
by its Russian acronym, *Goskomizdat*), radio and television broadcasting (through the State Committee for Television and Radio
Broadcasting), and censorship (the State Committee for the Protection of State Secrets, often called *Glavlit* but also sometimes
called *Goslit*).[29] Corresponding departments of local governmental

[28]See, for example, the account of a local controversy involving the pollution
of the Ob' River by oil and gas extraction in *Zhurnalist,* no. 9 (1981): 27–29.

[29]Information about censorship in the Soviet Union is extremely hard to come
by because the very topic of official secrecy or censorship is itself kept secret
through censorship. Certain pieces of information are available, however. Martin
Dewhirst and Robert Farrell, eds., *The Soviet Censorship* (Metuchen, N.J.: Scare-
crow Press, 1973) is a useful source. Also see Mark W. Hopkins, *Mass Media in
the Soviet Union* (New York: Pegasus, 1970). Paul Lendvai, *The Bureaucracy of Truth:
How Communist Governments Manage the News* (Boulder, Colo.: Westview Press,
1981) offers a helpful survey of media and censorship policies in the USSR and
Eastern Europe. More information pertaining to the mechanisms of censorship
in Eastern Europe, and especially Poland, has become available. See George
Schoepflin, ed., *Censorship and Political Communication: Examples from Eastern Europe*
(New York: St. Martin's, 1983). Recently a very important collection of materials
pertaining to censorship in Poland — smuggled out by a former employee of the
Polish censorship organs — was published. See Jane Leftwich Curry, trans. and
ed., *The Black Book of Polish Censorship* (New York: Vintage Books, 1984). The
editor's introduction is very informative about editorial and censorship policies
in Poland.

executive committees supervise broadcasting, publishing, and censorship in each territorial jurisdiction.

The Telegraph Agency of the Soviet Union (or TASS, by its Russian initials), is an agency without ministerial status of the Council of Ministers. It functions as a centralized source of authoritative information for media organizations as well as for many agencies of the party and government. Although it has branches in each union republic, it operates as a unified information channel for gathering and distributing information, primarily information of a political nature. It is an immense operation, one of the largest news agencies in the world. Its correspondents work in all republican and provincial capitals and in many other cities as well. It maintains offices in 110 foreign countries. As told, it transmits some 2.5 million words daily to its 20,000 subscribers, of which only about a fifth to a quarter are media organizations. An important function of TASS is to prepare specialized summaries of news, some of which are classified according to the sensitivity and objectivity of the reporting, for party officials, government offices, and other privileged subscribers. Although a few major newspapers, such as *Pravda* and *Izvestiia,* maintain their own foreign correspondents, nearly all Soviet media outlets depend almost exclusively on TASS's reporting for their own coverage of domestic and foreign affairs. Between a third and a half of the content of the average newspaper is supplied by TASS. In addition, TASS plays the crucial role of communicating official news about political events — the shooting down of the KAL airliner, the death of Chernenko and election of Gorbachev as general secretary, and similar occurrences — to foreign audiences. Thus TASS is, on most days and for most events, the official voice of the Soviet state for both domestic and international audiences.

Because of its exceptionally important role as a conduit of political information, TASS has been slow to develop as a source of softer news or fuller commentary on general topics. In 1961 an auxiliary news agency was formed specifically for this purpose. Called *Novosti Press Agency* (the news press agency, or APN in its Russian initials), APN supplements TASS by providing feature stories, commentary, interviews, and similar materials with the explicit goal of winning friends abroad and cultivating a favorable impression of Soviet society. It produces about 50,000 items per year and maintains its own string of branches and correspondents abroad. A recent function has been to enter foreign book markets with works in indigenous languages on a variety of social and political subjects as well as items of a lighter character. In 1979 it published 15 million copies of over 600 books and brochures.

The Soviet Union is covered with a network of newspapers, from the central papers such as *Pravda* and *Izvestiia,* which are distributed across the entire country, to newspapers produced in and for specific factories or farms. The organization of newspaper publishing is hierarchical. At the top of the pyramid are the approximately thirty central papers of all-union scope. These include *Pravda* (Truth), the daily newspaper of the party Central Committee, which speaks with the finality of the Politburo's will. Produced to be a model of thematic content, accuracy and quality of reporting, and authority of political line, it is available in most parts of the Soviet Union on the day of publication. The treatment *Pravda* gives to issues guides the content of all lesser papers. *Izvestiia* (News), the organ of the Supreme Soviet, is considered the second newspaper of the country. Important decrees and other materials are published simultaneously in *Pravda, Izvestiia,* and other central papers, but *Izvestiia* maintains its own reporting staff for national and some international matters. The All-Union Central Council of the Trade Unions publishes the newspaper *Trud* (Labor), which concentrates on industry and particularly labor union news. Probably as a consequence of the working class protest movement in Poland, *Trud* was singled out for criticism in a party resolution of September 1982, which demanded closer attention to letters and complaints sent in by workers.[30] The Komsomol publishes a widely read newspaper, *Komsomolskaya Pravda.* The Defense Ministry publishes the official central newspaper of the military, *Krasnaya zvezda* (Red Star), which is often studied for clues about current thinking among the top military command. The Union of Writers publishes a popular weekly newspaper aimed at intellectuals, *Literaturnaya gazeta* (Literary Gazette). Although its comments on foreign affairs generally reflect a harsh and polemical tone, it often opens its pages to discussions of substantial domestic problems. The medical profession, for example, was stung by a proposal aired in 1982 in the newspaper suggesting

---

[30]"O rabote gazety *Trud*" (On the Work of the Newspaper *Trud*), in *Spravochnik partiinogo rabotnika, 1983* (Handbook of the Party Employee, 1983) (Moscow: Izdatel'stvo politicheskoi literatury, 1983), pp. 463–68.

that a patient be allowed the right to dismiss a doctor and go to a different doctor. In an interview appearing in the monthly magazine of the Journalists' Union, *Zhurnalist,* a professor of medicine called the article disgusting and said that it should never have been published, even for discussion purposes.[31]

The thirty central papers together account for half of all copies printed of all newspapers, but lower-level papers are by far the most numerous category. Each union republic has newspapers aimed at the population of that republic. Every non-Russian republic publishes some newspapers in the languages of the indigenous ethnic population as well as in Russian (in some cases the Russian language paper is simply translated into the native language). As of 1981 there were 158 republic-level newspapers, some being published, as with the central press, by the central committees of the republican parties, others by the Supreme Soviets of the republics, others by the Komsomol, trade unions, or other organizations. Provincial, city, and district newspapers are usually published jointly by the party and government of the given unit.

The rural district newspaper (there are nearly 3000 of these) is the most common type and seeks to combine limited coverage of national and international events with attention to local problems. Frequent complaints about the quality of the district press, and even suggestions that it be abolished, indicate that most district newspapers are weak. They are often the starting point for a journalist's career, and it is the tedious and often dispiriting work of rewriting the letters and complaints from citizens that forms the first professional task of the beginning journalist. Soviet surveys of journalists have determined that the novice learns to depend heavily on the local party officials for guidance and information, which leads to the widespread impression that journalists have been coopted by the regime and possess no independent standards of professional judgment. Recent Soviet fiction (as well as émigré literature published in the last several years) paints an almost uniformly bleak picture of the Soviet journalist as one cranking out hackwork on any theme.[32]

---

[31]*Zhurnalist,* no. 7 (1982): 48.

[32]See the pained survey of recent Soviet stories and novels portraying journalists in *Zhurnalist,* no. 8 (1983): 20–21. For a bitter novelistic treatment of Soviet newspaper work by a former Soviet journalist, see Sergei Dovlatov, *The Compromise,* trans. Anne Frydman (New York: Knopf, 1983).

The lowest level of the pyramid is made up of the over 3500 papers put out by individual enterprises, institutions, and farms. For the most part they rely on activists to supply material, with full-time staff limited to an editor and one or two journalists to work up articles for publication. They are considered outlets for the constructive social energies of the masses but also help the regime spotlight problems and goals specific to particular industries.

All told, some 8000 newspapers are published in 55 languages of the Soviet Union and 10 foreign languages. Fewer than a quarter of these, however, appear daily, and almost none have as many pages as even a community newspaper does in the United States.[33] On the other hand, advertising takes up almost no space in the Soviet newspaper. Listings of television and radio programming are provided, as are notices of concerts, plays, and similar events; reviews of films, books, and other cultural productions are carried; there are even some dispatches about political news in and outside the Soviet Union. For the most part, however, the content of the Soviet press reflects the distinctive educational and propaganda functions that were assigned to the media by Lenin and help to build support for the political leadership and its policies.

Radio grew up concurrently with the Soviet regime; Lenin encouraged the development of radio for its enormous potential in reaching across vast distances and extending the voice of the press into remote corners of the country and to illiterate groups of the population. The most rapidly developing form of the mass media since the 1950s, however, has been television. As in the case with the other media, commercial considerations have played virtually no role in shaping this medium. On the other hand, as in the West, television viewers often regard the medium as a handy means of relaxation, a fact that limits its usefulness in education and mobilization.[34] Because of the power and popularity of the medium, however, it has expanded rapidly. Between 1950 and 1960 the number of program-generating television stations jumped from 2 to 82, and today has stabilized at around 120. Satellites

---

[33]Data about the press are taken from *Zhurnalist*, no. 5 (1981): 4.

[34]Ellen Mickiewicz, "Watching the Soviets Watch Television," *New York Times*, 9 July 1978; idem, *Media and the Russian Public*, ch. 2, "Watching Television in Russia."

have made it possible to broadcast from a single point to nearly the entire country. About 90 percent of the territory of the Soviet Union is now within range of television, and there is, on average, one television in use for every four persons. Nationally about 83 percent of families possess television sets.[35] In a major city such as Leningrad, over 95 percent of the households have at least one television set and nearly 10 percent have two. Surveys of viewing habits by the Leningrad sociologist Boris Firsov have found that, at least in Leningrad, 40 percent of the population watch over 15 hours of television per week, and three-quarters watch every day.[36] There are two all-union television channels. Besides these, republic-level and some provincial and city television studios produce programming as well, giving viewers some choice among the various types of programs including news, sports, comment, films, children's shows, dramas, variety shows, and concert or popular music. So popular is television that it is drawing audiences away from other forms of culture, such as theater and cinema, leading some Soviet social scientists to worry whether television is "privatizing" the culture and weakening social ties.[37] The Soviet Union continues, however, to seek to harness the popularity and immediacy of television by modernizing its technology, expanding, for example, the broadcasting done in color, the quantity of live coverage of sports events, and the variety of programming.[38] The more that television viewing spreads (and Firsov's Leningrad surveys have found that the proportion of heavy viewers has continued to grow) through the development of television technology, the more that viewers will adapt the medium to their own desires for passive, homebound entertainment at the expense of the collectivist political socialization that the regime seeks for the mass media. In television, more than any other medium, the regime's effort to use mass communications to construct an official political culture around approved values seems to have reached a point of diminishing returns.

---

[35]B. A. Miasoedov, *Strana chitaet, slushaet, smotrit: Statistichekii obzor* (The Country Reads, Listens, Watches: A Statistical Survey) (Moscow: Finansy i statistika, 1982), pp. 64–70.

[36]B. M. Firsov, ed., *Massovaia kommunikatsiia v usloviiakh nauchno-tekhnicheskoi revoliutsii* (Mass Communications in the Conditions of the Scientific-Technical Revolution) (Leningrad: Nauka, 1981), pp. 58–78.

[37]Mickiewicz, *Media,* pp. 38–39.

[38]*Zhurnalist,* no. 1 (1983): 20–22.

PUBLIC OPINION AND PARTY CONTROLS

In the last two decades, with the development of an empirical Soviet social science, authorities and scholars in the USSR have granted at least nominal recognition to the concept of public opinion, which is officially characterized as an active social force based on the exchange of information and ideas among citizens and elites.[39] Acknowledgment that the organized and expressed opinion of individuals in society properly exerts influence on decision making by the party and government represents a departure from the more stringent political centralism of the Stalin era, under which all organized social activities were treated as transmission belts that connected the directives of the central leadership with the thoughts and behavior of citizens. If we define public opinion as uncoerced expression on matters of concern to the nation by persons outside the ruling sphere who claim a right to influence decisions through their opinions, then, as Paul Kecskemeti wrote in 1950, public opinion cannot exist in a Stalinist system, since granting the right to ordinary citizens to influence policy would contradict the political monopoly possessed by the party leadership.[40]

Now, however, a liberal social scientist such as Rafael Safarov can write that public opinion is a factor of social progress in its own right, its role in the political system affirmed by the 1977 Constitution.[41] The constitution does specify the rights of citizens as individuals to take part in public discussions of laws (Article 48), to offer criticisms and suggestions for improvements concerning the activity of state and public organizations without fear

[39]On the Soviet conception of public opinion, see Elizabeth Ann Weinberg, *The Development of Sociology in the Soviet Union* (London and Boston: Routledge and Kegan Paul, 1974), esp. pp. 82–83; also see Zvi Y. Gitelman, "Public Opinion in Communist Political Systems," in Walter D. Connor and Zvi Y. Gitelman, with Adaline Huszczo and Robert Blumstock, eds., *Public Opinion in European Socialist Systems* (New York: Praeger, 1977), p. 5. An important statement of the theory of public opinion is by Herbert Blumer, "The Mass, the Public, and Public Opinion," in Bernard Berelson and Morris Janowitz, eds., *Reader in Public Opinion and Communication,* 2nd ed., (New York: Free Press, 1966), pp. 43–50.

[40]Paul Kecskemeti, "Totalitarian Communications as a Means of Control: A Note on the Sociology of Propaganda," *Public Opinion Quarterly* 14, no. 2 (Summer 1950): 224–34.

[41]See R. Safarov, "Obshchestvennoe mnenie: izuchenie i deistvennost'" (Public Opinion: Study and Impact), *Pravda,* 25 September 1981, pp. 2–3.

of reprisals (Article 49), to exercise freedom of speech as long as doing so does not injury society or the state (Article 50), and to file complaints about the actions of public officials (Article 58).[42] Indeed, in a book published in 1975, Safarov, a senior associate of the Institute of State and Law, urged that government organs — he did not include party bodies — be required to take polls of public opinion as part of the process of deliberating about laws. In some cases polls might determine the degree of public satisfaction or dissatisfaction with the quality of government efforts; in others, officials might submit two alternative versions of a proposed bill to a public referendum. Ascertaining the strength and direction of public opinion would, Safarov asserted, aid the legitimacy of government policy by arousing support for the implementation of decisions.[43] Safarov has gone as far as to hint that proper use of public opinion surveys can prevent the accumulation of social grievances to the point of explosion. There is a natural conflict, he states, between the "backward, conservative positions" of individuals and organs in power and the aspirations and desires of active citizens. Shortages of consumer products and other problems encountered in the course of daily life can be magnified in the public consciousness into generalized criticism of the system: "For example, the thoughts and judgments that shoppers have taken with them out of a store along with their purchases concern not so much the specific producers of a given good, as 'how are things generally?'" To resolve such frictions in socially constructive ways, regular means of sampling and expressing public opinion can serve as a "social vitamin" that invigorates policymaking.[44]

In the context of the Soviet system, which has emphasized the downward flow of propaganda and direction from elites to citizens more than the feedback flow of opinion back up the chain, such recommendations have a reformist and liberal ring. Nowhere, however, does Safarov call for institutionalized mechanisms of ac-

[42]See Robert Sharlet, ed., *The New Soviet Constitution of 1977: Analysis and Text* (Brunswick, Ohio: King's Court Communications, 1978), pp. 92–94.

[43]R. A. Safarov, *Obshchestvennoe mnenie i gosudarstvennoe upravlenie* (Public Opinion and the Government of the State) (Moscow: Yuridicheskaya literatura, 1975), esp. pp. 83–117.

[44]R. A. Safarov, "Sila obshchestvennogo mneniya" (The Force of Public Opinion), *Zhurnalist*, no. 6 (1981): 24–27.

countability that would make the preferences and desires of citizens binding on the behavior of officials, such as through competitive elections. At most, the modernized techniques for sampling citizen opinion are recommended for their ability to improve the work of existing structures of power through a more systematic flow of information about popular attitudes to party, government, security, and other officials. The responsiveness of government agencies to public opinion may be desirable because authorities need popular support for policy and for effective execution of policy, but it is not to be guaranteed through procedures requiring that officials derive their power from the expressed approval of the governed.

Despite these limitations, some within the party appear to resist the call for more effective means of linking expressed citizen preferences with the activity of the party and government. Safarov and others have urged that a nationwide system of regular opinion polling be instituted — a kind of Gallup or Louis Harris service. An important and unsigned article in the party's theoretical journal, *Kommunist,* called in 1980 for regular mass opinion surveys (*sistema massovykh oprosov*) on a national basis to gauge popular attitudes "on the most important questions of internal and foreign policy of the Soviet state."[45] A partial step toward this end was taken in 1979 when the Central Committee formed a group to study public opinion more scientifically and systematically than had been done in the past. Similar groups and councils have been created on an ad hoc basis in many union republics, provinces, cities, and districts. These initiatives reflect the belief among those who seek to modernize the techniques of ideological coordination in order to improve them that the older techniques for judging the public's views on policy, sources of discontent, and other issues were out of date and inadequate.[46] Leaders recognized that letters to the press and the party, comments made at public meetings, and other casual and ad hoc expressions of opinion did not always reflect the true distribution of beliefs. In addition, the so-

[45] "Sotsiologicheskie issledovaniia: rezul'taty, problemy i zadachi" (Sociological Research: Results, Problems, and Tasks), *Kommunist,* no. 13 (September 1980): 90.

[46] See Ellen Mickiewicz, "Feedback, Surveys, and Soviet Communication Theory," *Journal of Communication* (Spring 1983): 97–110.

cial effects of rising educational levels, large-scale internal migration, wider contacts with the outside world, and other changes
were not always well understood by decision makers. This failing
contributed to the belief in some sections of the party that more
sophisticated methods, using empirical sociology, were needed to
understand the trends caused by social development. Yet so far,
no major steps toward national opinion surveys have been taken.

Interestingly, Konstantin Chernenko was one of the officials of
the party apparatus most closely associated with support for modern techniques of public opinion research. In several of his
speeches and articles written before Brezhnev's death, he called
for better awareness on the part of party leaders of the moods and
interests of the grass roots. In this connection he advocated better
use of sociological methods and more systematic techniques for
receiving and studying mail from rank-and-file citizens. Responding to the political drama in Poland, Chernenko noted that the
Polish leadership's remoteness from the masses was a major and
avoidable cause of the weakening of party authority and the rise
of Solidarity. To prevent such a loss of party contact and vitality,
he demanded more effective and more open party work.[47] At the
time Chernenko died, in March 1985, no steps toward nationwide
survey research had been taken.

Public opinion polling on a large scale began in the 1960s, often
in the form of amateurish and unscientific attempts by magazines
to ascertain readers' tastes by asking them to fill out and return
questionnaires printed inside particular issues. As empirical sociology gained official recognition with the founding of the first
Institute of Sociological Research in 1968, the party endorsed the
social scientists' attention to questions of methodological validity

[47]An interesting and useful survey of Chernenko's writings is provided by Marc
D. Zlotnik, "Chernenko's Platform," *Problems of Communism* 31, no. 6 (November–December 1982): 70–74. Written at the time Brezhnev's health was fading
and Chernenko was clearly maneuvering for the succession, Zlotnik's article reviews the policy stands Chernenko had taken in the 1970s on which his campaign
for the succession was based. The relevance of these positions to Chernenko's
policies once he had finally attained supreme power is an open question. Certainly the removal of the celebrated and controversial director of the Taganka
theater in Moscow, Yuri Lyubimov, does not suggest openness on Chernenko's
part to cultural liberalism. On the Lyubimov affair, see the *New York Times,* 7
March 1984 and 15 March 1984.

in opinion surveys.[48] The party encouraged local party committees, factory managers, and evening party schools to employ survey methods in order to respond better to such problems as low
labor productivity and low levels of ideological knowledge among
the public. Modernizers within the leadership of the party at provincial and local levels linked improved social planning to better
use of survey techniques.[49] As sociologists acquired greater professional control over the design of opinion surveys, however, the
party — or conservative elements within the party officialdom —
became disturbed at the weakening of party control over the scope
of sociological research and the nature of the questions being investigated. A major purge of the sociological association and particularly the Institute of Sociological Research (formerly the
Institute of Applied [or Concrete] Social Research) was carried out
in 1972–1973 with the intention of reinforcing the policy utility
and ideological orthodoxy of survey research. In 1974, nonetheless, a journal devoted to the publication of empirical sociological
research was founded, entitled *Sociological Research (Sotsiologicheskie
issledovaniia)*, in which the methodological level of many contributions is relatively high. At the same time, however, in the more
restrictive and conservative political climate of the seventies, the
substantive reliability and scope of public opinion research has
suffered.

Among the doubts that may be raised about the validity of the
more recent surveys are suspicions about the willingness of citizens to express their true opinions to researchers who are obviously connected with the authorities. Many respondents think of
the surveys as part of the realm of the official and hence as calling
for the right response rather than the true one. Having internal-
ized the orthodox code of values and beliefs flowing from Marxism-Leninism, many citizens can readily and without apparent
thought formulate perfectly reasoned opinions that bear no relation to their actual views. Such stereotyped answers, which must
make up a varying proportion of the responses to any Soviet interview or survey, obviously invalidate the results of the survey

[48]A good account of the political controversies engendered by the development
of the sociological profession is Edward Beliaev and Pavel Butorin, ''The Institutionalization of Soviet Sociology: Its Social and Political Context,'' *Social Forces,*
61, no. 2 (December 1982): 418–35.
    [49]Ibid, p. 427.

to an unknown degree.[50] A second flaw in many Soviet surveys is bias in the very design of the study. Often questions and answers are worded in such a way as to yield desired results and to exclude unwanted findings. The structure of responses to a question may give the respondent a choice among a series of comments, some of which may be more ideologically acceptable than others but all of which are within the range of accepted behavior. Many surveys tapping the behavior and attitudes of citizens toward the mass media, for example, have sought to ascertain the sources of information used by citizens to obtain news about various types of social and political events. Despite the prevalent habit of listening to Western radio broadcasts, the surveys never include foreign radio stations as a possible source of information because of ideological hostility toward the penetration of Soviet society by imperialist intelligence services through radio broadcasting. Thus the actual distribution of information sources remains partially obscured.[51] Confronted with an artfully worded question and an artifically structured array of possible responses, even an individual who chooses not to give a stereotypically orthodox response may find it impossible to express his opinion truthfully and may opt instead for a "don't know" or "hard to say" response. Thus in various ways the selection of questions, their wording, and the structure of available responses may systematically, but to an unknowable degree, distort the validity of the findings. Finally, many surveys are not published or are conducted privately by the party or the KGB without distribution of their results.[52] Surveys that yield inconvenient results may be relegated to the files, or only parts of surveys may be published. In other cases, the reporting of survey findings may be partial and selective, with full description of the size of the sample, the survey instruments, and the results withheld. The surveys that are published may therefore represent that portion of the total range of surveys conducted that put Soviet society in the most favorable light.

[50]See the discussion of this phenomenon by Alexei Yakushev, "Are the Techniques of Sociological Surveys Applicable under the Conditions of Soviet Society?" *Archives Europeennes de Sociologie/European Journal of Sociology,* 13, no. 1 (1972): 149.

[51]See Ellen Mickiewicz, *Media and the Russian Public,* p. 139.

[52]Beliaev and Butorin, "Institutionalization of Soviet Sociology," p. 425; Yakushev, "Techniques of Sociological Surveys," p. 149.

Despite these hindrances, polls are now widely carried out. The boom in polling is such that it was estimated in 1982 that a half million citizens were surveyed each year.[53] The topics of the polls vary with the political needs of the sponsoring organizations. Some concern reasons for high labor turnover rates. Some determine citizen attitudes on social problems, such as drinking, divorce, and low birthrates. Some deal with job satisfaction and dissatisfaction, investigating the ways in which worker morale can be improved. Some test the effectiveness of party ideological work, judging by the degree of knowledge and the content of the answers whether citizens are being successfully molded by the methods of political socialization. Some party committees attach units for public opinion polling to their apparatus; others let out contracts for opinion studies to social science laboratories affiliated with local research institutes.[54]

To the extent that published poll data can be taken as accurate measures of public opinion, the findings are distributions of individual opinions more than they are the outcomes of exchanges among organized groups. Party control over access to the means of organization and communication suffices to prevent bodies of individuals without party license from establishing their own organizational structure, newsletters and journals, and paid lobbyists and publicists. As a result, comments and ideas published in the press and other outlets of communication only partially reflect the actual currents of opinion among larger aggregates in the society, such as ethnic, religious, or class groupings who share views on problems of considerable importance or delicacy. Calls by reformist figures such as Safarov for greater official attention to public opinion are always balanced by admonitions that the party's guidance is needed to give proper structure and direction to public opinion.

A recent Soviet book on party work and public opinion points out that public opinion is more than just the mechanical sum of a number of individual opinions. Rather, it is the outcome of mutual exchange and influence of views among many groups and

[53]D. D. Dzhamalova and G. S. Batygin, "Sotsiologicheskaya sluzhba gorkoma partii" (The Sociological Service of a City Party Committee), *Sotsiologicheskie issledovaniia* (Sociological Research), no. 1 (1982): 52.

[54]Darrell Slider, "Party-Sponsored Public Opinion Research in the Soviet Union," *Journal of Politics,* 47, no. 1 (February 1985): pp. 209–229.

individuals in the course of which a particular majority opinion, the concentrated expression of the collective mind, comes to prevail. In some cases, the author observes, a minority view may win out and persuade the majority of its correctness; this happened, he argues, when a small number of activists concerned about the pollution of Lake Baikal worked to swing public opinion around to the view that government measures to regulate the release of effluents into the lake were urgently required. A similar process whereby an unpopular view eventually won over the majority occurred in the discussion of the usefulness of private plots in agriculture, support for which at least at the level of official rhetoric has been a policy since the mid-1970s. There are also, the author states, "many other examples."[55]

To counterbalance the endorsement this analysis would seem to offer to political pluralism, however, the author asserts that public opinion derives its great moral and political authority from the unity with which it speaks: pluralism or multiplicity of views would detract from this force. Public opinion is evaluative, majoritarian, and dialectical ("distinguished by *diskussionnost'* ") and thus requires close and careful party direction to retain its high political status. Though the party monitors public opinion, seeking out the causes for this or that tendency, it also shapes it through propaganda and regulates the interplay between propaganda and opinion. Propaganda gives strength and influence to public opinion, connecting individual and group opinion with party policy.[56] According to this analysis, then, the link between individual and group opinion and policy formation is not established via elections, polls, or media discussions but rather through deliberate efforts by the party to mold public opinion with techniques of indoctrination and information control. In a similar vein, Rafael Safarov also stresses the importance of party control over public opinion, stating that the party's guidance keeps the impact and prestige of public opinion high by unifying it, reconciling diverse demands, and preventing opinion from slipping into consumerism and other regressive modes of consciousness.[57] From the fore-

---

[55]M. K. Gorshkov, *Partiinye organizatsii i obshchestvennoe mnenie* (Party Organizations and Public Opinion) (Moscow: Izdatel'stvo politicheskoi literatury, 1981), pp. 13–15.

[56]Ibid., pp. 24–37.

[57]Safarov, *Obshchestvennoe mnenie,* pp. 36–38.

going it is evident that even modernizers who seek greater scope for the expression and effect of public opinion in political life do not go so far as to advocate structural change that would allow public opinion autonomous means for expression or for institutionalized linkage between public opinion and public policy. In this respect, their approach is perfectly consistent with Article 6 of the 1977 Constitution, which calls the CPSU "the leading and guiding force of Soviet society, the nucleus of its political system and of state and public organizations." This article precedes Article 9, which describes the direction of political development of the Soviet state as movement toward greater socialist democracy characterized by "constant consideration for public opinion."[58]

In keeping with the role of the mass media as vehicles for the expression of complaints, ideas, and other comments from individuals, an important form of party influence on the expression of public opinion is party control over media content and party analysis of popular feedback. Balancing party controls over the content of published matter with the need to preserve the media's role as popular tribune and spokesman requires continuous consultation between media personnel and the party officials in the organization responsible for overseeing particular media organs. These groups decide how much and what kind of play to give popular opinion.

Under the time-honored tradition of the Soviet media, newspaper, magazine, radio, and television organizations receive an enormous number of letters from the public, some of which are printed in the newspapers or form the basis for articles by staff journalists. Most Soviet citizens write to newspapers rather than radio or television stations, believing — according to survey research that has been conducted on the subject — that newspapers are likely to be more effective in solving their problems.[59] All media organs handle an immense volume of mail, however. Provincial newspapers may get 30,000–35,000 pieces of mail each year; the central newspapers may each get half a million letters or more per year; the Central Television studios get some 2 million letters annually. A survey in the city of Taganrog found that about 10

---

[58]Sharlet, *New Soviet Constitution,* p. 79.

[59]L. G. Svitich and A. A. Shiriaeva, *Zhurnalist i ego rabota* (The Journalist and His Work) (Moscow: Izdatel'stvo moskovskogo universiteta, 1979), p. 79.

percent of the adult population had written a letter to the media, over half of whom had made specific suggestions about ways of improving conditions. At any given time, 2 to 3 percent of the mail responds directly to something published previously in the paper, and this figure rises when a particularly vigorous discussion is going on about a topic of common interest.[60]

In some cases, local or national authorities seek to stimulate a high volume of mail through an officially organized discussion. The national discussion of the draft 1977 Constitution was a carefully prepared publicity campaign. Every party committee, state institution, and social organization was instructed to set up special mechanisms for soliciting, recording, and forwarding suggestions about the constitution to a special commission in Moscow, which was charged with gathering and analyzing the comments that were received. In addition, the newspapers printed numerous letters concerning the constitution, and prominent legal scholars and officials published their own commentaries as part of the discussion. Between the publication of the draft document in May and the formal ratification of the revised final version in October, there were, according to Brezhnev's summary statistics, several million meetings held around the country to consider the constitution, in the course of which 140 million people had taken part; approximately 400,000 proposals for amending the draft had been received. Some, according to Brezhnev, were clearly "incorrect" (such as suggestions for abolishing the federal structure of the state, or prohibiting the private plot in agriculture), whereas others had yielded useful ideas about revisions, resulting in some 150 changes in substance or wording in the text.[61] The signal for an end to public proposals was a communiqué from the constitutional commission on September 28 announcing that the discussion had ended and the commission was now forwarding its proposals to the Supreme Soviet. As Robert Sharlet notes, a well-organized public discussion of this sort is a "leadership technique

[60]A. G. Mendeleev, *Chto za gazetnym slovom?* (What Is Behind the Newspaper's Printed Word?) (Moscow: Mysl', 1979), pp. 115–18.

[61]A thorough treatment of the constitutional discussion is presented in Robert Sharlet, *New Soviet Constitution,* pp. 24–50. Sharlet's analysis makes it clear that the 5 months of the campaign fell into distinct stages, with an early phase of ceremonial comment, followed by a longer middle phase of extensive substantive debate, after which a final, formal phase concluded the discussion.

for mobilizing the population and encouraging citizen participation in policy *implementation,* while the party uses the occasion for a mass political socialization campaign at the same time."[62]

Other media discussions assume a much less organized character and reflect spontaneous popular opinion. An issue of widespread popular interest may occupy the pages of the press for months or even years. When the weekly newspaper *Literaturnaya gazeta* (The Literary Gazette) ran a series called "If I Were Director," some 8000 people wrote in over the course of 3½ years, offering many thousands of suggestions about ways economic management could be improved.[63] Similar discussions about such topics as youth problems, drinking, and popular culture — which are much safer ideologically than questions concerning intellectual dissent, foreign policy, or the competence of the party leadership — attract a heavy volume of reader mail. Because such mail does measure, however imperfectly, the actual views and attitudes of citizens, party and government authorities do study it. *Pravda,* for example, prepares ten or twelve surveys of reader mail each month, broken down by subject, and forwards copies of the reports to appropriate departments of the Central Committee, government ministries, or lower levels of the party and government hierarchies.[64] The same practice on a smaller scale is followed by the editors of other newspapers.[65] In this way, a crude but effective means of judging the performance of agencies and officials as it affects the daily life of ordinary citizens can be constructed.

The ideologically imposed limits on the topics that can be raised

[62]Ibid., p. 27.

[63]Mendeleev, *Gazetnym slovom,* p. 67.

[64]S. V. Tsukasov, "Effektivnost' organizatsii — effektivnost' tvorchestva" (Efficiency of Organization Is Efficiency of Creativity), in K. K. Barykin et al., eds., *Problemy nauchnoi organizatsii zhurnalistskogo truda: ocherki teorii i praktiki* (Problems of the Scientific Organization of Journalistic Labor: Notes on Theory and Practice) (Moscow: Mysl', 1974), p. 31; S. V. Tsukasov, *Nauchnye osnovy organizatsii raboty redaktsii gazety* (The Scientific Foundations of the Organization of the Editorial Work of a Newspaper) (Moscow: Mysl', 1977), p. 30.

[65]B. S. Arkhipov, "Partiinyi komitet i organizatsiia raboty redaktsii" (The Party Committee and the Organization of Editorial Work), in K. K. Barykin et al., eds., *Problemy nauchnoi organizatsii zhurnalistskogo trudai ocherki teorii i praktiki* (Problems of Scientific Organization of Journalistic Labor: Sketches of Theory and Practice) (Moscow: Mysl', 1974), p. 104.

and the intensity of criticism in letters to the editor drive some forms of public opinion into alternative channels where they are harder for the authorities to police.[66] These include word-of-mouth conversation, samizdat, and the fine arts. At times, public pressure exerted through the mass media and the alternative channels may succeed in persuading the leadership to respond with a policy change that satisfies a public demand. Two significant recent examples are, first, the decision to permit large-scale Jewish and smaller-scale German and Armenian emigration (based largely on foreign policy considerations rather than public opinion), and the decision to allow the formation of the All-Russian Society for the Preservation of Historical and Cultural Monuments (the so-called Rodina, or Motherland, Society). Shortly after its formation in 1965, its membership swelled to three million in 1966 and seven million in 1972, suggesting the great base of public support for the organization's goals. The significance of this organization lies in the limited legitimacy it gives to sentiments of pride, love, and loyalty to the Russian national homeland, with the potential for competition between purely Russian national feeling and the values and emotions prescribed for the new Soviet person. John Dunlop describes this decision as a concession to public demands among Russian nationalists that helped relieve political tensions at a time of intensified repression of democratic intellectual dissent.[67]

The tradition in Russian arts of offering comment on social issues, of playing a role in forming the civic consciousness of the public, has also tended to make many of the works of Soviet writers, artists, novelists, filmmakers, musicians, and theatrical directors into major social events. Celebrated works such as the late Vassily Shukshin's *Red Snowball Tree* (*Kalina krasnaya*), a highly popular story that was turned into a smash movie for which he posthumously received the Lenin Prize, or Yuri Trifonov's novella *The Exchange* (*Obmen*), which became the basis for a long-running, sell-out production at Moscow's Taganka Theater under Yuri Lyubimov's direction, represent serious works of social com-

---

[66]See Thomas Remington, "The Mass Media and Public Communication in the USSR," *Journal of Politics* 43 (1981): 803–17.

[67]John B. Dunlop, *The Faces of Contemporary Russian Nationalism* (Princeton, N.J.: Princeton University Press, 1983), p. 38.

ment, raising moral questions about some of the most pressing dilemmas of society.[68]

The Red Snowball Tree, for example, raises the acute problem of the integration, or malintegration, of raw peasants into the Soviet cities. In the story a village boy who has been raised in an orphanage comes to the city, where he falls in with a gang of criminals. He is caught and jailed for his part in a robbery, and upon his release, despite his efforts to straighten himself out, his former comrades catch up with him and kill him. They are in turn killed by the brother of the young woman who tries to help him go straight: this scene in the movie, the settling of moral accounts, is greeted often with enthusiastic applause by the audience.[69] The story touches the problems of crime, love, and the fatal clash of village and city, doing so in ways acceptable to the censors but regarded as authentic and powerful by the public. After Shukshin's death in 1974, both the state and the public honored him with exceptionally warm tributes: editions of his works were published in the hundreds of thousands, a street in Moscow was renamed for him, and for weeks, mourners filed in long lines past his gravesite.[70]

Trifonov's story deals with the common practice of swapping urban apartments so as to split up a large household into several smaller apartments or trading several smaller apartments for a larger one. Although technically the practice is legal, it is typically accompanied by shadowy deals that may run afoul of the law. In *The Exchange,* an old woman dying of cancer occupies a single room on the other side of Moscow from her son and daughter-in-law and their daughter. The daughter-in-law, seemingly for the generous reason of wanting to help care for the dying woman, suggests that the two households exchange their separate rooms for a larger apartment together. The real reason, of course, is to obtain more living space for the family when the old woman is gone. The story and the play made from it were among the greatest cultural sensations of the 1970s (comparable, perhaps, to the suc-

---

[68]Both stories may be found in English translation in the anthology edited by the late Carl Proffer and Ellendea Proffer, *Contemporary Russian Prose* (Ann Arbor, Mich.: Ardis, 1982).

[69]Klaus Mehnert, *The Russians and Their Favorite Books* (Stanford, Calif.: Hoover Institution Press, 1983), pp. 175–76.

[70]Dunlop, *Faces of Russian Nationalism,* pp. 58–59.

cessful televised production of *Roots* in the United States) despite the grim light they shed upon the shallow and weak moral fabric of urban middle class life.[71]

These and other cultural artifacts, such as Solzhenitsyn's 1962 bombshell, *One Day in the Life of Ivan Denisovich,* are popular because they present honest and revealing portraits of the moral consequences of real, everyday social dilemmas, but they are permitted because they do not directly advocate policy changes or structural reform. More directly political expressions of an opinion that the authorities do not tolerate or on a topic that may not be treated publicly sometimes receive an outlet through samizdat. *The Chronicle of Current Events (Khronika Tekushchikh Sobytii)* has operated as a medium for the circulation of news about dissent and repression since its founding in 1968 despite the continuous stream of harassment and persecution to which the authorities have subjected its contributors. This periodical and others, together with individual works passed around in typescript from individual to individual, serve as alternative media for the articulation of otherwise unacceptable opinions. In fact, however, the number of people who rely on samizdat materials to express an opinion or receive information is relatively small. Mark Hopkins, in his recent study of the *Chronicle of Current Events,* estimates that the number of people who form the reading audience for any given issue of the *Chronicle* may range between 10,000 and 100,000.[72] As Hopkins points out, however, foreign radio broadcasts discussing items circulated in samizdat greatly magnify the audience size.[73] Thus, access of samizdat contributors to Western audiences becomes a means for reaching a broader domestic audience in the Soviet Union. For this very reason, authorities try to prevent contacts between Western journalists, scholars, and tourists, and Soviet dissidents. Such a motive was undoubtedly behind the decision to exile the leader of the Democratic Movement, Andrei Sakharov, to the closed city of Gorky in early 1980. Sakharov, who had gathered and related much information about dissent and repression in various parts of the country to both Soviet and Western citizens before his exile, has thus been placed in a po-

[71]Mehnert, *Their Favorite Books,* pp. 192–94.

[72]Mark Hopkins, *Russia's Underground Press: The Chronicle of Current Events* (New York: Praeger, 1983), p. 148.

[73]Ibid., p. 149.

sition of near total isolation from both his own countrymen and the West.

At the beginning of this section we defined public opinion as autonomous expression of views on matters of concern to society by people outside the ruling elite who claim a right to make their opinions influence government behavior. Under this definition does a Soviet public opinion exist? The evidence presented here that opportunities for the expression of opinion through opinion surveys, letters to the editor, and production or consumption of works of art that illuminate social issues coexist with restrictions on the freedom to express opinion suggests that public opinion exists in a partial or incomplete form. Its scope and force depend on the political climate. In the last 10 to 15 years legal channels for the expression of opinion that is critical of party policy or political structures may have narrowed and driven more opinion into silence, emigration, or samizdat. The role of the media as popular tribune serving the interests of criticism and self-criticism and the tradition (dating to prerevolutionary Russian culture) for the fine arts to be forums of civic comment and enlightenment will ensure, however, that some public articulation of opinions generated by the social and political strains of Soviet life will continue.

CHAPTER VI

Popular Participation and Elite Recruitment

POPULAR PARTICIPATION

Political elites in all political systems seek to activate citizens to assume roles of various kinds — as voters, supporters, taxpayers, jury members, performers of a large number of other political functions.[1] Differences among political systems in the citizens' ability to influence the choice of leaders and policies determine the degree of impact that popular political participation has on the policymaking and elite recruitment functions in any given political system. In some systems, sharp inequalities in the social and economic positions of different strata of the population are mitigated by their greater equality and influence as citizens in the political system. In others, relative equality in the social arena may prevail alongside a high degree of concentration of political power in a small elite group.[2]

In the modern age government stimulates a great deal of civic activity that is ceremonial in character. Ceremonial participation expresses in symbolic form the apparent cohesion and legitimacy of the political system through acts such as voting (often in plebiscitarian elections), rallies and parades, and membership in of-

[1]See the discussion of political recruitment in Gabriel A. Almond and G. Bingham Powell, *Comparative Politics: System, Process and Policy* (Boston, Mass.: Little, Brown, 1978), ch. 5.

[2]Sidney Verba, Norman H. Nie, and Jae-On Kim, *Participation and Political Equality: A Seven-Nation Comparison* (Cambridge, England: Cambridge University Press, 1978), p. 1.

ficially sponsored associations. Indeed, as Theodore Friedgut points out in his study of participation in Soviet local government, in the "participatory revolution" of our time, no less striking than the tendency for mass publics to assert themselves politically is the tendency for governments to enter the lives of ordinary citizens at an expanding number of points of contact, frequently drawing them into activity intended to elicit their awareness of and support for those in power.[3] Induced or coopted participation in political activity forms an especially common pattern in political systems dominated by communist parties because of their ambitious programs of social transformation and socialization and their claims to a monopoly on the policymaking function.

However extensive or limited the role of ordinary people in shaping policy, all societies are differentiated by the gap in power between the minorities who enjoy the privileges and bear the burdens of power and responsibility and the majorities who for the most part are subject to the will of the ruling few. Societies differ greatly, on the other hand, with respect to the paths that lead to membership in the political elite. In some societies, particularly those in which modern commercial and industrial organization has not penetrated deeply, the attributes of birth — one's family, class, region, religion, social connections, and other ascriptive traits — govern the selection of those who enter the political elite. In others, access to power is relatively open to those with the talents and interest to pursue a political career. In all societies, individuals of higher social status — as measured by levels of income, wealth, educational attainment, and occupational rank — tend to *participate* in political life more extensively and often more effectively and have higher chances of acquiring *elite* status, but in some the incumbents of the political elite turn over or circulate more rapidly than in those where a relatively closed political class dominates politics. In short, one important means of differentiating among political elites is by contrasting a one-time, snapshot examination of the composition of the elite with a longitudinal, cross-time perspective. In a society in which the elite is relatively open to new entrants, elite status might be compared to a bus that travels through time: various passengers get on the

[3]Theodore H. Friedgut, *Political Participation in the USSR* (Princeton, N.J.: Princeton University Press, 1979), p. 13.

bus at its stops, ride for differing lengths of time, and get out again. In a society in which the political elite is relatively closed, either because it is formed by traditional, ascriptive criteria or because it is made up of a power-monopolizing and self-selecting core, the membership of the elite is rather stable over time.

Other attributes of the political elite also vary greatly across societies. The roles played by different types of political leaders, officials, specialists, and other categories within the elite, the power and status relations among incumbents, the degree of answerability of incumbents of the elite to the public, and the manner in which political opposition is organized are among the most significant differences in the characteristics of elites across systems. In a pluralistic society, freedom to associate generates multiple opportunities for social organizations to form and to recruit individuals to political roles, for example, for the purpose of articulating the group's interests and pressuring government to respond favorably to its demands.[4] Competition among opposing political parties ensures that a set of political leaders, together with their supporting coteries of spokesmen, experts, clients, and allies, are always available to activate public dissatisfaction with the current incumbents, to formulate alternative policy programs, and to assume power in the next change of government. As Max Weber showed in his classic essay "Politics as a Vocation" (1918), in the democratic societies of the West, in which political power is acquired through mechanisms such as elections, a class of professional politicians arises that lives off politics and for politics, competing for public approval and maintaining loyal clients and associates by distributing patronage and other benefits attained by acquiring political power.[5]

One consequence of a pluralistic system, in which leaders of social and political associations and interest groups compete for popular approval as registered through actions such as elections, is to diversify and open the composition of the political elite. In

---

[4]Robert A. Dahl, "Pluralism Revisited," *Comparative Politics* 10, no. 2 (1978): 191–203; idem, *Dilemmas of Pluralist Democracy: Autonomy vs. Control* (New Haven, Conn.: Yale University Press, 1983); idem, *Polyarchy* (New Haven, Conn.: Yale University Press, 1971).

[5]Max Weber, "Politics as a Vocation," in H. H. Gerth and C. Wright Mills, eds., *From Max Weber: Essays in Sociology* (New York: Oxford University Press, 1958), pp. 83–86.

contrast, where popular participation has only a weak effect on the selection of leaders, the elite is relatively closed and homogeneous. A closed elite forms its own criteria for admitting new members and frequently is inclined to place the political security of its members ahead of other goals. Intent on preserving its power and privileges, a self-reproducing elite often seeks continual expressions of public support and esteem and devises means of eliciting them. These may include plebiscites and referenda in which the public is given a nominal opportunity to affirm regime policy by voting or political ceremonies ostensibly demonstrating the solidarity of the masses with their leaders. The greater the sense of insecurity of the political elite, the more zealous it is likely to be in rallying the masses to such symbolic forms of participation.

To be sure, even in a system in which popular participation can in principle influence the selection of leaders and the choice of policies, opportunities for meaningful participation may be restricted to a smaller segment of the public by various barriers imposed on the act of participation — such as raising the cost to citizens of acquiring information, limiting the freedom to organize in order to support or oppose particular individuals or causes, or placing artificial legal hindrances in the way of participating. Sheer indifference or alienation may reduce the level of popular participation and thus its effectiveness in determining the composition of the political elite. In addition, in pluralistic political systems, there continues to be a place for forms of popular participation that are largely or entirely symbolic, such as expressions of emotional protest against or support for public policies. Even in the most expressive of such political acts, however, there lies the aim of influencing government policy. In the strict sense, then, popular political participation refers to legal acts by private citizens intended to influence the selection of political elites and/or policy decisions by those in power.[6]

This definition of participation is not accepted by all who discuss the subject. Many pluralistic Western societies have relatively low levels of citizen involvement in political activity, whereas in systems of the Soviet type there are many forms of popular involvement designed to aid administrators in carrying out poli-

---

[6]Verba, Nie, and Kim, *Participation and Political Equality*, p. 1.

cies or to activate citizens to improve the performance of the economy. Noting this difference, some observers have adopted much broader views of the concept of participation. D. Richard Little considers it useful to regard participation as *all* roles played by members of society in their dealings with one another, with organized bureaucracies, and with those who make and carry out policy. By his definition, there are *no* nonparticipants in society: all are active to different degrees in performing their respective role functions as citizens, employees, family members, interest group members, and the like.[7] Though Soviet citizens have little or no opportunity to form associations through which to satisfy their common political interests, the many state-authorized organizations that they are pressed to join do, according to Little, provide some of the same opportunities to advance their interests. Moreover, levels of involvement in such organizations are typically higher than those in the United States. As to the relative significance of such participation, Little argues that it is comparable to mass-level participation in the United States, since the ordinary citizen has little influence in either system to influence policymaking.[8] This argument shifts the ground of comparison between the Soviet and American societies, however, from one of the degree of influence of civic organizations as such in the policymaking process to the marginal influence of the individual citizen in shaping government policy. In the pluralistic system, the individual may articulate interests by forming or joining any of the many associations that are subject to the freely expressed preferences of their members. In the Soviet system the political authorities determine what organizations may form and who their leaders will be and hence exercise controlling influence over both the nature of the interests articulated by organizations and the nature of the government's response. The large number of participatory bodies in the USSR no more testifies to the relative influence of the average citizen than it does to the degree of government accountability to the populace.

[7]D. Richard Little, "Bureaucracy and Participation in the Soviet Union," in Donald E. Schulz and Jan S. Adams, eds., *Political Participation in Communist Systems* (New York: Pergamon Press, 1981), pp. 86–87.

[8]D. Richard Little, "Mass Political Participation in the U.S. and the U.S.S.R.: A Conceptual Analysis," *Comparative Political Studies* 8, no. 4 (January 1976): 437–60.

The immense network of organizations through which Soviet citizens are mobilized to fulfill civic roles also performs crucial functions of political socialization and policy implementation. Many, such as the Komsomol, the committees of popular control, and local committees assisting the soviets, together with less institutionalized forms of participation such as letters to party and state bodies, contribute to the central authorities' ability to monitor the performance of bureaucratic agencies by exposing and inhibiting misbehavior by low-level officials and by helping to diffuse and direct popular criticism away from the top policymakers.[9] The utility to the central party leadership of such participatory acts may help explain the high degree of continuity in the forms and theory of mass participation from the Stalin period to the present.[10]

For many of those taking part in these activities, participation is not voluntary. A range of social pressures is brought to bear on individuals to ensure conformity with approved patterns. These patterns vary for different occupational and status groups, with those in higher-responsibility positions and higher social status being under heavy and usually inescapable pressure to take on "voluntary" social assignments. The degree to which political participation is in fact voluntary depends, therefore, on the nature of the activity, the position and status of the individual, and the strength of the individual's desire to determine his or her own role. In all cases, however, popular participation in politics occurs outside the regular occupational duties an individual fulfills and is unrewarded by material compensation.[11] Because of the prevalence of such spare-time semiobligatory activity, most observers are inclined to apply the term *participation* to include both purely ceremonial and ritualistic types of activity and assistance to government officials in policy implementation. Pressure to take part in these and other types of activity and the absence of participatory channels that challenge the authority of those in power make it evident that the elite deems it important to mobilize citizens to take on prescribed participatory roles.

[9] Merle Fainsod, *Smolensk under Soviet Rule* (New York: Vintage Books, 1958), pp. 407–8.

[10] See L. G. Churchward, "Public Participation in the USSR," in Everett M. Jacobs, ed., *Soviet Local Politics and Government* (London: Allen & Unwin, 1983), pp. 38–39.

[11] Friedgut, *Political Participation in the USSR,* p. 20.

It is very probable that mobilized participation in a communist regime, as Theodore Friedgut expresses it, is "one of the energizing mechanisms of the political system."[12] Thus the question appropriate to the analysis of popular political participation in the Soviet polity is not so much how and why people get involved in politics as it is how and why Soviet politics involve the people.[13] In the Soviet regime, political elites seek not merely the compliance of the citizenry with policy but also their eager and willing spare-time contributions to furthering the ends of policy by taking part in a variety of nominally voluntary activities connected with the determination, implementation, and supervision of policy.[14] The massive effort to turn out the populace for these forms of activity distinguishes communist systems from either those types of authoritarian polities in which citizen mobilization is low or pluralistic systems in which participation is concerned with the formulation of policy and the selection of elites.[15] Whether mobilized participation of these kinds, characterized by the low degree of choice citizens have over whether or not to take part as well as the low degree of influence these activities have over policymaking and elite selection, is indeed participation in the strict sense is doubtful, but the problem of definition should not be confused with the actual analysis of the nature of this activity.

Not all involvement by Soviet citizens in political activity is initiated or organized by the regime. As in all political systems, much takes the form of individually generated demands on political elites for action to remedy particular problems. In the last chapter we noted the prevalent habit of individuals' expressing their demands in letters to newspapers, television and radio stations, government and party leaders, and official agencies, or paying personal visits to the offices of official personages in order to seek redress of grievances. We noted that this habit imposes a very large volume of citizen-generated demands on the political system. We also noted that this highly institutionalized practice,

---

[12]Ibid., p. 17.

[13]Ibid, p. 14.

[14]D. Richard Little, "Political Participation and the Soviet System," *Problems of Communism* 29, no. 4 (July–August 1980): 62.

[15]Juan J. Linz, "Totalitarian and Authoritarian Regimes," in Fred I. Greenstein and Nelson W. Polsby, eds., *Handbook of Political Science*, vol. 3: Macropolitical Theory (Reading, Mass.: Addison-Wesley, 1975), pp. 175–411.

analogous to very similar patterns in tsarist Russia, reflects the lingering influence of patrimonial conceptions of government, under which absolute rule is tempered by the sovereign's willingness to hear and respond to the individual petitions of his subjects. *Parochial contacts,* as these types of articulated demands are called, do not hold elites accountable to citizens for their actions and generally have few means for enforcing the elite's obligation to respond to citizen demands. They do generate a stream of feedback information about problems that complements official directives and propaganda flowing from elites to masses. Moreover, they may offer citizens a way of forcing attention to particular issues. Not all parochial contacts concern purely personal matters. Many letters to the editor, for example, especially those from educated specialists and other high-status individuals, raise issues and suggest policy responses affecting general problems.[16] Moreover, though newspaper editors are free to ignore, publish, or refer letters to other agencies (only a tiny fraction of letters see publication and then often in rewritten form), those that appear in print are generally regarded as having some influence, since officials rarely enjoy seeing their efforts criticized in public.[17]

A study by James H. Oliver of the petitions placed before local soviets by citizens shows that although citizens vigorously exercise their right to petition government, many complaints are ignored or deferred by the officials who receive them because the officials lack the resources needed to resolve the problems. One of the institutionalized practices of Soviet government is the use of *electoral mandates* (*nakazy izbiratelei*). The mandate is a nominally binding list of demands that citizens direct their newly elected soviet deputies to deal with. To become part of the electoral mandate, a demand must meet certain criteria. It must be generally agreed upon in a meeting of one of the civic organizations that nominate candidates for the soviet so that it cannot be of interest purely to one or two individuals. It must also be approved by the party group present at the meeting, thus ensuring that the mandates are considered appropriate and acceptable from the standpoint of

[16]See Jan S. Adams, "Critical Letters to the Soviet Press: An Increasingly Important Public Forum," in Schulz and Adams, eds., *Political Participation in Communist Systems,* pp. 108–37.

[17]See Stephen Sternheimer, "Communications and Power in Soviet Urban Politics," in Everett Jacobs, ed., *Soviet Local Politics,* p. 145.

the party's political and ideological authority. Usually the electoral mandate concerns some specific demand, such as more convenient bus schedules or a new day care facility, that is not an element of the current local plan. Once adopted as part of the mandate, the demand is supposed to carry with it an obligation for the deputy to seek action. Yet Oliver's data suggest that mandates in practice often go unfulfilled.[18] That the system of mandates gives citizens some opportunity to articulate demands is indicated by the fact that when the initial draft of the 1977 Constitution omitted the article outlining the mandate system, popular concern succeeded in restoring it to the final draft, where it now stands as Article 102.[19]

We have outlined two predominant types of citizen involvement in Soviet politics: mobilized participation and parochial contacts. The latter has long been a fixed feature of the political landscape, but the former has recently undergone a major expansion, especially in the 1960s and 1970s. The tremendous growth of enrollment by citizens in the organizations formed by the regime to channel popular participation has stimulated political scientists to inquire whether it has affected the distribution of political power in a significant way or made Soviet political structures more responsive to the wishes of the public. Controversy has arisen over the degree of influence citizen participation has on policy decisions and the behavior of party and government officials. Some analysts agree with Jerry F. Hough's view that some forms of citizen involvement in the Soviet Union have greater impact on policy than in the United States.

> The Soviet Union obviously is a participatory society, with there being a very large number of settings in which citizen participation can take place. . . . First, the network of institutions to which a citizen can complain or appeal is extremely large — larger than in a western country — and large numbers of citizens make such appeals and complaints. . . . Second, although the right to present suggestions for change to the political authorities has been some-

[18]James H. Oliver, "Citizen Demands and the Soviet Political System," APSR 62, no. 2, pp. 465–475 (June 1969), reprinted in Lenard J. Cohen and Jane P. Shapiro, eds., *Communist Systems in Comparative Perspective* (Garden City, N.Y.: Anchor Books, 1974), pp. 379–99.

[19]See L. G. Churchward, "Public Participation in the USSR," in Jacobs, *Soviet Local Politics,* pp. 43–44.

what restricted, this type of communication has been freer than communication to fellow citizens. . . . Third, the individual citizen who is willing to make the effort and work through some committee, bureau, or council surely does have a real chance to affect the decisions of that group or to affect conditions over which it has jurisdiction.[20]

The final question Hough would pose — whether public opinion in a broad and collective sense influences policymakers in their deliberations, perhaps through the "law of anticipated reaction" — is one that he believes we have too little information at present to answer. Hough concludes that the absence of competing political parties and autonomous interest groups in the Soviet system does not prevent ordinary citizens and specialists from taking part in political life in a meaningful way, not different in kind from the forms of participation characteristic of liberal democracies. It is difficult to see, however, how this view can be reconciled with the lack of means by which ordinary Soviet citizens might exercise any influence over major policy decisions, such as in the foreign policy realm, that affect them.

Theodore Friedgut argues that the participatory forms in Soviet politics share both populist and totalitarian characteristics. Citizens have no opportunity to choose the structures and frameworks of participation. The importance of popular involvement in political life on a large scale, however, tends to provide opportunities for citizens to articulate demands and to give some credibility to the slogans that through involvement in the soviets, trade unions, production conferences, and the like, citizens in fact are governing themselves.[21] In these claims of self-government through volunteer participation, first Khrushchev, then less exuberantly and ambitiously the Brezhnev leadership, emphasized the progress the Soviet system was making toward the realization of the Marxist vision of the withering away of the state and its replacement by the organized initiative of society. Mobilized participation of the Soviet type is far from granting citizens the opportunity to govern themselves in fact, since, according to Friedgut, they enjoy little power to articulate or aggregate broad

[20]Jerry F. Hough and Merle Fainsod, *How the Soviet Union Is Governed* (Cambridge, Mass.: Harvard University Press, 1979), pp. 314–19.
[21]Friedgut, *Political Participation in the USSR,* pp. 22–30.

policy preferences. The involvement by the widest strata of the population in government rather concerns the outputs of the political process. That is, in the implementation of policy that has been decided by relatively limited groups of elites, many ordinary citizens take part in activity that assists organizational officials in applying and administering policy in their own workplaces and residences. The spectrum of such activities is, as Hough asserts, extremely broad.

Soviet constitutional specialists distinguish between two types of organizations in the political system through which civic participation occurs, *public,* or *mass,* organizations and *state,* or *governmental,* organizations. State organizations include the soviets, and bureaucratic arms of the state, such as the armed forces, the uniformed police, the security police, broadcasting facilities, book publishing, government ministries, economic enterprises, and state farms. Their authority is binding over citizens within certain legally defined limits. Public organizations (formerly called *mass* organizations) are self-forming and, though obliged under the constitution to observe the law, are said to be formally autonomous in their activity. Their membership is voluntary and they exist to serve the interests of their members while at the same time advancing the well-being of the whole society. Foremost among the public organizations is the Communist Party of the Soviet Union, which is, however, so dominant a body in the political system that in some respects it is clearly a state organization. Other major public organizations include the trade unions, the creative unions (unions of writers, composers, artists, journalists, and other creative intelligentsia), the Komsomol and its junior affiliate, the Pioneers, and a large number of other associations and groups, such as the Committee of Popular Control, the Voluntary Society for Assistance to the Army, Air Force and Navy (DO-SAAF), the Red Cross and Red Crescent, the Znanie Society, the All-Union Society for Inventors and Rationalizers (VOIR), and the All-Russian Society for the Preservation of Historical and Cultural Monuments (the Rodina Society — discussed in the last chapter). From the constitutional standpoint, the distinctive feature of such organizations is their formally voluntary character, in contrast to the inclusive and mandatory nature of the authority of state organizations.

Public organizations are generally constituted to parallel state organizations, combining a vertical delineation of authority (hierarchical subordination) with horizontal divisions by territorial-administrative units. In each case, the full-time executives managing a particular branch of the public or state organization are supplemented by a broader group of spare-time participants.

At the highest level of the vertical chain is the all-union, or Sovietwide, set of state and party offices. Examples of state bodies of all-union status include the Supreme Soviet, the highest level of elected parliament; the Council of Ministers, which operates as a government cabinet; Gosplan (the State Planning Agency), which under the supervision of the Council of Ministers sets binding production targets for all ministries and enterprises throughout the country; the KGB (Committee of State Security); the Supreme Court; the Procurator-General (chief prosecutor of the USSR); and a vast array of other agencies. The party also has deliberative and executive organs, the former role being nominally played by the party Central Committee, the latter by its Politburo and Secretariat. The jurisdiction of each of these bodies extends throughout the Soviet Union, and their authority in turn is binding on their counterpart organizations at the next level of the administrative-territorial hierarchy: the union republics.

In each of the fifteen union republics there is a full set of organs corresponding to the state organizations at the all-union level. Each republic has its own supreme soviet (with only one rather than two chambers, however), council of ministers, and branches of the planning and police agencies, together with the prosecutorial and judicial and other bodies. Their jurisdiction extends throughout the republic and is binding on equivalent agencies at the provincial and local levels. Most public organizations also have branches in each of the fifteen republics as well. We have already noted an important exception, however: the party lacks a network of Russian republic organs that would correspond to the governmental bodies of the Russian republic. Likewise the Komsomol, which is patterned on the party, maintains separate branches in each republic except for the RSFSR.

Next down the administrative ladder are the provinces into which some republics are divided. Most of these provinces are called *oblasti* (of which 122 exist throughout the USSR) but there are six large and sparsely settled regions that are given the name *krai,* or territory. In addition, where smaller ethnic groups inhabit a particular area, there may be a special ethnoterritory named for the nationality. Such ethnoterritories may be given the status of *autonomous republic,* or, for smaller groups, *autonomous province* or *autonomous circuit* (*autonomnyi okrug,* formerly called *national circuit*). We will treat all such territorial divisions as alternative types of provinces. Each province in the USSR possesses its own set of governmental bodies. Again, as at the higher levels, they are divided into deliberative and executive organs. Soviets of people's deputies are the deliberative bodies, the formal equivalent to legislatures or parliaments in democracies in that they are formed through popular election and are formally responsible for making laws. At the provincial level, these bodies are termed simply soviets rather than supreme soviets and, like the supreme soviets in the union republics, they are unicameral. Their executive organs are called executive committees and are formed by the vote of the soviet. The executive committees work through permanent departments that are subordinate both to the soviet and to government agencies at superior levels (this principle is called dual subordination). Likewise each province has its own branch of the party. Each province has its party committee, the equivalent of the central committee at the higher levels, and a smaller secretariat that carries out party policy on a day-to-day basis. Similarly, the Komsomol and the trade unions also have provincial branches with simplified deliberative and executive organs.

Subordinate to the provinces are 3199 *rural districts* and 2113 *cities* (data as of 1 January 1982). Rural districts (*raiony*) might be compared to counties; however, they are predominantly rural in character. Larger cities are administratively parallel to them. Some cities are large enough to permit further subdivision into *urban districts* (also called *raiony*). In each type of unit, rural district, city, or city district, a full set of soviet and party organs exists. The elected soviet works through its executive committee and departments, and the party committee works through its full-time secretariat and staff. Moreover, where villages and settlements exist in remote or rural districts, they, too, form soviets (though not, as a rule, party committees). Similarly, other public organizations, particularly the Komsomol and trade unions, often maintain branch offices in cities, rural districts, and urban dis-

tricts, which perform the role of liaison between the organizations
of their members in each workplace and the chain of territorial-
administrative command.

The bottom of the hierarchy as far as the party's organization
is concerned is the Primary Party Organization (PPO). Similarly,
most other public organizations also work through primary-level,
workplace-based units — for example, the Primary Komsomol
Organization and the factory trade union committee. It is noteworthy that the parallelism of all public organizations to the party
facilitates party supervision and direction of their activity. In each
case, the basis for forming the primary unit is occupational rather
than territorial. A PPO comprises all the party members employed at or affiliated with the particular workplace. A giant factory of 30,000 might therefore have a PPO with 3,000 or 4,000
members. A PPO of such size subdivides further into shop committees and party groups, which are small enough to allow the
members to know one another. Large PPOs form a governing
committee and maintain a full-time secretary to oversee their
work.

For both party and state organizations, the hierarchy just outlined provides a complete line of administrative control and subordination through which the will of policymakers at the top can
in theory be translated into the actions of administrators at each
level. At least in theory, the duplication of authority between government and party allows party officials to monitor and report on
the performance of government officials through a chain of authority and communication separate from (and superior to) the
chain of governmental-administrative power.[22] All organizations,
state and public, are said to be governed by the Leninist principle
of democratic centralism, through which democratic methods for
the formation of governing bodies and democratic respect for the
rights of each individual to take part in policy debate are com-
plemented by an equal (and in reality far more pervasive) principle of centralism: each organization is subordinate to the
organization immediately over it; no organization may counter-
mand instructions flowing from superior levels of authority; no
individual may publicly dissent from a policy decision once the
decision has been taken.

[22]Jerry F. Hough, *The Soviet Prefects* (Cambridge, Mass.: Harvard University
Press, 1969).

This complex system of state and public hierarchies affords citizens numerous opportunities to take on participatory roles, either through elective office — for example, as one of the more than 2 million deputies to the thousands of soviets throughout the country — or by assisting the work of public and state bodies. Within the party, about one-quarter of the more than 18 million members serve in the *elective party aktiv,* meaning that they are elected to one or more of the governing committees of the party. This means that about 4.5 million party members, nearly all of them holding jobs outside the party, take positions as members of party committees. This proportion appears to be a stable target of party policy: in any city or province, the number of party members elected to the party committees in the PPOs and higher bodies will equal approximately one-quarter of the total number of party members in that jurisdiction. In a similar way, activists in the Komsomol and the trade unions hold formally elective positions on the committees and councils of their respective organizations. Some especially active individuals serve on the committees of multiple organizations. In addition, each public organization relies upon a network of volunteer assistants in carrying out its duties and in providing communications links between the leaders in the organization and the general membership.

Within public organizations, individuals take on other types of elective posts as well. We will take the party as our example, but most other public organizations operate in the same fashion. Just as the membership of a PPO elects the governing committee and secretary (for smaller PPOs only a PPO secretary is elected), so the membership also elects delegates to the district party conference. Here the committee and inner governing bureau and secretariat of the district party organization are elected, and delegates to the provincial party conference are named. In turn, the provincial conference elects the members of the provincial party committee, its bureau and secretaries, and delegates to the republican party congress. The republican congress names the central committee of the republican party organization and the bureau[23] and the delegates who will travel to Moscow for the grand all-union congress of the party, held every 5 years.

Nominally the supreme seat of authority within the party, the

[23]Only the Ukrainian republican party organization is headed by a politburo; the rest are headed by bureaus.

party congress, consisting of 5000 delegates from all parts of the country, names the Central Committee of the all-union party, as well as approving the make-up of the Politburo and the Secretariat. Each party congress, or party conference at levels below the republic, serves as an occasion for the leadership of the party to report formally on how the Central Committee (or, correspondingly, the party committee) has performed its work: what successes have been achieved and what deficiencies remain to be overcome. The congress or conference votes formally on whether to accept the report and then, on the basis of the report, votes on a new resolution or set of resolutions about what needs to be done in the next term of office of the committee. In this way, party procedures offer a facade of democratic participation through which members formally elect their leaders and set their policies. The actual power relations within the party (as well as the Komsomol and trade union organizations), however, diverge sharply from this formally democratic structure.

In both state and public organizations, the apparent preponderance of power in the hands of part-time elected officials is in fact contradicted by the domination of full-time officials over elected bodies within the organization, by the domination of the party over other state and public organizations, and by the concentration of political power at the center of the political system. Within the party, full-time party officials manage the proceedings at every level of the election-and-reporting process and predetermine who is elected and what resolutions are adopted, thus vitiating the premise of democratic participation. Through their monopoly over the personnel selection system, party executives determine the slate of candidates for delegates to the conference or congress at the next higher level and for membership in the party committee, the bureau, and the secretariat. Only one slate is presented at the conference or congress, and no competition between opposing candidates is tolerated. To be sure, in a smaller PPO or party group, the closed and intimate nature of the party body may permit policy debates and even competition between candidates for secretarial posts. At the upper levels, however, discussion of policy resolutions and elections of the committee and its leadership are perfunctory and ritualistic, since the decisions have been reached beforehand and are presented to the conference for its unanimous endorsement. Party members and officials alike accept the ceremonial quality of these proceedings as justified by the need to display a united face to the country and the world.

Perhaps the most important point to make about popular participation of the kind just described is that it integrates executives from the most important sectors of society into a unified political elite. It would be a serious mistake to imagine that the domination by full-time party officials of the nominally democratic procedures for choosing policies and personnel means that those members of elected party committees and bureaus who are not full-time party officials are without power. On the contrary, the party's managers take pains to ensure that at each level the party committee and its bureau include the most powerful executives from party, government, Komsomol, media, military, police and economic and educational institutions in the jurisdiction of that unit. For these executives, participation in party committees may be regarded as a form of spare-time political activity, but its more important function is to ensure the coordination of policy in the principal organized spheres of social life.

An example of how this principle works may be seen in the provincial party organization studied by Philip D. Stewart, where the following officials were members of the bureau of the committee: the first, second, and third secretaries of the provincial party committee; the chairman of the provincial soviet executive committee; the first secretary of the party organization in the major city of the province; the head of the agriculture department of the provincial party committee; the chairman of the provincial trade union council; the head of the provincial unit of the KGB; and one man who was not identified but who may, according to Stewart, have been provincial military commander. The three nonvoting members of the bureau included the first secretary of the provincial Komsomol organization, the head of the propaganda and agitation department of the provincial party committee, and the head of the department of the provincial party committee that handles party, trade union, and Komsomol affairs. Thus the composition of the bureau was dominated by men who were full-time party officials. Those from other spheres — the KGB, the military, the Komsomol, and the trade unions —

all represented organizations over which the party exercises close daily supervision or that are vitally connected to internal security.[24]

Political participation in elective party bodies, particularly the bureaus and politburos, clearly serves functions connected with the coordination of policymaking and implementation and with the integration of elites across institutional sectors. In addition, serving on the larger, more honorific party committees and central committees helps to confer prestige and distinction upon political executives and grants them certain material privileges, such as special pension rights, access to certain channels of information, and special facilities for health care, shopping, and vacationing. An examination of the membership of the Central Committee of the all-union party indicates that Central Committee membership is closely correlated with incumbency in the institutional positions for which such membership is deemed desirable or appropriate. Generally these constitute the crucial levers of power in all-union, republican, and provincial political structures. Taken together, therefore, the officials holding these offices form the core of the Soviet political elite, with their elite status confirmed (and to a lesser degree, conferred) by their election to the party's Central Committee. The same point holds for republican party central committees and the party committees of local party units: the membership usually comprises leading officials from major bureaucratic sectors.

Robert V. Daniels analyzed the makeup of the Central Committee formed at the Twenty-third (1966) and Twenty-fourth (1971) Party Congresses and found that the Central Committee is "very carefully made up in accordance with a system of unwritten (or at least unannounced) rules." Under these rules, election to the Central Committee is assured

> to holders of elite-status bureaucratic offices — Party, governmental and military — with a sprinkling of the top figures in the other sectors of society (trade union, academic, cultural and so forth). There is in practice an organic and automatic connection between

---

[24]Philip D. Stewart, *Political Power in the Soviet Union: A Study of Decision-Making in Stalingrad* (Indianapolis, Ind.: Bobbs-Merrill, 1968), pp. 89–90.

this specific set of offices and the Central Committee status of their incumbents.[25]

Aside from a few individuals — honored manual workers or farmhands who are elected to the Central Committee to demonstrate the links of the party with the working masses — who do not fit into the elite categories Daniels describes, the membership of the Central Committee of the party comprises officials in party, other public, and state organizations from the all-union level as well as the more important officials in the party and state bureaucracies at republican and provincial levels. As a result, one very important attribute of political participation in the elective committees of the party is its function in interlocking members of the political elite across different institutions sharing the same rank in the administrative-territorial hierarchy and across administrative-territorial levels of the same institutional hierarchy. Thus one major function of this elite political participation is in representing the sectional and territorial interests of the major governing bureaucracies of the society within party committees and bureaus. This principle operates to prevent fragmentation of interest articulation and communication channels and to unify the elite recruitment process. In effect, although the political elite spreads across many fields of social activity, the co-optation and representation of the major institutional leaders on nominally elective party bodies help to establish common rules for recruiting members of the ruling group, common understandings about policy priorities, and a generalized elite political culture.

The other major form of mobilized participation besides taking elective office as a soviet deputy or as a member of the elective aktiv of a public organization consists of service as an activist helping one of the permanent state or public organizations. The aktiv of any given organization comprises the many people working in related occupations who can be counted upon to take on extra assignments to assist the organization. A provincial party committee will convene its economic aktiv — consisting of managers, engineers, planners, analysts, trade union organizers, bri-

[25]Robert V. Daniels, "Office Holding and Elite Status: The Central Committee of the CPSU," in Paul Cocks, Robert V. Daniels, and Nancy Whittier Heer, eds., *The Dynamics of Soviet Politics* (Cambridge, Mass.: Harvard University Press, 1976), p. 78.

gade leaders, and others in responsible posts — from time to time to explain a current policy drive and elicit their active support in carrying out the policy. The ideological aktiv of the same party committee will consist of a different set of individuals; it would include heads of Komsomol and trade union units, artists, writers and other creative intellectuals, journalists and editors, and agitators and propagandists. Broader or more narrow definitions of the aktiv might be supplied to fit a particular occasion or policy need. Similarly, the soviet executive committee of a particular jurisdiction maintains an aktiv to assist it. The aktiv is not so much a fixed category of individuals as it is an ideal whereby citizens in various occupations at different levels of responsibility are expected to become activists in furthering the work of full-time political institutions. Its ideal quality is borne out by the general expectation that as many citizens as possible should become activists in one or more spheres of political work.

The range of tasks that activists are called upon to perform is very broad, and in some cases activists assume major responsibilities. The importance of the aktiv is increased by rules that limit the number of full-time employees that party committees or government agencies may hire. The size of the full-time party apparatus, in relation to the size of both the party and the population that it ultimately rules, is strikingly small. Probably the number of apparatchiki lies between 150,000 and 200,000, fewer than at the peak under Stalin. Both Khrushchev and Brezhnev boasted of cutting down the number of full-time party officials as a token of the democratization of the party through the expansion of volunteer activism. At the same time restrictions on the growth of the apparatus help to hold down the growth of budget expenses on personnel. There are accordingly both normative and fiscal reasons for maintaining caps on the number of full-time officials that any given party organization may employ. The frankly economic reason for cutting down on the size of the state apparatus was acknowledged under Stalin, when, immediately after the war, expenditures on government staff were cut from 14 billion rubles in 1946 to 7.9 billion in 1953. A further cut after Stalin died released .75 million officials in 1954.[26]

[26]V. M. Ivanov et al., *Sovetskaia demokratiia: ocherk stanovleniia i razvitiia* (Soviet Democracy: A Sketch of Its Rise and Development) (Moscow: Politizdat, 1983), pp. 139, 148.

As a result, spare-time activist assistance to party and government bodies extends the work of full-time officials and creates opportunities for would-be officials to acquire experience, build ties to personnel managers, and prove their competence and reliability. Many activists, working as nonstaff officials, become eligible prospective recruits to full-time paid positions when vacancies open, and they are treated as if they were full-time officials: personnel records are maintained on them and their performance must match that of the paid staff. A report from the mid-1970s about ideological work in a provincial party committee in the Russian republic indicated that some 360 full-time staff employees working in the ideological sector of the provincial, city, and district party committees throughout the province were backed up by another 200 nonstaff officials. When staff positions opened up, these nonstaff activists were often hired to fill them.[27] Their work consisted of support for the department heads and instructors supervising ideological work. Thus they helped gather and analyze data, monitored the media, organized oral agitation and political work, and carried out other organizational and supervisory functions. Similar duties are performed by nonstaff activists who work with other departments of party committees or with departments of soviet executive committees. Aside from enabling individuals to discharge their obligation to do community-oriented political work on an unpaid basis, these highly visible forms of participation serve as channels for self-selection into the full-time ranks of the political elite by providing apprenticeships for ambitious would-be political executives.[28]

The majority of activist duties involve lower levels of responsibility. In the sphere of ideological work, for example, an individual might choose to serve as an agitator or political information specialist, often staying in that line of work for many years. For the more highly placed — such as scholars, factory managers, and government officials — teaching in the party's political education system or working as a propagandist becomes a "second profession." The party encourages continuity of service as a propagandist in order to allow individuals to cultivate depth of

---

[27] *Kompleksnyi podkhod v ideologicheskoi rabote* (A Complex Approach in Ideological Work) (Moscow: Izdatel'stvo politicheskoi literatury, 1976), p. 331.

[28] Cf. Bohdan Harasymiw, *Political Elite Recruitment in the Soviet Union* (New York: St. Martin's Press, 1984), ch. 6.

theoretical knowledge along with skill in explicating it. Thus, for example, *Kommunist* declared in 1979 that of the over 2.3 million party members teaching in the political education system, over half had been engaged in this work for over 10 years, making it "a second, public profession."[29]

The system of *social assignments* (*obshchestvennye porucheniia*), whereby party and Komsomol members as well as high-ranking managerial and scholarly personnel take on spare-time duties, has resulted in different levels and types of political participation for different strata of the population. The social and political status of an individual is correlated with the type of political assignment he or she performs. Retired citizens often take on assignments connected with their residential neighborhoods, assisting local soviets in the fields of retail trade, education, or housing. War veterans often participate in the military-patriotic education of the young. Skilled workers, shop foremen, brigade leaders, and other higher-status workers often become members of the trade union organization's aktiv or take part in popular control groups or other voluntary organizations based in the factory. All members of the work force may be called upon to patrol the streets at night every month or so as members of the *people's guards*. Similarly, the whole work force may be convened as a *comrade's court* to hear a case against a fellow worker on a charge of delinquency and to pass judgment and sentence. These institutions will be dealt with in more detail in a later chapter.

Virtually all party members have social assignments, and the tendency in the 1960s for a few superactivist party members to assume eight or ten different responsibilities while others took on few or none has been replaced by a tendency to spread the work out more evenly among all party members.[30] It is still the case, however, that individuals in higher-status social and political po-

---

[29]*Kommunist,* no. 9 (June 1979): 9; also see *Pravda,* 2 November 1979, p. 2, where a city party first secretary states that 75 percent of the propagandists in his organization are executives. In Vologda province, 90 percent of the engineering-technical personnel, specialists, and executives are active in ideological work. *Kompleksnyi podkhod,* p. 86.

[30]A. A. Korobeinikov and S. P. Goriunov, "Vazhnoe uslovie povysheniia roli partiinykh organizatsii" (An Important Condition for Raising the Role of Party Organizations), *Sotsiologicheskie issledovaniia,* no. 3 (July–August–September 1982): 89–96; also see the discussion of superactivists by Ellen Mickiewicz, *Media and the Russian Public* (New York: Praeger, 1981), ch. 8.

sitions perform a disproportionately large number of formal assignments. Most social-political volunteer work, for example, is conducted by individuals who are members of the elective party aktiv, which, as we saw, is dominated by political executives in key social sectors.[31] Among scientists and researchers, virtually all (98.6 percent) had public assignments, according to a survey of two research institutes in Moscow; most of these were elected to the committees of party, trade union, and Komsomol organizations, and others were elected to other positions, such as that of soviet deputy.[32]

Among engineering-technical personnel (middle management and the technical staff of enterprises), most possess multiple assignments, usually because they hold elective positions in party and workplace committees. Among rank-and-file workers, the fraction holding regular assignments varies between a third and a half. It should be borne in mind, however, in considering the high volume of formal participation that a significant amount of this work is not performed at all: studies show that the greater the number of assignments an individual is registered for, the greater the likelihood that some of the work is fictitious. A survey of over 3000 workers in a tractor factory in the Urals found that only about 60 percent of the persons formally listed as participating in social work actually did so.[33] In enterprises where figures for participation are higher, so is the proportion of fictitious participation.[34] Effectiveness of popular participation in social and political organizations is further hampered by the prevalent practice of performing the work on company time. This was found to be the custom among 80 percent of the engineering and technical per-

[31]A. T. Khlop'ev, "Obshchestvenno-politicheskaia aktivnost' trudiashchikhsia — vyrazhenie rosta sotsial'noi odnorodnosti sovetskogo obshchestva" (Social-Political Activeness of the Toilers — An Expression of the Growth of the Social Homogeneity of Soviet Society), in Zh. T. Toshchenko, ed., *Voprosy teorii i metodov ideologicheskoi raboty* (Questions of Theory and Methods of Ideological Work), vyp. 12 (Moscow: Mysl', 1980), p. 259.

[32]T. P. Arkhipova and V. F. Sbytov, *Voprosy teorii i praktiki politicheskogo rukovodstva: opyt deiatel'nosti raikoma partii* (Questions of Theory and Practice of Political Leadership: The Experience of the Activity of a District Party Committee) (Moscow: Izdatel'stvo politicheskoi literatury, 1981), p. 230.

[33]A. K. Orlov, *Sovetskii rabochii i upravlenie proizvodstvom* (The Soviet Worker and Management of Production) (Moscow: Profizdat, 1978), pp. 137-39.

[34]Ibid., p. 144.

sonnel and 60 percent of the manual workers in a survey conducted across several factories in the Urals and Siberia.[35]

As indicated, a great many of the public organizations through which individuals take on formally participant roles are based in workplaces and perform managerial or administrative functions in the economy. A prominent example is the popular control groups, in which some 9 million people are enrolled as members.[36] These groups have the duty of overseeing plan implementation, searching out labor and material reserves in order that the plan may be fulfilled more effectively, improving the quality and efficiency of production, helping to introduce new technology, and helping to expose violations of labor discipline or managerial standards. They investigate disputes, scandals, abuses, and errors, often submitting reports on findings to local newspapers for publication.[37]

The trade unions run a variety of workplace-based organizations, including the All-Union Society for Inventors and Rationalizers (VOIR), which numbered some 11 million members in 1982, and the Scientific-Technical Society (NTO), which began as an association of scientists and engineers, in 1954 was reorganized so as to open its membership to workers interested in technical innovation, and now numbers 8.5 million.[38] Many other workplace organizations exist as well: a medium-sized factory may have sixty or seventy organizations with mobilizing and socializing roles.[39] DOSAAF has exploded in formal enrollments, from 63.3 million in 1972 to 100 million in 1982. It operates several services of direct value to the Soviet military and civil authorities. In the 1981–1985 plan period, it planned to offer training or retraining to some 11.5 persons in military-related skills, such as truck driving and machine operation. Another 30 million people, including 11 million schoolchildren, take part in its sports pro-

---

[35]T. M. Novikova, "Obshchestvennaia deiatel'nost' v biudzhete vremeni promyshlennykh rabochikh" (Public Activity in the Time Budgets of Industrial Workers), *Sotsiologicheskie issledovaniia,* no. 2 (1981): 80–84; V. G. Britvin, "Proizvodstvenno-tekhnicheskaia sreda predpriiatiia i povedenie rabotnika" (The Productive-Technical Milieu of an Enterprise and Employee Behavior), *Sotsiologicheskie issledovaniia,* no. 2 (1982): 139–47.

[36]Jan S. Adams, *Citizen Inspectors in the Soviet Union: The People's Control Committee* (New York: Praeger, 1977.)

[37]Ivanov et al., *Sovetskaia demokratiia,* pp. 221–225.

[38]Ibid., pp. 153, 209.

[39]*Partiinaia zhizn',* no. 10 (May 1980): 38.

grams; as noted earlier, these, too, have direct military or military-technical application.[40] The Red Cross and Red Crescent have 95 million members. The Znanie Society (which enrolls persons willing to serve as lecturers) numbers over 3 million. The trade unions themselves have reached nearly total saturation of the working population: some 130 million individuals, virtually the whole labor force including most kolkhoz peasants, belong to trade unions. It is hard to consider trade union membership a form of mobilized participation, however, even in the Soviet sense, since the unions have assumed several functions on behalf of the state, such as allocating pension and disability payments.[41]

Other forms of organizational membership offer citizens outlets for the pursuit of relatively unpolitical social interests. Some organizations, such as the Rodina Society (numbering 14 million members as of 1982), the Society of Book-Lovers, or other hobby groups, do not represent mobilized participation. They, too, of course have full-time administrative staffs — often remarkably extensive ones (the Rodina Society spends more on full-time personnel than on preserving monuments)[42] — which afford the party further opportunities for surveillance and guidance of their activity. Still others, particularly religious organizations, are officially disapproved but tolerated. Public organizations, however, are noncompetitive and must receive party approval to exist, a phenomenon that John H. Miller refers to as "licensing."[43] Party approval of the goals and structure of the organization and of its leadership must be granted. Party and police control over voluntary associations is a vital form of system maintenance that helps prevent the pluralization and dispersion of political power to uncontrolled interest groups. Pluralization of social organizations was deemed a threat to the rule of the communist party in Czecho-

[40]See FBIS SU/6892/B/3 (28 November 1981) for a report on the meeting of the DOSAAF central committee in Moscow held in November 1981. The best study of DOSAAF is that of William E. Odom, *The Soviet Volunteers* (Princeton, N.J.: Princeton University Press, 1973), which deals with DOSAAF's predecessor organization, OSOAVIAKhIM.

[41]Ivanov et al., *Sovetskaia demokratiia*, p. 205.

[42]See the fascinating article by the late Soviet journalist Anatolii Agranovskii, "Reduction in Administrative Staff," *Izvestiia*, 13 May 1984, p. 2, in *Current Digest of the Soviet Press* 36, no. 19 (6 June 1984): 30.

[43]John H. Miller, "The Communist Party," in Archie Brown and Michael Kaser, eds., *Soviet Policy for the 1980s* (Bloomington: Indiana University Press, 1982), p. 2.

slovakia in 1968 and in Poland in 1980–1981.[44] The licensing of
social associations by the party ensures that organizations may not
form independent coalitions to articulate political interests or appeal directly for support to the general public.[45]

The socializing, mobilizing, and feedback functions of popular
participation supplement, as we saw, their role in integrating
social elites by linking political executives in the major bureaucracies of society. Through the system of social assignments, responsible individuals assume leadership positions in popular organizations, serving both as liaisons between the political
leadership and the general populace and as channels of upward
mobility for individuals seeking political careers. Thus for both
political executives and specialist elites, participation in social and
political activity contributes important services to the regime while
helping the party oversee the recruitment of individuals to elite
roles.

THE RECRUITMENT OF ELITES

We have emphasized the interlocking of political executives with
professional specialists by means of their common duties as social
activists and particularly through their participation in joint elective governing bodies in party, trade union, and other organizations. We observed that political executives, or full-time officials
who manage the key control bureaucracies of the political system — the party, the government, the mass media, the Komsomol, and the trade unions — form the core of the Soviet political
elite, controlling the process by which individuals assume executive positions. They may be distinguished from specialist members of the political elite by the breadth of their functions and
powers, which concern the aggregation of demands, policymak-

---

[44]On the liberalization of Czechoslovakia during the Prague Spring, see Vla-
dimir V. Kusin, *Political Groupings in the Czechoslovak Reform Movement* (New York:
Columbia University Press, 1972); idem, *The Intellectual Origins of the Prague Spring*
(Cambridge, England: Cambridge University Press, 1971); Galia Golan, *The
Czechoslovak Reform Movement* (Cambridge, England: Cambridge University Press,
1971); H. Gordon Skilling, *Czechoslovakia's Interrupted Revolution* (Princeton, N.J.:
Princeton University Press, 1976). On Poland, see Abraham Brumberg, ed., *Po-
land: Genesis of a Revolution* (New York: Vintage Books, 1983), and Radio Free
Europe Research, *August 1980: The Strikes in Poland* (Munich, 1980).

[45]Richard Lowenthal, "On 'Established' Communist Party Regimes," *Studies
in Comparative Communism* 7, no. 4 (Winter 1974): 346.

ing, and policy implementation. Specialists, on the other hand, enjoy powers connected with the exercise of their prescribed duties, such as enterprise management, economic planning, scientific research, troop command, artistic creation, or diplomacy. Through co-optation, specialist elites are sometimes drawn into full-time political executive positions; in other cases, political executives are recruited from among those who have been activists in Komsomol or other political organizations and who possess the necessary skills, experience, and reliability.[46]

The importance of close direction of elite recruitment ("work with cadres," in Soviet parlance) has long been recognized by Soviet leaders, and supervision of the system is entrusted to senior party and state administrators. At the highest levels of the political system, the executives who control the top executive bodies of the party and government, and the general secretary of the party himself, devote a good deal of attention to the selection, training, and deployment of leading personnel, or *rukovodiashchie kadry*. Record keeping on all party members throughout the country, appointments to positions of all-union significance, and direction of the personnel selection process at lower levels of the party apparatus are carried out through the organizational-party work department of the party Central Committee. Normally the head of this department is a member of the party Secretariat, and in the past, the secretary in charge of personnel has on occasion been a ranking member of the Politburo. Under Brezhnev, head of the organizational-party work department was I. V. Kapitonov, who was also a secretary of the Central Committee. Political direction of personnel work, though, was provided by Brezhnev's close associate Andrei P. Kirilenko, who was both a Politburo member and a member of the Secretariat. Through the 1970s, however, Brezhnev's associate Chernenko came to assume some of the duties of the personnel manager, overshadowing Kirilenko, who under the pressure of political (and probably also physical) ill health

[46]On co-optation, see Frederic J. Fleron, Jr., "Representation of Career Types in Soviet Political Leadership," in R. Barry Farrell, ed., *Political Leadership in Eastern Europe and the Soviet Union* (Chicago, Ill.: Aldine, 1970), pp. 108–39; idem, "System Attributes and Career Attributes: The Soviet Political Leadership System, 1952 to 1965," in Carl Beck et al., eds., *Comparative Communist Political Leadership* (New York: David McKay, 1973), pp. 43–85; also see the discussion by Robert W. Siegler, *The Standing Commissions of the Supreme Soviet: Effective Co-optation* (New York: Praeger, 1982), ch. 1.

was forced to resign his positions in November 1982, at the time Andropov was named to replace Brezhnev. At the same time Kapitonov was moved to unspecified duties, and the organizational-party work department was given in April 1983, after Andropov was named General Secretary, to Egor Ligachev. Born in 1929, Ligachev was one of the younger party officials who benefitted from Andropov's ascendancy. In December 1983, Ligachev was made a Central Committee Secretary, presumably still with responsibility for personnel selection, and in April 1985, with Gorbachev in power, Ligachev was named a full member of the party Politburo. Through 1985 Ligachev grew increasingly prominent, emerging as Gorbachev's "second secretary" with responsibility for ideology as well as personnel.[47] Equivalent departments at lower party committee levels perform the same recruitment functions within their jurisdictions.

Like most other political institutions in Soviet politics, the system of selecting and placing leading personnel is hierarchical. At each level of the administrative-territorial ladder, party officials regulate the recruitment process through several formal and informal mechanisms. The primary institution governing the selection of personnel is called the *nomenklatura* system. This refers to the maintenance of the table of appointments (the personnel nomenklatura) by which the party staff of a particular jurisdiction controls appointments to a listed set of major positions at its own and lower administrative-territorial levels. As we shall see, however, elite appointments are subject to a variety of informal forces, including clientelism, career specialization, and various kinds of preferences and barriers based on ethnicity, gender, and other ascriptive traits. These factors work under different circumstances both to advance and to hinder the career advancement of ethnic minorities and women. An important complement to the devices for identifying competent and reliable personnel for elite positions is the elaborate system for training elites in party doctrine. This

---

[47]On the work of the "organizational-party work departments" of the party apparatus, see Radio Liberty (RL) research reports 339/83 (9 September 1983); RL 6/84 (29 December 1983); and RL 2/84 (28 December 1983). Also see the interview with a self-described former Central Committee official, "A. Pravdin," by Mervyn Matthews, "Inside the CPSU Central Committee," *Survey* 20, no. 4 (Autumn 1974): 99, who calls the organizational-party work department the "brain and soul" of the party apparatus.

system, the political education system, will be discussed in the final section of this chapter.

The party's nomenklatura system is little discussed in Soviet literature and its workings are kept concealed from public or foreign inquiry. T. H. Rigby estimates that at present around 2 million employees are on the nomenklatura of one or another party committee.[48] The clearance that individuals must receive to secure such posts, together with the social prestige and privilege to which they are generally entitled, has prompted many in the Soviet Union and elsewhere to view the nomenclatured group as an identifiable class or stratum and even to refer to the nomenklatura as a kind of social caste.[49] The dissident scientist Andrei Sakharov characterized the nomenklatura group as possessing "its own lifestyle, its own sharply defined position in society. . . . The nomenklatura is virtually inalienable and is now becoming hereditary."[50] The nomenklatura system operates to ensure the political loyalty of elites appointed to a wide variety of executive positions in the party, government, trade unions, and other organizations and hence embraces the core of the Soviet political elite. Since political power in the Soviet system is the most important determinant of social distinction, it is common to refer to the nomenklatura as shorthand for the elite itself. As a structure, however, it serves the party by exercising political control over the recruitment of elites to leading positions.[51]

Each territorial party committee manages a list of positions over which it has appointment and veto power. Often it exercises this power by means of recommending comrades for particular positions, including elective posts. In addition, soviets and trade unions maintain their own nomenklatura lists, but actual appointments to the more important positions on their lists must apparently be cleared with the party.[52] There is evidently a tendency

---

[48]T. H. Rigby, "Introduction," in T. H. Rigby and Bohdan Harasymiw, eds., *Leadership Selection and Patron-Client Relations in the USSR and Yugoslavia* (London: Allen & Unwin, 1983), p. 3.

[49]See Michael S. Voslensky, *Nomenklatura: Die Herrschende Klasse der Sowjetunion* (Vienna: Molden, 1980).

[50]Quoted in Rigby, "Introduction," in Rigby and Harasymiw, eds., *Leadership Selection,* p. 5.

[51]See Harasymiw, *Political Elite Recruitment,* ch. 7.

[52]See Bohdan Harasymiw, *"Nomenklatura:* The Soviet Communist Party's Leadership Recruitment System," *Canadian Journal of Political Science* 2, no. 4 (December 1969): 505.

for party officials to seek nomenklatura powers over broader categories of executives, as attested by advice offered in a 1982 party handbook. The handbook asserts that enterprise directors should normally consult with the Primary Party Organization on making appointments within the enterprise but that it is not advisable for the PPO to maintain its own nomenklatura, which it defines as sets of positions that may be filled only with the PPO's consent. The nomenklatura system begins with the next level of party organization, the *raion* committee.[53] Moreover, although the practice clearly contradicts the nominally democratic facade, *elective* as well as appointive positions are subject to nomenklatura controls, including soviet deputies and members of party and other committees. The extraconstitutional status of the nomenklatura system is further underscored by the absence of any reference to it in the Soviet constitution.

One reason that the nomenklatura officialdom appears to form a social category is the job security that apparently accompanies appointment to a nomenklatura position. Once on nomenklatura lists, an individual rarely drops from them except in cases of gross political or professional misbehavior. For party members and nonmembers alike, appointment to a nomenklatura position becomes a powerful determinant of future career positions and an incentive for conformity to expected norms of behavior. By the same token, the system lends itself to the abuses and inefficiency that result from freeing elite recruitment of either accountability to the governed or independent publicity: the transformation of the nomenklatura group into a select coterie whose members regard themselves and their work as being above criticism and the retention of individuals who are professionally incompetent.[54] A newspaper in 1952, commenting on the self-protective behavior of local officialdom in a Ukrainian province, observed that the saying locally was that "once you've entered the *nomenklatura* of the *obkom,* even the devil can't hurt you." Rigby notes that "if this could be so even in the purge-prone conditions of the late Stalin period, how much more true must it be in the present

---

[53]*Organizatsionno-ustavnye voprosy KPSS: Spravochnik v voprosakh i otvetakh* (Questions of organization and regulations of the CPSU: a handbook in questions and answers) (Moscow: Izdatel'stvo politicheskoi literatury, 1982), p. 39.

[54]See Harasymiw, *"Nomenklatura,"* p. 510.

era.''[55] Through much of the Brezhnev era, when the watchword of policy was "stability of cadres," turnover and replacement of provincial-level officials were relatively low compared with the turbulent conditions of Khrushchev's rule. Andropov's brief rule brought a wave of turnover at provincial and local levels of the party apparatus, only to be followed by the return to Brezhnev-era security under Chernenko.[56] The degree of security the nomenklatura system affords to officials thus depends on the character of the central party leadership.

Important as nomenklatura is in forming and preserving the power of the political elite in the USSR, by itself it does not explain the particular attributes of the persons chosen. What are the chances, for example, that an ambitious female party official from a rural district in the Ukraine will ultimately be promoted to a position on the all-union Central Committee Secretariat, or that an Uzbek kolkhoz director will become agriculture minister of Uzbekistan? Empirical analysis of elite mobility has revealed certain patterns of recruitment that are outside the formally regulated procedures for personnel selection. One of the most important of these is clientelism, found to greater or lesser extent in elite recruitment in all political systems, which works to promote particular rather than general, impersonal loyalties. Patron-client ties are reciprocal relationships between two individuals, one of whom is superior in politically significant assets and is able to promote the interests of the inferior partner in return for the latter's loyalty and support. A powerful patron may form such relations with multiple clients; in turn, clients may cultivate their own networks of patronage.[57] Patron-client relations are characterized by personal loyalties that transcend the impersonal devotion to general rules that is essential to rational bureaucratic administration. To

[55]T. H. Rigby, "Introduction," in Rigby and Harasymiw, eds., *Leadership Selection*, p. 5.

[56]On patterns of appointment and careers of *obkom* party secretaries under Brezhnev, see T. H. Rigby, "The Soviet Regional Leadership: The Brezhnev Generation," *Slavic Review* 38, no. 1 (March 1978): 1–24.

[57]See the interesting studies of clientelism in the previously cited book edited by Rigby and Harasymiw, *Leadership Selection and Patron-Client Relations:* Shugo Minagawa, "Political Clientelism in the USSR and Japan: A Tentative Comparison," pp. 200–28; Gyula Jozsa, "Political *Seilschaften* in the USSR," pp. 139–73; and Daniel T. Orlovsky, "Political Clientelism in Russia: the Historical Perspective," pp. 174–99.

be sure, affective bonds may link equals as well as unequals, as is the case, for example, in an old-boy network of privilege that cuts across institutional sectors. These bonds may be converted into patron-client relations, however, when one of the members is in a position to aid the career positions of others.

The factors that facilitate the formation of patron-client ties in the Soviet system have been partially unearthed. Among the more important are common service in a particular region. For example, Konstantin Chernenko was serving as head of the agitation-propaganda department of the Moldavian Republic (newly annexed to the Soviet Union) when Leonid Brezhnev was named first secretary of the republican party organization in 1950. Although Brezhnev worked there only two years, he evidently formed a close and personal bond with Chernenko. When Brezhnev was brought to the Central Committee Secretariat in 1956, he secured as well Chernenko's transfer to Moscow, where he became head of the mass agitation section of the Propaganda Department. Then in 1960, when Brezhnev's career suffered a demotion (he was named to the figurehead position of Chairman of the Presidium of the Supreme Soviet), Chernenko became his chief administrative aide as chief of the secretariat of the Supreme Soviet Presidium. From that time until Brezhnev's death Chernenko loyally supported his patron, being rewarded by promotion to the Central Committee Secretariat in 1976, candidate membership in the Politburo in 1977, and full membership in the Politburo in 1978. Although Brezhnev appeared to favor Chernenko for succession to the party general secretaryship, he was passed over in the initial selection of a replacement for Brezhnev only to win the top post upon Andropov's death in 1984.[58] Other bases for patron-client ties include shared views, common generational or geographical background, marriage and kinship, and schooling. Sometimes the mere fact of an appointment creates a bond of loyalty and dependence between a subordinate and a superior official.[59] Party secretaries, particularly those in charge of per-

[58]See biographical details in Jerry F. Hough, "Soviet Succession: Issues and Personalities," *Problems of Communism* 31, no. 5 (September–October 1982): 30–31. A useful source for biographical background information on top Soviet leaders is Alexander G. Rahr, comp., *A Biographical Directory of 100 Leading Soviet Officials* (Munich: Radio Liberty Research, 1984).

[59]See Rigby, "Soviet Regional Leadership," p. 23.

sonnel, are in a powerful position to establish patronage networks because of their influence over the nomenklatura system. The important point to be made about patron-client relations is that they constitute reciprocal, personal bonds falling outside the purely meritocratic system for personnel decisions envisioned under party and government statutes. Clientelism can serve to ameliorate or lubricate processes grown stagnant or immobile; it can speed up the flow of information and decision making. Nonetheless, the aggregate effect of pervasive clientelism is to weaken central control over elite recruitment in a system in which controls over recruitment from below are weak or nonexistent.

A second informal pattern, now becoming more routine, is the specialization of political elites by career type.[60] The prevailing tendency for political executives to become *industrial administrators, agricultural administrators, ideological administrators, personnel administrators,* or *mixed generalists* may have less to do with formal education than with the predominant type of work to which the executive is attached over a succession of job assignments. The older view was that monopoly over policymaking and cadre selection by the party's full-time officials created a major line of cleavage between the party apparatus and the specialist elites in government, the economy, the military, science and technology, and other social sectors. In contrast to this idea, detailed research on elite career patterns has now determined that elite mobility tends to run within certain defined specialty tracks (industrial, agricultural, personnel, ideological, or general administration). In other words, political executives are more likely to move across party, government, and other sectors within their broad areas of specialization than they are to mix specialties within these sectors. Chernenko's career, again, provides both an example of this principle and an exception to it. In his early years, Chernenko held a series of positions in the ideological sector of the party. He first served in his native Krasnoyarsk territory in Siberia, and then, after attending Higher Party School, he became ideological secretary in Penza province in the Russian Republic before being named head of the agitation-propaganda department in the Mol-

---

[60]An excellent recent study of this phenomenon is Joel C. Moses, "Functional Career Specialization in Soviet Regional Elite Recruitment," in Rigby and Harasymiw, eds., *Leadership Selection,* pp. 15–61. The discussion that follows is based upon his research.

davian Republic in 1948. Even as Brezhnev's client, however, Chernenko remained concentrated in the ideological sphere as an official in the propaganda department of the Central Committee apparatus in Moscow from 1956 to 1960. Consonant with this specialization, moreover, once Brezhnev died and Andropov became general secretary, Chernenko gravitated to the ideological sphere for a brief but crucial period in 1983, assuming general responsibility for ideological matters until Andropov's death.[61]

Chernenko's career differs from that of most ideological specialists in that he ultimately attained the supreme prize despite the striking narrowness of his political experience. Industrial specialists and agricultural specialists, together with executives whose careers cross several functional categories ("mixed generalists," as Joel Moses terms them), are most likely to advance to other regions, acquiring experience and contacts crucial to promotion to higher levels. Industrial specialists, for example, may be moved among any of several positions within their specialization: secretary of a party committee responsible for local industry, first secretary of a party committee in an industrialized region, regional trade union council chairman. Their training for such positions often involves party or managerial work directly in industry — for example, as PPO secretary in an industrial enterprise, enterprise manager, or head of industrial department in a local party committee. Having risen to first to second secretaryship in an industrial region, they are likely to be moved later to other positions with predominantly industrial content: republican party secretary for industry, senior official in an industrial ministry, or first secretary in an industrialized province.[62] In a similar

[61]The position of general ideological arbiter was occupied for many years by Mikhail Suslov until his death in January 1982. In his capacity as Central Committee Secretary and Politburo member, Suslov oversaw the Central Committee departments dealing with agitation and propaganda, culture, education, foreign affairs, Komsomol, the mass media, the arts, and many other related spheres. Appointed head of the propaganda department of the Central Committee in 1947 and made a secretary, he wielded enormous power as secretary in charge of all ideological matters and became an extremely influential member of the ruling group of the Politburo throughout the Brezhnev period. See the description of his powers in Roy Medvedev, *All Stalin's Men,* trans. Harold Shukman (Oxford: Basil Blackwell, 1983), pp. 62–63. Chernenko was seeking to inherit Suslov's mantle while at the same time taking advantage of Andropov's failing health to position himself for the succession.

[62]See Moses, "Functional Career Specialization," p. 18.

way, an ideological specialist may have moved from Komsomol work, media work, education, or agitation-propaganda into the ideological departments of party committees, and future transfers may lead to higher-ranking positions in equivalent organizations. Identification with one of these de facto functional specialties becomes a major determinant of subsequent appointments under the nomenklatura system. Specialization may also cause political executives to identify with their counterparts working in other sectors in the same functional specialization.[63] Because of this tendency toward specialization among the political executives and because of the pattern of co-optation of specialists into political executive careers, the distinction between political elites and specialist elites is not absolute.

A final set of influences on elite recruitment comprises tacit barriers and preferments deriving from ascriptive traits such as ethnic identity, gender, or region of background. One of the most important contributions of a centralized, controlled nomenklatura system toward elite recruitment is its ability to maintain political dominance for the Slavic, and particularly Russian, national groups within the USSR. Within each national republic, cadres from the indigenous ethnic nationality have the opportunity to fill elite positions in every sector but seldom move out of their republic to other republics and are rarely transferred to work at the all-union level of the political system. On the other hand, Slavic and particularly Russian executives assume posts within both the Russian Republic and all other republics and thus acquire the breadth of experience needed for promotion to the all-union level. Within the national republics, Russians frequently hold key control positions in the party apparatus, the KGB, industry and agriculture, the media, and other sectors. In many cases, the first secretary of the party organization of national republics is a member of the indigenous nationality, and the second secretary is Russian.[64] Grey Hodnett's exhaustive research on the ethnic composition of leading positions in the fourteen non-Russian union republics over the 1955–1972 time period demonstrated that in spheres concerned with ideological, youth, labor, and health

---

[63]Ibid, p. 54.
[64]See Hélène Carrère d'Encausse, *Decline of an Empire* (New York: Newsweek Books, 1980), pp. 142–43.

affairs, indigenous elites held most or all of the key posts, but in the spheres relating to political security, industrial management, and cadre selection, Russians (or Russians and Ukrainians) often outnumbered members of the indigenous nationality. One example is the key position of head of the party organs department (or organizational-party work department), the department most concerned with supervising the nomenklatura system. In the Tadjik, Uzbek, Turkmen, Moldavian, and Estonian republics this post was not filled by members of the indigenous ethnic group at all during the period studied; it was held by natives for short spells only in Kazakhstan and Kirgizia.[65] Perhaps more significant is the evident barrier restricting mobility for ethnic elites *out* of their republics. Hodnett's findings show that elites of indigenous nationalities are far less likely than nonnatives to be transferred out of their republics.[66] Despite the nominal commitment to equal treatment of the members of all ethnic groups in the country, elite recruitment policies work to maintain political dominance of the Russians by such tacit rules on career mobility for ethnic elites.

A similar although perhaps more complex set of barriers affects mobility for women. The proportion of women on all-union political bodies such as the party Central Committee is many times lower than the proportion of women in the population or even the proportion of women who are members of the party. Though women comprise over 50 percent of the population, they constitute 28 percent of the party. A concerted effort by the party to recruit higher proportions of women has resulted in a slow but steady rise in this proportion. A sharp fall-off in female participation in elite party positions occurs, however, between the primary level and the lowest territorial levels of party organization. Fewer than 4 percent of the provincial party secretaries are women. A similar proportion of women are found as members of the Central Committee, not because women are barred from admission to the Central Committee but because the committee's membership reflects the composition of the all-union political elite, in which women make up a small minority. Of the women who are members of the Central Committee, about a third are mem-

[65]Grey Hodnett, *Leadership in the Soviet National Republics: A Quantitative Study of Recruitment Policy* (Oakville, Ontario: Mosaic Press, 1978), pp. 108–9.
[66]Ibid., pp. 306–9.

bers not by virtue of their political prominence but as token representatives of the working class or peasants or as outstanding representatives of nonpolitical occupations. The cosmonaut V. V. Nikolaeva-Tereshkova is an example of the last category.[67]

To be sure, in other social sectors and organizations women make up a higher proportion of leading officials. In the system of soviets women make up nearly half the deputies, although the proportions of women drop as one moves from local to provincial to republic and all-union levels. Women comprise 85 percent of all medical personnel and about half of chief physicians and executives of health institutions. They make up about 40 percent of the total number of specialists in the country but about 10 percent of full professors. Only 3 are full members of the Academy of Sciences out of 749 members. Women comprise nearly two-thirds of the administrative staff of industrial enterprises but only 9 percent of the directors of enterprises.[68] The influence of the traditional political culture is evident as well in the nature of the elite roles to which women are recruited: overwhelmingly the women in political executive positions are concentrated in so-called women's jobs in education, health, and social services and not in industrial administration, justice, and security.

The gap between women's participation in political life and their recruitment to elite positions in most politically significant sectors, a gap that remains even after educational differences are taken into account, has several explanations. The hold of traditional gender-based role norms on both men and women continues to be strong and is frequently perpetuated through the socialization process. In secondary school, for example, all girls receive nursing instruction and all boys receive basic combat training. A second explanation is the difficulty women experience in having to combine jobs outside the home with the primary or exclusive responsibility for housekeeping and child rearing: the double-burden problem, which we discussed in Chapter III. This pattern means that women on average have less time to devote to the extramural civic activism required of politically ambitious

---

[67]Gail Warshofsky Lapidus, *Women in Soviet Society* (Berkeley: University of California Press, 1978), ch. 6.

[68]Mary Ellen Fischer, "Women," in James Cracraft, ed., *The Soviet Union Today: An Interpretive Guide* (Chicago, Ill.: Bulletin of the Atomic Scientists, 1983), pp. 312–13.

elites. Together with this *supply-side* explanation, as Gail War-shofsky Lapidus terms it, however, are *demand-side* factors, in-cluding the reluctance of male elites to relinquish power to women. Finally, we should point out that these are aggregate trends, and major variations are found in the union republics or at the pro-vincial or local levels. Women's participation in political executive roles, for example, is more pronounced in some of the Central Asia republics than in some of the European republics, suggesting that no single set of all-union recruitment norms for women ap-plies and that lower-level personnel managers have some latitude in deciding how to employ the nomenklatura tables to advance or restrict women's opportunities for political careers.[69]

THE SYSTEM OF POLITICAL EDUCATION

Among the more important means by which the regime builds a common set of shared values among the political elite is the political education system, a vast network of settings for instruc-tion in political and related topics in which the majority of the country's political and social elites, and to a lesser extent much of the entire adult population, is, at least periodically, involved.[70] The courses and schools that offer training in political doctrine and applied subjects for elites form a highly elaborate, complex system performing several overlapping functions for the political system, including political socialization, elite recruitment, and communication. The ultimate rationale of political education stems from Lenin's injunction that party members should be mas-ters of Marxist theory as well as effective professional organizers.

As early as 1911 Lenin had organized schools in Paris and Ca-pri for training party propagandists, recognizing the need for sys-tematic instruction of party organizers in Marxist theory so that the fundamental principles of party doctrine would not be dis-

[69]On the proportions of women in top party positions in different republics, see Lapidus, *Women in Soviet Society,* p. 221; for data on membership rates of men and women in the different republics, see Ellen Mickiewicz, ''Regional Variation in Female Recruitment and Advancement in the Communist Party of the Soviet Union,'' *Slavic Review* 36, no. 3 (September 1977): 441–54. Mickiewicz finds that regional variation in women's party admission is so pronounced that only re-gional and republic-level policy can account for the trends rather than any single all-union policy governing such admission. See especially p. 453.

[70]The basic study of this system is that of Ellen P. Mickiewicz, *Soviet Political Schools* (New Haven, Conn.: Yale University Press, 1967); also see Gayle Durham Hollander, *Soviet Political Indoctrination* (New York: Praeger, 1972), pp. 146–49.

torted as they were applied to day-to-day problems. Thus arose the distinction between the simple, action-oriented exhortation known as *agitation* and the thorough exposition of doctrine called *propaganda*. Today's adult political education system grew out of the systematic training of party organizers in the theory of the Bolshevik movement. It has been greatly influenced, however, by the need to combine it with elementary political instruction for a largely uneducated population and, in more recent times, by the need to provide executives and specialists in a variety of fields with continuing education in both political and professional subjects. As a result, the adaptation of political education to the differing levels of prior education found in the adult population led to the adoption of a three-tiered, hierarchical framework for elementary, intermediate, and advanced levels of content, roughly paralleling the organization of the general educational system. The adaptation of the system to the functional needs of party rule over a highly diverse, complex society led to the horizontal segmentation of the system into forms serving multiple occupational specialties. Thus the system's vertical organization derives from its early role in providing mass-level political instruction to the general population, and its highly elaborate, differentiated contemporary structure owes much to its adaptation to the functional diversity of the Soviet political elite.

Over time the system has been pulled between mass and elitist orientations. The infusion of raw worker and peasant recruits into the party and the upper ranks of the professional, managerial, administrative, and political sections of the elite during the 1930s, together with the decimation of the Old Bolsheviks in the course of the Great Purges and terror, contributed to a weakening of the theoretical knowledge of the party membership. Stalin accordingly gave the political education system a more elitist, theoretical thrust in 1937 and 1938. A major Central Committee resolution of 1938 sharply criticized the existing system of political education for failing to train cadres adequately in Marxism-Leninism, a consequence of neglecting the intelligentsia while concentrating on rank-and-file worker indoctrination.[71] Under the resolution, 1

[71]"O postanovke partiinoi propagandy v svyazi s vypuskom 'Kratkogo kursa istorii VKP(b)' " (Concerning the Structure of Party Propaganda in Connection with the Publication of the "Short Course in the History of the All-Union Communist Party (of Bolsheviks)") (Moscow: *Pravda*, 1944).

year courses in doctrine were to be given to party propagandists and newspaper workers. A Higher School of Marxism-Leninism was to be formed under the Central Committee. It would offer a 3 year course for top-ranking party cadres. The intensity of emphasis given by party leaders to doctrinal training declined somewhat during the war years but revived shortly after the war in the form of a new Central Committee resolution, "On Training and Retraining Leading Party and Soviet Officials" (1946). This called for expansion of political education to include all senior party and government officials. The Higher Party School was reorganized and the 1 year courses were restructured to open a division specifically for government executives. Territorial party committees also opened their own schools for party and government officials.[72]

After Stalin's death unease within the leadership over the level of political knowledge and commitment among the general population and concern over the apathy displayed in many sections of society prompted a new round of reorganization of political education, this time directed toward the twin goals of reinvigorating it and broadening its scope. This effort was also undoubtedly stimulated by the challenge of ideological conflict with China and the growth of revisionism in Eastern Europe, together with the opening of Soviet society to contact with Western travelers and culture. Khrushchev's denunciation of Stalin's crimes and cult of personality necessitated a thorough rewriting of the existing textbooks dealing with party history and theory. These changes were reflected in a comprehensive directive on party propaganda of 1960. The resolution mooted Khrushchev's frequent demand that party propaganda be linked both with life (that is, it should have a practical character) and with the building of communism (the forward-looking programmatic goals that Khrushchev actively promulgated for Soviet society). Existing institutions of party propaganda were criticized for neglecting the masses and failing to raise "the workers in a communist spirit." Accordingly, propaganda should be "brought to every Soviet person" and should eliminate "abstractness." Moreover, party organizations were called on to provide a graded sequence of courses for party members, in which each member could proceed to a higher level of

[72]Ivanov, *Sovetskaia demokratiia,* p. 140.

instruction each year.[73] When implemented, the new system was said to reach over 22.5 million persons, fewer than a third of whom were party members.[74] This represented a tremendous increase in enrollment figures, a trend that continued until some 36 million persons were enrolled in 1964–1965. Khrushchev's successors then moved immediately to cut back enrollments sharply, emphasizing once again the primary role of the system in training political elites. Nonetheless, enrollment began to climb once again, from 13.5 million in 1966–1967 to 23 million in 1978–1979, despite continual pleas from party leaders against achieving higher enrollments for their own sake.[75]

The relative de-emphasis that theory received under Khrushchev, the practical and mass orientation of the system, and the search for high pro forma enrollments provoked a reaction from the Brezhnev leadership, which sought to restore the attention to doctrinal theory that had prevailed earlier and to balance theory with practical application. The new approach was signaled with an editorial in the Central Committee's main theoretical journal, *Kommunist,* in 1965.[76] Under new rules issued in 1967, evening universities of Marxism-Leninism would train propagandists in party doctrine, emphasizing the fundamentals of theory rather than the current line on applied problems. These universities, geared primarily to the training of propagandists, were one of several types of higher, or tertiary, political education provided under the post-Khrushchevian leadership. Along with them were schools for the party aktiv, which themselves came to be bifurcated into schools for the managerial and economic aktiv and schools for the ideological aktiv. In addition, for persons already possessing a sound grasp of theory, there are theory and methods

[73]"O zadachakh partiinoi propagandy v sovremennykh usloviiakh" (On Tasks of Party Propaganda under Present Conditions) in *Voprosy ideologicheskoi raboty* (Problems of Ideological Work) (Moscow: Izdatel'stvo politicheskoi literatury, 1961), pp. 144–64.

[74]V. I. Evdokimov, *Politicheskoe prosveshchenie — reshayushchee zveno propagandistskoi raboty* (Political Enlightenment — Decisive Link in Propaganda Work) (Moscow: Izdatel'stvo politicheskoi literatury, 1962), p. 20.

[75]Enrollment figures from *Spravochnik sekretaria pervichnoi partiinoi organizatsii* (Handbook of the Primary Party Organization Secretary), 2nd ed. (Moscow: Izdatel'stvo politicheskoi literatury, 1980), p. 353.

[76]"Aktivno formirovat' marksistsko-leninskoe mirovozrenie kommunistov" (Actively Shape the Marxist-Leninist World View of Communists), *Kommunist,* no. 13 (September 1965): 8–9.

seminars that depend upon independent study of the classic texts and current party literature.

The elementary level of the party education system, which since Khrushchev's time has consisted of *primary political schools,* has shown steadily declining enrollments, a consequence of increasing education and political education of the Soviet adult population. The term *school* is somewhat misleading in this context, since each school may be no more than a small circle of factory workers, meeting after work perhaps once a week for study and discussion under the tutelage of a trained propagandist. A good-sized enterprise is likely to have fifty or one hundred such schools, allowing teachers to monitor the attendance and progress of each class. Instruction in these schools covers subjects such as the life of Lenin, political and economic affairs, and current party policy.[77]

Besides these primary political schools under the party system, there are analogous forms of propaganda run by the Komsomol and the trade unions. Komsomol courses serve youth in VUZy, in the work force, and in the armed forces, and are a steadily expanding system of instruction, enrolling nearly 9 million persons at present.[78] The trade unions run classes called *people's universities* as well as *schools of communist labor.* The former deal with a variety of topics, from atheism to technology, and often enroll a single cohort, which advances from level to level. The trend of development of the people's universities, which are one of the few Khrushchevian forms of political education to survive the reorganizations of the Brezhnev period, is toward more specific and more vocational applications of training.[79] Schools of communist labor are oriented directly to problems of production. Lectures are supposed to deal with such themes as a communist attitude to labor, though sometimes they slip into purely practical, technical discussions instead.[80] Both Komsomol and trade union courses are designed to serve workers and peasants who may have

[77]Stephen White, *Political Culture and Soviet Politics* (London: MacMillan, 1979), p. 75.

[78]Ibid., p. 76; "KPSS v tsifrakh" (CPSU in Figures) *Partiinaia zhizn',* no. 14 (1981): 26.

[79]R. P. Skudra, "Narodnye universitety v sisteme ideino-vospitatel'noi raboty" (People's Universities in the System of Ideological Upbringing Work Questions of Theory and Methods of Ideological Work) in *Voprosy teorii i metodov ideologicheskoi raboty* (Questions of Theory and Methods of Ideological Work), no. 11 (1979): 121–30.

[80]*Zhurnalist,* no. 7 (1979): 12.

limited formal education and help prepare them for the more systematic instruction offered at the next levels of the system.

For those who have graduated from these schools there are *schools of the fundamentals of Marxism-Leninism,* which presuppose some knowledge of doctrine as well as some capacity to study independently. These are run by lower territorial party committees and by PPOs in enterprises and institutions. As with elementary schools, their average size is small, since a single enterprise may support several dozen such schools. Here instruction covers the essential points of party doctrine and takes the form of courses in party history, political economy, Marxist-Leninist philosophy, and the like. With time, the absolute and proportional numbers of individuals enrolled in these courses have grown. Typically these schools serve persons, both members and nonmembers of the party, who do not hold executive responsibility (as we shall see, managerial and professional elites commonly study in tertiary-level schools) but who may aspire to elite status. As an example, let us cite the story of a woman, an unskilled worker, who entered the study circles organized by Komsomol when she began working in a factory. From these she subsequently entered a school of fundamentals of Marxism-Leninism, later being admitted to the party, and finally being elected a member of the city party committee and the *oblast'* party committee.[81]

Because these schools sometimes experience difficulty in bridging the disparities in educational backgrounds that the listeners bring with them, the party moved in 1981 to create *schools for young communists,* designed to give basic political instruction to candidate members of the party as well as newly admitted members. At the same time, the schools of fundamentals of Marxism-Leninism are now to restrict enrollment to party members who possess at least a secondary education.[82]

From this intermediate tier, party members (and to a lesser degree, nonmembers) may undertake any of several forms of higher political education. Whether they avail themselves of these schools and which they enter apparently depends on a mixture of individual choice, the requirements of the person's occupation and auxiliary social commitments, and the preferences of the party

[81]*Pravda,* 23 August 1981, p. 2.
[82]*Pravda,* 11 August 1981, pp. 2–3.

committee and its personnel managers. The party generally requires that a person attend some form of higher schooling at least once every 5 years, a requirement that is hard to escape. Those working as instructors (propagandists) in lower links of the system attend universities of Marxism-Leninism, where they take a broad array of courses including revolutionary theory, party history, party policy, party and government organization, theory and methods of ideological work, economic management, and scientific-technical progress.[83] Those finishing these courses are qualified to serve as propagandists in the party, Komsomol, and trade union systems, as lecturers for the party, or as party group leaders or PPO secretaries.[84] Indeed, so extensive are the courses the propagandists are expected to master — numbering now some forty in all — that *Pravda* recently published a proposal that the number of required courses be reduced and the term of study be lengthened.[85]

More topical instruction is provided in other links of the system, such as the newly founded *schools of scientific communism, schools of the party-economic aktiv,* and *schools of the ideological aktiv.* These provide somewhat more specialized instruction. The schools of scientific communism deal with current events, including domestic and foreign policy and foreign affairs. In the case of the schools for the party-economic aktiv (for staff officials and activists in administrative and managerial branches), instruction covers party direction of trade unions, economic policy, and the theory of developed socialism; for PPO secretaries and group leaders, party lecturers, agitators, media workers and others, schools of the ideological aktiv cover questions directly relating to the party's supervision of ideological life.[86]

Finally, the seminars in theory and methods round out the system of party education at the tertiary level. These may be organized at the listener's place of work. Content varies with the occupations of those enrolled. Members of the scientific intelligentsia and VUZ professors study philosophical and social science topics connected with science, the scientific-technical revolution, and economics, as well as more directly political topics such as

---

[83]See the curriculum in *Partiinaia zhizn'*, no. 16 (1980): 12.
[84]*Pravda,* 23 August 1981, p. 2.
[85]*Pravda,* 11 June 1983, p. 2.
[86]See *Partiinaia zhizn'*, no. 16 (1980): 11; *Pravda,* 11 August 1981, pp. 2–3.

the theory of proletarian and revolutionary internationalism, socialist democracy, communist morality, education, and literature and art. Members of the cultural intelligentsia study similar questions as well as problems of cultural life under socialism, creativity, aesthetics, morality, and the world ideological struggle. In principle, those enrolled in such seminars design their own programs of study, meeting for periodic discussions with others. They follow guides published in party journals such as *Politicheskoe samoobrazovanie* (Political Self-Education) and *Partiinaia zhizn'* (Party Life), which provide syllabuses of topics and readings to direct their study.

For higher-level party and government officials, there remain party schools at province and republican levels, called *courses for raising the qualifications of party and soviet officials.* These offer continuous refresher training for officials at all levels of the territorial-administrative ladder. Alternatively, officials may enroll in courses by correspondence through the Higher Party Schools in each republic and under the Academy of Social Sciences of the Central Committee, the pinnacle of the entire party education system.[87] In this way the party ensures that each official can find training appropriate to the level of his knowledge and can keep up with courses year after year.

In 1971, after the Twenty-Fourth Party Congress, the party moved to form yet another category of political education by removing courses dealing with specifically economic subjects from the party schools and placing them under a rubric for schooling called *economic education.* Apparently designed for manual workers, the technical and managerial staff of economic enterprises, and others involved in economic planning, management, and administration, these complement the more directly political party courses. A separate economic system was created to emphasize the new post-Stalinist economic wisdom — to wit, that new advances in economic growth must derive from raising the productivity of capital and labor resources rather than from mobilizing large quantities of new resources into the relatively inefficient processes of production. (This lesson is customarily referred to in Soviet parlance as the stress on intensive as opposed to extensive factors of growth.) Recent party writing on the economic system

[87]*Partiinaia zhizn'*, no. 14 (1981): 25–26.

suggests that although its enrollments are quite impressive (38 million persons were enrolled in economic courses in the 1980–1981 academic year and 22.6 million in the party system,[88] its achievements are considerably less so.[89] A 1982 resolution issued jointly by the party, government, trade unions, and Komsomol expressed serious reservations about the system and gave it a more systematic framework, consisting of three tiers. The first level consists of the trade union schools of communist labor referred to above; new *schools of concrete economics* and *economic seminars* make up the second and third rungs. Concern at the highest levels of the leadership about the declining performance of the economy evidently has prompted continuing efforts to improve and restructure these economic schools, which are offshoots of the party education system and depend upon it for instructors. Establishment of this system may also be seen as a way of responding to the growing inefficiency of the economy while avoiding the politically difficult dilemma of structural reform.

Frequent criticism of the party and economic education systems in the Soviet press indicate that political education falls well short of achieving its avowed aims of arming the Soviet leadership and masses with a world outlook shaped by Marxism-Leninism. Several factors other than ideological zeal explain the high enrollment figures. Eager to report successful performance, party secretaries and particularly the party officials responsible for ideological work (including secretaries for ideology, heads of agitation-propaganda departments, instructors in such departments, and those working in local houses and offices of political enlightenment) pressure PPO organizers to sign up high numbers of party members and nonmembers in political education. The *Handbook of the Primary Party Organization Secretary* explains the "voluntary" nature of enrollment as follows:

> As is known, one of the basic principles in the organization of Marxist-Leninist study of communists is the *principle of voluntariness.* But sometimes it is incorrectly interpreted by some members of the party, who think, "well, I'll study if I want to." The party statutes oblige every communist to concern himself with raising his doc-

---

[88]See *Partiinaia zhizn'*, no. 14 (1981): 26.

[89]See *Spravochnik propagandista 1982* (The Propagandist's Handbook 1982) (Moscow: Politizdat, 1982), p. 118.

trinal-theoretical level, persistently to master Marxism-Leninism. But the party organization should strictly observe the principle of voluntariness in the choice of subject and the forms of study. . . . [90]

The resolution on reorganizing party education adopted in 1981 after the Twenty-sixth Party Congress stated, however:

> It is recommended not to be distracted by the broadening of the number of listeners in the party education system, but rather decisively to concentrate on raising its quality, strengthening its links with life and the practice of communist construction.[91]

Interestingly, after the resolution, some decrease in the number of persons enrolled in party study did occur, particularly among nonparty participants, evidently in connection with instructions that elite and theoretical goals were once again to be emphasized at the expense of the mass participatory character of the system.[92]

Thus in some cases high enrollments are purely formal and in others they reflect a good deal of less-than-voluntary participation. A second set of factors has to do with the motives of individual participants. Enrollment in political schools is a useful, often necessary, precondition to career advancement. The director of the university of Marxism-Leninism of the Briansk provincial party committee observed that a second secretary of a certain city party committee was recommended for attendance at the university of Marxism-Leninism, agreed to go, and was promoted to first secretary.[93] Discussions in the party press suggest that political education is often regarded as a kind of ticket punching, an

[90]*Spravochnik sekretaria pervichnoi partiinoi organizatsii,* p. 258.

[91]"O dal'neishem sovershenstvovanii partiinoi ucheby v svete reshenii XXVI s' ezda KPSS" (On the Further Improvement of Party Study in Light of the Decisions of the Twenty-sixth CPSU Congress), in *KPSS o formirovanii novogo cheloveka: sbornik dokumentov i materialov, 1965–1981*) (The CPSU on the Shaping of the New Person: A Collection of Documents and Materials, 1965-1981) (Moscow: Izdatel'stvo politicheskoi literatury, 1982), pp. 338–39.

[92]See V. N. Zaitsev, "Ideologicheskim kadram — postoiannuiu zabotu i vnimanie" (To Ideological Cadres — Continuous Concern and Attention), in V. I. Korzhov, comp., *Voprosy ideologicheskoi raboty: o kompleksnom podkhode k problemam kommunisticheskogo vospitaniia trudiashchikhsia Leningrada i oblasti* (Questions of Ideological Work: On a Complex Approach to the Problems of Communist Education of the Toilers of Leningrad and Leningrad Province) (Leningrad: Lenizdat, 1982), pp. 25–26.

[93]*Pravda,* 23 August 1981, p. 2.

essential credential that must be reflected on a career file before promotion to various elite positions can be considered.

From the standpoint of the regime leadership, a derivative but probably crucial consequence of the system is its function in forging a common consciousness of political responsibility among the political elite, quite apart from the rote learning of the specific ingredients of Marxism-Leninism that make up the formal curriculum. This becomes evident upon examining the composition of those attending party education courses in various localities. A secretary of Arkhangelsk obkom wrote that the party committee there sought to recruit all party officials, all members of elected party, soviet, and Komsomol committees, and all managers and specialists of economic enterprises in the province to the political education system.[94] The head of the agitation-propaganda department of the Kazakhstan party central committee noted that the party there was concerned to give a theoretical grounding to the republic's "leading cadres, especially those entering the *nomenklatura* of party committees."[95] In the Belorussian republic 41 percent of the students in the republic's sixteen universities of Marxism-Leninism were nomenklatura officials.[96] In Gurev province of Kazakhstan, about 30 percent of the nomenklatura officials of party committees in the province were enrolled in tertiary-level party schools, and another 23 percent had previously received higher party education.[97]

These and similar case materials indicate that political education is used to integrate the various sectors of the political and social elite, often by drawing them away from their places of residence and work for specialized instruction in common with their counterparts in other institutions and sectors of their province or republic. Such courses, therefore, probably help nurture a common awareness of their elite status as well as of the political skills and loyalties that are expected of them. For those attending courses at their places of work, the courses help to reinforce the party's authority by underlining the theoretical basis for its policies. The political education system need not be efficient in its ostensible aim of furthering an understanding of Marxism-Len-

[94]*Kompleksnyi podkhod,* p. 109.
[95]Ibid., pp. 218–19.
[96]Ibid., p. 196.
[97]Ibid., p. 356.

inism for these secondary benefits to be realized. Political education provides a consistent, uniform method for dealing with current events and policy issues throughout the entire country, counteracting potential tendencies toward pluralization of interest aggregation. It thus helps link the ideological foundations of the party's self-assigned authority with the day-to-day decisions that political executives and specialists must make in all the spheres of political action, and it integrates the elite groups differentiated by ethnicity, region, generation, and occupational branch. The oscillation between periods of populist expansion (as in the early 1930s and again in the early 1960s) and those of elitist retrenchment (after 1938 and again after 1964) indicates the difficulty the regime's leaders have in satisfying their twin goals: providing doctrinally grounded political socialization to the entire Soviet adult population and molding the collective consciousness of the Soviet political elite.

CHAPTER VII

Interest Articulation, Interest Aggregation, and Policymaking

INTRODUCTION

The political process is set in motion by interest articulation, or the making of political demands.[1] Almond and Powell define interest aggregation as "the function of converting demands into major policy alternatives," which can only occur when, for example, demands "are backed by substantial political resources" such as the "votes of citizens who support candidates, the votes of legislatures, the support of bureaucratic groups and the support of armed force that may be utilized in recruitment and policy making."[2] Policymaking is defined by the same authors as "the pivotal stage of the political process, the point at which political demands are converted into authoritative decisions."[3]

During roughly the last quarter century a substantial literature has been produced by Western scholars on the topics treated in this chapter. Its findings are varied and some are controversial, such as the respective roles of various actors, including top political leaders, bureaucratic hierarchies, interest groups, and other more or less organized generators, including influential individuals, of inputs to the Soviet political process, and the degree of change that has occurred in the system since the death of Joseph

---

[1]Gabriel Almond and G. Bingham Powell, *Comparative Politics,* 2nd ed. (Boston, Mass.: Little, Brown, 1979), p. 169.
[2]Ibid., p. 198.
[3]Ibid., p. 232.

Stalin. There is substantial agreement on certain points, however. Everyone recognizes that mass terror has been replaced by what has been termed selective terror, applied, for example, to persons who violate various loosely worded laws and the norms of public communication in the USSR by openly expressing opinions that the appropriate Soviet authorities have judged harmful or contumacious. A major difference between the way in which Stalin-era policy toward freedom of expression operated and the handling of such matters since the tyrant's death is that now, in contrast to the extremes of caprice and arbitrariness prevalent then, Soviet citizens as a rule recognize the boundaries separating what is permissible from what is likely to be punished. Under Stalin it was often desperately difficult to know whether or not one was saying or doing something entailing a high probability of self-destruction. In those days millions went to labor camps for alleged or suspected state crimes, in comparison with today's thousands.[4]

There is also relatively broad agreement on the beneficial but strictly limited results of this change. Certainly it appears to have provided a considerably enhanced measure of personal security for politically conformist Soviet specialists and experts and indeed for Soviet citizens generally. This, together with rising educational levels and steadily increasing appreciation in CPSU leadership circles of the dependence of national wealth and international influence on scientific and technological progress, has probably, within limits imposed by the hierarchical and centralist nature of the Soviet system, tended to improve the morale of Soviet professionals, emboldening them to press cautiously and prudently for increased autonomy. We shall return to these topics later.

Among informed students of Soviet politics, however, there is also a rather strong consensus that nothing resembling pluralism as it exists in Western democracies or *polyarchies,* to borrow a term apparently introduced by Robert Dahl and Charles E. Lindblom, exists or is likely to take shape in any foreseeable future in any country of the Soviet type. Some scholars, including us, however, see in communist Yugoslavia a political and especially an economic system that, though it is far from pluralist, has nevertheless

[4]On the abandonment of mass terror in the USSR and its consequences, see relevant chapters of Alexander Dallin and George Breslauer, *Political Terror in Communist Systems* (Stanford, Calif.: Stanford University Press, 1970).

moved substantially away from the Soviet model.[5] Perhaps the fact that Yugoslavs enjoy greater economic and cultural, if not political, freedom than do citizens of any other communist one-party, "Leninist" polity results from the existence in Yugoslavia of a partially "marketized" economy. The existence of such an economy, like the developments in Czechoslovakia and Poland referred to above, suggests the possibility that similar developments might someday occur in the USSR. For the foreseeable future, however — let us say at least the remainder of the twentieth century — neither pressure from below nor guidance from above seems likely to upset a political pattern characterized by centralized state control of economic and social life, strict censorship, and especially the all-pervasive leading role of the ruling CPSU.

In the Soviet Union and similar political systems, there is an absence of "organizational" pluralism, that is, "the existence of a plurality of relatively autonomous (independent) organizations (sub-systems) within the domain of a state."[6] Quoting the above statements from a recent book by the esteemed theorist of democracy, Robert Dahl, a leading analyst of communist. systems has expressed the view that, except for brief episodes in Czechoslovakia in 1968 and Poland in 1980–1981, no communist-ruled nation has thus far experienced anything remotely resembling pluralist government and politics of the type existing in what Dahl calls polyarchies.[7] Moreover, this scholar, Archie Brown, also rejects the view of a few Western scholars that the USSR is a "corporatist" polity.[8]

---

[5]For an original and stimulating but perhaps inevitably inconclusive attempt to find in the "marketization" of the Yugoslav economy a factor promoting political pluralism in that country and by extension in communist countries generally, see Wlodzimierz Brus, "Political Pluralism and Markets in Communist Systems," chapter 5 of Susan Gross Solomon, ed., *Pluralism in the Soviet Union* (London: MacMillan, 1983).

[6]The above quotations are in Robert Dahl, *Dilemmas of Pluralist Democracy* (New Haven, Conn.: Yale University Press, 1982), p. 5. Dahl asserts on p. 26 that "an organization is relatively autonomous if it undertakes actions that (a) are considered harmful by another organization and that (b) no other organization, including the government of the state, can prevent . . . except by incurring costs so high as to exceed the gains to the actor from doing so."

[7]See Archie Brown, "Pluralism, Power and the Soviet Political System: A Comparative Perspective," in Susan Gross Solomon, ed., *Pluralism in the Soviet Union*, pp. 61–107.

[8]Ibid., pp. 75–80.

Like many other well-informed Sovietologists, however, he finds abundant evidence of debates among Soviet scholars, usually in the pages of small-circulation specialist journals, on basic political concepts such as political power, the state, political parties, and "the relative autonomy of the state in political systems." This "somewhat esoteric debate," he asserts, "concerns not only the meaning of words and is not only about approaches to the study of politics," but sheds light on significant political differences; in general, those who "lay most emphasis on state power" are "more conservative Communists than those who emphasize *narodovlastie* [italics ours] or sovereignty of the people. . . . ''[9]

It should again be emphasized that the author whose views we have been summarizing and quoting in no way offers them as evidence of acceptance in the USSR of the merits of Western-style pluralism. On the contrary, in the course of his impressively documented presentation he offers a striking indication that even the highest-level ministers have relatively little influence by comparison with top party officials. (These ministers are roughly equivalent in status to heads of federal government departments in the United States.) Brown points out, for example, that a minister "cannot put an item on the Politburo agenda unless . . . he is himself a Politburo member."[10] More generally, he asserts that "while social and political forces within the broader society and opinion groupings within the party and within various other institutions do have an impact on public policy, the relative autonomy of institutions other than the highest party organs is (by comparative standards) fairly small and the relative autonomy of the supreme holders of political power at the apex of the party hierarchy is (again in comparative perspective) very great."[11]

It would be surprising if a political system in which the ruling few dominate and control access to the resources and processes of articulation and decision — not to mention goods, services, and perquisites — as the Politburo and Secretariat of the CPSU do in the USSR, operated as a Western pluralist democracy. To be sure, there is evidence that participation by loyal, conformist specialists — who by now are probably members of the party and hence

[9]Ibid., pp. 92-94.
[10]Ibid., p. 88.
[11]Ibid., pp. 94-95.

subject to party discipline — in articulating and aggregating demands and in shaping policy has gradually and substantially increased since Stalin's departure from the Soviet scene.[12] In evaluating this important and probably positive trend, it should be remembered that it is not entirely a post-Stalin development and that it has certain limits and even certain negative aspects. We agree with Archie Brown's judgment that "policies change and the limits of the permissible change as the result of the initiatives of individuals and the advocacy of opinion groupings within the networks of specialists without whose help the top party and government leadership would scarcely be in a position to govern," and also with his assertion that "there is a vast difference between the kind of specialist whom Stalin relied on — who were frequently charlatans, often more Stalinist than Stalin . . . and those who have been coming to the fore in the post-Stalin period."[13]

It is not at all certain that the apparently increasing influence of some Soviet scientists, for example, indicates increased influence for scientists as a profession, for specialists as an aggregate, or for members of the Soviet intelligentsia in general. It seems to be the case that since the ouster of Khrushchev, freedom of expression of unorthodox views about ethical values and aesthetic preferences has diminished sharply. This negative trend may adversely affect the ethical and aesthetic development of the USSR. Of course, an objective examination of such matters would require recognition that in the Western as well as in the Eastern industrial

---

[12]Archie Brown notes that the participants in the Soviet scholarly discussion he described were party members. Solomon, ed., *Pluralism in the Soviet Union,* p. 94. On the "restoration" of the "right of control" of party organizations in research institutes, etc., see F. Barghoorn, "Factional, Sectoral and Subversive Opposition in Soviet Politics," in Robert Dahl, ed., *Regimes and Oppositions* (New Haven: Yale University Press, 1973), pp. 27–88, at pp. 53–57. See also portions of George Breslauer, *Khrushchev and Brezhnev as Leaders* (London: Allen & Unwin, 1982).

[13]Archie Brown, "In the Corridors of the Kremlin," *London Times Literary Supplement,* 1 April 1983, pp. 333–34, at 334. Brown also here reminds us that the "arch-charlatan" Trofim Lysenko "succeeded in pulling the wool over the eyes of Khrushchev as well as Stalin," and that in some of the more "ideological areas" Stalin appointees are to this day forces to be reckoned with." On the rise of specialists and debates among them, see also Ronald Hill, *Soviet Politics, Political Science and Reform* (White Plains, N.Y.: M. E. Sharpe, 1980).

societies, progress in science and technology has been accompanied by development of deadly new military weapons and by other unfortunate consequences.[14]

In view of the clearly increasing concern in both Soviet and American polities with foreign policy and especially military issues, it is not implausible to hypothesize that the Soviet political leadership will increasingly give preferment to specialists who can demonstrate that their policy recommendations will increase the domestic and foreign power of the Soviet elite. If this proves to be the case, a favored few among the scientific and technical specialists may well be reaping the biggest rewards. Whatever the merit of such speculation, there are indications that in the period beginning in the late 1960s, the relative autonomy of specialists and professionals as a social group or stratum vis-à-vis that of the party leadership may have actually declined. One development that pointed in that direction was the restoration in 1971 by the Twenty-fourth CPSU Congress of the right of control over scientific and educational institutions to the primary party organizations within them. Following such other occurrences as the failure of the Twenty-third CPSU Congress in 1966 to reelect the liberal editor of the important literary journal *Novy mir,* as an alternate member of the party Central Committee, and the intensified repression of dissenters in the late 1960s, especially after Soviet action to crush the Czechoslovak reform movement, restoration of the "right of control" may have been a mainly symbolic measure. It was, however, an important part of the neo-Stalinist reaction that followed the ouster of Khrushchev.[15]

[14]These remarks are partially triggered by a series of articles in the *Wall Street Journal* in April and May, 1984, by William Kucewicz. An article dated May 1 features the Soviet biochemist Yuri Ovchinnikov, who, according to Kucewicz's substantial but necessarily inconclusive research, has become the most powerful member of the Academy of Sciences of the USSR. According to Kucewicz, Ovchinnikov's power appears to reflect the satisfaction of the top Soviet political leadership that Ovchinnikov's research in developing a gene-warfare program will confer great advantages upon the USSR in its military competition with the United States. See "Lead Scientist in a Scourge Search," *Wall Street Journal,* 1 May 1984, p. 24.

[15]On *Novy mir* editor Tvardovsky's role as a prudent and courageous champion of freedom of expression and inquiry, and particularly on the curbing of his influence under Brezhnev, see Dina Spechler, *Permitted Dissent in the USSR* (New York: Praeger, 1982), esp. pp. 218–30 and passim.

Another negative trend, to which a former Soviet sociologist, now an immigrant in the United States, has pointed as detrimental to the independence of the intelligentsia — which was growing in the 1950s and early 1960s — is "the overproduction of specialists," making them increasingly dependent for their life chances on party and state officials who control access to employment.[16]

We return here briefly to the decline that we perceive in freedom of expression regarding moral and other nontechnical, noninstrumental values in the post-Khrushchev era. Some writers, critics, and editors, particularly Tvardovski, his editorial colleagues at *Novy mir,* and such contributors as Solzhenitsyn, sought to revive the traditional role of Russian literature as the conscience of society. They were supported in their effort by other creative intellectuals, including performing artists such as the bards Alexander Galich and Vladimir Vysotski, the cellist Mstislav Rostropovich, and the Taganka theater director Yuri Lyubimov, and by some persons outside the literary-artistic community. The moderately critical and reformist views expressed by the liberal Soviet intellectual community — most of them doubtless readers of *Novy mir* — ceased to find an outlet in print after the forced resignation of Tvardovsky in February 1970. From 1965 on, especially after the arrest of the writers Yuli Daniel and Andrei Sinyavsky for sending abroad works of fiction objectionable to the Soviet authorities, both within-system liberals of the Tvardovski type and more radical open dissenters were under increasing harassment, pressure, and, in the case of the dissenters, repression by a regime that saw in all kinds of dissent a source of harm to the Soviet sociopolitical order.[17]

[16]Victor Zaslavsky, *The Neo-Stalinist State: Class, Ethnicity and Consensus in Soviet Soviety* (Armonk, N.Y.: M. E. Sharpe, 1982), pp. 16–21 and 147–51. Zaslavsky also refers to other relevant policies, such as official anti-Semitism, forced emigration of critically minded intellectuals, and drafting of a troublesome specialist into military-like exile to remote parts of the country. The counterpart of the latter policy, applied to workers, is assignment to "closed" enterprises, the raison d'être of which "lies in their genuine or fictitious participation in secrets of capital importance to the state." This practice exploits workers' pride and nationalism, isolates them from other elements of the population, and hence facilitates control and reduces possibilities for expression of discontent. See pp. 13–14. Zaslavsky believes that these factors, as well as relentless but skillfully applied repression, help explain the decline of dissent in the USSR after the mid- and late 1960s.

[17]For details, see Spechler, *Permitted Dissent,* and Edith Rogovin Frankel, *Novyi Mir: A Case Study in the Politics of Literature* (Cambridge, England: Cambridge University Press, 1981); also Stephen F. Cohen, "The Friends and Foes of Change:

Khrushchev's record was a mixed one. It would be a distortion of history to focus on his contributions in widening the boundaries of expression for loyal but in many cases highly critical reformist opinions while forgetting his limitations, such as the extraordinary harshness he displayed toward the rights of religious believers, his suppression by military force of a workers' demonstration in Novocherkassk in 1962, or his condoning the abuse of psychiatry against what he considered subversive dissent. Nevertheless, on balance, Khrushchev's leadership probably allowed the maximum freedom of expression and action possible without threatening the foundations of the Soviet system. His conservative opponents in the upper echelons of the party apparatus obviously thought that in such policies as tolerating publication of Alexander Solzhenitsyn's exposé of Stalin's gulag, *One Day in the Life of Ivan Denisovich*, Khrushchev had exceeded the boundaries of tolerable permissiveness. The attitude of those who pulled the rug from under Khrushchev in October 1964 and installed a new leadership in which Leonid Brezhnev, Aleksei Kosygin, and the venerable party ideologist Mikhail Suslov were perhaps the three most powerful figures, was reflected in subsequent actions. Brezhnev, for example, took as his title the one designated by Stalin — general secretary (Khrushchev had accented his break from Stalinism by using the new title of first secretary). About a month after the Brezhnev leadership assumed office, criticism of group attitudes among some Soviet writers began.[18]

Despite significant differences between the Khrushchev and Brezhnev administrations, however, their methods of rule differed vastly more from Stalin's than from each other's. Both renounced mass terror. Both, especially the Brezhnev leadership, were more oligarchical or collective than autocratic. Under both, especially that of Brezhnev, policies were often formulated after

---

Reformism and Conservatism in the Soviet Union," *Slavic Review* 38, no. 2, pp. 187–202 (June 1979). With some exaggeration, Cohen asserts on p. 202 of this article that "the overthrow of Khrushchev brought an end to reform and even some counter-reform in most areas of Soviet society."

[18]On the latter point, see *Pravda* lead editorial, 22 November 1964, cited in F. Barghoorn, "Soviet Russia: Orthodoxy and Adaptiveness," in Lucian Pye and Sidney Verba, eds., *Political Culture and Political Development* (Princeton, N.J.: Princeton University Press, 1965), pp. 450–511, at p. 484. Among other things this chapter briefly compared the new Brezhnev leadership's policies with those of Khrushchev and speculated about future development of the former.

extensive debate and discussion, partly outside the ruling Politburo. The Politburo, however, reserved to itself crucial prerogatives such as deciding whether to permit an issue to be placed on its agenda, not to mention retaining the sole right of final decision. In addition, under both regimes the incumbent leader felt constrained at times to alter or postpone adoption of policies in response to opposition from other members of the Politburo. Both leaders were able, however, when they considered it necessary, to engineer the ouster from the Politburo of some members of that body whose opposition they considered intolerable.

POLICYMAKING

PARTY CHIEFS AND OTHER TOP PARTY LEADERS

The Lenin Era. The major and dominant actors on the Soviet political stage were from the beginnings of the Soviet regime in 1917 leaders such as Vladimir Lenin, Leon Trotsky, Joseph Stalin, Grigori Zinoviev, and other members of the supreme decision-making body of the Russian (later the Soviet) Communist Party. Until the Politburo was formally established by the Eighth Congress of the party in March 1919, the supreme party decision-making body was the Central Committee. Paradoxically, however, despite the supremacy of the top party bodies, Lenin, the creator of the Communist Party and the only truly charismatic leader in Soviet history, preferred to rule through a state rather than a party body, namely, the Council of People's Commissars (*Sovnarkom*), which in its structure and procedures resembled the British Cabinet.[19] After a series of strokes first greatly curtailed Lenin's activity and finally killed him in 1924 at age 54, the pattern of policymaking established by Lenin in the Sovnarkom was replaced by policymaking overwhelmingly dominated by the Politburo and the party machine controlled by Stalin. T. H. Rigby appears to believe that if this had not happened, the development of Soviet politics might not have been as calamitous to the liberties of the peoples of the USSR as it turned out to be. Rigby is real-

---

[19]See T. H. Ribgy, *Lenin's Government: Sovnarkom 1917–1922* (Cambridge, England: Cambridge University Press, 1979). See also Barrington Moore, Jr., *Soviet Politics — The Dilemma of Power* (Cambridge, Mass.: Harvard University Press, 1951). Moore's book remains one of the best sources of history and analysis of Soviet politics under Lenin and Stalin.

istically aware that the outbreak of the civil war between the ruling but hard-pressed Bolsheviks in June 1918 facilitated emergence of what has been called (by Robert Tucker and Stephen Cohen) the "warfare state," an environment favorable to the development of extremes of dictatorship, coercion, and a siege mentality. This also was an environment in which the peculiar political personality of Stalin thrived.[20]

As perhaps the foremost historian of the Soviet Communist Party has written, the situation of non-Bolshevik political parties, including socialist ones such as the Mensheviks and the SRs (Socialist Revolutionaries), became after a few months of toleration so precarious that their relationship to Lenin's Bolsheviks "at any rate after 1918 was not oppositionist in the ordinary, Western political sense of that term at all; it was a struggle for survival."[21] Well before the situation described in the above quotation had developed, the violent dissolution engineered by Lenin of the democratically elected Constituent Assembly (in January 1918), in which the Bolsheviks constituted a minority, indicated Lenin's contempt for mere arithmetic majorities, composed of people whom he regarded as representatives of the bourgeoisie.

It did not take long for the communist rulers of Russia to add increasing elements of monolithism to the monopoly of power they claimed for their communist party. Only in the period of full Stalinism in the mid- and late 1930s, however, did the "cult of personality of J. V. Stalin," which Khrushchev condemned in 1956, fully flower. First Lenin and then Stalin expressed impatience with the early tendencies of some of their fellow Bolshevik leaders to engage in "endless theoretical discussion" of public policies, and by 1931 Stalin wrote to the editors of a theoretical journal warning of the dangers of "rotten liberalism" at the expense, as he put it, of "the vital interests of Bolshevism."[22] In the equally impor-

---

[20]See Rigby, *Lenin's Government,* esp. pp. 179–89 and 223–38. On Stalin's personality as the decisive factor in his political behavior see Robert C. Tucker, *Stalin as Revolutionary* (New York: Norton, 1973), esp. ch. 12, "The Decisive Trifle."

[21]Leonard Schapiro, *The Origins of the Communist Autocracy* (Cambridge, Mass.: Harvard University Press, 1955), p. xiii.

[22]Moore, *Soviet Politics,* p. 157. Moore notes: "It is perhaps in this statement that one finds for the first time the overt recognition of a monolithic dictatorship over intellectual and political life. In essence, Stalin was saying that certain theories of Bolshevism were above and beyond criticism, because such criticism endangered the foundations of the regime."

tant — perhaps even more important — sphere of organizational practice, the Tenth Party Congress in 1921 adopted a landmark resolution entitled "Concerning the Unity of the Party." This resolution, subsequently often cited against alleged factionalists by Stalin and his lieutenants in the party's "Leninist core," forbade organized political activity within the party by "factions" based on "special platforms" with their own "group discipline." In its final provision, published only in 1924, it empowered the Central Committee to expel from the party persons found to have been engaged in such activity. To a considerable extent, however, this "infamous" resolution was "a quixotic attempt by a panicky leadership to constrain, or legislate away, its own tradition" — which was one of factionalism and a struggle by whoever had succeeded in gaining control of the supreme party leadership to ward off challenges by other factions.[23]

As a rule, little detail is available on the activity of factions, especially defeated ones. A few years after the political crisis of June 1957, however, when what Khrushchev and his supporters termed "the antiparty group" (Georgi Malenkov, Vyacheslav Molotov, Lazar Kaganovich, and others) was defeated in its effort to overthrow Khrushchev, evidence of fierce factional strife was at least partially disclosed. (In October 1964, of course, most of Khrushchev's Politburo colleagues, headed by his erstwhile protégé and supporter Leonid Brezhnev and the veteran ideological specialist Mikhail Suslov, successfully conspired to oust Khrushchev.) In his speech at the Twenty-second CPSU Congress in 1961, A. N. Shelepin asserted that in June 1957 "when the factionalists went over to an open attack against the Central Committee," Nikolai Bulganin, then chairman of the Council of Ministers, had placed a guard in the Kremlin in such a manner that without his permission nobody could gain access to "the building where the session of the Presidium of the Central Committee of the CPSU was proceeding." Even more startling is the fact that Nikita Khrushchev and Frol Kozlov, then probably second-ranking CPSU leader, asserted at the same congress that if

---

[23]See, for example, Stephen F. Cohen, "Bolshevism and Stalinism," in Robert Tucker, ed., *Stalinism* (New York: Norton, 1977), pp. 3–29, footnote 50, at p. 17.

the antiparty group had gained power, it would have done away with "the honest leaders" of the party.[24]

Compared with the relative tranquillity of the Brezhnev leadership (1964–1982), Khrushchev's tenure as party leader (1953–1964) seems tempestuous. Under Khrushchev occurred, for example, the public humiliation and demotion of Nikolai Bulganin when he was replaced as chairman of the Council of Ministers (head of government) (and whose political career effectively ended in 1958 when Khrushchev took over his job), the unexplained disappearance from public life of Politburo member Aleksei Kirichenko in 1960 after only 5 years as a full member, and the startling rise and fall of Georgi Zhukov. Zhukov had emerged from World War II as Russia's most honored military commander but was exiled by a suspicious Stalin to a series of provincial posts; under Khrushchev he became the first genuinely professional military man to gain full Politburo rank, only to be relegated again to obscurity after he had helped Khrushchev beat back the 1957 challenge of the antiparty group. Most dramatic of all the political events of the Khrushchev era — at a time when, strictly speaking, it had not truly started — was the June 1953 arrest followed by execution of Lavrenti Beria, Stalin's long-time security chief. Among other things the hated Beria was accused of having been, from early in his career, an agent of British military intelligence. The pretext for his arrest, which occurred at a time when his political maneuvering, including an effort to curry favor with non-Russian elements in the political elite, had aroused suspicion that he might be planning a coup d'état, may have been an uprising of workers in East Germany, where the security service was dominated by officials close to Beria. The arrest was also part of a successful effort by the CPSU leadership, led particularly by Khrushchev, to put an end to a situation in which the security forces had been the main instrument of political leadership in the USSR under Stalin's rather than the Politburo's collective control.

Secretive and conspiratorial factional strife and accompanying

[24]See *Pravda,* 27 October 1961, and *Materialy XX s' ezda KPSS* (Materials of the 20th CPSU Congress) (Moscow: Izdatelstvo politicheskoi Literatury, 1961), p. 282.

purges were certainly a less conspicuous feature of Soviet politics under Brezhnev than they had been under Khrushchev. Still, the manner in which Politburo member Nikolai Podgorny's political career ended in 1977 should not be forgotten. Podgorny had come out of the Kharkov party organization, one that vied for a time with the immensely powerful Brezhnev faction, based originally in the coal and steel city of Dnepropetrovsk but expanded as Brezhnev rose through a series of posts — such as chief of the party in Moldavia, where he met and added to his clients Konstantin Chernenko. When in 1977, perhaps at the height of his power, Brezhnev chose to have a new constitution of the USSR adopted, replacing the "Stalin Constitution" in force since 1936, and also to take unto himself the position of chairman of the Presidium of the Supreme Soviet (now frequently referred to by Western news media as president), Podgorny's political career ended with his forcible retirement and removal from the Politburo. Available evidence indicates that he was a rather pathetic figure from then until his death a few years later.[25] Another Politburo member whose career ended abruptly under Brezhnev was Petr Shelest, removed in 1972, apparently because in the opinion of the Brezhnev faction he had excessively exalted the significance of Ukrainian culture and national consciousness in the very important Ukrainian Republic. Besides being a full member of the all-union CPSU Politburo, Shelest was until his removal also the first secretary of the Ukrainian Republic party organization. Somewhat similar, though less traumatic, was the fate of Andrei Kirilenko, who after years of being regarded by knowledgeable Western experts as the man most likely to succeed Brezhnev (he had been a full Politburo member since 1962 and was, with the exception of the veteran ideologist Mikhail Suslov, the ranking member of the Central Committee Secretariat), quietly faded from prominence in the last year of Brezhnev's leadership and retired from the Politburo on grounds of health. Thus, despite its relative tranquillity, even the long Brezhnev leadership (1964–1982) was not free of elements of secretiveness and arbitrariness. None of the events referred to were ever explained in any way in the Soviet media, thus leaving both the Soviet public and the outside world

[25]See John Löwenhardt, *The Soviet Politburo,* trans. Dymphna Clark (New York: St. Martin's Press, 1982), p. 64.

in virtually total ignorance of their causes, motives, and significance.

Stalin and Stalinism. To understand why elements of secrecy and conspiracy are still integral elements of Soviet high politics almost 70 years after the establishment of the Soviet regime in Russia, it is necessary to be familiar with at least the main features of the pattern of Joseph Stalin's rule in Russia. Opinion may legitimately differ as to the degree to which the Stalin pattern still influences policymaking in the USSR today, but it seems clear that the contemporary pattern cannot be understood without a good grasp of the terrifying struggles out of which the main lines of contemporary Soviet political institutions developed.[26]

Before presenting some salient features of the development of political institutions and practices during the Stalin era, at least a brief discussion of the part played by Stalin's peculiar personality in his political behavior will be useful. We believe that Robert Tucker's adaptation of the neo-Freudian psychoanalytic theories of Karen Horney constitutes an important contribution to the understanding of Soviet politics not only during but probably since the Stalin era, in view of the enormous and in some ways continuing influence of Stalin on Soviet political life. It seems to us necessary for the understanding of Stalin's political behavior to add to analysis based on political, historical, cultural, and other factors a special psychological component. We are inclined to this

[26]Robert Conquest, in his Foreword to Gavriel Ra'anan, *International Policy Formation in the USSR: Factional "Debates" during the "Zhdanovshchina"* (Hamden, Conn.: Shoe String Press, 1983), asserts that the late Dr. Ra'anan's book "has profound implications not merely for the period it covers," but also illuminates the "present Soviet background." One bit of evidence Conquest offers in support of his assertion is Yuri Andropov's promotion from Karelia to Moscow as a Central Committee inspector after the Leningrad Case purge, which led to the deaths of several former political allies of Andrei A. Zhdanov, former party leader of Leningrad, supporter of Tito of Yugoslavia, and ideological boss of the USSR in 1946–1948. Zhdanov died on August 31, 1948. His main opponent in Soviet factional politics was Georgi Malenkov. As Conquest puts it, Andropov "gave satisfaction" in "the events recounted" in Ra'anan's book. For a useful recent overview of Soviet policymaking during the period of Stalin's ascendancy (1934–1953), see Vernon Aspaturian, "The Stalinist Legacy in Soviet National Security Decisionmaking," in Jiri Valenta and William Potter, eds., *Soviet Decisionmaking for National Security* (London: Allen & Unwin, 1984), pp. 25–73. Aspaturian deals with the totality of the decision-making process, not merely with its national security aspects.

view by the pattern of Stalin's behavior, unique in Soviet history and Russian history generally. One can search in vain the record of Lenin's leadership, before Stalin fully established his dictatorship in the early 1930s, of Khrushchev's and Brezhnev's administrations, of the brief 15 months of Yuri Andropov's leadership, in 1982–1983, or of Konstantin Chernenko's even shorter tenure as General Secretary for any real parallel to the excesses that occurred under Stalin's rule. These included pervasive terror, widespread confinement in camps and prisons, and millions of deaths by starvation and disease or by execution. To be sure, every period of Soviet history has been highly repressive, both by comparison with the West in the nineteenth and twentieth centuries and by comparison with tsarist Russia. In comparison with Stalin's rule, however, the others have been mild, except of course the period of the revolution and civil war in 1917–1921.

According to Robert Tucker, after Stalin's death, "the terror-tinged atmosphere of the first months of the year evaporated like mist in the morning sun."[27]

The dynamics of the Stalin personality pattern at least partly responsible for Stalin's terror-driven rule seems to have been somewhat as follows.[28] Frequently beaten by his alcoholic shoemaker father but the darling of his strong-willed mother, bright, stubborn and himself strong-willed, Stalin learned to cope with an unfavorable environment at home and in the church school of his home town of Gori, where the school administration busied itself with attempting to Russify the mainly Georgian pupils. Early in life Stalin developed, according to Tucker, a "self-idealizing tendency, on the one hand, and a vengeful streak and indomitable will to fight and to win, on the other."[29] After he had become a Marxist and had "joined the Russian nation," rejecting his Georgian nationality, the adopted Lenin as his model, aspiring to become "Lenin II." A neurotic but a person of powerful will and vast ambition, he resorted to "repression, rationalization and

[27] Robert Tucker, "Memoir of a Stalin Biographer," *Princeton Alumni Weekly,* 3 November 1982, p. 24. During the time he writes about, Tucker and his Russian-born wife, Eugenia, were living in Moscow and waiting for visas to leave the USSR. Visas were not available as long as Stalin lived.

[28] What follows is based largely on Tucker, *Stalin as Revolutionary,* ch. 12, pp. 421–61, and ch. 3, esp. pp. 65–79.

[29] Ibid., p. 425.

projection" to preserve his "revolutionary self-image."[30] He lacked genuine self-confidence and was sensitive to whatever he perceived as a slight. Consequently, he was susceptible to the flattery lavished on him very early by the secret police operative Lavrenti Beria and later by the charlatan pseudo-scientist Trofim Lysenko. Stalin was good at hiding his "enormous ego-centricity," however. He liked to pose as a truly modest man, modeling himself in this respect as in so many others on Lenin. Eventually he became powerful enough to have the Soviet mass media proclaim him on the occasion of his fiftieth birthday as the "best Leninist" in Soviet Russia, a great revolutionary, the leader of the international communist movement, a great military strategist, an eminent Marxist theorizer, and the builder of socialism in the USSR.[31]

Consideration of Stalin's personality traits has led us to the subject of one of their most sinister manifestations, Stalin's "painful sensitivity to whatever he interpreted as a slight or aspersion."[32] Tucker cites numerous illustrations, including Trotksy's famous challenge at "a stormy Politburo session of 1926 attended by many Central Committee members," when he called Stalin the "gravedigger of the revolution," and "everyone realized instinctively that no matter how ill-disposed Stalin might have been toward Trotsky hitherto, his will to vengeance would now be utterly implacable.[33] As Stalin accumulated power and responsibilities for more and more spheres of Soviet life, he came increasingly to associate his self-image not only with his person but with such vast entities as communism in Russia and throughout the world and the Soviet system and foreign policy. Stalin regarded criticism of any cause, principle, or policy with which he identified himself as an affront to be punished. Often, as in the case of the victims of the purges of 1936–1938, the victims were political leaders, such as Grigori Zinoviev, Lev Kamenev, Nikolai Bukharin, and others, all of whom had opposed Stalin's policies in the 1920s. The fact that Stalin had put together his own policy packages largely by borrowing and using for his own purposes elements of policies

---

[30]Ibid., p. 431. Also see pp. 431–37.
[31]On these roles and the flowering of the Stalin cult, beginning in 1929, see Tucker, *Stalin as Revolutionary,* ch. 13, pp. 462–87.
[32]Ibid., p. 444.
[43]Ibid., p. 446.

earlier developed by former allies who later became opponents did not at all mitigate Stalin's hostility toward those who ended up at his rivals. In those who had wounded Stalin's pride, often unwittingly, Stalin saw not merely a personal enemy but also "an enemy of the Soviet cause."[34] Finally, says Tucker, Stalin "was driven by unconscious needs and drives to people the world around him with Stalin-hating enemies who pretended to be loyal Bolsheviks while waiting watchfully for an opportunity to strike a blow against the communist cause and against him as its leader. Were such enemies lacking in sufficient numbers, he would have to invent them. And invent them he did."[35]

We believe that Tucker's analysis of Stalin's personality helps us to understand the ferocity, unpredictability, and other peculiar and extreme aspects of political life under Stalin. Other factors played their parts, of course. They included the ideological gulf between the USSR and the bourgeois West and the special ideological tensions between Nazi Germany and Fascist Italy, on the one hand, and all the other great powers, on the other. Perhaps some attention should also be given to Theodore von Laue's view that "have-not" nations such as Russia behaved differently from rich, advanced nations such as Britain, France, or America because the have-nots "have had to adopt the alien institutions of the West often at breakneck speed and frightful sacrifice, a tempo largely dictated by Western rates of growth."[36] Certainly Russia's tradition of absolutism, the damage done to the economy and social structure by the years of revolution and civil war, and of course the extremely ambitious, unrealistic targets set by Stalin and his lieutenants for collectivization of agriculture and the first Five Year Plan of forced-draft industrialization played their parts in the pattern that was to become known as Stalinism. The latter two policies, constituting what Stalin himself characterized as a "revolution from above," were adopted in 1929 while Stalin

[34]Ibid., p. 449.

[35]Ibid, p. 461.

[36]Theodore von Laue, "Problems of Modernization," in Ivo Lederer, ed., *Russian Foreign Policy* (New Haven, Conn.: Yale University Press, 1962), p. 71. This chapter was one of the first of a long series of works in which von Laue has sought by reference to the disadvantages of Russia's relative underdevelopment to explain virtually all aspects of Russian domestic and foreign policy. We credit von Laue with eloquence and ingenuity in arguing a thesis that we regard as oversimplified but not without some merit if it is placed in proper context.

forced out of their former positions of power his erstwhile allies Bukharin, Rykov, and other right-wing Politburo members.[37]

For a student of Soviet politics, there can be few experiences more startling than to compare the records of the delegates to the Seventeenth and Eighteenth Party Congresses in 1934 and 1939, respectively. "Of the 1,966 delegates to the previous [Seventeenth] congress, only fifty-nine were re-elected as delegates to the Eighteenth Congress. . . . [Among delegates not in the top leadership, reelected were] only thirty-five of the 1,827 rank-and-file delegates to the 1934 Congress, that is, less than 2 percent"[38]

By the time of the Seventeenth Congress, "Stalin had already made enormous progress in substantially altering the decision-making process established by Lenin and in fastening his grip on the party."[39] The purges of the 1930s enabled Stalin to complete the process he had begun in the 1920s when he successfully played off his rivals against one another and paved the way for the terroristic dictatorship he established in the 1930s. According to Aspaturian, in the Stalin era and subsequently, Soviet political institutions "first degenerated, were regenerated and then entered a renewed phase of sustained degeneration until Stalin's death, when a new phase of regeneration and renovation was set in motion."[40] One might add that disintegrative tendencies again manifested themselves in the last few years of Brezhnev's leadership, after a long period of fairly effective functioning of the political system before Brezhnev's health began to decline noticeably. It may well be that the whole period from about 1976 to the early 1980s will be viewed as a period of decline, somewhat similar to, but of course also in some ways very different from, the post-World War II portion of Stalin's leadership. The most obvious difference of course between 1976–1984 and 1945–1953 is the absence in the more recent period of the threat of new and

---

[37]For an important collection of essays that sheds light on many aspects of the topics concerning us here, see Robert C. Tucker, ed., *Stalinism* (New York: Norton, 1977).

[38]Aspaturian, "Stalinist Legacy in Decisionmaking," p. 44, cites as his source Robert Conquest, *The Great Terror* (New York: Macmillan, 1968), p. 471. He also notes Roy Medvedev's assertion, in *Let History Judge* (New York: Knopf, 1971), pp. 309–10, that 70 percent of the full and candidate Central Committee members elected in 1934 "were arrested and shot."

[39]Aspaturian, "Stalinist Legacy," p. 34.

[40]Ibid., p. 33.

terrible purges that hung over the Soviet polity and people as Stalin fell deeper into the irrational suspicion that increasingly gripped him in his declining years.

Curiously enough, Stalin ruled Soviet Russia, formally at least, on the basis of his party posts (principally general secretary of the Central Committee, which he had first assumed in 1924) until May 6, 1941, when he replaced V. M. Molotov as Chairman of the Council of People's Commissars, or formal head of the Soviet government. (In 1946 this body was renamed Council of Ministers.) Stalin never assumed the position of formal chief of the Soviet state, although during the war he took over the supreme military and military-civil posts: chairman of the state defense committee, commissar of defense, chief of the general headquarters of the Supreme High Command, and commander-in-chief of the armed forces.[41] After 1958 Khrushchev followed Stalin's example in combining the top party post with that of head of government. Leonid Brezhnev, however, assumed the presidency after forcing Nikolai Podgorny to retire as chairman of the Supreme Soviet Presidium in 1977, the same year in which Brezhnev also had the 1936 Stalin Constitution replaced by a new constitution. It should be remembered, however, that unlike the American presidency, this Soviet post is a largely ceremonial one and is only nominally an elective office. In this way, Brezhnev at least partially resolved the anomaly in which hitherto the top Soviet party leader had been conducting the USSR's relations with foreign heads of state.

As Aspaturian points out, after Brezhnev became chairman of the Presidium in 1977, "he assumed the military rank of marshal of the Soviet Union, chairmanship of the constitutionally established Council of Defense of the USSR, and was formally and publicly appointed commander-in-chief of the Armed Forces."[42]

Despite the often stormy course of Soviet politics under

[41]Ibid., p. 51.

[42]Ibid., p. 29. The 1977 Constitution gave constitutional status to the Defense Council. Aspaturian observes that "while the new Constitution subordinates both party and state to its authority, it does little to clarify the institutional relationship between the two in the decisionmaking process." (p. 30) In this and other parts of his essay, Aspaturian offers interesting comments about various "constitutional" problems in the Soviet political system. Only time will tell whether such questions will become "operational" problems of Soviet politics.

Khrushchev, if one views the post-Stalin and especially the post-Khrushchev period as a whole, one can make a case for a trend that might be called creeping constitutionalism — but only, or at least mainly, at the highest levels of the political system. This has largely taken the form of vesting in institutions and offices created by Stalin fixed powers that they could not develop while Stalin lived because of the dictator's insistence on his own personal rule of the USSR. One aspect of this trend has been the growth in the significance of the Presidium of the Supreme Soviet, to which Brezhnev contributed so much by taking over this office in 1977. This dramatic, and in some ways highly unconstitutional act, had been foreshadowed by a development pointed out by T. H. Rigby as early as 1970.[43] The unconstitutional, or perhaps one should say nonconstitutional, aspect of Brezhnev's assumption of the "presidency" in 1977 is noted in Aspaturian's statement that as chairman of the Presidium of the Supreme Soviet "he [Brezhnev] literally appointed himself" to the positions of commander-in-chief of the Soviet armed forces, chairman of the Council of Defense of the USSR — a post created (or formally recognized) by the Constitution of 1977 — and marshal of the Soviet Union, all by signing a decree "investing himself with all these military positions." Incidentally, by one stroke of the pen Brezhnev thus gathered to himself approximately as impressive an array of military titles as Stalin, much more gradually, did during World War

---

[43]T. Harry Rigby, "The Soviet Leadership: Towards a Self-Stabilizing Oligarchy?" *Soviet Studies* 22 (October 1970): 167–91. In this important article Rigby argued among other points that a condition of Brezhnev's choice as general secretary by the other members of the Politburo that dismissed Khrushchev in October 1964 was a promise by Brezhnev not to seek the post of chairman of the Council of Ministers, which both Stalin and Khrushchev had eventually taken. Although agreeing with Rigby that the Brezhnev Politburo constituted an "oligarchy" and also that it was not part of the Soviet elite but *the* elite (italics in text), Harry Gelman, in his book *The Brezhnev Politburo and the Decline of Detente*, asserts that Brezhnev actually "spent most of his years as party leader vainly attempting to gain personal control of the Council of Ministers. . . ." Gelman also believes that Rigby overestimated the domestic importance of the functions of the Soviet presidency and underestimated its significance in foreign policy. Gelman also asserts that Rigby overstated the "seriousness of any private commitment that Brezhnev and his colleagues may have made to allow the ventilation of policy differences at Central Committee plenums." Harry Gelman, *The Brezhnev Politburo and the Decline of Detente* (Ithaca, N.Y.: Cornell University Press, 1984), pp. 230–31, 60.

II. To be sure, unlike Stalin, Brezhnev did not claim for himself the title of generalissimo, which for a few years Stalin shared with Francisco Franco of Spain, Chiang Kai-shek, and the dictator of the Dominican Republic, Rafael Trujillo.[44]

There are major elements of continuity as well as discontinuity in Soviet politics under Stalin and under his successors. Clearly, both Stalin and his successors clung to certain basic principles in directing the political, social, and economic life of the USSR. John Hazard, the dean of Western students of Soviet law, stated in 1983 that the two most fundamental are ''that the people need leadership in the form of a militant, disciplined elite Communist Party, still structured as Lenin thought it must be and still ruling alone; and that productive property cannot be left in private ownership but must be owned and controlled by society as a whole, represented by the state.'' [45] Of course doctrines of such vast and vague import as the above must be interpreted, applied, and implemented in the form of policies, practices and institutions if they are to have meaning. One such practice, and a major point of continuity between Soviet politics under Stalin and also under his successors is the dominant role played by full Politburo members who are at the same time senior secretaries of the Central Committee. A combination of seniority as a full Politburo member and as a Central Committee secretary seems to be a winning one in the struggle to become top leader, or general secretary of the Central Committee. After Stalin died, some Western students of Soviet politics thought that Georgi Malenkov, because of his vast experience as probably Stalin's most powerful assistant at the top level of leadership would succeed Stalin as general secretary. Among other things Malenkov, along with Vyacheslav Molotov, Lavrenti Beria, Lazar Kaganovich and other top Soviet leaders, including Stalin himself, had been a member of the State Defense Committee set up in June 1941 to direct and coordinate the Soviet war effort against Nazi Germany. Khrushchev had not belonged to this very important body, nor for that matter had Andrei Zhdanov, Malenkov's main rival in the struggle for Stalin's favor that raged during and after World War II. Zhdanov's early death at

---

[44]See Aspaturian, ''Stalinist Legacy,'' p. 29 and footnote 74, p. 72.

[45]John Hazard, *Managing Change in the USSR* (Cambridge, England: Cambridge University Press, 1983), p. 171.

the end of August 1948 left Malenkov and Khrushchev ultimately as the two main contenders to succeed Stalin. Khrushchev's victory, to be sure, was undoubtedly due in large part to his absence from the Moscow scene during many of the years in which Stalin's "crimes" against good communists (as Khrushchev labeled them in his 1956 secret speech) occurred. Another contributing factor was Khrushchev's wide contacts among and skill in appealing to provincial party secretaries, to whom Malenkov was a remote, perhaps somewhat discredited figure. Khrushchev's victory, however, may also have been due to the fact that he became a full member of the Politburo in 1939. Khrushchev outranked Malenkov in seniority on the Politburo, of which the latter became a full member only in 1946. Malenkov, however, outranked Khrushchev on the Central Committee secretariat, a fact that may have contributed to his strong position.

It should be noted that Lavrenti Beria made a brief bid for power — with all the earmarks of a potential coup d'état — in the first 3 months after Stalin's death, but the majority of the Politburo members, led by Khrushchev, uniting against what they felt was a threat not only to their political careers but to their very lives, arrested and executed Beria.[46] It seems likely that the "institutionalized procedure" of selecting as top leader the person who at the time of his predecessor's death — or as in the case of Khrushchev in October 1964, deposition — was next-ranking party secretary after the leader "may also have determined the succession to Khrushchev."[47] As we know from all available sources of information, Yuri Andropov, although at the time of Brezhnev's death in November 1982 he had been serving as a member of the Secretariat only since the spring of 1982, had been a Secretariat member in 1962–1967 and a full Politburo member since 1973. He had far greater seniority than his chief rival and the apparent closest associate of Brezhnev, Konstantin Chernenko, who achieved full Politburo membership in 1978 and be-

---

[46]On the above facts and events, see John Löwenhardt, *The Soviet Politburo* (New York: St. Martin's Press, 1982), pp. 40–44, 140–41.

[47]According to Zhores A. Medvedev, in his biography of Andropov, Brezhnev succeeded Khrushchev as First Secretary because he had been de facto "second" secretary and was a compromise figure acceptable to the rest of the leadership. Zhores A. Medvedev, *Andropov* (New York: Penguin Books, 1984), p. 48.

came a Central Committee secretary for the first time in 1976.[48]
Chernenko, who ranked second to Andropov in seniority and was
by wide agreement inferior to him in ability and reportedly suffering from emphysema, succeeded Andropov as general secretary in February 1984. More rapidly than Andropov, he then
became chairman of the Presidium of the Supreme Soviet (in April
1984).

Within 5 hours of the official announcement of Chernenko's
death on March 10, 1985, the Central Committee voted, upon
Andrei Gromyko's nomination, to approve the selection of Mikhail Gorbachev as general secretary. Distinguished by his youth
from the rest of the Politburo, Gorbachev had been considered a
likely but by no means certain choice. Forecasts as to the probabilities of succession are fraught with uncertainty. Even in the
post-Stalin period, when Soviet politics has been so much more
routinized than it was under Stalin, Andrei Kirilenko, for example, failed to succeed Brezhnev, although he had for years been
regarded by informed U.S. officials and academic and journalistic
specialists on Soviet affairs as the most likely successor. Apparently he fell out of favor with Brezhnev. In any case he resigned
from the Politburo in November 1982 in apparent political ill
health.[49] Somewhat different was the case of the long-time elder
statesman and ideological specialist Mikhail Suslov. Suslov, who
became a member of the Secretariat in 1947 and served on the
Politburo in 1952–1953 and then continuously from 1955 until
his death in January 1982, apparently was content with his immense influence. This extended beyond the field of ideology to
propaganda, Soviet relations with foreign communist parties, and
perhaps also matters of political succession — he apparently
played a major role in the overthrow of Khrushchev in October
1964.

Orthodoxy, in the sense of continued adherence to such practices and doctrines as democratic centralism, the leading role of
the party, and, as we have seen, the tradition of rule in Russia

[48]Löwenhardt, *Politburo,* p. 113, makes a strong case for the widely held view
among Sovietologists that Brezhnev wanted Chernenko to be his successor as
party leader.
[49]See *Pravda,* November 23 1982, where the announcement of his resignation — "due to the condition of his health and by his personal request" — appears, together with a tribute from the newly elevated Yuri Andropov.

by party secretaries who have served both in provincial party organizations and at the Politburo/Secretariat level in Moscow, has characterized Soviet politics both under Stalin and in the much more bureaucratic-routinized and far less revolutionary-transformational regimes that have been in power since March 5, 1953. At the same time, the Soviet system, as led both by Lenin and Stalin and by Stalin's successors, has displayed impressive capacity for adaptation to new pressures and requirements. As Aspaturian points out, while the Soviet Politburo "appears to have changed remarkably little since 1939," nevertheless, "its role and functioning have undergone tremendous, even perhaps fundamental, transformations over the past four decades." What was in 1939 the decision-making organ of "a semideveloped pariah state," today "makes decisions for a mighty global power." He adds that as Soviet influence has grown and "as Soviet society has continued to develop and modernize, this has been accompanied by an expansion in the complexity and differentiation of Soviet decision-making processes and institutions." He concludes: "Thus, while the Soviet political system institutionally is still the house that Stalin built, much of the potential that existed in these institutions has been developed through the generation of new processes and procedures. And even greater potential for development still exists."[50]

Another very important difference between the Stalin and post-Stalin leadership consists in "the subordination of security to party organs and of the KGB leadership to the Politburo collectively." Another is "the revival, including a return to regular meetings, of party committees at all levels." These developments were parts of a process that has been called "Khrushchev's revitalization of the party," following the long period under Stalin when, as Khrushchev pointed out in one of his major speeches, "over 13 years elapsed between the Eighteenth and Nineteenth Party Congresses, years during which our party and our country had experienced so many important events."[51]

---

[50]Aspaturian, "Stalinist Legacy," pp. 66–68.

[51]Archie Brown, "The Power of the General Secretary," in T. H. Rigby, Archie Brown, Peter Reddaway, eds., *Authority, Power and Policy in the Soviet Union* (New York: St. Martin's Press, 1980), pp. 137, 139.

COMPARATIVE POST-STALIN LEADERSHIP: KHRUSHCHEV,
BREZHNEV, ANDROPOV, CHERNENKO, AND GORBACHEV

Khrushchev and Brezhnev. Let us begin this section with what we consider the reasonable proposition that all post-Stalin leaders have resembled one another in style and substance far more closely than they resembled Stalin. In addition to the disappearance of mass terror — though not of selective terror directed against dissidents — for the most part the transformational component of Stalin's rule, or as Barrington Moore called it, the "revolution from above" is a thing of the past. The rapid, forcible herding of millions of peasant farmers into party- and state-directed collective farms and the almost equally coercive process of forced-draft industrialization are now history, though their impact has left a permanent mark on Soviet life. To be sure, George Breslauer, in the only systematic comparative study of the leadership of Khrushchev and Brezhnev, sees a "transformational" component in Khrushchev's but not Brezhnev's policy repertoire. Breslauer asserts that beginning in 1953 Khrushchev had been "attempting to demonstrate that political transformation could be made consistent with political stability, and could be used as a substitute for radical budgetary allocation." He did not, however, combine such aspirations with demands for "labor discipline," which as Breslauer points out is a Soviet euphemism for hierarchical controls, let alone with use of large-scale terror, although this most contradictory of Soviet leaders "would simultaneously lead the witchhunt against 'parasites' and sanction widespread use of the death penalty for economic crimes."[52]

[52]George W. Breslauer, *Khrushchev and Brezhnev as Leaders: Building Authority in Soviet Politics* (London: Allen & Unwin, 1982), pp. 106–7. See also pp. 269–75, rejecting, at least in its simple version, the widespread view that Khrushchev was an egalitarian reformer and Brezhnev was an elitist conservative. In a more balanced appraisal, Breslauer recognizes that both men operated within a "post-Stalin consensus," "avoiding either a return to Stalinism or a breakthrough toward liberalism," and that in certain respects, such as in his "advocacy of a reduction of dogma in technical, social, economic and scientific fields . . . and the creation of a less pressured and more predictable environment for the politically conformist," "Brezhnev stood further from the Stalinist pole than did Khrushchev." Breslauer's view on the "post-Stalin consensus" perhaps resembles somewhat John Lowenhardt's assertion in his *Decision Making in Soviet Politics* (New York: St. Martin's Press, 1981), pp. 125–26, that, "as far as internal politics are concerned, since the late 1950s nonincremental decisions have vanished from the Soviet political scene."

Breslauer's book, certainly one of the most valuable studies of Soviet politics and policymaking in recent years, is a contribution also to theory and methodology. As his major technique of analysis, Breslauer opts for a sophisticated version of Kremlinology, based on qualitative content analysis of Khrushchev's and Brezhnev's published speeches and other official Soviet sources and supplemented by careful study of Western scholarly literature as the only reliable way to study what Breslauer calls in his preface, "some of the central issues of Soviet domestic politics" and "the grand issues of Soviet domestic policy."[53] The policy issues on which the study focuses and that are treated within an explicit context of "political succession" are "consumer satisfaction," "administrative reform," and "political participation." From time to time, aspects of Soviet foreign policy relevant to policymaking on the above issues receive attention, but overwhelmingly this is a book about Soviet domestic policy. It has been criticized for failing to deal in detail with foreign policy on the ground that "a truly convincing analysis" of "authority building by top Soviet leaders" cannot be achieved without taking much fuller account than Breslauer did of events such as the Cuban missile crisis of 1962 under Khrushchev's rule, or the events in Czechoslovakia in 1968 under Brezhnev's, to which "the dilution and virtual abandonment of the Kosygin economic reform" contributed.[54] We believe that in spite of, indeed partly because of, the limits that Breslauer imposed on his study, its merits vastly outweigh its defects. It is true that in it Soviet domestic policies are treated much more fully than are foreign affairs. Breslauer often links domestic policy to the context of world affairs, however. He devotes considerable attention, for example, to interaction between U.S.-Soviet relations, Soviet (and American) military budgets, and the overall Soviet budget. It is appropriate to note that the top policy priorities of both Khrushchev's and Brezhnev's leaderships were building Soviet military power and improving the performance of Soviet agriculture. The latter was regarded by both as the main avenue to increased consumer satisfaction. It is obvious from

[53]Breslauer, *Khrushchev and Brezhnev as Leaders,* pp. ix, 116. On p. 116 Breslauer also offers his definition of policy as dealing "usually with the basic direction of policy, not the tactical details." He also declines to deal with the implementation of policy, asserting that that "would require another volume."

[54]See Archie Brown's earlier-cited review article in *Times Literary Supplement,* 1 April 1983.

Breslauer's study and from other major studies that military preparedness was given higher priority than was agriculture, although Brezhnev, much more than Khrushchev, was willing to allocate increased budgetary resources to agriculture. It is also apparent that the Soviet arms buildup was conducted more successfully than was the agricultural effort.[55] Breslauer's study makes little use of the writings of Soviet dissidents and relatively little of works by recent Soviet émigrés.[56] Breslauer, however, does refer to Alexander Yanov, *Detente after Brezhnev.*[57]

In our opinion the most serious defect of *Khrushchev and Brezhnev as Leaders* is probably its relative neglect of the crucial significance of de-Stalinization under Khrushchev and its replacement under

[55]Besides Breslauer, see Thane Gustafson, *Reform in Soviet Politics* (Cambridge, England: Cambridge University Press, 1981); and D. Gale Johnson and Karen Brooks, *Prospects for Soviet Agriculture in the 1980s* (Bloomington: Indiana University Press, 1983).

[56]See Breslauer, *Khrushchev and Brezhnev as Leaders,* p. 20, where the author comments that dissident sources "will at some point be useful but that at present they raise difficulties of interpretation."

[57](Berkeley, Calif.: Institute of International Studies, 1977.) While agreeing that such sources afford problems for interpretation, we would point out that the stringent censorship and self-censorship to which Soviet publications are subjected make knowledge of certain very important events virtually unobtainable through official sources. No mention is made, for example, of what was probably the most important manifestation of labor unrest in Russia since the 1920s, the strike and supporting demonstrations by hundreds of people at the Novocherkassk Electric Locomotive Plant in June 1962, which were put down by armed forces with heavy loss of life. By far the fullest account of the Novocherkassk events is in Alexander Solzhenitsyn, *Gulag Archipelago III* (New York: Harper & Row, 1976), pp. 506–14. Solzhenitsyn calls Novocherkassk "a turning point in the modern history of Russia." He may be right. This event was perhaps the most important of several that stimulated Khrushchev and Brezhnev to adopt measures such as buying grain abroad and to avoid repeating Khrushchev's folly in 1962 of combining a sudden increase in food prices and lowering of wages, which apparently triggered the protest of the Novocherkassk workers. On the recent efforts of Aleksei Nikitin and his fellow Donetsk miners to assert their rights and the authorities' brutal treatment of Nikitin, see Kevin Klose, *Russia and the Russians* (New York: Norton, 1984), chs. 2 and 3. Undoubtedly Novocherkassk and many other manifestations of labor unrest spurred efforts by Khrushchev and his successors not only to nip in the bud any organized labor movement but also to assure at least an adequate supply of bread and a modest improvement in the masses' standard of living. At least until perhaps the late 1970s these efforts and other reformist measures were sufficiently successful to keep popular discontent at a manageable level. Their impact may have been increased by propaganda calculated to blame external forces, particularly the United States, for international tensions that, so Soviet leaders said, required sacrifices by the Soviet people in the interests of national security.

Brezhnev and his successors by the end of overt condemnation of Stalin, combined with semicovert re-Stalinization. Probably this can be partly accounted for by the fact that Breslauer's categories, including "participation," under which he tends to treat the above topics, do not cover them very easily. They are of such enormous importance, however, that Stephen Cohen could write with only partial exaggeration that the Stalin issue "remains the most tenacious and divisive issue in Soviet political life."[58] The amazing — by Soviet standards — degree of freedom of expression that Khrushchev during his more liberal periods accorded to such writers, artists, and editors as Alexander Solzhenitsyn (forcibly expelled from the USSR in February 1974), Ernst Neizvestny, and Alexander Tvardovsky and, most important of all, Khrushchev's decisive role in the rehabilitation of millions of victims of Stalin's repression tend to be obscured in Breslauer's study.[59]

Another less significant but not unimportant topic somewhat insufficiently treated in *Khrushchev and Brezhnev as Leaders* is that of the vast expansion under Khrushchev and substantial contraction under Brezhnev of what we call adult political socialization, treated by Breslauer as an aspect of participation.[60] Also there is no mention of the very important topic of non-Russian nationalism, manifestations of which were involved in such events as the purge under Khrushchev of party leaders in a number of non-

[58]Stephen F. Cohen, ed., *An End to Silence* (New York: Norton, 1982), p. 23.

[59]On the above questions, see, for example, Roy Medvedev's tribute to Khrushchev as the only man who could bring about the rehabilitation of nearly 20 million people, "many of them, posthumously, alas," in his *Khrushchev* (Garden City, N.Y.: Anchor Press, 1984), p. 260; and the informative, insightful account in Ernst Neizvestny, *Govorit Neizvestny* (Neizvestny Speaks) (Frankfurt: Posev, 1984), ch. 1.

The very important story of Tvardovsky's powerful influence under Khrushchev, of his loss under Brezhnev of the editorship of *Novy mir,* and of his status as alternative member of the CPSU Central Committee is also absent from this study. For details on the Tvardovsky story, see the works by Edith Frankel, *Novy mir,* and by Dina Spechler, *Permitted Dissent,* as well as, especially for some remarks on fundamental differences between Khrushchev's relative cultural-ideological tolerance and the tightening of boundaries that followed his downfall, Frederick Barghoorn, "Regime-Dissenter Relations after Khrushchev: Some Observations," in Susan Gross Solomon, ed., *Pluralism in the Soviet Union,* pp. 136–39.

[60]The subject is dealt with in a sentence on p. 262, supported by, inter alia, a reference to the important article by Ellen Mickiewicz, "Policy Applications of Public Opinion Research in the USSR," *Public Opinion Quarterly* (Winter 1972–1973): 566–78.

Russian republics and, among other occurrences, the successful protests in 1978 in Georgia, Armenia, and (more muted) Azerbaijan against planned elimination of the status as state languages of the local, non-Russian languages of these three republics.

Despite these and other omissions, Breslauer's book is a distinguished and illuminating contribution to Soviet studies. It ably argues the thesis that interest aggregation and policymaking are to an overwhelming degree the prerogative of the top echelons of Soviet leadership, especially of the Politburo and the Secretariat, but that, at least in the post-Stalin era, Soviet leaders must not only use the traditional tools of politics, such as patronage, party intervention in the economic and other spheres, and "pulling rank," but must also take care to "build authority." This, says Breslauer, is the process by which Soviet leaders "seek to legitimate their policy programs and demonstrate their competence or indispensability as leaders." Soviet leaders build authority by playing the roles of "problem solver" and "politician," the first by forging policy programs "that promise to further the goals of the post-Stalin era," the second by creating "a sense of national elan, so as to increase the political establishment's confidence in [their] leadership ability." There is conflict within the post-Stalin consensus between performance of new tasks, such as "increased consumer satisfaction; greater material incentives for the masses; expanded political participation by social activists and specialists" and "ongoing elitist features of the Soviet tradition," including "heavy-industrial and military priorities, party activism and pressure as spurs to labor productivity."

In the absence of mass terror, party leaders "have had to worry more" since Stalin "about how to increase their authority in order to maintain their grip on office" and to "maintain control over the "policy agenda." In the post-Stalin setting "the perception that a leader is incompetent and dispensable — indeed threatening — can become so widespread that it can undermine his hold on office."[61]

Obviously both Khrushchev and Brezhnev developed more

---

[61]Breslauer, *Khrushchev and Brezhnev as Leaders,* pp. 4–8. It is worth noting that Robert Tucker, in his *Stalin as Revolutionary,* ch. 8, persuasively argued that Stalin, before he became a dictator, pursued legitimacy by playing skillful factional politics.

successful strategies for gaining and being confirmed in the top leadership than did their rivals. Khrushchev did not achieve this position until the spring of 1957, 4 years after Stalin's death and almost 4 years after his chief rival, Georgi Malenkov, was constrained to relinquish the post of first secretary of the CPSU in favor of Khrushchev. Khrushchev's period of ascendancy began only after he successfully crushed (politically, not physically) what he called the "anti-party group," made up of former Stalin lieutenants. This period lasted only until 1960, when it gave way to a period of "frustration and reaction," ending on October 12, 1964, with Khrushchev's dismissal by unanimous vote of the party Presidium (to be renamed Politburo in 1966) from his posts as first secretary and chairman of the Council) of Ministers. The next day Leonid Brezhnev was elected first secretary of the CPSU and Aleksei Kosygin was chosen chairman of the Council of Ministers (or Premier). Apparently Khrushchev had been aware a year before his dismissal that Brezhnev was the man most likely to succeed him.[62]

Brezhnev enjoyed his period of ascendancy in 1968–1972, and he experienced frustration and resorted to policies of reaction in 1972–1975. His authority was challenged at the Twenty-fifth Party Congress in 1976.[63] Brezhnev, however, unlike Khrushchev in 1960–1964, was able to recoup his authority by such measures as forcing out of office Chairman of the Presidium of the Supreme Soviet Nikolai Podgorny, who was replaced by the Brezhnev loyalist Nikolai Tikhonov. He also "seized the initiative" (1) by adding new features "geared toward securing a quick improvement in consumer satisfaction; (2) by preempting issues previously associated with Aleksei Kosygin" (as Khrushchev had in 1953–1955 seized upon issues that his rival Malenkov had sought to exploit); and (3) by "altering his strategy as politician" and keeping potential rivals off balance. Breslauer, however, having credited Brezhnev's "new, more conservative program" introduced in 1967 with restoring his shaken authority, then suggests that he may have been saved by the death a few months before the

---

[62]The foregoing account is based on Roy Medvedev, *Khrushchev,* p. 236. The meeting, reports Medvedev, included Minister of Foreign Affairs Gromyko, Minister of Defense Malinovski, and several *obkom* secretaries.

[63]Breslauer, *Khrushchev and Brezhnev as Leaders,* pp. 11–13.

Twenty-sixth Congress of Premier Kosygin, who had for some time intermittently criticized Brezhnev's economic policies.[64]

Why was Khrushchev dismissed from office in 1964? Why was Brezhnev after some damage to his authority in the mid-1970s able to stage at best a partial recovery of his power and authority? No full and definitive answer to these questions is possible. Breslauer's analysis and comparison of Khrushchev's confrontationist strategy and Brezhnev's consensual one go far in providing answers, however. It certainly seems to be true that Khrushchev's policies and rhetoric eventually alarmed, antagonized, or incurred the contempt of virtually all sectors of not only the Soviet political elite but even the creative intelligentsia, many of whose members wearied of his addiction to panaceas and the lack of dignity exemplified by his shoe banging at the United Nations General Assembly session in September 1960. Perhaps, however, he left a deeper imprint on the memory of ordinary Soviet people than did the more skillful politician Brezhnev. According to one well-informed author, Lenin's tomb and that of the unknown soldier are visited ritualistically, and "[t]ributes appear almost daily on Stalin's grave beside the Kremlin wall; generally these come from Georgia. And in the Novodevichy cemetery, on nearly every day of the year, fresh bunches of flowers are laid beside the impressive tombstone of Nikita Sergeyevich Khrushchev."[65]

It is important to note that in his struggle for the succession against Malenkov, Khrushchev was careful not to challenge traditional Stalinist doctrines, such as the priority of heavy over light industry; Malenkov, by contrast, incurred political vulnerability by, for example, "rejecting the Stalinist notion that heavy industry should always grow faster than light industry."[66] Even Khrushchev's famous crash program for a quick and partial fix for the grain crisis, one of the legacies of Stalinism, was in the Stalin tradition of grandiose, party-administered projects. As Khrushchev's stature grew, that of Malenkov diminished, espe-

---

[64]Ibid., pp. 230–31. Breslauer here also mentions the ouster of Kirill Mazurov from the Politburo in 1978, the attainment by Brezhnev's crony Chernenko of full membership, and other personnel changes, as major improvements in Brezhnev's power position, quite apart from new policies he concurrently introduced in his role as "problem solver."

[65]Roy Medvedev, *Khrushchev,* p. 260.

[66]Breslauer, *Khrushchev and Brezhnev as Leaders,* p. 25.

cially after the Twentieth Party Congress in 1956. At it, Khrushchev, who had largely confined his economic policy efforts to agriculture, "felt strong enough to expand his role decisively into the industrial realm." Among other things, he demanded "that party officials study and master the economies of industrial and agricultural management." "Given the low level of economic literacy among the Stalinist generation of party officials, however, many managers, specialists, and central leaders could legitimately have wondered how greater authority for that generation of apparatchiki would improve economic performance." According to Breslauer, Khrushchev answered that question in his secret speech after the congress. It, he asserts, implied a new era "of *physical security* [italics in original] for Soviet officialdom as a whole . . . but of *political insecurity* for entrenched Stalinist administrators in the party, state and police apparatuses." He was thus charting a course quite at variance from that of his colleagues in the leadership "and was offering himself as the leader with both the vision and the *power* to combine limited reconciliation, institutional transformation, and a sense of national purpose."[67] In the meantime, Malenkov and his associates, although they were prepared to "come to peace with the populace," did not, in contrast to Khrushchev, see this as a process requiring new attitudes toward the peasantry and the rural intelligentsia, expanded participation in public life by the masses, or increased material incentives, even for party officials, to spur their productivity.[68] But while sponsoring a "populist," egalitarian program, Khrushchev was "attempting to maintain his personal absolutism . . . and demanded that all groups — officials, specialists, and masses alike — follow his dictates."[69] In his main report (as distinguished from the secret speech) at the Twentieth Congress, Khrushchev broadened his call for increased mass political participation to include "new forms of participation in the urban-production and urban-public sectors."[70] In his secret speech he exploded a bombshell, by denouncing Stalin's crimes and, as Breslauer says, legitimizing "a form of systemic criticism."

During his period of ascendancy (1957–1960), Khrushchev set

[67]Ibid., pp. 47–49.
[68]Ibid., pp. 52–55.
[69]Ibid., p. 57.
[70]Ibid., p. 59.

forth a program, mainly at the Twenty-first Party Congress (1959), for "the attainment of levels of abundance, productivity and political participation associated with the vision of communism outlined in the work of Marx and Lenin." As he had done throughout his leadership, Khrushchev promised abundance without presenting any convincing explanation as to where the capital to produce it was to come from.[71] Among other things, Khrushchev promised in the above report that by 1970 American levels of per capita output and consumer affluence were to be attained. As Breslauer points out in beginning his presentation of the post-Khrushchev majority consensus, comparison with the U.S. levels of consumption, with their potential for arousing or preserving unsettling popular expectations, disappeared shortly after Khrushchev's ouster.[72]

As Breslauer presents it, Khrushchev's policy package fell apart from the end of 1959 on, although the previously ebullient, self-confident first secretary did not become aware that his domestic program was faltering until late in 1960. Like other analysts, Breslauer finds much cause for puzzlement in Khrushchev's impetuous and contradictory behavior during his last years in office. "Agriculture continued to stagnate; the rate of growth of light industry slowed to a near halt; the rate of expansion of heavy industry also slowed down markedly. . . . His authority as a problem-solver and as politician eroded precipitously" and in October 1964 he "was unceremoniously removed from office and exiled to his summer cottage."[73] Much has been omitted here from Breslauer's tightly packed account of the development and failure of Khrushchev's authority-building efforts, and that account omits or treats in a very condensed fashion many events treated, or even emphasized, in other sources. Perhaps enough has been presented, however, to indicate that Khrushchev, though in many ways an effective leader (Breslauer seems to think that at its height his "power over policy" was greater than that of Brezhnev) was also to some extent guilty of the charges leveled against him in the official press after his fall. He was accused of having forced "hare-brained schemes" upon his country and, as in his insis-

---

[71]Ibid., pp. 60–61.
[72]Ibid., p. 138.
[73]Ibid., p. 83.

tence upon planting corn on the best Ukrainian winter wheat land, of failing to heed either the lessons of experience or the advice of men of science. Perhaps, however, the most important element in the chorus of belittlement, which did not mention its target by name, was the thesis set forth in the important Central Committee journal, *Partiinaia zhizn'* (Party Life), no. 20 (October 1964), that even top leaders must justify their eminence by deeds and must consult with and heed the opinions of their colleagues. This oligarchic doctrine was not used to restore Malenkov and his supporters to power or respectability, however, though in July 1984, Molotov was to be reinstated in his membership in the CPSU.[74]

Such judgments appear to have reflected a strong desire among Politburo members and the Soviet elite generally for stability, tranquillity, and decorum after the hectic years of Khrushchev's leadership. Decorum ''in the new post-Khrushchev atmosphere'' meant, among other things, that ''when Brezhnev's various leadership opponents took their quarrels with him outside the Politburo walls, they generally found they had assumed a grave political liability. . . . ''[75] There were, according to Gelman, gradations of power among Politburo members. At any given time there was a core group of Brezhnev and a few other Moscow-based members. Brezhnev overshadowed his colleagues not only as senior member of the Secretariat but also through his chairmanship of the Defense Council, ''the joint organ of the Politburo and the defense establishment for defense policy.''[76]

Before the state of affairs just referred to could be attained,

[74]See F. Barghoorn, ''Soviet Russia: Orthodozy and Adaptiveness,'' in Lucian Pye and Sidney Verba, eds., *Political Culture and Political Development* (Princeton, N.J.: Princeton University Press, 1965), pp. 510-11, on Molotov's reinstatement in the party, see *New York Times,* 6 July 1984.

[75]Harry Gelman, *The Brezhnev Politburo and the Decline of Detente* (Ithaca, N.Y.: Cornell University Press, 1984), pp. 52-53.

[76]Ibid., p. 57. Gelman asserts that ''the evidence suggests that through much of the Brezhnev era senior Secretariat members other than Brezhnev were *not* [italics in original] admitted to the Defense Council.'' Gelman believes, however, that the Secretariat was ''Brezhnev''s primary base.'' On the subject of participation in policymaking at levels lower than the Politburo and Secretariat, Gelman's views are similar to those of Breslauer. According to Gelman, though the Brezhnev leadership ''thoroughly accepted the need for an expandable circle of expertise both within and alongside the central party apparatus in order to enrich Politburo decisions, ''it was ''resistant to any suspected efforts from below to modify its prejudices, let alone to alter those policy postulates . . . which were deeply intertwined with personal power relationships.'' Ibid., p. 54.

Brezhnev had to consolidate his power, as had Khrushchev and Stalin before him. The first and also most serious political threat to Brezhnev was posed by Alexander Shelepin, an ambitious man who sought to parlay momentum generated by his role in the betrayal and overthrow of Khrushchev and his impressive array of party and state posts, including membership in the Secretariat, into attainment of top political leadership. Foiling this effort by building a broad anti-Shelepin coalition, Brezhnev, who though a conservative was distinctly middle-of-the-road in comparison with the extreme hard-liner Shelepin, was able to strip Shelepin of his offices and effect his political annihilation, a process that was completed only in 1975 with the removal of Shelepin from the Politburo.[77]

Breslauer and Gelman agree that both Khrushchev and Brezhnev promoted the interests of the Soviet military-industrial complex, though Brezhnev did so much more effectively and enthusiastically than Khrushchev.[78]

---

[77]Ibid., pp. 76–78. Unaccountably, Breslauer does not deal with this episode, probably the most important threat to Brezhnev's tenure. The other cases in which he brought about the ouster from the Politburo of opponents such as Podgorny, Mazurov, and Shelest as well as his long dispute with Kosygin over economic policy, do not seem to have involved any threat to the security of Brezhnev's leadership.

[78]Breslauer, *Khrushchev and Brezhnev as Leaders,* p. 137, says Khrushchev in his last years in power "came to threaten the interests of the military-industrial complex without even a compensatory increase in productivity and consumer satisfaction." Gelman points out that although Khrushchev generally encouraged strategic missile programs, "it is only a modest exaggeration to say that he took a dim view of everything but missiles, air defenses and submarines." In sharp contrast, Brezhnev and the majority of the Politburo opted, beginning with a decision in 1965, for what Gelman calls the "all-service" approach to military funding. The shift to a massive, across-the-board military buildup, with its necessarily adverse consequences for the policies of greater abundance for the consumer that were advocated by Nikolai Podgorny and, more cautiously and tactfully, by Aleksei Kosygin, doubtless had a good deal to do with the gradual accretion of Brezhnev's authority and the steady political decline of Kosygin and Podgorny. Undoubtedly these trends owed something to developments in Vietnam and Czechoslovakia and, perhaps more important, in Sino-Soviet relations. See Gelman, *Brezhnev Politburo,* pp. 79–82, and Breslauer, *Khrushchev and Brezhnev as Leaders,* pp. 141–42, on the March 1965 and May 1966 adoption of "expensive, long-term programs of investment in agricultural machinery, irrigation, chemicals, land reclamation" — a field, incidentally, that Brezhnev had studied as a young man. In the competition of heavy and light industry, defense, and other interests for funds, Breslauer says, "Defense was the winner, in a big way." But he also notes that "Khrushchev's successors felt the need to sacrifice long-term growth in heavy industrial capacity to the short-term requirements of agriculture and current consumption."

It is important to keep in mind that, whereas Khrushchev had relied heavily on exhortation and social pressure in promoting his agricultural program, Brezhnev, from 1965 until he proclaimed his food program in 1982, displayed a realistic willingness to support his agricultural goals by allocation of very large financial resources. One important aspect of Brezhnev's agricultural policy was increased prices for collective farmers for deliveries of produce to the state, which was in turn an aspect of the post-Khrushchev leadership's increased reliance on material incentives as an economic stimulus; however, "Brezhnev's approach to incentive policy included a good deal of political mobilization as well."[79] One aspect of his use of "civic pride and Soviet nationalism was integrating this to rally the populace."[80] Especially in 1967–1968, Aleksei Kosygin, Chairman of the Council of Ministers, challenged Brezhnev's agricultural program; his speeches indicated that he spoke for elite elements that would have preferred reduced budget allocations for heavy industry and more for light industry and consumer goods. Kosygin's challenge was unsuccessful, but he was to return to it later, especially at the Twenty-fifth Party Congress in 1976. There, alluding to Brezhnev's tendency to blame bad weather for the mediocre performance of Soviet agriculture despite vast capital allocations, Kosygin made bold to remark that "everything cannot be attributed solely to the weather."[81]

In the area of administrative reform, a "majority coalition" appears to have agreed on "the desirability or the necessity of reconciling the search for administrative efficiency with a posture of accommodation and consensus-building toward Soviet officialdom" and on other related perspectives.[82]

[79]Breslauer, *Khrushchev and Brezhnev as Leaders,* p. 145.

[80]Ibid., pp. 146–47.

[81]Ibid., pp. 150–52, 226. For lack of space we have treated with extreme brevity the important Kosygin-Brezhnev polemic, which touched on a wide range of subjects, including economic reform and the necessity, as Kosygin saw it, of granting greater autonomy than Brezhnev was wiling to consider to Soviet industrial managers.

[82]Ibid., pp. 153–56. The new attitude was summed up in a *Pravda* article on June 11, 1966, which observed that "in the area of production it is necessary to strive for a more harmonious combination of the interests of the state, on the one hand, and the interests of the enterprise." It failed, notes Breslauer, to resolve key questions such as the relative roles of "party activism and political intervention," and "the role of the market." These issues were never resolved by Brezhnev and his colleagues and seem unlikely to be resolved in the foreseeable future by any Soviet leadership.

During his period of ascendancy, Brezhnev sought to exercise leadership through the synthesis of domestic political interests, by, for example, demanding increased production of consumer goods and reassuring the administrators of heavy industry that this did not represent a threat to their prestige.[83] At the Twenty-fourth Congress of the CPSU in 1971, Brezhnev proclaimed that great economic and political benefits could be derived from expanding economic relations with both Eastern Europe and the United States, Western Europe, and Japan.[84] His policy of increasing Soviet military might continued, however, as did his effort to improve the efficiency and production of Soviet agriculture. As Breslauer points out, "Brezhnev's program was ambitious: it would require both good luck and political leadership to sustain the momentum." It assumed good weather and Western credits, capital, and technology. The conditions necessary for its fulfillment proved to be only partially available, however. Despite the signing of trade agreements with a number of Western countries and a record harvest in 1973 (following a disastrous drought in 1972), a "drought of unprecedented intensity in 1975" led to "the most disastrous agricultural situation in decades."[85] Brezhnev increased investments in agriculture, partly for a program of long-term investment in the hitherto neglected non-Black Earth zone of central Russia, expanded programs for development of Siberia, the Russian Far East, and continued to seek foreign help for Soviet domestic economic development in Western Europe, but he cut back plans for increased development of consumer goods. In the meantime, he called for "expanded mobilizational pressure" in the economy; in December 1972, for example, he began, for the first time, to praise "socialist competition," and in other ways he agitated for increased labor discipline as well as increased coercion against unproductive workers. At the same time, Brezhnev supplemented these traditional mobilizational measures with "anti-egalitarian" projects, such as the Shchekino experiment,

---

[83]Ibid., p. 181. Breslauer says that Brezhnev, realizing the traditional low status of consumer goods production, coined the term *"industrial* [italics in original] consumer goods."

[84]Ibid., p. 182. Breslauer confines himself to a few words in the chapter where he first touches on this point but deals with it at slightly greater length in ch. 12, "Frustration and Reaction."

[85]Ibid., pp. 201–2.

first introduced in 1967 at the Shchekino Chemical Combine, which "called for the release of redundant labor, and the distribution of wages saved among the remaining skilled workers."[86]

Breslauer argues that in his retreat and redefinition of 1972–1975, Brezhnev, like Khrushchev earlier, had presented an ambitious program, "only to have it frustrated by circumstances at home and abroad over which he had little control." Whereas, "Khrushchev's response had been to launch a counteroffensive against the most powerful interests in the system," Brezhnev was more accommodating and adaptive, mixing partial retreat with "an attempt to maintain his image as an innovative problem-solver by coopting issues and redefining their thrust."[87] The challenge to some of Brezhnev's policies, begun in 1972–1975, reached its climax at the Twenty-fifth Party Congress in 1976, which saw, among other things, Aleksei Kosygin's "emphasis on the urgency of the consumer-goods situation."[88] It also saw on Brezhnev's part "threatening rhetoric against the cadres, "not yet a call for a purge," but "lacking in the balance and spirit of conciliation" of earlier Brezhnev statements.[89]

Apparently Brezhnev experienced an authority crisis in the late 1970s, with which he coped by a combination of advocacy of new policies, such as rapid oil extraction, broader introduction of the Shchekino experiment and new forms of agricultural management, as well as borrowing the "Khrushchevian tactic" of encouraging "the masses to criticize their hierarchical superiors within the state bureaucracy." The motivation for these tactics may have been "a desire to turn mass disaffection against local cadres . . . and thereby increase the political leverage of the central party secretariat with the continuing threat of purge."[90] In 1981, at the Twenty-sixth Party Congress, Brezhnev focused on

[86]Ibid., p. 190, note 32, on Shchekino; pp. 203–12 on retreat from previously proclaimed expanded consumer goods program, on labor discipline, and on new projects in Siberia, including "construction of the hugely expensive Baikal-Amur railway through Siberia."

[87]Ibid., pp. 201–2.

[88]Ibid., p. 227. Because of considerations of space, we do not here attempt to present details of the Brezhnev-Kosygin clash at the Twenty-fifth Congress, which, Breslauer emphasizes, did not imply that Kosygin was challenging Brezhnev's position as supreme leader. Ibid., p. 229.

[89]Ibid., p. 225.

[90]Ibid., pp. 233–35.

energy policy, particularly, in his words, "the rapid increase in extraction of Siberian gas."[91] One important study deals with the "gas campaign" and the energy policy of which this still continuing effort was a central component, signs of the harmful impact of Brezhnev's failure to alleviate tendencies of Soviet economic administration to focus so intensely on main targets that "product quality and reliability, spare parts, or auxiliary outputs" such as roads or housing for workers, are neglected.[92]

With Kosygin gone, the tone of Brezhnev's address to the Twenty-sixth Congress lacked the defensiveness, "the language of accusation and urgency," contained in his address at the Twenty-fifth Congress in 1976.[93] In 1981, Brezhnev paid noticeably less attention to foreign economic relations, though he was still "leaving his options open" in this area.[94]

We end this examination of Brezhnev as policymaker with two conclusions. First, Brezhnev was "far more than a broker among interests." Examination of Brezhnev's "assertive policy advocacy and changes in policies adopted by the Politburo" indicates that he was seldom defeated "on questions of priority and the direction of policy."[95] Second, "despite the great differences between their authority-building strategies, both Khrushchev and Brezhnev worked within the bounds of 'post-Stalinism,' avoiding either a return to Stalinism or a breakthrough toward liberalism."[96] Given Breslauer's conception of liberalism as including such things as

[91]Ibid., p. 238.

[92]See Thane Gustafson, *The Soviet Gas Campaign* (Santa Monica, Calif.: Rand Corporation, 1983), p. 14. Gustafson also asserts that despite the advantages of Soviet centralized decision making, such as "concentration of information and integration of political purpose," it was working more and more poorly in the late Brezhnev era. See p. 12. Gustafson's findings in this important case tally with Breslauer's observations on "widespread bottlenecks" and Brezhnev's effort to deal with this problem in the late 1970s. See *Khrushchev and Brezhnev as Leaders*, pp. 232–34.

[93]Ibid., pp. 240–41.

[94]Ibid., p. 240.

[95]In chapter 15, Breslauer presents substantial evidence of "correlations" between Brezhnev's demands and Politburo responses. He admits that "Brezhnev was surely not as powerful in 1971 as Khrushchev was in 1959," and also implies that Khrushchev's power over policy in 1961–1963, when he was confronting the most powerful interests in the Soviet system, was more impressive than was Brezhnev's ability to carry out his policies, which on the whole accommodated those interests.

[96]Ibid., p. 269.

"consumerism," "social pluralism," and "marketization," this statement is correct. It seems to us, however, that it exaggerates somewhat the similarities between the two leaders.[97] In the Khrushchev section of his book, Breslauer devotes several pages to Khrushchev's efforts in the spring 1963–fall 1964 period to promote such policies as "cuts in the defense budget to finance programs geared toward raising consumption" — something Brezhnev never did — "proposals for technocratic reform or decentralization of the economy," and "advocacy of formal accountability to the consuming masses on the part of enterprise managers." In connection with this last policy, Breslauer notes that "thus an element of consumer sovereignty had entered into Khrushchev's public statements." Perhaps most remarkable of all was Khrushchev's embracing the "link" (*zveno*) system in Soviet collective farm agriculture, which in contrast to the traditional brigade system, encourages "group efforts to find the most rational and productive means of working the land."[98]

On the whole, however, we accept Breslauer's view that Khrushchev failed to develop a coherent synthesis of new policies to deal with his authority crisis of 1961–1964, and in particular that Khrushchev apparently was unable to appreciate the logical contradiction between his simultaneous advocacy of policies promising increased autonomy and his continued reliance on intervention from the political center. Still, the changes in Khrushchev's apparent goals in his last 3 years in power were so great as to justify speculation about how he might have reformed the

---

[97]Breslauer in Table 1.1, p. 6, compares three Soviet "regime types:" "Stalinist," "Post-Stalinist," and "Liberal-Democratic."

[98]Ibid., pp. 95–101. On p. 101, Breslauer notes that though experiments with the link system had "produced phenomenal results," its use of far fewer workers than the brigade system "would threaten the sense of job security that Soviet leaders assured the masses is a distinguishing virtue of socialism." In addition, "producing far greater quantities of goods, and making the pay of remaining workers a reflection of those quantities," would increase inequality in the countryside. Finally, "giving autonomy to on-farm teams to run their fields as they see fit would diminish the interventionist prerogatives of local and central planners," but Breslauer points out that for Khrushchev "achievement was now more important than equality." See p. 103. Gelman, *Brezhnev Politburo,* pp. 239–40, says that the hostility that Brezhnev and others showed toward the link was "primarily political, not economic, and centered on their fear of loosening political controls over the countryside and their horror of tampering with the legacy of Stalin's collectivization."

Soviet system if he had retained that power. Probably, as events seemed to indicate, he could not have done so, but perhaps Breslauer is not sufficiently guided by the evidence in his own work of Khrushchev's radical reformist inclinations. If a leader with Khrushchev's values and with greater political skill and youth came to power, perhaps the outcome would be different. In his final chapter, Breslauer recapitulates the major themes in his study, such as the commonality of "the principles of party activism and pressure" in the Khrushchev and Brezhnev leaderships, offset to some degree, however, by "a persistent reform impulse" that has suffered "attenuation" over the course of the last 20 years.[99] According to Breslauer, "the strength . . . of conservatism . . . is easily explained as a product of the institutional and political legacy of Stalinism." The reform impulse persists because "conservative political constituencies are cross-pressured" by such factors as consensus in the Soviet political elite "since the disgrace of Molotov," commitment "to the post-Stalin goals of increasing consumer satisfaction and expanding political participation," fear of "popular responses to continued food shortages," and recognition "in the military-industrial complex" that "improvements in the standard of living are a prerequisite for making labor incentives effective as spurs to productivity."[100] In a brief speculative but not uninteresting section on "the international context," the author sees the possibility that it "may well have contributed to both the timing and the content of changes in domestic policy."[101]

Breslauer's concluding chapter, summarized here, is, a salutary offset to discussions of Soviet political problems that seem to suggest that the USSR faces imminent instability. It does, however, by stressing the durability and stability of the "post-Stalin consensus," perhaps somewhat unwarrantedly ignore the possibility that, if reform, especially in economic administration, is not more successful than it was under Khrushchev and Brezhnev, the future of the Soviet political system may be stormier than this remarkable study seems to envisage.

[99]Ibid., pp. 279–84.

[100]Ibid., pp. 284, 289.

[101]Ibid., pp. 290–92. Of four factors Breslauer considers relevant, perhaps the most intriguing is "the possibility that attempts to influence U.S. presidential elections . . . may have a major impact on the timing and content of Soviet domestic propaganda."

Brezhnev's Successors: Yuri Andropov, Konstantin Chernenko, and Mikhail Gorbachev. . Yuri Andropov held the post of general secretary of the CPSU from November 1982 until February 1984. Two questions about him are of great interest. How did he rise to the pinnacle of power in the USSR? What did he accomplish during his brief tenure in authority? An obvious but not fully satisfactory answer to the first question is that he was picked by his Politburo colleagues as the most competent and suitable candidate for the job. This answer is too simple, however. Like all top Soviet leaders, Andropov had to fight for his leadership post, and perhaps like all or most of them, he was aided by chance. It seems almost certain that the death of Mikhail Suslov, the most senior secretary of the Central Committee after Brezhnev (having first achieved this rank in 1947), helped pave the way for Andropov's meteoric rise in 1982 by creating a vacancy in the party Secretariat into which Andropov moved.[102]

---

[102]This point is stressed in William Odom, "Choice and Change in Soviet Politics," in Erik Hoffmann and Robbin Laird, eds., *The Soviet Polity in the Modern Era* (New York: Aldine, 1984), pp. 915–42, at pp. 915–20. Reprinted from *Problems of Communism* 32, no. 3 (May–June 1983): 1–21. Odom predicted that because an organizational structure existed that was capable of easily co-opting new members and that was motivated to continue to perform the task of "organizing society for military-command affairs," even in the event of "a series of deaths among Politburo members," a "break-up of the central policy-making system" was unlikely. The smoothness of the choice of Chernenko as Andropov's successor and the even greater rapidity with which Gorbachev was selected to succeed Chernenko confirmed the wisdom of Odom's prediction. Of course Odom's hypothesis was not tested as it would have been if such deaths had occurred during Andropov's 15 months of leadership. Odom also regarded other factors as key cards in Andropov's hand: his experience as head of the KGB, which gave him vast knowledge of the Soviet economy and "experience with the way the economic bureaucrats and factory managers cheat the system," and his experience and the contacts he made as a member of the Defense Council. The treatment of Andropov's rise in Gelman, *Brezhnev Politburo,* pp. 174–85, is compatible with Odom's account. On the other hand, Michael Voslensky, in *Die Nomenklatura* (Vienna: Molden, 1984), pp. 504–12, like a number of other authors, argues (1) that there was a struggle between Andropov, supported by Dmitri Ustinov, and Chernenko, favored by Brezhnev; and (2) that an indispensable role in Andropov's victory was played by a KGB campaign that undermined Brezhnev's authority by leaking information to Soviet and Western sources about intimate links between Brezhnev's daughter Galina and individuals with unsavory reputations for corruption. See also Gelman, *Brezhnev Politburo,* p. 182, asserting that Suslov's death, by "removing the primary guardian of Politburo decorum," "exposed Brezhnev to multiple indirect attacks that focused on the General Secretary's toleration and protection of corruption in the Soviet aristocracy," and seem "to have been engineered primarily by Andropov."

What did Andropov accomplish? For one thing, he added impetus to the trend already strong in the later years of Brezhnev's leadership of increasing power and influence for the KGB. Dissidents were if anything treated even more harshly under Andropov than under Brezhnev; the macabre episode of cutting off all communication between Andrei Sakharov and the outside world, beginning in June 1984, indicated that Andropov was further accentuating this area of KGB activity. Perhaps the single most important event indicating increased KGB power under Andropov was Vitali Fedorchuk's replacement, in early 1983, of Nikolai Shchelokov, a Brezhnev favorite, as Minister of the Interior (MVD). Shchelokov was one of a number of Brezhnev appointees who were swept up in Andropov's campaign for tightening civic discipline and punishing corruption. Fedorchuk, who had briefly replaced Andropov as head of the KGB when Andropov rejoined the CPSU Secretariat in the spring of 1982, was assigned the mission of cleansing the Soviet "militia," or ordinary police, of slackness and corruption. (As a national, centralized force, the militia were in charge of Soviet prisons and labor camps, among other activities.[103])

In fulfilling his major goal of improving the performance of the Soviet economy, Andropov achieved modest success. Overall, the economy grew in 1983 at a rate of about 3.2 percent — a sizable increase over the annual average growth of 1.6 percent for the period 1979–1982, though still below the 3.7 percent rate recorded through most of the 1970s. This spurt was due in large measure to a substantial improvement in the performance of agriculture, production in which had actually fallen in the dismal 1979–1982 period.[104] Higher economic growth reflected Andropov's demanding policies. In particular, the economy achieved some success in breaking the bottlenecks in transportation and in materials supply that had grown increasingly severe in the late 1970s and early 1980s. Of greater importance was a turnaround in the decline of productivity, evidently in part a product of Andropov's

---

[103]See John Burns, "Under Andropov Policeman's Lot Isn't Happy One," *New York Times,* 14 August 1983, and Amy Knight, "The Powers of the Soviet KGB," in Hoffman and Laird, eds., *Soviet Polity,* pp. 311–30, esp. 326–27.

[104]See Robert Gates, "Statement," Subcommittee on International Trade, Finance, and Security Economics of the Joint Economic Committee, U.S. Congress (21 November 1984), p. 2.

discipline campaign.[105] Economic performance in 1984, however, was not so favorable as in 1983, and it remains to be seen whether Andropov's policies produced no more than a short-lived and anomalous upturn in the secular decline of the economy or whether a period of modest but extended improvement is beginning.[106]

One leading British Sovietologist has offered a rather positive assessment of Andropov's overall performance, considering that "as Soviet officialdom acknowledged only after his death," Andropov was being treated by dialysis "from as early as February 1983." First Andropov succeeded in making substantial changes in personnel. When he died, "one quarter of the voting members of the Politburo, over a sixth of the top leadership team . . . over a third of the heads of departments of the Central Committee and over a fifth of the regional party secretaries were people who had not been in these posts at the time of Brezhnev's death." In addition, he notes, Andropov placed "greater emphasis on professional competence and less on long-standing acquaintanceship" and also selected "significantly younger men" than had Brezhnev. Moreover, he made other changes, such as permitting Mikhail Gorbachev "to introduce a significant agricultural reform (giving greater autonomy to groups of farmers) which he had not been able to push through under Brezhnev."[107]

Andropov's legacy may be significant in three important respects. First, though he failed to fulfill his apparent aspiration of "handling power over to the next generation of leaders," under his leadership "Mikhail Gorbachev and other younger leaders" were advanced to key positions, assuring them of a major role in the regime headed since February 14, 1984 by Brezh-

[105]Ibid., p. 23.

[106]For another relatively positive appraisal of economic performance under Andropov, see Marshall I. Goldman, prepared statement, *Political Economy of the Soviet Union* (Washington, D.C.: U.S. Government Printing Office, 1984), pp. 22–43. Also see Leonard Schapiro, "The Policeman's New Lot," *Times Literary Supplement*, 8 July 1983, dismissing Andropov's conception of economic reform as "a policeman's idea of reform." On the other hand, Fyodor I. Kushnirsky, "The Limits of Soviet Economic Reform," *Problems of Communism* 33, no. 4 (July-August 1984): 33–43, took a more positive view of the limited and experimental reforms enacted by Andropov in the summer of 1983, though arguing that even if they met their immediate goals, they were unlikely to achieve any long-run improvement in industrial productivity.

[107]Archie Brown, "Brief Authority," *Times Literary Supplement*, 6 July 1984.

nev's crony Konstantin Chernenko.[108] Second, under Andropov the issue of economic reform and the improvement of functioning of the economic mechanism was posed more forcefully than it had been for a number of years. Andropov took a harshly realistic look at the Soviet economic situation and sternly and insistently, even threateningly, called for improvement. He rejected the blandness and complacency of the late Brezhnev era. In an important article published under his name in the theoretical journal of the CPSU in early 1983, he wrote, among other things, that though "our concerns are focused on the effectiveness of production, of the economy in general," in the area of the practical solution of this problem, "matters are not moving as successfully as necessary."[109] Third, and this may have been most important, Andropov — partly perhaps because he had served longer as head of the KGB than anyone else — was able to project the image of a man who meant business, one who was impatient both with slackness and drunkenness among workers and with laziness and corruption among officials and executives.

The Politburo member who perhaps benefited most from Andropov's brief tenure was Mikhail Gorbachev (born March 2, 1931), who emerged as the effective head of the party during Chernenko's 13 month tenure as CPSU general secretary. Gorbachev had reportedly enjoyed Mikhail Suslov's patronage, which was responsible for his promotion to the position of Central Committee secretary in charge of agriculture in 1978, when Gorbachev was 47.[110] Under Andropov his power expanded. He gained general authority over economic matters, played a part in foreign affairs through a trip to Canada in May 1983, and assisted Andropov in carrying out the wide-reaching series of personnel changes in the Central Committee secretariat and among regional party secretaries. Particularly during the latter half of 1983, with

---

[108]See Marc Zlotnik, "Chernenko Succeeds," *Problems of Communism* 33, no. 2 (March–April 1984): 17–31, quotations on p. 17.

[109]Yuri Andropov, "Uchenie Karla Marksa i nekotorye voprosy sotsialisticheskogo stroitel'stva v SSSR" (The Teaching of Karl Marx and Some Problems of Building Socialism) in Andropov, *Izbrannye rechi i stati* (Selected Speeches and Articles) (Moscow: Izdatel'stvo politicheskoi literatury, 1983); reprinted from *Kommunist,* no. 3 (1983).

[110]See Serge Schmemann, "The Emergence of Gorbachev," *New York Times Magazine,* 3 March 1985, pp. 55–56.

Andropov critically ill, Gorbachev's position as the party secretary overseeing the economy and, probably, cadres gave him a powerful position from which to advance to the pinnacle.

In view of these facts, some observers expected that he would be named general secretary upon Andropov's death on February 9, 1984, but Konstantin Chernenko was named instead. Possibly Gorbachev's relative youth prevented his selection. Born in 1931, he was almost 5 years younger than the next youngest full member of the Andropov Politburo, Vitali Vorotnikov, and over 15 years younger than the average age of the remaining members. Alternatively, there might have been a rivalry between him and one or more other Politburo members, such as Grigori Romanov (born in 1923 and brought by Andropov to Moscow as a Central Committee secretary) that prevented his immediate selection. In any case, his fortunes generally prospered during the Chernenko interlude despite occasional odd signs of setbacks in his standing. One of the stranger of the latter signals occurred when a Central Committee plenum was held in October, 1984, that focused on agriculture. Despite Gorbachev's conspicuous association with agricultural policy, he did not address the plenum; instead the main report was delivered by the venerable chairman of the Council of Ministers, Nikolai Tikhonov (replaced in September 1985 by Nikolai Ryzhkev). Its content dealt primarily with the need for further expansion of the capital-intensive land reclamation program rather than with the organizational approach, relying on small independent work brigades and strengthening local agro-industrial administration, which was reputed to be Gorbachev's policy emphasis. If Gorbachev's status slipped in the fall, however, it clearly recovered by year's end. In December he delivered the main address to a conference of ideological officials, suggesting that he had assumed responsibility for this sphere; in the same month he made his highly publicized trip to Great Britain, meeting with Prime Minister Margaret Thatcher and members of Parliament to attack President Reagan's strategic defense program. His relaxed, confident air, his apparent vitality and intelligence, and his pragmatic style greatly impressed Westerners.

The extent of his power within the Soviet leadership was pointedly described in a remarkable speech by Foreign Minister Andrei Gromyko to the Central Committee, nominating Gorbachev for the post of general secretary. The speech was not published in the

Soviet press but appeared the following week in pamphlet form. In it, Gromyko informed the Central Committee that during Chernenko's illness, Gorbachev chaired meetings of the Politburo and was in charge of the party Secretariat, and, "without any exaggeration, he showed himself to be brilliant." The plea by Gromyko for unity made it clear that there were strong reservations about Gorbachev's reliability in some sections of the leadership, which Gromyko sought to counter by the unusual tactic of laying his own authority on the line for Gorbachev. Gorbachev quickly grasped the essential tasks in foreign policy: "Perhaps this is clearer for me than for some other comrades because of my long service," commented Gromyko. Gromyko called Gorbachev a man of principle and strong conviction and added, "I can personally vouch for this." Against those fearing that Gorbachev would be soft on defense, Gromyko offered the assurance that Gorbachev always stood up for the "holy of holies for us all, that is, fighting for peace and maintaining our defenses at the necessary level."[111] From the speed with which Gorbachev was named general secretary after the announcement of Chernenko's death, it seemed clear that the decision had been made beforehand, evidently with Gromyko playing a key role in arranging the succession.

INTEREST ARTICULATION AND AGGREGATION:
GROUPS AND TENDENCIES

Beginning in the 1950s and 1960s, some Western students of Soviet politics and even a few scholars in communist countries took notice of the existence of interest groups and other actors below the most exalted levels of the Soviet system, capable of influencing, or at least attempting to influence, policymaking. Gordon Skilling, by far the most influential proponent and disseminator of the interest group approach to Soviet and East

[111]See Charles Bremner, "Gromyko Speech Hints at Party Qualms over Gorbachev," Reuters News Service, 18 March 1985; Andrew Rosenthal, "Gromyko Speech Confirms Gorbachev's Top Role under Chernenko," Associated Press, 18 March 1985; and *New York Times*, 19 March 1985. It might be added that, again in evident response to the fear that he would cut military spending in his drive for economic modernization, Gorbachev confirmed in his acceptance speech that "our glorious armed forces will have, in future as well, everything necessary" to be able to deliver a crushing retaliatory blow upon any aggressor. *New York Times*, 12 March 1985, p. 6.

European politics, defined a "political interest group" as an "aggregate of persons who possess certain common characteristics and share certain attitudes on public issues and make definite claims on those in authority." He broke down the category of interest groups into "occupational" and "opinion" groups. The former, he asserted, included: (a) "intellectual" groups, such as writers, natural scientists and others, engaged in research or creative work, and (b) "official" or "bureaucratic" groups with "key positions in the power structure," such as party apparatchiki, state bureaucrats, managers, police officials, and the military. He recognized that within occupational groups it might be possible to identify "opinion groups" such as "liberal writers" sharing a viewpoint "usually in sharp conflict with that held by other members of the same occupation."[112]

It should be emphasized that the two editors and all the contributors to *Interest Groups in Soviet Politics* took pains to point out that within the groups analyzed in the book they found conflicts of interest. Thus Jerry Hough reported that in the CPSU apparatus, the "potential cleavages of greatest interest are those associated with the differentiated structure" of the apparatus.[113] Specifically, he identified differences between officials working in Moscow and those in the oblast committees "scattered across the country," as well as among those specializing either in Moscow or in the field on industrial, agricultural, or ideological matters. He found much evidence of support by local party organizations for the efforts of local economic administrators to obtain increases in funds from superiors in Moscow.[114] Hough also reported evidence of competition for funds among specialized officials of oblast and republic party organizations; officials concerned with agriculture, for example, might vie with those who focused on

[112]See H. Gordon Skilling, "Groups in Soviet Politics: Some Hypotheses," in H. Gordon Skilling and Franklyn Griffiths, eds., *Interest Groups in Soviet Politics* (Princeton, N.J.: Princeton University Press, 1971), pp. 19–46, at 24–25. Skilling indicates that the above definitions were formulated on the basis of the findings contained in the case studies that occupy most of the volume. Reprinted as the first chapter of the Skilling-Griffiths volume is a shortened version of Skilling's pathbreaking article, "Interest Groups and Communist Politics: An Introduction." The volume also contains a concluding article by Skilling, and Franklyn Griffiths' article, "A Tendency Analysis of Soviet Policymaking," pp. 335–78.

[113]Jerry F. Hough, "The Party *Apparatchiki*," in Ibid., pp. 47–92, at p. 52.

[114]Ibid., pp. 60–71.

ideological questions. Data on such competition at the Moscow level was, Hough indicated, virtually unavailable.[115] In this connection, Hough found that party and state officials working in the same special field are likely to cooperate with one another against party and state officials specializing in a different field. Though emphasizing highly competitive relations among different kinds of apparatchiki, Hough also acknowledged that "one would certainly expect the overwhelming majority to take for granted the wisdom" of central features of the Soviet system such as government ownership and planning of industry.[116] He ended on a skeptical note, asserting that only after a great deal of further research has been done will it be possible to answer the crucial question about interest groups in any country, namely "to what extent do they serve as channels through which all significant interests in society can be equitably represented in the political process?"[117] Later, however, Hough made statements indicating a very positive appraisal of the interest group approach. He averred, for example, that the ministries and other Soviet institutions "certainly are interest groups by the classical definition of such groups. . . ."[118]

Hough's contribution on the party apparatus to the Skilling-Griffiths symposium differed from those of the ohter contributors, both in the tentativeness of its findings and in its emphasis on the differences of perspective among the subgroups in the group he focused on. The others added fewer qualifications to their conclusions and found that "their" groups, or — and this is a crucially important distinction — a minority of their members could indeed be correctly characterized as interest groups. The authors of chapters on groups whose members were government officials, however (Roman Kolkowicz on the military, John Hardt and Theodore Frankel on industrial managers, Frederick Barghoorn on the security police) tended to attribute to their group a rather

---

[115]Ibid., p. 77.

[116]Ibid., pp. 69–71.

[117]Ibid., p. 91.

[118]Quoted by Skilling in "Interest Groups and Communist Politics Revisited," *World Politics* 36, no. 1 (October 1983): 1–27, at p. 3. This article, together with those by Skilling and Griffiths in the 1971 volume, provides a virtually complete bibliography of the available literature on interest groups in the USSR and on related topics.

high degree of solidarity in action and uniformity of perspective, goals, and values.[119]

Perhaps in part because their authors' tasks, though not easy, were less difficult than those of analysts confronted by such gigantic organizations as the party apparatus and the military, the essays on the more intellectual groups (writers, by Ernest Simmons; jurists, by Donald Barry and Harold Berman; and economists, by Richard Judy) found much sharper and clearer differences of characteristics, values, and demands between the more conservative and conformist and the liberal and reformist members of the groups that they studied. Judy, analyzing contributions by economists to the "debate of 1962–1965" on the role of profitability in the Soviet economy — opened by Khrushchev, significantly — found a "clustering of conservative opinion," and "clusterings of liberal opinion."[120] In his concluding speculations about the future, Judy asserted, among other things, that "the positions of any Soviet economist can be predicted with considerable accuracy if information is available on his age, his organization of primary affiliation and his degree of mathematical proficiency. Groups defined by these three characteristics engage in energetic struggle for influence with the top Soviet leadership." He foresaw continued penetration of Soviet economic thought by "the concept of optimality" and perhaps eventually "serious consideration of market socialism."[121]

Although the no-longer-young liberal-reformist mathematical economists have obviously so far been unable to exert much influence on Soviet policy, striving for fundamental economic reform persists. One of the most significant indications of this persistence was the critique by Tatiana Zaslavskaya of the obsolete

[119]Nevertheless, Hardt and Frankel suggested that the post-Stalin effort to create a new, less engineering-oriented and more entrepreneurially sophisticated manager type "ranges some professionals and party generalists . . . against a similar grouping on the other side." Skilling and Griffiths, eds., *Interest Groups,* p. 208.

[120]Ibid., pp. 236–40.

[121]Ibid., pp. 250–51. Judy conditioned his prediction regarding market socialism on the failure of mathematical methods and computers to produce optimal plans and prices. His speculations take on added interest in the light of Thane Gustafson's judgment, in *Reform in Soviet Politics,* p. 6, that "computerized management and planning . . . have led to little so far except expensive experiments and considerable disillusionment."

nature of the Soviet economic system in the Andropov era.[122] In her "Memorandum," Zaslavskaya observed that the "more qualified, energetic and active" members of enterprise administration as well as ordinary worker and engineering personnel groups would benefit most by fundamental structural and functional reform of the economy. In a comment on the memorandum appearing in the journal *Russia,* economist Igor Birman asserted that Zaslavskaya, who although she is a member of the economics division of the Novosibirsk branch of the USSR Academy of Sciences, is by profession a sociologist, was "the first in Soviet literature to speak of the various interests of different social groups," and thus recognizes that "contradictions of interest" among these groups are inevitable. Among Birman's numerous interesting comments, perhaps the most important is his opinion that the main reason for the failure of the Soviet leaders to introduce fundamental economic reforms is the fact, as he sees it, that "immediately after the reforms the situation will get even worse."[123]

John Löwenhardt's *Decision Making in Soviet Politics* is an important addition to the literature on groups as actors in Soviet politics (as well as on the role of "policy coalitions, institutions, and individuals") and also on categories such as issues, decisions, policy, agendas, and agenda building, and on the concept of influence. Lowenhardt devotes the first of his four chapters to criticism of other students of group influence in Soviet politics and to constructing a framework for what he hopes will be better, more systematic and "cumulative" research. His emphasis is on "what the Soviet citizen can do *within* [italics in original] the 'proper' channels, not with dissent." Borrowing from recent American theory on "agenda building," Lowenhardt recommends that Sovietologists dig deep into the early phases of the decision-making process, on pain of getting "an incomplete and inaccurate picture."[124] Having defined an issue as "a conflict," Lowenhardt turns to the concepts "public agenda" — "all issues that have been printed in publications which have been approved by the

[122]See pp. 102–3.

[123]See Igor Birman, "On Tatiana Zaslavskaya's Paper," *Russia,* no. 9 (1984): 43–50, at 46 and 48.

[124]John Lowenhardt, *Decision Making in Soviet Politics* (New York: St. Martin's Press, 1981), pp. 16–17.

censor'' — and formal agenda — ''the list of items which decision makers have formally accepted for discussion.''[125] There are, Löwenhardt avers, several modes of agenda building in the Soviet Union. There is, for example, the ''mobilization model,'' in which ''issues are placed on the formal agenda by decision makers and are soon expanded to the public agenda'' in order to generate public support. This technique was employed by Khrushchev in 1958 when he started his campaign to introduce ''production education.'' There are also the ''inside initiative model'' and the ''outside initiative model.''[126] Although there is not room to explain Löwenhardt's methodological framework thoroughly, we consider it necessary to say something about his discussion of the concept of influence. Löwenhardt interprets Robert Dahl's definition of ''manifest or actual influence'' as implying that the investigator of influence relationships ''has to show that the influencing actor has induced the other actor to act in a way that he would not otherwise, in the absence of the influence effort, have acted.''[127] It is very difficult, he admits, to demonstrate manifest influence reliably, but the attempt to apply this narrow definition of influence pays off because the investigator is forced to postpone conclusions until he has exhausted all the available evidence. In particular he will not be satisfied ''that the probability of a given outcome has been changed by the expression of a few demands in the press.''[128]

Löwenhardt applies the foregoing and other definitions, concepts, and caveats to the following ten cases, or as he calls them, issues, of decision making in the USSR:

1. Khrushchev's virgin lands campaign, 1953–54
2. The Sovnarkhozy (Regional Economic Councils) reform of 1957

[125]Ibid., pp. 9, 16–22. On p. 22, Löwenhardt agrees with Philip Stewart's ''hypothesis'' that interest groups will have little influence if the top leadership initiates the discussion of an issue but that ''societal groupings can exert influence over top policy makers if they initiate a discussion before the latter do.''

[126]Ibid., pp. 30–31. Löwenhardt borrows the above terms from Roger Cobb, Jennie Keith-Ross, and Marc Ross, ''Agenda Building as a Comparative Political Process,'' *American Political Science Review* 1 (1976): 126–38. One of Löwenhardt's interesting assertions is that Soviet decision makers use censorship to keep off the public agenda issues that ''could easily create an explosive situation.''

[127]Ibid., pp. 112–13.

[128]Ibid., p. 186.

3. Abolition of the machine-tractor stations, 1951–1958
4. Family law reform, 1954–1968
5. Introduction of governmental tort liability, 1956–1961
6. Antiparasite legislation, 1956–1965
7. Reform of primary and secondary education, 1952–1959
8. Opposing pollution of Lake Baikal, 1958–1978
9. Jewish emigration from the Soviet Union, 1967–1971
10. Reorganization of the Soviet Academy of Sciencies, 1954–1961[129]

Unlike the Skilling and Griffiths book, Löwenhardt's study does not consist of new research. Instead, Löwenhardt, in chapter 2, summarizes and reinterprets, using his own conceptual framework, already existing studies by Western scholars. In chapter 3, "Group Influence on Soviet Decision Making," he asks and attempts to answer a series of fundamental questions, such as what regularities can be established on the basis of the data in chapter 2 and what generalizations can be formulated on the role of individuals and groups. In chapter 4 the author presents his own study, "The Reorganization of the USSR Academy of Sciences, 1954–1961," and in chapter 5 he offers a few pages of conclusions.

Löwenhardt's book, especially chapters 3 and 5, is extraordinarily difficult to summarize. Its perspectives change as the author shifts from summarizing the results of other scholars' research to presenting his own views; he tends frequently to introduce concepts previously unmentioned and to alter his interpretations of events on which he has previously presented, apparently, his final opinion. This difficulty of summarization doubtless is a consequence of the methodological richness of the study. In any case, it forces us to limit further discussion of Löwenhardt to a few selected examples that we hope will highlight some of his more significant findings and opinions. Perhaps Löwenhardt's most significant finding was that in five of the nine cases he reanalyzed

[129]See pp. 8–10 for the above list as well as a breakdown of the list into the categories of first, economic policy and the subcategories agriculture/production (Virgin Lands); industry/organization (Sovnarkhozy) and agriculture/organization (MTS reform); second, law and social policy (family law reform and Academy of Sciences reform); third, science and education policy (educational reform, Academy of Sciences reform); fourth, Lake Baikal; fifth, the only issue involving both domestic and foreign policy — Jewish emigration.

(Jewish emigration, school reform, antiparasite legislation, family law reform, and governmental tort liability), actual influence on policy was exerted by policy coalitions. In the other four cases (Sovnarkhoz reform, abolition of MTS, Virgin Lands campaign, and Lake Baikal), only "possible influence" was exerted.[130] As for the group Lowenhardt studied, which succeeded between 1954 and 1961 in separating those of its branches that had engaged in technical, applied sciences research from the USSR Academy of Sciences, in order to improve performance in both pure science and technology, Löwenhardt seems to have demonstrated that many persons played important parts. These included not only Khrushchev, who has usually been regarded as the initiator of the move to reorganize, but also a host of other actors, including Alexander Nesmeyanov, the chemist president of the Academy, and the physicist Petr Kapitsa. In support of his opinion that "we cannot prove that the Communist Party would not have reorganized the Academy in the absence of the activities" of reform-oriented academicians, Lowenhardt points out, however, that "the success of the reformers was to some extent also wanted by Party authorities."[131]

Generally, Lowenhardt's study, though stimulating and thought-provoking, leaves us with the impression that effort by political actors below the top level of the Soviet system at best can be facilitative but not decisive, especially if the Politburo is not favorably disposed toward them. Almost all of the cases he examined related to the Khrushchev era, when conditions were more favorable to such efforts than after Khrushchev's ouster. The most successful external influence on Politburo policy was that exercised by Soviet Jewish emigration. As Löwenhardt points out, American Jews could help Soviet Jews because in conditions of détente the Politburo could logically calculate that in return for indulgence toward Jewish emigration the USSR might obtain valuable American technical and scientific information.

---

[130]See pp. 24–25, defining a policy coalition as alliances of opinion groups drawn from different interests and attitude groups, and p. 124, presenting Löwenhardt's verdict on the degree of influence exerted by the nine groups.

[131]For the account of the reorganization, see pp. 127–82. Löwenhardt's conclusion is on p. 183. It should be pointed out that Löwenhardt's research took off from Loren Graham's pioneer article, "Reorganization of the U.S.S.R. Academy of Sciences," in Peter Juviler and Henry Morton, eds., *Soviet Policy-Making* (New York: Praeger, 1967), pp. 133–62.

The ouster of Khrushchev, the decline of U.S.-USSR détente, the Soviet invasion of Afghanistan, and other events probably made it more and more difficult for actors below the Politburo-Secretariat-Council of Ministers level to lobby successfully for inclusion of their projects on the Politburo's agenda, unless they could demonstrate that their proposals had military value. Even in the post-Brezhnev era, however, reformist ideas were still to a limited degree being aired. The fact that from time to time Soviet media reiterated traditional strictures against ''group'' activity indicated that such activity, as always, persisted and that some of it may have been deemed unacceptable.[132]

[132]See, for example, *Pravda*'s leader of 25 June 1983, *''Zadachi obshchestvennykh nauk''* (Tasks of the Social Sciences), charging among other things, that institutes had withdrawn into their shells and arguing that the ''weakness of party influence'' therein could be explained by the mistaken propositions contained in certain articles and monographs.

CHAPTER VIII

Policy Implementation

IN HIS STUDY of the crash Soviet campaign to develop the natural gas reserves of Western Siberia, Thane Gustafson observes: "In decisionmaking, in the Soviet Union as elsewhere, nothing is ever finally settled. Issues keep resurfacing in different forms. . . . The problems encountered in carrying out a program frequently threaten the basic strategy, forcing decisionmakers to review their course as they go."[1] In this chapter, as we review the means by which Soviet political authorities carry out the policies they make, we will need to bear in mind Gustafson's observation. The preponderance of decision-making power at the central levels of the political system, the proliferation of bureaucratic agencies designed to execute the leaders' will, and the technical complexity of many modern issues challenge the political system's capacity to command and control the work of its policy-implementing agencies.

In the previous two chapters, we have seen that the CPSU, and particularly its full-time staff, monopolizes the processes of generating and controlling political power in the USSR, transmitting its binding decisions to elites in state and public organizations through its territorial party committees and primary organizations. Although the exact nature of the relationship between party and state is ambiguous in Soviet constitutional theory, broadly speaking, Soviet authorities assign the duties of political leadership to the party and the adoption of policy-implementing deci-

[1]Thane Gustafson, *The Soviet Gas Campaign: Politics and Policy in Soviet Decisionmaking* (Santa Monica, Calif.: Rand report no. R-3036-AF, June 1983), p. 10.

sions to the agencies of the state.[2] Party leaders distinguish between the functions of guidance, or direction, over political life (often expressed by the Russian term *rukovodstvo,* which refers to political leadership), which is the party's prerogative and responsibility, and the actual work of translating general policy guidelines into the directives, rules, and regulations that control citizens' behavior. The latter sphere of tasks (in Russian, *upravlenie,* meaning management or government) belongs to the agencies of the state. The party also *supervises* the work of state agencies, verifying that their actions conform to the policies and principles enunciated by the party. This power, which extends even to the activity of the Primary Party Organization in the enterprise, is called *the right of oversight (kontrol').* In this chapter we shall discuss the state administrative organs that carry out policy, leaving discussion of the judicial process and the roles of police, courts, prosecutors, and other related structures to the next chapter.

Although party leaders frequently inveigh against excessive involvement by party officials in the work of implementation, a practice that detracts from their ability to perform their other duties, the parallel and overlapping organization of party and state institutions together with the pressure on CPSU officials to achieve ambitious policy goals often leads in practice to a blurring of the lines distinguishing the party's directing and supervising responsibilities from the duties of the government officials in executing policy.[3] The party's coordination of policy implementation is further complicated when lines of political control are multiplied by creating redundant bureaucratic hierarchies. These include the local soviet and executive committee — the seat of formal government power in each jurisdiction — with its departments and agencies, as well as the local offices of a number of national min-

---

[2] A good discussion, drawing out the many sides of party-state relations, is provided by Ronald J. Hill and Peter Frank, *The Soviet Communist Party,* 2nd ed. (London: Allen & Unwin, 1983), ch. 5, "Party-State Relations."

[3] The problem of *podmena,* or improper interference by party officials in domains that are rightfully those of state officials, is mentioned often in Soviet literature. A good analysis is found in Hill and Frank, who identify several causes for the problem's persistence. These include the tendency for state administrators to refer even minor decisions to party officials, the lack of adequate training for state officials (an especially acute problem in the periods during and after the civil war and World War II), and ultimately the party's higher policymaking authority. Hill and Frank, *The Soviet Communist Party,* pp. 118–21.

istries, state committees, and other organizations, some created for the purpose of coordinating others. The nominal unity of political interest of all state bureaucracies through *democratic centralism* distinguishes the Soviet pattern of public administration from the pluralistic patterns prevalent in the United States. Nevertheless, the multiplication of separate lines of control creates fertile ground for interagency disputes, power aggrandizement, and other forms of bureaucratic politics that tend to subvert rational, coherent administration.

Some degree of coordination of the work of many governmental agencies in each territorial jurisdiction is provided by the concentration of power in the party committee and particularly in its first secretary, who serves as a "prefect," to use Jerry Hough's analogy, riding herd on the field representatives of most other bureaucracies.[4] The local branches of some security-related bureaucracies however, are largely exempt from local party supremacy. These include the KGB and the armed forces (which divide the territory of the country into military commissariats with responsibility for conscription), ultimate control over which rests in the Politburo of the CPSU Central Committee. These agencies excepted, the party secretary in each area exercises general supervision over all government decision-making and executing bodies, setting goals that sometimes override existing institutional routines and powers. Though parallelism in party and state organization, which seems sometimes to divide power from responsibility and thus to promote inefficiency in the work of administrative agencies, appears needlessly wasteful at times to outside observers, it is also capable, as Jerry Hough concludes, of promoting economic development and responding flexibly to shifting policy priorities.[5] Many analysts, however, both Soviet and Western, now argue persuasively that the top-heavy Soviet administrative structure is increasingly dysfunctional. Though it may have been effective in accomplishing the rapid mobilization of human and natural resources for a few basic industrial and military goals, this essentially Stalinist system is unable to achieve the third-generation tasks that the Soviet system today confronts. Policy goals

---

[4]See Jerry F. Hough, *The Soviet Prefects* (Cambridge, Mass.: Harvard University Press, 1969.

[5]Ibid., chs. 14–15.

requiring the close coordination of multiple agencies and the fine-tuning of general policy to different local circumstances appear to be beyond the capacity of the existing bureaucratic system to achieve effectively.[6] Many observers believe that only a major overhaul of the political system that would decentralize decision-making power will suffice to remedy these problems.[7]

The soviets, executive committees, ministries, state committees, and other organizations in the system of state organs are important for another reason besides their function in implementing policy. They also serve to mobilize public support for policy, in part through the channels they create for popular participation. Millions of Soviet citizens serve as deputies to the soviets and millions more work as unpaid assistants to the commissions of soviets and other formal bodies of government.[8] Through the communications system, through regular meetings and contacts with citizens, and by means of extensive popular assistance to government bodies, government agencies carry out the crucial functions of informing citizens about policies and building support for them. Moreover, through such bodies as the popular control committees, which are set under the jurisdiction of the soviets, several million activists act as a further check upon the power of government bureaucracies, also helping to legitimate Soviet power by allowing citizens some opportunity to monitor the performance of executive agencies. Even the representative and participatory bodies in the state, not simply those concerned primarily with the execution of policy, function as policy-implementing rather than policy-setting institutions.

At each level of the territorial-administrative pyramid, the structure of government in the USSR resembles a parliamentary system, in which power is divided between an elected, representative, deliberative organ holding legislative power and a smaller executive organ, answerable to the former, which formulates and proposes policy measures to the legislative body and simulta-

[6]Thane Gustafson, *Reform in Soviet Politics* (Cambridge, England: Cambridge University Press, 1981), esp. ch. 10.

[7]Marshall I. Goldman, *The USSR in Crisis: The Failure of an Economic System* (New York: Norton, 1983); cf. Timothy J. Colton, *The Dilemma of Reform in the Soviet Union* (New York: Council on Foreign Relations, 1984).

[8]See Theodore H. Friedgut, *Political Participation in the USSR* (Princeton, N.J.: Princeton University Press, 1979), pp. 211–19.

neously supervises the bureaucratically organized agencies that translate policy into specific and binding rules. The applicability of the parliamentary analogy, even as far as the outward forms of the governmental apparatus are concerned, is limited by the crucial role of the party in selecting the personnel who fill both elected and appointed positions in the government and by the extensive use of unpaid activists to supplement the work of government.

The pyramid of soviets, which are organized in descending order from the USSR Supreme Soviet down to the grass-roots village and district soviets (soviet means council), is the backbone of the formal governmental structure. At each level, the popularly elected soviet formally approves the makeup of the executive committee (*ispolkom*, in Russian, short for *ispolnitel'nyi komitet*, or executive committee) that holds executive power in the locality. At the level of the union republics and of the all-union center, the top executive authority is not an executive committee but a council of ministers, which corresponds to the cabinet of a parliamentary system. At each level, therefore, the soviet constitutes the formal legislative power, and the executive committee or council of ministers the executive power. Executive bodies, however, are constitutionally subject to the rule of dual subordination: in keeping with the principle of a unitary state (contradicting the federal principle that is also said to apply to the Soviet state), Article 150 of the Soviet constitution specifies that the executive committees "are directly accountable to both the Soviets that elected them and to higher executive and administrative bodies."[9] The ability of the elected deputies in any jurisdiction to set local policy is thus limited by the subordination of their executive organs to higher-level agencies for policy implementation.

In keeping with the role of soviets as bodies for mass representation, certain territorial jurisdictions have been created specifically to give recognition to ethnic groups residing in the area. As we have seen, the USSR itself is divided into fifteen nominally sovereign national republics, each named for the predominant ethnic group in its territory. Besides the provinces into which the union republics are subdivided, there are special ethnoterritories that provide representation for certain smaller nationalities. Some

[9]Robert Sharlet, *The New Soviet Constitution of 1977: Analysis and Text* (Brunswick, Ohio: King's Court Communications, 1978), pp. 124–25.

national minorities (Jews, Germans, Crimean Tatars and some others), lacking a territorial base, do not have the corresponding governmental institutions, however.[10] As of January 1, 1983, the USSR contained, in addition to its fifteen union republics and lesser administrative subdivisions, twenty autonomous republics, eight autonomous provinces (*oblasti*), and ten autonomous circuits (*okruga*) representing minority national groups; nearly all of these are located in the Russian Republic.[11] Each national unit possesses its separate set of soviet and executive organs, staffed to a large extent by members of the indigenous nationality. Political representation by nationality is further provided in the Council of Nationalities, one of the two chambers of the USSR Supreme Soviet. Unlike the Council of the Union, deputies to which are elected on a one-person one-vote basis in electoral districts of equal population, the Council of Nationalities employs a weighted voting system in which each nationality unit elects a set number of deputies. The electorate of each union republic elects thirty-two deputies, each autonomous republic eleven, each autonomous province five, and each autonomous circuit one.[12]

Several rounds of legislation, affirmed and strengthened in the language of the 1977 Constitution, have sought to give soviet deputies added stature in their representative and constituent service functions. A 1972 law giving deputies the right to make inquiries of administrative and public bodies at the request of their

[10]The Jews are a partial exception to this exception; in 1928 a Jewish autonomous province was set up in Siberia with its capital at Birobidzhan. Few Jews migrated to the province and even fewer live there today. It is not actively considered a Jewish homeland within the Soviet Union. Indeed, the large-scale emigration of Soviet Jews during the 1970s, permitted primarily to allow the reunification of divided families, was given further legislative legitimacy by Soviet recognition that the Jews had no national territory within the Soviet Union. The same principle applied to the 80,000–90,000 Soviet Germans who were allowed to emigrate during the same period. On the Birobidzhan experiment, see Chimen Abramsky, "The Biro-Bidzhan Project, 1927–1959," in Lionel Kochan, ed., *The Jews in Soviet Russia since 1917,* 3rd ed. (New York: Oxford University Press, 1978), pp. 64–77.

[11]A complete listing of the territorial-administrative units of the USSR, with population figures, is provided in the reference book, *SSSR: Administrativno-territorial'noe delenie soiuznykh respublik na 1 ianvaria 1983 goda* (The USSR: The Administrative-Territorial Division of the Union Republics as of 1 January 1983) (Moscow: Izvestiia, 1983).

[12]Article 110 of the 1977 Constitution. Sharlet, *The New Soviet Constitution,* p. 109.

constituents was confirmed in the 1977 Constitution, which also obliged officials to respond promptly: "executives of the state and public agencies, enterprises, institutions and organizations in question are obliged to receive Deputies without delay and to examine their proposals within the established time periods."[13] As Jan Adams observes, however, in surveying these legislative changes, the *actual* powers of soviet deputies are not expanded: for the most part, deputies are still mainly concerned with the implementation of policy rather than with making it.[14] Indeed, empirical investigation of the work of deputies reveals that they devote relatively little time to their duties as deputies. Since they continue to hold their regular jobs and perform other social service work, it is not surprising that the average deputy gives around 10 hours per month to his work as deputy, as against a suggested norm of 30 hours.[15] Few citizens know the names of the deputies representing their districts in the district, city, province, republican, and all-union soviet bodies, and deputies tend to spend rather little time meeting with their constituents (on average, around half an hour per month).[16] The weakness of the representative function of soviet deputies is reinforced by the noncompetitive nature of elections to soviets. In the course of the nomination process, a single candidate for each constituency is chosen to run. Proposals to allow contested elections (as have occurred in other members of the socialist fraternity, such as Poland and Yugoslavia) have not so far been accepted.[17] The role of soviets as representative organs is more symbolic than political. Deputies are chosen according to certain norms of demographic representation — so many women, so many nonparty members, so many workers, so many with particular educational levels.[18] Care is taken to ensure that a certain number of deputies have good pro-

---

[13]Article 105. Sharlet, *The New Soviet Constitution*, p. 107.

[14]Jan S. Adams, "Citizen Participation in Community Decisions in the USSR," in Peter J. Potichnyj and Jane Shapiro Zacek, *Politics and Participation under Communist Rule* (New York: Praeger, 1983), p. 184.

[15]Friedgut, *Political Participation*, pp. 220–21.

[16]Ibid., p. 231.

[17]See Ronald J. Hill, *Soviet Politics, Political Science and Reform* (White Plains, N.Y.: Sharpe, 1980), pp. 23–30; and Friedgut, *Political Participation*, p. 146.

[18]See Hill and Frank, *The Soviet Communist Party*, p. 111.

duction records or are distinguished in their fields.[19] A nominating meeting described by a recent émigré went as follows. At a certain Leningrad factory a representative of the factory party committee addressed the workers and explained that the candidate nominated should meet the following criteria: the person should be a woman, a blue-collar worker, of Russian nationality, not a party member, and 35–40 years of age. Having considered these criteria (which had undoubtedly been passed down to the party committee from higher party levels), the party committee had decided to nominate Comrade S. A short description of Comrade S.'s qualifications followed. Those present were polled and Comrade S. was accepted without dissent.[20]

Soviet discussions of the socialist conception of democracy usually emphasize such features as high turnover rates among deputies, the large number of persons who serve as deputies and unelected assistants, and the occasional recall of an unfit deputy to demonstrate the democratic character of the soviets.[21] The power of soviets as policymaking bodies is limited by several factors. One is the fact that much power over the production and distribution of local goods and services, including housing, education, consumer goods, and municipal utilities, remains vested in powerful enterprises or in the ministries to which the enterprises are subordinate (a situation that might be compared to the

[19]Everett M. Jacobs, "Norms of Representation and the Composition of Local Soviets," in Everett M. Jacobs, ed., *Soviet Local Politics and Government* (London: Allen & Unwin, 1983), p. 78.

[20]Victor Zaslavsky and Robert J. Brym, "The Structure of Power and the Functions of Soviet Local Elections," in Jacobs, ed., *Soviet Local Politics,* p. 76. A young worker who attended the meeting remarked to her friends afterward that the meeting was purely a charade; her fellow workers reportedly replied that undoubtedly it was all for show but that fortunately the meeting had been held during work hours and now the workers were allowed to go home early.

[21]A good example is F. Burlatskii, "Politicheskaia sistema razvitogo sotsializma" (The Political System of Developed Socialism) *Kommunist,* no. 12 (1166) (1979): 62–73; also V. M. Ivanov, et al., *Sovetskaia demokratiia: ocherk stanovleniia i razvitiia* (Soviet Democracy: A Sketch of its Rise and Development) (Moscow: Politizdat, 1983), esp. pp. 195–96. An important discussion of the various conceptions of political representation, which brings out the distinction between representation as standing for a constituency and representation as acting for it, is Hannah Fenichel Pitkin, *The Concept of Representation* (Berkeley: University of California Press, 1967).

company-town character of some American localities).[22] Another is the dependence of the soviet at any given level for the greater part of its budget on allocations from higher levels of government. In the urban district observed by Theodore Friedgut, 88 percent of the district soviet's budget represented an allocation from the budget of the city soviet.[23] Two additional factors in the relative weakness of soviets as policymaking bodies are the frequently apathetic or uninformed responses of citizens to soviet activity and, of course, the predominant decision-making role of the party committee in each jursidiction.[24]

As the legislative matters with which soviets at all levels have to deal grow more complex, the societs have increased the number of standing commissions that play a role similar to that of a legislative committee in a parliament except that they depend upon an unelected aktiv of citizens, including specialists, to advise them. The standing commissions of the Supreme Soviet help to draft or refine the language of legislative proposals, and those at lower levels help to oversee the work of local government agencies in such areas as health care, education, and public catering.[25] Friedgut observes that although the committees and commissions in lower-level soviets are supposed to exercise supervision (*kontrol'*) over the work of the local bureaucracy, they appear to provide more support than oversight; this fact suggests again the importance of the soviets as agencies for legitimating policy as it is implemented. Such bodies, however, may also serve as channels of information and demands from citizens about the work of gov-

[22]See William Taubman, *Governing Soviet Cities* (New York: Praeger, 1973); David T. Cattell, "Local Government and the Provision of Consumer Goods and Services," in Jacobs, eds., *Soviet Local Politics,* p. 182; and Carol W. Lewis, "The Economic Functions of Local Soviets," in Jacobs, ed., *Soviet Local Politics,* p. 65.

[23]Theodore H. Friedgut, "A Local Soviet at Work: The 1970 Budget and Budget Discussions of the Oktyabr Borough Soviet of Moscow," in Jacobs, ed., *Soviet Local Politics,* pp. 158–62.

[24]Ronald J. Hill, "The Development of Soviet Local Government since Stalin's Death," in Jacobs, ed., *Soviet Local Politics,* p. 30.

[25]On the standing commissions and committees of the local soviets, see Friedgut, *Political Participation,* pp. 186 ff.; on those of the Supreme Soviet, see Robert W. Siegler, *The Standing Commissions of the Supreme Soviet* (New York: Praeger, 1982). Also see Peter Vanneman, *The Supreme Soviet: Politics and the Legislative Process in the Soviet Political System* (Durham, N.C.: Duke University Press, 1977).

ernment agencies. Participation by specialists in the work of leg-islative commissions makes expertise available to leaders for the purposes of drafting legal acts but does not widen the arena for policymaking. Legislative enactment of measures decided upon by the political elites in party and state administrative organs pri-marily serves to lend them the legitimacy of formal legality. The soviets themselves have little opportunity to play a significant role in policymaking. The twice-a-year meetings of the Supreme So-viet, for example, last only 2 or 3 days. (The soviets at lower levels typically meet for 1 day or at most 2 days, four to six times a year.)[26] They provide a forum for the presentation of reports by the chairman of Gosplan, the minister of finance, and other of-ficials, but they invariably affirm the budget and plan proposals presented. Individually and collectively, deputies have very few resources with which to cultivate expertise or influence in shaping legislation.

Managing the business of the Supreme Soviet is the task of its Presidium, headed by a chairman, a first deputy chairman, and fifteen deputy chairmen (the chairmen of each of the Supreme Soviet presidia of the union republics). The Presidium does not exercise governmental power — that is the domain of the vastly more powerful Council of Ministers. Rather, it supervises the meetings of the Supreme Soviet, setting the dates of elections and coordinating the legislative committees, as well as performing other functions on behalf of the Supreme Soviet in the intervals between sessions. Chairmanship of the Supreme Soviet Presidium is a position equivalent to a titular head of state in a parliamentary system. It is not in itself powerful, but it symbolizes the power and continuity of the state. Between 1938 and 1946, Stalin found it expedient to assign this job to the harmless, fatherly, and rel-atively popular M. I. Kalinin, and between 1960 and 1964, in disfavor with Khrushchev, Leonid Brezhnev was given the post as a kind of administrative exile. Since 1977, however, when Brezhnev removed the incumbent Nikolai Podgorny and occupied the position again himself, the party general secretary has found it more convenient to hold both positions. This is undoubtedly connected with the diplomatic embarrassment created when

---

[26]Everett M. Jacobs, "Introduction: The Organizational Framework of Soviet Local Government," in Jacobs, ed., *Soviet Local Politics,* p. 11.

Brezhnev negotiated on behalf of the Soviet state during the period of détente but could not, under the standing rules of protocol, be accorded the same rights of treaty making as a head of state. Replacing Podgorny thus simultaneously eliminated a rival and gave Brezhnev the symbolic powers he desired. As Mikhail Gorbachev remarked when he nominated Konstantin Chernenko for the position immediately after Chernenko replaced Andropov as general secretary, the party general secretary's occupancy of the chairmanship of the Supreme Soviet presidium bears "enormous significance for the conduct of the Soviet Union's foreign policy."[27] Under Brezhnev, Andropov, and Chernenko, a first deputy chairman — a post newly created in the 1977 Constitution — took over much of the chairman's work. The inference that the practice of combining the titular state presidency with the party secretaryship had become institutionalized was disproven, however, when Andrei Gromyko left his post as Foreign Minister to become head of the Supreme Soviet in July 1985.

Circumscribed though the legislative powers of the soviets are, it would be a mistake to overlook their functions as agencies of socialization and regime legitimation. The opportunities they offer to two million people to serve as deputies and another 30 million people to be volunteer assistants to the soviets,[28] help to generate support for the system. The educational mission of soviets is best displayed during elections to the soviets, which are treated as important political ceremonies. Elections to the lower soviets are held every two and one-half years, to the Supreme Soviets every five years. Propaganda ties the act of election (the very word does violence to the meaning of election, since there is no choice involved) to the expression of symbolic identification with the regime by casting a vote for the candidate of the bloc of party and nonparty candidates. Posters extolling the merits of the candidates, agitation explaining the importance of the vote, and heavy media attention all help foster an atmosphere of festive solemnity. The most strenuous efforts are made by activists to turn out all eligible voters. Komsomol members, for example, take bal-

---

[27]*Pravda,* 12 April 1984.

[28]See Burlatskii, "Politicheskaia sistema," p. 71; Jan Adams, "Citizens Participation," pp. 179–80.

lot urns around to hospital patients. Urns are set up on long-distance trains and airplanes. Activists visit the homes of those who have not voted early in the day. A high turnout is considered an essential feature of the symbolism of voting.[29] The pressure to achieve 100 percent turnouts is intense. At the Third International Sakharov Hearings in Washington, D.C., Tatiana Khodorovich testified about the consequences of her deliberate refusal to vote, an act treated by local party authorities as an expression of opposition to the state.[30] To be sure, a voter has the option of crossing out the name of the candidate listed and of inserting another name before dropping it in the ballot urn, but to do so would be to call unwelcome attention to oneself. Still, in some localities, especially in villages, some candidates do fail to receive the required majority of ballots cast and hence are considered defeated. Moreover, in a few hundred cases each year, deputies who fail to meet the expectations held of them are recalled.[31] Thus, though the principle of accountability of the elected deputies to the electors is honored to a limited degree, the essential lesson that the authorities seek to inculcate through the voting process is the theme of solidarity between the populace and its rulers.

The pyramid of soviets is nominally the institutional structure for rule making in the USSR. In performing administrative functions, the soviets act as rule-applying bodies, and in fact, at the lower levels they are the organs of government that impinge most directly on the citizens' daily lives. The most powerful organs of government in the USSR, however, are those, such as ministries and state committees, with a distinctively bureaucratic structure — that is, they are "departments of the state staffed by appointed and not elected functionaries, organized hierarchically,

---

[29]Citizens who wish to may cast the equivalent of absentee ballots by registering that they will be away from their regular polling place on election day. This procedure enables them to evade the election, since it is impossible to check to determine whether all absentees have voted. For this and other administrative reasons, the reports of 99.98 percent turnout that invariably follow elections must be treated with considerable skepticism. Perhaps 5 to 15 percent of the electorate in cities manages to avoid voting. Victor Zaslavsky and Robert J. Brym, "The Structure of Power and the Functions of Soviet Local Elections," in Jacobs, ed., *Soviet Local Politics,* p. 70.

[30]Dorothy Rabinowitz, "Notes on the Soviet Union," *Wall Street Journal,* October 10 1979; see also Max E. Mote, *Soviet Local and Republic Elections* (Stanford, Calif.: Stanford University Press, 1965), p. 78.

[31]Friedgut, *Political Participation,* pp. 109–34.

and dependent on a sovereign authority" which carry out the "articulated ends of government."[32] Characteristic of the Soviet political system is the large number of such ministries and state committees, most of which have responsibility for administering individual branches of the economy. Of the sixty-four ministries and twenty-two state committees whose heads are represented on the Council of Ministers of the USSR, thirty-eight operate as all-union organs. In other words, as Leonard Schapiro explains it, they are "in sole charge within their field of competence of the sphere of administration entrusted to them, without reference to the republican governments."[33] They set up local branches as needed. The other category of agencies under the Council of Ministers is the union-republic bodies. These have central offices in Moscow, and in each of the fifteen republics they function through counterpart ministries in the republican capitals. Examples of the latter include the Ministry of Education, the Ministry of Justice, the Ministry of Ferrous Metallurgy, and Gosplan (the State Committee on Planning). The Ministries of Defense, Foreign Trade, and the Petroleum Industry, as well as the State Committees on Science and Technology and Foreign Economic Relations, operate as all-union agencies.[34] In addition, the governments of the union republics have certain ministries dealing with linguistic and other local matters that exist only at the republican level.

Centralization of administrative authority is furthered by the establishment at the all-union level of certain agencies that lack

[32]The first quotation is from Michel Crozier, *The Bureaucratic Phenomenon* (Chicago, Ill.: University of Chicago Press, 1967), p. 3. The second is from Joseph LaPalombara, "Bureaucracy and Political Development: Notes, Queries and Dilemmas," in Joseph LaPalombara, ed., *Bureaucracy and Political Development* (Princeton, N.J.: Princeton University Press, 1963), p. 49.

[33]Leonard Schapiro, *The Government and Politics of the Soviet Union* (New York: Vintage, 1965), p. 127.

[34]According to a Soviet writer, the functional difference between all-union and union-republican ministries is that the former run branches requiring higher levels of centralization. See N. A. Volkov, *Vysshie i tsentral'nye organy gosudarstvennogo upravleniia SSSR i soiuznykh respublik v sovremennyi period* (Supreme and Central Organs of State Government of the USSR and the Union Republics in the Contemporary Period) (Kazan: Izdatel'stvo kazanskogo universiteta, 1971), p. 111. This assertion is untenable, however. The constitutional distinction between all-union and union-republican ministries and state committees counts for little in terms of actual powers. Such highly centralized agencies as the Ministry of Foreign Affairs and the State Committee on Security (KGB) have formal status as union-republic agencies.

formal ministerial status. These include the State Bank, the Central Statistical Administration, the Academy of Sciences, and TASS, the Telegraphic Agency of the Soviet Union. These and similar organizations oversee systems of local branches under the general supervision of the Council of Ministers and of the departments of the Central Committee with functional responsibility for their fields of activity. Still other units, including various commissions of the Council of Ministers, operate as high-level advisory and coordinating boards. One of these, the Military-Industrial Commission, supervises the ties among defense industries and ensures that defense-related production contracts involving multiple ministries are fulfilled smoothly and satisfactorily. In turn, this commission is probably overseen by yet another body, the Defense Council. Formed, according to the Constitution, by the Presidium of the Supreme Soviet, the Defense Council is the equivalent of a special arm of the Politburo linking several of the ministries and party bodies concerned with military and defense issues. Many observers believe it to be a powerful unit in its own right that bridges Politburo decisions on strategic policy with the administration of the defense industries and other organs concerned with shaping the nation's military capability.[35] Thus the top echelon of governmental power in the USSR consists of large, vertically organized bureaucracies administering individual economic and social branches as well as of coordinating, interagency bodies lacking bureaucratic machinery.

Formally the Council of Ministers oversees all the governmental agencies established at the all-union level. The large number and massive size of these bodies, however, necessitate a smaller body, formed from the Council of Ministers, to coordinate their efforts. This is the herculean task of the Presidium of the Council of Ministers, headed by a chairman, the first deputy chairmen, and regular deputy chairmen. Just as the chairman of the Presidium of the USSR Supreme Soviet corresponds to the president or

[35]See Ellen Jones, "Defense R & D Policymaking in the USSR," in Jiri Valenta and William C. Potter, eds., *Soviet Decisionmaking for National Security* (London: Allen & Unwin, 1984), p. 122; also see, in the same volume, Jerry F. Hough, "The Historical Legacy in Soviet Weapons Development," p. 106. The contributions by Jones and Hough are extremely helpful in clarifying the roles of the many administrative bodies concerned with formulating and implementing security-related policy in the USSR.

head of state in a parliamentary system, so the chairman of the Presidium of the Council of Ministers holds a position equivalent to that of prime minister or premier. He supervises the entire machinery of government, translating general party directives into the specific decisions that keep the ministries and state committees functioning in accordance with the party leadership's will. The enormous power of this position — it is, next to the role of party general secretary, the most influential post in the political system — has made it a coveted prize for ambitious party leaders, who have sought either to hold it or to control it by placing trusted clients in it. Having deposed his rivals in the antiparty group in 1957, Party Secretary Khrushchev, for example, took over the chairmanship of the Council of Ministers himself the next year, thus combining party and government power in his own person. His alleged misuse of this power led to the practice, followed since his expulsion, of a division between party and government offices. Under Brezhnev, Alexei Kosygin served as chairman of the Presidium of the Council of Ministers for virtually the entire Brezhnev era, from 1964 until his illness-related retirement in October 1980 (which was followed 2 months later by his death). After Kosygin's retirement, the chairmanship was held by the aging Brezhnev crony Nikolai Tikhonov, who was pensioned off in September 1985, and replaced by the considerably younger Nikolai Ryzhkov.

A crucial task of the government machinery is administration of the economy. Since virtually all economic production and exchange lies under government control, the sphere of legal economic activity for private profit is extremely narrow and circumscribed.[36] Under the Soviet system of socialism the marketplace has been superseded by administrative mechanisms as a means of allocating basic goods in the economy, leaving the agen-

---

[36]It includes private provision of certain services, such as handicrafts and household repairs as well as the practice under specified limits of professional services, such as legal consultation, tutoring, and dentistry; certain types of hunting and prospecting in remote wilderness areas; and the sale of agricultural surpluses at farmers' markets (see Gregory Grossman, "The 'Second Economy' of the USSR," *Problems of Communism*, no. 5 (September–October 1977): 25–27.) Legal activity frequently shades off into gray or black markets: the various shades of legality are surveyed in a valuable article by a former Soviet economist, Aron Katsenelenboigen, "Coloured Markets in the Soviet Union," *Soviet Studies* 29, no. 1 (January 1977): 62–85.

cies of government to perform the managerial tasks that private individuals and corporations perform in capitalist economies.[37] In theory, a planned economy in which the units of production and exchange are fulfilling directive targets set by the central planners is a perfect system for carrying out socially agreed-upon policy goals, since all economic activity embodies the wishes of the political authorities. In practice, achievement of such a degree of centralization of planning power has proven impossible, in part because of difficulties associated with plan implementation. As a result, the history of Soviet politics is filled with attempts to increase actual central control over the economy by reorganizing the agencies concerned with formulating plans and executing them.

THE TREADMILL OF ADMINISTRATIVE REFORM

The existing model of centralized, vertically organized branch ministries dates to Stalin's era. Khrushchev mandated a radical decrease in the number of economic ministries and instead created a network of regional economic councils, which lasted from 1957 until soon after his fall, although even during Khrushchev's tenure the number of central ministries crept back up, sometimes under the guise of state committees. Despite this short hiatus, however, the system has continued to suit the powerful vested interests that favor the concentration of bureaucratic power at the center. Khrushchev's successors reconcentrated economic administration in a major reform package in 1965, and since then the functions of planning, price setting, research and development, and supply have been managed by separate state committees (Gosplan for planning, Gostsen for price setting, Gostekhnika for R&D, and Gossnab for supply); the actual oversight of production is performed by the individual branch ministries.

Although the separation of production administration from the logistical functions that support it is supposed to improve the ability of the Politburo and the Council of Ministers to maintain centralized control over the enterprises, in practice the system has created enormous rigidities and tensions. Interenterprise and in-

[37]A thorough discussion of the mechanics of the marketplace as an allocator of economic resources and the nature of the replacement of market mechanisms by government in socialist economies is Charles E. Lindblom, *Politics and Markets: The World's Political-Economic Systems* (New York: Basic Books, 1977).

terbranch relations are marked by continuous conflict caused by bottlenecks in the provision of scarce resources; these in turn, because of the general tautness of the planning system, produce further distortions. Enterprise managers typically respond to the demands imposed on them by their branch ministries by means of a variety of devices, some of which are irrational from the standpoint of the economy as a whole, such as the hoarding of spare parts and raw materials, maintaining needlessly large work forces so that they can respond to any unexpected contingencies, shading the figures in their reports, and cutting corners on quality of output. The enterprise manager's unwillingness to assume risk means that the propensity to innovate is, by capitalist standards, very low.[38] Another problem is a systematic bias in favor of those types of products and those criteria of performance that serve goals inherited from the Stalin era of rapid mobilization: centralized control and rapid development of producers' goods and defense industries. Thus, when in doubt, the manager will generally choose to shortchange consumer goods rather than producers' goods and will stress quantitative targets, such as gross output, over qualitative ones, such as efficiency and quality.

The inefficiencies and distortions caused by this system, the lack of competitiveness of Soviet manufactured goods on the world market, and the decline in the rate of Soviet economic growth have prompted the leaders to embark on a succession of piecemeal reforms. Each reform stimulates further reforms to correct the distortions it has caused. In all, the series of measures taken by the leaders to ameliorate the most acute defects of the Stalinist system of economic administration without ever dealing with their fundamental causes is well described by Gertrude Schroeder as a "treadmill of reforms."[39] Since the early 1970s, even the term *reform* has been avoided by the conservative leadership in favor of the euphemism *measures to further perfect the economic mechanism.*

All of these corrective measures, however, essentially aim to

[38]See Joseph S. Berliner, *The Innovation Decision in Soviet Industry* (Cambridge, Mass.: MIT Press, 1976).

[39]See Gertrude E. Schroeder, "The Soviet Economy on a Treadmill of 'Reforms,' " in *Soviet Economy in a Time of Change* (Washington, D.C.: Joint Economic Committee of the U.S. Congress, 1979), pp. 312–40; also by the same author, "Soviet Economic 'Reform' Decrees: More Steps on the Treadmill," in *Soviet Economy in the 1980's: Problems and Prospects, Part 1* (Washington, D.C.: Joint Economic Committee of the U.S. Congress, 1982), pp. 65–88.

preserve the system of central planning and to improve the implementation of plans.[40] They represent responses to four sets of problems resulting from the branch-ministry-centered, planned economy: the excessive centralization of authority, the tendency for plans to be continuously subverted by administrative intervention, the problem of carrying out programs requiring the cooperation of multiple branches, and the tendency for the economy to respond only to one-time, high-priority, crash projects.

CENTRALIZATION VERSUS DECENTRALIZATION

Although the issue of decentralization is a perennial one in all administrative systems, the Soviet authorities have proved to be far more cautious about loosening the grasp of the central government over the economy than have the socialist systems of Poland, Hungary, East Germany, and Bulgaria, not to speak of Yugoslavia and China, which have experimented widely with elements of market socialism. Although, as Jerry Hough points out, there may be sound economic reasons for the leadership's reluctance to decentralize (such as the fear of strong inflationary pressures)[41], the hold of conservative views on the political dangers of decentralization remains strong, especially among such powerful sectors as the planning and ministerial bureaucracies and the armed forces. Fears of uncontrollable social pressures caused by unemployment and inequality that would be let loose by allowing greater play to market forces undoubtedly lie behind the leaders' reluctance to tolerate any but the most modest changes in the direction of economic decentralization. Enterprise managers have been given somewhat greater latitude in using enterprise resources to reward employees for good performance, but actual measures increasing managerial discretion have been more modest than some social experiments. Experimentation in turn has been more cautious than some of the theoretical propositions advanced by liberal-minded economists.

Under Khrushchev wide-ranging economic discussion was once

---

[40]See the stimulating overview of reform attempts since Khrushchev by Joseph S. Berliner, "Planning and Management," in Abram Bergson and Herbert S. Levine, eds., *The Soviet Economy: Toward the Year 2000* (London: Allen & Unwin, 1983), pp. 350–90, esp. pp. 351–61.

[41]Jerry F. Hough, *Soviet Leadership in Transition* (Washington, D.C.: Brookings Institution, 1980), pp. 135–36.

again encouraged after the dogmatism of the Stalin years. Some of the bolder spirits in the economic profession began to explain poor enterprise performance as a consequence of misplaced success indicators. Managers were being rewarded, as under Stalin, for sheer quantity of output, often regardless of other characteristics of the production that affected its usefulness to buyers. Bad success indicators, the argument of the reformers went, led to managerial decisions that served the interests of the enterprises but harmed the interests of society as a whole. Needed instead were economic (market-oriented) rather than administrative levers to shape managerial decision making. The 1965 reforms, often associated with the name of Alexei Kosygin, then chairman of the Council of Ministers, substituted a new performance criterion, based on profit, for the old indicator of gross output. Now enterprises were expected to satisfy the demands of buyers, and revenue from sales would be used to calculate whether the enterprise was functioning efficiently; efficiency as evidenced by a profit on the accounting books would be rewarded with greater managerial discretion over a bonus fund for the employees. As conservatives feared, the reform did not improve matters. The price system was arbitrary and materials were in tight supply. As a result of the first problem, profit was a poor measure of efficiency, and as a result of the second, buyers had little choice over whether to accept or reject goods, since they were still constrained to meet their own plan targets. Moreover, managers could resort to devices with which to raise the ostensible prices of their goods and thus artificially inflate profits. In essence, managers were responding to a different set of incentives than the branch ministries that oversaw them; the enterprises were in a position to frustrate fulfillment of the plan and ministries lacked the means to hold them responsible. To remedy the many unforeseen consequences of the reform, the planners gradually imposed many new plan targets on managers to curb their freedom. By the early 1970s, the manager's position was essentially the same as it was under Stalin, and talk of decentralizing reform all but ended.[42]

---

[42]See the discussion of the Kosygin reform of performance indicators in Schroeder, "The Soviet Economy on a Treadmill of 'Reform,' " pp. 324–29; Joseph S. Berliner, "Planning and Management," in Bergson and Levine, eds., *The Soviet Economy,* pp. 353–55.

In 1967, a potentially significant experiment widening managerial autonomy well beyond what was allowed under the Kosygin reforms was adopted. The new method substantially raised the manager's rights to reduce the size of the enterprise labor force and to use the savings to increase wages and benefits for the remaining employees and invest in new plant and equipment. Since it was introduced at the Shchekino Chemical Combine, it became known as the *Shchekino experiment*. It was the most widely publicized of a variety of social experiments — small-scale reforms tried out to test the effects of a novel concept. The initial results of the Shchekino experiment were highly encouraging: the work force was cut by about half (the workers released usually found new jobs in other sectors of the expanding chemical industry), and productivity rose. The experiment quickly ran out of steam, however. Despite the favor of senior party leaders, including Brezhnev, it has not spread widely, and where it has been adopted, it has been hedged with various restrictions and requirements that weaken its force. Among the reasons its impact has been slight are the difficulties for managers of obtaining scarce modern equipment in which to invest their retained savings; resistance from the ministries to the diffusion of the experiment has also been substantial.[43] Perhaps the underlying, unstated threat posed by the experiment is to security of employment for industrial workers, one of the major props of the regime's support among the populace. Workers know that however stern and demanding the regime may be, the labor supply is insufficient and managers are reluctant to lose workers. The Shchekino experiment introduces an element of capitalist anxiety about job tenure that could potentially upset the social contract between regime and working class.[44]

Going further than the Kosygin reforms, with their limited and flawed introduction of economic levers, and the Shchekino experiment, which introduced just one market element into a plan-

---

[43]On the Shchekino experiment, see Schroeder, "The Soviet Economy on a Treadmill of 'Reforms'," pp. 329–30. On the use of social experiments in the Brezhnev period, see Darrell L. Slider, "Social Experiments and Soviet Policymaking," Ph.D. diss., Yale University, 1981.

[44]See George W. Breslauer, "On the Adaptability of Soviet Welfare-State Authoritarianism," in Karl W. Ryavec, ed., *Soviet Society and the Communist Party* (Amherst: University of Massachusetts Press, 1978), pp. 3–25.

dominant environment,[45] was a proposal drafted at the Institute of Economics and Organization of Industrial Production of the Siberian Branch of the Academy of Sciences and offered for discussion at a high-level economic conference. A copy was (doubtless intentionally) leaked to Western sources and published abroad. The Novosibirsk memorandum, as the document has come to be called, sheds interesting light on the types of thinking that can be given limited expression by established specialists. The premise of the report was quite radical: the current system of economic administration established under Stalin was "a social system, in the framework of which people were consistently regarded as 'cogs' in the economic mechanism and behaved almost as obediently and passively as machines and materials." Since that time, however, the economy has changed enormously. Accordingly, "the complexity of the economic structure has long since passed the threshold at which it could be effectively regulated from a single center. The deepening of the regional, branch, and economic disproportions in the USSR's economy, which has been observed in the last Five Year Plan periods testifies more clearly than anything else to the exhaustion of the possibilities of the centralized-administrative management of the economy and the necessity of more active use of 'automatic' regulators for balancing production, *tied with the development of market relations.'*[46] Hanson observes that the report was probably too far-reaching in its theoretical criticism of the system to have permitted open publication but be-

[45]A widely circulating Soviet anecdote of the early 1980s neatly captures the absurdity of folding one or two market features into an economy that is still governed largely by administrative fiat. It seems that the Soviet traffic authorities have determined that the British system of driving on the left side of the road is preferable to the old system of right-side driving. They have therefore decided to adopt the British system. To allow drivers time to gain familiarity with the system, however, it will be introduced in stages. First, all truck traffic will be required to drive on the left; 3 months later, so will all private vehicles.

[46]Our translation and italics. The full Russian-language text is found in Tat'iana Zaslavskaya, "Doklad o neobkhodimosti bolee uglublennogo izucheniia v SSSR sotsial'nogo mekhanizma razvitiia ekonomiki" (A Report on the Necessity of Deepened Study in the USSR of the Social Mechanism of Economic Development), *Materialy samizdata,* no. 35/83, Arkhiv Samizdata no. 5042 (26 August 1983): 7. See the discussion of the document by Philip Hanson, "The Novosibirsk Report: Comment," *Survey* 28, no. 1 (120) (Spring 1984): 83–87. An English translation of the full text appears in the same issue of *Survey,* pp. 88–108.

lieves that it reveals ideas currently under discussion in top economic and policy circles.

On the other hand, the report is notably devoid of concrete proposals for ways of decentralizing the economy and introducing greater freedom for market principles. Indeed, despite the general philosophical and economic critique of overcentralization, the author ultimately concludes that what is needed is more academic study of the problems discussed. There is no mention of what forms of ownership might be needed to implement market relations. Above all, although the ministries come in for sharp criticism for foot-dragging and resistance to change, there is no mention, let alone criticism, of the party.[47] The absence of specific recommendations and the recognition of the political obstacles standing in the way of greater market freedom probably reflect well the dilemma of many intellectuals who lament the stifling overcentralization but see no obvious way out of the current impasse.

STRENGTHENING PLAN INTEGRITY

It is a paradox of hypercentralized systems that the apparently all-powerful plans under which their organizations operate are constantly upset by unforeseen contingencies. Plan goals must be revised so frequently as information from the field comes in that the final plan is an improvised compromise between what was originally intended and what was found to be possible or expedient over the course of the plan period. This principle is all the more true in an economy of the Soviet type, where certain key resources — transportation, raw materials, energy, and sophisticated equipment — are so scarce that the planners must give them special attention for allocation. The execution of the plan then becomes a series of ad hoc, individual decisions by high-level administrators about how to allocate scarce goods. In order to be able, at the end of the plan year, to show figures proving 100 percent or more fulfillment of the plan, the original plan target figures are officially revised — almost always downward — during the period of the plan's implementation.[48]

[47]Hanson, "Novosibirsk Report," p. 86.
[48]See Raymond P. Powell, "Plan Execution and the Workability of Soviet Planning," *Journal of Comparative Economics* 1, no. 1 (March 1977): 51–76. Powell quotes Clausewitz on the inevitable modifications of a plan as it is executed in

Exhaustive research on the plan process during the Stalin era has shown that the seeming draconian pressure that accompanied the issuing of plans could not in fact protect them from these adjustments and modifications by administrative decision.[49] It should therefore come as no surprise that today despite the political leaders' ceaseless admonitions that the plan must not be watered down in the course of the plan period, Soviet plans are rarely fulfilled as originally projected; in fact, it is hard to identify any single draft of the plan as *the* authoritative version.[50] The process of plan formulation is extremely complex, and, like the process of formulating the federal budget in the United States, it takes the form of a continuous cycle of drafting estimates of availability and expenditure of resources.[51] In fact, the annual plans that enterprises receive from their branch ministries are invariably given out late, often in the spring of the year, so that ministries must estimate what their actual final targets are for the year and must then often scramble to satisfy the plan targets by the end of the year. On the other hand, rarely are managers greatly surprised by the plans that are eventually passed down to them. Soviet plans are assembled by a process of tacking a small percentage of growth over the previous year's achieved output, which makes plans relatively predictable. In fact, incrementalism in planning,

---

war. Powell's article details ways in which managers and administrators satisfy basic plan goals at the expense of secondary goals, such as by substituting more accessible for less accessible inputs in production.

[49]See the exhaustive study by Eugene Zaleski, *Stalinist Planning for Economic Growth, 1933–1952*, trans. and ed. Marie-Christine MacAndrew and John H. Moore (Chapel Hill, N.C.: University of North Carolina Press, 1980).

[50]One should be wary of taking this argument too far. Some theorists have argued that in view of these continuous administrative interventions in the execution of nominal plans, the Soviet economy runs by a series of ad hoc microbalances that never meet the equilibrium between resources and uses that the planners decree, and that as a result, the Soviet economy is not, in a true sense, planned. This is the view of Paul Craig Roberts, the theorist of supply-side economics, who bases his case partly on philosophical, partly on empirical grounds. See his *Alienation and the Soviet Economy* (Albuquerque: University of New Mexico Press, 1971), chs. 3–5. We regard this view as extreme. Soviet plans are significant, not because in the legal sense they are binding on the ministries and enterprises to which they apply but because they provide the essential information, replacing market cues, on which managers base their decisions.

[51]J. Michael Montias, "Planning with Material Balances in Soviet-Type Economies," *American Economic Review* (December 1959): 963–85. Reprinted in Alec Nove and D. M. Nuti, eds., *Socialist Economics* (Baltimore, Md.: Penguin, 1972), pp. 223–51.

though it violates the very purpose of central planning, is so well established that it is called "planning from the achieved level."[52]

Soviet planners, aware of these deficiencies, have formulated a number of proposals to strengthen planning. Some of the measures involve lengthening the time horizon of plans, for example by making the Five Year Plan, rather than its annual segments, the true *operational* plan. Such was one of the provisions of the Kosygin reforms of 1965.[53] In the early 1970s the authorities began drafting elements of a 15 year plan to run until 1990, but the effort languished in the late 1970s. Several measures announced as part of a comprehensive reorganization package promulgated in 1979 declared that the operational Five Year Plans for production were to be based on a 20 year program of scientific-technical development as well as a 10 year plan for social development. Moreover, plans were to incorporate both branch production targets and regional developmental perspectives, the latter of which were to be approved by republican councils of ministers. The production-branch plans and the regional development plans were, of course, to be reconciled with each other.[54] So far, these ambitious projects do not seem to have greatly increased the leaders' capacity for comprehensive planning.

Many attempts to improve planning revolve around the effort to find better plan targets than simply gross output or profit. In 1979, the authorities introduced a new performance indicator called *normative net output* designed to become a master indicator and to replace the previous criteria for measuring enterprise performance. Together with a number of other measures tightening plan discipline, the reform package was, writes Nancy Nimitz, "a respectable third-best reform in a world where the first-best never comes and the second-best comes too late."[55] The 1979 package of economic measures aimed at improving the collection of planning data, devising new and better performance indicators, step-

[52]Its mechanism is well described by an émigré economist who formerly worked in the Soviet planning apparatus. See Igor Birman, "From the Achieved Level," *Soviet Studies* 30, no. 3 (April 1978): 153–72.

[53]Schroeder, "The Soviet Economy on a Treadmill of 'Reforms'," p. 318.

[54]See the discussion of these measures in Berliner, "Planning and Management," pp. 358–59.

[55]Nancy Nimitz, "Reform and Technological Innovation in the 11th Five-Year Plan," in Seweryn Bialer and Thane Gustafson, eds., *Russia at the Crossroads: The 26th Congress of the CPSU* (London: Allen & Unwin, 1982), p. 141.

ping up intrabranch and intraenterprise financing, and stiffening pressures to fulfill supply and construction contracts properly and on time.[56] The full range of information necessary to integrate all aspects of central planning is beyond the capacity of the ministry officials to collect. As a result, according to Morris Bornstein, coordination of effort across branches and regions continues to suffer. Rather, the 1979 program has tended simply to increase the number of conflicting performance indicators to which managers must respond. Preliminary indications are that it has not improved the effectiveness of planning and that, indeed, it may have increased the administrative burden on already overloaded planning and ministerial bureaucracies and therefore made matters worse.[57] New plan indicators have not improved the overall quality of planning because the old indicators seldom disappear, leaving managers and ministers to cope as well as possible with an even broader array of directive targets. Plan integrity suffers as managers choose which targets to meet.[58]

Despite the evident lack of success the 1979 measures have had in improving the quality of planning and administration, their essential features have been included in an economic experiment being tried out in five ministries. On 1 January 1984, two all-union ministries and three republic-level ministries[59] began to apply the new principles of planning at the level of the production association. As Bornstein points out, any intent of the central party leadership to improve economic performance by using this reform to decentralize managerial power is contradicted by the reform's stated goal of strengthening centralized management. Although it is still too early to make a definitive judgment about the effect of this experiment, there is little reason to expect that it will enjoy greater success than the 1979 program.[60]

The quality and predictive accuracy of central plans are also to

---

[56]This "Program to Improve the Economic Mechanism" is analyzed in detail by Morris Bornstein, "Improving the Soviet Economic Mechanism," *Soviet Studies* 37, no. 1 (January 1985): 1–30.

[57]Schroeder, "Soviet Economic 'Reform' Decrees," p. 88.

[58]Bornstein, "Improving the Soviet Economic Mechanism," pp. 16, 22–23.

[59]These are the USSR Ministry of Heavy and Transport Machinery, the USSR Ministry of the Electrical Equipment Industry, the Ukrainian Ministry of the Food Industry, the Belorussian Ministry of Light Industry, and the Lithuanian Ministry of Local Industry.

[60]Bornstein, "Improving the Soviet Economic Mechanism," p. 24.

be enhanced by modern mathematical methods using automated high-speed data-processing technology. Much effort has been made to computerize enterprise management, branch administration, statistical collection, and central planning. For the most part, however, computers have apparently been used only for accounting and statistical analysis, not mathematical modeling or forecasting for plan purposes. Moreover, despite an ambitious project to integrate all economic computation in a single, integrated national network (the OGAS project), different ministries and agencies have acquired their own individual hardware and operating systems, so that actual interbranch networking is very limited. Although great advances have been made by Gosplan's analysts in the modeling of optimal resource allocation within various branches, these sophisticated models tend not to be used in current operational plans, which still rely to a large extent on the old incremental planning "from the achieved level."[61] Probably the most productive way in which to strengthen the integrity of central plans would be to simplify them radically by reducing the number of plan targets set by Gosplan, grouping product targets into large aggregates, and even replacing the practice of planning by physical units of goods (tons of steel; meters of cloth) with the use of value measures (the ruble value of goods produced).[62] The problem with value-based planning — which is used, for example, in Hungary — is that if the measures are to be meaningful, prices must be true scarcity prices, reflecting cost. The structure of Soviet prices is still, despite many comprehensive price reforms, far from an accurate picture of true cost.[63] The Kosygin reforms of 1965 did attempt to improve planning by simplifying it and reducing the number of directive targets set by the plan-

[61]Schroeder, "The Soviet Economy on a Treadmill of 'Reforms'," pp. 319–22; on OGAS, see William J. Conyngham, "Technology and Decision Making: Some Aspects of the Development of OGAS," *Slavic Review* 39, no. 3 (September 1980): 426–45; also see Kathryn M. Bartol, "Soviet Computer Centres: Network or Tangle?" *Soviet Studies* 23, no. 4 (April 1972): 609–19.

[62]At present, value terms are used as a supplement to production plans to help measure the consistency and fulfillment of plans, but the primary units for plans are still physical.

[63]On pricing policy, see Berliner, "Planning and Management," pp. 355–56. Berliner especially points out the detrimental effect of a distorted price structure on incentives for the introduction of new and more efficient technology. He generalizes that "central planning is at its best with well-known technologies, and at its worst with technologies not yet fully developed or even yet unknown."

ners. The decentralizing effect of the reform dissipated within a few years, however, as the planners began reinstating various additional targets for the enterprises.

INTERSECTORAL AND INTERREGIONAL COORDINATION

We noted above that one of the objectives of strengthened central planning was to give the central leadership a better grasp on plans involving multiple branch ministries. Integrated plans requiring the close coordination of several branches in order to bring about comprehensive growth in a locality have proved to be difficult to attain because of the persistent fragmentation of authority among vertically organized branches. Nevertheless, the practice of social planning, which takes into account all the economic and infrastructural needs of a particular locality or region over a plan period, has been widely promoted. In mature cities such as Leningrad it has been a tactic used by the local party and government authorities to enhance the economic strength of the city.[64] In raw areas rich in mineral resources, interbranch plans are essential in order to provide simultaneously for the construction of infrastructural facilities, such as rail and other transportation lines, worker housing, schools, medical care facilities, cultural amenities, and retail trade facilities, and for the capital investment needed for extraction of minerals and production of goods. In these areas the challenge is defined as complex planning, program-goals planning, or the creation of territorial-production complexes. In each case, the common problem is finding a means for integrating planning and administration across sectoral lines and bringing them to bear on a single developmental goal.

Traditionally, the Soviet system has performed relatively poorly at interbranch coordination, since the central authorities have tended to reserve the power to coordinate branch production at the very top of the system, especially in matters related to defense industries. The increasing exhaustion of natural resources in the heavily settled regions of the country, however, above all in areas west of the Urals, and the difficulty of inducing workers to settle in the inhospitable regions where the great mineral wealth is deposited (largely east of the Urals) have required the authorities to

[64]Blair A. Ruble, "Romanov's Leningrad," *Problems of Communism* 32, no. 6 (November–December 1983): 40–45.

vest great authority in regional development projects requiring coordination among ministers. A prime example is the effort to develop the oil and gas industries of Western Siberia, centered in Tyumen province. To facilitate the regional approach to planning and administration for this project, Gosplan created a special department for Western Siberian oil and gas that set up its office directly in Tyumen. The Council of Ministers formed a special council to oversee the development of the oil and gas complex in the region, and established an office linking the relevant energy development ministries.[65] In addition, the Central Committee Secretariat has assumed general direction of energy development, singling it out for special priority and assigning responsibility for the program to Central Committee Secretary Vladimir Dolgikh. In the field, the first secretary of the Tyumen *obkom* plays a crucial role in coordinating the many government agencies and bodies that are overseeing energy development.[66]

Implementation of the Tyumen energy program has not only *not* ended the policy debates relating to Western Siberian regional development, but it has posed new questions even more acutely. How much capital, for example, should be sunk into the construction of permanent cities in the marshy and forbidding territories where the oil and gas fields lie? The debate between those seeking to develop Western Siberia for long-term settlement and those emphasizing rapid but temporary exploitation of its natural resources continues. The local officials seeking more investment in housing, transportation, and other local infrastructures argue that without such development, the bottlenecks that are created by the hasty stripping of Siberia's resources will lead to their early exhaustion and over the long run will damage the country's overall interests. There is some evidence that they are right. Thane Gustafson points out that the push to pump as much natural gas as possible out of the Tyumen deposits is reducing total usable output and may be damaging the pipelines and compressors through which the gas is shipped westward.[67] On the other hand, long-term infrastructural development of Tyumen, which will be extremely

---

[65]Gustafson, *The Soviet Gas Campaign,* pp. 23–24; Schroeder, "Soviet Economic Reform Decrees," pp. 80–81.

[66]Gustafson, *The Soviet Gas Campaign,* pp. 23–25.

[67]Ibid., pp. 79–81.

costly, may not be able to overcome the climatic disadvantages that deter permanent settlers. Many Moscow officials accordingly argue that Siberia should simply be treated as a source of wealth for the country.

As Gustafson observed in the remark we quoted at the outset of this chapter, policy implementation raises new issues for policymakers: policymaking and policy implementation are closely intertwined; we can separate them analytically but not in practice. Special efforts to make branch agencies focus on regional development do not eliminate the choices policymakers must make. Each administrative decision implicitly involves clashes among alternative values in which institutions have political interests, such as short-term versus long-term benefits or maximizing branch output versus building up a region. The natural gas campaign provides a clear example of how difficult it is for Soviet authorities to make the planning and administration system a mechanism for implementing their will. In practice, each implementing unit develops policy goals of its own and uses the policy-implementation process to advance them.

MOBILIZATION VERSUS SYSTEM BUILDING

Gustafson has pointed out that the Soviet system has performed most effectively at two kinds of tasks: accomplishing a small number of large-scale, customized projects and turning out a large number of a highly standardized systems.

> Its [the Soviet system's] great weakness lies in its lesser ability to produce quickly large numbers of custom-made systems, each one adapted to a highly individual setting (computer software systems, small and medium research instruments, novel architectural design, automation of local workplaces and auxiliary tasks, and imaginative use of new construction materials). The general reasons are well known: Vertical segmentation prevents customers from obtaining components and materials quickly from several ministries simultaneously.[68]

Yet these are the very tasks that the system must learn to cope with effectively in the vastly more complex modern era if it is to compete with capitalist systems and avoid internal decay.

[68]Gustafson, *Reform in Soviet Politics,* pp. 138–39.

Soviet scholars and leaders have not been blind to these problems and have attempted to find theoretical solutions. Aware that the complex and shifting needs of the society require sophisticated managerial techniques, Soviet thinkers have drawn on Western management research and other sources to derive new understandings of the importance of good organization to achieve good results. As a result, the study of organizational design is becoming an important area of specialized study.[69] Under the new conception of management, political goals determine organizational structure rather than becoming adapted to the interest of organizations. The theorists recognize that policy-setting and coordinating functions must be separated from operational management in order to allow central levels of the system to provide proper overall direction. Moreover, management must become far more adept at knitting vertically organized hierarchies together, creating flexible and adaptable horizontal structures. In this way, questions arising from conflicts among vertically built agencies do not constantly need to be referred to top officials, a process that overloads the officials' ability to govern.[70]

In a few cases, new units to study and improve organizational structure within exising administrative agencies have been set up. The Ministry of Ferrous Metallurgy has formed a new Department for Improving the System of Management, and the Ministry of Electrical Engineering has established a Department of Organization on Management Systems and Processes.[71] These are still exceptional cases, however; most ministries lack such units. The Tenth Five Year Plan (1976–1980) required each ministry to come up with a master plan for improving its internal organization by 1980, and many did so. Some, however, were limited to modifications of the existing branch structure.[72] So far, the awakened interest shown by top party leaders and some modernizing management experts in redesigning administrative structures has failed

[69]See Paul Cocks, "Rethinking the Organizational Weapon: The Soviet System in a Systems Age," *World Politics* 32, no. 2 (January 1980): 228–57; reprinted in Erik P. Hoffman and Robbin F. Laird, eds., *The Soviet Polity in the Modern Era* (New York: Aldine, 1984), pp. 331–58.

[70]Cocks, "Rethinking the Organizational Weapon," pp. 333–40.

[71]Ibid., p. 343.

[72]Ibid., p. 344.

to overcome the pervasive fragmentation of authority among multiple bureaucratic agencies that, as we have seen, undermines the leadership's capacity for centralized rule.

In fact, the dilemma of constructing sound organizations to make and carry out policy is not so new as the systems theorists contend. It originated in the revolutionary period when the Bolshevik leaders sought to concentrate maximum political power in their hands to defeat internal and external enemies and move to the transformation of society along socialist lines. Through a far-reaching mobilization of society, they turned existing social institutions into units of government, suppressing others by force and seeking to institute centralized control over virtually the entire economy and culture.[73] The result was a chaotic sprawl of bureaucratic institutions at the center of the political system that were resistant to political control or rational planning and driven by multiple conflicting interests. New attempts to centralize power over various problems by creating new super-bureaucracies ended up by producing redundant parallel lines of control that only compounded the problem of control. Just as the accumulated crisis brought about by these problems threatened to bring down the regime, the Bolshevik leaders obtained a respite by a radical act of decentralization: through the New Economic Policy (NEP) they relinquished a great deal of their claimed power over economic production and trade, allowing free markets first in agriculture and later in many manufacturing industries and retaining socialist ownership largely over the commanding heights of the economy, which included basic industries and large enterprises. The Bolsheviks had not, however, despite some interesting advances in organizational theory, resolved the dilemma of establishing functional institutional authority while trying to centralize power.

Under Stalin, the dictator's unchallengeable personal authority replaced institutional authority as the supreme arbiter of policy. Although policymaking and implementation were once again chaotically diffused among a variety of competing institutions,[74] Sta-

---

[73]See Thomas F. Remington, *Building Socialism in Bolshevik Russia* (Pittsburgh, Pa.: University of Pittsburgh Press, 1984).

[74]See Vernon V. Aspaturian, "The Stalinist Legacy in Soviet National Security Decisionmaking," in Valenta and Potter, eds., *Soviet Decisionmaking for National Security*, pp. 42–47 and passim.

lin's own power and his penchant for close involvement in the most minute details of administration allowed the system to function more or less effectively during the war. After the war, however, as Stalin's health failed and the need for effective coordination of administrative bodies was less acute, administrative confusion grew again.[75] The problem, therefore, of institutionalizing authority in a system intent on mobilizing power was left unresolved by the elevation of the dictator to supreme authority over party, armed forces, and government. In the post-Stalin era, with Stalin's successors determined not to allow a new Stalin to dominate the political system as Stalin had, the problem resurfaced; it was simply more acute as the number of organizational bodies that comprised the political system proliferated.

As Gustafson observes, the power lost to the center by the diffusion of decision making to a variety of bureaucratic and local agencies is not necessarily delegated, claimed, or exercised by independent centers. Competing bureaucracies can block one another's actions by obstruction, which need not take the overt form of declarative policy. Bureaucratic veto power, in turn, frustrates the leaders' ability to accomplish policy goals by employing the centralized administrative framework.[76] Their characteristic solution, as a result, is the same as that of the early Bolsheviks or of Stalin: to force intermediate units of the system to turn their attention to one or a few top-priority goals, even to the detriment of other and longer-term policy objectives.

One of Lenin's Bolshevik colleagues once diagnosed the dilemma of Bolshevik power as a clash between the *dubinushka,* or cudgel — with which political leaders clubbed intransigent bureaucrats into doing their will — and the *mashinushka,* or little machine, by which he meant the kind of harmonious, smoothly ordered functioning of the Ford Motor Company, where every worker or manager knows and performs his defined role in the production process. Today's theory of the scientific-technical revolution and of organizational design resembles the early Bolshevik search for the model of the perfect mashinushka that would eliminate friction in carrying out central policy. Bureaucratic resistance, however, to any organizational solutions that injure the

[75]Aspaturian, "The Stalinist Legacy," p. 60.
[76]Gustafson, *Reform in Soviet Politics,* pp. 145–46.

interests of powerful institutions has weakened and distorted even those modest reforms that the leaders have adopted as remedies. It is important to recognize that a reform that significantly restructured the system of policy implementation would necessarily entail the reduction of the policymaking power of central party and government leaders. Whether the new leadership around Gorbachev has the political power to carry out so far-reaching a reform remains to be seen.

CHAPTER IX

Rule Adjudication:
Soviet Justice in Action

INTRODUCTION

The term *rule adjudication* usually refers to the process by which courts or other specialized autonomous legal institutions decide civil and criminal issues. In the case of criminal proceedings, with which we shall be mainly concerned in this chapter, adjudication refers to the process of deciding whether individuals or corporate entities have violated a law and, if so, what penalty must be applied. Since the end of Joseph Stalin's dictatorship, justice dispensed by courts has to a considerable degree replaced terror applied by security police officials as one of the major methods of "managing change" in the USSR.[1]

Progress toward what in pluralist democracies is often called the *rule of law* has been severely limited, however. We shall presently examine in some detail the course of law reform in the USSR. In evaluating the state of legality in Soviet adjudication, we shall draw upon the testimony of a former member of the Soviet bar, Dina Kaminskaya, as well as upon studies by Western scholars of Soviet law. The most experienced of the handful of

---

[1]See, for example, John Hazard, *Managing Change in the USSR* (Cambridge, England: Cambridge University Press, 1983); Robert Sharlet, ed., *The New Soviet Constitution of 1977: Analysis and Text* (Brunswick, Ohio: King's Court Communications, 1978); and Sharlet's highly informative paper "Law, Discipline and the Economy in the USSR," Sixteenth Annual Convention of the American Association for the Advancement of Slavic Studies (New York, 3 November 1984). For a published version of Sharlet's paper, see "Soviet Legal Policy under Andropov: Law and Discipline" in Joseph Nogee, ed., *Russia After Brezhnev* (Praeger: New York, 1985), pp. 85–106.

defense attorneys who took on the risky task of defending dissenters (for which she, like a handful of other such defense attorneys, suffered disbarment), Kaminskaya also had extensive experience in defending persons accused of having committed ordinary crimes such as theft and murder. Both her accounts of individual cases in which she was involved and her general, apparently well-grounded evaluations of Soviet justice as she observed it in 37 years as a defense lawyer demonstrate that Soviet prosecutors, criminal investigators, and judges often violated the legal rights of the accused, occasionally, but at times flagrantly, in nonpolitical cases, systematically in political ones. According to the official Soviet position, there are no political trials in the Soviet Union. Rather, in most cases, political offenders are accused of violating laws against "especially dangerous state crimes" (*osobo opasnye gosudarstvennye prestupleniya*), such as "anti-Soviet agitation," which is covered by the well-known Article 70 of the Russian Republic Criminal Code (a model for corresponding articles in the criminal codes of the non-Russian republics). A systematic effort is made to portray dissidents, for example, as criminals of a kind particularly dangerous to Soviet society. It would not be too much of an exaggeration to say that in the case of persons whose opinions, in the view of the party and KGB, are highly objectionable, Soviet justice functions according to the principle of sentence first, trial later.[2]

In general, Kaminskaya argues convincingly that an alert and skillful Soviet defense attorney can see to it that his client is justly treated. Her position is somewhat similar to that of one of the leading American students of Soviet law, Harold Berman, who wrote some 20 years ago that under Stalin

---

[2]See Dina Kaminskaya, *Final Judgment: My Life as a Soviet Defense Attorney* (New York: Simon & Schuster, 1982), describing a conversation she had with the KGB investigator assigned to replace an investigator on the staff of the Moscow city procuracy — roughly equivalent to a district attorney's office in the United States. The KGB man, commiserating with Kaminskaya on the difficulty of her task of defending the prominent dissident Vladimir Bukovsky, said to her before Bukovsky's trial, "You and I both know that Bukovsky's fate has already been decided." See p. 188. On the illegality committed by the Moscow procurator's office in transferring Bukovsky's case to the KGB, see p. 176. Kaminskaya devotes about a hundred pages to a vivid and chilling account of her successful but extremely arduous effort to see that justice was done in the case of two boys falsely accused by an unscrupulous prosecutor of raping and murdering a girl. See pp. 65–160.

Law was for those areas of Soviet life where the political factor was stabilized. Terror, whether naked or (as in the purge trials of the late 1930s) in the guise of law, was applied when the regime felt itself threatened. But these two spheres were not easy to keep separate either in theory or in practice. It was not a peaceful coexistence.[3]

As Berman added, terror under Stalin had "a deleterious effect" on the Soviet legal system. Because efforts to reform that system might arouse suspicion of "deviationism," reform efforts were "sidetracked." Since the publication of Alexander Solzhenitsyn's *Gulag Archipelago* and numerous works of similar content by Soviet and Western authors, we know how nearly completely in the Stalin era law was overshadowed by terror. The definition of terror that seems most useful to us is "the arbitrary use, by organs of political authority, of severe coercion against individuals or groups."[4] There is no doubt that even after the important reforms of the Soviet legal system in the late 1950s and early 1960s, since the adoption of the 1977 Constitution, and during Yuri Andropov's brief leadership, selective terror has been an important instrument of Soviet government. It has been used especially against dissidents and perpetrators of economic crimes, such as bribery and counterfeiting, to whom in 1961 and 1962 the death penalty was extended, shortly after a trend toward "greater leniency in penal policy" had set in.[5] In the period after the fall of 1979, when Soviet-Western (and especially Soviet-American) relations deteriorated sharply, there was a resurgence of neo-Stalinist practices such as allowing dissidents in labor camps to die prematurely by failing to provide medical care that might have saved their lives, resentencing others after falsely accusing them of having committed ordinary, nonpolitical crimes in camps, and seeing to it that some were tortured by common criminals in camps. A notable victim of the latter practice was the psychiatrist Anatoli Koryagin, sentenced to a camp after he incurred official wrath for zeal in protesting the commitment of dissenters to mental institutions. Perhaps even more significant as an indicator of the So-

---

[3]Harold Berman, *Justice in the USSR,* rev. ed. (Cambridge, Mass.: Harvard University Press, 1963), p. 66.

[4]See Alexander Dallin and George Breslauer, *Political Terror in Communist Systems* (Stanford, Calif.: Stanford University Press, 1970), p. 1.

[5]Berman, *Justice in the USSR,* p. 69.

viet leadership's hostility toward nonconformity and of its disregard for due process and guarantees of legal rights has been the treatment during the period since 1979 of Andrei Sakharov and his wife Elena Bonner. Sakharov was abducted early in 1980 and transported to the city of Gorki, 400 miles from Moscow. For the next several years the couple was constantly harassed, until in 1984 they were isolated from and deprived of communication with the outside world. These events constituted the single most important blow to the freedom movement in the USSR since it began in the 1960s. The muzzling of the Sakharovs was enormously significant because, among other important activities, they had functioned for years as the link between numerous human rights activists and the foreign press and diplomatic communities in Moscow.[6]

Concurrent with these regressive tendencies in the judicial field came the diminution to a thin trickle of emigration from the USSR (mostly Jewish but with significant Armenian and German streams), which had reached its height in 1979.

DEVELOPMENT OF JUDICIAL POLICY SINCE STALIN

Defective as Soviet justice seems to most informed citizens of polyarchies, particularly those with legal systems shaped by Anglo-Saxon traditions, it is vastly superior to the system that the Soviet people endured during the harshly coercive and often frighteningly arbitrary rule of Stalin. This is true even though ever since the substantial reforms that occurred during Nikita Khrushchev's leadership and remain basically intact — in some ways in improved form, in other ways watered down — such features of British and American law as trial by jury, presumption of innocence, judicial review, and habeas corpus are lacking in Soviet law. Such features however, were and still are absent from

---

[6]On the above-mentioned topics, see, for example, Serge Schmemann, "Soviet Dissidents Fear New Law May Add to Sentences," *New York Times,* 5 December 1983, concerning a law that took effect October 1, 1983 and provided terms of up to 5 years "for prisoners who refuse to renounce their activities or causes while in camps." Schmemann reported that this law apparently gave Soviet authorities, in effect, "arbitrary power to extend the sentences of dissidents." His dispatch referred to other important topics, such as publication of the third edition of a book by Nikolai Yakovlev, which "traced the entire dissident movement to a CIA conspiracy." See also David Satter, "The Kremlin Tortures a Psychiatrist," *Wall Street Journal,* 29 December 1983.

the continental European legal systems upon which the legal system brought to the Russian Empire as one of Emperor Alexander II's (1856–1881) Great Reforms was modeled. After a brief period during which the communist rulers flirted with ideas derived from an extremely utopian version of Marxism, such as the withering away of state, law, and even marriage and schools, they realized that — at least until socialism had been built — law and law enforcement were necessary if a measure of social stability was to be achieved. In so doing they tended to revive tsarist institutions but with new names. For example, hated words such as *gendarme* and *police* were replaced by *militia* (*militsiya*), which is still the term that describes the uniformed police, as distinct from the secret police (KGB). Another link with the tsarist past was the communists' practice of declaring off limits to routine law enforcement crimes against the new revolutionary authority and the new socialist property — nationalized mines, factories, and the like.

Until Stalin consolidated his power in the 1930s, however, the Soviet authorities were embarrassed by the use of law, which was still regarded by the regime's authoritative theorists, such as Pashukanis and Stuchka, as quintessentially a part of the capitalist superstructure, an instrument developed by the bourgeoisie to exploit the proletariat, to govern a society aspiring to the building of socialism. Stalin, ably assisted by Andrei Vyshinsky, the prosecutor of former close associates of his in the communist leadership and the chief ideologist of the legal revolution in the 1930s, proclaimed that the Soviet Union was henceforth to be governed by a new, uniquely superior socialist law. The first period of flourishing of socialist law coincided, ironically, with the mass terror of the 1930s.[7] Terror, masquerading as law, reigned supreme. Although this was less true in relatively unpolitical fields, the ability of the authorities, especially of Stalin himself, to designate anything as political inspired pervasive anxiety. What Stalin — and more moderately and rationally, his successors — tried to do was to combine the intimidating force of exceptional measures administered by the secret police with the persuasive force of legal processes and symbolism. In addition, the new Stalinist legality was a useful instrument of Soviet propaganda abroad.

[7]For historical background on the above-mentioned developments, see Berman, *Justice in the USSR*, pp. 24–65, and Peter Juviler, *Revolutionary Law and Order* (New York: The Free Press, 1976), pp. 16–67.

It may be difficult to understand how the post-Stalin Soviet legal system, containing so few safeguards for the rights of individuals against the coercive powers of the state, can be considered an improvement over the Stalinist system. A brief examination of the changes that occurred in the structures and practices of Soviet justice in the Khrushchev era, however, is enough to convince even a skeptical student that the role of law increased substantially after Stalin. Several of Khrushchev's moves were important contributions to the new atmosphere that made legal reform possible by discrediting Stalin and the defenders of his legacy. Among these were denunciations of Stalin's arbitrary and cruel actions, Khrushchev's "secret" but widely known speech of February 1956, his public address at the October 1961 Twenty-second Party Congress (which unlike the 1956 speech went beyond castigating the late dictator for his mistreatment of communists to speak of "evil caused to our Party, the country and the Soviet people"), and his clearance for publication of Solzhenitsyn's famous novella *One Day in the Life of Ivan Denisovich.*[8] Fundamental to the revival of law was the reduction in the scope of the punitive functions of the political police. They lost their role as Stalin's principal instrumentality of rule and became (and seem to have remained) clearly subordinate to the CPSU Politburo. Perhaps of even greater significance in the lives of Soviet citizens was the dismantling of most of the economic empire based on forced labor, administered by the security police and at the labor camp level by the militsiya, under the Ministry of Internal Affairs, or MVD. It was the labor camps, especially death camps such as those in Kolyma, that had been responsible for the premature deaths of millions of Soviet people by malnutrition, hardship, and lack of medical care.

Major events involved in these developments included the abolition in 1953 of the special board (*osoboe soveshchanie*) of the Ministry of Internal Affairs, which on the basis of a 1934 statute had been empowered to sentence suspects, in absentia and without counsel or trial, to terms of up to 25 years in labor camps; the

---

[8]On the creation of an anti-Stalinist, reformist atmosphere under Khrushchev and its vulnerability to neo-Stalinist resistance, see Stephen Cohen, *An End to Silence: Uncensored Opinion in the Soviet Union* (New York: Norton, 1982). The quotation above from Khrushchev's Twenty-second Congress address is on p. 37 of that work.

execution of Lavrenti Beria and many of his former associates in the security services; denunciation of arbitrary actions by police personnel; and amnesty and release of many innocent victims of injustice or their posthumous "rehabilitation."[9]

The most positive developments in Soviet law after Stalin were doubtless those categorized by Berman as reflecting the "tendency toward the elimination of terror," some of which we have already mentioned. Others included abolution of the provision for punishment of "relatives of one who deserts to a foreign country from the armed forces — though they knew nothing of the desertion" and Vyshinski's doctrine that confessions had special evidentiary force in cases of trial for alleged counterrevolutionary crimes or that in such cases the burden of proof shifted to the accused.[10]

Also salutary were such changes as the elimination of the principle of *analogy.* In the first Soviet Criminal Code of 1922 and until its elimination in the 1958 Fundamental Principles of Criminal Law, which replaced the 1922 Code, this doctrine, as Hazard puts it, authorized a "judge who found an act to be socially dangerous to take protective measures against the actor, even if no article of the code defined the act as criminal." Borrowed from a tsarist concept, analogy was extensively applied during the purges of the 1930s.[11]

Although Soviet law today does provide a set of rules defined clearly enough for citizens to know what they must avoid doing in order not to run afoul of the law and its enforcers, it is necessary to keep in mind that the language of many key articles of the criminal codes is vague. Among these are articles 65 and 70 of the RSFSR criminal codes, dealing respectively with espionage

---

[9]See Berman, *Justice in the USSR,* pp. 66–96, enumerating "seven tendencies" in law reform, including "liberalization" of the law and the tendencies toward "the elimination of terror," "systematization and rationalization" of the legal system, "popular participation" in administering justice, and threatening "those who will not cooperate in building communism" with harsh penalties. In addition, says Berman, "a new Soviet theory of law" developed, "which rejected some of the Stalinist innovations in Leninist doctrine."

[10]Berman, *Justice in the USSR,* pp. 70–71.

[11]Hazard, *Managing Change in the USSR,* pp. 202–3. Hazard also notes on pp. 61 and 103 that two articles of the Stalin era criminal code under which "thousands were condemned to serve terms in labor camps," namely, those concerning wrecking and sabotage, "survive from Stalin's time," but that they "are not being applied," "as far as is known."

and anti-Soviet agitation and propaganda, and the even more loosely worded articles 190/1, 190/2, and 190/3. More important is the fact that the KGB security police continue to have jurisdiction over the detection and pretrial investigation of crimes against the state (often referred to in Soviet terminology as especially dangerous state crimes). Although the KGB is not legally empowered to investigate alleged violations of articles 190/1, 190/2, and 190/3, it has done so, as in the case referred to earlier, in which Dina Kaminskaya acted as defense attorney for Vladimir Bukovsky.[12]

Regarding the post-Stalin legal reforms, Berman asserts that they might "prove to have been the most significant aspects of Soviet social, economic and political development in the decade after Stalin's death."[13] He also states, however, that Soviet law remained a "totalitarian law" that sought "to regulate all aspects of economic and social life, including the circulation of thought"; its "primary function" was to discipline, guide, train, and educate Soviet citizens to be dedicated members of a collectivized and mobilized social order."[14] As Berman adds in a later publication, the "long-range problem of the development of Soviet law is "whether Soviet leaders are willing and able to establish not merely a season . . . of freedom and initiative but also a legal and institutional foundation" that would secure these values from the intervention of the leaders themselves.[15] By the late 1960s it was clear that innovative legal reform, at least in the sense of the liberalization that Berman had earlier pointed to as one of the major tendencies at work in the judicial field, had languished. It was

[12]On the history and functions of the KGB, which is the latest in the series of Soviet political security agencies that began with the Cheka (Extraordinary Commission to Combat Counterrevolution and Sabotage) in 1917, see, for example, F. Barghoorn, "The Security Police," in M. Gordon Skilling and Franklyn Griffiths, eds., *Interest Groups in Soviet Politics* (Princeton, N.J.: Princeton University Press, 1971), ch. 4, and Amy Knight, "The Powers of the Soviet KGB," in Erik P. Hoffmann and Robbin F. Laird, eds., *The Soviet Polity in the Modern Era* (New York: Aldine, 1984), ch. 12. Also see John Barron, *KGB* (New York: Reader's Digest Press, 1974), and Barron's *KGB Today* (New York: Reader's Digest Press, 1983). These books focus mainly on the KGB's foreign activities, reflecting its increasing role in foreign espionage, especially in the technology field.

[13]Berman, *Justice in the USSR,* p. 67.

[14]Ibid., p. 68.

[15]Harold Berman, "The Dilemma of Soviet Law Reform," *Harvard Law Review* 76 (March 1963): 950.

clear that for the foreseeable future, political considerations inherent in the doctrine of socialist legal consciousness as interpreted by the CPSU leadership, would largely determine the significance and application of legal rules.[16] Doubts about the quality of Soviet justice and prospects for future improvement, at least in the area of expression and independent, critical thought, were reinforced by such events as sentencing the writers Andrei Sinyavski and Yuli Daniel to labor camps in February 1966 for allegedly slandering Soviet society in creative literary work published abroad. To be sure, the two authors were treated much more humanely than they would have been before Stalin's death, when they would almost certainly have died either in arranged automobile accidents — as happened to numbers of victims of Stalin's anti-cosmopolitan campaign in 1949–1952 — or in camps. Sinyavski and Daniel were tried in court, defended by counsel, and allowed to plead not guilty. On the other hand, they were sentenced not for any illegal actions but for publishing works of fiction deemed by KGB investigators and by prosecutor and judge to fall into the category of anti-Soviet propaganda. Moreover, they were subjected to a long, secret pretrial investigation; with considerable justification it could be said that their case was really tried long before their sentencing by vilification in the Soviet press.[17]

[16]On the last-mentioned doctrine, see the still valuable contribution by Stephen Weiner, "Socialist Legality on Trial," in Abraham Brumberg, ed., *In Quest of Justice* (New York: Praeger, 1970), pp. 39–51. As Weiner points out, this doctrine in effect requires that judges be guided by party policy in deciding "whether a given statute governs a certain pattern of established facts." Thus even if a defendant's procedural rights are not violated, his fate may be decided on the basis of "the political preferences of the regime." This certainly seems to have been the case in many trials of Soviet dissidents.

[17]The protests against the Sinyavski and Daniel trial in the USSR and the Kremlin's embarrassment at the negative reactions abroad, even from some communist intellectuals, led not to a change of policy toward dissent in the USSR but among other things to enactment of Article 190 of the RSFSR Criminal Code, which does not require the prosecutor to prove, even formally, that a person or persons charged with violating it have acted with the purpose of "subverting or weakening Soviet power." For the text in English of Article 70, see Harold J. Berman and James W. Spindler, *Soviet Criminal Law and Procedure,* 2nd ed. (Cambridge, Mass.: Harvard University Press, 1972), pp. 153–54. Articles 190/1, -/2, and -/3, will be found on pp. 180–81 of the same volume. The Sinyavski-Daniel trial, more than any other event, spurred the open expression of critical thought known as the democratic movement and the determined repression thereof by the Soviet authorities, which were striking features of Soviet political and intellectual life in the years after 1966.

CRIME AND THE SOVIET REGIME

According to Leninist doctrine, crime is a product of capitalist society. Its persistence in the Soviet Union was long attributed to survivals in the consciousness of Soviet people inherited from the tsarist heritage or to influences emanating from the bourgeois outside world. Today there is less of the traditional propaganda proclaiming the superiority of humane Soviet justice to the allegedly antiblack, antilabor, antipeace, and antisocial progress brand of justice that Soviet judicial officials have often portrayed as reigning supreme in the imperialist West, especially in the United States.[18]

Vitali Fedorchuk, whom the late CPSU General Secretary Yuri Andropov briefly installed as his replacement as head of the KGB and then in December 1982 put in charge of the Ministry of the Interior (MVD), held a "businesslike and frank" discussion about a wide range of problems, such as corruption, theft, and numerous other kinds of crime, alcoholism, juvenile delinquency, and the quality of police work, in the editorial offices of the important weekly newspaper *Literaturnaya gazeta* in August 1984.[19] Fedorchuk's remarks, which, according to the reported statement of editor-in-chief Chakovsky, dealt with problems that were "troubling . . . readers and our public," comprised only one of several public statements by the tough new law enforcement chief.[20]

[18]But see, for example, A. Sukharev, first deputy minister of justice of the USSR, "V interesakh obshchestva i grazhdanina" (In the Interests of Society and the Citizen) *Pravda,* 15 June 1982, which was published in connection with the 1982 campaign for election of judges and before Yuri Andropov launched his effort to restore discipline to all spheres of Soviet life. The article largely glossed over the defects that were to be acknowledged by the Andropov leadership with perhaps unprecedented candor.

[19]Reported in *Literaturnaya gazeta,* 29 August 1984, and translated in *Current Digest of the Soviet Press* 36, no. 34 (September 19, 1984). The statement characterizing the style of Fedorchuk's discussion was reportedly made by editor-in-chief, A. B. Chakovsky.

[20]See, for example, Fedorchuk's article, "Na sluzhbe pravoporyadka: grazhdanin, obshchestvo, zakon" (In the Service of Legality: the Citizen, Society and the Law), *Pravda,* 10 August 1983; John Burns, "Under Andropov, Policeman's Lot Isn't Happy One," *New York Times,* 14 August 1983, and "A Fraudulent Trial Sets Off Wide Purge in a Soviet Republic," *New York Times,* 16 March 1984; Dusko Doder, "Purge Is Upgrading Police Forces, Soviet Internal Affairs Minister Says," Washington Post Service, in *International Herald Tribune,* 12 August 1983. According to Doder, the former minister of the interior, Nikolai

The public statements of Fedorchuk in the context of Andropov's broad, multifaceted discipline campaign amounted to admitting that crime and other problems were a serious potential threat to the vitality of the Soviet system and in particular to an increasingly stagnant Soviet economy. By implication at least, the new frankness cast doubt on the capacity of Soviet socialism to solve problems that Soviet leaders had usually asserted were, if not nonexistent in the USSR, of diminishing concern. In addition, the revelations that surfaced of corruption and scandal in high places, involving not only Leonid Brezhnev's friend Shchelokov but also his daughter Galina, tarnished the image of Soviet leadership. In the judgment of Andropov and his former KGB associates, whom he and Fedorchuk assigned to the task of rooting out incompetence and corruption in the MVD, the Ministry of Justice, the Procuracy, and other branches of public administration, stern corrective measures were required. These were effected through penalties ranging from demotions and dismissals of personnel from the Ministry of the Interior and other agencies to executions of some officials directly involved in large-scale corruption. Equally or even more important was the significant and extensive legislation enacted during Andropov's leadership. This completed the drafting of laws on which the Brezhnev leadership had embarked but was proceeding at a snail's pace. It affected every aspect of Soviet life — political, economic, and administrative — and agencies such as the police and procuracy, many of whose high-ranking officials were forced to engage in public self-criticism for slack work in the past. A major trend in the field of criminal law was increased harshness of penalties. Penalties were, reports Sharlet, reduced for less than a dozen offenses but increased for scores of other crimes. In some cases, such as *parasitism* — roughly definable as failure of citizens to satisfy the

---

Shchelokov, who had held his post for 16 years prior to his dismissal in December 1982, had managed to acquire four Mercedes-Benz sedans and more than ten other Western-made cars that he had distributed among members of his family. Burns, in the second of his cited articles, reported that the minister of internal affairs of the Belorussian Republic and his deputy, as well as the chief prosecutor, his deputy, the judge in the first "fraudulent" trial, and other officials, were dismissed.

authorities they had done all they should have to get a job in which they could perform socially useful labor, the language of the law was tightened up to make it easier to apply. Some new legislation further enhanced the power of the authorities to combat dissent; other laws increased the pressure on labor to increase productivity.[21]

With the exception of certain continued investigations into corruption in the Uzbek and other national republics, Chernenko's 13-month rule brought about a relaxation of the discipline campaign launched by his predecessor. Traditional exhortation and a don't-rock-the-boat mentality had replaced the effort made by Andropov to, as Sharlet puts it, "revitalize" the Soviet system by "juridization."[22] If in comparison to the stern Andropov, Chernenko seemed easygoing about problems of crime and discipline in general, however, the treatment of dissidents in his regime was, if anything, even harsher than it had been under Andropov. Examples of this attitude include the increasing violence in labor camps against victims such as the psychiatrist-prisoner Anatoli Koryagin and the adamant insistence on holding Andrei Sakharov and Elena Bonner behind a blackout of ominous silence.

LAW AND THE ECONOMY

Largely because the Soviet state administers almost all economic activity — at least *legal* economic activity, as distinct from the generally illegal activity of the underground *second economy* — the range of activities defined as criminal is very wide. Severe penalties are provided for economic crimes against the state. Thus criminal responsibility has been imposed for production of poor

---

[21]On the foregoing, as well as other aspects of the sociopolitical uses of legislation under Andropov, see Sharlet, "Law and Discipline," pp. 11–25.

[22]See Sharlet, "Law and Discipline," pp. 25–37. Here Sharlet points out, inter alia, that the Chernenko leadership was downplaying major economic crime and shifting legal attention from high-ranking to lower-ranking bureaucrats, while at the same time emphasizing upbringing (*vospitanie*) for discipline as a means of correcting the economic and administrative weakness that Andropov had attacked in a harsh, but in many ways serious and systematic, fashion.

quality, for failure to supply certain enterprises with certain products according to plan, and for poor performance.[23]

In Stalin's time it was in fact virtually impossible to run an industrial or agricultural enterprise without violating some law. After Stalin's death accounts of criminal proceedings against workers, farmers, and managers continued to be published.[24] Andropov dramatized the issue of industrial discipline, which of course includes scrupulous respect for law, by his famous unannounced visit to a Moscow factory, in the course of which he reminded managers and government ministers, as well as ordinary workers, of their production obligations.[25]

Perhaps the most significant application of law to the Soviet economy since the 1960s has been as a means of disciplining Soviet labor. It had been Soviet practice to treat workers permissively as long as they in no way challenged the party, state, or management. This means that as a rule, as John Hazard points out, "voluntary choice of a job" was the "basic principle governing employment" in the USSR. This principle was violated on a gigantic scale during the Great Purge by deportation of millions of people to gulag camps as well as by 1940 decrees, issued when war threatened, that sharply tightened labor discipline. Among other things, the new decrees rendered tardiness to work punishable by a fine; three instances of tardiness by over 20 minutes was punishable by a prison term. The new decrees also instituted a labor draft, which allowed the state to assign young people to jobs. Although these laws were repealed in 1955 and

[23]A. V. Venediktov listed thirteen categories of "criminal responsibility" for acts such as "output of poor quality of production." See A. V. Venediktov *Grazhdansko-pravovaya okhrana sotsialisticheskoi sobstvennosti v SSSR* (Civil Law Protection of Socialist Property in the USSR) (Moscow: Izdatelstvo akademii nauk, 1954), p. 264. A decree of April 26, 1958, imposed "criminal responsibility" for the failure of enterprises to supply other enterprises with various materials and products. On this, see A. E. Lunev, *Obespechenie zakonnosti v sovetskom gosudarstvennom upravlenii* (Assurance of Legality in Soviet State Administration) (Moscow: Iuridicheskaia literatura, 1963), pp. 89–95; and George L. Kline, "Economic Crime and Punishment," *Survey*, no. 57 (October 1965): 67–72.

[24]Joseph Berliner, *Factory and Manager in the USSR* (Cambridge, Mass.: Harvard University Press, 1957), chs. 10–12. See also A. N. Vasilev, *Razvitie sovetskoi demokratii i ukreplenie pravoporyadka na sovremennom etape* (Development of Soviet Democracy and Strengthening Legality at Present) (Moscow: Izdatelstvo moskovskogo universiteta, 1967), ch. 4.

[25]See Serge Schmemann, "Andropov on Plant Tour, Tells Workers to Produce," *New York Times*, 2 January 1983.

1956, internal passport regulations continued to restrict the mobility of workers and especially collective farmers, and the job assignment system for graduates of universities, technical schools, and vocational training schools still required 3 years of labor at a state-assigned job.[26]

Hazard mentions several important laws and decisions designed "to strengthen labor discipline with a view to increasing productivity," such as a 1977 ruling of the Russian Republic Supreme Court against a mechanic who had been transferred against his will to unskilled work and a 1980 statute according to which work norms are set "not for the individual workbench" but for the Production Brigade, or team of workers, making each member "responsible for the action of all other members."[27]

The fragility and narrow limits of the legal position and rights of labor in the USSR are emphasized in a study published in 1982 by Yuri Luryi.[28] On the basis of his experienced observations as a Soviet jurist and with impressive documentation, Luryi demonstrates that, for example, the right to unite in social organizations such as trade unions, granted to Soviet citizens by the 1977 Constitution, is by no means equivalent in practice to the right to organize or establish associations, which in effect the USSR granted when it signed the International Covenants and Conventions on Human Rights. To be sure, as Luryi points out, Soviet laws and the constitution do not prohibit establishment of associations. As Luryi asserts, "Therefore a social organization without a party nucleus may also exist in the USSR." All efforts to establish such free, nonparty trade unions in the USSR have been harshly penalized, but the participants in these efforts were either confined to psychiatric institutions or charged

[26]See Hazard, *Managing Change in the USSR,* pp. 84–86.

[27]Ibid., pp. 90–91, citing as a source the Soviet emigrant legal scholar, Yuri Luryi. It should be noted that Hazard perceives not only labor but also Soviet management as hampered, the latter in contributing to professed regime objectives of utilizing science and technology to the full in raising productivity. Both labor and management suffer from continued centralized bureaucratic controls, but Hazard appears to think that lawyers may be able to help the Soviet leadership to develop new institutions capable of coordinating administration with accelerated application of new technology. See especially pp. 49–57, 83, 88.

[28]See his chapter "Three Years of the New USSR Constitution: the Soviet Approach to Human Rights," in F. J. M. Feldbrugge and William Simons, eds., *Perspectives on Soviet Law for the 1980s* (The Hague: Martinus Nijhoff, 1982), pp. 53–75.

with stealing, hooliganism, or disseminating "false distortions which defame the Soviet system"; they were not charged with violating any legal prohibition of the right to organize a union, since formally there is none.[29]

From time to time lead newspaper editorials are published on the importance of law and its strict enforcement as a factor in the performance of the economy, and indeed the functioning of the social and political system in general.[30]

A large branch of Soviet civil law deals with economic relations between enterprises and other state organizations. In addition, a vast body of administrative regulations governs such matters as

---

[29]Luryi discusses the above question on pp. 53–58. The remainder of his essay is devoted to an equally realistic analysis of violations by Soviet authorities of two aspects of the right to work, namely, the right to just and favorable conditions of work and the right of free choice of work without discrimination. See pp. 58–72. Among other things, Luryi accuses the KGB in several cases that he cites of applying the principle of analogy, officially repealed in 1961. One of these was the notorious case in which Arseni Roginski, a secondary school teacher, a man of an independent, critical turn of mind and a highly respected historian, was dismissed from his teaching job after the KGB, in two searches of his home, found books it considered subversive; however, the charge employed to bring about his dismissal by the principal of the school where he worked — in violation of the Fundamental Principles of Labor Legislation and with the passive assent of the trade union to which Roginski belonged — was that he had, among other things, violated an article of the RSFSR Criminal Code by allegedly forging letters recommending that he be allowed to use for his research certain archival materials in libraries. According to Luryi, this article was, in any case, inapplicable to Roginski's case, and the proceedings against him "contradicted the norms of Soviet criminal law" and violated the Soviet constitution. For an excellent, concise history of the movement for socioeconomic rights in the USSR, see Ludmilla Alekseeva, *Istoriya inakomysliya v SSSR* (History of Dissent in the USSR) (Benson, Vt.: Khronika Press, 1984), pp. 379–95; see also F. Barghoorn, "Regime-Dissenter Relations after Khrushchev," in Susan Gross Solomon, ed., *Pluralism in the Soviet Union* (London: MacMillan, 1983), pp. 139–46.

[30]See, for example, "Pravovaya kultura" (Legal culture), *Pravda,* 19 July 1981, which begins by saying that Lenin considered law the "highest measure of rational behavior." Also see "Pravovye rychagi ekonomiki" (Legal Levers of the Economy), *Pravda,* 27 November 1984, a much meatier, more powerful piece, presumably reflecting the continued impact of Andropov's (and perhaps Gorbachev's) concern for the uses of law as an instrument of social and political control. This dealt briefly with a series of important topics, such as the application of law to increasing labor productivity by rendering the brigade form of work organization as effective as possible, assuring fulfillment and overfulfillment of the production plan, and fighting such crimes as bribery and "speculation, waste and theft of socialist property, abuse of official positions, etc." Its optimistic tone regarding what had allegedly been accomplished in respect to ending economic crime probably reflected the difference in the outlook of the Chernenko leadership from that of Andropov.

preparing and executing contracts among productive units, supply agencies, transport and warehousing organizations, and the like. The desire to use formally codified law as an instrument of central control is thwarted by the immense complexity of the system of rules and regulations that have accumulated over time and the resulting need by managers to bend the rules in order to meet their plan targets. Accordingly, a long-standing debate among Soviet jurists concerns whether all economically related civil and administrative law provisions should be unified and codified in a separate branch of law called economic law. Those favoring the reform intend economic law to strengthen plan discipline and ensure the conformity of managerial behavior with the letter and intent of the authorities. Opponents evidently fear the consequences of giving bureaucratic officials new grounds justifying administrative interference in the operations of the economy. As Harold Berman comments in discussing this debate, the paucity of general principles pertaining to economic relations — above all the near absence of the concept of the reciprocity of rights and obligations vis-à-vis subordinate and superior organizations — in Soviet civil law and the abundance of references in civil law to particular administrative regulations make it likely that movement in the direction of the proposed reform would further strengthen bureaucratic power at the expense of law.[31]

JURISCONSULTS AND ARBITRATORS

A late 1984 scholarly study provides the first substantial information in English on the functions and significance of two hitherto little studied elements of the legal system, jurisconsults and arbitrators.[32] Louise Shelley based her informative study partly on interviews with twenty-five individuals in Israel and North America who had worked in the USSR either full time or part time as jurisconsults (*iuriskonsulty*) or arbitrators (*arbitry*) and partly on published Soviet and Western sources. Jurisconsults ''are the lawyers employed on a full-time or part-time basis by ministries, local Soviet enterprises, and educational and medical institu-

[31]Harold J. Berman, "The Concept of Soviet Economic Law and Its Implications for the Operation of the Soviet Planned Economy," in Feldbrugge and Simons, eds., *Perspectives on Soviet Law for the 1980s,* pp. 197–200.

[32]Louise I. Shelley, *Lawyers in Soviet Work Life* (New Brunswick, N.J.: Rutgers University Press, 1984).

tions." Their formal responsibilities include "insuring that the law is upheld . . . in organizational operations, improving the economic indicators of their enterprise, and providing legal assistance to employees of their organization and its trade union." As Shelley points out, jurisconsults are not members of the bar, unlike defense lawyers, some of whom, as she also indicates, are sometimes employed part time by enterprises.[33] Arbitrators "act as judges in a system of economic courts with powers of both a judicial and administrative character. It is to them that iuriskonsults must turn to resolve the economic disputes involving their organizations."[34]

The study finds that the "resolution of the daily legal problems of Soviet citizens" by "free legal assistance that employees receive at their workplace on such work-related problems as pensions and vacation leave as well as on such personal matters as divorce, child support, inheritance and housing . . . is an important source of stability for the Soviet regime." It observes, however, that the "widespread habit of evading and even violating the law," common to management, lawyers and workers, "makes it difficult for law to realize its potential role in Soviet society."[35] In addition, "the manager of an organization determines the role law assumes in his institution." Many jurisconsults have low pay and relatively poor working conditions, and since they are subordinate to their managers, "they must be careful not to . . . antagonize them." Indeed, jurisconsults "can be fired at the whim of the director."[36]

In a chapter entitled "Law and the First Economy," the study shows that the "enterprise lawyer who effectively uses all available legal tools can improve the economic indicators of his organization," if, for example, he or she is alert and knowledgeable about the preparation of contracts or has the requisite knowledge,

[33]Ibid., pp. 4, 13.

[34]Ibid., p. 4.

[35]Ibid., pp. 4–5.

[36]Ibid., pp. 4–6, where Shelley also notes that female jurisconsults have more limited possibilities of promotion than males. In contrast to jurisconsults, arbitrators are better paid, hence not forced to seek outside employment to supplement their regular pay, but the major drawback of their work is its "perceived futility," rooted "often in the Soviet economic system rather than in specific management practices." See pp. 50–52 for last-quoted assertion.

skill, and courage successfully to sue the Soviet railroads ''for their failure to provide prompt service,'' thus preventing the enterprise from receiving supplies on time to maximize its efficiency and fulfill its plan.[37] Managers appreciate the ability of a skilled jurisconsult to find needed flexibility in the maze of rules and regulations that confront him, even though this frequently means finding loopholes in the law or covering up for minor violations.

A series of laws in the 1960s and 1970s that were aimed at raising the level of legality in the economy accentuated the ambiguous role played by law in the first, or legal, economy. A 1963 decree made enterprise jurisconsults watchdogs over the propriety of managerial acts and was followed by a 1972 law obliging them not only to ensure that the actions of enterprise administrators conformed to the law but also to assist in exposing inefficiency and ensuring the fulfillment of duties. These and other enactments required the enterprise lawyers to assist management in preventing, filing, and defending against suits by other enterprises, which could potentially be costly for the enterprise. The jurisconsult advises on the drafting of contracts and counterplans, represents management in arbitration, and helps in disputes between management and labor. All of these duties place the jurisconsult in the position of representing management; according to Louise Shelley's interviewees, jurisconsults are part of management. On the other hand, the requirement that they stand outside management in order to expose waste, inefficiency, and criminal acts creates conflicting pressures. Similarly, the jurisconsult frequently presents lectures to the workers and holds private consultations with workers informing them of their legal rights and advising them on their problems. In cases of conflict between workers and management, however, jurisconsults generally take the side of management against workers. Even where managers directly violate labor law, the jurisconsult and trade union together have little power to check them.[38] In the second, or illegal, economy, ''all levels of employees are involved,'' in-

[37]Ibid., pp. 58–63. Shelley reports that most jurisconsults ''are unaware of the railroads' complex operating regulations or are afraid to confront an organization with strong government protection.''

[38]Ibid., pp. 3–5, 32–33, 48–49, 53–55, 79–89, 96–118, 145–49 and passim.

cluding, according to Shelley, "managers, workers, supervisory personnel and sometimes the jurisconsults."[39]

Apparently the efforts of jurisconsults to reduce the losses to their enterprises caused by theft by employees, for example, and other forms of illegal economic activity, achieve very limited success; indeed, in the interests of their own safety, as Shelley puts it, "most legal advisers keep both their avaricious and their altruistic instincts in check." By remaining detached from the second economy, lawyers "maintain their moral principles, avoid arrest, and may gain rewards from managers appreciative of their unseeing eye."[40]

In her last chapters — "Law and the Employee," "Lawyers in Social and Governmental Organizations," and "The Role of Law in Soviet Work Life" — she holds that the law governing the "behavior of management and workers is more closely obeyed than the legislation that regulates economic performance" and that the jurisconsult "is often the individual to whom workers and service personnel turn when they need assistance in both their work-related and their personal problems."[41] In social service organizations, city government departments, arts institutions, and so on, the work of the jurisconsult is in many respects "more like that of a social worker than a lawyer." In these organizations, a large share of the lawyers employed are female, "reflecting the

[39]Ibid., p. 79. The author also points out that there are frequent conflicts between the private interests and the public responsibilities of the jurisconsult, who "is often at the same time a participant in illegal activities and the individual responsible for upholding the law." Managers frequently find jurisconsults useful either in colluding with their illegal actions or in supplying legal camouflage for them. Jurisconsults appear, however, to be less involved in illegal economic activity than directors, bookkeepers, and warehouse managers and even than legal professionals employed in the criminal justice system, but they often are "rewarded in semi-legal ways" by directors for "turning their energies to the benefit of their organizations." She cites the startling case of one of her interviewees who, though his salary hardly exceeded 2000 rubles a year, had accumulated well over 100,000 rubles — approximately $130,000 — by accepting bribes, buying and selling houses, and similar activities (p. 81).

[40]Ibid., p. 86. See also p. 95, where Shelley asserts that "the second economy has survived because it provides tangible benefits to millions of individuals." Its "major beneficiaries," she writes, "are management and the Party apparatus that rules the Soviet state." Hence, "until the . . . bureaucratic and Party elite identify their welfare with that of their enterprises, law will remain an ineffective weapon . . . and iuriskonsults and arbitrators will be permitted only to remedy the damage inflicted by the second economy instead of fighting to eradicate it."

[41]Ibid., pp. 119–20.

lesser prestige accorded to those who work in these areas.''[42] The case studies examined of jurisconsults ''employed outside the economic sector reveal that their patterns of behavior . . . were strikingly different from those . . . employed in factories and trade organizations.'' The jurisconsults employed in noneconomic spheres, less likely to be forced to ''participate in the illegal activities of their coworkers,'' ''could obtain a sense of personal accomplishment from their work.''[43]

In her concluding chapter, the author again emphasizes the considerable significance of the work of lawyers in the Soviet workplace. For example, she regards their responsibilities as broader than those of corporate counsel in the West, although she also again asserts that though in the USSR ''the scope of the lawyer's responsibilities is broader,'' ''he can actually carry out only a portion thereof.''[44] She speculates, however, that as ''the Soviet administrative apparatus comes to appreciate'' ''the economic and social gains that can be achieved through the medium of the law,'' jurisconsults may come ''to play a more vital role.''[45]

She poses the interesting question, ''Why is it that legal violations destabilize Western societies but are a source of stability for the Soviet regime?'' The answer, she believes, is that the West has a tradition of ''codified law'' and of viewing violations of the law as threats to ''basic societal tenets,'' but in Russia and the USSR, ''the force of law rests not on a written code but on the ability of individuals to personalize authority.'' In addition, however, ''established legal procedures do govern the daily economic transactions of Soviet business life and the domestic problems of primary concern to Soviet workers.''[46]

Although the claims Shelley makes for the role of ''personalized'' and ''flexible'' law in the USSR may be a bit optimistic (considering, for example, that ''more than half the enterprises and organizations do not yet have a full-time iuriskonsult''[47]) nevertheless this absorbingly interesting study is a valuable corrective to the widespread view in the West that law and lawyers

[42]Ibid., p. 121.
[43]Ibid., p. 141.
[44]Ibid., p. 143.
[45]Ibid., pp. 143–44.
[46]Ibid., p. 149.
[47]Ibid., p. 37.

are of no significance in Soviet life. It is also an indirect source of much valuable information on many hitherto obscure aspects of daily popular life in the Soviet Union.

STRUCTURE OF THE LEGAL SYSTEM

In the Soviet Union the legal profession comprises more than 150,000 individuals working in law-related occupations. These include some 20,000 *advokaty* (defense attorneys), 100,000 jurisconsults, 13,500 judges, 17,000 procurators (comparable to public prosecutors), and 3,255 notaries. (Unlike their American counterparts, Soviet notaries are degreed lawyers who perform many of the routine legal functions, such as drafting wills, that would be performed by attorneys in the United States, while also performing standard notarial functions such as certifying documents.[48]) Although when compared with the 6 million persons with higher degrees in engineering or the nearly 1.5 million scientific workers employed in the Soviet Union, the legal profession is small, its members can rise to high rank and influence, especially in the procuracy and the KGB.[49] Excepting Lenin, probably the most politically successful lawyer in Soviet history is Mikhail Gorbachev, who graduated from the Law Faculty of Moscow State University in 1955. Gorbachev, however, did not enter the legal profession after graduation but immediately undertook Komsomol and then party work. Lawyers also find increasing demand for their services in government, especially in local soviets, where the lack of such people leads frequently to decisions "not grounded in law."[50] Nonetheless, in spite of their improved education, their greater professional cohesiveness and their "common vested interest in the preservation of legality," members of the legal profession have generally achieved only limited success in preventing negative developments in the law.[51]

[48]W. E. Butler, *Soviet Law* (London: Butterworth, 1983), pp. 78, 87, 95, 103, 110.

[49]T. Harry Rigby, *Communist Party Membership in the USSR, 1917–1967* (Princeton, N.J.: Princeton University Press, 1968), p. 439.

[50]V. A. Lebin and M. N. Perfilev, *Kadry apparata upravleniya v SSSR* (Cadres of the Administrative Apparatus of the USSR) (Leningrad: Nauka, 1970), pp. 131–34.

[51]The cohesiveness of the legal profession rises in the face of any attempts — more common under Khrushchev than now — to replace professional law enforcement with lay assemblies and community vigilante groups. See Peter H. Juviler, "Criminal Law and Social Control," in Donald D. Barry, William E.

Judges, advocates, and procurators are trained members of a profession that, in spite of small modifications, is basically under the control of the party. The most powerful of the three is the procurator, who serves as the prosecuting arm of the government and as one of its legal watchdogs. Though not enjoying a very favorable official image, the advocate may nevertheless be relatively well off and a member of the elite. His role in court as a defense counsel, however, is overshadowed by that of the procurator. The judge dominates the proceedings — in keeping with the continental, or civil law, tradition, as opposed to the common law, or Anglo-Saxon, tradition that prevails in the United States[52] — but generally conducts them on the basis of materials prepared by the procurators. (Jurisconsults, notaries, and other members of the legal profession will not occupy our attention, except insofar as we mention individual legal scholars who have played a major role in proposing legal reforms.[53])

JUDGES

Although they are formally elected — directly by the citizenry at the lowest (city or district) level, that of the people's court, and by the soviets at higher levels — Soviet judges are essentially civil servants, "promoted from lower to higher courts on the basis of ability."[54] Most judges today have a higher legal education (in contrast to the situation in 1936, when only 7.6 percent had a higher legal education), but they are not required to be degreed lawyers. All Soviet courts, whether people's courts or higher-level courts, may serve as courts of first instance, depending on the type of case, but in practice it is the people's courts that are the courts of first instance in the vast majority of cases. Soviet law requires that all cases heard in courts of the first instance be heard

---

Butler, and George Ginsburgs, eds., *Contemporary Soviet Law: Essays in Honor of John N. Hazard* (The Hague: Martinus Nijhoff, 1974), p. 54. On the Soviet legal profession as an "interest group," see Donald D. Barry and Harold J. Berman, "The Jurists," in Skilling and Griffiths, *Interest Groups in Soviet Politics,* pp. 291–334.

[52]See John Henry Merryman, *The Civil Law Tradition* (Stanford, Calif.: Stanford University Press, 1969).

[53]Descriptions of the major structures of the legal system, written by leading Western scholars, may be found in F. J. M. Feldbrugge, ed., *Encyclopedia of Soviet Law* (2 vols.) (Dobbs Ferry, N.Y.: Oceana Publishers and Leiden: A. W. Sijthoff, 1973).

[54]Barry and Berman, "The Jurists," p. 308.

collegially. This means that judges in people's courts, and occasionally in higher-level courts, are joined in hearing cases by members of the public termed *people's assessors*. Two people's assessors — who are equivalent to juries in the Anglo-American system — are elected laypersons who have equal rights with the judge in deciding verdicts and sentences. The lay assessors are elected for two and one half years and serve no more than two weeks per year, whereas judges are elected for five years; thus it is likely that judges, by reason of their legal experience and training and longer tenure, exercise decisive influence over judicial decisions.[55]

Above the level of the people's courts, regular courts exist at the provincial, republican, and all-union levels of the political system. Autonomous and union republics and the federal government of the USSR all have supreme courts, which oversee the lower courts. All courts above the people's courts hear appeals from lower-level courts and in certain types of cases (especially complex ones, for example) exercise original jurisdiction, but about 95 percent of all cases are heard initially by the people's courts.[56] City and province-level courts, which Barry and Berman term "intermediate appellate courts," have original jurisdiction over cases such as murder with aggravating circumstances, counterfeiting, and desertion. Supreme courts of the fifteen republics can review decisions of the intermediate courts. The Supreme Court of the USSR, the only all-union court, has original jurisdiction in cases appealed from decisions of republic supreme courts. An extremely important function of the supreme courts is that of guiding the work of lower courts; their "guiding explanations," according to Butler, provide important and binding instruction on how to apply current law and are published in regular bulletins. Although not formally considered law, these instructions have the force of law and help to ensure that lower courts adjudicate cases according to party policy and uniform legal standards.[57]

According to the constitution, "Judges and people's assessors are independent and subordinate only to the law."[58] Direct in-

[55]On the structure of courts, see Butler, *Soviet Law,* pp. 94–101.
[56]Ibid., p. 96.
[57]Ibid, p. 98.
[58]Sharlet, ed., *The New Soviet Constitution of 1977,* p. 126 (Article 155).

terference by party organizations in particular cases is condemned. Judges are expected, however, to adhere to the spirit of
party policy in their decisions, and through a variety of methods
the party exercises supervision over judicial activity.[59] Nevertheless, in a substantial minority of cases, party supervision takes the
form of direct instruction to judges on the disposition of individual
cases, through hints or advice on verdicts or sentences. Because
party officials may at any time interfere in particular cases, it is
hard to separate broad party oversight of the judicial process from
intervention, since judges must always keep the wishes of the party
organization in mind.[60] The great majority of judges are CPSU
members and hence subject to party discipline and, in particular,
to the influence of the doctrine of socialist legal consciousness.[61]
The careers of both members and nonmembers of the party are
subject to the controls the party wields over personnel through the
nomenklatura system. Moreover, the party *apparat* possesses several
means of influencing the judicial process. All courts have primary
party organizations, which constantly seek ways of upholding the
goals and interests of the party in the judiciary. In addition, the
party maintains close contact with the bench through periodic regional conferences of legal cadres, at which the current party line

[59]A comprehensive survey of the modes of party supervision over and inter-
ference into the legal process is provided in Robert Sharlet, "The Communist
Party and the Administration of Justice in the USSR," in Donald D. Barry et
al., eds., *Soviet Law After Stalin, Part III: Soviet Institutions and the Administration of
Law* (Alphen aan den Rijn, The Netherlands and Germantown, Md.: Sijthoff
and Noordhoff, 1979), pp. 321–92. Also see F. J. M. Feldbrugge, "Law and
Political Dissent in the Soviet Union," in Barry, Butler, and Ginsburgs, eds.,
Contemporary Soviet Law, pp. 55–68; also see Christopher Osakwe, "Due Process of
Law and Civil Rights Cases in the Soviet Union," in Donald D. Barry, George
Ginsburgs, and Peter B. Maggs, eds., *Soviet Law after Stalin, Part 1: The Citizen
and the State in Contemporary Soviet Law* (Leyden: A. W. Sijthoff, 1977), pp. 179–
221. Osakwe believes there is a clear distinction between political and ordinary
cases, the former being any that the authorities deem politically significant. Although violations of the legal rights of individuals may occur in the operation of
the legal system in ordinary cases, the latter are characterized, he believes, by a
good-faith effort to apply the laws. In political cases, however, "the rule of law
gives way to unbridled arbitrariness both at the operational and planning levels
of government." Thus he finds a "double standard" in the legal system. See
Osakwe, pp. 214–15. The evidence cited in Sharlet's article, however, suggests
that party intervention occurs routinely in certain kinds of nonpolitical cases as
well, as will be detailed below.

[60]Sharlet, "The Communist Party and the Administration of Justice," p. 332.

[61]On the party membership of judges, see Rigby, *Communist Party Membership*,
pp. 424–25.

on matters of both law and policy are discussed and conveyed to judges.[62] Instructors from the party organization and from state agencies (particularly the Ministry of Justice and its local branches), consult with judges, inspect their work, and offer both professional and political direction. Through all these channels, party officials inform judges of the nature and goals of current political campaigns, such as the 1966 campaign against hooliganism and alcoholism or the 1969 and 1974–1975 waves of prosecution against economic violators.[63] During campaigns, both the high rates of convictions obtained and the severity of sentences meted out against offenders who fall into the highlighted category are expected to serve a widely educational purpose, persuading the public that the authorities are taking action against a major form of crime and deterring others from following a criminal path. Judges are expected to take their cue from the party during such campaigns, which, as Sharlet points out, may push adjudication across the boundary from full and vigorous enforcement of the law to abandonment of the law in pursuit of political aims.[64]

In cases when party supervision of the judicial process shades into interference, verdicts and even sentences are decided well before a trial begins. The types of cases in which direct party interference occurs vary. One category consists of offenses committed by party officials and other members of the nomenklatura stratum and even by ordinary party members. In such instances, it is apparently the rule that the party first decides on the fate of the offender, and only with the party committee's permission may the judicial process unfold. Obviously, law-breaking officials enjoying high-level protection may be able by this means to escape prosecution for their crimes for years. In the notorious case of the first secretary of the Communist Party of the Georgian Republic, V. P. Mzhavanadze, who until exposed and replaced in 1972 was involved in large-scale racketeering with many of the

[62]Sharlet, ''The Communist Party,'' p. 332.

[63]On the effect of political campaigns on judicial behavior, see Sharlet, ''The Communist Party,'' pp. 355–56. An informative analysis of the rates of procuratorial representation during the peaks and troughs of particular campaigns is provided by Gordon B. Smith, ''Procuratorial Campaigns against Crime,'' in Barry et al., eds., *Soviet Institutions and the Administration of Law,* pp. 143–67.

[64]Sharlet, ''The Communist Party,'' p. 356.

republic's top officials, only a decision at the level of the All-Union CPSU Politburo to punish him finally ended his career.[65]

In other instances, the party deems a case politically significant. No one accused of violating the statutes of the criminal codes against ''anti-Soviet agitation and propaganda'' has yet been acquitted in court; in practice, therefore, the party decides the outcomes of all trials of dissidents beforehand. Even an unexpectedly vigorous defense offered by the accused's *advokat* has no effect on the outcome. Usually in fact, the role of the defense lawyer is confined to pleading for leniency from the court rather than seeking to refute the procurator's case. An excessively energetic defense in a political case may result in the lawyer's disbarment.[66] The rigged quality of trials against dissidents is reinforced by the practice of selective admission to the courtroom; besides close family members, the public in attendance frequently consists of loyal Komsomol youth or KGB informers, who can be counted upon to evince their hostility to the defendant.

On occasion party officials may intervene in other, nonpolitical cases. These may involve well-known offenders or highly visible crimes, or the cases may be important as object lessons in the course of a current anticrime campaign. Sometimes a party official exercises personal authority and intercedes to protect an ally or settle accounts with an enemy. When a party official lacks approval or justification for interfering with justice, however, he may provoke the righteous indignation of the party, which periodically holds up instances of unjustified meddling in the legal process as examples of unparty-like behavior. Then the party's condemnation of the individual act of intervention is shown to be further confirmation of the party's respect for the inviolate independence of the judiciary from political pressure.

In a variety of ways, therefore, the CPSU exercises close control over both the adjudicative and socializing functions of Soviet courts. It is not only political forces, however, that affect the role Soviet judges play. Traditional Russian concepts of law, together with the principles of the continental legal tradition (also sometimes called the civil law, Napoleonic, or Romanist tradition),

[65]Ibid., p. 362.
[66]Ibid., pp. 367–68.

strongly influence the behavior of judges. In some ways, their role is broader than that of judges in the Anglo-American tradition. In keeping with the structure of judicial process in the continental system, for example, Soviet judges are expected to take an active part in ascertaining the facts in a given case; they do not sit as umpires in an adversarial proceeding between prosecution and defense, as do British and American judges. In addition, in keeping with a prerevolutionary Russian tradition, they are expected to represent society in its educational and parental role vis-à-vis the defendant (and the public generally). In other words, the judge exercises a good deal of discretion — guided, of course, by the spirit of party-mindedness — over the fate of the accused. The vagueness and breadth of many legal statutes create ample opportunity for arbitrary decisions.[67] During a trial, the court will try to teach the transgressor the error of his ways and point out to him the path he must follow if, after serving his sentence, he is to be an honest, public-spirited Soviet citizen.[68] The message of the courts is underlined by their authority to impose a large array of sanctions, including sentences that strike the citizen of a Western system as extraordinarily harsh.[69] In keeping with the educational mission of the court, which, as Harold Berman observes, is an end in itself in Soviet justice and not merely a hoped-for byproduct of the process,[70] the court proceedings often receive wide publicity in the press. Press commentary about cases even before they are heard in court, often written in a tone of sententious moralism that would be considered prejudicial to a defendant's rights in a democratic system, is also considered part and parcel of the socially educational function of courts. Indeed, the concept that pretrial publicity may be injurious to the defendant's rights is alien to Soviet thinking. Judges, advocates, procurators, and all other members of the legal profession are also expected to write and lecture before the public.

On the other hand, the position of the judge is quite limited in some ways. Obviously, as we have seen, judges are subject to both

---

[67]Osakwe, "Due Process," p. 215.

[68]Berman, *Justice in the USSR,* pp. 282–84, 299–308.

[69]George Feifer, *Justice in Moscow* (New York: Delta, 1965), pp. 217–18 and passim.

[70]Berman, *Justice in the USSR,* p. 283; and idem, "The Educational Role of Soviet Criminal and Civil Procedure," in Barry, Butler, and Ginsburgs, eds., *Contemporary Soviet Law,* p. 13.

direct and indirect political pressure from the CPSU and perhaps from the KGB as well. The constitutional position of the Soviet judge is also weak, however.[71] Judges are not empowered to refuse to enforce statutes on constitutional grounds, and they lack jurisdiction over major economic disputes. Finally, judges are overshadowed in prestige, and often in training and experience, by procurators. It attests to the stature of the procuracy in relation to the bench that the conviction rate in the USSR is about 90 or 95 percent.[72]

PROCURATORS

In application and interpretation of the law, procurators are second only to the KGB in real power, and even the KGB cannot initiate an investigation or make an arrest without permission from the appropriate officer of the procuracy. Historically, the procuracy goes back to the time of Peter the Great, although its present legal roots derive from a statute passed in 1955. If the rate of male saturation can be taken as an index of the power and prestige of an occupation, then the procuracy has the highest status of all the legal professions, being at least 95 percent male. This compares with a rate of 63.5 percent for judges, 60 percent for advocates, and 20 percent for notaries. Moreover, some 83 percent of procurators are party members.[73]

The procuracy is a kind of bureaucratic-legal hydra. Its most important administrative function is to fight graft and corruption in the economy, a function that has come to occupy a growing portion of procurators' time.[74] In its legal aspect, the procuracy seeks to ensure that high-level party and state policy is carried out and that officials of middle and low rank do not exercise their

[71]See Leonard Schapiro, "Prospects for the Rule of Law," *Problems of Communism* 14, no. 2 (March–April 1965): 2–7.

[72]See Butler, *Soviet Law,* p. 317.

[73]These figures and other information about the procuracy are drawn from Butler, *Soviet Law,* pp. 79, 95, 103, 110. For a history and analysis of the procuracy's role, also see Glenn G. Morgan, *Soviet Administrative Legality* (Stanford, Calif.: Stanford University Press, 1962), and D. S. Karev et al., *Organizatsiya suda i prokuratury v SSSR* (Organization of Court and Procuracy in the USSR) (Moscow: Gosiurizdat, 1961), chs. 9–10. A recent study of the role of the procuracy in enforcing standards of administrative legality is Gordon B. Smith, *The Soviet Procuracy and the Supervision of Administration* (Alphen aan den Rijn, The Netherlands: Sijthoff and Noordhoff, 1978).

[74]Smith, *The Soviet Procuracy,* p. 132.

power arbitrarily. For this purpose it has departments charged with general supervision over the legality of all governmental operations, including the courts (except the USSR Supreme Court) and other economic and administrative agencies. The Council of Ministers of the USSR and the CPSU are exempt from its supervision, however. Finally, the procuracy is expected to protect the rights of citizens by receiving and responding to grievances submitted by individuals about possible violations of the law, which may prompt official investigations. In this range of powers and duties, the Soviet procurator has a broader role than does the prosecutor in the American system.

Because of its formidable role, strong efforts have been made to keep the procuracy free of local party and government links that might compromise its independence and integrity. According to the constitution, the USSR Supreme Soviet appoints the general procurator of the USSR, who in turn appoints the procurators of the union republics, autonomous republics, territories, provinces, and autonomous provinces.[75] They appoint the procurators of autonomous regions, rural districts, and cities. The current procurator general, Alexander Mikhailovich Rekunkov, has held his position since 1981, when he also became a full Central Committee member. He had served as first deputy procurator general under R. Rudenko, and upon the latter's death, Rekunkov moved to replace him. Unlike his predecessor, Rekunkov has a law degree, though received through correspondence courses. Born in 1920, he entered the procuracy after the war and worked his way up the ladder, holding posts of procurator in two provinces and serving as first deputy procurator for the RSFSR before moving to the all-union level of the procuracy.[76] He thus has a considerable degree of professional experience for his current post.

Since Khrushchev, the powers of professional law enforcement agencies, including the procuracy as well as the Ministry of Internal Affairs, have been expanded in keeping with the emphasis under Brezhnev and his successors on greater centralization and professionalization.[77] At the same time, however, the procuracy's

[75]Sharlet, *The New Soviet Constitution,* p. 128 (Articles 165 and 166).

[76]Biographical details are taken from Alexander G. Rahr, *A Biographical Directory of 100 Leading Soviet Officials* (Munich: Radio Liberty Research, 1984), pp. 164–65.

[77]Juviler, "Criminal Law and Social Control," p. 54.

functions for upholding legality in the government and economic bureaucracy overlap with those of other agencies, including the Ministry of Internal Affairs, the KGB, the OBKhSS department of the uniformed police, and the People's Control Committees. Although a study of the actions brought by the procuracy has found that the number of actions seeking to preserve the state's economic interests has increased while the number of investigations prompted by citizens' complaints has declined,[78] the rising current of criticism of slack and corrupt performance by bureaucratic officials, especially prominent during Andropov's short reign, indicates serious regime dissatisfaction with the work of the procuracy. The procuracy has always found supervision over the activities of economic enterprises difficult. It usually lacks the economic and accounting skills needed to cope with the refined evasive techniques often put to use by administrators (often abetted by jurisconsults). The procurators are not supposed to interfere with the work of agencies that check on economic performance and are supposed to confine their investigations to possible legal violations.[79] In fact, the discovery of illegal economic activities has never been carried out to the satisfaction of the party.

ADVOCATES

The position of the advocate, or trial lawyer, in the Soviet legal system and in society is somewhat ambiguous. It was only in the post-Stalin period that the view that defendants were entitled to a vigorous legal defense in court became widely accepted, and not until the 1977 Constitution did the institution of the *advokatura* gain constitutional status. Advocates make up only about 12 percent of all legal professionals, and with the increase in numbers and stature of the jurisconsult, both their role and numbers may now be slipping below those of other groups.[80] About 60 percent of advocates are party members, and nearly all by now have a higher legal education. On the other hand, they receive fees for services, a quasi-bourgeois practice that casts a capitalist shadow on their public image. The government sets fee schedules and keeps them low so as to maximize the availability of legal services

[78]Smith, *The Soviet Procuracy*, p. 132.

[79]Smith, "Procuratorial Campaigns against Crime," p. 162.

[80]Zigurds L. Zile, "Soviet *Advokatura* Twenty-Five Years after Stalin," in Barry et al., eds., *Soviet Institutions and the Administration of Law*, p. 230.

to the public. For example, drawing up a will may cost 6 rubles, representing a client in a suit for a claim of 501–1000 rubles might net only 30 rubles, and representing a defendant in a criminal case for one day brings in 25 rubles. As much as a third of the fee is retained by the legal consultation office for overhead expenses. The state requires that certain services be offered free of charge, such as claims for disability compensation or alimony. Average official earnings for advocates are around 250 rubles per month.[81] Consequently, many practitioners supplement their legal earnings with additional remuneration in the form of gifts and other considerations, a practice that allows an advocate to earn considerably more than a jurisconsult or a people's court judge. In fact, according to Dina Kaminskaya, this practice is now well institutionalized. "Supplementary, unrecorded fees which the client pays directly to the advocate" may comprise the greater portion of the advocate's earnings.[82]

Advocates perform four basic types of service to clients: giving advice to citizens, preparing declarations and petitions of grievance, participating in the pretrial investigation in a limited proportion of criminal cases, and serving as counsel in most criminal and perhaps 5 to 6 percent of civil cases.[83] Most services are rendered through legal consultation offices set up in cities and districts, of which there are approximately 20,000 throughout the country,[84] that serve the legal needs of individual citizens; but by agreement between the legal consultation office and an organization such as an enterprise, advocates can also represent organizations as clients. Perhaps as much as one-third of the advocates' earnings come in this way.[85] In addition, like other members of the legal profession, advocates are called upon to give a large number of lectures to the public about law.

Unlike other professions, the advokatura is treated as a self-administering body, though it is subject to party and government control. The 1962 statute on the advokatura placed ultimate power

[81]Butler, *Soviet Law,* pp. 80–81.

[82]Kaminskaya, *Final Judgment,* pp. 29–30. She notes that such payments go by the jargon term *mixt. Mixt* is often unconcealed from procurators and judges, who, according to Kaminskaya, privately consider it just and reasonable.

[83]Zile, "Soviet *Advokatura,* " p. 215.

[84]See the editorial "Pravovaya kultura," (Legal Culture), *Pravda,* 19 July 1981).

[85]Butler, *Soviet Law,* pp. 80–81.

over the enforcement of professional standards and decisions about the schedule of fees and conditions for gratuitous service into the hands of the government. In November 1979 a new law on the advokatura was adopted by the USSR Supreme Soviet, followed by equivalent republican laws adopted in 1980–1981 by all fifteen union republics, which further strengthened central direction of legal advocacy.[86] Soviet advocates are organized in colleges that monopolize and regulate the practice of law. These colleges, composed of the duly trained and qualified defense attorneys of a given area, elect a governing board, called a presidium, to manage their own affairs, subject, of course, to state supervision. The presidia of the colleges recruit advocates, discipline erring members, and handle other professional matters.[87]

The ability of persons accused of crimes to retain an advocate is hampered by certain restrictions. For example, *special courts* — closed courts operating under rules of secrecy — exist to hear cases involving employees of closed (secret) installations, such as defense industries. Individuals tried by special courts do not have the right to hire advocates of their choosing but are defended by advocates on the staff of the special courts.[88] Certain categories of cases tried in regular courts may also restrict the defendant's right to choose an advocate, since the authorities may limit participation in the trial only to those lawyers possessing special clearance and hence considered politically reliable. Perhaps the most notable exception to the post-Stalin observance of the right to a defense concerns the pretrial investigation, during which, except in rare cases, a person suspected or accused of a crime may not hire an advocate to defend him. This point warrants further examination.

THE PRETRIAL INVESTIGATION

Soviet criminal cases move through several stages before being heard and decided by a court. Once a case has been initiated and an inquiry determines that a preliminary investigation is war-

[86]Ibid., p. 78.

[87]Ibid., pp. 79–80; see also Lawrence M. Friedman and Zigurds L. Zile, "Soviet Legal Profession: Recent Developments in Law and Practice," *Wisconsin Law Review*, no. 1 (1964): 32–77, esp. pp. 66–67.

[88]Yuri Luryi, "The Right to Counsel in Ordinary Criminal Cases in the USSR," in Barry, Ginsburgs, and Maggs, eds., *The Citizen and the State*, pp. 106–7.

ranted, the procurator sanctions the formal arrest of a suspect (who until that time may be detained by the police). The preliminary investigation may be conducted by the procuracy, the KGB, or the investigators working for the Ministry of Internal Affairs.[89] In cases of especially serious state crimes, which include political dissent, it is the KGB that normally conducts the pretrial investigation. During this period, while the arrested person is held in the state's custody, the procurator is expected to protect the accused person's rights, since only in exceptional instances may a defense attorney be admitted to the case before the indictment is handed down. These are circumstances when minors or persons who are mentally or physically handicapped are accused. In 1970 an all-union edict authorized the procuracy to admit defense counsel from the beginning of the preliminary investigation but did not require it. The same edict also required the participation of an advocate to defend an accused person who did not speak the same language as that in which the proceedings were held, but this latter provision was annulled in 1972, leaving defendants with scarcely more legal protection than they had previously enjoyed. It is very exceptional for a procurator to permit a defense attorney to enter the case before he draws up the indictment.[90] Even though many eminent Soviet legal scholars have argued forcefully in public and private for extension of the right of counsel to the pretrial investigation, the authorities have so far resisted.[91]

Because the senior author of this book was himself the subject of a pretrial investigation on trumped-up charges of espionage in 1963, it may be instructive to review the details of this incident. Since the charge of espionage meant that the offense was political, the questioners were from the KGB. The investigation may not typify those held where the charges are nonpolitical.

The incident began without warning. In the evening of October 31, 1963, Professor Barghoorn was abducted from in front of his

[89]Butler, *Soviet Law*, p. 310.

[90]For a discussion of this question, see Harold J. Berman's introduction to Harold J. Berman and James W. Spindler, *Soviet Criminal Law and Procedures: The RSFSR Codes*, 2nd ed. (Cambridge, Mass.: Harvard University Press, 1972), pp. 84–85.

[91]It should be noted that the colleges of advocates have had little interest in extending their role this way, in part perhaps because they see little material gain to themselves. Such pressure as there has been on this point has come from legal scholars.

hotel in Moscow just after a stranger had planted supposedly incriminating papers on his person. He was immediately taken by car to the Inner Prison of the KGB (the infamous Lyubyanka of earlier days, still in use). For the next 16½ days he was held in absolute isolation, and all requests for contact with the United States embassy and with counsel were denied in what appeared to be amused explanations that both were contrary to Soviet law. Throughout the period of confinement there was no torture or physical violence such as had been common in Stalin's era. Except for a period of about 6 hours, during which he had to wear very tight handcuffs, Professor Barghoorn was not physically restrained, in a narrow sense. The interrogators have so many advantages, however, that physical abuse really does not seem necessary. The prisoner is kept isolated and helpless. He may be told that failure to answer questions will result in imprisonment (in Barghoorn's case, 6 months) and that false answers will be punished by a longer sentence (in this case, 2 years), despite the fact that under Soviet law the accused may remain silent without any adverse implications being drawn.[92] Throughout his ordeal, every effort was made to convince Barghoorn that he would actually come to trial and that his fate would be easier if he confessed his guilt. During the entire time, he never saw another prisoner, never had contact with any persons outside, and never heard about the reaction of the outside world to his disappearance.

The educational side of Soviet justice was evident. After formal interrogation, the chief investigator (a man of wit and humor) would often engage Professor Barghoorn in long, speculative conversations setting forth the official Soviet view on all questions discussed. For the most part conducted in Russian, these conversations were more informal and relaxed and less rigid than might have been expected. Thus, in spite of the threat implicit in the situation and annoyances such as 24 hour illumination of the cell and extremely frequent inspection through a peephole, the experience was not without its interesting moments. President Kennedy's personal intervention ended this chapter. Only on the plane flying from Moscow to London did Professor Barghoorn learn how his imprisonment had been received outside.

In certain ways, the legalities had been observed throughout.

[92]Butler, *Soviet Law*, p. 311.

The administrative regulations posted in the cell had been carefully carried out.[93] On the other hand, the entire case rested on a flagrant breach of legality. Although he knew nothing of military affairs, Barghoorn was accused of having in his possession military intelligence data (photographs), which a stranger had thrust on him moments before the arrest. He never saw his alleged accomplice. Other charges were based on his alleged activities as a diplomat with the United States embassy (from 1943 to 1947), as a State Department officer interviewing Soviet refugees in West Germany (from 1949 to 1951), and as a tourist. All were supposedly based on materials carefully gathered over a period of years to form a dossier of background information. Perhaps the Soviet government wanted to use him as a hostage. Perhaps there were other reasons.

In Professor Barghoorn's case, of course, the preliminary investigation was not completed with the usual official presentation of an indictment, officially called the *conclusion to indict*. Once the investigator finds sufficient grounds to try the arrested person, he issues a decree to prosecute. The pretrial investigation is supposed to be concluded in two months, but it may be extended under certain circumstances for up to nine months (during which time the prisoner still is denied counsel). Once the conclusion to indict is issued, however, the defendant must be informed of the charges and at that point may bring in a defense attorney. The attorney may petition for modification of the charges, introduce counterevidence, or suggest that additional witnesses be called. The procurator has a certain amount of leeway at this point. He may decide to refer the case to a comrade's court (if a relatively minor offense), to change or even drop the charges, or to confirm the indictment and present it to a court. The court receives the indictment in an administrative session, and once having decided to accept the indictment, it must begin hearing the case within two weeks.[94]

The trial rests largely on the materials collected during the preliminary investigation, together with whatever evidence the de-

---

[93]One regulation, which prohibited tapping to communicate with other prisoners, was reminiscent of accounts of prison life in the tsarist and Stalinist past, when tapping was a usual method of communication among prisoners.

[94]Butler, *Soviet Law*, pp. 312–13.

fense can present. The decision of the procuracy to turn the case over to the court for hearing is often considered a strong indication of guilt, despite the assertion in the code of criminal procedure that no one may be found guilty of a crime except by a court.[95] The advantages enjoyed by the procuracy in preparing a case tend to influence the outcome of the court trial. George Feifer, who observed a number of Soviet trials, found that the "trial is a reconstruction not so much of the crime as of an earlier reconstruction of it. . . . [One feels] that it has all been said before."[96] To be sure, the procurator's case must rest on evidence proving the charges, and a confession from the defendant is not considered proof in and of itself of the validity of the charges; this provision, of course, is a far cry from the legal practices of the Stalin era, when confession — no matter how obtained — was called "the queen of evidence." Nevertheless, although the procurator is obliged to prove the case of guilt through evidence presented at the trial and the accused is not obliged to prove innocence, and despite arguments by prominent Soviet jurists, there is still no explicit clause in Soviet law providing that a person is deemed innocent until proved guilty or that the burden of proof rests with the prosecution.[97] The fact that, for example, a deputy of the USSR Supreme Soviet wrote in *Pravda* in 1958 that the presumption of innocence was a "worm-eaten dogma of bourgeois doctrine," and the resistance to any amendment of criminal law or procedure that would make the presumption of innocence explicit suggest how weakly rooted in Soviet legal practice are procedural guarantees of a defendant's rights. Further testimony to the advantage of prosecution over defense is provided by the reversal in 1972 of the 1970 law permitting participation by defense counsel in certain preliminary investigations and by the almost total nonuse of the provision allowing the procurator on his own discretion to authorize the participation of defense counsel during the preliminary investigation.

The relative unimportance of the defense counsel can also be measured in another way. The ablest law school graduates go into

[95]On this point, see the discussion by Harold J. Berman, "Introduction," in Berman and Spindler, eds., *Soviet Criminal Law and Procedure,* pp. 57–58.

[96]Feifer, *Justice in Moscow,* p. 239.

[97]Berman, "Introduction," in Berman and Spindler, eds., *Soviet Criminal Law and Procedure,* p. 59.

the bureaucracy as members of the procuracy or into graduate school to train for careers in scholarship or teaching.[98] Outstanding legal researchers become members of the Institute of State and Law of the Academy of Sciences. Celebrated *advokaty* — famous trial lawyers who might correspond to a Clarence Darrow or an F. Lee Bailey — are not to be found in the Soviet Union, any more than are Wall Street law firms. According to Andreas Bilinsky, a German specialist on Soviet law, Soviet law school graduates who seek admission to the colleges of advocates are often either mediocrities or idealists.[99] Some who belong to the latter category defend their clients with spirit and skill, despite the risks inherent in boldly opposing procurators and judges, who are powerful state bureaucrats. In this connection the defenses offered by attorneys Melamed and Kaminskaya in defending Vadim Delone and Vladimir Bukovsky, respectively, against the charge that they had engaged in a criminal demonstration in January 1967, even though cautious, must be regarded as courageous. These attorneys vigorously defended their clients and strongly criticized not only the prosecution's arguments but also public policies that, in their opinion, had caused their clients to behave improperly.[100] For this behavior, though, Kaminskaya and other such advocates were subsequently barred from taking on political cases.[101]

THE CONFLICT BETWEEN POPULAR PARTICIPATION AND SUBORDINATION

Leon Lipson has made an acute analysis of the divergent objectives of Soviet law.[102] Two of them are the desire — particularly strong when Khrushchev was in power — to increase popular participation in the judicial process and the desire to re-

[98]Barry and Berman, "The Jurists," pp. 311–12.

[99]Andreas Bilinsky, "The Lawyer and Soviet Society," *Problems of Communism* 14, no. 2 (March–April 1965): 62–71, esp. p. 67.

[100]See Pavel Litvinov, comp., *The Demonstration in Pushkin Square* (Boston, Mass.: Gambit, 1969), pp. 102–3, 105–8.

[101]See "Interview with D. I. Kaminskaya and K. M. Simis," Radio Liberty Special Report, RL 10/78 (11 January 1978), pp. 12–13. Also see Kaminskaya's defense of Galanskov, one of the four arrested for circulating material on the Sinyavsky/Daniel case, as presented in Pavel Litvinov, comp., *The Trial of the Four* (New York: Viking, 1972), esp. her long closing argument for Galanskov's acquittal on pp. 184–97.

[102]Leon Lipson, "Law and Society," in Allen Kassof, ed., *Prospects for Soviet Society* (New York: Praeger, 1968), p. 106.

press any deviant trends threatening the party's control. The shifts in emphasis that occur in this struggle and its outcome can have a significant impact on the direction of future Soviet development.

Soviet doctrine posits the eventual withering away of the state. Progress toward this goal will involve the gradual replacement of administrative and coercive government agencies by the more democratic machinery of a developing all-people's state and the limited transfer of law enforcement from the regular police, court, and prosecution agencies to the public. If political and social stability and prosperity at home increase, if peaceful coexistence with the outside world develops, and if progress toward communism continues, then it is logical to assume that noncoercive citizen activity in the interpretation and application of norms of behavior should increase, and both the regular judicial system and the political police will fade into the background and eventually disappear.

Khrushchev said in his report to the Twenty-first Party Congress in 1959 that the withering away of the state, if understood "dialectically," involved "the problem of the development of socialist statehood into communist public self-government."[103] He went on to suggest that "social organizations" such as the people's guards, "comrades' courts," and "organs similar to them," had means for coping with "violators of socialist legal order" that were not inferior to those of the regular police, the courts, and the procuracy. He added the hope that the regular organs and the social organizations might work in parallel to assure public order and security. Finally, he said that the process of transfer of power was already occurring: "The apparatus of the militia has been sharply cut and the apparatus of the organs of state security has been especially sharply curtailed."[104]

Let us now see how what Lipson called the "noncourts and impolice" actually operate.[105] Since Khrushchev, the emphasis on social self-government has withered away and the powers of the

---

[103]*Vneocherednoi XXI s''ezd kommunisticheskoi partii sovetskogo soyuza* (Extraordinary Twenty-first Congress of the Communist Party of the Soviet Union), vol. 1 (Moscow: Izdatelstvo politicheskoi literatury, 1959), p. 102.

[104]Ibid., p. 104.

[105]Leon Lipson, "Hosts and Pests: The Fight Against 'Parasites,' " *Problems of Communism*, 14, no. 2 (March–April 1965): 72–81, esp. p. 73.

regular institutions of law enforcement have been reinforced. The institutions Khrushchev mentioned, however — the people's guards, the comrades' courts, and the social organizations participating in the administration of justice — have been preserved and expanded. Public participation in the legal process is not totally new to the Soviet system; some participatory adjudicative bodies have existed since the revolution and in fact are rooted in traditional Russian practices of informal community courts and councils. Under Khrushchev, however, the principle of popular participation in the legal system was given widespread application and intense propaganda; it remains important today, although the forms of popular participation have been modified by various legal enactments that have tended, on the whole, to strengthen legal formality at the expense of popular discretion.

THE PEOPLE'S GUARDS

People's guards (*narodnye druzhiny*) are a kind of auxiliary police force, intended to assist the uniformed police.[106] Early in 1972 it was reported that the number of these guardians of public order was almost 7 million.[107] People's guard units are formed in enterprises, neighborhoods, Komsomol organizations, or other social units; under the Model Statute on Voluntary People's Guard Detachments for the Protection of Public Order, adopted jointly by the party and government in 1974, these units must be composed of volunteers, over 18 years of age, who have agreed to form patrols to help reinforce public order and "struggle against violations of law."[108] While on patrol, *druzhinniki* wear red armbands to distinguish them. Their functions are quite broad. They are involved in maintaining order at public gatherings, assisting with traffic control, giving first aid to accident victims, breaking up street fights, preventing crimes and apprehending criminals, and combating hooliganism and public drunkenness. They have

[106]For the early history of the people's guards, see Dennis M. O'Connor, "Soviet People's Guards: An Experiment with Civic Police," *New York University Law Review* 39 (June 1964): 579–614.

[107]Yu. Feofanov, "Patrul dobra" (Patrol of the Good), *Izvestiya* (8 January 1972). In this long article Feofanov urges more formal organization and supervision in the guards.

[108]Butler, *Soviet Law*, p. 131.

assisted the security police in preventing and breaking up public demonstrations by dissenters, and, according to Kevin Klose, have kept close watch over petitioners who bring their appeals for redress of grievance to the halls of the Central Committee, the Supreme Soviet, the Supreme Court, and other top official agencies in Moscow.[109] They have the right to demand identity documents and even to detain citizens and take them to a police station, if deemed necessary. Resistance to a member of the people's guard is tantamount to resisting a uniformed policeman, and in case they are injured in the course of executing their proper duties, they are extended the same protection received by the regular police.[110]

Sometimes members of people's guards units abuse their powers, and some have clashed with the regular police. Despite problems, however, the institution has proven to be useful, both in popularizing law enforcement and in backing up the regular police in keeping public order. Though claims that the people's guards are strictly voluntary must be taken with a certain amount of skepticism, this form of participation has struck at least something of a responsive note among some in Soviet society. A survey of workers' attitudes toward various forms of administrative participation found that the people's guards received the second highest rating of those listed.[111] Closely overseen by the party, Komsomol, trade unions, and local soviets, they constitute a useful extension of the state's power to channel popular participation.[112]

---

[109]Kevin Klose, *Russia and the Russians* (New York: Norton, 1984), p. 67.

[110]O'Connor, "Soviet People's Guards," pp. 593–610; Butler, *Soviet Law,* p. 132.

[111]A. K. Orlov, *Sovetskii rabochii i upravlenie proizvodstvom* (Moscow: Profizdat, 1978), p. 102. The people's guards received a favorable rating by 45.9 percent of the respondents and were exceeded only by the general workplace meeting (51 percent). Considerably lower ratings were received by such institutions as people's control committees (37 percent), comrades' courts (33.1 percent), and permanently operating production conferences (28.4 percent).

[112]A *Pravda* report of January 14, 1984, summarizing the CPSU Politburo's deliberations noted that the Politburo had adopted a resolution commemorating the twenty-fifth anniversary of the formation of the people's guards, praising their contribution to the strengthening of public order and law enforcement and calling for improvement in their work. See *Current Digest of the Soviet Press* 36, no. 2 (8 February 1984): 20.

COMRADES' COURTS

Like people's guards, which in their contemporary form were first organized in 1958 at the peak of Khrushchev's campaign to enlist mass participation in state administration, the comrades' courts were revived by Khrushchev in a drive to transfer to social institutions some of the functions heretofore reserved for the state. The initial objective of the comrades' courts is conveyed in the text of the 1961 statute adopted by the RSFSR in 1961:

> Comrades' courts are elected social agencies charged with actively contributing to the education of citizens in a spirit of a communist attitude toward labor and socialist property and the observance of the rules of socialist community life, and with developing among Soviet people a sense of collectivism and comradely mutual assistance and of respect for the dignity and honor of citizens.[113]

When first formed in the late 1950s, the comrades' courts were intended as an instrument of peer justice, their authority social rather than state in character. Penalties meted out by comrades' courts were called *measures of social pressure* rather than *punishment;* their power was considered persuasive rather than coercive.[114] They wield the power, however, to impose sanctions ranging in severity from reprimands to fines and, formerly, the eviction of a person from his home. Like other Khrushchevian innovations, the mixture of popular and formal elements in the comrades' courts has shifted with time toward codification, systematization, and formality. The principle of layman's justice remains, but regulations — particularly a 1977 statute adopted by the RSFSR Supreme Soviet Presidium — have tightened its procedures.

Comrades' courts are convened generally either in workplaces or in places of residence and are directed primarily at cases involving infractions of labor discipline or of standards of communal living. The jurisdiction covers a wide range of petty and moderately serious offenses, such as absenteeism and tardiness, dam-

---

[113]See Harold J. Berman and James W. Spindler, "Soviet Comrades' Courts," *Washington Law Review* 38 (Winter 1963): 587–88.
[114]Butler, *Soviet Law,* p. 128.

age to equipment, negligence, theft of state property, hooliganism, drunkenness, insults, and slander; offenses committed in residences include child or wife abuse, damage to communal property, theft, and speculation. Small-scale civil disputes may also be heard.[115] The court is elected and must consist of at least three members of the collective. The case itself may be initiated by various social organizations or by courts or other state agencies; people's courts may review the decisions of the comrades' courts and must give their approval to any imposition of financial sanctions.[116] Further oversight over the conduct of the comrades' courts is exercised by Social Councils for the Work of Comrades' Courts, which are attached to soviets and trade union committees and which coordinate and publicize the work of comrades' courts.

In the early days of comrades' courts, proceedings were apt to be rough and ready, since the emphasis was not on formal legality but on the collective determination of justice for a peer whose entire life and pattern of behavior could be reviewed by the court; coworkers and neighbors were encouraged to attend and comment freely on the trial. With time, though, as greater legal institutionalization has been imposed on the comrades' courts, the element of spontaneity appears to have diminished, perhaps thereby strengthening observance of the legal rights of accused persons. The 1977 statute on comrades' courts requires that the courts reach their decisions without regard to "extraneous circumstances,"[117] although this presumably does not apply to advice offered by party activists and officials, who seek to make the proceedings socially educational.[118] Efforts have been made to give members of comrades' courts some rudimentary legal training, and in many cases lawyers and other members of the legal profession have taken part, lending the proceedings the benefit of legal expertise. With greater supervision over comrades' courts by state bodies such as courts, soviets, and procuracy, the comrades' courts seem to be evolving into "state bodies on a lower level."[119]

[115]Ibid., p. 129.
[116]Ibid., p. 130.
[117]Ibid., p. 129.
[118]Sharlet, "The Communist Party," p. 351.
[119]Frits Gorle, "The Latest Developments in Comradely Justice," in Feldbrugge, ed., *Perspectives on Soviet Law for the 1980s,* pp. 171–80.

POPULAR PARTICIPATION IN REGULAR LEGAL INSTITUTIONS

Besides the people's guards and the comrades' courts, several established channels for popular participation in regular judicial proceedings provide additional contacts between the public and the state. Among these are the involvement of public accusers and public defenders in court trials, visiting sessions of people's and higher courts held at places of work and residence, officially recognized participation in court proceedings by representatives of social organizations, and new social centers for the protection of order.

All of these institutions integrate organized nonstate activity into the regular functioning of the state's legal institutions. Public defenders and accusers and representatives of social organizations present testimony in trials as spokesmen for an officially recognized community opinion.[120] They may offer opinions as to the character of the accused or the background of the case at hand. An accused person may officially invite a representative of a social organization, such as a trade union, to assist him in his defense. These representatives supplement rather than replace the parts played by procurator and advocate. Another means of drawing the public into the work of judicial agencies is the practice of holding regular sessions of court directly in an enterprise or neighborhood so that the peers of the victim or the accused may observe the trial. In this case, as Robert Sharlet points out, the educational purpose of the session is lost if the facts or the law in the case are muddy; the issues should be clear-cut so as to enlist the sympathies of the public on the proper side. Perhaps because of the difficulty of arranging for the regular occurrence of such cases, this practice seems to be falling into disuse.[121] More recently, the state has established "social centers for the protection of order," governed by a statute adopted in 1980. These are agencies combining social and state authority. They are operated by councils formed by local soviet executive committees and are made up of representatives of social and state agencies such as trade unions, enterprises, police, and courts. Their purpose is to coordinate the efforts of the many public law-related institutions in a given area, such as comrades' courts, people's guards, neighborhood com-

---

[120]Berman and Spindler, *Soviet Criminal Law and Procedure,* pp. 69–70.
[121]Sharlet, "The Communist Party," pp. 347–48.

mittees, and the like. Though they enjoy no formal law enforcement power themselves, they are intended to assist the state in shaping and guiding the numerous forms of quasi-public participation in law enforcement.[122]

One of the best illustrations of the tension between the aims of Soviet law cited earlier — popular participation and the desire to suppress any politically threatening deviant behavior — is the history of antiparasite laws. One of the innovations of the Khrushchev era was the enactment, in varying forms by the different union republics, of laws providing that persons who led "an antisocial, parasitic way of life" — even if, for appearances' sake, such a person held a regular job — or who lived on the proceeds of activities such as "the exploitation of land plots, automobiles, or housing," were subject to prosecution. Under the law, such a person would be warned by "a social organization or state agency." Ignoring this warning would be followed either by a "social" punishment handed down by a labor collective, or, for the unemployed, by a people's court order for "resettlement in specially designated areas."[123] The breadth of the statute, which applied to a way of life rather than to any definable crime, made it a ready tool for use by the authorities against individuals whose political views were deemed unacceptable. A notorious instance of this kind was the case of the Leningrad poet Joseph Brodsky, now an immigrant in the United States, who in 1964 was sentenced to serve 5 years in Arkhangelsk for "parasitism."[124]

[122]Butler, *Soviet Law,* pp. 132–33.

[123]Quotations are taken from the 1961 law passed by the RSFSR, which, according to Harold Berman, for all its vagueness was somewhat more restrictive than equivalent laws passed in several other union republics. The quotations are drawn from the lengthy citation in Berman, *Justice in the USSR,* pp. 291–94.

[124]He was released in September 1965. See Berman and Spindler, *Soviet Criminal Law and Procedure,* p. 78; a transcript of the Brodsky trial may be found in *The New Leader,* 31 August 1964, pp. 6–17. It includes remarkable exchanges between Brodsky and the judge, such as the following:

Judge: "But in general what is your specialty?"
Brodsky: "I'm a poet, a poet-translator."
Judge: "And who said that you were a poet? Who included you among the ranks of the poets?"
Brodsky: "No one." (Unsolicited) "And who included me among the ranks of the human race?"

On the early application of the parasite laws, see two articles by Leon Lipson: "The Future Belongs to . . . Parasites?" *Problems of Communism* 12, no. 3 (May-June 1963): 1–9; and "Hosts and Pests: The Fight against Parasites," *Problems of Communism* 14, no. 2 (March-April 1965): 72–82.

Until 1965 the basic sanction against social parasites was exile for from two to five years, with compulsory labor at the place of exile. In September 1965 the Supreme Soviet of the RSFSR drastically amended its 1961 law, limiting and tightening the definition of the type of behavior to which the law was to apply. It also took a significant step in the direction of legality by requiring that only administrative agencies of government or regular courts could punish persons who willfully refused to perform socially useful labor. The 1965 law considerably reduced the number of parasite cases that made their way to the courts.[125] Difficulties in applying the law remained, however. There was inadequate judicial supervision over the process by which social organizations such as labor collectives issued warnings and punishments to parasites; there was also little control over the individual once he had been assigned a job elsewhere.[126]

In 1970 the antiparasite law was made part of the criminal code for the first time, making it a crime, rather than simply an administrative offense, to avoid socially useful labor. The law further tightened the provisions, requiring that the individual must be given an official warning, must be given time to find a job, and, failing that, must be assigned to a job by the soviet executive committee. Refusing to obey the order of the soviet, not the initial parasitism, was the criminal offense. The law also specified that certain categories of individuals were exempt from its effect, including housewives, pensioners, and persons temporarily out of work.[127] Violation was punishable by imprisonment or correctional labor for up to 1 year. The law was modified once again in 1975, when parasitism was incorporated into the article of the criminal code that made it an offense to engage systematically in begging or in vagrancy, either of which could be punished by imprisonment or correctional labor.[128] As before, the person must refuse to obey an order to cease his parasitic existence for the law

---

[125]Berman and Spindler, *Soviet Criminal Law and Procedure,* p. 79.

[126]Ibid, p. 79.

[127]Ibid, p. 80.

[128]See ibid., p. 187, for texts of Articles 209, on vagrancy and begging, and the old Article 209-1, on refusing to discontinue a parasitic way of life. This latter article was abolished in 1975 and incorporated into the immediately preceding article.

to apply. Similar exemptions for housewives, pensioners, disabled persons, and others remain in the new law.[129]

More recently the antiparasitism statute was revised again in an effort to stiffen penalties and close loopholes for evasion. Revisions in the language of Article 209 of the RSFSR Criminal Code, adopted in October 1982 (shortly before Brezhnev's demise), aimed at strengthening the punishments for repeat offenders and at ensuring that individuals assigned to jobs by local soviet executive committees did not escape their obligation to take, and remain at, their assigned work. The new language also specified that local soviet executive committees were responsible for finding jobs for ex-convicts and others freed from state custody. Moreover, employers could not refuse to hire parasites and vagrants whom the local soviet assigned them. Press comment early in 1983 — shortly after Andropov's rise to power and the beginning of his highly publicized crackdown on crime and other social pathologies — also attempted to pressure local government and law enforcement agencies to step up the fight against parasites.[130]

During the successive stages of legalizing the provisions that prohibited the parasitic way of life, most of the law's Khrushchevian populism was removed. In its earliest form, for example, cases involving parasites were to be adjudicated by assemblies of peers who, under guidance from the party, were free to apply harsh penalties of banishment to individuals who had committed no positive criminal act.[131] Officially this was an administrative rather than a legal proceeding, and the individual lacked such protections as the right to counsel or the right to appeal.[132] Now the provision is treated in much the same way as any other criminal offense, yet its foundation is ultimately not a crime but a way of life deemed offensive to the community. It can be, and is, used

---

[129]Butler, *Soviet Law,* pp. 276–77.

[130]See the articles in *Current Digest of the Soviet Press* 35, no. 2 (9 February 1983): 5–6, including the text of the new language of Article 209 and a commentary on the new law appearing in *Sovetskaya Rossiya,* the newspaper of the Supreme Soviet of the Russian Republic. On the crackdown on crime launched by Andropov, see the article by A. Rekunkov, Procurator-General of the USSR, "The Citizen, Society and the Law: Without Leniency," *Pravda,* 9 January 1983, translated in the same issue of *Current Digest,* pp. 1–4.

[131]Sharlet, "The Communist Party," pp. 353–54.

[132]Berman, *Justice in the USSR,* p. 295.

as a weapon against socially marginal persons whom the authorities wish to punish for political or other reasons.

MILITIA

Like the KGB, the militia, or regular police, is semimilitary in its training, organization, and ranks. Also like the KGB, the militia is under strict party and government control, exercised by the Ministry of Internal Affairs (MVD).

In some ways the Soviet militia resembles police forces in noncommunist states. Its work includes traffic control, maintaining public order, and apprehending criminals. At the same time, both its functions and its organization have some important peculiarities. The militia, for example, administers crucial instruments of social control such as the internal passport system. Established in 1932, this system (like so much else in Soviet administrative and police practice) closely resembles the prerevolutionary system controlling movement and residency once so fiercely denounced by the Bolsheviks. All citizens who have reached the age of 16 and who reside in specified categories of communities must have an internal passport and must, upon demand, present the passport to the militia and other appropriate authorities. Standard Soviet legal textbooks say the passport system is important for preserving public order and state security.[133] The passport system was expanded, beginning in the mid-1960s, to include collective farm peasants, who were previously ineligible to hold them without special need; the change meant that they now possessed the right to move legally away from the farm and to a city. All Soviet citizens, however, face additional restrictions on residence in another control on the population administered by the police. Certain cities have "closed" status, meaning that legal permission to reside there requires a permit (*propiska*), which may be obtained only if a person holds a job entitling him (and his family) to receive it. Some individuals, eager to live in such cities as Moscow and Leningrad, accept the types of jobs that authorize receipt of a residency permit (typically jobs in construction and other

---

[133]See V. A. Vlasov and S. S. Studenikin, *Sovetskoe administrativnoe pravo* (Soviet Administrative Law) (Moscow: Gosudarstvenoe izdatelstvo yuridicheskoi literatury, 1958), pp. 272–75.

physical labor); others evade the law and live in fear of exposure by the militia.[134]

In addition to the strict and complicated passport and residency controls, the militia administers many other controls, including procedures for obtaining permission to have and use printing, mimeographing, typewriting, and other reproduction and communication equipment, as well as photographic equipment, guns, and explosives.[135] Such police controls over communication reinforce the control exercised by the party and the censorship, as well as that of editors.

Another of the unusual features of the militia is that it, in common with the military, maintains an internal hierarchy of political officers who are responsible for ensuring that the behavior of the militia conforms to the party's political and professional standards. This system of political organs, created with great fanfare in July 1983, has been assigned the tasks of conducting political education for the militia and of upholding professional standards among uniformed personnel in the performance of their duties.[136]

In addition, as part of Andropov's campaign to crack down on the widespread corruption within the militia, top MVD officials were replaced with former KGB officials. As has been stated earlier, one of Andropov's first actions as general secretary was to sack the minister of internal affairs of the USSR, Nikolai A. Shchelokov, for corruption and to replace him with Andropov's former subordinate in the KGB, Vitalii V. Fedorchuk. Upon An-

---

[134]This can lead to Catch-22 dilemmas. Some jobs are available only if the individual already holds a permit, but the permit may not be issued until the individual holds a job. Not surprisingly, many people resort to various ruses and devices to get around the restrictions and to obtain the all-important permit.

[135]Vlasov and Studenikin, *Sovetskoe administrativnoe pravo*, 1958, p. 276; also Yuri Kozlov, *Sovetskoe administrativnoe pravo* (Moscow: Iuridicheskaya literatura, 1964), p. 264. Secret, unpublished restrictions on printing presses also apparently exist. In 1977 an Estonian law tightening control over printing and engraving equipment was passed that referred to an as-yet unpublished USSR law. See Radio Liberty Research, RL 8/78, "Decree to Tighten Control over Printing Presses," 9 January 1978.

[136]See Amy Knight, "Soviet Politics and the KGB-MVD Relationship," *Soviet Union/Union Soviétique* 11, part 2 (1984): 180. The author points out that political organs had existed in the militia prior to 1956 but were abolished by Khrushchev in an effort to strengthen the power of local party organs over law enforcement. The reestablishment of these bodies therefore suggested the desire to place greater control over the police in the hands of the central party apparatus.

dropov's transfer to the party secretariat in May 1982, Fedorchuk had succeeded him as chairman of the KGB between May and December 1982. Then, when Andropov succeeded Brezhnev as general secretary, he transferred Fedorchuk to the MVD, evidently with a charge of cleaning up the lax and corrupt organs of the police. Disgracing Shchelokov had the additional effect of removing one of Brezhnev's cronies — and his network of political clients — since Shchelokov had been a Brezhnev ally since the 1930s. Placing a top KGB official in charge of the uniformed police also helped centralize control over the competing MVD and KGB bureaucracies.[137]

THE COMMITTEE FOR STATE SECURITY: THE KGB

More formidable than the Ministry of Internal Affairs and the regular police is the Committee for State Security (KGB), the current designation for the powerful national political police agency. In its present form, the agency dates from a decree of the Council of Ministers of March 13, 1954, as amended by a law of July 1978.[138] Although the KGB continues to operate in great secrecy and its governing statute remains unpublished, its status remains considerably inferior to that of Stalin's era, when it administered punishments and managed the gulag system independently of the legal system and, except for Stalin himself, independently of al-

---

[137]On the careers of Shchelokov and Fedorchuk, see Alexander G. Rahr, *A Biographic Directory of 100 Leading Soviet Officials* (Munich: Radio Liberty, 1981), pp. 186–89; and idem, *A Biographic Directory of 100 Leading Soviet Officials* (Munich: Radio Liberty, 1984), pp. 65–67. On KGB-MVD rivalry, see below.

[138]Similar agencies under different names have existed since the first weeks of the Soviet regime. The first Soviet state security agency was the Cheka (short for Extraordinary State Commission to Combat Counterrevolution and Sabotage), established in December 1917 to perform intelligence and counterintelligence functions and to administer summary justice to enemies of the revolution. See George Leggett, *The Cheka: Lenin's Political Police* (London: Oxford University Press, 1982). The Cheka was superseded by the State Political Administration (GPU) in 1922, which was under the People's Commissariat of Internal Affairs. The republican GPU hierarchies were unified in the all-union GPU, or OGPU, in 1923. From 1934 to 1941 the security organs operated as the Chief State Security Administration under the People's Commissariat of Internal Affairs (NKVD). Subsequently the state agency became a separate commissariat, the People's Commissariat for State Security (NKGB). This was then replaced with the Committee of State Control, attached to the Council of Ministers of the USSR, in 1954. The KGB was promoted in July 1978, when its official status was no longer described as being "under" the Council of Ministers; it was simply "the Committee of State Security of the USSR." See Butler, *Soviet Law,* pp. 125–26.

most any political authority. After the post-Stalin reforms of 1954, the security police were subjected to the same pattern of supervision in their investigative work as the regular police.[139] It is not used to instill terror among Soviet citizens. Nevertheless, the political and quasi-judicial powers of the KGB remain formidable, probably far more so than some Soviet jurists would wish.[140] Observers agree, however, that it retains the right to take over the pretrial investigation of persons suspected of dissident activity or other political offenses. It also assumes leadership in detecting and investigating persons suspected of crimes such as currency speculation, large-scale embezzlement of state property, and smuggling. For years the KGB has administered the highly trained and honored frontier guards (*pogranichniki*). The KGB has the duty to bring suspects to justice in cases involving espionage, anti-Soviet agitation and propaganda, and foreigners. Because these crimes are vaguely defined in the law, the investigators often gather an extraordinarily broad range of evidence as proof of an individual's anti-Soviet activity. In conjunction with the censorhip organs, for example, the KGB has an elaborate classification scheme for evaluating the degree of harmfulness of published and unpublished literature found in a suspect's apartment. Works by Solzhenitsyn, for example, and especially his *Gulag Archipelago,* are considered extremely damaging; works by other published Soviet and Western authors may be considered "damaging," "tendentious," or "nonrecommended."[141] The KGB carries out its functions in part through a vast network of informers, often recruited from among loyal citizens or individuals who fear exposure and punishment for some wrongdoing. Emigrants often testify to the difficulty of turning down a KGB request to keep an eye on one's peers, whether coworkers, neighbors, or fellow students.

---

[139]Berman and Spindler, *Soviet Criminal Law and Procedure,* p. 49.

[140]In 1957 and 1958 some legal scholars argued unsuccessfully that all pretrial investigations should be turned over to the procuracy.

[141]See Yuri Lurii, "Three Years of the New USSR Constitution: The Soviet Approach to Human Rights," in Feldbrugge and Simons, eds., *Perspectives on Soviet Law for the 1980s,* pp. 68, 75; also see the interview with Dina Kaminskaya and Konstantin Simis shortly after their departure from the USSR, in Radio Liberty Special Report RL 10/78 (11 January 1978), where Kaminskaya comments that when their apartment was searched, books published abroad by Solzhenitsyn were discovered, together with books by Akhmatova, Mandelstam, and Nabokov; of these Solzhenitsyn's works were "the most incriminating by far of all the things found." Pp. 4–5.

To its weighty domestic responsibilities, the KGB also adds important foreign policy functions. The KGB is the main counterintelligence and foreign espionage agency of the Soviet state, although other agencies, such as the counterintelligence unit of the armed forces (GRU), also perform intelligence and security functions. It is likely that at times the semiautonomous activities of the KGB influence Soviet foreign policy. By arresting or detaining foreign citizens, even those with diplomatic passports, and accusing them of espionage, the KGB, perhaps in collusion with one or another faction of the party leadership, may be able to heighten tension between the USSR and foreign powers. As an interest group, the KGB seems to have played a role in the downfall of Khrushchev by allying with those in the party Presidium and Secretariat who opposed Khrushchev's liberalizing reforms; more recently, it has been suggested that the KGB, under Andropov, played a role in discrediting Brezhnev during the latter's final year.[142] The KGB works closely with the party to keep alive among the populace emotions of fear and hostility toward the capitalist world and vigilance toward the putative struggle of imperialism to subvert the Soviet order. KGB leaders and party ideologues seek to invoke an atmosphere of suspicion among Soviet citizens toward foreigners in their midst, frequently warning in the press or in lectures that foreign tourists, journalists, students, and diplomats may be spies in disguise. Their shady and subversive deeds are periodically exposed by Soviet writers. The KGB encourages citizens to be watchful of communication between Soviet citizens and visitors from imperialist countries. As bureaucratic interest group, as ally in top-level factional strife, and as loyal executor of the policies of the party leadership, the KGB is associated with the never-flagging ideological struggle between socialism and imperialism.

The broad powers and mandate of the KGB have frequently led it to clash with the MVD. In fact, according to Amy Knight, the relationship between the KGB and the MVD "has been fraught with tension and conflict over the years," reflecting conflict between the Soviet regime's professed effort to fit law enforcement to crime in a precise, orderly, and predictable fashion, and its demands for total political conformity and other party val-

---

[142]On this affair, see Knight, "KGB-MVD Relationship," pp. 176–77.

ues incompatible with the smooth functioning of a regular professional police force. Often the KGB, as the party's prime agency of political control when other means have been exhausted, has been called upon to intervene in the work of the militia. If to this inferior status of the militia is added its relatively poor pay and perquisites, it is understandable that some observers, especially in recent years, have reported that relations between the regular and the political police are far from harmonious.[143]

CONCLUSIONS

Since the death of Stalin, law and law enforcement in the USSR have been instruments of a political system increasingly controlled by influence rather than restraint and by material and symbolic power more than coercion.[144] Neither a society in which the rule of law prevails nor one ruled as overwhelmingly by terror as was Stalin's USSR, the post-Stalin system has maintained numerous means of overriding the constitutional and legal protections on citizens' rights when the political authorities believe their interests to be threatened.[145] The 1977 Constitution, though going some distance to close the gaping chasm between constitutional law and actual practice that existed when Stalin's constitution was promulgated in 1936, still left the party ample room to make law an instrument for serving political ends, including social control and political socialization. The progressive encroachment of legal formality upon many of the popularizing innovations of the Khrushchev era has had the effect, as Robert Sharlet puts it, of "routinizing the governance process," but this has been done "in such a manner as to [leave the party] sufficient ambiguity to circumvent the system of 'legality' [*zakonnost'*] when necessary."[146] Although the new constitution strengthens the "position of individuals in the criminal justice process," and offers "participatory rights" to the Soviet citizen, it also responds to the "strongly articulated and widespread demands for more discipline of all kinds"

[143]See Knight, "KGB-MVD Relationship," pp. 158, 181.

[144]On the distinction between control by "influence" and by "restraint," see Felix Oppenheim, *Dimensions of Freedom* (New York, 1961), ch. 2.

[145]A good German-language study of the degree of Soviet observance of civil and legal rights is Otto Luchterhandt, *UN-Menschenrechtskonventione: Sowjetrecht-Sowjetwirklichkeit* (UN Human Rights Conventions: Soviet Law–Soviet Reality) (Baden-Baden: Nomos Verlagsgesellschaft, 1980).

[146]Sharlet, *The New Soviet Constitution,* p. 8.

that were voiced in the organized public discussion that preceded adoption of the final version.[147]

Also reflecting the highly authoritarian nature of the 1977 Constitution is its Article 6, which states that the "CPSU is the leading and guiding force of Soviet society, the nucleus of its political system and of [all] state and public organizations."[148] This article also asserts that "all party organizations operate within the framework of the USSR Constitution," surely a logically contradictory statement, since the party itself is given the right to interpret the constitution. The party obviously does not consider itself bound by any constitutional provisions, as was demonstrated by the events of 1977, when Brezhnev summarily expelled Nikolai Podgorny from the chairmanship of the Presidium of the Supreme Soviet of the USSR and from the party Politburo.[149]

There is much justification for Sharlet's assertion that the outcome of the constitution-drafting process was "a Soviet-style *Rechtsstaat,* a legal framework through which the party can govern its vast domain without irrevocably limiting its ultimate power of action." Law and legality exist, according to Sharlet, on one side of a "magic wall," which separates and conceals the sphere of untrammeled party authority from the realm of regular, predictable, legal procedures and rights.[150] On one side of the wall are the legally codified relations among citizens and between citizens and the state, in which by and large the rule of law is respected. On the other are the instances of arbitrary and unaccountable interventions into legality by the party and its representatives. At one time many Soviet citizens and foreign observers hoped that as the post-Stalin era benefited from growing internal and international security and the growth of its material well-being, the magic wall would be pushed back and the realm of legally regulated social relations would expand. Despite the increasing application of legal formality, as evidenced by the rapid growth in the numbers of jurisconsults and the "juridization" of many forms of popular participation in the legal system, such hopes now appear unduly sanguine.

---

[147]Ibid., pp. 13, 16, 54–55.

[148]Ibid., p. 78.

[149]The new Article 6 of the 1977 Constitution, laying out the party's role and introducing an apparent limitation of the constitutional status of the party, makes more explicit than did the equivalent articles of the 1936 constitution the dominant role of the CPSU in all spheres of Soviet life.

[150]Sharlet, *The New Soviet Constitution,* p. 56.

CHAPTER X

Political Performance

EVALUATING SYSTEM PERFORMANCE

The performance of a political system, according to Almond and Powell, is best conceptualized as a sequence of distinct though overlapping stages in the policy process: policymaking, policy implementation, policy outputs, policy outcomes, and feedback.[1] They remind us that the actual outcomes of policy may be somewhat different from the intentions of policymakers. The interaction of a political system with the domestic and international environments in which it is situated is extraordinarily complex, and the outcomes of policy acts frequently reflect the unplanned short- and long-term influence of environmental forces on the political system. In comparison with liberal democracies, a political system of the Soviet type is distinctive for the far greater control over the domestic environment that is claimed by the political leadership in order to accomplish its policy objectives. Extractive, distributive, and regulative policy is notable for the breadth of social activity it affects and the rapidity with which it has brought about change. Not surprisingly, therefore, the performance of the Soviet political system has been subjected to the most widely varied assessments since the inception of the Soviet regime in 1917. So, too, has the question of the criteria or measures that are to be used in evaluating the policy intentions, acts, and outcomes of the Soviet leadership.

Some observers claim that owing to Russia's initial backwardness, its suffering at the hands of others during civil war and World

---

[1]Gabriel A. Almond and G. Bingham Powell, *Comparative Politics: System, Process, and Policy* (Boston, Mass.: Little, Brown, 1978), p. 284.

War II, and the necessity for creating a national network of educational, cultural, and health care facilities, the actual performance of the system should be judged by comparison less with the economic successes of the more advanced capitalist systems of the West than with the least developed nations on Europe's periphery. Siding with them are many who believe that the Stalinist model of development, for all its undeniable brutality, represents the only chance for developmental breakthroughs in the contemporary Third World.[2]

Alternatively, in earlier decades the argument was often made that the commitment of the Soviet system to equality of condition for all toilers, elimination of class exploitation, and provision of the benefits of modern socialism to all ethnic and religious groups in the multi-national Soviet state was its most important achievement and that the system's accomplishments in the realm of social and economic rights, as opposed to civil and political liberties, represented a significant triumph over poverty and despotism. (This argument is made less frequently today.)[3] Often such assessments were coupled with efforts to rationalize the existence of mass terror and with exaggerated claims as to the achieved level of social welfare.

In contrast to the ethical criteria for judging performance advanced by some Westerners sympathetic to the avowed goals of Stalin's social revolution, Soviet political leaders from the Bolsheviks forward have generally adhered to pragmatic views about the political importance of rapid economic growth in ensuring a strong industrial and military base for the state's power so as to match and exceed the industrial and military power of its surrounding enemies. Perhaps the most straightforward expression of this view was Stalin's famous speech about the need for rapid fulfillment of the Five Year Plan — a rapid *tempo*, as it was called at the time — before a gathering of industrial administrators in 1931:

> To slacken the tempo would mean falling behind. And those who fall behind get beaten. But we do not want to be beaten. No, we

[2]See Charles K. Wilber, *The Soviet Model and Underdeveloped Countries* (Chapel Hill, N.C.: University of North Carolina Press, 1969).

[3]See evaluations by Western intellectuals as cited in Paul Hollander, *Political Pilgrims* (New York: Oxford University Press, 1981), esp. ch. 4, "The Appeals of Soviet Society: The First Pilgrimage."

refuse to be beaten! One feature of the history of old Russia was the continual beatings she suffered for falling behind, for her backwardness. She was beaten by the Mongol Khans. She was beaten by the Turkish beys. She was beaten by the Swedish feudal lords. She was beaten by the Polish and Lithuanian gentry. She was beaten by the British and French capitalists. She was beaten by the Japanese barons. All beat her — for her backwardness: for military backwardness, for cultural backwardness, for political backwardness, for industrial backwardness, for agricultural backwardness. She was beaten because to do so was profitable and could be done with impunity. . . . That is why we must no longer lag behind. . . . Do you want our socialist fatherland to be beaten and to lose its independence? If you do not want this you must put an end to its backwardness in the shortest possible time and develop genuine Bolshevik tempo in building up its socialist system of economy. There is no other way. That is why Lenin said during the October Revolution: ''Either perish, or overtake and outstrip the advanced capitalist countries.''[4]

Quite unequivocally Stalin identified the success of the crash program to industrialize backward Russia with the ultimate test of war. When that test came 10 years later, Stalin's regime belied the expectations of many (including some of Germany's political and military leaders) and retained sufficient political cohesiveness and economic resilience to withstand the shattering losses sustained at the outset of the war and to create a powerful military and industrial force capable of defeating Germany's armies in the east. Quick to construe victory in war as vindication of the Soviet political system per se, Stalin in a major 1946 address claimed that the outcome of the war had proved the superiority of the Soviet socialist political model, which nevertheless faced new threats from the encircling imperialist powers in the future. It must therefore be raised to yet higher levels of economic production so that it would be invulnerable in the face of any war that might yet be unleashed.

So, how must we understand our victory over our enemies, what can this victory mean from the standpoint of the condition and development of the internal forces of our country? Our victory indicates, first of all, that our Soviet *social* order won, that the Soviet

[4]Quoted from ''The Tasks of Business Executives,'' in Joseph Stalin, *Selected Writings* (New York: International Publishers, 1942), p. 200.

social order successfully met the test in the fire of war and proved its viability. . . . The war showed that the Soviet multinational state order successfully met the test, grew yet stronger during the war and proved itself a fully viable state order. . . . Now there can be no question as to the viability of the Soviet state order, for its viability cannot be doubted. . . . With the help of what policy did the communist party succeed in securing these material possibilities in the country in so short a time? Above all with the help of the Soviet policy of the industrialization of the country. . . . Second, with the help of the policy of collectivization of agriculture. . . . We must see to it that our industry can produce up to 50 million tons of iron a year, up to 60 million tons of steel, up to 500 million tons of coal, up to 60 million tons of oil. Only under these conditions can we say that our Motherland will be guaranteed against all eventualities.[5]

It is, therefore, by the criteria of economic, and particularly industrial, production and of military power and preparedness that the Soviet leadership has judged the performance of the political system as a whole. Individual sacrifice and deprivation in the present are justified first by the necessity to create the mighty economic and military base required by Soviet power (which in turn is also the economic and military base for socialism everywhere), and second by the ambition to convert the collective labor of the present generations into a future society of abundance, equality, and justice. This is a utopian dream whose force is evidently so spent by now that the idea has been savagely satirized by the brilliant former Moscow University professor of mathematic logic, Alexander Zinoviev, in his novel *The Radiant Future* (*Svetloe budushchee*).[6] Let us therefore examine the record of Soviet economic performance since the war before turning to the more specific dimensions of system performance, namely extractive, distributive, and regulatory policy.

In an important comparative study of the process of modernization in Russia and Japan, Cyril Black and a group of distinguished historians and social scientists point out certain similarities

[5]Joseph Stalin, ''Rech' na predvybornom sobranii izbiratelei stalinskogo izbiratel'nogo okruga goroda Moskvy'' (Speech at the pre-electoral meeting of voters of the Stalin electoral district of the city of Moscow), 9 February 1946, in I. V. Stalin, *Sochineniia* (Works), vol. 3, ed. Robert H. McNeal (Stanford, Calif.: Hoover Institution, 1967), pp. 1–22.

[6]Alexander Zinoviev, *The Radiant Future,* trans. Gordon Clough (New York: Random House, 1980).

between the two nations: both were "late modernizers," seeking to catch up with the more powerful nations of Europe and America; both employed methods involving centralized political power to mobilize resources and direct the development process; both achieved notable successes in their development drives. With respect to the premodern social endowments the two nations possessed, however, and, more important for our purposes, the effect of the destruction caused by World War II on their postwar performance, the two cases differ significantly. The authors note that in the premodern period, Japan, with its high population density and the pressure of limited arable land, stressed "intensive" development of its resources — that is, higher levels of literacy and education, higher levels of social organization and coordination, and a larger proportion of its population belonging to the administrative elite. Russia, however, traditionally adopted a strategy of "extensive" development, in which quantities of inputs to the economy — namely manpower, natural resources, and land — were mobilized by central authority.[7]

More important, however, for comparing the post-1945 performance of the two systems is the different effect the war had on the two societies. In Japan, the war shattered the traditional social and political institutions that had brought the country into the modern world but had launched it on a disastrous course of military expansion. In Russia, by contrast, the war (as Stalin also noted in the latter of the two speeches quoted above) had the effect of strengthening the Soviet social and political order. As a result, the hypercentralized administrative structures through which Stalin had implemented his industrializing policies were not seriously reformed by the war, nor were they, the authors point out, significantly affected by Stalin's passing. The consequence has been that the rigidity of Soviet administrative and political institutions has increasingly become a brake on further growth. The contrast between the two nations' performance is illustrated by Table 1, showing both the higher average annual growth of Japan's economy since the war and the more modern and growth-oriented structure of that economy.

Note in particular that despite the high extractive capability achieved by the authoritarian Soviet polity, Japan's economy de-

[7]Cyril E. Black et al., *The Modernization of Japan and Russia: A Comparative Study* (New York: The Free Press, 1975), p. 342 and passim.

TABLE 1: *Comparative Economic Performance, Japan and USSR (in Percentages)*

	Japan		USSR	
Average annual rates of growth:	1950–1973		1950–1973	
Gross National Product	9.9		5.5	
GNP per capita	8.7		4.0	
National Product by Sectors of Origin:	1940	1970	1940	1970
Agriculture	16	6	29	24
Manufacturing	53	50	45	47
Services	31	44	26	29
Share of Labor Force Employed in:				
Agriculture	44	19	54	27
Manufacturing	31	41	28	45
Services	25	40	18	28
National Product by End Uses:				
Consumption	65	52	63	58
Gross Capital Formation	24	40	26	30
Government	11	8	11	12

Source: Reprinted with permission of The Free Press, a Division of Macmillan Inc., from *The Modernization of Japan and Russia: A Comparative Study* edited by Cyril E. Black. Copyright © 1975 by The Free Press.

voted a higher share of national product to investment in capital in 1970 than did that of the USSR. Both this higher investment rate and the higher degree of efficiency with which capital generates output in Japan help account for the faster economic growth observed in Japan.

Japan's postwar economic record is, of course, unique among the developed nations of the world and hence may exaggerate the contrast between Soviet economic performance and that of other societies. The comparison does provide evidence for the proposition that, for a society entering the process of modernization in a competitive international environment, Stalinist methods of development are not alone in yielding high rates of economic growth. Moreover, by comparison with the record achieved by Soviet society in the decades of the thirties, forties, and fifties, Soviet performance in the sixties, seventies, and eighties has shown signs of a long-term, secular decline. Table 1 illustrates this point.

Table 2 indicates the overall trend in aggregate economic performance in the two decades following 1960, a period of unusual domestic political tranquillity by comparison with any previous 20 year period. The data show a sharp, unmistakable decline in

TABLE 2: *Growth of Output and Productivity (Average Annual Rates of Growth in Percentages)*

	1960–65	1965–70	1970–75	1975–80	
Gross National Product [1]	5.0	5.2	3.7	2.7	
Labor productivity [2]	3.4	3.2	2.0	1.3	
Total factor productivity [3]	0.6	1.1	−0.5	−0.8	
Industrial Production	6.6	6.3	5.9	3.6	
Industrial labor productivity [2]	3.6	3.1	4.4	2.0	
Industrial total factor productivity [4]	−0.1	0.5	1.1	−0.6	

	1976	1977	1978	1979	1980
Gross National Product [1]	4.8	3.2	3.4	0.8	1.4
Labor productivity [2]	3.6	1.7	1.7	−0.7	0.2
Total factor productivity [3]	1.2	−0.4	−0.3	−2.7	−1.9
Industrial Production	3.9	4.0	3.5	3.0	3.4
Industrial labor productivity [2]	1.6	2.4	1.8	1.6	2.4
Industrial total factor productivity [4]	−1.0	−0.4	−0.7	−1.1	−0.2

Notes:

1. Based on indexes of GNP (in 1970 rubles), by sector of origin, at factor cost.

2. Output per man-hour.

3. Output per combined input of man-hours, capital and land.

4. Output per combined inputs of man-hours and capital.

Source: Herbert S. Levine, "Possible Causes of the Deterioration of Soviet Productivity Growth in the Period 1976–1980," in *Soviet Economy in the 1980's: Problems and Prospects,* vol. 1 (Washington, D.C.: Joint Economic Committee of the U.S. Congress, 1982), p. 154.

the growth rate of GNP as well as of its most important component — industrial production. Paralleling and partly causing this general downward trend is the worsening performance of the factors of production, including labor. The productivity of labor, capital, and land (measured as output per unit of input) not only ceased growing but actually declined each year in the latter half of the 1970s. Many factors account for this record, including unfavorable weather conditions and difficulties in the world market, but the most important causes arise from policy decisions, including the slow rate of replacement or modernization of capital, the high priority given to investment in military industry, the disruption caused to the economy by crash programs to develop individual sectors or regions, the slackening of labor discipline, and the siphoning of a greater share of the nation's goods and services into the second economy.[8] These causes may, in turn, be regarded as the consequences of other problems. The spread of the second economy, for example, is in part a response to the growing gap between rising money incomes and officially available supplies of consumer goods and services.[9] Keeping in mind the model presented in the first chapter of a system interacting with its environment, we would conclude that the policies implemented by the regime in such areas as investment priorities are preventing the system from achieving major long-term goals set by the leadership.

As the economy's growth slows, the difficulty of the political choices faced by the leadership increases.[10] One problem is the fact that, as Seweryn Bialer points out, an economy growing very slowly is more susceptible to the effects of year-to-year fluctuations in the performance of any single sector, such as agriculture or energy.[11] In turn, this means that plans calling for steady increases in the resources devoted to any single sector, such as defense, will pose a heavy burden on the capacity of the economy. At the macrosystem level, Soviet leaders are faced with the problem of allocating an ever smaller increment of economic growth among three major sectoral claimants: economic investment, consumption (referring to consumption of goods and services by in-

---

[8]See Herbert Levine, "Possible Causes of the Deterioration of Soviet Productivity Growth in the Period 1976-1980," in *Soviet Economy in the 1980's,* part 1, pp. 155-68.

[9]Michael Kaser, "Economic Policy," in Archie Brown and Michael Kaser, eds., *Soviet Policy for the 1980s* (Bloomington: Indiana University Press, 1982), p. 190.

[10]Seweryn Bialer, *Stalin's Successors: Leadership, Stability, and Change in the Soviet Union* (Cambridge, England: Cambridge University Press, 1980), ch. 15, "The Politics of Stringency," pp. 283-305.

[11]Bialer, *Stalin's Successors,* p. 290.

dividuals and households), and military spending. Competition among these and hence the political consequences of intersectoral competition will increase correspondingly.[12] Regarding the painful dilemma of choosing among these three sectors, Bialer writes:

> Reducing growth in investment below current rates seems difficult in view of vast needs for new, more energy-efficient investment goods throughout the country and the already slow pace of investment (3 percent per year). Reducing growth in consumption would have a negative impact on workers' morale and productivity, just when a boost in both is needed most. Reducing growth in defense spending at a time of leadership transition would be equally difficult since those vying for power will probably be reluctant to press for actions that might alienate the military. In the absence of any reduction in the pace of defense expenditures, however, the burden of slowing economic growth would fall squarely on the consumer, whose standard of living would stagnate after more than a decade of continued improvement.[13]

Elsewhere Bialer argues that although the legitimacy of the Soviet system is stronger than is often assumed, both among Soviet elite groups and among the populace at large, declining economic performance undermines popular legitimacy. Since Stalin, according to Bialer, rising living standards have become a substantially more important source of political legitimacy for the nation's leadership. Hence, as performance stagnates, this source of legitimacy is jeopardized. Bialer believes it likely that the regime has responded to seriously weakened popular support by inflaming national fears of war and inducing a sense of threat associated with the cold war.[14]

So far we have considered the dysfunctional consequences of decisions taken by the supreme leadership at the policy level of the political system — particularly choices concerning the allocation of national resources among competing claimants. A more far-reaching argument about declining performance, however, attributes the worsening of performance to degeneration of the system itself. In a controversial essay published in 1966, not long

---

[12]Bialer, *Stalin's Successors,* p. 292.
[13]Ibid.
[14]Seweryn Bialer, ''The Dilemmas of Soviet Foreign Policy under Andropov,'' in *The Political Economy of the Soviet Union* (Washington, D.C.: Joint Economic Committee and House Committee on Foreign Affairs, 1984), pp. 84–86.

after Brezhnev had assumed power, Zbigniew Brzezinski asserted that since decision making had gradually become routine since Stalin's death, the supreme leader no longer had the capacity to prevent a stultifying bureaucratization of the system. Indeed, Brezhnev and Kosygin, whom Brzezinski termed *apparatchiki,* were incapable of breaking the grip of the powerful bureaucratic organizations through which the party leadership ruled:

> [Brezhnev and Kosygin] are still part of an extremely centralized and rigidly hierarchical bureaucratic organization, increasingly set in its ways, politically corrupted by years of unchallenged power, and made even more confined in its outlook than is normally the case with a ruling body by its lingering and increasingly ritualized doctrinaire tradition.[15]

Although disputes now arise, according to Brzezinski, between contending institutional interests and are resolved by compromise, the bureaucratic nature of the system and the ideological limits of allowable policy positions tend to deter individuals of talent and creativity from seeking political careers. Hence the newer generations of leaders will be drawn from the most mediocre, conformist elements of society rather than from among able innovators. Finally, the role of the party becomes increasingly dysfunctional in such a system. In early years the party performed a mobilizing role, providing "leadership, and a dominant outlook for a rapidly changing and developing society."[16] Today, however, the society's complexity and institutional diversity make the party's demands for ideological uniformity restrictive on change and development and hence a retarding factor in growth. Only through specific mechanisms for the replacement of leadership (such as that required of the Mexican president, for example) and the institutionalization of forums for *political* participation — demand articulation and political deliberation — can the system successfully cope with the dilemma of change.[17]

Brzezinski's analysis was widely regarded as unduly pessimistic and overstated at the time. As Brezhnev gradually acquired personal authority and political power, formulating and implementing large-scale programs such as the agricultural modernization

---

[15]Zbigniew Brzezinski, "The Soviet Political System: Transformation or Degeneration?" *Problems of Communism* 15, no. 1 (1966): 5.

[16]Ibid., p. 11.

[17]Ibid., p. 15.

campaign and the expansion of trade and diplomatic contact with the outside world, Brzezinski's dismissal of the Brezhnev regime as "high level clerks" seemed at odds with the effective leadership exercised by the ruling Politburo. Moreover, Brzezinski appeared to be overlooking the expanded forum for the articulation and mediation of political interests that had gradually been established as mass terror and Stalinist dogmatism were dismantled. In a major rebuttal to Brzezinski, Jerry F. Hough argued that the clash of bureaucratic interests that Brzezinski had identified as the consequence of the single leader's loss of effective political authority over the party and government machinery had become one of the most important characteristics of the political system — a characteristic that Hough termed "institutional pluralism." Hence pluralization of interests, enhanced by the party's role as a broker among competing interests and by incrementalism in policymaking, had fundamentally altered the system and created the conditions for adaptive policy change. Far from attesting to the petrification of the system, such change, Hough argued, was best revealed in three important spheres of policy: the increasing rationalization and modernization of managerial technique, a stronger voice for those political forces seeking faster growth of consumer goods and services at the expense of producer and military industries, and the equivalent of a war on poverty, which had significantly closed the gap between highest and lowest income levels in society and produced a marked increase in overall living standards for the population.[18]

Judging today with the benefit of hindsight, each of these three areas of policy now appears to have been given a stimulus by initiatives undertaken by the Brezhnev leadership in the late 1960s and early 1970s but to have ceased undergoing meaningful change thereafter. Despite a great deal of *discussion* about the modernization of organizational structure — referred to in the chapter on policy implementation — we have seen that few actual institutional changes have resulted. Powerful administrative units, particularly branch ministries, have succeeded in weakening the effect of modest attempts to strengthen horizontal and program-ori-

---

[18]See Jerry F. Hough, "The Soviet System: Petrification or Pluralism?" *Problems of Communism* 21, no. 2 (March–April 1972): 25–45; reprinted in Lenard J. Cohen and Jane P. Shapiro, *Communist Systems in Comparative Perspective* (Garden City, N.Y.: Anchor Books, 1974), pp. 449–86, at pp. 474–75.

ented links in administration. Second, the growth targets for the ninth Five Year Plan (1971–1975), which reversed the traditional priority given Group A (producer goods and military industries) over Group B (light and consumer goods) industries, were left unfulfilled and soon reverted to the traditional, Stalinist pattern.[19]

Finally, the effects of the various measures adopted under the Brezhnev regime to improve the social welfare of peasants and lower-stratum blue-collar workers and to equalize income levels have tended to level off and have even in some respects exacerbated shortages of food and other necessities. Although differentials in income levels have been narrowed, particularly by raising the incomes of the least well-off strata, the trend toward equalization has slowed.[20] In part this is a function of the slowing growth of government spending on social welfare. According to Alastair McAuley, the growth of government spending on what is termed *social consumption* (a category of outlays for such collective goods as education and health care as well as transfer payments to pensioners and others) slowed sharply in the late Brezhnev period.[21] Moreover, the trend under both Khrushchev and Brezhnev to increase cash payments to individuals in the form of pensions, minimum wages, and other benefits, together with the faster rate of growth of money incomes than of consumer goods and services, has created inflationary pressure and shortages in some important categories of consumer necessities, including meat and dairy products. This means that higher income may not be readily translatable into desired goods and services.[22]

Today Soviet economic discussion centers around ways of link-

---

[19]See, on this point, Alexander Yanov, *Detente after Brezhnev: The Domestic Roots of Soviet Foreign Policy* (Berkeley, Calif.: Institute of International Studies, 1977), pp. 16–20; and George W. Breslauer, *Khrushchev and Brezhnev as Leaders: Building Authority in Soviet Politics* (London: Allen & Unwin, 1982), pp. 180–81, 203.

[20]Abram Bergson, "Income Inequality under Soviet Socialism," *Journal of Economic Literature* 22 (September 1984): 1052–99, Table 3, p. 1063, and pp. 1092–93. This article is a comprehensive survey of relevant available data and findings bearing on income levels of the Soviet population.

[21]Alastair McAuley, "Social Policy," in Archie Brown and Michael Kaser, eds., *Soviet Policy for the 1980s* (Bloomington: Indiana University Press, 1982), p. 153.

[22]See statements by Robert W. Campbell and Marshall I. Goldman in *Political Economy of the Soviet Union*, pp. 11, 45–46. Note the difference in emphasis between economists who stress the "monetary overhang" of rising disposable income over less rapidly rising supply and those who attribute supply shortages to failures in the production and distribution of consumer necessities. The consequence is the same in either case: long lines for basic goods, shortages, and black markets.

ing pay and benefits more effectively to actual output per worker. As Andropov said in a speech to the Moscow machine-tool factory workers, "Miracles, as they say, don't happen. You understand yourselves that the Government can give only so many goods as are produced. The growth of wages — if it is not accompanied by needed wares, of good quality, if, finally, services are suffering — cannot give a real improvement in material well-being."[23] Current reform proposals aimed at raising levels of labor productivity by rewarding individual or small-group effort will almost surely increase rather than diminish income differentials among social strata.

In a recent study comparing the effects of executive succession in the political systems of East and West, Valerie Bunce asked, Do new leaders make a difference?[24] The foregoing discussion suggests that new leaders may alter policy priorities but that the political system within which they operate retards the effectiveness and duration of their policies. As George Breslauer notes, the political system generates impulses for reform but also restricts and blocks the implementation of any reform that a new leadership group adopts.[25]

We conclude, therefore, that the institutionalization of political competition, which Hough associated with legitimate and invigorating institutional pluralism, has not progressed very far in the Soviet system. To create legitimate political mechanisms for the open articulation and aggregation of demands through which the competition for power could be regulated would be to widen institutionalized political participation; this would undercut, at least in the short run, the power of the central party and governmental elite. In the absence of public arenas for political contests, intra- and interbureaucratic relations frequently become arenas for what T. H. Rigby has termed "crypto-politics."[26] Despite the

[23]See the account in the *New York Times,* 1 February 1983, and *Pravda,* February 1, 1983.

[24]Valerie Bunce, *Do New Leaders Make a Difference?* (Princeton, N.J.: Princeton University Press, 1979).

[25]Breslauer, *Khrushchev and Brezhnev as Leaders,* pp. 280–88; on the conservative behavior of quasi-autonomous bureaucracies in the military-industrial sphere, see Arthur Alexander, *Decisionmaking in Soviet Weapons Procurement,* Adelphi Papers, no. 147–48, (London: International Institute for Strategic Studies, 1978).

[26]See, for example, his essay, "Politics in the Mono-Organizational Society," in Andrew C. Janos, ed., *Authoritarian Politics in Communist Europe* (Berkeley, Calif.: Institute of International Studies, 1976), esp. pp. 37, 61–64.

ostensible integration of the activity of such organizations as research institutes, industrial associations, branch ministries, and police agencies, the behavior of state officials commonly reflects internecine squabbles and alignments through which disputes over power and policy are played out. The difference between bureaucratic politics in, say, the executive branch of the U. S. government and in the Soviet system, as Rigby points out, lies in the fact that the Soviet "mono-organizational system" "seeks to direct the *whole* social life of its members." Since outside the bureaucracy political mechanisms for voicing demands and resolving conflicts are weak, the channels of communication and action designed to implement policy are subverted by their covert political functions. New policies aimed at reorganizing bureaucratic powers and tasks rarely resolve long-standing power struggles and are often drawn into them, limiting or distorting their effects. Central control therefore is undermined by the unpredictability of outcomes.[27]

Thus bureaucratic resistance to reform policies undercuts the potential for significant improvement of the system at the policy level. In the absence of a Stalin-like political leader at the top, therefore, the system is chronically susceptible to immobilism — an inability to formulate and execute policies capable of substantially improving the performance of the system.[28] Many observers would agree that the solution lies in system-level change. Thane Gustafson writes:

> [T]he success of the next generation of Soviet leaders in matching the evolution of their increasingly modern society and economy with modern political instruments will depend less on their ability to launch new programs and reorganizations, incentive systems and indexes, than on their capacity to rethink the inherited relations between knowledge and power, between control and autonomy, and between a safe conservatism and progress.[29]

[27]See also the final chapter of William E. Odom, *The Soviet Volunteers* (Princeton, N.J.: Princeton University Press, 1973), for a strong plea to analyze organizational dynamics in Soviet life in political terms.

[28]William Odom, "Choice and Change in Soviet Politics," *Problems of Communism* 32, no. 3 (May-June 1983): 1-21; reprinted in Erik P. Hoffmann and Robbin F. Laird, *The Soviet Polity in the Modern Era* (New York: Aldine, 1984), pp. 915-942, at p. 920.

[29]Thane Gustafson, *Reform in Soviet Politics* (Cambridge, England: Cambridge University Press, 1981), p. 161.

Brzezinski, however, concluded that only increased popular political participation through institutions for the mediation of group interests could overcome the petrification of the system: "Obviously, the implementation of such institutional reforms would eventually lead to a profound transformation of the Soviet system."[30]

EXTRACTIVE PERFORMANCE

Comparison of public policy in diverse political systems must reflect the fundamental differences between socialist societies of the Soviet type, where the vast bulk of economic activity occurs under the ownership and control of the state, and others in which the role of government is far narrower. To be sure, even in the most market-oriented capitalist societies, governments use their power to command and distribute goods and services according to established policies, and in the contemporary Western world, the economic role of governments is imposing.[31]

Nevertheless, the difference between a political system in which government is only one of many employers and consumers and one in which government is the major employer and consumer, as in the Soviet Union, requires us to distinguish types of extractive policies in market-oriented societies from the administrative control government exercises over resources in socialist systems. In the former, government obtains needed goods and services by means of purchases at market value, supplementing these with extraction of labor, goods, and money through administrative force. Military conscription and taxation are probably the most important of these forms of extraction. In the Soviet type of system, however, the state is the major property owner in society, and hence most economic exchanges are transactions between units of the state.

Not all economic resources are state property, however. Labor, except for that of such institutionalized persons as prisoners and soldiers, is private. Thus for the most part labor services must be either paid for through wages or extracted through conscription. Since much consumption is by private persons rather than state

[30]Brzezinski, "Transformation or Degeneration?" p. 15.

[31]Andrew Shonfield, *Modern Capitalism* (New York: Oxford University Press, 1969); Edward P. Tufte, *Political Control of the Economy* (Princeton, N.J.: Princeton University Press, 1978).

enterprises, another form of government resource extraction is the taxation of goods sold to consumers as well as other imposts (such as income taxes). In addition, certain forms of productive property are not state-owned. A sphere of cooperative ownership is recognized legally by the state, and its most important form is the collective farm, or *kolkhoz*. Since Stalin's time, however, such cooperative production organizations, along with the cooperatives retailing food and other products, have been subject to such extensive state control that they are scarcely distinguishable from types of property that the state owns outright. Finally, there is a modestly important sphere of legal private property, including the private plots maintained by collective and state farmers, from which the government extracts taxes. In all, because of the predominance of the state as employer, producer, and consumer, the extraction of economic resources from outside the political system plays a smaller role in determining the amounts and kinds of economic resources in Soviet society than does the flow of goods and services within the state sector. In this section we shall examine the policy objectives of the regime as embodied in plans for resource allocation, including extractive fiscal policy such as wage setting, price setting, and taxation as well as the extraction of manpower through military conscription and penal labor.

In contrast to a market-based economy, in which goods and services take the form of purchasable commodities that can be commanded through the interchangeable and fungible medium of money, the Soviet socialist economy has been characterized since the great industrialization and collectivization drives beginning in 1928–1929 by extensive reliance on central planning to allocate economic resources.[32] The marketplace does play a role in the economy, however. Consumers have some freedom to choose how to spend their incomes on the range of goods and services available through state-regulated outlets, although the selection, quantity, prices, and quality of these goods and services are largely undetermined by consumer preferences. The other realm in which limited play for market forces exists is that of labor. In principle, workers are free to find and change jobs as they wish. The state, however, sets wage levels, using the structure of pay and benefits

---

[32]A lucid explanation of the ways in which market and administrative devices differ in their allocative functions is provided by Charles E. Lindblom, in *Politics and Markets* (New York: Basic Books, 1977).

as incentives to direct the flow of workers into regions and occupations.

In the crucial sphere of relations among enterprises and ministries, however, transactions are largely determined by administrative decisions over the quantity, assortment, and value of production, as well as over the supply of inputs and the distribution of the finished goods. The effectiveness of central planning is enhanced by the control the planners exercise over especially scarce goods (called *deficit* goods) needed by producers to meet their planned output targets. Although since the Stalin era, enterprises, government agencies, and other organizations have somewhat greater freedom to dispose of their money revenues, their opportunity to invest in new capital or in schools, housing, hospitals, and the like is severely constrained by the shortage of available physical resources and the tight controls over scarce goods that the planners maintain.[33]

The persistent domination of administrative or command mechanisms in the economy over market mechanisms, the consequence of Stalin's imposition of a centralized planning and administrative bureaucracy over most spheres of economic activity, continues to be justified by the goal to redirect society's product into capital investment and government (including military) spending rather than into consumption. Through command and the manipulation of prices, moreover, the authorities also determine the structure of consumption, emphasizing collective forms such as education, communications, and physical culture over more personal and individual forms such as household goods, clothes, and entertainment. The limited supply of such goods and the vigorous demand for them (fed partly by knowledge of Western tastes and styles), together with rising disposable incomes, have created flourishing black markets in the goods and services least available through official channels, such as blue jeans, records, books, automotive parts, construction materials, medical supplies and services, and foodstuffs. Under the official structure of economic administration, overall consumption is held down in

---

[33]On the structure of the economy and the relationship of administrative and market channels for economic allocation, see Alec Nove, *The Soviet Economic System*, 2nd ed. (London: Allen & Unwin, 1980); James R. Millar, *The ABC's of Soviet Socialism* (Urbana: University of Illinois Press, 1981); Raymond Hutchings, *Soviet Economic Development*, 2nd ed. (New York: New York University Press, 1982).

favor of allocating national resources to high-priority sectors: government and military spending in the present and investment for future growth. Second, the structure of consumption also reflects government-imposed priorities, which economize on national resources and also divert consumption into more politically acceptable forms. Third, the effort to limit and channel supply of consumer goods, combined with higher overall income levels, has led to the expansion of black markets, through which consumers circumvent these administrative controls.

The use of administrative controls over the flow of physical resources, money, and manpower for the purpose of building a powerful industrial-military base has persisted despite the increase in the total size of the economy. Overall, gross national product has risen about four times since 1950, according to Western measures.[34] During this period, the share of national product devoted to investment — the extraction of resources for the creation and renovation of productive capital — has *risen,* from 14 percent to 33 percent (at 1970 prices) of GNP. Meanwhile the percentage of the national product given over to consumption — which includes such collective goods as education, health services, and transportation — has *fallen* from 60 percent to 53 percent. Though the rising levels of total national production have enabled per capita consumption to rise (though at a slowing rate) over this period, the increase in the share of the national product devoted to investment in capital suggests that the Soviet administrative mechanisms have effectively maintained the traditional priority of investment over consumption. It should also be noted that the share of GNP devoted to military spending has increased at a rate slightly faster than that of the overall economy since 1965, and hence that the defense burden has risen in this period.[35]

Table 3 indicates the allocation of national income among the three aggregate sectors into which the national product is channeled: government spending, investment, and consumption. It also draws comparisons between Soviet performance in this respect and that of selected other industrialized nations.

Some interesting comparisons may be drawn from these data.

[34]John Pitzer, "Gross National Product of the USSR, 1950–1980," in *USSR: Measures of Economic Growth and Development, 1950–1980* (Washington, D.C.: Joint Economic Committee of the U.S. Congress, 1982), p. 15.

[35]Ibid., pp. 18–19.

TABLE 3: *Percentage Distribution of National Product by End Use in Selected OECD Countries (GDP) and in the USSR (GNP)*

	Consumption				Investment				All Other Expenditures			
	1950	1960	1970	1979	1950	1960	1970	1979	1950	1960	1970	1979
USSR	59.9	57.7	54.2	53.2	14.2	24.2	28.2	32.5	25.8	18.1	17.6	14.3
US	62.1	60.9	62.2	64.6	19.5	18.2	18.4	17.4	18.4	20.9	19.4	18.0
Japan	63.2	63.2	54.4	55.4	15.1	23.1	34.9	33.2	21.7	13.7	10.7	11.4 (a)
Finland	52.8	54.4	55.1	54.1	25.5	30.1	28.6	23.2	21.7	15.5	16.3	22.7 (b)
Italy	66.1	59.4	63.6	62.4	15.6	26.0	24.4	18.9	18.3	14.6	12.0	18.7 (b)

a. Figures in 1950 column actually pertain to 1952.

b. Figures in 1950 column actually pertain to 1951.

Source: Table 2 in Pitzer, "Gross National Product of the USSR," p. 21.

First, despite the extensive and cumbersome administrative mechanisms that keep consumption in the USSR to a relatively low level, the consumption levels of Scandinavian countries are comparable or even lower (as in the cases of Finland, seen in the table, or of Norway and Sweden), evidently as a consequence of the combination of welfare state policies with relatively abstemious habits among the populace. Second, as we noted previously, the relatively high investment rates of the Soviet socialist model are not unique to the Soviet system: Japan has shown comparable, and in 1970 higher, rates of investment realized through voluntary savings and government policies designed to reward investment over consumption. Thus, although Soviet policy overall has been to divert resources for productive investment and spending on immediate governmental needs such as defense, it has not proved notably more efficient in doing so than some of its capitalist rivals. The political costs of suppressing potential opposition to the party's priorities and the administrative costs of maintaining the extensive bureaucratic apparatus needed to control the economy have been high.

The administrative controls over the flows of goods and services, money, and manpower need fuller description. Decisions about production, pricing, and supply are all embodied in binding economic plans issued by the state planning authorities and broken down into more specific plans for each branch of the economy and ultimately each enterprise and organization. The plan is considered a legally binding document, vesting responsibility for its fulfillment in the managerial staff of each organization, which then must fulfill the plan or satisfy the authorities that non-fulfillment was the fault of other organizations. In principle, all goods and services have an intended or at least permitted purpose in accordance with the general policies adopted by the party leadership. Some physical goods and some surplus manpower always evade official supply channels, to be sure, as is attested by the common managerial practice of hoarding scarce inputs and of keeping needlessly large staffs of workers on the payroll. In these ways managers protect themselves against arbitrary or changing demands from superiors. The most important form of administrative control over resources, including labor services, however, remains the system of planning material production.

The state extracts revenues from the population by means of pricing, wage setting, and taxation. Tax revenues from the sale of alcoholic beverages, for example, yield, it is estimated, some 11 percent of total state money revenues, a sizable proportion but somewhat lower than those yielded by the tsarist state monopoly on spirits.[36] (Lenin and his fellow Bolsheviks roundly denounced these revenues as a means by which the state exploited workers by profiting on their degradation.) A large share of government revenues is derived from a tax imposed on goods, particularly consumer goods, called the *turnover tax,* which is paid when goods are produced or when they reach the wholesalers but before they reach the consumer.[37] Individual enterprises, associations, and ministries are expected to be monetarily self-sufficient — that is, their incomes are expected to suffice to cover their expenditures — thus minimizing the need for state subsidies to failing organizations.

On the other hand, government pricing policies ensure low prices on several goods and services directly affecting the daily life of the population. Bread is kept at low prices (despite the widening gap, made up by growing state subsidies, between the prices paid by the government to farmers for their produce and the prices set for food in the stores), as are meat — when it is available — and dairy products.[38] Similarly, the costs to consumers of housing

[36]Vladimir G. Treml, *Alcohol in the USSR* (Durham, N.C.: Duke University Press, 1982), pp. 29–32.

[37]See Nove, *Soviet Economic System,* p. 238.

[38]On the consequences of increasing the subsidies needed to cover low retail food prices, see Vladimir G. Treml, "Subsidies in Soviet Agriculture: Record and Prospects," in *Soviet Economy in the 1980's,* part 2, pp. 171–86.

and utilities are low, a situation that, given the continuing shortage of housing, creates secondary markets in rented or purchased housing space. The costs to consumers of education, health services, urban transportation, and cultural goods such as books, records, and tickets to theatrical performances are also kept low. Relatively low prices for such goods and services combined with high demand produce lines and shortages, which are compensated for by the ubiquitous second economy. Through influence, bribes, barter, or payments, consumers obtain such goods and services "on the left." The prevalence of such transactions is important in its own right, although efforts to measure the size and scope of the second economy have been frustrated by the absence of firm systematic data published on the subject.[39] Of greater interest to us is the question of whether its operations widen or narrow the disparities between rich and poor among the population. Official taxation and pricing policy is set to ensure a certain minimum standard of living even to the lowest-paid strata in the economy — an opportunity to enjoy such benefits of socialism as free or nominally priced food, shelter, basic medical services, and education. When the supply of these and other goods is diverted into illegal markets, however, those groups with the fewest resources (including money, influence, or access to pilfered materials) may have a lower standard of living than they otherwise would. Those with resources convertible into black-market commodities may enjoy a higher standard. On the other hand, the second economy also works to circumvent supply shortages and thus lubricate the operation of an economy in which supply of consumer products often does not equal demand.

The government also uses taxation policy to prevent legal forms of private economic activity from exacerbating inequality, taxing earnings from such petty bourgeois work as private dental, tutorial, or legal services at a high and progressive rate. On the other hand, those privileged few in the Soviet Union with high money incomes from the socialist sector, such as famous writers (who may earn royalties on their books), high-ranking military officers, star performers, and senior scientists, are allowed both to accumulate large sums, taxed at rather nominal rates, and to

[39]See Gregory Grossman, "Notes on the Illegal Private Economy and Corruption," *Soviet Economy in a Time of Change* (Washington, D.C.: Joint Economic Committee, U.S. Congress, 1979), pp. 834–55.

pass on their fortunes to their heirs.[40] Even middle-income Soviet families, if they live modestly, may accumulate large bank savings, which may go toward a car, a cooperative apartment, or an expensive household appliance, when the desired item becomes available. The rather steep prices for long-distance domestic travel and for automobiles, jewelry, and other goods officially considered luxuries tend to diminish the demand for them. Yet even in the case of automobiles, unsatisfied demand has created a thriving black market in new and used cars as well as in the supplies needed to run them, such as spare parts, repair services, and gasoline. The discrepancy between demand and official supply is illustrated by the fact that on the unofficial market, prices for secondhand automobiles are considerably higher than official prices for new ones.[41]

Thus, of the administrative controls over the extraction of economic resources, including material production planning, taxing, wage setting and pricing policies, and appropriation of labor services, the extraction of monetary income is least significant, first, because it is continually superseded by administrative interventions commanding resources and second, because it is widely subverted by illegal and quasi-legal private exchanges.[42]

In allocating manpower, the government employs a mixture of controls to generate a high volume of labor for the state, including the structure of wages and benefits in state-owned enterprises and extraction of manpower through coercive and normative power. Coercive forms of power include military conscription and the compelled labor of prisoners and other persons subject to mandatory labor assignments, such as those serving terms of exile or probation. Normative incentives include exhorting citizens to donate labor to social causes. As noted above, though the basic mechanism for allocating labor consists of responses by laborers to pay incentives associated with various occupations and regions,

---

[40]Nove, *Soviet Economic System,* pp. 239–40; Bergson, "Income Inequality," pp. 1085–89.

[41]On the role of the automobile in the second economy, see the paper by Michael Alexeev, "The Automobile and the Soviet Second Economy," paper presented at the Southern Conference on Slavic Studies, Lexington, Ky., 1981.

[42]On the varieties of quasi-legal markets, those lying between fully legal "red" markets and fully illegal "black" markets, see Aron Katsenelinboigen, "Coloured Markets in the Soviet Union," *Soviet Studies* 29, no. 1 (January 1977): 62–85.

the government (with some participation by the trade unions) sets pay and benefit levels in order to induce the desired response on the part of the work force.[43] These devices have been inefficient in distributing the populace among jobs and regions, partly because despite high wage and benefit levels for labor in such places as western Siberia, where rapid energy development is proceeding, laborers are notoriously reluctant to settle in such inhospitable climates, where amenities such as housing, schools, and cultural life are still few. On the other hand, low overall income levels are one reason for the nearly universal participation by women in the labor force, a fact noted in the chapter on social structure and political subcultures. Despite nearly full employment in the economy for both men and women, a grave shortage of labor exists and is growing, in part because of the inefficiency with which labor is used. Improvement in the productivity of labor — recognized as an indispensable condition for improvement in the performance of the economy — will require both more rapid mechanization of production and the elimination of the drag on labor productivity caused by absenteeism, drinking, indifference, and other behavioral problems.[44] Most current discussions of labor productivity have centered around finding ways to apply material rewards and disincentives to the efforts of individuals or small groups (such as the labor brigade, which receives intensive

[43]On the role of trade unions, see Blair Ruble, *Soviet Trade Unions: Their Development in the 1970's* (Cambridge, England: Cambridge University Press, 1981); also see the interesting attempt by the same author to test the "corporatist" theory of Soviet politics by examining the political role of trade unions. Idem, "The Applicability of Corporatist Models to the Study of Soviet Politics: The Case of the Trade Unions," *Carl Beck Papers in Russian and East European Studies,* no. 303 (Pittsburgh, Pa.: University of Pittsburgh, 1983).

[44]The address given by Yuri Andropov at the first plenary meeting of the Central Committee of the CPSU after his accession to the post of general secretary represented a bolder acknowledgment than had previously been permitted by the party leadership of the fact that labor productivity, which he called the main indicator of economic performance, was unsatisfactory. He also directly referred to the subjective factors hindering improvement in this area when he stated: "It is essential to create the conditions, economic and organizational, to stimulate high-quality, productive labor, initiative, and enterprise. And by the same token, bad work, sloth, and irresponsibility, should have an immediate and irreversible effect on material compensation, on occupational status, and on the moral authority of officials." *Pravda,* 23 November 1982. Other press articles had also made the case that inadequate technological advancement in industry had accounted for the decreasing rate of productivity growth. See the article by V. Trapeznikov, a member of the Academy of Sciences, in *Pravda,* 7 May 1982.

press publicity). This would change the wage system from one tending to equalize income within occupational categories to one that would reward the more efficient workers at the expense of their less efficient comrades. Since it is likely that powerful latent interests, such as those of the lower-skill groups of workers themselves as well as the administrators and managers of relatively inefficient enterprises, would oppose vigorous implementation of such a policy reform, current efforts in this direction are unlikely to make much impact on overall levels of labor productivity.

The government also sets the stage for the play of market forces in another way besides setting wages. By determining the number of educational spaces for the training of specialists of every type, the government exercises some control over the supply of trained specialists turned out by vocational-technical schools, specialized secondary schools, institutes, and universities.[45] In this way it avoids the gross overproduction of, say, automobile repairmen or lawyers and underproduction of railroad engineers and machine tool operators. A rough balance between the supply of specialists and the demand for them by branch is achieved on a short-run basis, as each ministry supplies information about the current and projected need for specialists in its field.

Governments faced by a need for rapid deployment of manpower for military or economic purposes or by the reluctance of a population to respond satisfactorily to material incentives can in theory turn to two other categories of incentives: coercion and exhortation. All governments use both to some degree. Military conscription — the draft — is the most familiar and obvious form of the extraction of manpower by coercion. In addition, in wartime or times of emergency, governments may also draft laborers. Another form of forced labor is penal labor, which has been employed for the performance of hard physical labor since the inception of the Soviet regime. All these types of manpower allocation represent the use of administrative force rather than market wages in order to put manpower to some government-established use. When a government places its armed forces on a voluntary rather than conscripted basis, it is likely to find that

[45]See Mervyn Matthews, *Education in the Soviet Union* (London: Allen & Unwin, 1982), pp. 169–74.

appeals to patriotism must be backed up with high pay to attract youth in sufficient numbers. The difference between the pay levels of American privates, who volunteer for service, and Soviet privates, who are conscripted, makes this point dramatically: the Soviet private receives about 4 rubles per month, enough perhaps for cigarettes and postage stamps, whereas the American private receives about $600 per month.

Traditionally, coerced labor has played a very important role in the extraction of manpower in the Soviet Union, a pattern that also applies to the prerevolutionary Russian state with its institutions of serfdom and of mandatory service by the nobility to the state (the former abolished in the nineteenth century, the latter in the eighteenth). The Bolshevik regime established labor conscription in the earliest days of the revolution, combining several methods of coercion: one was the "labor book" certifying that the bearer was performing productive labor, without which food rations could not be received; another was binding laborers at their places of work such that leaving one's job was equivalent to military desertion; and the last was rounding up workers to perform certain jobs.[46] Similarly, in 1940 Stalin restored the practice of the "labor draft" with a law aimed primarily at drawing rural youth between the ages of 14 and 17 into vocational training for certain industrial occupations. The system was not abolished until 1955.[47]

Far greater in scope under Stalin was the system of labor camps run by the NKVD, administering many millions of inmates who provided inexpensive labor for the great construction projects to fulfill plan targets assigned by Gosplan.[48] Although, as is generally true of coerced labor, the work of convicts was extremely inefficient, the Soviet attitude probably continued to be that

[46]See Thomas F. Remington, *Building Socialism in Bolshevik Russia* (Pittsburgh, Pa.: University of Pittsburgh Press, 1984), ch. 4.

[47]See Alex Inkeles, *Social Change in Soviet Russia* (New York: Simon & Schuster, 1981), pp. 162–63.

[48]On the labor performed by the prisoners of the gulag, see Robert Conquest, *The Great Terror* (New York: Collier, 1973), pp. 481–86; also see S. Swianiewicz, *Forced Labor and Economic Development* (New York: Oxford University Press, 1965). Of course, Alexander Solzhenitsyn's *Gulag Archipelago* (New York: Harper & Row, part 1, 1973; part 2, 1975; part 3, 1978) is the most important source on the labor camp system from the revolution forward.

expressed by Trotsky when he justified the system of "labor armies" during the civil war period: the armies accomplished relatively little, considering their large size and potential, but on the other hand, they cost the state little, since they were composed of conscripts receiving little pay.[49] This argument ignores the cost to the society of diverting labor from uses where it might be far more productive to uses where it was largely wasted. Inefficiency of course resulted from the fact that prisoners were overworked and underfed, exhausted by the conditions of incarceration, and placed in situations in which their actual results had to fall well below the planned work norms; accordingly, these results were falsely reported all the way up the chain of command.[50]

Not only hard physical labor was extracted from camp prisoners. Accounts of camp survivors make it clear that significant scientific and technical research was carried out in specially outfitted camps (the *sharashka*s such as the one Solzhenitsyn describes in *The First Circle*[51]). In other cases companies of performing artists — including all-prisoner jazz bands made up of some of the best jazz musicians in Russia — were formed for the entertainment of camp administrators and other high officials.[52] Moreover, when it served the needs of the regime, individual prisoners might be released in order to fulfill an assignment of high honor and trust. Konstantin Rokossovsky, later a marshal of the Soviet Union and still later defense minister of communist Poland, was arrested and beaten during the terror in the late 1930s and incarcerated in labor camps until he was suddenly released at the beginning of the war and placed in command of an army on the German front.[53] Practices such as these, blurring the distinction between free and not free service to the state, suggest how arbi-

[49]See Remington, *Building Socialism in Bolshevik Russia,* p. 90.

[50]On the falsification of production reports, a practice called *tufta* or *tukhta,* see Solzhenitsyn, *The Gulag Archipelago,* Part 2, pp. 160–67. Note that Conquest estimates that the *average* mortality rate for those incarcerated in the labor camps under Stalin was 10 percent per year. Conquest, *The Great Terror,* p. 454.

[51]Aleksandr I. Solzhenitsyn, *The First Circle,* trans. Thomas P. Whitney (New York: Harper & Row, 1968).

[52]S. Frederick Starr, *Red and Hot: The Fate of Jazz in the Soviet Union, 1917–1980* (New York: Oxford University Press, 1983), pp. 224–26.

[53]Timothy Colton, *Commissars, Commanders, and Civilian Authority: The Structure of Soviet Military Politics* (Cambridge, Mass.: Harvard University Press, 1979), pp. 72, 263.

trary was the line between penal labor and the conscription of military or labor manpower.

The dismantling of mass terror under Khrushchev in the mid-1950s and the release of the greater part of the camp population into the mainstream of the economy did not entirely eliminate penal labor. The CIA estimates that some 4 million individuals either are in labor camps or are ex-convicts on probation or parole and obliged to perform some form of forced labor. Of these, 10,000 are estimated to be political prisoners.[54] Although this figure is small in comparison with the millions of forced laborers under Stalin, it is not negligible.

Of greater scope today is coercively extracted manpower for the armed forces. The Soviet military establishment maintains the largest standing force in the world, estimated currently to comprise 4.8 million men.[55] (The Chinese People's Liberation Army is currently estimated to have 4.5 million; the United States armed forces have approximately 2 million.) Although most of these troops are assigned to units with directly combat-related missions, others are assigned to units that perform auxiliary and support roles, including construction and transportation duties. Some of the latter are used for civilian purposes, such as aiding in the construction of the Baikal-Amur Mainline (BAM), the great Siberian rail line linking the northern tip of Lake Baikal with the Amur River in the Far East. Thus these forces may be considered to contribute constructive, low-cost labor to the civilian economy. Nonetheless, specialists on Soviet manpower questions believe that the large size of the armed forces puts a strain on the economy because of the increasing shortage of manpower. Murray Feshbach has suggested that the minimum term of service may be lengthened from 2 to 3 years in order to compensate for the dwindling pool of Russian-speaking youth eligible for recruitment.[56] Interestingly, one of the reasons for reducing the minimum term of mandatory service for recruits from 3 to 2 years in 1967 was

[54]*New York Times,* 7 November 1982.

[55]Murray Feshbach, "The Soviet Union: Population Trends and Dilemmas," *Population Bulletin* (Washington, D.C.: Population Reference Bureau, 1982), p. 29.

[56]See Murray Feshbach, "Statement," in *The Political Economy of the Soviet Union,* p. 123.

to stimulate labor productivity by releasing a larger number of youth into the economy.[57]

A final method for extracting manpower resources is through moral incentives — appeals to the population's sense of patriotism, ideological zeal, or fear. This type of extracted labor is used most of all to generate volunteer service for socially approved activity, including aid to party and government bodies or participation in one of the voluntary societies, such as DOSAAF, which train and channel the spare-time energies of citizens. In addition, Komsomol summons the idealism and adventuresomeness of its members when calling for volunteers to work on great construction and agricultural projects for little or no pay: such was the ostensible nature of the campaign for volunteers to help cultivate the virgin lands in the mid-1950s, to construct the Bratsk Hydroelectric Dam, or more recently, to work on the BAM railroad construction project. Adults, especially those in nomenklatura positions, are expected to attend adult political schools on a volunteer basis. It will be recalled, however, that in discussing elite recruitment and training, we quoted a resolution that cautioned local party committees not to take the voluntary principle too literally. Individuals have some choice over the form and level of schooling that is appropriate for them, but enrollment in political education is expected.[58] Likewise, voting for deputies to the soviets is nominally voluntary, but intense and personal pressure is applied to persuade individuals to exercise their civic duty. Particularly in the small-group settings of workplace and organization, the regime is still capable of exerting strong pressure on individuals by mobilizing feelings of obligation to the peer group (the collective), the community, and the nation. It is likely that the appearance of voluntary spare-time political education or social activism where, as we have seen, truly remarkable rates of participation have been achieved is maintained through considerable doses of administrative pressure, though these fall well short

[57]See the report on the new draft law of 1967 presented by then Defense Minister Andrei Grechko to the Supreme Soviet in *Zakon SSSR o vseobshchei voinskoi obiazannosti* (The Law of the USSR on Universal Military Conscription) (Moscow: Voennoe izdatel'stvo, 1967), pp. 40–41. Grechko observed that by cutting down the length of service and inducting and discharging recruits twice rather than once a year, the new law would give youth two years of military training and discipline and still allow them to enter the labor force before age 20.

[58]See chapter 6.

of the draconian forms that coercion took in earlier periods of Soviet rule. Maintaining the pretense of voluntary participation in such activity seems to be another part of the drive for the appearance of unanimous consent and solidarity, of conformity and total commitment that, along with considerable private skepticism and indifference, distinguishes the Soviet political culture.[59]

DISTRIBUTIVE PERFORMANCE

In the realm of distributive policy it is particularly difficult to choose appropriate criteria for evaluating the performance of the system. The sustained policy of emphasizing capital investment and military spending at the expense of consumption, which was demonstrated in Table 3, indicates the continuing importance to the Soviet leadership of building the mighty industrial and military base considered necessary to protect and advance the interests of the Soviet state. Khrushchev's ascendancy, however, as noted in Chapter VII, brought with it a considerable change in the stated distributive goals of the system. Having defeated the apparent heir to Stalin's power, Georgi Malenkov, at least in part by attacking Malenkov's alleged willingness to place the interests of consumer satisfaction ahead of the military-industrial sector, Khrushchev adopted a policy of ameliorating the drab life of ordinary citizens by improving the supply of food and other consumer products and services. Under Khrushchev, regime propaganda sought to revive the national spirit of rapid progress that had been dulled and ritualized in the more than two decades of rapid forced-draft industrialization. In 1961, at the Twenty-second Party Congress, Khrushchev boldly and confidently predicted that within 20 years Soviet society would achieve the fundamental features of communist society, providing to everyone the blessings of material abundance and freedom from want. Several quotations from Khrushchev's address to the congress, in which he presented the new party program, will indicate the ambitious and risky character of these promises:

> In the coming 20 years the output of all the consumer goods industries is to increase approximately 5-fold. . . . The output of

[59]See the discussion of the "dualism" of Soviet behavior — the combination of a loyal outward or public demeanor with private views substantially at variance with the public face — in Stephen White, *Political Culture and Soviet Politics* (London: MacMillan, 1979), p. 111.

cultural and household goods, the demand for which is rising rapidly, will increase 10-fold. . . . The concern shown for consumer
and household goods, for domestic appliances, for all the things that
make the life of Soviet people easier and more attractive, should
not be less than, say, the concern shown for metallurgical equipment. . . . The draft Programme envisages that in twenty years the
aggregate agricultural output will rise about 3.5-fold, the aggregate
output of grain more than 2-fold, of meat nearly 4-fold and of milk
nearly 3-fold. . . . Within the first ten years already all sections of
the Soviet people will be enjoying sufficiency, and will be well provided for. . . . In the coming 10 years all Soviet people will be able
to acquire consumer goods in adequate quantities, and in the subsequent 10 years the consumer demand will be met in full. . . . In
the course of the next 10 years we must put an end to the housing
shortage. At the close of the second decade every family will have
a separate comfortable flat.[60]

In subsequent years, as system performance fell grossly short
of these expectations — which were tied to specific deadlines —
the leadership sternly instructed its propagandists to refrain from
overpromising as a means of boosting popular morale. In his major address on ideological matters at the June 1983 Central Committee plenum, for example, Konstantin Chernenko alluded to
Khrushchev's grand visions:

[A]t a certain time, as you know, a simplified conception about the
paths and term of the transition to the highest phase of communism
was common. Hastening, so to speak, our dream, certain theorists
and propagandists smoothed over, so to speak, the uneven places
in the path we are taking, cutting themselves off from the real conditions of life. Yet without fully and consciously overcoming the
"flight" of propaganda from reality, it is impossible to attain unity
of word and deed — which is the most important source of our
strength.[61]

Khrushchev evidently intended to use the vision of rapid fulfillment of the utopian promises of the socialist revolution as a means
to stimulate a renewed burst of popular energy and enthusiasm
in the society, as well as to recreate positive bonds of popular loy-

[60]*The Road to Communism: Documents of the 22nd Congress of the Communist Party
of the Soviet Union, October 17–31, 1961* (Moscow: Foreign Languages Publishing
House, 1961[?]), pp. 206–35.
[61]*Pravda*, 15 June 1983.

alty to the party regime and its post-Stalin leadership. He made similar propagandistic use of the successful launch of a space satellite in 1957 to symbolize the soaring prospects lying ahead for the country.[62] His successors, however, forced to excuse the failure of society to reach these prospects, above all in the sphere of consumer goods, had to develop new theoretical concepts to explain the current stage of development. The theory of *developed socialism,* which gained currency in the Brezhnev era, referred to the maturation of the existing post-Stalin sociopolitical order as opposed to the imminent passage of the society to full communism.[63]

Distributive policy since Khrushchev, therefore, has aimed at a slower but steadier improvement of popular welfare without allowing the development of the consumer sector to detract from growth in the crucial sectors of heavy industry, military power, and, particularly through the Brezhnev period, investment in agricultural infrastructure. As a result, the standard of living of the Soviet population — expressed as per capita consumption — rose by nearly three times between 1950 and 1980, though the growth slowed markedly in the 1970s.[64] The growth of services available to consumers such as transportation, communications, and utilities rose rapidly in this period. The supply of housing grew more slowly, and in urban areas it still falls "below the minimum norm for health and decency set by the government in 1928."[65] The

[62]For example, Khrushchev, in the speech quoted above, noted that the party program currently before the congress was the third party program: "The Programmes of the Party may be compared to a three-stage rocket. The first stage wrested our country away from the capitalist world, the second propelled it to socialism, and the third is to place it in the orbit of communism." *The Road to Communism,* p. 188.

[63]See Roy A. and Zhores A. Medvedev, *Khrushchev: The Years in Power* (New York: Norton, 1978), for a fascinating account of the disastrous results of Khrushchev's campaigns to reach extraordinary production targets in food products. The disruptive and destructive consequences of the fraud needed to report fulfillment of these goals made it correspondingly more difficult to achieve even realistic growth. See especially the tragicomic tale of the Ryazan fiasco, ch. 9. On the concept of developed socialism, see Donald Kelley, "Developments in Ideology," in Donald Kelley, ed., *Soviet Politics in the Brezhnev Era* (New York: Praeger, 1980), pp. 182–99.

[64]The following discussion is based on Gertrude E. Schroeder and M. Elizabeth Denton, "An Index of Consumption in the USSR," in *USSR: Measures of Economic Growth and Development, 1950–1980,* pp. 325–26 and passim.

[65]Ibid., p. 325.

provision of communal services such as education and medical care has risen on a per capita basis at an uneven rate. Quantitative measures of the rise in health services, such as the number of doctors and hospital beds per 10,000 population, do not offer an accurate indication of the quality or effectiveness of health services. As we shall see, there is substantial reason to believe that despite the doubling of the number of doctors and hospital beds per capita over the 1950–1980 period, the actual performance of the health care system is declining.[66] This contradiction alerts us to the need for caution in judging the quality of performance by quantitative measures or the actual *outcomes* of policy by observing its formal *outputs*.

Over time, the average consumer has come to expend a larger share of his or her income on household goods and less on food and beverages, a larger share on services such as transportation and communications and a smaller share for education and health.[67] The use of *average* consumption figures conceals, of course, wide differences in the structures and levels of consumption between city and village and between rich and poor strata. Aggregate measures also mask the planned diversion of certain scarce goods and services into closed distribution channels, such as the system of *raspredeliteli* (discussed in Chapter III), closed stores at which selected members of the elite may shop. If the political system increases the supply of goods to these channels or increases the number of people eligible to receive goods through them, then the overall growth in consumption for the rest of the population is correspondingly diminished. Moreover, if the second economy is disposing of an increasing supply of goods and services leaked out of the official economy, average consumers may suffer from the declining availability (and higher prices) of these resources despite the supposed increase in their supply. For these reasons it would be fallacious to infer from the record of aggregate growth in consumption that ordinary consumers are actually benefiting from rising living standards to the same degree.

Moreover, the comparison of 1980 consumption levels with those of 1950 sheds little light on the serious decline in performance since the 1960s in some critical areas of popular welfare.

[66]Ibid., p. 325.
[67]Ibid., pp. 325–27.

These include rising levels since 1964 of male mortality (death rates) in most age categories and a serious and disturbing increase in infant mortality.[68] Much discussion in recent years has centered on findings that the rate of infant mortality, a sensitive and widely used index of a nation's health and one in which economic development almost universally brings about improvement, has risen to a level about three times that of the United States, after steadily falling until about 1964.[69] Even after taking account of the possibility that improvement in the system of reporting infant deaths may undermine the accuracy of these figures, Soviet sources have acknowledged a disturbing increase. In addition, the incidence of premature mortality among young to middle-aged males has risen since the early 1960s and has brought male life expectancy at birth down from about 67 to about 62, lower than that of men in Mexico.[70] Women's life expectancy has fallen as well but less sharply. What reasons account for these trends? As in other developed countries, heart disease is the leading cause of death. The incidence of heart disease in the USSR is rising, whereas it is falling in the United States. Between 1960 and 1979, the rates of heart disease-related deaths in the USSR doubled.[71] The great underlying cause of the rise in mortality rates, however, appears to be growing alcohol abuse and alcoholism.[72] Soviet publications reveal that drunkenness and alcohol addiction are increasing and that the increase in alcoholism is rising faster among women than among men, with corresponding effects on the health of women

[68]See Christopher Davis and Murray Feshbach, "Rising Infant Mortality in the USSR in the 1970's," Series P-25, No. 74 (Washington, D.C.: US Bureau of the Census, September 1980); Murray Feshbach, "Issues in Soviet Health Problems," in *Soviet Economy in the 1980's,* part 2, pp. 203–27; in the same volume, see also Christopher Davis, "The Economics of the Soviet Health System," pp. 228–64, and Murray Feshbach, prepared statement in *Political Economy of the Soviet Union,* pp. 127–37. These articles provide estimates based on Soviet statistical reports of the increase in mortality and, for certain diseases, morbidity rates, as well as a discussion of the reason that death rates have risen and life expectancy has fallen despite the increase in the numbers of doctors and health care facilities. For a general discussion of quality-of-life problems in the USSR, see Nick Eberstadt, "Overview," in *Soviet Economy in the 1980's,* pp. 187–202.

[69]See Feshbach, prepared statement, in *Political Economy of the Soviet Union,* p. 131.

[70]Eberstadt, "Overview," pp. 193–94.

[71]Feshbach, "Issues in Soviet Health Problems," p. 206.

[72]Feshbach, prepared statement in *Political Economy,* p. 89; Feshbach, "Issues in Soviet Health Problems," pp. 225–27.

and of their children. Alcohol abuse is associated with the large number of deaths from accidents, poisoning, and injuries, as well as those from heart-related disease.

The figures, based on reports published in primary and secondary Soviet sources, suggest that the rise in the physical availability of health care has not prevented a worsening in the overall state of the nation's health. Perhaps the long-term growth in the number of doctors, nurses, and paraprofessionals (there are twice as many doctors in the Soviet health care system as there are in the United States), the growth in the number of hospital beds, and the rise in the number of patient visits to doctors cannot compensate for the very slow and inadequate growth in the supply of equipment and medication. Though the wages paid to medical personnel increased, the average wage between 1965 and 1980 fell from 82 percent of the national average to 75.[73] As Christopher Davis points out, the low wages paid to health care professionals tend to lower the quality of entrants to the field and to affect adversely the quality of the care given by medical practitioners.[74] Moreover, stinting on investment in medical facilities has meant that existing health care capacity falls short of demand.[75] In addition, severe shortages continue to undermine the distribution of drugs and medical supplies. Thus difficulties in the health care system, though certainly not a cause of the increase in mortality, have failed to prevent it.[76]

We have dwelt on the subject of performance in the distribution of medical goods and services both because of the evidence of serious and growing problems in this area and because it provides an illuminating insight into the discrepancy between certain quantitative indexes of increasing popular well-being (such as hospital beds per 10,000 population; number of doctors, nurses, and paraprofessionals; number of visits to medical facilities; and the like) and the actual performance in this area. The discussion underlines an important point raised by the theoretical perspective used in this volume. Seen as a dynamic system, the Soviet political system interacts with its foreign and domestic environments. The consequence of policy outputs in certain areas, such

[73]Davis, "Economics of the Soviet Health Care System," p. 243.
[74]Ibid., pp. 251–52.
[75]Ibid., p. 253.
[76]Ibid., p. 261.

as the priority placed on investment in certain industrial, agricultural, and defense sectors at the expense of increases in outlays on, say, pharmaceuticals production and distribution, is that ultimately the system cannot provide an adequate standard of living for a population that still largely depends on the planned rationing of many basic goods and services. In turn, deterioration in the overall health of the population impedes the leadership's efforts to restore higher rates of economic growth, which is an essential precondition for its long-term success in meeting stated goals. The relationship between the distribution of material and intangible resources to society and the pressures to which the political leadership must respond forms a complex feedback loop, which belies the apparent concentration of decision-making power at the center.

REGULATIVE PERFORMANCE

Perhaps the most notable aspect of regulative activity in the Soviet system, aside from its close link to the extraction and distribution of resources by the state, is its pervasiveness. The immense scope of social activity for which the party and government take directing responsibility, including the vast majority of economic transactions and nearly all cultural life, imposes a burden on the state for social regulation that is far more encompassing and intrusive than is the case in democratic systems. In addition, the vastness of government bureaucracy generates recurrent pressures for external supervisory controls, exercised by agencies independent of the authority of the branch hierarchies they oversee. These external monitoring agencies include the KGB, the uniform police and procuracy, and a system of special agencies called the *OBKhSS,* or Department for Struggle against Theft of Socialist Property and Speculation (*Otdel bor'by s khishcheniiami sotsialisticheskoi sobstvennosti i spekuliatsiei*), which is especially active in investigating abuses in retail trade, uncovering fraud and theft of state goods.

In addition, a substantial part of the role of party committees, including Primary Party Organizations in the workplaces, consists of *kontrol,* or oversight of the activity of the organization in which the committee is located or the government and public bodies in the party committee's jurisdiction. Moreover, the regime emphasizes the importance of popular involvement in the work of kontrol, encouraging the masses of citizens to take part in the popular control committees and to send letters and articles to the mass media detailing cases of misbehavior by officials and citizens. If the concerted efforts of all these forms of regulation from above as well as from below fail to prevent a good deal of illegal political and economic activity, they at least provide a steady stream of information about infractions of law. Indeed, public awareness of the need for vigilance and heightened moral consciousness is an instrument wielded by the central leadership in its constant effort to regain effective control over policy implementation. It therefore resorts to periodical publicity campaigns in which accounts of the arrests, trials, convictions, and punishment of lawbreakers are recounted, often in lurid detail. Details of a crackdown in the Uzbek Republic were published intermittently over the summer of 1984, for example, educating the public about corruption at the highest levels of republican leadership and creating the impression of a Watergate-style succession of impending arrests of ever higher-ranking officials. A provincial executive committee chairman was dismissed for illegally building a luxurious mansion with a swimming pool, using dishonestly acquired materials. As the investigation proceeded, the minister of the cotton industry of the republic, together with two other top officials in the ministry, were dismissed. Newspaper accounts made it clear that the investigation was continuing and that individuals apprehended were being offered incentives to provide information about those with whom they worked.[77] The execution of the former head of a major Moscow food store, on grounds of large-scale economic wrongdoing, provided an even more graphic example of the regime's seriousness in cracking down on corruption.[78]

The current campaign against corruption in high places — reminiscent of a campaign under Khrushchev in the early 1960s but not close to it in scale — was launched by Andropov and, despite these few spectacular examples, seems to have lost momentum. Accounts by some observers and émigrés indicate that the scale of official corruption is immense[79] and that many of the

[77]*Soviet Analyst* 13, no. 16 (8 August 1984): 6–8.

[78]See Frederick Kempe, ''You Can't Get Caviar at Gastronom No. 1, But Goodies Abound,'' *Wall Street Journal,* 12 September 1984.

[79]See, for example, Konstantin Simis, *USSR: The Corrupt Society* (New York: Simon & Schuster, 1982).

organs charged with administering the law have themselves been corrupted. On the other hand, the power of the state to regulate behavior, particularly in the areas where the political and ideological interests of the leadership are at stake, remains formidable. The special force with which the repression of political dissent has been conducted since early 1980 (a period beginning with the invasion of Afghanistan and preparations to clear Moscow of potential troublemakers in advance of the Moscow Olympics) affords ample evidence of the undiminished power of official agencies to suppress challenges to their political hegemony.[80] Moreover, the scope of regulatory authority claimed by the regime extends into areas of private life quite apart from private political conviction or expression, such as family relations. Through a series of laws governing marriage, divorce, and abortion, the state has attempted to regulate the family's role in producing and rearing children. At times state policy and legislation have been hostile to the stability of family life, at other times so favorable as to make divorce and abortion virtually unobtainable. Current policy seems to assume that given the continuing shortage of men relative to the number of unmarried women and the severe decline in the birthrate in the Slavic nationalities, it is desirable to provide incentives to women to bear children regardless of their marital status.[81]

The regime's efforts in regulatory policy are cumbersome, far-reaching, and relatively inefficient. As we have seen, *planning* embodies official determinations of targets for the production and distribution of most goods and services — including, besides the physical output of steel mills and oil wells, such indexes as the number of passenger miles each taxicab will drive, the number of articles dealing with Lenin a newspaper intends to publish, and incalculable numbers of other physical quanta. It thus serves to guide the administrative agencies concerned with the control of all resources under official authority. The problem of ensuring full and timely fulfillment of all these interlocking plans, of overseeing the implementation of policy decisions they embody, is a major

[80]See Julia Wishnevsky, "The Rise of Dissidence in the Brezhnev Era," RL 453/82 (15 November 1982), esp. pp. 7–8.
[81]See Peter H. Juviler, "The Family in the Soviet System," *Carl Beck Papers in Russian and East European Studies* no. 306 (Pittsburgh, Pa.: University of Pittsburgh, 1983).

preoccupation of the regulatory agencies we have listed. Beyond this task, however, lies the goal of regulating the private behavior of the citizenry by means of education, indoctrination, and sanctions to induce in them a generalized sense of identification with the regime that transcends their mere compliance with its various rules and requirements. The panoply of these channels and forms of regulation imposes heavy and continuous pressure on Soviet citizens to conform with a multiplicity of sometimes contradictory rules and to meet goals that are frequently and even deliberately unrealistically high.[82]

In every enterprise and office, institute and farm, the organization with final responsibility for coordinating the many forms of regulatory policy that bear on the political and social behavior of individuals is the Primary Party Organization. Made up of the party members employed in a given workplace — including a high proportion of those in managerial, technical, and other influential posts — the PPO is charged with providing the political leadership needed to ensure smooth operation of the unit and fulfillment of its major assigned targets. Its power over personnel selection, its responsibility for ideological-political affairs, and its regular contact with party offices at higher territorial levels are to be used to see to it that the workplace effectively carries out the party's goals.

A useful illustration of the regulatory power of the Primary Party Organization is the role it plays in scientific and educational institutions. Concerned that scientific and technological research was not contributing adequately to economic progress, the Brezhnev leadership in 1971 extended to PPOs the same rights of control over management in research institutes that they had long possessed in economic enterprises and other production organizations. Intended to supplement the self-regulating mechanisms of science such as peer review, the party's political influence over science through such means as supervision of the internal administration of research institutions, instilling appropriate ideological consciousness through the political education system, and overseeing personnel matters often tends to weaken the quality of sci-

[82]See Michel Crozier, *The Bureaucratic Phenomenon* (Chicago, Ill.: University of Chicago Press, 1964), pp. 228–31.

ence. In selecting individuals to head laboratories, departments, institutes, or other research and educational organizations, for example, the party takes into account both professional and political qualifications. Similarly, in determining who may attend foreign scientific conferences, the party inspects applicants' political records and uses the opportunity for contact with foreign scientists as an incentive for political conformity. According to a careful recent study of the relationship between scientific research and the party by Peter Kneen, these political considerations injected into science tend to be counterproductive by weakening the conditions necessary for fruitful scientific research.[83]

One should not, however, exaggerate the power of the PPO in a scientific or educational institution as an instrument of political control. The party secretary generally does not overshadow the authority of the director, who normally belongs to the committee or bureau of the PPO. A survey of approximately 200 former Soviet scientists and technical specialists found that few believed the PPO had the last word in day-to-day decisions in their organizations or that it made the most important decisions; former party members were the most emphatic in denying that the PPO was so important. On the other hand, there was general agreement that the party organization was responsible for keeping up the political-ideological climate, for resolving personal disputes, and for approving all personnel evaluations (*kharakteristiki*) submitted to higher authorities as well as approving all administrative appointments.[84] Most respondents believed that party involvement increased in the late 1960s and 1970s, with greater interference in technical matters as well as closer control over personnel decisions.[85] At the same time, the party often assisted with obtaining scarce materials at short notice or in solving other problems. Though most respondents believed that the PPO secretary and director worked together harmoniously, many claimed that a strong director could appeal to the next higher territorial level of

[83]Peter Kneen, *Soviet Scientists and the State: An Examination of the Social and Political Aspects of Science in the USSR* (Albany: State University of New York Press, 1984), esp. pp. 95–99.

[84]Robert F. Miller, "The Role of the Communist Party in Soviet Research and Development," *Soviet Studies* 37, no. 1 (January 1985): 39–45, 55.

[85]Ibid., p. 45.

the party — generally the district committee, or *raikom* — for backing against a PPO secretary. The administrators, as the respondents pointed out, hold their posts with the approval of the raikom and hence know and accept the rules of party authority.[86] The party's regulatory power in the workplace is thus exercised not solely through the PPO in the organization but also through injecting political criteria into the activity of the director and other managerial personnel and selecting administrators and other nomenklatura officials.

In pluralistic societies, the power of government to control the lives of private citizens is counterbalanced by the variety of groups and organizations that individuals may join to advance their common interests. The more diverse the types of social interests, the more difficult it is for them to be incorporated into a few large categorical organizations, such as Catholic or Protestant churches, labor unions or owners' associations, liberal or conservative parties. At one time, political theorists concerned with the problem of totalitarianism rooted its rise in the breakdown of associations that mediated between individuals and the state.[87] Certainly in political systems of the Soviet type, not all mediating social organizations are eliminated, but to the extent possible they are penetrated by the party and made instruments for carrying out its goals. In recent years this principle has been applied with growing intensity to the workplace, or labor collective, which is treated as the fundamental organizational unit for coordinating the individual's multifaceted relations with the state. Through the workplace the individual receives not just pay but often also such necessities as housing, medical care, and vacations.[88] Although the 1977 Constitution and a 1983 law recognize the labor collective as a legal entity with distinctive rights and powers, a close examination of regime policy in this area indicates that the new attention to

[86]Ibid., pp. 42–43.

[87]Cf. William Kornhauser, *The Politics of Mass Society* (Glencoe, Ill.: Free Press, 1959).

[88]See Louise I. Shelley, *Lawyers in Soviet Work Life* (New Brunswick, N.J.: Rutgers University Press, 1984), p. 96. Shelley's book is a valuable treatment of the role played by legal advisers — *iuriskonsul'ty* — and arbitrators in the administration of the Soviet economy. She points out that the importance of the workplace for individuals' welfare gives the enterprise lawyer a good deal of influence over whether and how severely they may be penalized for infractions of the rules.

the collective is connected with a desire to increase the regime's regulation of the public and private behavior of its citizens.[89]

According to some Soviet constitutional theorists, it was a notable sign of progress that the 1977 Constitution treated the article dealing with labor collectives under the heading of *the political system* (this term itself being an innovation imported from bourgeois political science) rather than under that of *economic system*.[90] The 1977 Constitution assigned vague powers to the labor collective, both in articulating policy demands in the political system and in implementing regime policy within the collective. According to Article 8 of the Constitution:

> Labor collectives participate in the discussion and resolution of state and public affairs, in the planning of production and social development, in the training and placement of cadres, and in the discussion and resolution of questions of the management of enterprises and institutions, the improvement of working and living conditions, and the use of funds earmarked for the development of production and for social and cultural measures and material incentives. [91]

The breadth of these rights necessitated legislation specifying and enacting them, and the events in Poland, in which unofficial sources of organizational authority seized the political initiative from the government, may have spurred the promulgation of the draft legislation granting Soviet labor collectives specific rights and powers. By the same token, the events of 1980–1981 must have indicated to the Soviet leadership how vital it was to retain the ideological and political upper hand within each enterprise. Indeed, this point has been expressed with increasing force by Soviet ideological authorities and by social scientists studying the structure of public opinion in the Soviet Union. The 1979 edition of

[89]A very useful discussion of the 1983 law on labor collectives is Elizabeth Teague, "The USSR Law on Work Collectives: Workers' Control or Workers Controlled?" RL Bulletin 184/84 (10 May 1984); also see the article on the new law by Darrell Slider, "Reforming the Workplace: The 1983 Soviet Law on Labour Collectives," *Soviet Studies*, 37, no. 2 (April 1985): 173–183.

[90]On this point and on the spread of Western political science terminology into the writing of Soviet scholars who identify themselves as "political scientists," see Archie Brown, "Political Science in the Soviet Union: A New Stage of Development," *Soviet Studies* 36, no. 3 (July 1984): 317–44.

[91]Robert Sharlet, *The New Soviet Constitution of 1977: Analysis and Text* (Brunswick, Ohio: King's Court Communications, 1978), p. 78.

the *Handbook of the Party Group Leader* instructs communists to seek to influence public opinion in the collective, using their personal authority among their fellow workers to explain party policy and build support for it. They must, according to the handbook, take the initiative in conversations so that attitudes of indifference, parochialism, and passivity do not gain ground.[92] Likewise, Soviet research on the effectiveness of workplace-based agitation and propaganda reveals that the climate of opinion fostered by the daily face-to-face contact of primary groups, especially labor collectives, serves to mediate official messages.[93] These mediating influences may undercut or strengthen the idea an official speaker seeks to convey, and hence authority within the collective group is essential if messages are to have impact. There are various explanations for the prevalent habit of sharing news and opinion within the workplace: the closeness of social relations, the failure of many blue-collar workers to comprehend political events, and dissatisfaction among more highly educated groups with the insufficiency of objective information in the official media. These factors lead many to form their opinions in the course of direct conversation with other members of the labor collective.[94]

Because the labor collective plays such an important role in the formation of public opinion, Soviet authorities seek to capture and direct its moral influence. Both Article 8 of the 1977 Constitution and the new law on labor collectives, together with another 1983 law on labor discipline, call attention to the vital role of the labor collective as a source of labor discipline and political consciousness. "Labor collectives," reads the constitution, "instill in their members a spirit of communist morality and show concern for increasing their political consciousness. . . ."[95] The law on labor collectives specifies both the duties to be assigned to the collective in enforcing labor discipline and the sanctions available for enforcement, such as turning over cases of rules infraction to the

[92]*Sputnik partgruporga, 1979* (Moscow: Izdatel'stvo politicheskoi literatury, 1978), pp. 129–34.

[93]G. T. Zhuravlev, *Sotsiologicheskie issledovaniia effektivnosti ideologicheskoi raboty* (Moscow: Mysl', 1980), p. 154.

[94]On this point, see the references listed in Thomas Remington, "Soviet Public Opinion and the Effectiveness of Party Ideological Work," *Carl Beck Papers in Russian and East European Studies* (Pittsburgh, Pa.: University of Pittsburgh, 1983).

[95]Sharlet, *The New Soviet Constitution,* p. 79.

comrades' court in the workplace, recommending demotion or dismissal, or levying fines.[96]

That a significant aspect of the new law's impact was supposed to be stiffening the collective's role as an enforcer of discipline was suggested by subsequent press articles detailing the effects it had stimulated in various enterprises. Commenting on the various reports, an article in the trade union newspaper *Trud* on November 5, 1983, asserted: "[T]he USSR law on work collectives has significantly raised the workers' activity in the management of production and in the resolution of social problems, but the role of the collective has particularly grown in the strengthening of labor discipline."[97] Later in the summer the regime moved again to emphasize the importance of tightening up on labor discipline and again linked the labor collective with this effort. The decree issued by the party Central Committee, the USSR Council of Ministers, and the All-Union Central Council of Trade Unions on strengthening labor discipline in August 1983 asserted: "The CPSU Central Committee, USSR Council of Ministers, and AUCCTU consider increasing the role of labor collectives, and their effective use of the rights granted them, to be the most important direction of work in education and strengthening labor discipline. It is in the labor collective where the personality of a toiler of socialist society is molded and forged."[98]

The law on labor collectives and decree on labor discipline of the summer of 1983, promulgated shortly before Yuri Andropov's long and final seclusion, clearly reveal the link that leaders envisioned between the labor collective as an educational and disciplinary force and the campaign for higher labor productivity that the Andropov leadership placed as one of its top priorities. Seen in this light, the new emphasis on making labor collectives effective units for social regulation (or social self-regulation) derives above all from the need for higher levels of social discipline, which, the leadership hoped, could be enforced most effectively by building on the recognized power of each collective to generate

[96]"Zakon o trudovykh kollektivakh i povyshenii ikh roli v upravlenii predpriiatiiami, uchrezhdeniiami, organizatsiiami" (The Law on Labor Collectives and Strengthening Their Role in Managing Enterprises, Institutions, and Organizations), *Pravda,* 19 June 1983.

[97]Quoted in Teague, "Law on Work Collectives," p. 14.

[98]*Pravda,* 7 August 1983.

its own climate and culture. The regime's activists were admonished to seize the initiative in shaping the moral climate in the enterprise on the grounds that, as the party journal *Partiinaia zhizn'* (Party Life) wrote in 1982, there is never an ideological vacuum — any weakening of socialist ideology automatically leads to the strengthening of an alien and hostile doctrine.[99] In other ways as well the regime has made the workplace a basic unit for social control. The enterprise is — increasingly, it would appear — the site for distribution of basic economic goods, including food and durable goods such as automobiles. Goods in short supply are apparently distributed through the enterprises, one reason meat and other foodstuffs may be less scarce than the empty shelves of retail stores would suggest.[100] The use of the workplace to provide food is further enhanced by the growing practice of allowing enterprises to maintain their own farms and even food-processing facilities, reducing the dependence of their workers on regular state channels of supply but further binding the workers to the work collective. A *Pravda* article of September 8, 1984, indicates another way in which authority within the work collective can be used to regulate the private behavior of members. It discusses the work of an activist in a Moscow-province plant whose social assignment it is to advise and encourage her fellow workers in choosing which newspapers and magazines to subscribe to in the coming year. She urges all workers to receive a central newspaper such as *Pravda* and is especially eager to help recently admitted members of the party choose which party papers and magazines to receive.[101]

As these examples indicate, the regime seeks to incorporate the role the labor collective plays as a social collectivity, a primary group, and reference group for its members into the party's devices for wielding political authority in society. The party welcomes certain customs and ceremonies as positive educational

[99]"Kommunisticheskaia partiia vysoko neset znamia Lenina," (The Communist Party Carries High the Banner of Lenin) *Partiinaia zhizn'*, no. 2 (1982): 7.

[100]See statement by Robert W. Campbell, in *Political Economy of the Soviet Union*, p. 11. According to Professor Campbell, "distribution of some important commodities has been shunted to a considerable extent out of normal market channels to workplace channels."

[101]G. Savel'ev, "I pomozhet, i podskazhet" (She helps and she hints), *Pravda*, 8 September 1984.

experiences, such as the initiation of new workers into the group, although party writers inveigh against the tradition of getting the initiate as intoxicated as possible. Similarly, various officially encouraged institutions, such as "mentorship" (*nastavnichestvo*) by older workers who instill good work habits into younger workers, or the "adoption" of a lagging collective by an advanced one (*sheftstvo*), and the omnipresent institution of "socialist competition" (*sotsialisticheskoe sorevnovanie*) among enterprises, are ways of cultivating a collective sense of aspiration toward higher achievement and common responsibility for results. In addition, in the realm of its ideological work — including agitation, political education, clubs, circles, evenings, meetings, ceremonies, and recreation — the party lays greater emphasis on the workplace than on the residential neighborhood or town as the primary site of indoctrination. Again, this is connected with the desire to employ the authority of the collective as a social unit for the ideological goals of party work.

In addition, each enterprise or organization contains a multitude of public organizations, membership in which is nominally voluntary. After the party and the Komsomol, the most important of these is the trade union. Normally all members of a particular enterprise belong to the same union, since Soviet unions are based on the industrial rather than craft principle of organization. Since 98 percent of the Soviet work force belongs to unions, membership is a matter of course. The trade union maintains its own organization in each enterprise, with a defined sphere of administrative rights and duties; normally the union looks after social amenities, such as day care facilities and often housing, and administers benefits such as vacations, sick pay, and social insurance. The many dozens of formal organizations within each labor collective that create channels for mass and elite participation help reinforce the social bonds linking members of the collective to one another and, ultimately, to the political and administrative authorities within the workplace. All forms of authority — the manager as a representative of the state, the engineers and technicians as experts, the party committee representing the political and ideological authority of the socialist regime, the moral influence of the collectivity as a community, and the nominally self-generated authority of the public bodies — are expected to be reciprocally reinforcing. Deviant behavior can be checked and reversed much more easily in a system in which all forms of social authority are made one seamless whole than in the more individualized and fragmented culture of liberal democracies, as long as ideological control over the work force is maintained. When this breaks down, as it occasionally does, a counterelite is produced and organized protest results, in the form of strikes and demonstrations.

Just such a counterleadership is said to have formed, for example, in the auto plant at Togliatti, on the Volga, in the 1980 disturbances that occurred there.[102] A Soviet citizen told a *New York Times* correspondent that "an unofficial worker leadership" had formed at the auto plant and "had become more influential than the official labor union." It had organized the strike only after earlier attempts to present grievances to management had gone unanswered and after several previous brief work stoppages had proved unavailing. Very much the same process has occurred in the enterprises of other socialist countries, with Poland the most outstanding example. In these cases, the very forces that create the capacity for internal cohesion are turned against the authority of the regime but, lacking intermediate arenas for the resolution of grievances, are treated as political challenges to the regime. In this way, economic or material grievances are readily politicized; in Poland the workers immediately after striking over rises in food prices articulated demands for political rights, including the right to organize and to maintain independent communications media. The Polish example clearly indicates the reasons for the seriousness with which the Soviet authorities treat the question of ideological authority within the labor collective, but it also points up the almost total absence of opposition among the Soviet workers. Whatever this fact may owe to the ubiquity of regulatory controls in the workplace, it also must be explained in part as the product of a very different political culture.

Perhaps the best way of summing up our discussion of regulatory performance and of the extractive and distributive activity that it enforces is to conclude that the vast network of political and administrative controls through which the Soviet authorities

[102]See Betsy Gidwitz, "Labor Unrest in the Soviet Union," *Problems of Communism* 31, no. 6 (November–December 1982): 34. Also see Frederick C. Barghoorn, "Regime-Dissenter Relations after Khrushchev: Some Observations," in Susan Gross Solomon, *Pluralism in the Soviet Union* (London: MacMillan, 1983), pp. 141–43.

carry out their aims works most effectively when the controls are not at cross-purposes and when they are congruent with values and beliefs embedded in society. The evidence presented in this chapter of a decline in the performance of the system in the three major domains discussed here accords with the diagnosis of some observers, such as the author of the "Novosibirsk memorandum" discussed earlier or Western authors such as Timothy Colton, who assert that only significant administrative decentralization can solve the problems causing this decline.[103] We should not, however, underestimate the adaptiveness of the Soviet political system, particularly adaptation occurring with a change of leadership. The sharp turns in policy associated with Lenin and Stalin and the important phase of de-Stalinization under Khrushchev suggest that the impulse for radical policy change is frequently accompanied by major changes in the structures of political leadership and authority. Though we do not rule out the possibility of significant reform in the coming decade, current trends of development point unmistakably to a weakened capacity of the central leadership to carry out any policy- or system-level reform that weakens the power of the central bureaucracy.

[103]Timothy J. Colton, *Dilemma of Reform in the Soviet Union* (New York: Council on Foreign Relations, 1984), pp. 71–74.

CHAPTER XI

Soviet Foreign Policy: Conflict and Coexistence

INTRODUCTION: ORGANIZATION FOR FOREIGN POLICYMAKING

In the conduct of its foreign relations, perhaps even more than in the management of domestic affairs, Soviet policymaking is characterized by an intense striving for unity of perspective and of hierarchical and centralized organization. This does not preclude, however, increasing use of expert information supplied by academic specialists. The hallmarks of Soviet foreign policy are centralism of decision making, secrecy, and, as a rule, coherence of perspectives and strategy. It appears, however, that when the top leadership is relatively weak and less than normally capable of enforcing an informal consensus on the policymaking process, Soviet foreign policy may lose some of the advantages normally conferred by unity of command. This may have been the case in the last months of the leadership of Yuri Andropov and during much of the 13 months of Konstantin Chernenko's term as CPSU General Secretary. We should also keep in mind that in the East-West rivalry, the USSR and its bloc are at a substantial economic disadvantage in competition in the Third World and with advanced industrial nations such as the United States, Japan, and West Germany. Finally, it must be recognized that the anarchic, largely lawless nature of the international arena forces all states, regardless of ideology and organization (particularly the United States, USSR, and the People's Republic of China), to devote enormous resources to achieve national security. This effort paradoxically heightens insecurity but also has given rise to such potentially tension-reducing measures as nuclear arms reduction negotiations and to the precarious security derived from fear of nuclear war.

As far as the Soviet leadership is concerned, its perspective on the international situation, at least in the period since the Soviet invasion of Afghanistan in 1979 and the retaliatory U.S. grain embargo imposed by President Carter but lifted by President Reagan, is illustrated by a statement in a publication of the authoritative Institute of State and Law of the Soviet Academy of Sciences. According to this publication, written by and for Soviet scholars and officials,

> World imperialism has not only not lost its aggressiveness, but yet more intensively conducts a policy of accumulating deadly weapons, a reactionary policy toward the socialist countries and toward peoples struggling for national and social liberation. Carrying out the peaceful policy of the USSR under these circumstances becomes a more and more complicated process, requiring a strictly scientific approach to the analysis of the phenomena of contemporary international life, properly taking account of the objective and subjective factors involved. The communist party, armed with advanced theory, capable of predicting and laying the foundation of the path of the development of human history, disposes of such possibilities.[1]

More propagandistic than empirical-analytic, the foregoing typical statement offers a view of Soviet foreign policy behavior and that of the "imperialist" powers that Soviet leaders may partly believe or at least hope to persuade mass audiences, at home and abroad, to accept. In its emphasis on the "peaceful" nature of Soviet foreign policy, the statement reiterates a claim that has characterized Soviet propaganda for both domestic and foreign audiences since the inception of the Soviet state. It is advisable, therefore, for readers of such statements to be aware that this of-

---

[1] Quotation from *Materialy XXV S"ezda KPSS* (Materials of the Twenty-fifth Congress, CPSU), in *Sovetskoe administrativnoe pravo* (Soviet Administrative Law) (Moscow: Yuridicheskaya literatura, 1979), p. 281. The above quotation is followed on the next few pages by references to articles of the 1977 Soviet Constitution emphasizing the principles and tasks of Soviet foreign policy as "strengthening the positions of world socialism," "defining the line for the victory of communism," etc.

ficial propaganda is the only kind of expression of devotion to the cause of peace permitted in Soviet communications media. A small number of Soviet citizens, mostly scientists and other members of the creative intelligentsia, organized the Group of Trust, which sought to promote mutual understanding between Soviet private citizens and their counterparts abroad. Shortly afterward, persecution of the sort that usually befalls persons who express independent opinions, particularly if they form organizations and get in touch with people abroad, followed.[2]

Even more important is the emphasis in the above declaration on the guiding role of the CPSU in Soviet foreign relations, without, however, any indication of the organizational structure that exercises this guidance. Nothing is said anywhere in the book from which the above quotation was taken about a Central Committee Secretariat department that is probably more influential in Soviet foreign policy than the USSR Ministry of Foreign Affairs, namely, the International Department. To be sure, between 1973, when he became a member of the Politburo, and 1985, when he was named Chairman of the Presidium of the Supreme Soviet and was replaced by Eduard Shevardnadze as Minister of Foreign Affairs, Andrei Gromyko may well have been the most powerful Soviet leader concerned with foreign affairs next to the party's general secretary. In part, Gromyko's influence reflected his personal stature, acquired through long political service and formidable ability. It did not necessarily mean that the power of the ministry he headed increased. In fact, the Foreign Ministry may have lost influence relative to the Central Committee's International Department, headed by Boris Ponomarev, a long-time candidate member of the Politburo and former high official of the Communist International (Comintern). Some years ago, a leading expert on Soviet affairs, the late Leonard Schapiro, expressed the opinion that the International Department exercised, "subject to the Politburo, decisive influence on Soviet foreign policy."[3]

[2]See, for example, Lyubov Potekhina, "Bortsy za mir v sovetskoi tyurme" (Fighters for Peace in a Soviet Prison), *Novoe russkoe slovo* (The New Russian Word), 17 December 1983.

[3]Leonard Schapiro, "The International Department of the CPSU: Key to Soviet Policy," *International Journal* (Winter 1976–1977): 40–55, at p. 44. See also the valuable study by Elizabeth Teague, "The Foreign Departments of the CPSU," supplement to Radio Liberty Research Bulletin, October 1980, and relevant parts of Richard Shultz and Roy Godson, *Dezinformatsia: Active Measures*

There are several other Central Committee departments concerned with foreign policy, including the Department for Relations with Communist and Workers' Parties of Socialist Countries; the Department for Cadres Abroad, closely linked with the KGB; and the International Information Department, about which little is known abroad. In general, the International Department and these others supervise the work of the Ministry of Foreign Affairs. More important, there appears to be a division of labor between party and government agencies, with the party agencies performing — often in collaboration with the KGB, which puts International Department policies into operation after their approval by the Politburo — not only overall supervisory functions but also policymaking functions involving covert, subversive operations. On the other hand, in general, the Ministry of Foreign Affairs conducts more conventional diplomatic activities. In a sense, the International Department, as the heir to the functions of the Comintern, plans those activities that are designed to promote the cause of revolution now largely conducted by a combination of Soviet-aided, Soviet-oriented national liberation and other movements deemed useful and hence worthy of support by Moscow. By contrast, official, overt Soviet diplomacy and much Soviet foreign propaganda seek to reassure noncommunist publics that Soviet objectives are not incompatible with peace, international order, and other cherished values. In fact, the underlying strategy of Soviet foreign policy represents a challenge to the values central to Western democracy and in general to the established order in most of the world. Concealment of this fact is clearly regarded by the Soviet leaders as essential to the successful conduct of Soviet policy — hence the elaborate mechanisms for concealment and camouflage represented by the administrative mechanism briefly described here and by such tactics as "active measures" (in Russian, *aktivnye meropriyatiia*). According to Shultz and Godson, "active measures may entail influencing the policies of another government, undermining of confidence in its leaders and institutions . . . and discrediting and weakening governmental and

---

in Soviet Strategy (Washington, D.C.: Pergamon-Brassey, 1984). Most recently, see the detailed information on the International Department in Robert Kitrinos, "International Department of the CPSU," *Problems of Communism* 33, no. 5 (September–October 1984): 47–75.

non-governmental opponents.''[4] One might perhaps speak of positive and negative active measures. The former often include using ostensibly objective, independent sources, who, sometimes under KGB instruction, disseminate disinformation disguised as truthful reporting or comment. A notable example was the activity in France for several years in the 1970s of the ''Parisian insider'' and Soviet ''agent of influence,'' Pierre-Charles Pathé. In his newsletter, *Synthesis,* Pathé, who received ''partial funding from the Soviets,'' disseminated themes calculated to foster disunity among Western nations, portray the United States as the primary threat to world peace, and discredit Soviet dissidents and other ideological opponents of Moscow. In 1979 he was convicted of espionage.[5]

Besides ''agent of influence'' operations, such as the one involving Pathé, the USSR and other Soviet bloc countries have frequently employed the techniques of forgery. Among the many forgeries described in *Dezinformatsia,* ''one of the most successful'' apparently was a forged U.S. Army Field Manual that ''purportedly provided guidance to Army intelligence personnel regarding interference in the affairs of the host country, the subversion of foreign officials and military officers'', and other matters.[6] It should not be supposed that the open, noncovert Soviet communications media are free of the element of deception, which reaches its fullest development in the types of activity referred to above. Distortion is habitual in Soviet journalism, especially when allegedly imperialist or anti-Soviet governments, policies, or persons whom the Soviet authorities choose to denigrate are concerned. Sometimes, as in a case involving one of the authors of this book, distortion is linked with outright falsification.[7]

One of the most important International Department activities is direction of the work of international fronts, such as the World Peace Council, the World Federation of Trade Unions (WFTU), the Afro-Asian People's Solidarity Organization (AAPSO), the

[4]Shultz and Godson, *Dezinformatsia,* p. 2.
[5]On the Pathé affair, see ibid., pp. 132–49.
[6]Ibid., p. 157.
[7]See Chapter IX.

World Federation of Democratic Youth (WFDY), the International Union of Students (IUS), and many others.[8]

Among other important functions of the International Department are the following: disbursement of financial aid to some nonruling communist parties (apparently not to large parties such as the French), control of bodies such as the Afro-Asian Solidarity Committee "which serve a useful purpose for maintaining relations with liberation movements to which the Soviet Union does not yet wish to award diplomatic recognition — such as the Palestine Liberation Organization," keeping tabs on some foreign socialist parties, holding theoretical conferences on foreign policy problems, and producing and distributing the interparty theoretical journal, *Problems of Peace and Socialism,* published in Prague since 1958 in numerous languages (the English language edition is called *World Marxist Review*).[9]

A word on the personal role of Ponomarev should be added to the foregoing. Teague sees Ponomarev playing a foreign affairs "elder statesman" role since 1972, operating not only as head of the International Department but also as chairman of the Commission for Foreign Affairs of one of the two chambers of the USSR Supreme Soviet. Despite the Supreme Soviet's relative powerlessness, this position enables him to travel abroad "in nonparty roles."[10] The frequency of Ponomarev's participation in meetings between Soviet and foreign officials and public figures is striking. In 1984 Ponomarev participated in the high-level Soviet delegation (including Prime Minister [Chairman of the Council of Ministers and Politburo member] Nikolai Tikhonov, Deputy Prime Minister Nuriev, and several officials such as Higher Education Minister Elyutin) that received the chairman of the Council of Ministers of the People's Republic of Kampu-

---

[8]Ten of the most important front organizations, including those mentioned here, are listed on pp. 24–25 of Shultz and Godson, *Dezinformatsia.* Considerable information on Soviet-directed, or Soviet-linked, front organizations is available in the annual yearbooks (*Ezhegodniki*) of the *Bolshaya sovetskaya entsiklopediya* (Great Soviet Encyclopedia) and in Richard Staar, ed., *Yearbook on International Communist Affairs* (Stanford, Calif.: Hoover Institution Press, annual.)

[9]The above is based on Schapiro, "International Department of the CPSU," p. 43, and on Teague, "Foreign Departments of the CPSU," pp. 14–16.

[10]Teague, "Foreign Departments of the CPSU," p. 22.

chea, and he was present when a Soviet group headed by Chernenko met with the chairman of the Social Democratic Party of Finland.[11]

Besides the International Department of the Central Committee, there also exists a Central Committee International Information Department, which appears to have the responsibility of coordinating the foreign policy-related work of TASS (Telegraphic Agency of the Soviet Union), the unofficial Novosti Press Agency, the vast Soviet international radio broadcasting output, prestige publications such as *Pravda,* and a number of periodicals dealing with foreign affairs such as *New Times* and *International Affairs.* It is also important to realize that the covert and overt realms of Soviet activity are interconnected and frequently overlap: "TASS, Novosti and vehicles of Soviet journalism in general are known to harbor a percentage (sometimes quite large) of KGB officers among their domestic and overseas personnel."[12] The available evidence, including a statement in a 1981 speech by Chernenko, indicates that the International Department, not the International Information Department, "sets the overt propaganda line."[13] It is worth noting here that members of the Politburo, some of whom travel frequently to foreign nations, often make public speeches in which they voice the official Soviet policy line. For many years, former Foreign Minister Gromyko was doubtless the best-known traveling mouthpiece of Soviet propaganda. In March 1984, then Defense Minister Dimitri Ustinov, visiting New Delhi, praised India for its contribution to the "struggle for peace and disarmament" and lashed the "American military" for "sowing death and destruction" in Lebanon, conducting an "undeclared war" in Afghanistan, threatening Cuba, supporting South African "aggression" against Angola, invading the "independent state of Grenada," and among other charges, bringing the world ever closer to the "atomic brink."[14]

As external relations have become an increasingly important sphere of Soviet policymaking in the post-Stalin era, the Politburo has sought to improve the quality and scope of the information

---

[11]*Pravda,* 2 July 1984 and 27 September 1984.
[12]Shultz and Godson, *Dezinformatsia,* chart 1, p. 20, and pp. 26–31. Quotation, p. 30.
[13]See ibid., p. 27, and p. 47, footnote 63.
[14]*Pravda,* 6 March 1984.

on which Soviet foreign policy is based. This is indicated by the reported "marked increase in the consultative role played by academic institutes, which advise not only the Secretariat and the Ministry of Foreign Affairs, but also the members of the Politburo directly."[15]

The comments made in previous chapters about limitations on the role of academic and journalistic experts in articulating interests and shaping policy are, perhaps, particularly pertinent with respect to matters of foreign policy, defense, and national security. Nevertheless, even in these extremely sensitive domains, differences of viewpoint are expressed, sometimes in important ways. For example, after the treaty restricting the deployment of ABM (antiballistic missile) weapon systems in the USSR and the United States was reached in SALT I,[16] civilian Soviet writers began describing the strategic posture of both superpowers as essentially parallel, and as one of a mutual hostage relationship. Formerly, Soviet writings had rejected the view that the Soviet Union had to accept mutual deterrence. Whether, however, the analyses published by observers such as Georgi Arbatov, Alexander Bovin, Genrikh Trofimenko, and others had any actual influence on leadership policy or whether these were merely intellectual rationalizations of the Politburo-level decision to renounce large-

[15]Teague, "Foreign Departments of the CPSU," p. 23. Teague here mentions the Institute of the World Economy and International Relations (IMEMO), set up immediately after the 1956 Twentieth Party Congress, the Institute of the USA and Canada, established in 1967, and the Institute of the International Workers' Movement (IMRD), "reactivated" in 1971. She cites articles on IMEMO by Jerry Hough, in *World Politics*, no. 4 (July 1980) and on IMRD by Joan Barth Urban in *Orbis* (Winter 1976). A great deal of information on the USA Institute is contained in Morton Schwartz, *Soviet Perceptions of the United States* (Berkeley: University of California Press, 1978). On Soviet research institutes for the study of the politics of international relations of Asia, Africa, and Latin America, see Elizabeth Kridl Valkenier, *The Soviet Union and the Third World: An Economic Bind* (New York: Praeger, 1983), esp. pp. 41–59. An informative survey of the major Soviet research institutes providing expertise on foreign areas is presented by Daniel C. Matuszewski, "Soviet International Relations Research," in Walter Connor, Robert Legvold, and Daniel Matuszewski, eds., *Foreign Area Research in the National Interest: American and Soviet Perspectives* (New York: IREX Occasional Paper, 1982).

[16]Under the terms of the treaty signed in 1972, each side was limited to two ABM systems; by an amendment to the treaty signed in 1974, each side was limited to one. The USSR continued to deploy and improve an ABM system around Moscow, but the United States discontinued its ABM program entirely, continuing only to conduct research on ABM concepts.

scale ABM deployments is disputed. Moreover, most Western analysts note that the monopoly on data and analyses relating to matters of national security and defense possessed by the Soviet military establishment relegates Soviet civilian experts on foreign affairs to a minor role in policymaking. (In the United States, by contrast, civilian research and analysis are strongly influential in strategic policymaking.) To the extent that experts on nuclear disarmament discuss the arms race and the strategic competition between the superpowers, the information and analysis presented treat developments in the West only as posing a threat to world security.[17]

An aspect of Soviet foreign policy that perhaps deserves more attention than it usually receives from foreign observers is the systematic Soviet effort to reap political benefits from carefully controlled contacts with foreigners. For example, from almost the earliest days of Soviet power, there have been Soviet organizations whose function has been to practice what Paul Hollander has called the "techniques of hospitality." Under this tactic ordinary tourists are sometimes treated to food and lodging in a manner beyond

[17]Much has been written about Soviet national security decision making in recent years. An account by a former employee of the Disarmament Section of the Institute of the World Economy and International Relations (IMEMO) is Igor S. Glagolev, "The Soviet Decision-Making Process in Arms Control Negotiations," *Orbis* (Winter 1978): 767–76. On Soviet views of SALT, deterrence, and nuclear strategy, see the important articles by Raymond L. Garthoff, "Mutual Deterrence and Strategic Arms Limitation in Soviet Policy," *International Security* (Summer 1978): 125–32, and idem, "The Soviet Military and SALT," in Jiri Valenta and William Potter, eds., *Soviet Decisionmaking for National Security* (London: Allen & Unwin, 1984). A sound recent book on Soviet nuclear policy and strategy is David Holloway, *The Soviet Union and the Arms Race* (New Haven, Conn.: Yale University Press, 1983). Also see the special issue of the journal *Soviet Union,* edited by Ellen Mickiewicz and Roman Kolkowicz, entitled "The Soviet Calculus of Nuclear War," vol. 10, parts 2–3 (1983). Andrei Sakharov contributed an important article to the discussion over strategic competition between the United States and the Soviet Union, entitled "The Danger of Thermonuclear War," *Foreign Affairs* (Summer 1983): 1001–26. A conservative view of Soviet nuclear strategy is presented by Francis P. Hoeber and Amoretta M. Hoeber, "The Soviet View of Deterrence: Who Whom?" *Survey* (Spring 1980): 17–31. A review of Soviet policy debates over strategy vis-à-vis the West is provided in Thomas N. Bjorkman and Thomas J. Zamostny, "Soviet Politics and Strategy toward the West: Three Cases," *World Politics* (January 1984): 189–214. An interesting attempt to classify Soviet views more generally on U.S. policy and the nature of U.S.-Soviet relations is by Franklyn Griffiths, "The Sources of American Conduct: Soviet Perspectives and their Policy Implications," *International Security* (Fall 1984): 3–50.

the dreams of most Soviet citizens, and particularly lavish treatment is accorded to distinguished foreign visitors whom the Soviet authorities consider it politically profitable to cultivate.[18]

One of the most effective forms of face-to-face propaganda used by communist countries, especially the USSR and Cuba, may well be the instruction and training of foreign students. Much of this is aimed at poor students from less-developed countries (for example, at Patrice Lumumba Friendship University in Moscow), and some is provided at the elementary and secondary level, especially in Cuba. It should be noted that the USSR and its allies, unlike the United States, where leading universities play a major role in the admissions process for foreign students, do not insist on strict academic standards for admissions. One author believes that "with time . . . Soviet programs for educating students from less-developed countries may well bring rich political dividends to the USSR and contribute to the spectacular success that its schools have already enjoyed in furthering the spread of communism."[19]

---

[18]See Paul Hollander, *Political Pilgrims* (New York: Harper & Row), esp. ch. 8, where Hollander describes such modes of political seduction as the "ego massage," "selective exposure and display," and "rearranging reality." See also Frederick Barghoorn, *The Soviet Cultural Offensive: The Role of Cultural Diplomacy in Soviet Foreign Policy* (Princeton, N.J.: Princeton University Press, 1960), and Sylvia Margulies, *The Pilgrimage to Russia: The Soviet Union and the Treatment of Foreigners* (Madison: University of Wisconsin Press, 1968). A good brief recent account of Soviet techniques of showing visitors the best the USSR has to offer and preventing their seeing anything that might tarnish the desired positive image is John F. Burns's article, "For Moscow's Guests, Life in a Luxurious Cocoon," *New York Times,* 15 May 1982.

[19]Quotation in Edward Raymond, "Education of Foreign Nationals in the Soviet Union," in Richard Merritt, ed., *Communication in International Politics* (Urbana: University of Illinois Press, 1972), pp. 120–45, at pp. 144–45. In the last part of the quoted statement, Raymond refers to the program of training for foreign communist leaders and potential leaders that flourished before World War II and, according to sources cited by Raymond, was later revived, especially for Chinese and Germans (mostly POWs). See also Jo Thomas, "Marxism," *New York Times Magazine,* 4 October 1981. The author reports that "since 1977, some 26,000 children from Cuba, Africa and Central America have been brought to a Cuban island for . . . a program that is a mixture of general education and Marxist indoctrination"; Fred Hechinger, "Latin Region Focus of Aid by East Bloc," *New York Times,* 25 September 1984; Logan Robinson, *An American in Leningrad* (New York: Norton, 1982); Andrea Lee, *Russian Journal* (New York: Random House, 1979). The last two books, especially Robinson's, reveal a great deal about the rewards and frustrations of study in the USSR for American graduate students; Robinson ably describes the endless runaround to which *Inotdel* (short for *Inostrannyi otdel,* or foreign department, the department at any Soviet

The administrative and political machinery described above has as its purpose the maximization of Soviet influence on the non-Soviet world. It is supported by controls, touched on above only tangentially, such as border controls, censorship, and prevention of unfettered contacts between Soviet citizens and foreigners, designed to minimize the flow of influence from the non-Soviet world to Soviet society. The machinery is formidable, though it sometimes fails; for example, it has not prevented the loss by defection to the West of a large proportion of the most creative Soviet writers, dramatists, performing artists, and other highly skilled professionals in recent years. Though it is a manifestation of power, it also bespeaks the weakness of a system that cannot bear free discussion and critical examination. It is, however, a formidable weapon of ideological struggle and political warfare and has perhaps contributed to the expansion of Soviet power and influence.

EXPANSIONISM AND NATIONALISM

In its intentions and, to a significant degree, in its capabilities, the foreign policy of the USSR is expansionist. The USSR's expansionist urge has led to impressive acquisitions of territory in areas contiguous to the Soviet borders and, especially since World War II, to influence in numerous overseas areas. Since 1939, the USSR has incorporated territories taken from Poland (1939), Finland (1940), Romania (1940), China (Tannu-Tuva, 1944), Czechoslovakia (1945), Germany (1945), and Japan (Southern Sakhalin and the Kuril Islands — particularly four small islands very near the large northern island of Honshu — 1945), and it incorporated as union republics the whole of the formerly independent states Latvia, Lithuania and Estonia, the latter having been ruled by Russia until the collapse of the tsarist empire in 1917.[20]

---

university that administers contacts between foreign students and the university, subjects non-Soviet students. It rules on matters "presumed by Westerners to be automatic — such as leaving the city, changing dormitory rooms or visiting a historical archive." Robinson, pp. 29–31.

[20]Lists and classifications of territories taken from various nations by Soviet Russia are in the Appendix to Chapter VIII of Maurice Tugwell, David Charters, Dominick Graham, eds., *No Substitute for Peace* (Frederickton, New Brunswick, Canada: Centre for Conflict Studies, University of New Brunswick, 1982), and in Nick Eberstadt and Tom Ricks, "The Costs of Pax Sovietica," *New Republic* (30 December 1981): 13–18.

As a leading expert on Soviet policy in Asia pointed out in 1982, since 1975 armed force has played an increasing role in the expansion of Soviet power and influence. During this period, "seven pro-Soviet communist parties have seized power or territory . . . with armed force." These countries were South Vietnam, Laos, Angola, Ethiopia, Afghanistan, South Yemen, and Cambodia. As the same author noted, "the Russians were active players in each of the above-mentioned cases."[21]

In addition the USSR has acquired preponderant power over the states of Eastern Europe, except for Yugoslavia (which is careful to refrain from actions that might seriously irritate Russia) and Albania. Of course, by comparison with the situation in the Stalin era, the East European allies have acquired a certain measure of autonomy, but, as such events as the invasion of Czechoslovakia in 1968 and the imposition of martial law in Poland in 1981 showed, Moscow has circumscribed their freedom of development. Cuba, since Fidel Castro took power in 1959 and especially since the late 1960s, has been a semiautonomous ally of the USSR, useful to its mighty patron as an assistant in projecting and consolidating Soviet influence in far-flung areas of the Third World.

In Afghanistan a conspiracy led by the little-known communist Noor Mohamed Taraki engineered a coup d'état in April 1978, that established a socialist republic closely allied with Moscow. In December 1979, after a new leader, Hafizullah Amin, who had come to power by murdering the author of the 1978 coup, came to be regarded as unreliable by the Politburo, Soviet forces moved in. They installed as nominal head of state the highly subservient Babrak Karmal. Six years later, however, Soviet efforts to reestablish undisputed control in Afghanistan remained frustrated. Nonetheless, strategically located Afghanistan furnishes significant evidence of the persistence of the expansionary urge in Soviet foreign policy. The Mongolian People's Republic and the Democratic Republic of Vietnam (and its Laotian and Kampuchean satellites) round out the list of countries ruled by Soviet-oriented Marxist-Leninist one-party states.

In addition to the above group, called by some Western authors

[21]See Donald Zagoria, "The Strategic Environment of East Asia," in Zagoria, ed., *Soviet Policy in East Asia* (New Haven, Conn.: Yale University Press, 1982), p. 1. We should add that as of the fall of 1985 the USSR was actively seeking close relations with North Yemen and tightening its relations with Syria and Ethiopia.

"colonies" of the USSR but in Soviet terminology members of the "socialist commonwealth," there are the client states: South Yemen (since 1970), Laos (since 1973), Angola (since 1975), and Ethiopia (since 1976). In 1984 Ethiopia established a Soviet-style ruling communist party.[22]

Vast as the area ruled or swayed by Moscow is, what some experts refer to as the Soviet empire would have been even bigger had the Soviet leaders, beginning with Lenin, had their way.[23]

There have of course been retreats on the road to what contemporary Soviet doctrine calls the "revolutionary transformation of the world" — a process in which "proletarian internationalism" is called "a mighty instrument."[24] However, the doctrine as set forth in the authoritative work by Fedoseev, a prestigious ideologist, which is studded with quotations from Soviet leaders from Lenin through Brezhnev, presents Soviet foreign policy within the context of "the tendency toward the uniting of the communists of the world in the struggle against the common enemy," and, more to the point, of the "faithfulness of the CPSU and the Soviet people to its international duty." This duty consists of such activities as providing economic, ideological, and diplomatic aid to Iraq, Angola, Mozambique, Ethiopia, the People's Republic of Yemen, and other countries.[25]

The Fedoseev book acknowledges that the USSR, as in the case of Afghanistan, provides military assistance if needed to "independent countries that have embarked on the path of social progress" — aid that "imperialist reaction" falsely describes as "inter-

---

[22]Unlike Tugwell et al., we have not included Cuba among the client states because of its fully communist internal structure and its very close foreign policy collaboration with the Soviets. Eberstadt and Ricks offer a third category of "Soviet allies," namely the "radical" but "non-Leninist" leaders in the Third World such as Qaddafi in Libya, Hafez Assad of Syria, and Palestine Liberation Organization leader, Yasir Arafat. They correctly note that though without the help of such nations and men, many Soviet objectives could not be achieved, these "ideological friends" nevertheless sometimes also present Moscow with problems.

[23]Scholars such as Robert Conquest, Richard Pipes, Teresa Rakowska-Harmstone, and Hélène Carrère d'Encausse call the USSR an empire, and Alvin Rubinstein titles his book *Soviet Foreign Policy Since World War II: Imperial and Global.*

[24]See, for example, Academician T. N. Fedoseev et al., *Proletarskii internatsionalizm — moshchnoe oruzhie revoliutsionnogo preobrazheniia mira* (Proletarian Internationalism — A Mighty Weapon for the Revolutionary Transformation of the World) (Moscow: Mysl, 1980).

[25]See ibid., pp. 119, 152.

vention.''[26] The CPSU, however, also considers it an international obligation to defend socialism throughout the entire socialist camp. This principle, used to justify the Warsaw Pact invasion of Czechoslovakia in 1968, is often referred to as the Brezhnev Doctrine.[27] Moreover, contemporary Soviet sources assert with pride that there is no part of the globe where problems of foreign relations can be resolved without the participation of the USSR.[28]

Such pronouncements tend to confirm the views of Western specialists who find in the ideological-cultural foundations of Soviet foreign policy a mixture of Marxist-Leninist and Russian nationalist influences. A vigorous expression of this view is Adam Ulam's statement that ''Marxism, the most internationalist of nineteenth century ideologies, has merged with Russian nationalism, their synthesis being Soviet communism, which is internationalist in form and nationalist in essence.''[29] Ulam reminds us that the primary task of foreign communists, under the direction of the Comintern (Communist International) with its headquarters in Moscow, was to ''defend and support the USSR.'' If the Soviet leaders, however, have found it expedient to subordinate a nominally internationalist Marxism-Leninism to the Russian nationalism that Ulam and others regard as the wellspring of Soviet foreign policy, why do they bother to retain as their professed official ideology an increasingly ritualized, obsolete, and irrelevant Marxism? The answers may well be (1) that the Soviet elite could not secularize the Soviet state by abandoning its justifying ideology and still preserve its power and (2) that if the veneer of Soviet ideology is removed from Russian nationalism, ''the problem of preserving the territorial integrity of what is now the Soviet Union becomes well-nigh impossible.''[30]

Doctrinal claims that imperialism is retreating while Soviet power is growing may encourage at least a passive acceptance of the Soviet system among Soviet citizens, despite the difficulties and frustrations of daily life in the USSR. Thus, ideology is the

---

[26]Ibid., p. 152, citing a statement by Leonid Brezhnev.

[27]Ibid., p. 186.

[28]Ibid., pp. 127, 136–37.

[29]Adam Ulam, ''Russian Nationalism,'' in Seweryn Bialer, ed., *The Domestic Context of Soviet Foreign Policy* (Boulder, Colo.: Westview Press, 1981), p. 3.

[30]Ibid., p. 14.

servant of Russian nationalism but a servant, says Ulam, who cannot be dismissed "without gravely imperilling the position of the master." Insofar as this judgment is based on the assumption that most Soviet people see in the success of Soviet foreign policy evidence that history is on the side of the USSR in the East-West struggles, it seems somewhat oversimplified. For one thing, does Soviet influence in Angola, Ethiopia, Mozambique, and South Yemen, even with a favorable trend from Moscow's point of view in Central America, really counterbalance reverses since the mid-1960s in Indonesia, Egypt, and Somalia, not to mention the Soviet loss of China? Occasionally individual Soviet citizens express outright hostility to Soviet Third World adventures on the grounds, apparently, that they waste resources that could better be employed to raise the standard of living of the Soviet people. Relatively little can be known about the effects of Soviet foreign policy propaganda on Soviet mass opinion, but the fear the Soviet authorities display toward the potentially subversive effects that the knowledge of freedom and prosperity in the West might have on Soviet people makes us skeptical about hypotheses such as Ulam's. Moreover, events such as casualties in and foreign criticism of the "Soviet Vietnam" in Afghanistan and the relatively poor performance of Soviet arms in the Israeli-PLO and Israeli-Syrian fighting in Lebanon in the summer of 1982 may well have diminished the appeal Soviet foreign policy expansiveness may have for the Soviet man in the street. As for the Soviet elite, they know too much about the possible dangers of East-West military conflict to take a positive attitude toward a policy likely to provoke it. In fact, we believe that both elites and masses in the USSR desire peace, and that Soviet propaganda on foreign affairs achieves its greatest impact if it can persuade Soviet people that the Politburo is working for peace while the imperialists plot war. This hypothesis, which must remain speculative in the absence of adequate studies of Soviet public opinion, perhaps derives support from such facts as the prominence in Soviet propaganda of Brezhnev's "Peace Program" (*Programma mira*), proclaimed at the Twenty-fifth Congress of the CPSU in 1976 and subsequently, and the persistent effort of the KGB to portray dissenters such as Sakharov and Solzhenitsyn as enemies of peace. Nevertheless, chauvinistic nationalism is a strong sentiment in some segments of Soviet society, particularly in organizations concerned with foreign policy, intelligence, defense, heavy industry, and propaganda. There are also undoubtedly many who, without much enthusiasm for an expansionist foreign policy, are partial to widening contacts with the outside world so as to make possible the attainment of one of the most coveted prizes that civil service in the USSR can bestow — travel and residence abroad, especially in the West.

Seweryn Bialer agrees with Ulam on the importance of nationalism as a driving force of Soviet foreign policy. Bialer has written that "the mainstay of the Soviet political elite's sense of common purpose is provided more than ever by nationalism."[31] This nationalism, asserts Bialer, "constitutes the major effective, long-lasting bond within the political elite and between the elite and the masses."[32] Like most knowledgeable students of Soviet foreign relations, Bialer also believes that the pride in national power and prestige shared among Soviet elites is a special kind of nationalism. It is characterized by four traits: (1) it is braced for potential disaster emanating from a potentially hostile external world; (2) it is an imperial nationalism, committed to the retention of the empire that Stalin built in Eastern Europe; (3) it is "the nationalism of a great power that is still young, growing, ambitious and assertive;" and (4) it represents a combination of the universalistic elements present both in the communist world outlook and in prerevolutionary Russian thought.[33]

Insightful though the views of Ulam and Bialer are on the role of Russian nationalism as a driving force of Soviet foreign policy, they underestimate the difficulties of harnessing it to Soviet goals. Official Soviet patriotism is certainly a form of nationalism, with its stress on centralism, unity, and, paradoxically, on internationalism: all of these are code words for Russian domination of the USSR and USSR domination of the socialist community and the international revolutionary movement. Soviet patriotism, however, is inextricably linked to a world outlook deeply antithetical

[31]Seweryn Bialer, "Soviet Foreign Policy: Sources, Perceptions, Trends," in Bialer, ed., *Domestic Context of Soviet Foreign Policy,* pp. 409–41, on p. 426.

[32]Ibid., p. 426.

[33]Ibid., pp. 427–28. Incidentally, on this last point, Bialer's views resemble those set forth by Philip E. Mosely in his very important 1948 article, "Aspects of Russian Expansion," reprinted in Philip Mosely, *The Kremlin and World Politics* (New York: Vintage Books, 1960), pp. 42–66.

to the religious and folk cultural roots of Russian national identity. The assertion of historic Russian values by Solzhenitsyn and other traditionalistic Russian patriots presents a threat to Soviet power and inevitably leads to repression of its articulators by the regime, as does the voicing of other traditional ethnic values. In addition, even when disguised as Soviet patriotism and proletarian internationalism, Russian nationalism in practice is offensive to both non-Russians (unless they are assimilated into the Russian culture pattern or are sufficiently cowed or opportunistic to ignore it) and foreign communists, radicals and patriots who still care about the promises of ethnic equality to which Moscow pays lip service.

Of greater significance even than controversy over the role and significance of nationalism as an influence on Soviet foreign policy is the conflict between the "macroanalytic" and "microanalytic" approaches. The former, as Morton Schwartz puts it in the introduction to a very useful book, focuses on "variables external to the Soviet Union," and the latter "explains Soviet foreign policy primarily in terms of internal needs." Only understanding the interplay of domestic and external factors, however, can satisfactorily explain Soviet foreign policy.[34] William Zimmerman, in particular, argues that Soviet foreign policy behavior is adaptive and is at least potentially responsive to reassuring or threatening behavior on the part of the United States.[35]

Such hypotheses are interesting but so far have proved difficult to support with convincing evidence. An impressive recent study by Hannes Adomeit finds that neither in the crucially important Berlin Blockade crisis of 1948–1949 nor in the equally significant Berlin crisis of 1961 can it be persuasively argued that Stalin's or Khrushchev's policies, respectively, were influenced by identifiable group or organizational pressures.[36] It is clear, however, that among the Soviet elite and foreign policy specialists there are dif-

[34]Morton Schwartz, *The Foreign Policy of the USSR: Domestic Factors* (Encino, Calif.: Dickenson, 1975), pp. 1–4. See also Alexander Dallin, "Domestic Sources of Soviet Foreign Policy," in Bialer, ed. *Domestic Context,* as well as the contributors to Parts I and II, entitled, respectively, "The Study of Soviet Foreign Policy" and "Domestic Policies and the Formation of Soviet Foreign Policy," in Erik Hoffman and Frederick Fleron, eds., *The Conduct of Soviet Foreign Policy,* 2nd. ed. (New York: Aldine 1980).

[35]See, for example, the opposing views of Zimmerman and Charles Gati reprinted in Hoffman and Fleron, eds., *Conduct of Soviet Foreign Policy,* pp. 644–72.

[36]Hannes Adomeit, *Soviet Risk-Taking and Crisis Behaviors: A Theoretical and Empirical Analysis* (London: George Allen & Unwin, 1982), pp. 340–42.

fering opinions as to what the foreign policy line of the USSR should be, although it is very difficult because of the poor quality of data available to demonstrate just how conflicting preferences actually affect specific decisions.

Another important subject that was mentioned in the first section of this chapter is the impressive improvement since the death of Stalin in the resources of information, research, and professional training at the disposal of Soviet foreign policy decision makers. To Americans the best-known manifestation of this development is the activity of the Institute of the USA and Canada, a large and, at least in terms of access to Soviet policymakers, influential organization, which publishes the important journal *USA (SShA)* and has sent its experts, including its director, Georgi Arbatov, on a number of visits to the United States. Arbatov's visits fell victim, probably temporarily, to the increasing coolness of U.S.-Soviet relations in 1983–1984.[37]

SOVIET FOREIGN POLICY IN ACTION: COLD WAR, DÉTENTE, AND COEXISTENCE

We regard as realistic Ulam's judgment that "it is clear that few developments in modern times bear such an air of inevitability as the melancholy turn of events we describe as the cold war."[38] This is not to deny the value of inquiring into what could have been done in the past, or, more important, might be done in the future to prevent Soviet-American crises. A recent study by a group led by Alexander George takes an imaginative and realistic approach to this important question. Though he does not assume that a comprehensive end to the competitive behavior of the superpowers is likely in the foreseeable future, George takes the position that some confrontations may be prevented and the severity of others mitigated by such measures as improved communications, agreement on rules to regulate conflict in particular cases, and the moderation of competition.[39]

[37]Morton Schwartz's study, *Soviet Perceptions of the United States,* based largely on analysis of the content of *USA,* is a useful source of information on the results of the work of the institute headed by Arbatov. See also relevant portions of Jan F. Triska and David Finley, *Soviet Foreign Policy* (New York: Macmillan, 1968).

[38]Ulam, *Expansion and Coexistence* (New York: Praeger, 1968), p. 398.

[39]Alexander L. George, ed., *Managing U.S.-Soviet Rivalry: Problems of Crisis Prevention* (Boulder, Colo.: Westview Press, 1983), esp. ch. 15, "Crisis Prevention Reexamined," pp. 365–98.

The cold war was a state of relations with minimal communication and continuous hostile propaganda exchanges between the United States and Soviet Union. It was also a time when fear of a direct Soviet-American military clash was intense. A recent study of Soviet foreign policy in the Stalin era argues that both détente and cold war were instruments of Stalin's foreign policy. This point appears to be valid still. A state approaching cold war tends to develop when Western governments after a period of failed détente become convinced that they must stiffen resistance to Soviet efforts to take advantage of Western accommodativeness, perceived by Moscow as weakness. This resistance in turn arouses irritation in the Kremlin.[40] The foregoing does not mean that we attribute to Soviet leaders a grand design for speedy world conquest. In fact, we see in Soviet policy intense determination, infinite patience, and unlimited persistence, buttressed by confidence that history is on the side of socialism, as interpreted by the Soviet Politburo, in the struggle against the still dangerous but waning forces of imperialism.

Crucial to understanding Soviet foreign policy behavior is comprehension of the Soviet approach to détente and peaceful coexistence of states with different social systems, which since the death of Stalin have been increasingly invoked by the Soviet authorities to characterize Soviet goals. An authoritative party training textbook published in 1978 describes peaceful coexistence as a "form of class struggle between socialism and capitalism." Although this text asserts that the USSR, in keeping with Lenin's precepts, seeks to settle international disputes by peaceful negotiation and to broaden scientific, cultural, and trade relations, it also points out that peaceful coexistence is not applicable to "the internal processes of class and national-liberation struggle in capitalist countries," or to "relations between oppressors and oppressed, colonizers and victims of colonial oppression."[41]

Upon close examination, the contemporary uses of the concepts of détente and coexistence in Soviet diplomacy and propaganda differ little from those applied, on the basis of far less material power, by Lenin and Stalin. They are instruments for convincing domestic and foreign audiences of the Soviet leadership's desire

---

[40]See William Taubman, *Stalin's American Policy: From Entente to Détente to Cold War* (New York: Norton, 1982).

[41]*Vneshniaia politika sovetskogo soiuza* (The Foreign Policy of the Soviet Union) (Moscow: Politizdat, 1978), pp. 34–35.

for peace and ultimately for minimizing the costs of preserving and expanding the USSR's influence abroad.

Years ago Kurt London sensibly pointed out that Khrushchev's proclamation of peaceful coexistence, which under Lenin and Stalin had been regarded as a short-term tactic, as the long-term strategy of Soviet foreign policy, in reality was an adaptation of Lenin's dualistic foreign policy approach to the new conditions of the nuclear age. Under this approach Lenin and his successors simultaneously pursued both revolutionary and pragmatic policies. In other words, through agents of the CPSU and by whatever other overt or covert agencies were available, they could promote the world revolutionary process, and through the Ministry of Foreign Affairs and other state agencies, they could practice respectable, conventional diplomacy.[42]

CONFRONTATION AND DÉTENTE IN EUROPE

There is wide agreement among students of Soviet foreign policy, including Soviet scholars, that the most important issue in Soviet-Western relations since the end of World War II has been the destiny of Germany. What rendered the German question particularly acute was the fact that as a result of the outcome of the war, Germany was divided into three Western zones of occupation (American, British, and French) and a Soviet zone. This division plus the location of Berlin about 100 miles inside the Soviet-occupied portion of Germany made Berlin (also divided into four parts, or sectors) vulnerable to pressure by the Soviet occupation authorities.[43]

[42]See Kurt London, "Soviet Foreign Policy: Fifty Years of Dualism," in Kurt London, ed., *The Soviet Union — A Half Century of Communism* (Baltimore, Md.: Johns Hopkins Press, 1968), pp. 327–66. The fullest historico-theoretical study of the uses of peaceful coexistence is in Paul Marantz, "Peaceful Coexistence: From Heresy to Orthodoxy," in Paul Cocks et al., eds., *The Dynamics of Soviet Politics* (Cambridge, Mass.: Harvard University Press, 1976), pp. 293–308. Among other things, Marantz's extensive documentation demolishes the Soviet propaganda claim that coexistence was a Leninist doctrine; on this point also see F. Barghoorn, *Soviet Foreign Propaganda* (Princeton, N.J.: Princeton University Press, 1964), esp. pp. 87–98.

[43]The centrality of Germany may help to account for the fact that Soviet experts are more in agreement on the Western military alliance than, for example, on policy toward the Third World. On the Western alliance, see Michael Sodaro, "Soviet Studies of the Western Alliance," in Herbert Ellison, ed., *Soviet Policy Toward Western Europe* (Seattle: University of Washington Press, 1983), pp. 234–65. According to Sodaro, on U.S.-Western European relations the spectrum is "narrow, with divergent viewpoints hugging close to a central point." P. 239.

Top leaders of the German Communist Party arrived in Berlin with the victorious Soviet troops and under the supervision of Moscow's representatives quickly established a new German regime, known since 1949 as the German Democratic Republic (GDR). The GDR's dependence on Soviet military and diplomatic power against pressures and blandishments from the far more populous, prosperous, and free Federal Republic and its enormous strategic importance to the USSR (indicated in part by the very large Soviet military strike forces always on duty in the GDR) are among many reasons that the leadership of the GDR has usually worked more closely with the USSR than has any other East European state with the possible exception of Bulgaria. This fact made all the more striking the limited tendency toward independence displayed for a while by the GDR in 1984. According to Milovan Djilas, a former close associate of Yugoslav communist leader Josip Broz-Tito, Stalin said in April 1945, that "this war is not as in the past: whoever occupies a territory imposes his own social system."[44]

Djilas's statement identifies one of the two major aspects of Soviet policy in East Germany and Eastern Europe in general. Wherever Soviet armed forces took control of a country's territory, a Soviet-style regime was, after a relatively short time, installed. Moreover, these regimes were not permitted to alter either their stance of loyalty to Moscow or the essential structure and functioning of their domestic political systems. The exceptions are tiny Albania and, more important, Yugoslavia, neither of them contiguous to the USSR and neither possessing the strategic significance of the other East European states, especially the GDR, the Polish People's Republic, and Czechoslovakia.

By the 1970s, negotiations begun in 1954 through a series of agreements and treaties led to the Helsinki Conference on Security and Cooperation in Europe (CSCE). Besides the United States and USSR, thirty-three other Eastern and Western European countries and Canada took part. By that time Soviet hegemony over Eastern Europe had been accepted by the West. The Final Act of CSCE, signed August 1, 1975, was a somewhat vague document. It gave satisfaction, however, both to the USSR and to the West by subscribing to such principles as nonintervention

[44]Quoted here from Adomeit, *Soviet Risk-Taking*, p. 67.

in the internal affairs of other countries and renunciation of the use of force to change frontiers. From the Soviet point ot view, its most important point was one that Moscow has sought since at least 1954, to wit, agreement on the inviolability of frontiers in Europe. The Helsinki affirmation on frontiers may have appeared to the Soviets to satisfy the demand voiced by Khrushchev earlier for the West to "accept the results of World War II." All of these and other provisions were included in the so-called Basket 1 of what are often referred to as the Helsinki Accords (they are not formal treaties). Basket 2 is concerned with economic cooperation. The only negative feature of CSCE, from the standpoint of Soviet interests, is Basket 3, regarding human rights. Included largely at the insistence of Western European countries, particularly small countries such as Holland and Denmark, it was to furnish a basis for subsequent criticism of what the Western nations regarded as obvious violations by the USSR of its obligations respecting human rights. Of course, the collectivist USSR and the individualist West proceeded from very different conceptions of human rights.

Ironically, by the time the Helsinki Final Act was signed in 1975, détente, which seemed for a time to represent the beginning of a new and higher stage of international relations, was already being viewed, especially in the United States but probably also in the USSR, with a more and more jaundiced eye. The summit conferences between Brezhnev and Nixon in 1972 and 1973 and the signing of the SALT (Strategic Arms Limitation Talks) Agreement in 1972 probably marked the high point of Soviet-American détente, which was struck a mortal blow by the Soviet invasion of Afghanistan in the week between Christmas and New Year's Day 1979. The invasion followed on the heels of other developments in the Third World (e.g., the establishment of Marxist governments in Ethiopia, Angola, Mozambique, and South Yemen) and the failure of trade with the United States to provide the economic benefits that Moscow hoped to receive.

Oddly, in view of the deep Soviet suspicions and antipathy toward Germany in the 1940s, 1950s, and 1960s, détente between West Germany and the USSR and Eastern Europe generally was stronger than the relationship achieved between the United States and Russia. The same was true to a lesser degree of Franco-Soviet relations, but the socialist president of France, Francois Mitter-

and, was to take a much harder line than his Gaullist predecessor, Valéry Giscard d'Estaing. Gradually, following the erection of the Berlin Wall in 1961, the GDR, no longer suffering the drain of many of its most enterprising young workers and professionals to West Germany, experienced rapid economic growth. The West Germans, like the East Germans, adjusted successfully to the new situation created by the sudden end to emigration from the GDR. Trade between West and East Germany, as well as between the Federal Republic and the USSR, grew rapidly. A somewhat similar pattern prevailed between France, under a succession of conservative governments, and the Soviets. Western Europeans in the 1970s, although by no means unsympathetic to Soviet human rights defenders, came to feel that they could develop a relationship of live and let live with the Soviets.

Nevertheless, fear of the military power of the USSR, nowhere so massive and menacing as on the European continent, continued strong in the European consciousness. In the fall of 1979, following a rapid buildup of a large force of mobile, intermediate-range Soviet SS-20 missiles targeted on Europe, the United States, at the behest of NATO, undertook to deploy in Western Europe a total of 572 intermediate-range ballistic missiles of the Pershing 2 and cruise types unless the USSR agreed to remove its SS-20 IRBMs. Opposition to deployment of the American missiles soon developed, especially in the Federal Republic. The USSR brought to bear on the peoples and governments of the NATO and other European countries its formidable arsenal of instruments of propaganda and psychological warfare to persuade them that the United States was planning to make them the victims of an American-Soviet war that, as Soviet propaganda presented the story, Washington hoped could be fought in Europe.

The Soviet leadership under Andropov tried to intensify this pressure in order to sap Western public acceptance of NATO's plans, a tactic used in earlier peace-and-disarmament campaigns led by Soviet-dominated front groups and their sympathizers. Soviet peace propaganda was accompanied by thinly veiled threats that the USSR would match any deployments by America with new deployments of its own. The new European peace movement, strongest in Germany but also vigorous in other countries, was more radical and far more naive than any comparable one in the United States. Many of its adherents, unlike most members of the counterpart American nuclear freeze movement, were advocates of unilateral disarmament. Though Soviet propaganda undoubtedly played a part, the rapid growth of the new antinuclear mood in both Europe and America can also be attributed to what appeared to be incautious rhetoric in Washington and to the belief in some quarters that American strategic weapons policy had shifted from deterring nuclear war to fighting and winning such a war. In any case, Soviet intimidation efforts largely failed, at least for the time being, in preventing the deployment of the first contingents of new missiles. In November 1983, shortly after the West German parliament voted to accept deployments of the modern intermediate-range missiles, the USSR suspended both the INF and START (strategic arms reduction talks) negotiations in Geneva. Late in 1984, however, the USSR signaled its willingness to resume negotiation as long as the issue of space-based and defensive weapons was included on the agenda, and in March 1985 a new round of strategic arms talks began; almost simultaneously, Mikhail Gorbachev assumed the leadership of the Soviet regime.

ASIA AND THE THIRD WORLD

Since President Nixon's dramatic visit to China in 1972, a triangular relationship among the Soviet Union, the People's Republic of China (PRC), and the United States has emerged. After Mao's death in 1976 and again after the election of President Reagan in 1980, Soviet hopes for better relations with the PRC led to exploratory feelers and renewed negotiations. Whether the round of Sino-Soviet consultations that began in March 1983 would significantly reduce the level of antagonism was doubtful. The issues that have divided the two communist giants since Khrushchev exposed the conflict to world view in 1960 by abruptly withdrawing Soviet technical advisers from China have included disputes over demarcation of their common border, the presence of Soviet forces in the Soviet-dominated Mongolian People's Republic, Soviet influence in Vietnam, Vietnamese domination of Kampuchea (Cambodia), and of course the Soviet military occupation of Afghanistan. Although the extreme hostility expressed by the Chinese toward Soviet social imperialism and hegemonism during the Cultural Revolution of 1966–1969 has abated, and no repetition of the Sino-Soviet military clashes of

1969 has occurred, relations remain wary and occasionally tense, as when China attacked the border provinces of Vietnam in the spring of 1979. For their part, the Soviet divisions stationed in the vicinity of the Chinese border have risen since the mid-1960s from about twelve or fifteen to over forty-six, or between a half million and a million men. The Soviets have also built up their forces on the four small Kuril Islands seized from Japan at the end of World War II over Japanese protests. One scholar sees Moscow as having gained considerable advantage over the PRC because of the Soviet-Vietnamese alignment. A hostile front "had been opened up on the PRC's southern borders," and, among other benefits, "the new strategic ties have provided the Russians with base facilities at . . . Cam Ranh bay and Danang."[45]

Both the Soviet Union and China seek to retain the freedom to improve relations with the United States should circumstances be propitious. The Chinese denounced U.S.-Soviet détente as a fraud perpetrated by Moscow, much as the Soviet Union warned the United States against deals with China regarded as inimical to Soviet interests. Likewise, the initiatives each side took to improve relations with the other could be seen as a means of courting Washington's favor.[46] In December 1984, during the visit of a deputy Soviet premier to Beijing, the Soviet Union signed a long-term economic and technological cooperation agreement with China, indicating a partial return to the former amity between them. Soon afterward, upon Chernenko's death, the Chinese press referred to Chernenko as an "outstanding leader of the party and the state" under whose leadership relations between the two countries had improved "noticeably."[47] That the evident rapprochement between China and the USSR can advance much further seems unlikely, however, in view of Soviet unwillingness to offer concessions on the points that the Chinese consider essential to

[45]Robert Scalapino, "The Political Influence of the USSR in Asia," in Donald Zagoria, ed., *Soviet Policy in East Asia* (New Haven, Conn.: Yale University Press, 1982), pp. 57–92, at p. 71. Scalapino finds three sets of objectives behind Soviet policy in Asia: to contain China, to vie with the United States for influence, and to project a "dual image" of a "revolutionary society and a developmental model" and at the same time "that of a responsible but formidable world power;" p. 64.

[46]See Leslie H. Gelb, "U.S.-China Ties: Lower Expectations," *New York Times,* 2 February 1983, p. 3.

[47]*New York Times,* 12 March 1985.

further improvement of relations: withdrawing Soviet forces from Afghanistan, reducing the size of Soviet standing forces on Chinese frontiers, and ceasing support for Vietnamese occupation of Cambodia.[48]

Despite Soviet signals of an interest in a solution to its quagmire in Afghanistan, few experts expect the Soviet Union to find an acceptable solution in the near future. Through the United Nations, Soviet diplomats (indirectly, by speaking through their Afghan allies) negotiated with Pakistan to find a way of neutralizing Afghanistan and thus of withdrawing their 100,000 troops without having to fear the collapse of the Babrak Karmal regime and its replacement by an anti-Soviet Moslem government. To be sure, the Soviet Union appears to be overextended in the country, capable of controlling only the major cities and suffering significant levels of casualties. The current regime under Babrak Karmal, however, is fractured by internal dissension between its two factions, the Khalq and the Parcham, and is unlikely to be capable of ruling without major assistance from the Soviet Union.

The Afghan venture — the first commitment of Soviet forces since World War II to combat outside the European theater — has been interpreted in the light of both offensive and defensive motives. Most observers agree that direct intervention was the only means of saving the weak government of Hafizullah Amin, even though rescuing his government meant killing him in a palace shootout on December 27, 1979. Soon Soviet propaganda was calling him a CIA agent. The invasion also put the Soviet Union in a stronger position eventually to dominate or even occupy Iran, an outcome that could enable Moscow to control the strategic oil routes through the Persian Gulf.[49] Regardless of whether Afghanistan turns out to have been Russia's Vietnam, clearly the operation has been more costly and perhaps divisive than the Politburo calculated in 1979. Like the Cuban missile crisis of 1962 or the Berlin blockade of 1948–1949, perhaps the Afghan invasion will be resolved only by skillful negotiation combined with significant concessions.

[48]*New York Times,* 16 March 1985.

[49]See Vernon V. Aspaturian, "Moscow's Afghan Gamble," *The New Leader,* 28 January 1980, pp. 7–13; for background to the invasion, see Anthony Arnold, *Afghanistan* (Stanford, Calif.: Hoover Institution Press, 1981.)

Neither the military aid given to the Soviet Union's Middle Eastern allies nor military pressure of the type directed toward Japan has been wholly successful in influencing the politics of the states that neighbor the Soviet Union. Soviet protests did not deter Japan from slightly increasing its defense spending (which remains, however, near the benchmark of one percent of its growing GNP), nor did a stream of military equipment and advisers prevent President Sadat of Egypt from realigning his country with the United States in 1972. The destruction of an unarmed civilian KAL airliner over Sakhalin Island on September 1, 1983, and the repeated overflights of Japanese territory in October–November 1984 by Soviet bombers showed the limits of Moscow's means for cultivating Japanese public opinion and its continuing reliance on heavy-handed tactics of intimidation. Soviet foreign policy seeks opportunities for the expansion of Soviet influence and strengthens the effect of diplomatic and propaganda instruments by a steady and substantial increase in its military power. Despite the slowdown in Soviet economic growth in the late 1970s and early 1980s, the Soviet Union has acquired parity with, and in some areas superiority to, American military power over the period since the mid-1960s. At that time defense spending entered a phase of sustained growth, averaging perhaps 4–5 percent between 1965 and 1976 and perhaps 2–3 percent per year since then. The challenge for the Soviet Union has been to convert its vast nuclear and conventional force into commensurate political power. The fragmentation of the PLO following Israel's invasion of Lebanon in 1982 and the failure of Soviet efforts to cultivate Iran in its long war with Iraq demonstrated, as did the Camp David agreements between Egypt and Israel, that the Soviet Union did not participate in the main arena of Middle Eastern peace or war except as a supplier of arms to its Arab clients. The lack of success with which Syria and the PLO performed against Israel in 1982 prompted the Soviets to issue an unusually defensive statement to the effect that, contrary to rumor, the arms provided to its allies were not second-rate in quality.

Where possible, the Soviet Union has avoided direct military involvement in Third World countries, preferring instead to use proxy forces, often Cubans and East Germans. Such is the case with Soviet support for Marxist-Leninist forces in the former Portuguese colonies of Angola and Mozambique and for insurgencies in Central America. The aim of such activity is to undermine and eliminate American influence and to establish footholds for the further growth of Soviet influence. There is no question but that the Soviet Union has responded to political opportunities that local instability or power vacuums — such as the collapse of the Portuguese empire in Africa following the military coup in Lisbon in 1975 — have presented to it. Whenever local conditions generate movements hostile to capitalism, the USSR seeks to turn these conditions to its advantage and to draw revolutionary movements under its wing once they have become significant forces or, better still, have achieved power.

It is important to remember, however, that it is the enormous difficulties confronting less developed countries, far more than Soviet politico-military activity, that produce the political turmoil exploited by Soviet policy. As long as problems generated by the vulnerability and instability of developing nations remain acute, the relatively wealthy industrial societies will face difficult choices, requiring not only the will to utilize economic and, if necessary, military power under certain circumstances to counter Soviet expansionism but also patience, knowledge, skill, and sympathetic understanding of customs different from their own. A Western policy that assumes that the Third World's ills result mainly from communist plots and propaganda will be worse than futile. It may drive people whose values, at least in the early stages of their struggle for justice and well-being, resemble those of Western democracies into the arms of communist states. These states may appear more aware of and receptive to the needs of contemporary reform, not to mention revolutionary movements, in poor underdeveloped countries than are the political elites and governments of relatively rich industrialized democracies.[50] An important point, often overlooked, is that the official Moscow-oriented communist parties, perhaps especially in Latin America, have often been far less radical and less enthusiastic about early revolutionary action than have movements such as Fidel Castro's in Cuba or that of

[50]In the case of the United States, both the difficulties of devising an effective policy responsive to the needs of Central American nations for economic development and social justice and the consequences of the policy, including revolutionary movements seeking aid from communist states, are among the subjects of Walter Lafeber's study, *Inevitable Revolutions: The United States in Central America* (New York: Norton, 1983).

the Nicaraguan Sandinistas.[51] The foregoing should not be construed as advocacy of indiscriminate granting of funds to the governments of underdeveloped countries. Aid money has too often found its way to the pockets of corrupt officials. Wherever possible, aid should be granted, preferably by nongovernmental organizations, to small businesses for carefully supervised projects that will help to strengthen the development of an indigenous middle class, thus indirectly promoting the growth of democratically inclined elements.

There is a growing body of evidence indicating the emergence in the Soviet Union, especially among some Soviet experts professionally engaged in analyzing the economies and political systems of less developed countries, of pragmatic modernizers who seek to introduce new ideological formulations for explaining trends in the Third World. Sympathetic to the need in developing countries for extensive institutional reform, the members of this new group may be seen as relatively realistic and more aware than their orthodox colleagues of the difficulties in Soviet relations with the Third World; they are even willing to recognize conflicts of interest between the Soviet bloc and underdeveloped countries.[52]

Dealing with Western policy toward both Third World countries and the USSR poses supremely difficult problems because of the combination of vast power and a strange mixture of inferiority and superiority complexes. Such policy must combine hardheaded realism with a search for cooperation on issues and problems when and if it can be negotiated.

---

[51]See, for example, Stephen Kinzer, "Marxist's Mission: Defeat Sandinistas," *New York Times,* 7 October 1984, reporting expression of a "sense of betrayal" on the part of a Moscow-oriented Nicaraguan communist because Moscow "opportunistically" ordered his party in 1979 to join the Sandinista Front, obviously because the Soviets thought it had the best chance to gain power.

[52]On this trend toward realism and pragmatism in Soviet thinking about socialist relations with less developed nations, see Valkenier, *Soviet Union and the Third World,* ch. 4, "The New International Economic Order: The Parting of the Ways."

CHAPTER XII

Gorbachev and the Soviet Future

KONSTANTIN CHERNENKO, fifth general secretary of the Central Committee of the CPSU and sixth of the men who have headed the party, died on March 10, 1985.[1] Andrei Gromyko, Politburo member since 1973 and from 1957 until July 1985 Soviet minister of foreign affairs, nominated Mikhail Sergeievich Gorbachev as Chernenko's successor, a motion that was adopted unanimously. The fact that Gromyko was chosen by the Politburo to nominate Gorbachev can probably be seen as evidence of his stature in an era when foreign affairs — particularly the complex and tense state of relations between the USSR and states dominated by or associated with it, the United States, and its NATO allies — had become more important than ever. More important, it showed support for Gorbachev by the surviving members of the Politburo whose careers began under Stalin and Brezhnev. It also indirectly called attention to the fact that although Gorbachev had given proof during his rapid rise to the top that he was a fast learner, nevertheless, despite a number of journeys to Asian and Western nations (including a highly successful one to Britain in December 1984), his mastery of foreign affairs was still considerably more limited than his experience in general party affairs and particularly in agriculture and the economy generally.[2]

---

[1]*Pravda,* 12 March 1985.

[2]For biographical information on Gorbachev, including data on his relations with figures such as Fedor Kulakov, his predecessor as Central Committee agriculture secretary; Mikhail Suslov, top-level Central Committee ideological expert; and Yuri Andropov, who played an important part in smoothing Gorbachev's path to power, see Harry Gelman, *The Brezhnev Politburo and the De-*

Important aspects of Gorbachev's political personality and experience justify the widespread view that his selection as general secretary was an event of unusual significance. Indeed, it could turn out to have been the most important event in Soviet politics since the death of Stalin. After the debilitating effects of the years after 1977 when Brezhnev lost physical and intellectual vigor and the uncertainty and embarrassment generated by Andropov's and Chernenko's frequent inability to perform their leadership functions effectively because of poor health (information about which was largely concealed by the Soviet authorities from the Soviet and foreign publics), not to mention the extraordinary brevity of each man's tenure in office, a healthy, vigorous Gorbachev might well herald a period of energy, stability, and substantive achievement that had long been lacking in the Soviet leadership. At 54, Gorbachev was 4 years younger than Brezhnev had been when he became general secretary in 1964. His other assets included health, energy, and a span of political experience as a line party secretary in the tradition that had produced previous general secretaries Stalin, Khrushchev, Brezhnev, Andropov, and Chernenko. Gorbachev was also free of the shadow of long years of service under Stalin's terror-ridden regime, and hence seemingly free of complicity in the liquidation of colleagues and competitors and of other acts common in Stalin's Russia.

Though like his predecessors at the apex of the Soviet system, Gorbachev's claim to leadership is based primarily on experience in party secretaryships, and he also shares Russian nationality with all top leaders excepting Stalin, he differs, as the leading British expert on Soviet affairs, Archie Brown, points out, in several respects. Perhaps the most important of these is the fact that "no one before Gorbachev has become top leader as the youngest

cline of Detente (Ithaca, N.Y.: Cornell University Press, 1984); Alexander G. Rahr, *A Biographical Directory of 100 Leading Soviet Officials* (Munich: Radio Liberty, RFE/RL, 1984); "Vashe mnenie o novom genseke" (Your opinion of the new general secretary), *Posev,* no. 4 (Frankfurt/Main: April 1984): 18–27, containing interviews with A. Avtorkhanov, Georgi Vladimov et al. on the significance of Gorbachev's accession to power; Serge Schmemann, "The Emergence of Gorbachev," *New York Times Magazine,* 3 March 1985, pp. 40–57; "Ready, Steady Gorbachev," *Economist* (London), 27 April 1985; John Löwenhardt, *The Soviet Politburo,* trans. Dymphna Clark (New York: St. Martin's Press, 1982); Archie Brown, "Gorbachev: New Man in the Kremlin," *Problems of Communism* 34, no. 3 (May–June 1985): 1–23.

member of both the Politburo and Central Committee Secretariat.''[3] Gorbachev's attributes and past record may afford some comfort to his fellow members of the Soviet nomenklatura and to some extent to the Soviet people, who might a few years from now enjoy a higher standard of living if Gorbachev can reform the sluggish Soviet economy. For the West, however, particularly the United States, the outlook is less hopeful in view of a series of harshly anti-American statements made by Gorbachev during his first two months in office.[4]

[3]Archie Brown, "Gorbachev: New Man in the Kremlin," p. 3. As of late August 1985, all full and candidate Politburo members and new Central Committee secretaries continued to be older than Gorbachev, though some, such as the 57-year-old Eduard Shevardnadze, were only slightly older than the new general secretary. Brown presents many interesting details on Gorbachev's family background — such as his statement that "both his parents and grandparents were peasants" — and on his relationship to rising figures such as Ryzhkov and Ligachev, Andropov and Chernenko, and on his personal attributes and policy inclinations. He is cautiously optimistic about the prospects for significant economic reform under Gorbachev, but also asserts that "to attempt to foist upon him notions of pluralistic democracy would be wrong and misleading." See pp. 9 and 21, respectively. Brown's portrait of Gorbachev is based partly on interviews with persons who met Gorbachev on his 1984 visit to Britain and partly on an article by Zdenek Mlynar, a former Czechoslovak reform leader who knew Gorbachev at the Moscow University Law Faculty. Brown depicts Gorbachev as a politician with charm laced with determination who is anxious to introduce reforms compatible with Soviet doctrine and institutions. Without rejecting this image, we are also struck by the persistence of less attractive features of Soviet political life since Gorbachev's accession to power, such as continued persecution of dissenters, including the members of unofficial peace groups, the extolling of Stalin's methods of pressuring workers for ever-higher output norms reflected in the campaign surrounding the fiftieth anniversary of the birth of the Stakhanovite movement, and the evident requirement that professionals in all fields of endeavor echo Gorbachev's call for "intensification" of economic development. An example of the latter is a lengthy article by the chief director of the Moscow Komsomol Theater, Mark Zakharov, on economic problems of the theater; this is followed by an editorial note requesting that directors, actors, playwrights and audiences join in a discussion of "new economic incentives" in the theater, which, it explained, are needed just as much in the arts as in science and technology. See Mark Zakharov, "Aplodismenty ne deliatsia" (Applause Is Not Divided), *Literaturnaya gazeta,* 31 July 1985, p. 8.

[4]In probably the most important statement of Gorbachev's first two months as general secretary, his report to the April 23, 1985, party plenum, he asserted that imperialism was to blame for the "alarming and dangerous" state of world affairs, for which he also asserted that the "governing circles" of the United States bore prime responsibility. Text in *Pravda,* April 24, 1985. It is also highly significant that in the same speech, Gorbachev included a paragraph accusing imperialism of having in recent years intensified its "subversive work" against socialist countries. Since Soviet officials and the censored official Soviet press frequently accuse dissidents and protesters of being agents of foreign intelligence

One factor in Gorbachev's unusually rapid rise to power seems to have been a series of lucky breaks. There can be little doubt, however, of the greater importance of his ability — the product of shrewdness, tact, ambition, and energy — to capitalize on good fortune. It is known that three powerful Politburo members who had close ties with the important Stravropol grain and livestock region where Gorbachev in a 22 year period of Komsomol and party work laid the foundations of his eminence, made significant contributions to his success. The first, chronologically, was Fedor Kulakov, who as head of the Stavropol regional party organization and later as a Politburo member with his power base in the Stavropol area, facilitated Gorbachev's rise to the top of the Stavropol party unit. His death at an early age in 1978 paved the way for Gorbachev's replacing Kulakov as Central Committee secretary with responsibility for agriculture. It is impressive that in spite of the poor performance of Soviet agriculture during the years after 1978 while Gorbachev was in charge of this increasingly crucial sector, neither his physical nor his political health seems to have suffered. Mikhail Suslov, for years the leading figure in the Soviet ideological realm, appears also to have had a hand in promoting Gorbachev's progress. According to Serge Schmemann in a *New York Times Magazine* article, "probably the most significant aspect of Gorbachev's 22 year service in Stavropol" was "the patronage of Mikhail A. Suslov, the powerful ideologue and kingmaker in Brezhnev's Kremlin, whose power base was in Stavropol." "One sign of special favor," notes Schmemann, was

---

services, Gorbachev's statement warning about the danger of foreign subversive activity may have been a veiled attack on Soviet dissidents and their alleged foreign masters, or it may have constituted a rebuff to Westerners who have expressed the view that one way for the USSR to demonstrate its desire to restore détente would be to ease the plight of Soviet dissidents and would-be emigrants. While as of mid-August, 1985, Gorbachev had not undertaken any significant measures of this kind, it is interesting that Julia Wishnevsky, Radio Liberty's expert on dissent in the USSR, pointed out that although Gorbachev is considered to have been a protégé of Andropov, there might be at least some grounds to hope that because Gorbachev brought to his new eminence "a remarkably clean record," he would be "glad to use the emigration of Jews and dissidents as a bargaining chip in securing closer trade relations with the West." Letting Sakharov and his wife emigrate, for example, would be an effective good will gesture. See Wishnevsky, "Dissent under Three Soviet Leaders: Suppression Continues, the Style Changes," RL Research Bulletin, 27 March 1985. Wishnevsky devotes most of this study to Brezhnev, Andropov, and Chernenko, emphasizing Andropov's particularly fierce policies against dissenters.

Gorbachev's direct election to full Central Committee membership, enabling him to skip the usual stage of candidate status.[5]
Suslov's favorable attitude toward Gorbachev of course does not
necessarily mean that the latter fully shared the former's predi-
lection for coercion and guile or his responsibility for political operations that helped create Suslov's sinister reputation. It should
be remembered that Khrushchev, for example, though he had
been a trusted lieutenant of Stalin, was able once he consolidated
his power to become a significant force for reform, though this
was a major factor in his downfall. Still, in pondering possible
formative influences on Gorbachev's political personality, it would
be imprudent to overlook the reputations of mentors such as Suslov and Andropov for toughness and cunning. Suslov, for example, played a leading role in such operations as the dissolution
of the Kalmyk republic and the deportation of the Kalmyk people
to Central Asia in 1943. Similarly, he oversaw the pacification of
Lithuania in 1944–46, which entailed mass executions, deportations, and agricultural collectivization.[6]

As for Andropov, to a considerable extent he must be credited
with the making of Gorbachev. Although Andropov's period of
leadership was marred by, among other events, the Soviet shooting down of a Korean Airlines passenger jet with a loss of 269
persons in September 1983, Soviet suspension of U.S.-Soviet arms
control negotiations, and the fiercest campaign against all forms
of dissent and unorthodox opinion in the post-Stalin history of the
USSR, nevertheless, as one leading Kremlinologist asserted, the
"advent of Andropov to the General Secretaryship apparently enhanced, at least to some degree, the personal position of certain
individuals who have long seemed exceptionally moderate in the
Soviet context and who probably all along privately desired that
improvement of relations with the United States be given a priority higher than the consensus of the Brezhnev Politburo thought
appropriate."[7] Gorbachev benefited greatly by the replacement
under Andropov of one-fifth of the regional party first secretaries

---

[5]Schmemann, "The Emergence of Gorbachev."

[6]On Suslov's role in these events, see Löwenhardt, *The Soviet Politburo*, p. 130.

[7]See Gelman, *The Brezhnev Politburo*, p. 215, mentioning, as examples, Yuri
Arbatov, Alexander Bovin, and Fedor Burlatsky. Gelman, however, is skeptical
about the likelihood that such elements will enjoy increased influence in the foreseeable future.

and nine of the twenty-three Central Committee department heads. According to Schmemann, "as Andropov's health deteriorated, Gorbachev's role expanded, until at the end, he was the sole link between the dying leader and the party hierarchy."[8] Perhaps even more important were the changes in the Politburo under Andropov, involving promotion to candidate Politburo membership of three Andropov choices, Viktor Chebrikov, whom Andropov named Chairman of the KGB almost immediately after becoming general secretary and made a candidate member of the Politburo in 1983; Egor Ligachev, who appears to have been even more a client of Gorbachev than of Andropov and who in 1983 became chief of the very important Central Committee Department of Party Organizational Work (if Gorbachev feels it necessary to launch a purge, Ligachev presumably would be his main assistant in the operation); Nikolai Ryzhkov, only two years older than Gorbachev, who became chief of the Central Committee's Economic Department.[9]

The promotion of all three of the above men to full Politburo membership at Gorbachev's April 1985 plenum not only significantly reduced the influence of the remaining "Brezhnevites" in the Politburo but also added considerably to Gorbachev's influence. Other full Politburo members, who as of the April 1985 plenum had reached that level since Brezhnev's death, include the only full member from the Caucasus, the Azeri Geidar Aliev, elected in 1983 under Andropov and, like Andropov, experienced in both party and KGB work; Mikhail Solomentsev, Chairman of the CPSU Committee for Party Control since the death of Arvid Pelshe in 1983; and Vitali Vorotnikov, characterized by Rahr as an industrial specialist who was "evidently Andropov's man" in the Politburo, of which he became a full member in 1983. Gorbachev also named three new Central Committee secretaries in his first four months: Viktor Nikonov to oversee agricultural policy; Boris Yeltsin, who was also named head of the Construction

[8]Schmemann, "Emergence of Andropov," p. 56. Schmemann here also asserts, as seems to be confirmed by all available evidence, that "Gorbachev emerged" — from the process of replacing Andropov with Chernenko as general secretary — as "the effective second in command, with more responsibility than any previous leader in a similar position."

[9]A full list of Politburo and Secretariat members will be found in the Appendix.

Department of the Central Committee apparatus; and Lev Zaikov, formerly first secretary of the Leningrad party committee.

More dramatic than these changes was the fall of Grigori Romanov, who had been a Politburo member since 1976, and until June 1983, when Andropov made him a Central Committee secretary, the long-time first secretary of the Leningrad party organization. Many considered Romanov a possible successor to the post of general secretary and therefore a rival to Gorbachev. After the Lenin birthday observance in April 1985, however, Romanov disappeared from public view until the startling announcement, on 1 July 1985, that his request for retirement for health reasons had been granted — language that has become customary in reporting the political demise of Soviet leaders, especially if they are not to be granted honors upon their retirement.[10]

What caused the elimination of the man who as a full member of the Politburo and Secretariat during the period of Chernenko's leadership had performed the very important function of riding herd over military affairs? In part, Romanov's fall can plausibly be attributed to personal characteristics and to behavior that struck a dissonant note under a leadership that valued sobriety along with efficiency and serious-mindedness. Everything known to foreigners about Romanov indicated that he was a tough, hard-driving, and hard-drinking party boss. It is perhaps not entirely fanciful to speculate that Gorbachev's antialcoholism campaign was inaugurated, in part, to justify Romanov's removal. Romanov's ouster also may have been motivated by an imperious new leader's desire to remove a potential threat to his own power and the fulfillment of his ambitious and far-reaching policy goals. Also, reports after Romanov's fall in a number of leading Western press organs suggested that the innovating and relatively outspoken Soviet Marshal Nikolai Ogarkov had been "rehabilitated" and appointed to a new high military post after a period of apparent disgrace that had been due in part, according to these reports, to action taken by Romanov against Ogarkov. Romanov may have unwisely used his influence against one of the USSR's most talented military leaders — and suffered a heavy pen-

---

[10]The sole breach in Romanov's lengthy disappearance was the publication of his name among the signatories of an obituary for Marshal Kirill Moskalenko. See *Pravda,* 19 June 1985.

alty therefore. Whatever may have been the reason for this star-tling development, there is no doubt that its outcome seems to have left Gorbachev vastly strengthened.[11]

Perhaps equally impressive as evidence of Gorbachev's power and possibly of even greater potential significance, especially in the area of foreign policy, was Gorbachev's replacement of Gro-myko as Minister of Foreign Affairs by Eduard Shevardnadze with the simultaneous transfer of Gromyko to the symbolically impor-tant post of Chairman of the Presidium of the Supreme Soviet. At the CPSU Plenum immediately preceding the Supreme Soviet session of early July, Shevardnadze became a full Politburo mem-ber.

These moves surprised Western specialists, who expected that Gorbachev would follow the example of previous general secre-taries, beginning in 1977 with Brezhnev, by assuming the post of head of the Supreme Soviet chairmanship. It was also a stunning move because, despite the nominal honor it gave Gromyko — who after all had helped Gorbachev by delivering a strong speech nominating him as general secretary — it also deprived him of much of his power by removing him from operational control of foreign policy. Among the possible explanations of these displays of Gorbachev's power, the following are perhaps among the most plausible. The removal of Gromyko as foreign minister would en-able Gorbachev, with some assistance from Shevardnadze as well as Gromyko, still evidently a Politburo member in good standing, gradually to become the dominant figure in foreign policy mak-

---

[11]See, for example, Hedrick Smith, "Shuffle in the Soviet Military Under Way," *New York Times,* 19 July 1985. Smith reported that according to "reliable information" reaching Washington, Ogarkov was slated to replace Marshal Vik-tor Kulikov as Warsaw Pact forces commander and, among other things, that Ogarkov had for some time been advocating "more spending on high technology and conventional forces" and had "opposed a nuclear buildup." Smith also cited such leading Sovietologists as Arnold Horelick of the Rand Corporation and Pro-fessor Thane Gustafson of Georgetown University as agreeing that Ogarkov and Mikhail Gorbachev "seemed to have common views on the need for high tech-nology." Articles in *Novoe russkoe slovo* (The New Russian Word), a New York Russian-language daily, reported assertions by the Soviet affairs analyst Albert Weeks to the effect that Grigori Romanov, allegedly a close friend of the late Soviet Defense Minister Dmitri Ustinov, helped arrange the removal of Ogarkov from his post as Chief of the Soviet General Staff in 1984. See "Chto proizoshlo s Grigoriem Romanovym?" (What Happened to Grigori Romanov?), *Novoe rus-skoe slovo,* 22 June 1985; and "Zakat Grigoriya Romanova" (The Fall of Grigori Romanov), *Novoe russkoe slovo,* 2 July 1985.

ing. Moreover, as one American correspondent in Moscow speculated, Shevardnadze's debut might "be the capstone of a major Soviet effort . . . to project a more open public image."[12]

Without denying the charm of "Easy Ed," as Thatcher dubbed Shevardnadze, it is well to recall that his career included seven years in his native Georgia as minister of internal affairs (i.e., chief of police) and that he was also associated with an important Soviet "front" organization, the Afro-Asian Solidarity Committee. While head of the Georgian party organization, he displayed a combination of firmness and flexibility in the management of public opinion, and contributed substantially to the application of public opinion polls and other social science techniques to guiding public opinion. It is possible to speculate that Shevardnadze's background and attributes would make him useful in conducting a foreign policy emphasizing, more than did Gromyko, an all-out effort to isolate the United States from its NATO allies, and also one that would seek to play on sources of Third World animosity toward the West — the whole being presented as an effort to promote fear of the war-like potential of "imperialism" and the exploitation of worldwide yearnings for peace and for social justice.

It is also noteworthy that the elevation of Shevardnadze to full membership in the Politburo, and his appointment as foreign minister, increased the visibility of the non-Russian membership of the ruling elite. As of the July 1985 Central Committee Plenum, five of the thirteen full members of the Politburo were non-Russians: the Azeri Aliev, the Kazakh Kunayev, the Ukrainians Shcherbitsky and Tikhonov, and the Georgian Shevardnadze. In addition, full member Vorotnikov is sometimes identified in Soviet sources as Ukrainian, sometimes as Russian.

On the whole, it appears that Gorbachev partly inherited from Andropov and partly formed by his own efforts a strong leadership team. Together with his record as a party executive, his demonstrated political skills and effective personality, and also his unusually good education by comparison with previous general

[12]Gary Thatcher, "Shevardnadze's Style is Easy and Open," *Christian Science Monitor*, 2 August 1985, pp. 9–10. Thatcher quoted positive statements about Shevardnadze by the British and West German foreign ministers and reported apparent Soviet efforts since Shevardnadze's appointment indicating an effort to convince world public opinion of Soviet flexibility in arms negotiations in the face of "American truculence."

secretaries (with a degree from the law faculty of Moscow State University in 1955 and one in agricultural economics in 1967), this bodes well for his future prospects as the USSR's seventh party leader. Moreover, Gorbachev's skills in political maneuvering were highly impressive, as the new leader moved quickly to replace incumbents and fill vacancies in senior party and government posts at central and provincial levels. By the end of July 1985, less than five months after his election as general secretary, Gorbachev had brought about an exceptionally large turnover in the Soviet party and government leadership. Besides the four voting members of the Politburo who had been added and the one removed and the three new Central Committee secretaries, five department heads in the Central Committee apparatus had been named, along with nine government ministers, eleven ambassadors, and eighteen province-level party first secretaries. In addition, there were significant shifts in senior military posts.[13] Moreover, it seemed likely that a further set of changes, perhaps even more sweeping than these, would occur at the time of the Twenty-seventh Party Congress, scheduled for February 1986, when a new Central Committee will be elected.[14]

While moving fast to consolidate power and establish their legitimacy, Gorbachev and his lieutenants have expressed sharp dissatisfaction with the performance of the Soviet economy as well as confidence that a newly energized party-state machine could cope with mounting problems at home and abroad. In the first two and a half months of Gorbachev's leadership the focus was mainly on simultaneously readying the party and the country for the Twenty-seventh CPSU Congress to be held in February 1986, and on taking the first steps toward preparing an agenda for urgently needed programs to reorganize agriculture and industry. Like Andropov but unlike the complacent, enfeebled Brezhnev of the late 1970s and the early 1980s, Gorbachev in his April plenum speech presented a long list of defects in economic performance, ranging from waste of resources by ministries and enterprises to more serious matters such as the fact that the "productive ap-

---

[13]These changes are enumerated in Alexander Rahr, "Personnel Changes since Gorbachev Came to Power," RL Research Bulletin 243/85 (30 July 1985).

[14]See Terry McNeill, "Gorbachev Strengthens His Hold," RL Research Bulletin 134/85 (26 April 1985).

paratus of the country had seriously aged" and must be replaced, beginning in 1986, by "a new generation of machines and equipment." He demanded "revolutionary" changes and the discipline necessary to achieve them. To be sure, Gorbachev's approach was more hortatory than specific. Still, his address did touch on most of the problems that both reform-minded Soviet economists and sociologists and Western analysts of the Soviet economy and society have identified, such as lack of sufficient autonomy for industrial managers, work collectives, and scientists to generate a high level of initiative, efficiency, and innovation.[15]

Will Gorbachev seriously attempt to fundamentally reform the Soviet economy? There are statements in his April plenum address indicating that he will, enormous though the effort obviously will be and discouraging though the record of previous attempts has been, as we have pointed out in our chapters on

[15]It is interesting to compare the defects in Soviet economic performance and the remedies Gorbachev recommended with, for example, the cogent and succinct discussion in Ed. A. Hewett, *Energy, Economics, and Foreign Policy in the Soviet Union* (Washington, D.C.: Brookings Institution, 1984), ch. 1, "Overview," esp. pp. 7–8 and 15–23. Hewett finds Soviet leaders in an economic bind: having profited from the high price of energy, exports of which had in the late 1970s and early 1980s helped to pay for food imports, they have faced, since about 1981, difficult, unpleasant choices. Among these are whether to cut subsidized energy supplies to Eastern Europe and run the risk of further worsening the economic situation there, possibly leading to "serious political instabilities in the region," or whether to respond to "lower energy-supply growth rates by reducing exports for hard currency," which, he says, "would considerably reduce Soviet capabilities to import food, capital goods, and intermediate products. . . . " He sees little hope for improved economic performance until Soviet leaders "increase enterprise autonomy — simultaneously increasing pressure on enterprises to make profits — and revive the price system as a useful guide to social costs and benefits." This, he notes, "is what the Hungarians are doing."

On the background to an extensive debate that went on in the USSR from the late 1960s to the adoption in 1983 of a law on plant work collectives, see Maria Huber, *Betriebliche Sozialplanung und Partizipation in der UdSSR* (Enterprise Social Planning and Participation in the USSR) (Frankfurt/Main: Campus Verlag, 1983). The 1983 law was, as a Radio Liberty researcher has pointed out, "formulated in such a way as to allow managers to circumvent or ignore its provisions if they so wished." See Elizabeth Teague, "Gorbachev Criticizes Implementation of USSR Law on Work Collectives," RL 88/85, 19 March 1985. Teague criticizes Gorbachev, in remarks he made in December 1984, before he became CPSU general secretary, for failing to take account of the crippling effect of the loose drafting of a law ostensibly intended to enhance the rights of workers to participate in production decisions. Interestingly, Gorbachev included remarks to which Teague's criticism seems to be applicable in his April 1986 plenum address.

policy formation and policy implementation. Perhaps the clearest indication is his reference in the April plenum address to efforts begun in 1983 but not completed, said Gorbachev, probably with Chernenko in mind, to "somewhat improve the situation" of the economy. So important was this effort, asserted Gorbachev, that "the historical destiny of our country, the position of socialism in the contemporary world depend in large measure on how we conduct matters henceforth." To listeners familiar with the speeches of Joseph Stalin, this assertion may have stirred memories of Stalin's warning, in his famous speech to Soviet economic leaders in 1931 (quoted in Chapter X), of the dire consequences of failing to catch up economically with the capitalist world. In assessing the probabilities that Gorbachev might go significantly beyond tinkering with the economy, beyond further muddling through, it may be useful to look briefly at his previous record and experience as an economic policymaker. Terry McNeill, one of whose analyses of Gorbachev's potential was cited earlier, pointed out in an earlier study the important fact that Gorbachev had never publicly said that he favored a radical restructuring of the Soviet economy. His emphasis has been more on "streamlining and optimizing the functioning of the present system."[16] On balance, we are inclined to accept this appraisal as it applies to industry but not as applied to agriculture. During the period of "panic" (McNeill's word) in the Kremlin caused by President Carter's grain embargo, Gorbachev attempted unsuccessfully to institute a "mini-NEP," "in effect exempting farming from the dictates of central planning," as McNeill, perhaps with some exaggeration, asserts. He also, at least in his former Stavropol bailiwick, went far in experimenting with policies that encouraged use of the link system ("link" is the English translation of the term *zveno*, referring to a small and relatively autonomous farm work team). Previous experiments had proved the link system to be effective but objectionable to most party bureaucrats because it reduces party and government control over collective farmers. Even Andropov, though obviously favorably disposed toward Gorbachev's experimental approach, did not permit him to extend the experiment outside the Stavropol area, and Gorbachev felt constrained

[16]Terry McNeill, "Mikhail Gorbachev — Just Another *Apparatchik?*" RL 464/84, December 1984, pp. 13, 18.

while he was serving as number two man to General Secretary Konstantin Chernenko.[17]

It may also be instructive to compare Gorbachev's early economic policies with the economic reforms being undertaken in China, where entrepreneurs have been given wide scope to exercise private initiative. By contrast with the leadership of Deng Xiaoping, that of Gorbachev seems considerably less bold, at least so far, in exposing managers, workers and farmers to the benefits and risks of a Western-style market economy. Moreover, current Soviet writing on the Chinese experiments has been overwhelmingly hostile.[18]

Nonetheless, it would be unwise to minimize the significance of the modest initiatives Gorbachev has launched in the economic sphere. Some indication of the new leader's priorities in economic policy was provided by visits he paid on April 16 and 17, 1985, to the Likhachev automotive plant in Moscow and, in the same district of the city, to a school, a retail store, a hospital, and a young couple's apartment. After the highly publicized factory visits of Andropov and Chernenko shortly after their rise to the leadership, the first call might have been considered obligatory. At the auto plant, he emphasized, as in each speech, the importance of stepping up scientific-technical progress, addressing such points as reconstruction of machinery, introduction of new models, use of better incentives such as rewarding long job tenure with extra pay, and the problem of production quality. The latter visits, however, suggested that Gorbachev sought to place problems of living standards and daily life of Soviet citizens near the top of his economic agenda. At the school, Gorbachev was reported to have discussed matters of curriculum with the teachers — reminding the public of his highly visible role in implementing the 1984 school reform — and stressed the importance of introducing computer education into the schoolroom. At the hospital, he discussed the sensitive subjects of the quality of health care, the availability of drugs and equipment, the levels of pay for health care personnel, and the need to improve the care of the ill with patients and medical staff. He also signaled his concern for two other areas of

---

[17]Ibid., pp. 10–12.

[18]See, for example, the nearly full-page article by Vladimir Kulikov, "Pekinskie zarisovki" (Peking Sketches), *Literaturnaya gazeta*, 31 July 1985, p. 14.

popular welfare, retail trade and housing, through his visits to a store and a private apartment. These visits indicated a change in the traditional priorities of Soviet politics.[19]

It appears highly probable that some time after the Twenty-seventh Congress Gorbachev will be in a position to institute some serious, even drastic economic reforms. Most of the Western economists qualified to forecast the future of Soviet economic policy believe that Gorbachev is unlikely to have achieved enough organizational consolidation or to have gained high enough stature as a leader to attempt the risky and even dangerous task of institutional reform. If, however, he is sufficiently convinced that this is necessary for the effective performance of the Soviet system and perhaps for its viability as a competitor in world affairs with the United States, and if he is willing to engage in the bruising political battles that reform may entail, he may move sooner than most anticipate. Gorbachev will of course have to choose carefully the timing of his forthcoming policy initiatives. If he waits too long, he may lose momentum and may eventually become another Brezhnev. If he moves too fast, he may experience a fate similar to Khrushchev's, or worse. Thus far he seems to have gained considerable momentum, but the policy he has enunciated in his speeches and in *Pravda* and other Soviet sources has seemed somewhat vague, eclectic, and contradictory. Stalinist notes, such as a campaign to revive the spirit of Stakhanovism, have been struck.[20] Also not encouraging to those inside and outside the USSR who may hope for a less harsh relationship between regime

[19]See "Vstrecha M. S. Gorbacheva s trudiashchimsia Proletarskogo raiona g. Moskvy" (Meeting of M. S. Gorbachev with the Toilers of the Proletarian district of Moscow), *Pravda,* 18 April 1985.

[20]See, for example, the lead editorial "Stakhanovskii pocherk" (The Stakhanovite Handwriting), *Pravada,* 19 May 1985. Another example of the publicity surrounding the Stakhanov anniversary is a long article by I. Vorozheikin, "Prodolzhaya slavnye traditsii: o pyatiletii stakhanovskogo dvizheniya," *Pravda,* 26 July 1985, linking Stakhanovism to contemporary "socialist emulation" campaigns. The article emphasized party leadership in socialist emulation so heavily as to make a reader suspect that this orthodox principle was in danger of being neglected. Stakhanov was the coal miner selected for outstanding performance to encourage miners and workers in general to exceed production norms. The reactionary aspect of the Stakhanov movement consisted in its potential for pressure on and exploitation of labor by management. Perhaps not much significance should be attributed to Gorbachev's use of a traditional mobilizational measure (Brezhnev also used it), but it is hardly compatible with the image of Gorbachev as a liberal reformer that his advent to power seemed to evoke in some Western circles.

and people, especially in the area of freedom of expression and organization, was an article on "The Rights on Man and the Ideological Struggle" in *Pravada*.[21]

A more positive indication of Kremlin concern about popular welfare was the announcement in mid-May 1985 that pay scales for scientific-technological workers were to be adjusted to strengthen "material and moral" incentives of such workers, both in industry and in scientific research establishments. It should be kept in mind, however, that Gorbachev himself (in his April plenum address, for example), has joined forces with those demanding that the practical application of scientific work be stressed, and this emphasis is not necessarily propitious for scientific progress. The same report on the last Politburo session meeting before May 15 also announced a modest increase in old-age and some other categories of benefits, including those for single mothers. It was noted that pensions below 60 rubles per month for "workers and employees and their families," which were to be raised — the amount of the increase was not reported — had not been increased in more than ten years.[22]

There have also been indications that the new leadership intends to expand worker participation, if not in the making, then at least in some manner in the implementation of economic policy. This is suggested by a spate of publicity demanding fuller implementation of the 1983 law on labor collectives.[23] The evidence

[21]V. Kudryavtsev, "Prava cheloveka i ideologicheskaia bor'ba," *Pravda,* 17 May 1985. Kudryavtsev attacked as slander of socialism the attitude of the United States toward human rights in the USSR. In societies where "socialist democracy" prevails, wrote the author, a leading commentator on legal matters, life demands, "organizational order, the strict observance of state and labor discipline, connected with the increasing complexity of the tasks of economic and social development and the course of the scientific and technological revolution." This sort of hard-line rhetoric, together with continued tough treatment of Andrei Sakharov and other dissidents, indicates determination to punish severely any behavior on the part of Soviet citizens that could be construed by the authorities as interfering with whatever policies the latter might regard as in the interests of the party and state. The official doctrine that rights are contingent on duties, stressed by Kudryavtsev, provides a rationale by which the authorities can expand or restrict rights at their convenience.

[22]See "V Politburo Ts.K. KPSS" (In the Politburo of the C. C. of the CPSU) *Pravda,* 15 May, 1985.

[23]See, for example, the lengthy article by B. Mochalov, entitled "Trudovoi kollektiv v upravlenii proizvodstvom" (The Labor Collective in the Management of Production), *Pravda,* 19 July 1985. The article cautiously endorsed the "collectivist" and "democratic" principles of production relations which Marx, ac-

cited, it seems to us, supports the assessment that Gorbachev's initial policies are attempting to strengthen both the powers of the central planners and those of the enterprises. Gorbachev has appeared to place his hopes in what the editors of the British weekly *The Economist* called "more whiz-kids, higher tech, smoother streamlining."[24]

In view of the persistent difficulties Soviet leaders have faced in ensuring the implementation of even the limited reorganizational measures that have been adopted over the last two decades, it is more than possible that the actual effect of Gorbachev's programs will amount to minor but beneficial operational adjustments rather than to risky fundamental innovations and reconstruction. If so, there may be a great deal of tightening of controls, of high pressure for intensified effort, saving of fuel and raw materials, crackdown upon crime, and so forth, but "leaving the fundamentals of the system untouched."[25]

Despite the agreement between the United States and Soviet

---

cording to the author, had set forth. Mochalov criticized the slow implementation of the new law. Although expressing satisfaction that more than 60 percent of workers in industry were enrolled in production brigades, Mochalov asserted that many executives remained unfamiliar with the law's provisions and hence still relied excessively on "administrative" methods. Mochalov stressed the importance of improving labor discipline as well as the "moral-psychological climate" of the collectives, and called for a type of managerial leadership that combined "one-person authority (*edinonachalie*) with broad participation by the workers in management." Despite the importance he assigned to collectivism, however, Mochalov's major point was the necessity of rewarding workers differentially. Those who perform best must receive superior material rewards, he argued: it is not sufficient that all members of the most productive enterprises be paid more than those of other collectives. Ways must be found to reward those individuals whose efforts are decisive in expediting the introduction of new technology while those who waste materials or electricity must be made to feel the effects in their pocketbooks. It is doubtless no accident that one month before Mochalov's article, the top echelon of Soviet media officials were summoned to Central Committee headquarters and instructed by Gorbachev to give "systematic airing" to "the work of the party organizations, labor collectives, soviets and economic organs, intended to intensify social production and disseminate advanced management experience." See "Vstrecha v Ts.K. KPSS" (Meeting in the Central Committee of the CPSU), *Pravda,* 19 June 1985.

[24]"The Gorbachev Effect . . . Won't Turn Russia into an Economic Superpower," *The Economist,* 3 August 1985, pp. 13–14.

[25]See Hewett, *Energy, Economics, and Foreign Policy,* pp. 22–23. Hewett warns his readers not to "underestimate the ability of the Soviets to muddle through in situations that appeared to require drastic action," but he also asserts that muddling through will be far more difficult in the future than in the past.

Union on a summit meeting between President Reagan and General Secretary Gorbachev to be held in Geneva in November 1985 (and which Gorbachev will precede with a meeting with French President Mitterrand), there appears little likelihood of an early agreement on arms control or other major issues. Mutual mistrust and intransigence on the part of both superpowers, together with harsh rhetoric, remained prominent in the U.S.-Soviet relationship. There were some positive notes in the relationship as well, however, including U.S. Secretary of Commerce Malcolm Baldridge's talks with Gorbachev and other Soviet officials in Moscow. According to Baldridge, "the main achievement had been to restore high-level trade contacts after a seven-year suspension."[26] Each side proclaimed a desire for improved relations yet expressed determination not to permit its adversary to achieve military superiority. The Soviet side, in particular, sought to convince the world that it was the true champion of peaceful coexistence and détente and that, as Gorbachev claimed in his address on the eve of the fortieth anniversary of the Soviet victory over Nazi Germany (Soviet Victory Day is celebrated on May 9, whereas May 8 is the date Germany surrendered to the Western allies), "American militarism is at the cutting edge of the threat of war to mankind."[27]

Soviet use for propaganda purposes of the different observances

[26]See Serge Schmemann, "Talks Aid U.S.-Soviet Trade," *New York Times,* 22 May 1985, pp. D-1, D-5. The same issue also reported renewed agreement on the sale of Pepsi-Cola in the USSR and Soviet Stolichnaya vodka in the United States.

[27]See Gorbachev's address, "Bessmertnyi podvig sovetskogo naroda" (The Immortal Feat of the Soviet People), *Pravda* and other Soviet newspapers, 9 May 1985. In the same address Gorbachev paid high tribute to the "gigantic work" of the State Defense Committee and the then general secretary of the party, Joseph Stalin; following Gorbachev's mention of Stalin, there was, the papers reporting Gorbachev's address noted, "prolonged applause." One of the main themes of Gorbachev's address was that just as the success of the USSR and its allies in World War II had shown that states with different social systems could act together to deal with a common threat, so today it was necessary and feasible to unite against the "common enemy," the threat of nuclear war. He also sharply criticized U.S. foreign policy, including "state terrorism" against Nicaragua and "undeclared war" in Afghanistan. He expressed confidence, however, that there were "completely realistic possibilities" to "restrain the forces of militarism" and to achieve peace. Among other things, he called for cooperation in the cause of peace between the "most varied social and political forces," beginning with a return to the détente [*razryadka*] of the 1970s.

by the United States and the Soviet Union of the fortieth anniversary of the war's end was indicated in Gorbachev's above-noted Victory Day address and also in a short commentary in *Literaturnaya gazeta* for May 15, by Fedor Burlatsky.[28]

The autumn of 1985 became a season of active public diplomacy by the two superpowers, offering some hope of eventual improvement in the U.S.-Soviet relationship. The new Soviet leadership took advantage of the opening of the United Nations General Assembly session in New York to publicize a major new strategic arms proposal presented by Foreign Minister Eduard Shevardnadze to President Reagan in a meeting on 27 September 1985. The first major counterproposal to the negotiating position tabled by the American delegation at the arms talks in Geneva, it was characterized by Secretary of State George Shultz as potentially constructive but also "deeply flawed and self-serving."[29] In particular, the Soviet proposal was apparently aimed at preventing the administration from carrying out its long-term program of research and development in strategic defenses, which observers agree represents the single greatest strategic issue dividing the two countries. Whether sufficient room for compromise on this and the other differences in the two sides' positions existed to permit an agreement was a matter over which informed opinion varied. It is possible that the initial bargaining postures of the two sides were being presented in such a way as to ensure the best possible outcome of a later compromise. In the period before the Reagan-Gorbachev summit meeting, both sides sought

[28]See Burlatsky, "Tsena 'peremiriya' " (The Cost of "Reconciliation"), *Literaturnaya gazeta*, 15 May 1985. Burlatsky contrasted Gorbachev's statements in his May Victory Day address expressing gratitude and respect for the valor of American, British, and French forces and for allied material aid during the war against Hitler's forces with Mr. Reagan's silence in his address at Strasbourg regarding "the role of the USSR in the struggle against the Hitlerite occupiers and the Japanese militarists." The reference to the Japanese is rather odd in view of the fact that the Soviet Union was involved in the war against Japan for only a few days. Burlatsky rejected Presidential Press Secretary Larry Speakes's complaint regarding the "tough speech" by Gorbachev — a reference to Gorbachev's expression of determination not to allow the "military balance" between the two countries to be broken — with the statement that "our country" [the USSR] "will not emulate the United States in its policy of confrontation, nor in the rhetoric of enmity." Burlatsky also, like Gorbachev a week earlier, accused the United States of appeasing the surviving elements of Nazi "revanchism" in Germany.

[29]*New York Times,* 15 October 1985.

to define the agenda of the meeting through widely publicized appeals to world opinion — Gorbachev, for example, through a lengthy interview with *Time* magazine in September and a visit to France in early October; President Reagan through an address to the United Nations General Assembly on 24 October 1985.[30] If these statements indicated that the two leaders remained far apart in their expectations about the agenda and significance of their meeting, there were grounds for hope in the fact that it was to be held and that other links between the two major ideological and power blocs were being restored.

As the deadlock in arms limitation negotiations continues, both sides have proceeded with the development of new types of weapons systems. As General William E. Odom pointed out in an informative and provocative article in the summer of 1985, United States and the USSR face a future of continuous competition in new weaponry, increasingly shaped by technological advances that threaten the security of each. Particularly interesting were Odom's assertions that increased Soviet-Western trade could foster rather than hinder the arms race, and that qualitative, though not quantitative, arms competition "is likely to make the use of nuclear weapons both less attractive militarily and less probable."[31] Still, significant progress in breaking the current impasse in arms negotiations between the two countries will require of both sides creativity and political will, as well as a shared recognition that the preservation of the world's security rests in their common power.

[30] *Time,* 9 September 1985. During his visit to France 2–5 October 1985, Gorbachev made an appeal to France and Britain for a separate agreement to reduce the number of European nuclear weapons. He ensured intense press coverage for his initiatives by holding, just before leaving for France, a press conference for French and Soviet correspondents on 30 September, which was broadcast in both France and the USSR, then, in France, addressing the French National Assembly, and finally, holding a news conference with President Mitterrand following his talks with the French leader. His deft and informed answers to a wide-ranging array of questions impressed Western audiences. See *Pravda,* 2 October 1985; *New York Times,* 5 October 1985; and *Wall Street Journal,* 7 October 1985.

[31] Lt. Gen. William E. Odom, "Soviet Force Posture: Dilemmas and Directions," *Problems of Communism,* v. 34, no. 4 (July–August 1985), pp. 1–14, esp. "Conclusions," pp. 12–14. Quotation on p. 13.

Organization of the Soviet Communist Party and Government

Chart 1 Integration of CPSU and Soviet Government (April 1954)

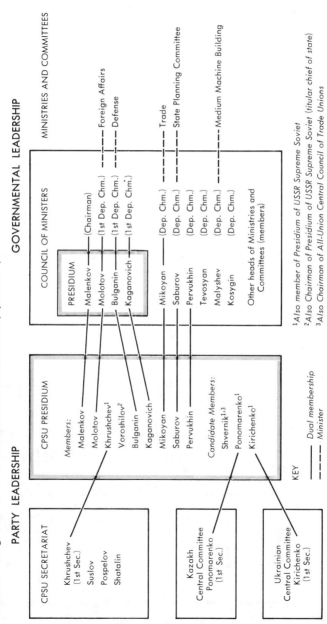

PARTY LEADERSHIP

GOVERNMENTAL LEADERSHIP

CPSU SECRETARIAT

Khrushchev
(1st Sec.)
Suslov
Pospelov
Shatalin

CPSU PRESIDIUM

Members:

Malenkov
Molotov
Khrushchev[1]
Voroshilov[2]
Bulganin
Kaganovich
Mikoyan
Saburov
Pervukhin

Candidate Members:

Shvernik[1,3]
Ponomarenko[1]
Kirichenko[1]

Kazakh
Central Committee
Ponomarenko
(1st Sec.)

Ukrainian
Central Committee
Kirichenko
(1st Sec.)

COUNCIL OF MINISTERS

PRESIDIUM

Malenkov — (Chairman)
Molotov — (1st Dep. Chm.) ---- Foreign Affairs
Bulganin — (1st Dep. Chm.) ---- Defense
Kaganovich — (1st Dep. Chm.)

Mikoyan — (Dep. Chm.) ---- Trade
Saburov — (Dep. Chm.) ---- State Planning Committee
Pervukhin — (Dep. Chm.)
Tevosyan — (Dep. Chm.)
Malyshev — (Dep. Chm.) ---- Medium Machine Building
Kosygin — (Dep. Chm.)

Other heads of Ministries and
Committees (members)

MINISTRIES AND COMMITTEES

[1] Also member of Presidium of USSR Supreme Soviet
[2] Also Chairman of Presidium of USSR Supreme Soviet (titular chief of state)
[3] Also Chairman of All-Union Central Council of Trade Unions

KEY

———— Dual membership
---- Minister

Chart 2 Interlocking Directorate—USSR Party and Government (May 1, 1962)

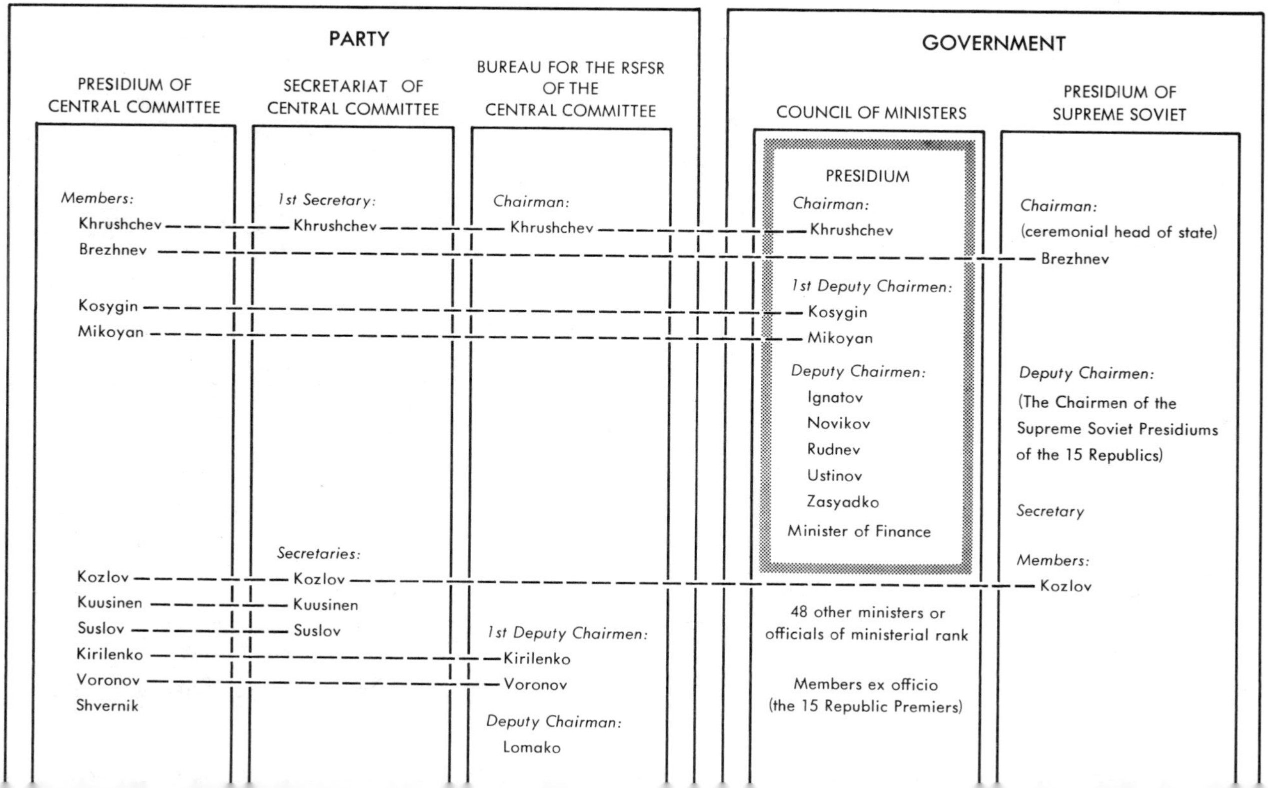

PARTY

PRESIDIUM OF CENTRAL COMMITTEE

Members:
Khrushchev
Brezhnev

Kosygin
Mikoyan

Kozlov
Kuusinen
Suslov
Kirilenko
Voronov
Shvernik

SECRETARIAT OF CENTRAL COMMITTEE

1st Secretary: Khrushchev

Secretaries:
Kozlov
Kuusinen
Suslov

BUREAU FOR THE RSFSR OF THE CENTRAL COMMITTEE

Chairman: Khrushchev

1st Deputy Chairmen:
Kirilenko
Voronov

Deputy Chairman:
Lomako

GOVERNMENT

COUNCIL OF MINISTERS

PRESIDIUM

Chairman: Khrushchev

1st Deputy Chairmen:
Kosygin
Mikoyan

Deputy Chairmen:
Ignatov
Novikov
Rudnev
Ustinov
Zasyadko
Minister of Finance

48 other ministers or officials of ministerial rank

Members ex officio
(the 15 Republic Premiers)

PRESIDIUM OF SUPREME SOVIET

Chairman: (ceremonial head of state)
Brezhnev

Deputy Chairmen:
(The Chairmen of the Supreme Soviet Presidiums of the 15 Republics)

Secretary:

Members:
Kozlov

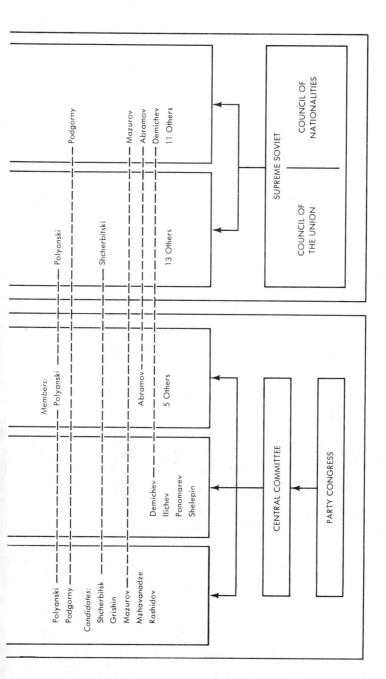

Members:

Polyanski — — — — — Polyanski — — — — — Polyanski — — — — — Polyanski — — — — — — Polyanski
Podgorny — Podgorny

Candidates:
Shcherbitsk — — — — Shcherbitski — — — Shcherbitski
Grishin
Mazurov — — — — — — — — — — — — — Mazurov — — — — — — — — — — — — — Mazurov
Mzhavanadze — — — — — — — — — — — — Abramov — — — — — — — — — — — — Abramov
Rashidov — — — — — — — — Demichev — — — — — — — — — — — — — — — — — — — Demichev
                        Ilichev
                        Ponomarev   11 Others
                        Shelepin   5 Others   13 Others

CENTRAL COMMITTEE

PARTY CONGRESS

SUPREME SOVIET

COUNCIL OF   COUNCIL OF
THE UNION   NATIONALITIES

Chart 3 CPSU Central Committee Apparatus (April 9, 1966)

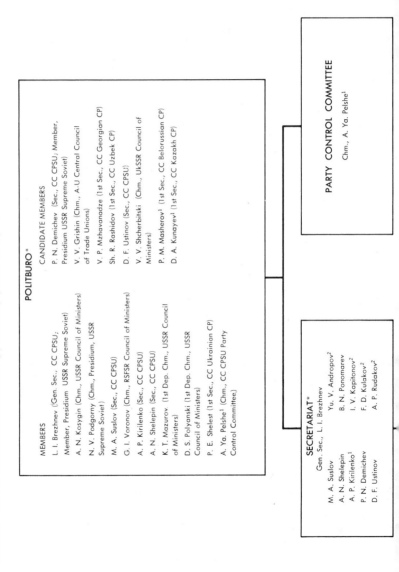

POLITBURO*

MEMBERS

L. I. Brezhnev (Gen. Sec., CC CPSU; Member, Presidium USSR Supreme Soviet)

A. N. Kosygin (Chm., USSR Council of Ministers)

N. V. Podgorny (Chm., Presidium, USSR Supreme Soviet)

M. A. Suslov (Sec., CC CPSU)

G. I. Voronov (Chm., RSFSR Council of Ministers)

A. P. Kirilenko (Sec., CC CPSU)

A. N. Shelepin (Sec., CC CPSU)

K. T. Mazurov (1st Dep. Chm., USSR Council of Ministers)

D. S. Polyanski (1st Dep. Chm., USSR Council of Ministers)

P. E. Shelest (1st Sec., CC Ukrainian CP)

A. Ya. Pelshe[1] (Chm., CC CPSU Party Control Committee)

CANDIDATE MEMBERS

P. N. Demichev (Sec., CC CPSU; Member, Presidium USSR Supreme Soviet)

V. V. Grishin (Chm., A-U Central Council of Trade Unions)

V. P. Mzhavanadze (1st Sec., CC Georgian CP)

Sh. R. Rashidov (1st Sec., CC Uzbek CP)

D. F. Ustinov (Sec., CC CPSU)

V. V. Shcherbitski (Chm., UkSSR Council of Ministers)

P. M. Masherov[1] (1st Sec., CC Belorussian CP)

D. A. Kunayev[1] (1st Sec., CC Kazakh CP)

SECRETARIAT*

Gen. Sec., L. I. Brezhnev

M. A. Suslov	Yu. V. Andropov[2]
A. N. Shelepin	B. N. Ponomarev
A. P. Kirilenko[1]	I. V. Kapitonov[2]
P. N. Demichev	F. D. Kulakov[2]
D. F. Ustinov	A. P. Rudakov[2]

PARTY CONTROL COMMITTEE

Chm., A. Ya. Pelshe[1]

DEPARTMENTS OF CENTRAL COMMITTEE

MAIN POLITICAL ADMINISTRATION OF SOVIET ARMY AND NAVY
Chm. A. A. Epishev

CULTURE
Chm. V. F. Shauro?

PROPAGANDA AND AGITATION
Chm. V. I. Stepakov

SCIENCE AND EDUCATION
S. P. Trapeznikov

CADRES ABROAD
Chm. A. S. Panyushkin

ECON. REL. WITH SOCIALIST COUNTRIES
Chm.?

INTERNATIONAL AFFAIRS
Chm. L. D. Shevlyagin ?

RELATIONS WITH BLOC PARTIES
Chm. Yu. V. Andropov[3]

AGRICULTURE FOR UNION REPUBLICS
Chm. F. D. Kulakov

CHEMICAL INDUSTRY
Chm. V. M. Bushuyev

CONSTRUCTION
Chm. A. E. Biryukov

DEFENSE INDUSTRY
Chm. I. D. Serbin

HEAVY INDUSTRY
Chm. A. P. Rudakov

LIGHT AND FOOD INDUSTRIES
Chm. P. K. Sizov

MACHINE BUILDING
Chm. V. S. Frolov

TRADE AND DOMESTIC SERVICES
Chm. Ya. I. Kabkov[1]

TRANSPORT AND COMMUNICATIONS
Chm. K. S. Simonov

ADMINISTRATIVE ORGANS
Chm.?

ADMINISTRATION OF AFFAIRS
Chm. G. S. Pavlov

GENERAL
Chm. K. V. Chernenko[1]

ORGANIZATIONAL-PARTY WORK
Chm. I. V. Kapitonov

Unidentified Sections

[1]New incumbent
[2]Also heads of other agencies
[3]Tenure in doubt

* Listings as in Brezhnev's April 8 closing speech
to the Twenty-third Party Congress.

493

Chart 4   CPSU Central Committee Apparatus (November 23, 1971)

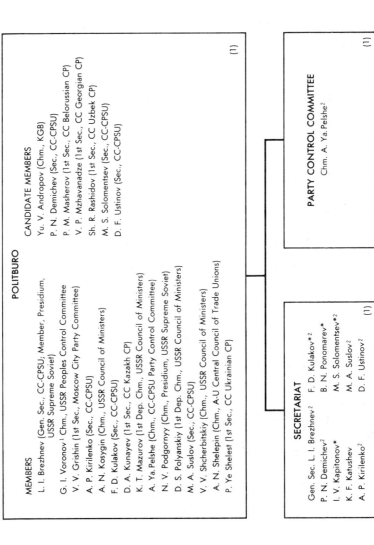

POLITBURO

MEMBERS

L. I. Brezhnev (Gen. Sec., CC-CPSU; Member, Presidium,
USSR Supreme Soviet)

G. I. Voronov[1] Chm., USSR Peoples Control Committee

V. V. Grishin (1st Sec., Moscow City Party Committee)

A. P. Kirilenko (Sec., CC-CPSU)

A. N. Kosygin (Chm., USSR Council of Ministers)

F. D. Kulakov (Sec., CC-CPSU)

D. A. Kunayev (1st Sec., CC Kazakh CP)

K. T. Mazurov (1st Dep. Chm., USSR Council of Ministers)

A. Ya. Pelshe (Chm., CC-CPSU Party Control Committee)

N. V. Podgornyy (Chm., Presidium, USSR Supreme Soviet)

D. S. Polyanskiy (1st Dep. Chm., USSR Council of Ministers)

M. A. Suslov (Sec., CC-CPSU)

V. V. Shcherbitskiy (Chm., USSR Council of Ministers)

A. N. Shelepin (Chm., A-U Central Council of Trade Unions)

P. Ye Shelest (1st Sec., CC Ukrainian CP)

CANDIDATE MEMBERS

Yu. V. Andropov (Chm., KGB)

P. N. Demichev (Sec., CC-CPSU)

P. M. Masherov (1st Sec., CC Belorussian CP)

V. P. Mzhavanadze (1st Sec., CC Georgian CP)

Sh. R. Rashidov (1st Sec., CC Uzbek CP)

M. S. Solomentsev (Sec., CC-CPSU)

D. F. Ustinov (Sec., CC-CPSU)

(1)

SECRETARIAT

Gen. Sec. L. I. Brezhnev[2]   F. D. Kulakov*[2]

P. N. Demichev[2]   B. N. Ponomarev*

I. V. Kapitonov*   M. S. Solomentsev*[2]

K. F. Katushev   M. A. Suslov[2]

A. P. Kirilenko[2]   D. F. Ustinov[2]

(1)

PARTY CONTROL COMMITTEE

Chm. A. Ya. Pelshe[2]

(1)

DEPARTMENTS OF CENTRAL COMMITTEE

MAIN POLITICAL ADMINISTRATION OF SOVIET ARMY AND NAVY (1) Chm. A. A. Yepishev	CADRES ABROAD (4) Chm. A. S. Panyushkin [1]	AGRICULTURE (1) Chm. F. D. Kulakov
CULTURE (1) Chm. V. F. Shauro	INTERNATIONAL (1) Chm. B. N. Ponomarev	CHEMICAL INDUSTRY (3) Chm. V. M. Bushuyev
PROPAGANDA (1) Vacant	RELATIONS WITH BLOC PARTIES (1) Chm. K. V. Rusakov	CONSTRUCTION (3) Chm. I. N. Dmitriyev
SCIENCE AND EDUCATIONAL INSTITUTIONS (1) S. P. Trapeznikov		DEFENSE INDUSTRY (2) Chm. I. D. Serbin
		HEAVY INDUSTRY (1) Chm. M. S. Solomentsev [1]
		LIGHT AND FOOD INDUSTRIES (4) Chm. P. K. Sizov [1]
		MACHINE BUILDING (2) Chm. V. S. Frolov
		TRADE AND DOMESTIC SERVICES (2) Chm. Ya. I. Kabkov
		TRANSPORT AND COMMUNICATIONS (3) Chm. K. S. Simonov
		PLANNING AND FINANCIAL ORGANS (3) Chm. B. I. Gostev

ADMINISTRATIVE ORGANS (2) Chm. N. I. Savinkin
ADMINISTRATION OF AFFAIRS (1) Chm. G. S. Pavlov
GENERAL (1) Chm. K. V. Chernenko
PARTY ORGANIZATIONAL WORK (1) Chm. I. V. Kapitonov
UNIDENTIFIED SECTION (4) Chm. N. N. Organov [1]

All names in Russian alphabetical order

[1] Future tenure in doubt

[2] Also on Politburo

[*] Also head of CC section

National Party status

(1) Member, CC-CPSU

(2) Candidate Member, CC-CPSU

(3) Member, CPSU Central Auditing Commission

(4) None

Chart 5 CPSU Central Committee Apparatus (December 1, 1985)

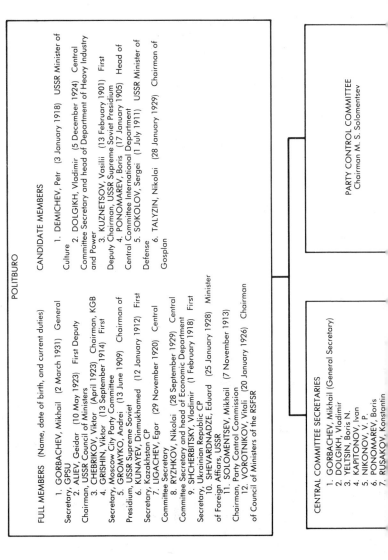

POLITBURO

FULL MEMBERS (Name, date of birth, and current duties)

1. GORBACHEV, Mikhail (2 March 1931) General Secretary, GPSU
2. ALIEV, Geidar (10 May 1923) First Deputy Chairman, USSR Council of Ministers
3. CHEBRIKOV, Viktor (April 1923) Chairman, KGB
4. GRISHIN, Viktor (13 September 1914) First Secretary, Moscow City Party Committee
5. GROMYKO, Andrei (13 June 1909) Chairman of Presidium, USSR Supreme Soviet
6. KUNAYEV, Dinmukhamed (12 January 1912) First Secretary, Kazakhstan CP
7. LIGACHEV, Egor (29 November 1920) Central Committee Secretary
8. RYZHKOV, Nikolai (28 September 1929) Central Committee Secretary and head of Economic Department
9. SHCHERBITSKY, Vladimir (1 February 1918) First Secretary, Ukrainian Republic CP
10. SHEVARDNADZE, Eduard (25 January 1928) Minister of Foreign Affairs, USSR
11. SOLOMENTSEV, Mikhail (7 November 1913) Chairman, Party Control Commission
12. VOROTNIKOV, Vitali (20 January 1926) Chairman of Council of Ministers of the RSFSR

CANDIDATE MEMBERS

1. DEMICHEV, Petr (3 January 1918) USSR Minister of Culture
2. DOLGIKH, Vladimir (5 December 1924) Central Committee Secretary and head of Department of Heavy Industry and Power
3. KUZNETSOV, Vasilii (13 February 1901) First Deputy Chairman, USSR Supreme Soviet Presidium
4. PONOMAREV, Boris (17 January 1905) Head of Central Committee International Department
5. SOKOLOV, Sergei (1 July 1911) USSR Minister of Defense
6. TALYZIN, Nikolai (28 January 1929) Chairman of Gosplan

CENTRAL COMMITTEE SECRETARIES

1. GORBACHEV, Mikhail (General Secretary)
2. DOLGIKH, Vladimir
3. YELTSIN, Boris N.
4. KAPITONOV, Ivan
5. NIKONOV, V. P.
6. PONOMAREV, Boris
7. RUSAKOV, Konstantin

PARTY CONTROL COMMITTEE
Chairman M. S. Solomentsev

Administration of Affairs
N. F. Kruchina

Administrative Organs
N. I. Savinkin

General
A. I. Lubyanov

Letters
B. P. Yakovlev

Organizational-Party Work
G. Razumovsky

Trade and Domestic Services
N. A. Stashenkov

Agriculture and Food Industry
V. A. Karlov

Agricultural Machine Building
I. I. Sakhnyuk

Chemical Industry
V. G. Afonin

Construction
B. N. Yeltsin

Defense Industry
O. S. Belyakov

Economic
B. I. Gostev

International
B. N. Ponomarev

International Information
L. M. Zamyatin

Cadres Abroad
S. V. Chervonenko

Liaison with Ruling
Communist
Parties
K. V. Rusakov

Machine-Building
A. I. Volsky

Main Political Administration
of Soviet Army and Navy
A. D. Lizichev

Culture
V. F. Shauro

Propaganda
A. N. Yakovlev

Science and Educational
Institutions
V. A. Medvedev

Heavy Industry and Power
I. P. Yastrebov

Light Industry and Consumer Goods
F. I. Mochalin

Transport and Communications
K. S. Simonov

Chart 6   Structure of the Central Committee of a Republic Party

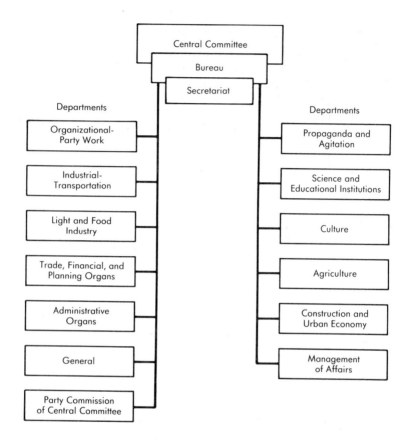

Note: In many union republic central committees there are also departments for the most highly developed industrial and agricultural branches of the republic. In some central committees instead of a department for trade, finance, and planning organs there is a department of trade and services.

Chart 7 Structure of a Province (*Krai* or *Oblast*) Committee of the Party

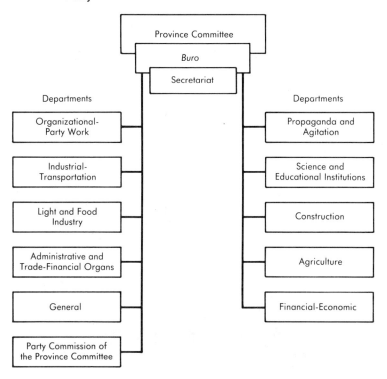

Note: In many province committees there are departments for the most highly developed industrial branches of the province. In some committees instead of an industrial-transport department there are a department for industry and a department of transportation and communications; instead of a department of administrative and trade-financial organs, there are departments of administrative organs and trade-financial organs. Many province committees have a department for light and food industry and trade.

Chart 8   Structure of a City Party Committee

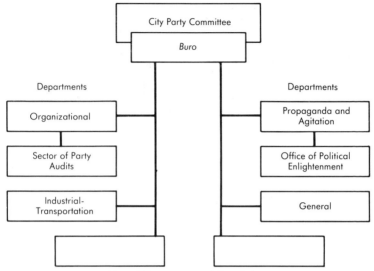

City Party Committee

Buro

Departments

Organizational

Sector of Party Audits

Industrial-Transportation

Departments

Propaganda and Agitation

Office of Political Enlightenment

General

Nonstaff Departments and Commissions

Note: In many larger cities, party committees have departments for construction and urban economy, science and educational institutions, and administrative and trade-financial organs. City committees that incorporate rural party organizations have agricultural departments.

Chart 9 Structure of a District Committee of the Party

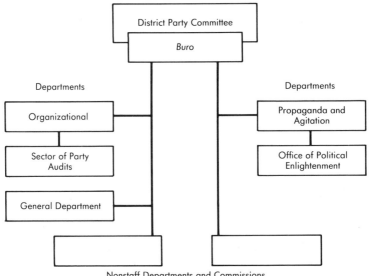

Nonstaff Departments and Commissions

Note: Some district party committees, particularly those in urban districts, also have industrial-transportation departments.

Chart 10 Organizational Structure of the CPSU

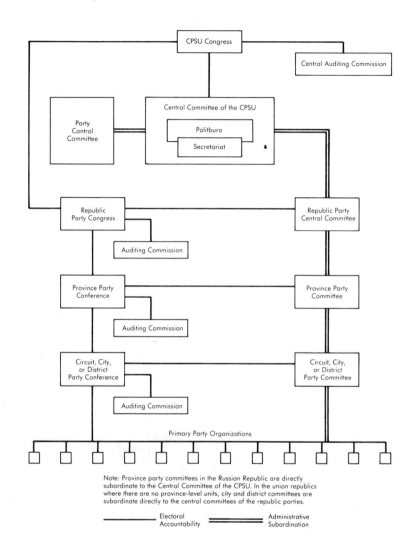

Note: Province party committees in the Russian Republic are directly subordinate to the Central Committee of the CPSU. In the union republics where there are no province-level units, city and district committees are subordinate directly to the central committees of the republic parties.

———— Electoral Accountability   ═══════ Administrative Subordination

Chart 11 Organization of USSR Council of Ministers (January 1963)

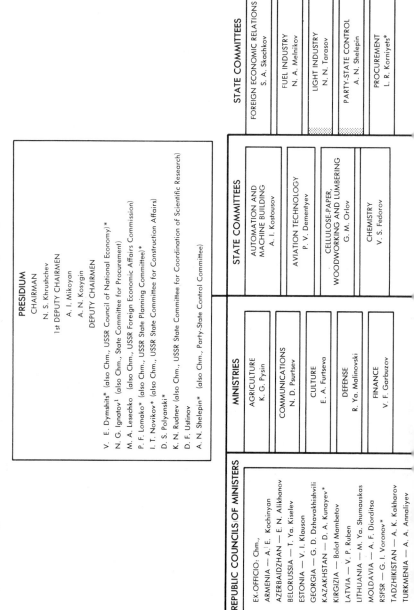

PRESIDIUM
CHAIRMAN
N. S. Khrushchev
1st DEPUTY CHAIRMEN
A. I. Mikoyan
A. N. Kosygin
DEPUTY CHAIRMEN

V. E. Dymshits* (also Chm., USSR Council of National Economy)*
N. G. Ignatov[1] (also Chm., State Committee for Procurement)
M. A. Lesechko (also Chm., USSR Foreign Economic Affairs Commission)
P. F. Lomako* (also Chm., USSR State Planning Committee)*
I. T. Novikov* (also Chm., USSR State Committee for Construction Affairs)
D. S. Polyanski*
K. N. Rudnev (also Chm., USSR State Committee for Coordination of Scientific Research)
D. F. Ustinov
A. N. Shelepin* (also Chm., Party-State Control Committee)

REPUBLIC COUNCILS OF MINISTERS	MINISTRIES	STATE COMMITTEES	STATE COMMITTEES
EX-OFFICIO: Chm.,	AGRICULTURE	AUTOMATION AND	FOREIGN ECONOMIC RELATIONS
ARMENIA — A. E. Kochinyan	K. G. Pysin	MACHINE BUILDING	S. A. Skachkov
AZERBAIDZHAN — E. N. Alikhanov		A. I. Kostousov	
BELORUSSIA — T. Ya. Kiselev	COMMUNICATIONS		FUEL INDUSTRY
ESTONIA — V. I. Klauson	N. D. Psurtsev	AVIATION TECHNOLOGY	N. A. Melnikov
GEORGIA — G. D. Dzhavakhishvili		P. V. Dementyev	
KAZAKHSTAN — D. A. Kunayev*	CULTURE		LIGHT INDUSTRY
KIRGIZIA — Bolot Mambetov	E. A. Furtseva	CELLULOSE-PAPER,	N. N. Tarasov
LATVIA — V. P. Ruben		WOODWORKING AND LUMBERING	
LITHUANIA — M. Ya. Shumauskas	DEFENSE	G. M. Orlov	PARTY-STATE CONTROL
MOLDAVIA — A. F. Diorditsa	R. Ya. Malinovski		A. N. Shelepin
RSFSR — G. I. Voronov*		CHEMISTRY	
TADZHIKISTAN — A. K. Kakharov	FINANCE	V. S. Fedorov	PROCUREMENT
TURKMENIA — A. A. Annaliyev	V. F. Garbuzov		L. R. Korniyets*

504

SPECIALIZED AGENCIES

USSR COUNCIL OF NAT'L ECON. Chm., V. E. Dymshits*
1st Dep. Chm., A. A. Etmekdzhiyan
1st Dep. Chm., V. M. Ryabikov
Dep. Chm., N. I. Strokin
Dep. Chm., V. P. Zotov

STATE PLANNING COMMITTEE Chm., P. F. Lomako*
1st Dep. Chm., A. A. Goreglyad
Dep. Chm., N. A. Tikhonov

FOREIGN ECONOMIC AFFAIRS COMMISSION Chm., M. A. Lesechko

STATE BANK Chm., A. K. Korovushkin

CONSTRUCTION BANK Chm., G. A. Karavayev

MAIN ADMINISTRATION OF GAS INDUSTRY Chm., A. K. Kortunov

ALL-UNION ASSOCIATION FOR AGRICULTURAL EQUIPMENT Chm., J A. A. Ezhevskii*

CENTRAL STATISTICAL ADMINISTRATION Chm., V. N. Starovski

FOREIGN AFFAIRS A. A. Gromyko

FOREIGN TRADE N. S. Patolichev

GEOLOGY AND PROTECTION OF NATURAL RESOURCES A. V. Sidorenko

HEALTH S. V. Kurashov

HIGHER AND SPECIALIZED EDUCATION V. P. Elyutin

MARITIME FLEET V. G. Bakayev

MEDIUM MACHINE BUILDING E. P. Slavski

POWER INDUSTRY AND ELECTRIFICATION P. T. Neporozhny

RAILWAY TRANSPORT V. P. Beshchev

TRANSPORT CONSTRUCTION E. V. Kozhevnikov

V. N. Novikov* (without portfolio)*

COORDINATION OF SCIENTIFIC RESEARCH K. N. Rudnev

CULTURAL RELATIONS WITH FOREIGN COUNTRIES S. K. Romanovski

CONSTRUCTION AFFAIRS I. T. Novikov*

DEFENSE TECHNOLOGY L. V. Smirnov

ELECTRICAL INDUSTRY N. Obolenski

ELECTRONIC TECHNOLOGY A. I. Shokin

FERROUS AND NON-FERROUS METALLURGY V. E. Boyko

FISHING INDUSTRY A. A. Ishkov

FOOD INDUSTRY P. V. Naumenko

PROFESSIONAL-TECHNICAL EDUCATION G. I. Zelenko

QUESTIONS OF LABOR AND WAGES A. P. Volkov

RADIO BROADCASTING AND TELEVISION M. A. Kharlamov

RADIO ELECTRONICS V. D. Kalmykov

SHIPBUILDING B. E. Butoma

STATE CONTROL G. B. Enyutin

STATE SECURITY V. E. Semichastny

TRADE A. I. Struyev

UTILIZATION OF ATOMIC ENERGY A. M. Petrosyants

Abolished agency

All-Union ministries

*New incumbent

‡Replaced

Pre-existing agencies

Reorganized agencies

New agencies

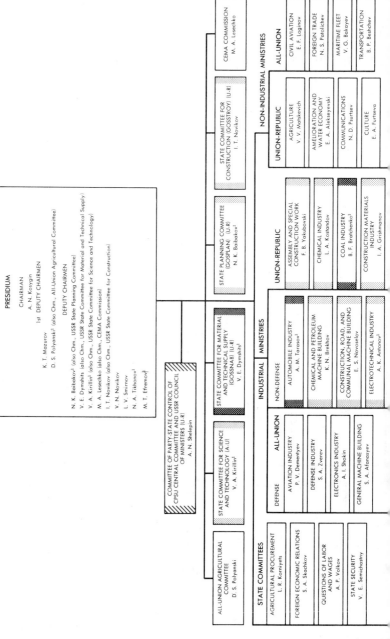

SPECIALIZED AGENCIES

MEDIUM MACHINE BUILDING E. P. Slavski	GAS INDUSTRY A. K. Kortunov	FERROUS METALLURGY I. P. Kazanets[1]	DEFENSE R. Ya. Malinovski
RADIO INDUSTRY V. D. Kalmykov	HEAVY, POWER, AND TRANSPORT MACHINE BUILDING V. F. Zhigalin[1]	FISHING ECONOMY A. A. Ishkov	FINANCE V. F. Garbuzov
SHIPBUILDING B. E. Butoma	INSTRUMENT-MAKING, AUTOMATION, AND CONTROL SYSTEMS K. N. Rudnev[1]	FOOD INDUSTRY V. P. Zotov[1]	FOREIGN AFFAIRS A. A. Gromyko
	MACHINE BUILDING FOR LIGHT AND FOOD INDUSTRIES AND HOUSEHOLD APPLIANCES V. N. Doyenin[1]	LIGHT INDUSTRY N. N. Tarasov	GEOLOGY A. V. Sidorenko
	MACHINE TOOL BUILDING AND INSTRUMENT INDUSTRY A. I. Kostousov	MEAT AND DAIRY INDUSTRY S. F. Antonov[1]	HIGHER AND SECONDARY SPECIALIZED EDUCATION V. P. Elyutin
	TRACTOR AND AGRICULTURAL MACHINE BUILDING I. F. Sinitsin[1]	NON-FERROUS METALLURGY P. F. Lomako[1]	PUBLIC HEALTH B. V. Petrovski[1]
	TRANSPORT CONSTRUCTION E. F. Kozhevnikov	PETROLEUM EXTRACTION INDUSTRY V. D. Shashin[1]	TRADE A. I. Struyev
		PETROLEUM PROCESSING AND PETROCHEMICAL INDUSTRY V. S. Fedorov	
		POWER AND ELECTRIFICATION P. S. Neporozhny	
		TIMBER, CELLULOSE-PAPER, AND WOODWORKING INDUSTRY N. V. Timofeyev[1]	

SPECIALIZED AGENCIES
CENTRAL STATISTICAL ADMINISTRATION V. N. Starovski
STATE BANK A. A. Poskonov

EX-OFFICIO MEMBERS: CHM. OF THE REPUBLIC COUNCILS OF MINISTERS

ARMENIA — A. E. Kochinyan
AZERBAIDZHAN — E. N. Alikhanov
BELORUSSIA — T. Ya. Kiselev
ESTONIA — V. I. Klauson
GEORGIA — G. D. Dzhavakhishvili
KAZAKHSTAN — M. B. Beysebayev
KIRGIZIA — B. M. Mambetov
LATVIA — V. P. Ruben
LITHUANIA — M. Ya. Shumauskas
MOLDAVIA — A. F. Diordiitsa
RSFSR — G. I. Voronov
TADZHIKISTAN — A. K. Kakharov
TURKMENIA — M. N. Gapurov
UKRAINE — V. V. Shcherbitski[1]
UZBEKISTAN — K. K. Kurbanov

AGENCIES FORMERLY PART OF COUNCIL OF MINISTERS

SUPREME ECONOMIC COUNCIL V. N. Novikov	STATE COMMITTEE FOR CINEMATOGRAPHY A. V. Romanov	STATE COMMITTEE FOR PRICES (UNDER GOSPLAN) V. K. Sitnin[1]	STATE COMMITTEE FOR THE UTILIZATION OF ATOMIC ENERGY A. M. Petrosyants
COUNCIL OF NATIONAL ECONOMY V. E. Dymshits	STATE COMMITTEE FOR CIVIL CONSTRUCTION AND ARCHITECTURE (UNDER GOSSTROY) M. V. Posokhin	STATE COMMITTEE FOR PUBLISHING N. A. Mikhaylov[1]	STATE COMMITTEE FOR VOCATIONAL-TECHNICAL EDUCATION A. A. Bulgakov[2]
ASSOC. FOR AGRICULTURAL EQUIPMENT AND SUPPLIES (SOYUZSELKHOZTEKHNIKA) A. A. Ezhevski[2]	STATE COMMITTEE FOR CULTURAL RELATIONS WITH FOREIGN COUNTRIES S. K. Romanovski	STATE COMMITTEE FOR RADIO BROADCASTING AND TELEVISION N. N. Mesyatsev	COMMITTEE FOR PEOPLE'S CONTROL P. V. Kovanov[1,2]

New agencies

Reorganized agencies

Abolished agencies

[1]New incumbent

[2]Agencies headed by "Members of Government"

(A-U) All-Union

(U-R) Union-Republic

Chart 13 Organization of USSR Council of Ministers (July 28, 1971)

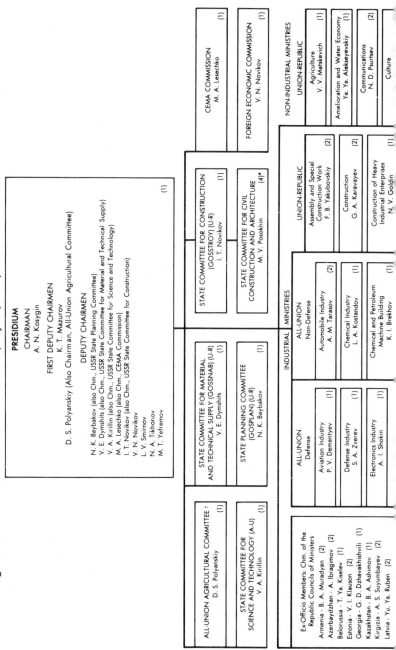

PRESIDIUM

CHAIRMAN
A. N. Kosygin

FIRST DEPUTY CHAIRMEN
K. T. Mazurov
D. S. Polyanskiy (Also Chairman, All-Union Agricultural Committee)

DEPUTY CHAIRMEN
N. K. Baybakov (also Chm., USSR State Planning Committee)
V. E. Dymshits (also Chm., USSR State Committee for Material and Technical Supply)
V. A. Kirillin (also Chm., USSR State Committee for Science and Technology)
M. A. Lesechko (also Chm., CEMA Commission)
I. T. Novikov (also Chm., USSR State Committee for Construction)
V. N. Novikov
L. V. Smirnov
N. A. Tikhonov
M. T. Yefremov   (1)

CEMA COMMISSION   (1)
M. A. Lesechko

FOREIGN ECONOMIC COMMISSION   (1)
V. N. Novikov

STATE COMMITTEE FOR CONSTRUCTION   (1)
(GOSSTROY) (U-R)
I. T. Novikov

STATE COMMITTEE FOR CIVIL   (4)*
CONSTRUCTION AND ARCHITECTURE
M. V. Posokhin

STATE COMMITTEE FOR MATERIAL   (1)
AND TECHNICAL SUPPLY (GOSSNAB) (U-R)
V. E. Dymshits

STATE PLANNING COMMITTEE   (1)
(GOSPLAN) (U-R)
N. K. Baybakov

ALL-UNION AGRICULTURAL COMMITTEE †   (1)
D. S. Polyanskiy

STATE COMMITTEE FOR   (1)
SCIENCE AND TECHNOLOGY (A-U)
V. A. Kirillin

INDUSTRIAL MINISTRIES

ALL-UNION MINISTRIES

ALL-UNION
Defense

Aviation Industry   (1)
P. V. Dementyev

Defense Industry   (1)
S. A. Zverev

Electronics Industry   (1)
A. I. Shokin

ALL-UNION
Non-Defense

Automobile Industry   (2)
A. M. Tarasov

Chemical Industry   (1)
L. A. Kostandov

Chemical and Petroleum   (1)
Machine Building
K. I. Brekhov

UNION-REPUBLIC

Assembly and Special   (2)
Construction Work
F. B. Yakubovskiy

Construction   (2)
G. A. Karavayev

Construction of Heavy   (1)
Industrial Enterprises
N. V. Goldin

NON-INDUSTRIAL MINISTRIES

UNION-REPUBLIC

Agriculture   (1)
V. V. Matskevich

Amelioration and Water Economy (1)
Ye. Ye. Alekseyevskiy

Communications   (2)
N. D. Psurtsev

Culture

Ex-Officio Members: Chm. of the
Republic Councils of Ministers
Armenia - B. A. Muradyan (2)
Azerbaydzhan - A. Ibragimov (2)
Belorussia - T. Ya. Kiselev (1)
Estonia - V. I. Klauson (2)
Georgia - G. D. Dzhavakhishvili (1)
Kazakhstan - B. A. Ashimov (1)
Kirgizia - A. S. Suyumbayev (2)
Latvia - Yu. Ya. Ruben (2)

508

Moldavia - P. A. Paskar (2)
RSFSR - M. S. Solomentsev[1] (1)
Tadzhikistan - A. K. Kakharov (2)
Turkmenistan - O. N. Orazmukhamedov (2)
Ukraine - V. V. Shcherbitskiy (1)
Uzbekistan - N. D. Khudayberdyyev (1)

STATE COMMITTEES

- Foreign Economic Relations S. A. Skachkov (1)
- Forestry G. I. Vorob'yev[1] (4)
- Labor and Wages A. P. Volkov (4)
- People's Control G. I. Voronov[1] (4)
- Prices V. K. Sitnin (4)
- Radio Broadcasting and Television S. G. Lapin (1)
- Standards V. V. Boytsov (4)
- State Security Yu. V. Andropov (1)
- Vocational-Technical Education A. A. Bulgakov (1)

SPECIALIZED AGENCIES

- Assoc. for Agricultural Equipment and Supplies (Soyuzselkhoztekhnika) A. A. Yezhevskiy (1)
- Central Statistical Administration V. N. Starovskiy (3)
- State Bank M. N. Sveshnikov (4)

- General Machine Building S. A. Afanas'yev (1)
- Machine Building V. V. Bakhirev (1)
- Medium Machine Building Ye. P. Slavskiy (1)
- Radio Industry V. D. Kalmykov (1)
- Shipbuilding B. Ye. Butoma (1)

OTHER AGENCIES WITHOUT MINISTERIAL STATUS

- Committee for Cinematography A. V. Romanov (2)*
- Committee for Physical Culture and Sport S. P. Pavlov (3)*
- Committee for Publishing B. I. Stukalin (4)*
- State Committee for Safe Practices in Industry and Mining L. G. Melnikov (4)*
- State Committee for the Use of Atomic Energy A. M. Petrosyants (4)*
- Committee for Inventions and Discoveries Yu. Ye. Maksarev (4)*
- State Commission for Stockpiling Useful Minerals I. I. Malyshev (4)*

- Construction, Road and Communal Machine Building Ye. S. Novoselov (3)
- Electrotechnical Industry A. K. Antonov (1)
- Gas Industry A. K. Kortunov (2)
- Heavy, Power, and Transport Machine Building V. F. Zhigalin (1)
- Instrument-Making, Automation and Control Systems K. N. Rudnev (1)
- Machine Building for Light and Food Industries and Appliances V. N. Doyenin (2)
- Machine Tool Building and Instrument Industry A. I. Kostousov (1)
- Petroleum Industry V. D. Shashin (2)
- Tractor and Agricultural Machine Building I. F. Sinitsyn (2)
- Transport Construction Ye. F. Kozhevnikov (1)
- Medical Industry P. V. Gusenkov (4)

- Coal Industry V. F. Bratchenko (1)
- Construction Materials Industry I. A. Grishmanov (1)
- Ferrous Metallurgy I. P. Kazanets (1)
- Fishing Economy A. A. Ishkov (2)
- Food Industry V. P. Lein[1] (2)
- Industrial Construction A. M. Tokarev (1)
- Light Industry N. N. Tarasov (2)
- Meat and Dairy Industry S. F. Antonov (3)
- Non-Ferrous Metallurgy P. F. Lomako (1)
- Petroleum Processing and Petrochemical Industry V. S. Fedorov (2)
- Power and Electrification P. S. Neporozhniy (2)
- Rural Construction S. D. Khitrov (1)
- Timber and Woodworking Industry N. V. Timofeyev (3)

- Defense A. A. Grechko (1)
- Education M. A. Prokofyev (1)
- Finance V. F. Garbuzov (1)
- Foreign Affairs A. A. Gromyko (1)
- Geology A. V. Sidorenko (2)
- Higher and Secondary Specialized Education V. P. Yelyutin (1)
- Internal Affairs N. A. Shchelokov (1)
- Justice V. I. Terebilov (3)
- Procurement Z. N. Nuriyev (1)
- Public Health B. V. Petrovskiy (2)
- Trade A. I. Struyev (1)

ALL-UNION

- Civil Aviation B. P. Bugayev[1] (1)
- Foreign Trade N. S. Patolichev (1)
- Maritime Fleet T. B. Guzhenko[1] (2)
- Railways B. P. Beshchev (1)

New agencies
[1] New incumbent
A-U All-Union
U-R Union-Republic

National Party Status
(1) Member, CC, CPSU
(2) Candidate member, CC CPSU
(3) Member, CPSU Central Auditing Commission
(4) None
* Officials not Members of Council of Ministers
† No constitutional status

Chart 14   USSR Council of Ministers (January 1, 1983)

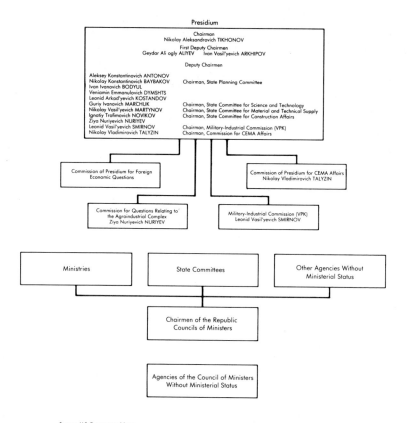

Presidium

Chairman
Nikolay Aleksandrovich TIKHONOV

First Deputy Chairmen
Geydar Ali ogly ALIYEV   Ivan Vasil'yevich ARKHIPOV

Deputy Chairmen

Aleksey Konstantinovich ANTONOV
Nikolay Konstantinovich BAYBAKOV — Chairman, State Planning Committee
Ivan Ivanovich BODYUL
Veniamin Emmanulovich DYMSHTS
Leonid Arkad'yevich KOSTANDOV
Guriy Ivanovich MARCHUK — Chairman, State Committee for Science and Technology
Nikolay Vasil'yevich MARTYNOV — Chairman, State Committee for Material and Technical Supply
Ignatiy Trofimovich NOVIKOV — Chairman, State Committee for Construction Affairs
Ziya Nuriyevich NURIYEV
Leonid Vasil'yevich SMIRNOV — Chairman, Military-Industrial Commission (VPK)
Nikolay Vladimirovich TALYZIN — Chairman, Commission for CEMA Affairs

Commission of Presidium for Foreign Economic Questions

Commission of Presidium for CEMA Affairs
Nikolay Vladimirovich TALYZIN

Commission for Questions Relating to the Agroindustrial Complex
Ziya Nuriyevich NURIYEV

Military-Industrial Commission (VPK)
Leonid Vasil'yevich SMIRNOV

Ministries

State Committees

Other Agencies Without Ministerial Status

Chairmen of the Republic Councils of Ministers

Agencies of the Council of Ministers Without Ministerial Status

Source: U.S. Department of State

Adapted from Gabriel Almond and G. Bingham Powell,
Comparative Politics Today: A World View, 3rd ed.
(Boston, Mass.:   Little, Brown), pp. 338–339.

510

Ministries

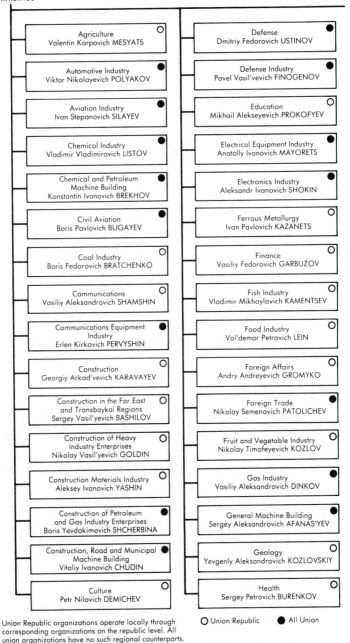

Agriculture Valentin Karpovich MESYATS ○	Defense Dmitriy Fedorovich USTINOV ●
Automotive Industry Viktor Nikolayevich POLYAKOV ●	Defense Industry Pavel Vasil'vevich FINOGENOV ●
Aviation Industry Ivan Stepanovich SILAYEV ●	Education Mikhail Alekseyevich PROKOFYEV ○
Chemical Industry Vladimir Vladimirovich LISTOV ●	Electrical Equipment Industry Anatolly Ivanovich MAYORETS ●
Chemical and Petroleum Machine Building Konstantin Ivanovich BREKHOV ●	Electronics Industry Aleksandr Ivanovich SHOKIN ●
Civil Aviation Boris Pavlovich BUGAYEV ●	Ferrous Metallurgy Ivan Pavlovich KAZANETS ○
Coal Industry Boris Fedorovich BRATCHENKO ○	Finance Vasiliy Fedorovich GARBUZOV ○
Communications Vasiliy Aleksandrovich SHAMSHIN ○	Fish Industry Vladimir Mikhaylovich KAMENTSEV ○
Communications Equipment Industry Erlen Kirkovich PERVYSHIN ●	Food Industry Vol'demar Petrovich LEIN ○
Construction Georgiy Arkad'vevich KARAVAYEV ○	Foreign Affairs Andry Andreyevich GROMYKO ○
Construction in the Far East and Transbaykal Regions Sergey Vasil'yevich BASHILOV ○	Foreign Trade Nikolay Semenovich PATOLICHEV ●
Construction of Heavy Industry Enterprises Nikolay Vasil'yevich GOLDIN ○	Fruit and Vegetable Industry Nikolay Timofeyevich KOZLOV ○
Construction Materials Industry Aleksey Ivanovich YASHIN ○	Gas Industry Vasiliy Aleksandrovich DINKOV ●
Construction of Petroleum and Gas Industry Enterprises Boris Yevdokimovich SHCHERBINA ●	General Machine Building Sergey Aleksandrovich AFANAS'YEV ●
Construction, Road and Municipal Machine Building Vitaliy Ivanovich CHUDIN ●	Geology Yevgenly Aleksandrovich KOZLOVSKIY ○
Culture Petr Nilovich DEMICHEV ○	Health Sergey Petrovich BURENKOV ○

Union Republic organizations operate locally through
corresponding organizations on the republic level. All
union organizations have no such regional counterparts.

○ Union Republic   ● All Union

continued

Ministries   (*continued*)

Heavy and Transport Machine Building ● Vladimir Fedorovich AHIGALIN	Medium Machine Building ● Yefim Pavlovich SLAVSKIY
Higher and Secondary ○ Specialized Education Vyacheslav Petrovich YELYUTIN	Mineral Fertilizer Production ● Aleksey Georgiyevich PETRISHCHEV
Industrial Construction ○ Aleksandr Maksimovich TOKAREV	Nonferrous Metallurgy ○ Petr Fedeyevich LOMAKO
Installation and Special ○ Construction Work Boris Vladimirovich DAKIN	Petroleum Industry ● Nikolay Alakseyevich MALTSEV
Instrument Making, Automation ● Equipment and Control Systems Mikhail Sergeyevich SHKABARDNYA	Petroleum Refining and ○ Petrochemical Industry Viktor Stepanovich FEDOROV
Internal Affairs ○ Vitalii V. FEDORCHAK	Power and Electrification ○ Petr Stepanovich NEPOROZHNIY
Justice ○ Vladimir Ivanovich TEREBILOV	Power Machine Building ● Viktor Vasil'yevich KROTOV
Land Reclamation and ○ Water Resources Nikolay Fedorovich VASIL'YEV	Procurement ○ Grigoriy Sergevich ZOLOTUKHIN
Light Industry ○ Nikolay Nikiforovich TARASOV	Radio Industry ● Petr Stepanovich PLESHAKOV
Machine Building ● Vyacheslav Vasil'yevich BAKHIREV	Railways ● Ivan Grigor'yevich PAVLOVSKIY
Machine Building for Animal ● Husbandry and Fodder Production Konstantin Nikitovich BELYAK	Rural Construction ○ Stepan Dmitriyevich KHITROV
Machine Building for Light and Food ● Industry and Household Appliances Ivan Ivanovich PUDKOV	Shipbuilding Industry ● Mikhail Vaili'yevich YEGOROV
Machine Tool and Tool ● Building Industry Boris Vladimirovich BAL'MONT	Timber, Pulp and Paper, and ○ Wood Processing Industry Mikhail Ivanovich BUSYGIN
Maritime Fleet ● Timofey Borisovich GUZHENKO	Tractor and Agricultural ● Machine Building Aleksandr Alekandrovich YEZHEVSKIY
Meat and Dairy Industry ○ Sergey Fedorovich ANTONOV	Trade ○ Aleksandr Ivanovich STRUYEV
Medical Industry ● Afanasiy Kondrat'yevich MEL'NICHENKO	Transport Construction ● Ivan Dmitriyevich SOSNOV

State Committees

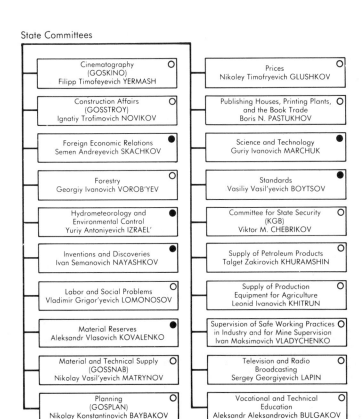

Cinematography (GOSKINO) Filipp Timofeyevich YERMASH ○	Prices Nikoley Timofryevich GLUSHKOV ○
Construction Affairs (GOSSTROY) Ignatiy Trofimovich NOVIKOV ○	Publishing Houses, Printing Plants, and the Book Trade Boris N. PASTUKHOV ○
Foreign Economic Relations Semen Andreyevich SKACHKOV ●	Science and Technology Guriy Ivanovich MARCHUK ●
Forestry Georgiy Ivanovich VOROB'YEV ○	Standards Vasiliy Vasil'yevich BOYTSOV ●
Hydrometeorology and Environmental Control Yuriy Antoniyevich IZRAEL' ●	Committee for State Security (KGB) Viktor M. CHEBRIKOV ○
Inventions and Discoveries Ivan Semanovich NAYASHKOV ●	Supply of Petroleum Products Talget Zakirovich KHURAMSHIN ○
Labor and Social Problems Vladimir Grigor'yevich LOMONOSOV ○	Supply of Production Equipment for Agriculture Leonid Ivanovich KHITRUN ○
Material Reserves Aleksandr Vlasovich KOVALENKO ●	Supervision of Safe Working Practices in Industry and for Mine Supervision Ivan Maksimovich VLADYCHENKO ○
Material and Technical Supply (GOSSNAB) Nikolay Vasil'yevich MATRYNOV ○	Television and Radio Broadcasting Sergey Georgiyevich LAPIN ○
Planning (GOSPLAN) Nikolay Konstantinovich BAYBAKOV ○	Vocational and Technical Education Aleksandr Aleksandrovich BULGAKOV ○

○ Union Republic   ● All Union

continued

513

Other Agencies Without Ministerial Status

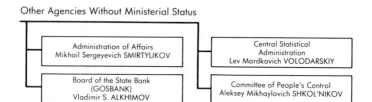

Administration of Affairs
Mikhail Sergeyevich SMIRTYUKOV

Central Statistical
Administration
Lev Mordkovich VOLODARSKIY

Board of the State Bank
(GOSBANK)
Vladimir S. ALKHIMOV

Committee of People's Control
Aleksey Mikhaylovich SHKOL'NIKOV

Chairmen of the Republic Councils of Ministers

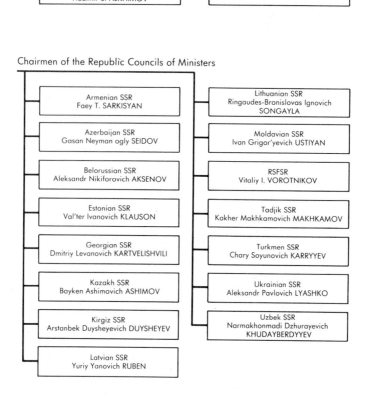

Armenian SSR
Faey T. SARKISYAN

Lithuanian SSR
Ringaudes-Bronislovas Ignovich
SONGAYLA

Azerbaijan SSR
Gasan Neyman ogly SEIDOV

Moldavian SSR
Ivan Grigor'yevich USTIYAN

Belorussian SSR
Aleksandr Nikiforovich AKSENOV

RSFSR
Vitaliy I. VOROTNIKOV

Estonian SSR
Val'ter Ivanovich KLAUSON

Tadjik SSR
Kakher Makhkamovich MAKHKAMOV

Georgian SSR
Dmitriy Levanovich KARTVELISHVILI

Turkmen SSR
Chary Soyunovich KARRYYEV

Kazakh SSR
Bayken Ashimovich ASHIMOV

Ukrainian SSR
Aleksandr Pavlovich LYASHKO

Kirgiz SSR
Arstanbek Duysheyevich DUYSHEYEV

Uzbek SSR
Narmakhonmadi Dzhurayevich
KHUDAYBERDYYEV

Latvian SSR
Yuriy Yanovich RUBEN

Agencies of the Council of Ministers Without Ministerial Status

Academy of Sciences
Anotoliy Petrovich ALEKSANDROV

All-Union Bank for Financing Capital Investments
(STROYBANK)
Mikhail Semenovich ZOTOV

Committee for Lenin and State Prizes
in Literature, Art and Architecture
Georgiy Mokeyevich MARKOV

Committee for Lenin and State Prizes
in Science and Technology
Anotoly Petrovich ALEKSANDROV

Committee for Physical Culture
and Sports

Council for Religious Affairs
Vladimir Alekseyevich KUROVEDOV

Higher Certification Commission
(VAK)
Viktor Grigor'yevich KIRILLOB-UGRYUMOV

Main Administration for
Foreign Tourism
Sergey Sergeyevich NIKITIN

Main Administration of Geodesy and Cartography
(GUGK)
Il'ya Andreyevich KUTUZOV

Main Administration of the
Microbiological Industry
Rostislav Sergeyevich TYCHKOV

Main Administration for Safeguarding
State Secrets in the Press
(GLAVLIT)
Pavel Konstantinovich ROMANOV

Main Archives Administration
(GAU)
Filipp Ivanovich DOLGIKH

State Board of Arbitration
(GOSARBITRAZH)
Yevgeniy Vasil'yevich ANISIMOV

State Commission for
Stockpiling Useful Minerals
Aleksey Mironovich BYBOCHKIN

State Committee for the
Utilization of Atomic Energy
Andronik Mel'konovich PETROSYANTS

Telegraphic Agency of the Soviet Union
(TASS)
Sergey Andreyevich LOSEV

515

Chart 15   Structure of All-Union Industrial Branch Ministry

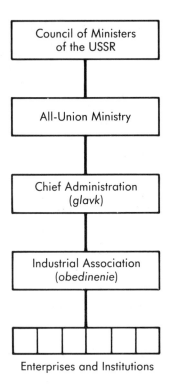

Enterprises and Institutions

Chart 16 Elections to Supreme Soviet of USSR

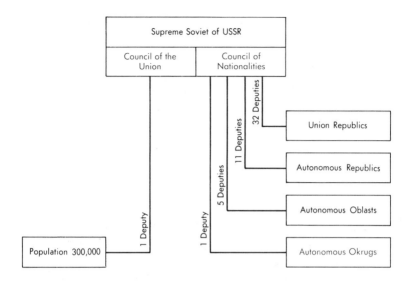

Chart 17 Soviet Nationality Structure of Union Republic

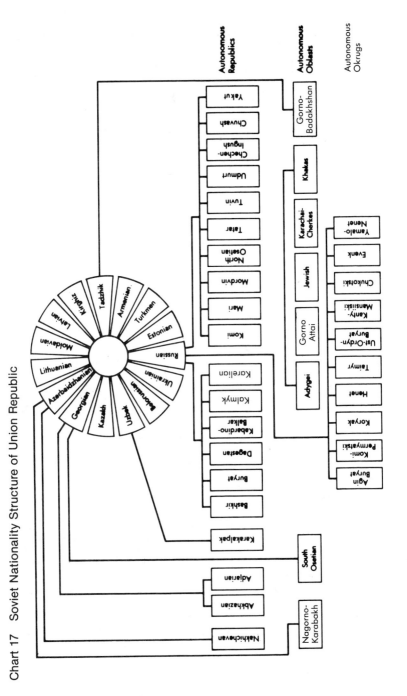

518

Chart 18   USSR—the Union Republics

Designation of Union Republics	Dates of formation	Capital	Area (sq. km)	1983 Population (thousands)
RSFSR	November 7, 1917	Moscow	17,075.4	141,012
Ukrainian SSR	December 25, 1917	Kiev	603.7	50,461
Belorussian SSR	January 1, 1919	Minsk	207.6	9,807
Uzbek SSR	October 27, 1924	Tashkent	449.6	17,039
Kazakh SSR	December 5, 1936	Alma-Ata	2,715.1	15,452
Georgian SSR	February 25, 1921	Tbilisi	69.7	5,134
Azerbaidzhanian SSSR	April 28, 1920	Baku	86.6	6,399
Lithuanian SSSR	July 21, 1940	Vilnius	65.2	3,506
Moldavian SSSR	August 2, 1940	Kishinev	33.7	4,052
Latvian SSSR	July 21, 1940	Riga	63.7	2,569
Kirghiz SSSR	December 5, 1936	Frunze	198.5	3,801
Tadzhik SSSR	October 16, 1929	Dushanbe	143.1	4,239
Armenian SSR	November 29, 1920	Erevan	29.8	3,219
Turkmen SSSR	October 27, 1924	Ashkhabad	488.1	3,042
Estonian SSR	July 21, 1940	Tallin	45.1	1,507

A sixteenth republic (the Karelo-Finnish) existed from 1940 until 1956, when it was redesignated an autonomous oblast.

Index